MEDICAL LIABILITY AND TREATMENT RELATIONSHIPS

ASPEN SELECT SERIES

MEDICAL LIABILITY AND TREATMENT RELATIONSHIPS

Fourth Edition

Mark A. Hall
Fred D. and Elizabeth L. Turnage Professor of Law and Public Health
Wake Forest University

David Orentlicher
Cobeaga Law Firm Professor of Law
UNLV William S. Boyd School of Law

Mary Anne Bobinski
Professor
Allard School of Law University of British Columbia

Nicholas Bagley
Professor of Law
University of Michigan

I. Glenn Cohen
Professor of Law
Harvard University

Wolters Kluwer

Published by Wolters Kluwer in New York.

Wolters Kluwer Legal & Regulatory U.S. serves customers worldwide with CCH, Aspen Publishers, and Kluwer Law International products. (www.WKLegaledu.com)

To contact Customer Service, e-mail customer.service@wolterskluwer.com, call 1-800-234-1660, fax 1-800-901-9075, or mail correspondence to:

Wolters Kluwer
Attn: Order Department
PO Box 990
Frederick, MD 21705

Printed in the United States of America.

2 3 4 5 6 7 8 9 0

ISBN 978-1-4548-9024-9

About Wolters Kluwer Legal & Regulatory U.S.

Wolters Kluwer Legal & Regulatory U.S. delivers expert content and solutions in the areas of law, corporate compliance, health compliance, reimbursement, and legal education. Its practical solutions help customers successfully navigate the demands of a changing environment to drive their daily activities, enhance decision quality and inspire confident outcomes.

Serving customers worldwide, its legal and regulatory portfolio includes products under the Aspen Publishers, CCH Incorporated, Kluwer Law International, ftwilliam.com, and MediRegs names. They are regarded as exceptional and trusted resources for general legal and practice-specific knowledge, compliance and risk management, dynamic workflow solutions, and expert commentary.

To Larry C. Hall, Ph.D., for showing me the joys of an academic life.
— *M.A.H.*

To the memory of Prof. Herman I. Orentlicher, for his commitment to "neutral skepticism," rigorous standards, and, above all, decency.
— *D.O.*

To my partner, Holly, and our daughter, Anna, and to my parents, for their encouragement.
— *M.A.B.*

To Celia and Sebastian, who have brought so much joy and meaning to my life.
— *N.B.*

To Jesse. You and I and no one else.
— *I.G.C.*

To Bill Curran, for his guiding light.

Summary of Contents

Contents

2

■

The Treatment Relationship: Formation and Termination   *55*

3

■

The Treatment Relationship: Confidentiality, Consent, and Conflicts of Interest

4

■

Preface

The Content and Organization of This Book

This book contains the materials from *Health Care Law and Ethics* (9th ed. 2018) that are focused on medical liability and treatment relationships. As the larger book passes its half-century anniversary, we pause to reflect on the remarkable metamorphosis of health care law from a subspecialty of tort law, to a mushrooming academic and practice field whose tentacles reach into myriad scholarly disciplines and areas of substantive law. This book's eight prior editions reflect important stages in this evolutionary growth. Health care law originated as a separate field of professional practice and academic inquiry during the 1960s, when this book was first published. Under the somewhat grandiose label of "medical jurisprudence," the primary focus at first was on medical proof in all kinds of criminal and civil litigation, on medical malpractice actions against physicians, and on public health regulation. The principal concern was how traditional bodies of legal doctrine and practice—such as criminal, tort, and evidence law—should apply in medical settings.

During the 1970s, bioethics became a major additional area of concern as a consequence of the right to die movement spawned by the *Quinlan* case, and the focus on individual autonomy contained in the informed consent doctrine and the landmark decision on reproductive decisionmaking in Roe v. Wade. Law courses during this and earlier periods were taught under the heading of "law and medicine."

In the 1980s, economic and regulatory topics formed the third component of health care law, as exemplified by the increasing application of antitrust laws to the health care industry and the growing body of legal disputes under Medicare and Medicaid. This newer dimension accelerated its growth into the 1990s with the spread of HMOs and other managed care organizations, which propelled various corporate and contractual restructurings. These newer topics found their way into courses described as "health law."

New developments present continuing challenges to each of these areas of health care law and ethics. Biotechnology, consumer-driven health care, and bioterrorism are examples of emerging issues that receive increased attention in the previous edition. Currently, there is an explosion of interest in health care public policy, coinciding with Affordable Care Act, whose importance reverberates throughout the field yet whose survival remains uncertain.

This path of development has resulted in an academic discipline defined more by an accretion of topics drawn from historical events than by a systematic conceptual organization of issues. Each of the four major branches—malpractice, bioethics, public health, and financing/regulation—stands apart from the others and is thought to be dominated by a distinct theme. The principal concern of malpractice law is quality of care; bioethics is concerned with individual autonomy; public health poses the rights of patients against the state; and the primary focus of financing and regulatory law is access to care and the cost of care. As a consequence, health care law has yet to become a truly integrated and cohesive discipline.[1] It is too much the creature of history and not of systematic and conceptual organization.

Our major ambition in this book is to improve this state of disarray. This field has reached a stage of maturity that calls for stepping back and rethinking how all of its parts best fit together as a conceptual whole. In our view that conceptual whole is best organized according to the fundamental structural relationships that give rise to health care law. These relationships are:

1. The patient/physician relationship, which encompasses the duty to treat, confidentiality, informed consent, and malpractice
2. State oversight of doctors and patients, which encompasses the right to die, reproductive rights, physician licensure, and public health
3. The institutions that surround the treatment relationship, encompassing public and private insurance, hospitals and HMOs, and more complex transactions and organizational forms

We develop the traditional themes of quality, ethics, access, and cost throughout each of these three divisions. We also address cutting-edge and controversial topics such as health care reform, genetics, managed care, and rationing, but not as discrete topics; instead, we integrate these developments within a more permanent,

---

1. This disarray is reflected by the ongoing confusion over competing names for the field. Although "law and medicine" and "health care law" appear to signify the same topic, the first term is understood to mean older style malpractice subject matter, and the second term is used to refer to newer economic and regulatory issues. Paradoxically, whereas "health care law" and "health law" might be thought to signify somewhat different fields—the latter is not restricted to medical treatment and therefore encompassing public health issues—in fact they are taken to mean the same thing.

overarching organizational structure, which is capable of absorbing unanticipated new developments as they occur.

In deciding which topics to present in each section and in what depth, our basic guide has been to focus on the essential attributes of the medical enterprise that make it uniquely important or difficult in the legal domain. Health care law is about the delivery of an extremely important, very expensive, and highly specialized professional service. If it were otherwise, this book would likely not exist. Some lawyers and scholars maintain that there is no unifying concept or set of ideas for health care law; instead, it is merely a disparate collection of legal doctrines and public policy responses, connected only by the happenstance that they involve doctors and hospitals in some way—much as if one had a course on the law of green things or the law of Tuesdays. It would be far more satisfying to find one or more organizing principles that explain not only what makes the disparate parts of health care law cohere, but also why that coherence distinguishes health care law from other bodies of integrated legal thought and professional practice.

We believe those organizing principles can, in part, be found in the phenomenology of what it is to be ill and to be a healer of illness. These two human realities are permanent and essential features that distinguish this field from all other commercial and social arenas. They permeate all parts of health care law, giving it its distinctive quality and altering how generic legal doctrine and conventional theories of government respond to its problems and issues. Health care law might still be worth studying even without these unique attributes of medical encounters, but it is much more engaging and coherent because of them. It is these attributes that give rise to an interrelated set of principles that justify classifying health care law as a coherent and integrated academic and professional discipline. Elaborating this perspective, see Mark A. Hall, The History and Future of Health Care Law: An Essentialist View, 41 Wake Forest L. Rev. 347 (2006).[2]

Accordingly, we stress the essential attributes of medical encounters throughout these materials by incorporating insights from other academic disciplines and

---

2. For additional discussion of the overall content of health care law and approaches to teaching and understanding it, see Clark Havighurst, American Health Care and the Law: We Need to Talk!, 19(4) Health Aff. 84 (July 2000); William M. Sage, Relational Duties, Regulatory Duties, and the Widening Gap Between Individual Health Law and Collective Health Policy, 96 Geo. L.J. 497-522 (2008); Theodore W. Ruger, Health Law's Coherence Anxiety, 96 Geo. L.J. 625-648 (2008); Wendy Mariner, Toward an Architecture of Health Law, 35 Am. J.L. & Med. 67 (2009); M. Gregg Bloche, the Emergent Logic of Health Law, 82 S. Cal. L. Rev. 389-480 (2009); Andrew Fichter, The Law of Doctoring: A Study of the Codification of Medical Professionalism, 19 Health Matrix 317-385 (2009); Sandra Johnson, Regulating Physician Behavior: Taking Doctors' "Bad Law" Claims Seriously, 53 St. Louis U. L.J. 973 (2009); Maxwell Mehlman, Can Law Save Medicine?, 36 J. Leg. Med. 121 (2015); Teaching Health Law, J.L. Med. & Ethics (recurring column); Symposium, Teaching Health Law , 61 St. Louis U. L.J. 371 (2017); Symposium, Jurisprudence and the Body, 63 Syracuse L. Rev. 327 (2013) Symposium, 19 Ann. Health L. 1 (2010); Symposium, Patient-Centered Law and Ethics, 45 Wake Forest L. Rev. 1429 (2010); Symposium, Rethinking Health Law, 41 Wake Forest L. Rev. 341 (2006); Symposium, The Field of Health Law: Its Past and Future, 14 Health Matrix 1 (2004); William J. Curran, Titles in the Medicolegal Field: A Proposal for Reform, 1 Am. J.L. & Med. 1 (1975).

theoretical perspectives. Behavioral disciplines such as psychology, sociology, and anthropology help to illuminate the nature of medical knowledge and the lived experience of illness, dependency, and trust as they occur in real-life medical encounters. Findings from health services research published in the health policy literature create a stronger empirical and theoretical base for exploring health care law, one that better exposes its broad social impact. Analytical disciplines, such as economics and moral and political theory, create the foundation for understanding developments in financing, regulation, and bioethics. And, the perspectives of feminist, communitarian, and critical race theory demonstrate the limitations of conventional analytical models and help us understand how health care law must evolve to accommodate viewpoints and concerns that have been excluded in the past.

The 1992 death of Bill Curran, the original author of this casebook, left us with a considerable burden to shoulder. Although Prof. Curran was involved in the conceptual reorganization of these materials, he was unable to contribute to their selection and editing. Still, his presence is felt in every part of these materials through the inspiration of his mentoring, his friendship, and his vast body of work.

We intend that this book will continue to serve as both a teaching tool and an ongoing resource for conducting research in health care law. To that end, we provide substantial bibliographic notes in each section. Also, we have created a dedicated Web site to serve this book: www.health-law.org. It extends the book's content with interesting background materials, updates of important events since publication, additional relevant topics that were excluded due to space constraints, and links to other resources on the internet.

The following is a bibliography of resources and readings that relate to research in health care law generally. Additional bibliographic references can be found at page 294, and on the casebook Web site.

Treatises and Texts: Barry Furrow et al., Health Law (2d ed. 2001); Mark A. Hall, David Orentlicher, and Ira Mark Ellman, Health Care Law and Ethics in a Nutshell (3d ed. 2011); Eleanor Kinney, Administrative Law of Health care in a Nutshell (2016); Hooper, Lundy & Bookman, Treatise on Health Care Law; John H. Robinson, Roberta M. Berry & Kevin McDonnell, eds., A Health Law Reader: An Interdisciplinary Approach (1999); World Health Organization, International Digest of Health Legislation.

Health Care Law Journals: American Journal of Law and Medicine (Boston Univ.); Annals of Health Law (Loyola-Chicago); DePaul Journal of Health Care Law; Food, Drug and Cosmetic Law Journal; Health Law & Policy Abstracts and Public Health Law Abstracts (SSRN online journals); Health Matrix (Case Western Univ.); Houston Journal of Health Law & Policy; Indiana Health Law Review (Indiana Univ.-Indianapolis); Journal of Contemporary Health Law and Policy (Catholic Univ.); Journal of Health & Biomedical Law (Suffolk), Journal of Health and Life Sciences Law (St. Louis Univ., AHLA); Journal of Health Care Law & Policy (Univ. of Maryland); Journal of Law and Health (Cleveland-Marshall); Journal of Law, Medicine and Ethics (ASLME); Journal of Legal Medicine (So. Illinois Univ.); Medical Trial Technique Quarterly; Journal of Medicine and Law; St. Louis Univ. Law Journal (recurring symposia); Seton Hall Law Review (same); Quinnipiac Health Law Journal; Whittier Law Review; Yale Journal of Health Policy, Law and Ethics.

Leading Medical, Industry, and Health Policy Journals: American Journal of Public Health; American Medical News (AMA); Health Affairs (published by Project Hope); Health Care Financing and Delivery (SSRN online journal), Medicare & Medicaid Research Review (DHHS/CMS); Health Economics, Policy and Law (Cambridge Press); Health Services Research; Inquiry (published by Excellus, a Blue Cross plan in Rochester, NY); Hospitals and Health Networks (AHA); Journal of the American Medical Association; Journal of Health Politics, Policy and Law; Medical Care; Milbank Quarterly; Modern Healthcare; New England Journal of Medicine.

Health Law Societies, Digests, and Newsletters: ABA Section on Health Law (newsletter and journal); American College of Legal Medicine (journal); American Society of Law, Medicine, and Ethics (two journals); BNA Health Law Reporter (weekly); American Health Lawyers Association (monthly digest and newsletter, bimonthly journal).

Acknowledgments

This manuscript could not have been prepared without the diligent help of those students and staff who assisted us over the past few years (Hailey Cleek, Travis Edwards, Victoria Hall-Palerm, Dorothy Hector, Colin Herd, Amy Lai, John Minkley, Robert Petito, Lena Rieke, Michael Shapiro, and Jacob Steiner), and without the superhuman patience of our families (who, curiously, wish to remain anonymous). We also thank the authors and publishers who granted permission to use each of the excerpts of copyrighted material in these readings.

Baker, Tom, The Medical Malpractice Myth (2005). Copyright © 2005 by the University of Chicago Press. Reprinted by permission. All rights reserved.

Beauchamp, Tom L., and James F. Childress, "The Right to a Decent Minimum of Health Care" in Principles of Biomedical Ethics (4th ed. 1994). Copyright © 1994 by Oxford University Press. Reprinted by permission. All rights reserved.

Bennett, Amanda, "End-of-life Warning at $618,616 Makes Me Wonder Was It Worth It." Bloomberg News (March 4, 2010). Copyright © 2010 by Bloomberg BNA. Reprinted by permission. All rights reserved.

Blumenthal, David, "Making Medical Errors into 'Medical Treasures.'" JAMA 272, no. 23 (1994): 1867-68. Copyright © 1994 by the American Medical Association. Reprinted by permission. All rights reserved.

Bobinski, Mary Anne, "Autonomy and Privacy: Protecting Patients from Their Physicians." University of Pittsburgh Law Review 55 (1993): 291. Copyright © 1993 by the University of Pittsburgh Law Review. Reprinted by permission. All rights reserved.

Buckman, Robert, and Karl Sabbagh, Magic or Medicine? An Investigation of Healing and Healers (1995). Copyright © 1995 by Prometheus Books. Reprinted by permission. All rights reserved.

Butterfield, Bruce, and Gerard O'Neill, "Regulatory System in Shambles; Negligent Doctors Stay on Job." Boston Globe (October 2, 1994). Copyright © 1994 by the Boston Globe. Reprinted by permission. All rights reserved.

Eddy, David M., Clinical Decision Making: From Theory to Practice (1996). Copyright © 1996 by Jones & Bartlett. Reprinted by permission. All rights reserved.

Mark Hall
David Orentlicher
Mary Anne Bobinski
Nick Bagley
Glenn Cohen

April 2018

1

■

Introduction

These readings introduce background information and overarching perspectives that are important for understanding the legal issues developed throughout this book. All of us have had some exposure to the world of medicine, but few law students have reason to understand the intricacies of this financing and delivery system and how it has developed. This understanding is essential in a course that focuses on the full range of legal and public policy issues pertaining to the delivery and payment for medical care. Those issues have naturally taken shape according to the structural components and historical growth of the health care sector and its various institutions.

As you read through what sometimes seems to be an alphabet soup of actors, institutions, and acronyms, rather than memorizing all the details, try to construct a coherent story line of how the health care sector took shape over time and how its various pieces interconnect at present. You don't need to master all the details now, as they will reemerge throughout the course, but it will be easier to remember them at the end if you have an initial framework to which you can attach them.

A. THE NATURE OF MEDICAL PRACTICE

We begin with a description of the human condition of illness and the professional practice of medicine, since these are what distinguish health care law from other fields of legal study. It is essential throughout this book to have some appreciation of the impact that illness has on how people function, the intricacies of medical decisionmaking, and how doctors and patients interact. To focus your thoughts on these issues, reflect on your own experiences with medical care, and consider the following list of popular "misconceptions" (developed by Alain Enthoven). What observations and evidence emerge from these readings to rebut or qualify each of these commonly held notions?

1. The doctor should be able to know what conditions the patient has, to answer the patient's questions precisely, and to prescribe the right treatment. If the doctor doesn't, that is incompetence or even malpractice.
2. For each medical condition, there is a "best" treatment. It is up to the doctor to know about that treatment and to use it. Anything else is unnecessary surgery, waste, fraud, or underservice.
3. Medicine is an exact science. Unlike 50 or 100 years ago, there is now a firm scientific base for what the doctor does. Standard treatments are supported by scientific proof of efficiency.
4. Medical care consists of standard products that can be described precisely and measured meaningfully in standard units such as "inpatient days," "outpatient visits," or "doctor office visits."
5. Much of medical care is a matter of life and death or serious pain or disability.
6. More medical care is better than less care.
7. People have no control over the timing of their need for medical care. Whatever care is needed is needed right away.

1. Patients, Doctors, and Hospitals

■ HEALTH CARE PAST AND PRESENT
Robert Rhodes
Health Care Politics, Policy, and Distributive Justice:
The Ironic Triumph*

Death before the nineteenth century was an ever-looming presence in our ancestors' thoughts and a frequent visitor to their families. They feared it and had little control over it. Sudden death was as central to attitudes prior to the twentieth century as the cemetery was to every village and town. . . .

Resignation and fatalism toward natural occurrences characterize preindustrial societies, just as a sense of self-direction and control characterize modern society. . . . Modern societies have faith that they can control the future. A futurist orientation allows for savings, capital formation, long periods of education, and lifestyles that deny instant gratification for future health. Preindustrial conditions do not reward such faith. . . . Uncontrollable natural or supernatural forces took away life, and one needed to reconcile one's fate to the four horsemen of the apocalypse: disease, famine, pestilence, and drought.

The twentieth century represents perhaps the clearest triumph of science over fatalism. . . . The modern hospital, the professionalism of physicians and nurses, and effective pharmaceuticals have dramatically altered mortality rates and improved the quality of life in postindustrial states.

For those entering a hospital prior to 1900, the probability of treatment help-ing, rather than harming, would be less than fifty-fifty, and the odds would be con-siderably poorer prior to 1870. Today, we identify hospitals as technologic citadels of sophisticated medical practice. But their preindustrial origins were as religious and charitable institutions for the hopelessly sick and poor. They were places to comfort the indigent dying.

For the first three quarters of the nineteenth century, medical personnel were not in charge of hospitals. . . . In the main, hospitals at that time were places for the homeless poor and insane to die. The affluent classes were treated at home. For a variety of reasons, however, hospitals became central to medical practice and edu-cation between 1870 and 1910.[1] . . .

[T]he development of the medical profession parallels particular develop-ments of the hospital. This is especially true of surgery, which enjoyed a dramatic increase of prestige and precision during this time. Technological advances played a major role in changing surgery. Before painkilling drugs, surgical methods in the first half of the nineteenth century depended upon powerful and swift physicians whose craft and tools were closer to the corner butcher. Mortality rates of about 40 percent followed amputation.

Three developments altered the brutality and mortality rates and allowed abdominal surgery, which was rarely performed prior to 1890. Dentist William Morton's demonstration of ether at Massachusetts General Hospital in 1846 ush-ered in a means of eliminating pain and allowed more careful and delicate sur-gery. Joseph Lister's discovery of antisepsis in 1867 gradually led to new procedures during surgery to prevent infection. However, antisepsis was poorly understood. Lister's technique was based on the use of carbolic acid spray, but his methods were adopted only over a long period of time. Fatal infections continued even after using the spray because antiseptic procedures were not followed carefully until after 1880. Soon, sterile procedures were properly followed and surgery rapidly expanded. Finally, the development of the X-ray in 1895, along with other diagnostic tools, opened the way for abdominal surgery for appendicitis, gallbladder, and stomach ulcers. Thoracic surgery and surgery of the nervous and cardiovascular systems developed in the early 1900s.

TRIUMPH AND TRAGEDY

By 1950, the cliché a "medical miracle" had rich meaning. Infant mortality rates in the United States were fewer than 15 per 100,000 births, down from 300 or so per 100,000 at the turn of the century. Pneumonia, once whispered by medi-cal staff who witnessed the suffering of the dying to be the "old man's relief," now was easily controlled with penicillin. Infectious diseases in particular dramatically declined in the first half of the twentieth century. Improvement in health was a triumph of modernity, and part of that triumph was a consequence of modern

1. Paul Starr, The Social Transformation of American Medicine 151 (1982).

medicine. There is, however, much debate about the weight of medicine's contribution, compared to other modern factors. . . .

Our dramatic advances in health are also related to improved nutrition, lifestyle, and education, as well as to medical advancements. The literature of health care points, in particular, to . . . proper diet, minimal tension, absence of smoking or heavy drinking, daily exercise, and a life-style that provides low-risk factors for accidents. Advances in health and longevity are more closely tied to higher income, better diets, and especially greater education than to advances in medicine. . . .

Yet, American perception of well-being is closely identified with medicine. Paradoxically, much of the public's present disenchantment with medicine is the consequence of this identification. Modern medicine has advanced to the frontiers of preserving life, but only by increasingly more expensive therapies and diagnoses to preserve life "on its margins." That is, additional expenditures and efforts to treat disease produce diminishing results in proportion to the effort. We are just beginning to learn that our scientific capacity to triumph over illness, physical anomalies, and death, on many occasions with medical miracles, brings with it a special brand of tragedy.

We have become totally modern. No more can we explain death and suffering as a consequence of fate. It is our medicine, or lack of it, that denies death and suffering. We know we must choose who receives scarce resources and who does not. No longer can we attribute to fate or to God the responsibility for making life-and-death decisions. Yet, these life-and-death decisions involve very expensive procedures and technologies and often contribute only marginally to extending life. Examples are well known and regularly make front-page newspaper drama: organ transplants, aggressive treatment of terminal patients, neonates under 750 grams, or long-term comatose patients.

These new choices challenge our basic values and frequently produce conflict. . . . Conflict is father to politics and law, and politics determines who gets what, when, and how. Conflict also forces moral reassessment of traditional attitudes and postures, including the justice question: "Who *should* get what, when and how."

How do we distribute health care? How should we? How does political power within the present economic system determine the distribution of health care? These questions obviously spill over the boundaries of economics, politics, sociology, law, medicine, history, and philosophy. In particular, looming over the politics of health care is a sense of the tragic, as well as the majestic. Tragedy points to human endeavors that are virtuous and honorable, yet carry the seeds of their own downfall. Our efforts to lessen the suffering and lengthen the lives of Americans through accessible, affordable, quality health care represent the best of our traditions and have been, on balance, an American success story. Sometimes we fall short in that effort because some group is unreasonably left behind in the political shuffle. The [45] million Americans who [have] no health coverage represent[] such a group. At other times, our very success leads to exasperating dilemmas of bioethics and distributive justice that would cross the eyes of a Solomon. Our dilemma over public financing for costly organ transplants at the expense of other badly needed programs or continued aggressive treatment of comatose or terminally ill loved ones are poignant, modern examples. It is here where triumph merges with tragedy.

■ END-OF-LIFE WARNING AT $618,616 MAKES ME
WONDER WAS IT WORTH IT
Amanda Bennett
Bloomberg News, Mar. 4, 2010*

It was some time after midnight on Dec. 8, 2007, when [the doctor] told me my husband might not live till morning. The kidney cancer that had metastasized almost six years earlier was growing in his lungs. He was in intensive care at the Hospital of the University of Pennsylvania in Philadelphia, and had begun to spit blood.

Terence Bryan Foley, 67 years old, my husband of 20 years, father of our two teenagers, a Chinese historian who earned his Ph.D. in his 60s, a man who played more than 15 musical instruments and spoke six languages, a San Francisco cable car conductor and sports photographer, an expert on dairy cattle and swine nutrition, film noir and Dixieland jazz, was confused. He knew his name, but not the year. He wanted a Coke.

Should Terence begin to hemorrhage, the doctor asked, what should he do? This was our third end-of-life warning in seven years. We fought off the others. Perhaps we could dodge this one too. [Terence's oncologist] and I both believed that a new medicine he had just begun to take would buy him more time. Keep him alive if you can, I said. Let's see what the drug, Pfizer Inc.'s Sutent, can do.

Terence died six days later, on Friday, Dec. 14, 2007. What I couldn't know then was that the thinking behind my request—along with hundreds of decisions we made over seven years—was a window on the impossible calculus at the core of the U.S. health-care debate.

EXPENSIVE LAST CHANCES

Terence and I didn't have to think about money, allocation of medical resources, the struggles of [millions of] uninsured Americans, or the impact on corporate bottom lines. Backed by medical insurance provided by my employers, we were able to fight his cancer with a series of expensive last chances like the one I asked for that night.

How expensive? The bills totaled $618,616, almost two-thirds of it for the final 24 months, much of it for treatments that no one can say for sure helped extend his life. In just the last four days of trying to keep him alive—two in intensive care, two in a cancer ward—our insurance was charged $43,711 for doctors, medicines, monitors, X-rays and scans. Two years later, the only thing I know for certain that money bought was confirmation that he was dying.

Some of the drugs probably did Terence no good at all. At least one helped fewer than 10 percent of all those who took it. Pharmaceutical companies and insurers will have to sort out the economics of treatments that end up working for only a small subset. Should everyone have the right to try them? Terence and I answered yes. Each drug potentially added life. Yet that too led me to a question I can't answer. When is it time to quit?

---

*Excerpted with permission. For a fuller account, see Amanda Bennett, The Cost of Hope (2012).

SCIENCE, EMOTION, COSTS

Congress didn't touch the issue in [the Patient Protection and Affordable Care Act of 2010]. The mere hint of somehow limiting the ability to choose care as aggressively as Terence and I did, created a whirlwind of accusations that the ill, aged and infirm would be forced before government "death panels."

As the debate heated up, I remembered the fat sheaf of insurance statements that arrived after Terence's death . . . [from] six hospitals, four insurers, Medicare, three oncologists, and a surgeon. Those papers tell the story of a system filled with people doing their best. And they raise complex questions about a health-care system that consumes 17 percent of the economy. As I leafed through the stack of documents, it was easy to see why 31 percent of the money spent on health care goes to paperwork and administration. . . .

The documents revealed an economic system in which the sellers don't set and the buyers don't know the prices. The University of Pennsylvania hospital charged more than 12 times what Medicare at the time reimbursed for a chest scan. One insurer paid a hospital for 80 percent of the $3,232 price of a scan, while another covered 24 percent. Insurance companies negotiated their own rates, and neither my employers nor I paid the difference between the sticker and discounted prices.

'IT'S COMPLETELY INSANE'

In this economic system, prices of goods and services bear little relation to the demand for them or their cost to make — or, as it turns out, the good or harm they do. "No other nation would allow a health system to be run the way we do it. It's completely insane," said Uwe E. Reinhardt, a political economy professor at Princeton University. . . . Taking it all into account, the data showed we had made a bargain that hardly any economist looking solely at the numbers would say made sense. Why did we do it?

I was one big reason. Not me alone, of course. The medical system has a strong bias toward action. My husband, too, was unusual . . . in his passionate willingness to endure discomfort for a chance to see his daughter grow from a child to a young woman, and his son graduate from high school.

After Terence died, [his doctor] drew me a picture of a bell curve, showing the range of survival times for kidney cancer sufferers. Terence was way off in the tail on the right-hand side, an indication he had indeed beaten the odds. An explosion of research had made it possible to extend lives for years — enough to keep our quest from having been total madness.

Terence used to tell a story, almost certainly apocryphal, about his Uncle Bob. Climbing aboard a landing craft before the invasion of Normandy, so the story went, Bob's sergeant told the men that by the end of the day, nine out of 10 would be dead. Said Bob, on hearing that news: "Each one of us looked around and felt so sorry for those other nine poor sonsabitches."

For me, it was about pushing the bell curve. Knowing that if there was something to be done, we couldn't not do it. Believing beyond logic that we were going to escape the fate of those other poor sonsabitches. It is very hard to put a price on that kind of hope.

PRICING HOPE

We found the cancer by accident [a decade ago]. . . . Within a month, Terence was in surgery, and [another doctor] had taken out the diseased kidney. . . . "We got it all," he said. Terence was visibly moved. "Thank you for saving my life," he said. . . . The statistics looked good. By the traditional method of staging—a 7-centimeter tumor with no sign of having spread—Terence had an 85 percent chance of surviving five years.

The bills from Regence Blue Cross & Blue Shield of Oregon show the operation was relatively inexpensive, too, just over $25,000, or only about 4 percent of the total [eventually] charged to keep Terence alive. Insurance paid a discounted $14,084. Terence and I paid $209.87. The lab soon cast a chill on our optimism.

Terence had "collecting duct" cancer, the rarest and most aggressive form. . . . If that was correct, Terence had almost no chance of making it to the end of the year. . . . "Watchful waiting" was the recommended path. Waiting for him to die was what we feared. He didn't die. He got better. We didn't know why. We tried not to think about it. . . .

Then, on May 6, 2002, I was at work when [our son] Terry called, panic in his voice. "Mom, come home. Dad is very sick." . . . His father was in bed, his face flaming with fever, shaking with chills under a pile of blankets. He could barely speak. "The cancer is in my lungs," he said. "I've got six to nine months left."

A scan had spotted the cancer's spread. Not wanting to worry us, Terence had secretly begun taking Interleukin-2. If he recovered, he figured, we would never know how close he came; if he died, he would have spared us months of anguish. . . . What he didn't reckon on was that the drug would make him violently ill. But it was the only possible therapy at that time. Injections of the protein—at $735 a dose—were intended to stimulate the immune response to help fight off the cancer's invasion. The overall response rate was about 10 percent. For most, it did nothing.

That evening, for the one and only time, I felt pure terror. I spent the night awake in our dark living room. . . . Knowing the long odds, [the oncologist later] told me he had prescribed Interleukin-2 simply because it was all there was. Terence stopped taking it after just a few weeks, unable to stand the side effects.

I shook off my fear and plunged into the Internet. If there was something out there that could save him, I was going to find it. One colleague had been snatched from dying of AIDS by a chance introduction to a doctor who prescribed an experimental antiviral cocktail. Another had beaten leukemia with a cutting-edge bone marrow transplant. We could defeat this, too. . . .

The entire medical bill for seven years . . . was steeply discounted. The $618,616 became $254,176 when the insurers paid their share and imposed their discounts. Of that, Terence and I were responsible for $9,468—less than 4 percent. . . .

[A]s summer in Philadelphia turned to autumn. Terence resumed [another treatment which he had ceased earlier due to side effects]. Because he wasn't in a clinical trial, our insurance company was billed: $27,360 a dose, for four treatments. [But that also failed to stop the cancer's spread.] . . .

READING THEIR GOODBYES

[A few months later] I signed the papers transferring Terence to hospice. The next day, Tuesday, the hospital staff took away the machines and the monitors. The oncologists and radiologists and lab technicians disappeared. Another group of people — hospice nurses, social workers, chaplains and counselors for me and the children — began to arrive one by one, as the focus shifted from treating Terence to easing our transition.

For the next three days, with Terence in the same hospital bed, we spent $14,022 on [pain and anxiety medications], and on monitoring for him and counseling for a different kind of pain management for the children and me. The cost was less than a third of the previous four days' $43,711.

Terence drifted into a coma on Tuesday. I e-mailed his friends and read their goodbyes aloud, hoping he could hear and understand. I slept in a chair. At about 2:30 A.M. Friday, a noise in the hall startled me. I awoke just in time to hold his hand as he died. They gave me back his wedding ring the next day.

Looking back, memories of my zeal to treat are tinged with sadness. Since I didn't believe my husband was going to die, I never let us have the chance to say goodbye. . . .

Would I do it all again? Absolutely. I couldn't not do it again. But I think had he known the costs, Terence would have fought the insurers spending enough, at roughly $200,000, to vaccinate almost a quarter-million children in developing countries. That's how he would have thought about it. . . .

Did we help Terence? Or harm him? . . . [His doctor] and I looked at the numbers. The average patient in his [clinical] trial got 14 months of extra life. Without any treatment, [his doctor] estimates that for someone at Terence's stage of the disease it was three months. Terence got 17 months — still within the realm of chance, but way, way up on the bell curve.

There's another bell curve that starts about where Terence's left off. It charts the survival times for patients treated not just with [the dugs Terence received] but also Novartis's Afinitor and GlaxoSmithKline's Votrient, made available within the past three years. Doctors and patients now are doing what we dreamed of, staggering one drug after another and buying years more of life. . . .

[Terence's] 17 months included an afternoon looking down at the Mediterranean with Georgia from a sunny balcony in Southern Spain. Moving Terry into his college dorm. Celebrating our 20th anniversary with a carriage ride through Philadelphia's cobbled streets. A final Thanksgiving game of charades with cousins Margo and Glenn.

And one last chance for Terence to pave the way for all those other poor sonsabitches.

■DOCTORS, PATIENTS, AND HEALTH INSURANCE: THE ORGANIZATION AND FINANCING OF MEDICAL CARE
Herman Miles Somers & Anne Ramsay Somers
1961

. . . The popular conception of the doctor-patient relationship is a mixture of fact and fancy. Until World War II the general practitioner family doctor was still in the majority. The one-to-one relationship of a personally chosen physician — where economic and other factors permitted any choice — with his patient was the most common form of medical practice. In big cities, the doctor had an office, usually mahogany and leather, sparsely equipped with simple diagnostic aids, a few surgical tools, and some antiseptic drugs. But, especially in rural areas and suburbs, he was more often found in the homes of his patients doing his rounds, working àt the bedside of the sick and injured. His black bag held almost all his equipment. His records were kept partly in a small notebook, mostly in his mind and heart. He appeared indefatigable, compassionate, and available wherever and whenever needed. . . .

This doctor of the past has been idealized in story, picture, and legend. . . . Despite its apparent anachronisms, the picture still appeals to people's sentiments—even to those fully aware of its use as a public relations device. It has the warmth and intimate concern that no hypodermic needle—no complex of steel and tubing—can replace, however effective they may be. Although medical miracles are now performed successfully between strangers, doctors and patients both believe that the absence of continuity, personal concern, and individual attention are detrimental to the best medical care. This is not without foundation.

The origin of the "traditional" doctor-patient relationship reaches deep into the past. From the beginning of medical history, the practicing physician has been part priest, part technician, part personal or family counselor. In early days, when medicine had very little in the way of scientific knowledge to rely on, it was inevitable that the subjective priestly element should be dominant. . . .

In modern times medicine has become more scientific. But the traditional reliance on mystical forces and a highly authoritarian doctor-patient relationship persists to a degree unknown in other contemporary human relations. . . . The relationship of citizen and state, of employer and employee, of teacher and pupil, parent and child, even of husband and wife, have undergone profound and acknowledged changes as a result of the technological and socio-economic trends of the past few centuries. But there is no general acknowledgment or acceptance of the significant change that has, in fact, been taking place in the doctor-patient relationship. Of the manifold and complex reasons, only a few of the more important can be noted here.

First and basic is the persistence—in spite of scientific progress—of large elements of uncertainty and fear regarding illness and medical care which are conducive to continued reliance on hope, faith, confidence and other subjective factors on the part of both doctor and patient. "Honor thy physician because of the need thou hast of him," so said apocryphal Ecclesiastes to the Hebrews thousands of years ago. And still, today, patients yearn to have confidence in their doctors, to idealize them, to endow them with superhuman powers. Talcott Parsons, the Harvard sociologist, reconciles the use of such subjective factors—the use of "modern magic"—with the scientific basis of modern medicine by calling it a "functional bias."

> The basic function of magic is to bolster the self-confidence of actors in situations where energy and skill *do* make a difference but where, because of uncertainty factors, outcomes cannot be guaranteed. This fits the situation of the doctor, but in addition on the side of the patient it may be argued the *belief* in the possibility of recovery is an important factor in it. If from purely a technical point of view both the individual doctor and the general tradition are optimistically biased it ought to help. . . . Of course, this argument must not be pressed too far.

As the boundaries of medical ignorance and uncertainty are pushed back, one would expect this resort to supra-scientific factors to decline, and, indeed, it has in the case of bacterial and other diseases where the cause and cure are clearly established. But the reduced role of subjective factors in the treatment of specific cases has been more than offset by an increasing interest in the role of the emotions in illness. A widespread increase in psychotherapy and psychosomatic medicine has renewed the emphasis on a personal doctor and a personal doctor-patient relationship of a type that permits knowledge of the "whole [person]." . . .

Moreover, it is now widely believed that illness, *per se*, tends to create—even in the most intellectual of patients—an attitude of dependence, of "regression" to helplessness, and perhaps to childlike behavior. . . . In this state, confidence in the authority and benevolence of the doctor, as well as in his scientific knowledge and technical skill—the now-familiar "father-image"—is generally desired and often desirable.

Finally, there is the impenetrable mystery of death. The physician's relation to this event—however helpless he in fact may be—has endowed him, in the eyes of centuries of patients, with an aura of the mystery. To the extent that the physician identifies himself with this priestly role and takes on himself the burden associated therewith, or at least appears to do so through the gravity of his personal demeanor and behavior, his supra-scientific role continues to be respected and perpetuated, reinforcing in the eyes of individual patients and society at large his status as a dispenser of increasingly scientific medicine.

■ COMPETING SOLUTIONS: AMERICAN HEALTH CARE PROPOSALS AND INTERNATIONAL EXPERIENCE
Joseph White
1995

America's systems for delivering and paying for medical care are notably more complex than those of most other countries. Many doctors work in more than one hospital, making governance of medical staffs difficult; specialists are harder to coordinate because there are more of them; and the proliferation of forms of managed care means rapid change in patterns of gatekeeping and referral.

PHYSICIANS

American doctors go through extensive training to work long hours for high pay. The typical medical school program requires, after four years of college, four more years of "undergraduate" medical education. During the final two years, students receive some clinical training. Virtually all graduates then must complete some graduate medical education in order to be licensed to practice medicine. This education is obtained in residency programs, mainly in hospitals affiliated with medical schools. Normally only one year of residency (as an intern) is needed for licensure, but up to eight years (for neurosurgeons) may be required for certification as a specialist.

. . . Given the length of their training and the size of their debts, it is understandable that most physicians feel entitled to incomes that are much higher than those of most other Americans. . . . [The median physician salary is about $200,000, roughly five times that of the average American worker. The range across specialties is broad. Pediatricians and general practitioners typically earn around $175,000, common medical specialists (cardiology, dermatology, anesthesiology) are in the $250,000-$350,000 range, while heart surgeons and brain surgeons can earn well over $500,000. Some doctors earn substantially more from entrepreneurial activities such as medical patents and investments in various health care organizations.]

An unusually high proportion of American doctors are trained to specialize. Fewer than 10 percent of American doctors [call] themselves general practitioners (GPs), the standard term for primary care physicians. But because a specialist such as a family practitioner, internist, pediatrician, or obstetrician-gynecologist may be a person's regular physician, between 33 and 40 percent of physicians (depending on who is counting) are mainly primary care providers. [Specialists who receive several years of extra training and pass additional exams are designated as "Board Certified," meaning that they comply with voluntary, private standards set by the American Specialty Boards, which operate under the auspices of the AMA. At one time, board certification was relatively rare, but now the vast majority of new doctors obtain certification. About two dozen boards now exist, covering not only standard specialties but also areas of general practice such as family medicine and internal medicine.] . . .

Two-thirds of physicians practice in offices, the vast majority with admitting privileges to a hospital. Many practice in more [than one hospital] (for example, a nice suburban hospital for simple cases, and a high-tech academic medical center for difficult ones). Hospitals therefore must compete for admissions by making those physicians happy, such as by having the fanciest equipment. . . .

INSTITUTIONAL CARE

Long-term or chronic care, especially for the aged, is a complicated system on its own, and the potential expenses of long-term care are so great that it is highly unlikely that any reform will do much about it. [Therefore, the focus here is] on the costs of the current American health care system, of which one major component is hospital services for acute care.

The American supply of hospitals is dominated by private nonprofit hospitals—many owned by religious organizations. [About two-thirds] of hospital beds [are] provided by the nonprofits, 10 percent by the for-profit sector. The rest, just over a quarter of the beds, [are] in federal, state, or local facilities. It is hard to identify much difference between the behavior and efficiency of the for-profit and private nonprofits. If private institutions are more efficient, the savings go largely or entirely to investors.

Americans spend a great deal of money on hospitals: [about 40 percent] of all spending on patient care. But . . . the hospital is not as dominant a provider as it once was or still is in other countries. Hospitals and doctors tried to avoid regulation by moving care to ostensibly freestanding ambulatory care facilities. Examples include kidney dialysis units, and radiology group practices with close relations with hospitals. Some payers encouraged the shift, believing those facilities would be cheaper. . . .

Back in the traditional hospitals, the nature of care depends greatly on hospitals' relationships with doctors and medical schools, and on hospitals' catchment areas — the areas from which they get most of their patients. . . .

A suburban hospital can generally provide sophisticated care, such as cardiac bypass surgery, but it is not as likely to have clinical professors who are able to provide extremely specialized care for "interesting" cases. All hospitals want the most advanced equipment, but the academic medical centers must have it for research and training. These centers rely heavily on residents and interns for delivery of care and, most important, are likely to have a much lower-class population of patients.

Many of the [academic medical centers] are in inner cities. They are likely to have large outpatient departments to train the students (residents) and serve the local population, which feeds into the inpatient wards; the emergency room not only gets emergencies but also serves as an outpatient clinic for some of the population. All of this is the good news: If a major teaching hospital is in the inner city, then either a large and endowed institution or a state government pays for some care for the inner-city poor.

When local hospitals receive little funding for education, poor populations must frequently rely on a hospital financed by a strapped city or county budget. Such hospitals — for example, Cook County in Chicago, Boston City, and Charity in New Orleans — have interns and residents to do the work because of their relationship with a training program, but nowhere near the resources of a freestanding university hospital. All hospitals in the inner city try to convince Medicare that they deserve an extra subsidy for treating a poorer, less-insured, and often sicker population. The federal government calls these disproportionate share payments. One of the huge issues for American health care reform is what will happen to the academic medical centers and the remaining urban public hospitals if payment systems allow competing insurers to favor hospitals that are less expensive because they have lesser teaching and subsidy burdens.

Another major issue is how a bias toward specialized, high-technology medicine, created in part by how medical education is financed and how physicians are paid, is reinforced by arrangements for capital investment in American medicine. There are hardly any measures in place to prevent a "medical arms race" among hospitals that seek the most advanced technology in order to attract physicians and generate revenue. . . .

Because for years insurers would pay whatever physicians and hospitals billed, and hospitals relied on physicians to provide patients, hospitals competed for patients by having the best equipment, and insurers ended up paying for excess treatments and higher charges per treatment. Also, at one time, physicians could refer patients to any specialist they wished, and patients could go directly to a specialist without referral.

The rise of managed care and of more aggressive bargaining by insurers has change[d] this basic pattern. Insurers have become more likely to refuse to approve a given service or to insist on a lower price. Hospitals still need to attract physicians by offering the best equipment, however, so they are caught between the demands of doctors and payers. Meanwhile insurers are limiting choice of and access to specialists by building closed panels, in which a person covered by a plan either cannot use or must pay a surcharge to use any provider who is not on special contract to the plan. A patient might find that her doctor of 20 years' standing is no longer part of her insurance plan; a physician might find that many of his patients can afford referral only to three nephrologists whom he does not know. One of the key issues in reform is whether these . . . restrictions on choice of physician are necessary.

■DOCTORS, PATIENTS, AND HEALTH INSURANCE: THE ORGANIZATION AND FINANCING OF MEDICAL CARE
Herman Miles Somers & Anne Ramsay Somers
1961

[T]he conflict between [hospital] medical staff and [hospital] management has become both sharper and more open in recent years. The roots of this conflict—the basic dichotomy in hospital organization—go back to eighteenth century Britain and the establishment of the Anglo-American tradition of voluntary hospitals. There was no such dichotomy in medieval days when hospitals were operated, with little medical assistance, by monastic orders for the sick poor. There is generally no such duality in the major Continental hospitals which are usually run, with unquestioned authority, by full-time chiefs of medical services. The distinguishing feature of the Anglo-American voluntary hospital, however, has been its use by private physicians for private patients with little or no accompanying administrative or financial responsibility. . . .

Recent developments—the hospital's changing role, its increase in size, complexity, utilization, cost, and its greatly altered financial base—have intensified the inherent instability of this administrative structure. . . . Lay influences on hospital administration and policy are clearly increasing. Ultimate policy responsibility has always rested with lay trustees. Traditionally, they limited their oversight to balancing the books. With the tremendous increase in hospital costs, however, this single concern has led to increasing surveillance over the hospital's total functioning, including the organization of the medical staff. The hospital administrator, traditionally an untrained individual content to play a fairly subservient role and socially outranked by doctor and trustee alike, is being transformed into a professional with increasing self-confidence and authority. . . .

At the same time the hospital has become an indispensable workshop for the modern physician, who finds it virtually impossible to practice good medicine without hospital affiliation. The hospital is the center of his professional world, and he is acknowledged to be its key figure. Fully 40 percent of private physician income is now earned in the hospital. Naturally he wants "his" institution equipped with the latest scientific and technological facilities. But the doctor's relationship to the hospital is peculiarly ambiguous. As a rule he assumes neither administrative nor financial responsibility. Yet, in practice, his is the most powerful voice in the organization. He alone admits and discharges patients; he alone can diagnose, prescribe, and treat patients—still the chief purpose for which the hospital exists. With his high professional status, he may, in most hospitals, countermand administrative orders and defy lay authority with relative impunity. The result is the confusing duality that prevails today throughout the hospital system, public and private. . . .

It is sometimes proposed that hiring the medical staff on a salary or contract basis would increase the doctors' sense of responsibility for hospital administration and help clarify lines of accountability. It could integrate the administrative structure without restricting professional integrity. This is the general pattern in a few of the nation's best hospitals, such as the Henry Ford in Detroit and the Cleveland Clinic Hospital. Most of the profession is, however, vigorously opposed to such practice, alleging "hospital domination," "lay control," or the "corporate practice of medicine." Some hospitals have taken a middle road—employing full-time medical directors (this is frequently the practice in government hospitals) and in a few instances, full-time chiefs of medical services. This too is generally frowned on by physicians in private practice. . . .

Many hospital spokesmen, however, content themselves with pleading for physician cooperation in assuring some responsibility for hospital operations and costs. . . . But such recommendations are usually set in a purely hortatory context. It is not clear how such preachments are to influence the individual doctor. The "medical staff" of which he is a member is in most instances simply a term for the collectivity of physicians authorized to practice in a particular hospital. The staff can be as disciplinary an instrument as it chooses to be, but in most places it has chosen minimal responsibility. . . . By and large the staff still prefers not to interfere with the practices of the individual physician.

■ CLINICAL DECISION MAKING: FROM THEORY TO PRACTICE
David M. Eddy
1996

Medical practice is in the middle of a profound transition. Most physicians can remember the day when, armed with a degree, a mission, and confidence, they could set forth to heal the sick. Like Solomon, physicians could receive patients, hear their complaints, and determine the best course of action. While not every patient could be cured, everyone could be confident that whatever was done was the best possible. Most important, each physician was free, trusted, and left alone to determine what was in the best interest of each patient.

All of that is changing. . . . Now physicians must deal with second opinions, precertification, skeptical medical directors, variable coverage, outright denials, utilization review, threats of cookbook medicine, and letters out of the blue chiding that Mrs. Smith is on two incompatible drugs. Solomon did not have to call anyone to get permission for his decisions. What is going on?

What is going on is that one of the basic assumptions underlying the practice of medicine is being challenged. This assumption is not just a theory about cholesterol, antiarrhythmia, or estrogens. This assumption concerns the intellectual foundation of medical care. Simply put, the assumption is that whatever a physician decides is, by definition, correct. The challenge says that while many decisions no doubt *are* correct, many are not, and elaborate mechanisms are needed to determine which are which. Physicians are slowly being stripped of their decisionmaking power.

Notes: Doctors and Hospitals

1. *The Two-Headed Monster.* The unique structure of American hospitals, in which doctors are independent but essential to their financial well-being, has been described as "attractive as a two-headed monster" and as "stable as a three-legged stool." See H. L. Smith, Two Lines of Authority Are One Too Many, 84 Modern Hosp.

59 (Mar. 1955). This division of authority is mirrored throughout the organizational structure of the health care system. For instance, hospitals, unlike any other business organization, are required by state licensure laws and private accreditation standards to have *two* sets of corporate bylaws; one for the hospital administration and a second for the medical staff. Similarly, health insurance traditionally pays hospitals separately from doctors, as reflected in the distinctions between Blue Cross (hospital insurance) vs. Blue Shield (physician insurance) and between Medicare Part A vs. Part B.

2. *Power Relationships in Medicine.* Medical sociologists and organizational theorists have produced a rich literature discussing the role of physicians within medical institutions. Leading examples are Eliot Freidson, Doctoring Together (1975); Eliot Freidson, Profession of Medicine (1970); Paul Starr, The Social Transformation of American Medicine (1982); Jeffrey Harris, The Internal Organization of Hospitals: Some Economic Implications, 8 Bell J. Econ. 467 (1977). For an exploration of how these insights illuminate a variety of legal doctrines and public policy debates, see Mark A. Hall, Institutional Control of Physician Behavior: Legal Barriers to Health Care Cost Containment, 137 U. Pa. L. Rev. 431 (1988) ("Because the law absorbs and reflects the values and relationships of traditional medicine, it has codified the ethic of professional dominance, effectively shielding physicians from the institutional influence contemplated by revolutionary changes in health care policy."); Sara Rosenbaum, The Impact of United States Law on Medicine as a Profession, 289 JAMA 1546 (2003); Symposium, 29 J. Health Pol. Pol'y & L. 557 (2004); Symposium, 4 Ind. Health L. Rev. 205-286 (2007).

3. *History and Description.* For **general histories and descriptions** of the health care delivery system, see David Smith & Arnold Kaluzny, The White Labyrinth: A Guide to the Health Care System (2d ed. 2000); Kristina M. Young & Philip J. Kroth, Health Care USA: Understanding Its Organization and Delivery (9th ed. 2018); David Johnson & Nancy Kane, The U.S. Health Care System: A Product of American History and Values, *in* E. Elhauge ed., The Fragmentation of U.S. Health Care (2010); Hamilton Moses et al., The Anatomy of US Health Care, 310 JAMA 1947 (2013). For more extensive historical accounts of the transformation of hospitals and their role in modern medicine, see Guenter B. Risse, Mending Bodies, Saving Souls: A History of Hospitals (1999); Charles Rosenberg, The Care of Strangers (1987); David Rosner, A Once Charitable Enterprise (1982); Rosemary Stevens, In Sickness and in Wealth: American Hospitals in the Twentieth Century (1989).

2. *Medicine, Illness, and Healing*

■ MAGIC OR MEDICINE? AN INVESTIGATION OF HEALING AND HEALERS*
Robert Buckman & Karl Sabbagh
1995

[S]ome may find surprising . . . that the exact definition of what constitutes a disease or an illness is determined not by biology but by society. Certainly, there is a class of health problems that are seen in a similar way in all societies. For instance, if a previously fit man suddenly clutches his chest, looks white and sweaty and is acutely short of breath even at rest, then in Western society we would say that this man has probably had a heart attack, and we would prove it with ECGs and blood tests. It might be that in another society that episode is regarded as a visitation from a malevolent spirit . . . .

Some [diseases] are far more difficult to define and pigeon-hole and are classified differently in different societies. In Germany, for example, doctors prescribe six times the amount of heart drugs per person than in England or France. This is not because of a greater incidence of coronary artery disease in Germany . . . . One of the major reasons is that the German language doesn't have a way of distinguishing heart problems from any other kind of chest pain. . . . Thus, *Herzinsuffizienz* is an illness-label that is almost exclusive to Germany . . . .

In the same way, in France, a large number of nonspecific symptoms are attributed to a *crise de foie*—a "crisis of the liver." In fact, approximately 80 percent of problems attributed to a crisis of the liver are actually migraine. . . . Similarly, in the American medical view, minor illnesses are much more likely to be ascribed to (unspecified) viral illnesses. This is in line with the prevailing mood of the times in America in which disease is seen as an external invasive threat and there is a predilection for diagnosing infections since they can often be dealt with actively and quickly. . . .

Now consider a common event—bereavement. We expect to be sad after the death of someone we love—if the bereaved person cries continuously for a week, is that an illness? If he or she cries for six months, is that an illness? And what about adolescence? In Montana, a change in financing of private hospitals led to many general hospitals quickly changing themselves into psychiatric hospitals. Unfortunately, there were not enough patients to fill them, so there was a sudden epidemic of new diagnoses. Teenagers who had falling grades at school were now diagnosed as psychiatrically disturbed (with a major advertising campaign to get the point across to the parents) and were admitted to a hospital—at four times the rate that occurred in neighboring Utah. . . .

These [examples] again emphasize the partly arbitrary—and rather parochial—definitions of disease and illness. Each society decides for itself at the time what are legitimately regarded as diseases or illnesses. Those definitions vary from culture to culture. Furthermore, those conditions that we regard as normal today may be diagnosed as illnesses tomorrow.

■ THE TYRANNY OF HEALTH*
Faith T. Fitzgerald
331 New Eng. J. Med. 196 (1994)

There has recently been much in both lay and medical literature on the promotion of healthy lifestyles. Once upon a time people did not have lifestyles; they had lives. Those lives were filled with work and play, battle and respite, excitement and boredom, but principally with the day-to-day struggle for existence, centered largely around the family, birth, death, disease, and health. What is the difference between a lifestyle and a life? Central to it, I believe, is the concept that lifestyle is something one chooses, and life is something that happens to one. This distinction will affect the future of medicine, and certainly health care reform, in this country. The emphasis on healthy lifestyles, although salutary in many ways, has a very dark side to it and has led to the increasing peril of a tyranny of health in the United States. To explain the potential dangers of the emphasis on healthy lifestyles, I here review the concept of health and its role in the fabric of our society.

A healthy lifestyle is said to be essential to the promotion of wellness. What is wellness? In 1946, the World Health Organization, largely in revulsion against the activities of Nazi physicians and the creatures who worked with them, redefined health as "a state of complete physical, mental, and social well being, and not merely the absence of disease or infirmity." This has become known as "wellness," a highly desirable state. A well or healthy person is one who is not only physically whole and vigorous, but also happy and socially content. What a good idea! . . .

Concurrently, and perhaps naively, both the lay public and the medical profession began to confuse the ideal of health with the norm for health. That is, we went from "Wouldn't it be great to have this be the definition of health" to "This *is* the definition of health." Having accepted the view that health should be a perfect state of wellness, we went on to declare that it was. But if one accepts the idea that physical vigor and emotional and social contentment are not only desirable, but also expected, there is a problem. If health is normal, then sickness and accidents are faults. Who or what is at fault varies: environmental pollution, for example, or government plots, doctors themselves, diet, radon, or political bias. We now act as if we really believe that disease, aging, and death are unnatural acts and all things are remediable. All we have to do, we think, is know enough (or spend enough), and disease and death can be prevented or fixed. . . .

In his paper "Medical Nemesis," [Lancet 1974;1:918-921,] Illich wrote in 1974 that classifying all the troubles of humanity as medical problems is actually antithetical to true health, in that it limits the ability of people to learn to cope with pain, sickness, and death as integral parts of life. Health, he maintained, is not freedom from the inevitability of death, disease, unhappiness and stress, but rather the ability to cope with them in a competent way. If this is true, then the more medicine and society direct individual behavior, the less autonomous, and therefore the less healthy, the individual may become.

We must beware of developing a zealotry about health, in which we take ourselves too seriously and believe that we know enough to dictate human behavior, penalize people for disagreeing with us, and even deny people charity, empathy, and understanding because they act in a way of which we disapprove. Perhaps the health care crisis could be resolved, in part, if we [health care professionals realized that] . . . we cannot fix everything (though we do some things marvelously well), nor can our patients—no matter how intelligent or attentive—prevent all disease and death. We may be trying to do too much and thus diluting an awareness and application of what we can do well.

▮ THE MACHINE AT THE BEDSIDE*
Stanley Joel Reiser & Michael Anbar
1984

Technology has altered significantly the form and meaning of the medical relationship. It allows us to direct our vision and attention to variables singled out by it as significant. Thus, stethoscopes increase the significance of chest sounds, X-rays of anatomic shadows, electrocardiograms of waves on a graph, computers of printouts, dialysis machines of chemical balances, and so forth. Such evidence is important for diagnosis and therapy, and the more precisely it can be stated, the more valuable it becomes. In comparison, evidence given by patients, and altered by its passage through the prism of their experience and personality, has seemed to the technological age of the past two centuries less substantive, accurate, and meaningful as a basis for clinical decisionmaking and actions. Increasingly, practitioners encounter patients for relatively brief and intermittent periods—such as the consultant visiting a hospitalized patient whom he or she has never before met. In such visits the technical aspects often dominate, for there is no time or prior relationship to determine much about who the patient is, or what the patient thinks about the illness or the needs it engenders. And even in medical relationships that are not so discontinuous, technological measurements and measures tend to crowd out other dimensions of evaluation and therapeutics. To speak so of the attention focused on the technological features of practice does not diminish their great significance and benefit. Rather, it points out that they do not encompass all critical aspects of diagnosis or treatment. . . .

From the beginning of their introduction in the mid-nineteenth century, automated machines that generated results in objective formats such as graphs and numbers were thought capable of purging from health care the distortions of subjective human opinion. They were supposed to produce facts free of personal bias, and thus to reduce the uncertainty associated with human choice. This view, held by both practitioners and patients, stimulated the intense use of these devices, sometimes to excess. This excess has been characterized by overreliance on technologically depicted features of illness, inadequate understanding of the capabilities and limits of machines and the information they generate, and relative inattention to those aspects of medicine learned by inquiry into the patient's experiences and views. Machines can seem so accurate, so right. They can make us forget who made them, and who designed into them—with all the possibilities of human frailty and error—the programs that dictate their function. They can make us forget the hands and minds behind their creation; they can make us forget ourselves.

Notes: The Social Construction of Disease

1. *Is Anyone Healthy?* Students, especially younger ones, often fail to appreciate the extent to which health issues pervade society. According to one survey, in a typical *month,* 80 percent of adults report some type of medical symptom, 20

percent visit a doctor, 6 percent visit an alternative (nontraditional) health care provider, and 4 percent go to a hospital. Larry Green et al., The Ecology of Medical Care Revisited, 344 New Eng. J. Med. 2021 (2001). See also H. Gilbert Welch et al., Overdiagnosed: Making People Sick in the Pursuit of Health (2011); Nortin M. Hadler, Worried Sick (2008); Otis Brawley & Paul Goldberg, How We Do Harm: A Doctor Breaks Ranks About Being Sick in America (2012); Nortin M. Hadler, The Last Well Person (2004); Clifton Meador, The Last Well Person, 330 New Eng. J. Med. 440 (1994).

2. For additional views on the meaning of health and illness and the impact of medical technology, see Peter Conrad, The Medicalization of Society (2007); Nancy King et al. eds., The Social Medicine Reader (2d ed. 2005); R. A. Deyo & D. L. Patrick, Hope or Hype: The Obsession with Medical Advances and the High Cost of False Promises (2005); Robert A. Aronowitz, Making Sense of Illness: Science, Society, and Disease (1998); Daniel Callahan, False Hopes: Why America's Quest for Perfect Health Is a Recipe for Failure (1998); Rene Dubos, Man, Medicine, and Environment (1968); Michel Foucault, The Birth of the Clinic (1963); David Mechanic, Symptoms, Illness Behavior, and Help Seeking (1982); Roy Porter, The Greatest Benefit to Mankind (1998); David Rothman, Beginnings Count: The Technological Imperative in American Health Care (1997); Wm. B. Schwartz, Life Without Disease: The Pursuit of Medical Utopia (1998); Susan Sontag, Illness as Metaphor (1988); Richard A. Miller, Extending Life: Scientific Prospects and Political Obstacles, 80(2) Milbank Q. (2002); Lars Noah, Pigeonholing Illness: Medical Diagnosis as a Legal Construct, 50 Hastings L. Rev. 241 (1999); Talcott Parsons, The Sick Role and the Role of the Physician Reconsidered, 53 Health & Soc'y 257 (1975); Symposium, The Price of Medical Technology, 27(6) Health Aff. (Nov. 2008); Symposium, 21(2) Health Aff. (Mar. 2002); Symposium, 20(5) Health Aff. (Sept. 2001); Symposium, 25 J. Med. & Phil. 519 (2000); Developments, Medical Technology and the Law, 103 Harv. L. Rev. 1519 (1990).

■MAKING MEDICAL SPENDING DECISIONS*
Mark A. Hall
1997

THE ONTOLOGICAL ASSAULT OF ILLNESS

Illness is frequently described as an "ontological assault." It undermines one's personal identity by attacking the fundamental unity of mind and body. In a state of health, our body is part of an integrated sense of self that responds instinctively to our will and serves our inner purposes almost effortlessly. When illness strikes, our body becomes an enemy of self. It does not respond as we wish and its frailties dominate our conscious thoughts. Illness strikes at one of our most fundamental assumptions in everyday life—that we will continue to exist and function much as we have in the past. Serious illness shatters our "primordial sense of invulnerability" (Silberman 1991).

The profound incapacitating effect of this assault on our very being is much more debilitating than any of life's other major disruptions, whether they be divorce, incarceration or impoverishment. Physician and philosopher Edmund Pellegrino observes correctly that:

> In no other deprivation is the dissolution of the person so intimate that it impairs the capacity to deal with all other deprivations. The poor man can still hope for a change of fortune, the prisoner for a reprieve, the lonely for a friend. But the ill person remains impaired even when freed of these other constraints on the free exercise of his humanity. (Pellegrino 1982, at 159)

Consider also this account by a philosopher and patient who herself suffers from a severe chronic illness, multiple sclerosis:

> The most deeply held assumption of daily life is the assumption that I, personally, will continue to be alive and it is in light of this assumption that one engages in daily activities. The onset of illness, however, brings one concretely face-to-face with personal vulnerability. . . . Thus, the person who is ill . . . is unable readily to fit illness into the typified schema used to organize and interpret experience. . . . One finds oneself preoccupied with the demands of the here and now, confined to the present moment, unable effectively to project into the future. (Toombs 1992, at 21, 69)

In addition to these profound internal effects, . . . when ill we are often immobilized and confined to bed in a prone position and subjected to mind-altering medications. This compromises our physical ability to act and deliberate and places us in a psychological state of dependency. Treatment also compromises physical integrity and exposes us to singular vulnerability by giving physicians unprecedented access to our bodies and personal histories. Treatment requires us to expose every part of ourselves, down to our very blood and guts, while we remain prostrate or unconscious.

Typically, when ill, we do not resist what would otherwise be viewed as utterly repugnant invasions and vulnerabilities. Sickness returns us to an infantile state where our strongest desire is usually to be cared for and to be relieved of the responsibility and anxiety of deciding and acting. "Such sick people . . . may plausibly prefer not to take on any kind of work, much less the fierce, foreign, and forbidding labor of medical decisions" (Schneider 1997). This is true even for the most knowledgeable of patients—physicians themselves. Franz Ingelfinger, M.D., long time editor of the eminently prestigious New England Journal of Medicine and an expert in diseases of the esophagus, found himself in a dilemma of how best to treat his own difficult case of cancer of the esophagus. His doctors, respecting their patient's world renowned expertise, were leaving this vexing decision to him:

> As a result, not only I but my wife, my son and daughter-in-law (both doctors), and other family members became increasingly confused and emotionally distraught. Finally, when the pangs of indecision had become nearly intolerable, one wise physician friend said, "What you need is a doctor." . . . When that excellent advice was followed, my family and I sensed immediate and immense relief. . . .

[M]y description of the real experience of illness applies to simple and serious conditions alike. Sickness does not have to be life threatening for it to profoundly affect thinking and functioning. A bad flu bug, a relentless shooting pain, a case of food poisoning, an inconsolable child, or even an unexplained lump or a persistent bad cough can have these menacing and incapacitating effects at least to some degree. Even if this state of mind is the exception in medical treatment encounters, it nevertheless is the dominant explanation of why the medical system exists. . . . Medical ethics and health care policy should have its primary focus on the quintessential features of the treatment relationship even if those features account for only a fraction of [medical] decisions.

THE MYSTICAL POWER OF HEALING

[The condition of illness is only half of the story in a medical encounter. We must also understand something about the experience of healing. Modern medicine thinks of healing as occurring mainly through biochemical processes activated by medical interventions chosen based on diagnostic analysis and professional experience.] . . . Much of medicine is of this rational quality, but [this account ignores] an essential nonrational component of medicine. . . . This essential component is the mystical power of healing. By this, I mean the hidden elements of the treatment encounter that result in healing through what might be termed charismatic or self-healing means. The power of healing I refer to is the dimension of doctoring that enables physicians to confer relief through spiritual or emotional means akin to those used by parents or priests.[2]

Before alienating the skeptical reader entirely, let me illustrate with an everyday example from my own experience. Last year when my six-year-old daughter was suffering from a common ear ache, her distress brought her to inconsolable tears while waiting more than an hour to be seen by the doctor. I convinced a nurse to take her temperature, give her an aspirin, and say a few kind words of reassurance. Instantaneously, my daughter felt much better, far quicker than any possible pharmacological effect could have taken hold. I was puzzled by this abrupt improvement until I had my own excruciating ear ache a few weeks later and experienced exactly the same sort of instantaneous relief as soon as the doctor examined me and wrote a prescription. Knowing that I was in the good hands of a trained professional who offered the prospect of relief produced in me a sense of exhilaration and a release of anxiety accompanied by a pronounced improvement of my symptoms. This instantaneous recovery might be attributed simply to excessive nerves or to a more complex type of placebo effect but, however labeled or explained, it was effective. The pain was not just more bearable; it went away.

Researchers and physicians have documented countless similar examples of mundane and miraculous relief caused by a largely nonscientific or "nonspecific" process of healing. This placebo effect is not limited to purely psychological states, bizarre conditions, especially susceptible patients, or to manipulative physicians. This effect has been documented in the treatment of diabetes, cancer, and heart disease, for instance, and without the physicians even intending to cause the effect. In one scientific study, two sets of patients were subjected to different surgical operations to treat angina (chest pain), one that performed the standard chest

2. On the prevalence of the image of physician as parent or priest, see May 1983.

operation, and the other that only pretended to do so by cutting the skin under anesthesia. Both the sham and the real procedure produced equal relief of physical symptoms (Beecher 1961). A review of other surgical and medical procedures once firmly believed to be effective but later discarded as entirely unfounded led one author to speculate that placebo healing effects may be present to a significant extent in 70 percent of clinical encounters (Roberts 1993).

Those who have studied this nonspecific healing effect conclude that it pervades medicine, both in modern times and in prescientific and primitive cultures. This is because the effect is connected more to the intervention of the healer than it is to the particular therapeutic agent used. Put another way, the doctor himself is a therapeutic agent, regardless of the actual effectiveness of the particular drug or procedure (Suchman & Matthews 1988; Houston 1938). In each culture and each era, there has been a prevailing theory of medical treatment, many of which are pure fantasy if not dangerous, yet remarkably few have been proven to be wholly without benefit. Doctors and healers have been universally respected throughout the ages and across primitive and advanced societies; we can only assume that most of them have offered some form of relief despite the now apparent quackery they once practiced. Indeed, it has often been commented that the history of medicine until this century has been the history of the placebo effect. Now that medicine has a firm scientific foundation, this mystical or charismatic element has been surpassed by technological skill, but it will never be entirely displaced. One of the prominent trends in modern medicine is the revival of both popular and scientific interest in these poorly understood domains of caring for patients through alternative or holistic schools of medicine (Frohoch 1992; Cousins 1979).

The best scientific explanation for this charismatic healing effect is that the process of treatment, and not its specific content, has universal benefit for many or most illnesses, regardless of the specific physiological effects of the treatment. The treatment process has this universal healing power by virtue of the archetypal characteristics that activate the patient's own healing mechanisms—mechanisms that are still largely undiscovered and unexplained. This is best demonstrated by the fact that the basic structure of the treatment encounter is remarkably the same across all systems of medicine, including Western, Eastern, religious, herbal, and primitive. In each of these belief systems, society recognizes the healing powers of a professional elite (physicians or shamans), who administer personally to the patient with physical touching and healing agents (drugs or herbs), often in a dramatic and cathartic ritualistic setting (surgery or exorcism) specially designed for the purpose (hospital or bonfire). In the process, patients feel cared for (nurses or mystics), they are given an explanation for their condition (diagnosis or demonization) that is consistent with their prevailing belief system (scientific medicine or spirit worship), and they are assigned tasks of self care in which they take responsibility in part for their own improvement (dietary regimen or prayer).[3]

These many symbolic structural elements are thought to activate patients' internal healing powers through a variety of psychological channels. A patient who knows someone is devoted to caring for him is able to release the dread and anxiety

3. The leading work developing this explanation is Frank 1973. See also Brody 1992; Novack 1987.

that may be heightening discomfort and weakening the body's resistance. Believing in the power of the healer may enable the patient to regress to an earlier, more infantile state of mind that enhances this release and the resulting comfort. This confidence in the healer is elevated by the healer's status in society, his invocation of methods consistent with that society's belief system, and his offering an explanation of the otherwise troubling and disorienting disease that makes sense to the patient. And, this belief is further cemented by the ritualistic and dramatic elements of laying on of hands, taking of medication, climactic performance, and hallowed setting. . . .

Critical to this healing power is the patient's confidence and trust in the healer. "The image of omnipotence is an essential component of the healer" (see Cassell 1991). The healer appears able to activate the patient's own healing mechanisms because the patient turns himself over both in mind and body to the healer. "A patient's hope and trust lead to a 'letting go' that counteracts stress and is often the key to getting well" (Siegel 1986). Psychiatrists, starting with Freud, have described this phenomenon as "transference," in which patients foist on their healers qualities they formerly attributed to their parents in infancy when parents were viewed as all powerful and all knowing. "Deep in patients' unconscious, physicians are viewed as miracle workers, patterned after the fantasied all-caring parents of infancy. Medicine, after all, was born in magic and religion, and the doctor-priest-magician-parent unity that persists in patients' unconscious cannot be broken" (Katz 1984, at 142-47, 192). . . .

I hasten to concede that none of these assertions are known with any degree of empirical confidence. We are forced into this highly speculative reading of anecdotal accounts from physicians, anthropologists, and ethnographic researchers since empirical testing of this nonspecific healing power is very difficult and has not been widely attempted.[4] Nevertheless, many informed observers and patients view the charismatic dimension of healing as fundamental to the treatment relationship (e.g., Brody 1992; Schenck & Churchill 2011).

[PARTIAL BIBLIOGRAPHY, UPDATED]

Beecher, H. (1961). "Surgery as Placebo," 176 JAMA 1102.
Brody, H. (1992). The Healer's Power (New Haven, CT: Yale Univ. Press).
Cassell, E.J. (1991). The Nature of Suffering and the Goals of Medicine (Oxford Univ. Press).
Cousins, N. (1979). Anatomy of an Illness as Perceived by the Patient: Reflections on Healing and Regeneration (New York: W.W. Norton).
Frank, J.D. (1973). Persuasion and Healing: A Comparative Study of Psychotherapy (Baltimore: Johns Hopkins Univ. Press).
Frohoch, F.M. (1992). Healing Powers: Alternative Medicine, Spiritual Communities, and the State (Univ. Chicago Press).
Houston, R. (1938). "The Doctor Himself as a Therapeutic Agent," 11 Annals Int. Med. 1415.
Katz, J. (1984). The Silent World of Doctor and Patient (New York: The Free Press).

4. There are some scattered scientific studies demonstrating the placebo effect and the effect of certain of these healing rituals, but no scientific studies exploring what ingredients make this process work . . . [or are counterproductive].

Kleinman, A. (1988). The Illness Narratives: Suffering, Healing, and the Human Condition (Basic Books).

Miller, F. et al. (eds.). The Placebo (2013).

Novack, D.H. (1987). "Therapeutic Aspects of the Clinical Encounter," 2 J. Gen. Intern. Med. 346.

Pellegrino, E.D. (1979). "Toward a Reconstruction of Medical Morality: The Primacy of the Act of Profession and the Fact of Illness," 4 J. Med. & Philo. 32.

Pellegrino, E.D. and Thomasma, D.C. (1981). A Philosophical Basis of Medical Practice (Oxford Univ. Press).

Roberts, A.H. et al. (1993). "The Power of Nonspecific Effects in Healing," 12 Clin. Psychol. Rev. 375.

Schenck, D. & Churchill, L. (2011). Healers: Extraordinary Clinicians at Work.

Schneider, C.E. (1997). The Practice of Autonomy: Patients, Doctors, and Medical Decisions (Oxford Univ. Press).

Spiro, H.M. (1986). Doctors, Patients, and Placebos (New Haven, CT: Yale Univ. Press).

Suchman, A.L., and Matthews, D.A. (1988). "What Makes the Doctor-Patient Relationship Therapeutic? Exploring the Connexional Dimension of Medical Care," 108 Ann. Intern. Med. 125.

Toombs, S.K. (1992). The Meaning of Illness, A Phenomenological Account of the Different Perspectives of Physician and Patient (Boston: Kluwer Academic Publishers).

Notes: The Phenomenology of Sickness and Healing

1. *Illness.* Does your own experience with illness confirm or rebut the incapacitating and dehumanizing effects described by Mark Hall? Consider the additional accounts, both analytical and narrative, on the Web site for this book, www.health-law.org.

2. *Doctors, Patients, and Placebos.* These readings explain that the placebo effect is not isolated to a few psychologically susceptible individuals or conditions. It permeates medical encounters and typifies the doctor-patient relationship in ways that scientific medicine tends to ignore or deny. The mere encounter with a doctor appears to activate internal, self-healing mechanisms across a wide range of medical conditions, regardless of the actual treatments rendered. In short, doctors do not just administer placebos; they *are* placebos. Considering this, should the FDA deny approval for a drug because it acts "only" as a placebo? How does a doctor obtain informed consent from a patient when he knows the treatment is partially or totally intended to invoke a placebo effect?

In 2006, the AMA issued an ethics opinion that it is unprofessional to use placebos deceptively. Taking issue with this position, see Adam J. Kolber, A Limited Defense of Clinical Placebo Deception, 26 Yale L. & Pol'y Rev. 75-134 (2007); Rachel Sherman & John Hickner, Academic Physicians Use Placebos in Clinical Practice and Believe in the Mind-Body Connection, 23 J. Gen. Intern. Med. 7 (2007).

3. *Alternative and Conventional Healers.* There is now widespread social interest in alternative healing, both as a separate area of professional practice and as a component of conventional scientific practice. For further exploration, see the casebook Web site, www.health-law.org and the sources in note 5.

4. *Therapeutic Jurisprudence.* Consider the various implications these provocative readings have for law and public policy. Do they alter conventional legal

notions about who should control decisionmaking in the treatment encounter? Do they suggest that health insurance should more freely cover untested or unorthodox therapies? When disputes arise over treatment decisions or insurance coverage, are patients capable of aggressively pursuing their legal rights? Are patients capable of acting as informed consumers in a medical marketplace in which they evaluate the costs and benefits of different treatment options? Questions like these are addressed by a branch of legal thought known as "therapeutic jurisprudence," which views law as a therapeutic agent. This perspective asks whether normal social and behavioral assumptions realistically fit the medical arena, and whether legal rules do a good job of fostering the therapeutic goals of medicine.

5. *Bibliography.* For additional descriptions and analyses of the **phenomenology of illness (note 1)**, see Howard Brody, Stories of Sickness (1987); Kathy Charmaz, Good Days, Bad Days: The Self in Chronic Illness and Time (1991); Norman Cousins, The Healing Heart (1983); Michael C. Dohan, Reflections on a Bone Marrow Transplant, 132 Annals Intern. Med. 587 (2000). Discussing how issues of trust and vulnerability affect a number of issues in health care law, see Mark A. Hall, Law, Medicine, and Trust, 55 Stan. L. Rev. 463 (2002); Robert Gatter, Faith, Confidence, and Health Care: Fostering Trust in Medicine Through Law, 39 Wake Forest L. Rev. 395 (2004).

For additional discussion of the **placebo effect (note 2)**, see Anup Malani, Regulation with Placebo Effects, 58 Duke L.J. 411 (2008); Kathleen M. Boozang, The Therapeutic Placebo: The Case for Patient Deception, 54 Fla. L. Rev. 687 (2002); Anne Harrington, The Placebo Effect: An Interdisciplinary Exploration (1997); The Science of the Placebo (Harry A. Guess et al. eds., 2002). See generally Amitai Aviram, The Placebo Effect of Law: Law's Role in Manipulating Perceptions, 75 Geo. Wash. L. Rev. 54 (2006) (discussing how, "like the placebo effect of medicine, a law may impact social welfare beyond its objective effects by manipulating the public's subjective perception of the law's effectiveness").

On **alternative medicine (note 3)**, see Anne Harrington, The Cure Within: A History of Mind-Body Medicine (2007); Michael H. Cohen, Complementary and Alternative Medicine: Legal Boundaries and Regulatory Perspectives (1998); Michael Ruggio & Lauren DeSantis-Then, Complementary and Alternative Medicine: Longstanding Legal Obstacles to Cutting Edge Treatment, 2 J. Health & Life Sci. L. 137 (2009); Barbara L. Atwell, Mainstreaming Complementary and Alternative Medicine in the Face of Uncertainty, 72 UMKC L. Rev. 593 (2004); Symposium, 31 J.L. Med. Ethics 183 (2003); Michael H. Cohen & Mary C. Ruggie, Integrating Complementary and Alternative Medical Therapies in Conventional Medical Settings, 72 U. Cin. L. Rev. 671-729 (2003); Joseph A. Barrette, The Alternative Medical Practice Act, 77 St. John's L. Rev. 75 (2003); James A. Bulen, Complementary and Alternative Medicine: Ethical and Legal Aspects of Informed Consent to Treatment, 24 J. Leg. Med. 331 (2003); Kathleen M. Boozang, Is the Alternative Medicine? Managed Care Apparently Thinks So, 32 Conn. L. Rev. 567 (2000).

For leading examples of **therapeutic jurisprudence (note 4)**, focused mainly on mental health and criminal law, see Law in a Therapeutic Key (David B. Wexler & Bruce J. Winnick eds., 1996); Marshall B. Kapp, The Law and Older Persons: Is Geriatric Jurisprudence Therapeutic? (2003). For an attempt to further develop this perspective in health care law, see Hall, supra, 55 Stan. L. Rev. 463 (2002).

3. The Nature of Medical Judgment

■ CLINICAL DECISION MAKING: FROM THEORY TO PRACTICE
David M. Eddy*
1996

. . . Why do physicians vary so much in the way they practice medicine? At first view, there should be no problem. There are diseases—neatly named and categorized by textbooks, journal articles, and medical specialty societies. There are various procedures physicians can use to diagnose and treat these diseases. It should be possible to determine the value of any particular procedure by applying it to patients who have a disease and observing the outcome. And the rest should be easy—if the outcome is good, the procedure should be used for patients with that disease; if the outcome is bad, it should not. Some variation in practice patterns can be expected due to differences in the incidence of various diseases, patients' preferences, and the available resources, but these variations should be small and explainable.

The problem of course is that nothing is this simple. Uncertainty, biases, errors, and differences of opinions, motives, and values weaken every link in the chain that connects a patient's actual condition to the selection of a diagnostic test or treatment. . . . Uncertainty creeps into medical practice through every pore. Whether a physician is defining a disease, making a diagnosis, selecting a procedure, observing outcomes, assessing probabilities, assigning preference, or putting it all together, he is walking on very slippery terrain. It is difficult for nonphysicians, and for many physicians, to appreciate how complex these tasks are, how poorly we understand them, and how easy it is for honest people to come to different conclusions.

DEFINING A DISEASE

If one looks at patients who are obviously ill, it is fairly easy to identify the physical and chemical disorders that characterize that illness. On the other hand, a large part of medicine is practiced on people who do not have obvious illnesses, but rather have signs, symptoms, or findings that may or may not represent an illness that should be treated. Three closely related problems make it difficult to determine whether or not a patient actually has a disease that needs to be diagnosed or treated.

One problem is that the dividing line between "normal" and "abnormal" is not nearly as sharp as a cursory reading of a textbook would suggest. . . . A second problem is that many "diseases," at least at the time they are diagnosed, do not by themselves cause pain, suffering, disability, or threat to life. They are considered diseases only because they increase the probability that something else that is truly bad will happen in the future. . . .

The difficulty of defining a disease is compounded by the fact that many of the signs, symptoms, findings, and conditions that might suggest a disease are extremely

*Reprinted with permission. Dr. Eddy is a physician researcher, formerly on the faculty of Duke University, and now a consultant in Jackson Hole, Wyoming.

common. If a breast biopsy were performed on a random sample of senior citizens, fully 90 percent of them could have fibrocystic disease. If obesity is a disease, the average American is diseased. . . . Morbid obesity is defined as 100 percent above the ideal weight. But what is "ideal," and why 100 percent? The lesson is that for many conditions a clinician faces, there is no clear definition of disease that provides an unequivocal guide to action, and there is wide room for differences of opinion and variations in practice. . . .

[E]ven when sharp criteria are created, physicians vary widely in their application of these criteria—in their ability to ask about symptoms, observe signs, interpret test results, and record the answers. The literature on "observer variation" has been growing for a long time. . . . Thirteen pathologists were asked to read 1,001 specimens obtained from biopsies of the cervix, and then to repeat the readings at a later time. On average, each pathologist agreed with himself only 89 percent of the time (intraobserver agreement), and with a panel of "senior" pathologists only 87 percent of the time (interobserver agreement). Looking only at the patients who actually had cervical pathology, the intraobserver agreement was only 68 percent and the interobserver agreement was only 51 percent. The pathologists were best at reading more advanced disease and normal tissue, but were labeled "unsatisfactory" in their ability to read the precancerous and preinvasive stages.

Similar studies have been reported for . . . many other signs, symptoms, and procedures. Even if there were no uncertainty about what constitutes a disease and how to define it, there would still be considerable uncertainty about whether or not a patient has the signs, symptoms, and findings needed to fit the definition.

SELECTING A PROCEDURE

The task of selecting a procedure is no less difficult. There are two main issues. First, for any patient condition there are dozens of procedures that can be ordered, in any combination, at any time. The list of procedures that might be included in a workup of chest pain or hypertension would take more than a page, spanning the spectrum from simply asking questions, to blood studies, to X-rays. Even for highly specific diagnostic problems, there can be a large choice of procedures. For example, if a woman presents with a breast mass and her physician wants to know its approximate size and architecture, the physician might contemplate an imaging procedure. The choice could include mammography, ultra-sonography, thermography, diaphanography, computed tomography, lymphography, Mammoscan, and magnetic resonance imaging. . . . And why should a diagnostic workup be limited to one test? Why not follow a negative mammogram with a computed tomogram (or vice versa)? For the detection of colorectal cancer, a physician can choose any combination of fecal occult blood tests (and there are more than a dozen brands), digital examination, rigid sigmoidoscopy, flexible 30 cm sigmoidoscopy, flexible 60 cm sigmoidoscopy, barium enema (either plain or air contrast), and colonoscopy. These choices are not trivial. Most procedures have different mechanisms of action and a long list of pros and cons. . . . These procedures are for relatively well-defined diseases; imagine the problems of selecting procedures to evaluate symptoms like fatigue, headache, or fever that can have about a dozen causes. . . .

In theory, much of the uncertainty just described could be managed if it were possible to conduct enough experiments under enough conditions, and observe the outcomes. Unfortunately, measuring the outcomes of medical procedures is one of the most difficult problems we face. The goal is to predict how the use of a procedure in a particular case will affect that patient's health and welfare. Standing in the way are at least a half dozen major obstacles. The central problem is that there is a natural variation in the way people respond to a medical procedure. Take two people who, to the best of our ability to define such things, are identical in all important respects, submit them to the same operative procedure, and one will die on the operating table while the other will not. Because of this natural variation, we can only talk about the probabilities of various outcomes — the probability that a diagnostic test will be positive if the disease is present (sensitivity), the probability that a test will be negative if the disease is absent (specificity), the probability that a treatment will yield a certain result, and so forth.

One consequence of this natural variation is that to study the outcomes of any procedure it is necessary to conduct the procedure on many different people, who are thought to represent the particular patients we want to know about, and then average the results. . . . Some diseases are so rare that, in order to conduct the ideal clinical trials, it would be necessary to collect tens of thousands, if not hundreds of thousands, of participants. A good example concerns the frequency of the Pap smear. One might wonder why the merits of a three-year versus one-year frequency cannot be settled by a randomized controlled trial. Because of the low frequency of cervical cancer, and the small difference in outcomes expected for the two frequencies, almost one million women would be required for such a study. . . .

Finally, even when the best trials are conducted, we still might not get an answer. Consider the value of mammography in women under fifty, and consider just one outcome — the effect on breast cancer mortality. Ignore for the time being the radiation hazard, false-positive test results, inconvenience, financial costs, and other issues. This is one of the best-studied problems in cancer prevention, benefiting from the largest (60,000 women) and longest (more than 15 years) completed randomized controlled trial, and an even larger uncontrolled study involving 270,000 women screened for five years in 29 centers around the country. Yet we still do not know the value of mammography in women under 50. . . .

Unable to turn to a definitive body of clinical and epidemiological research, a clinician or research scientist who wants to know the value of a procedure is left with a mixture of randomized controlled trials, nonrandomized trials, uncontrolled trials, and clinical observations. The evidence from different sources can easily go in different directions, and it is virtually impossible for anyone to sort things out in his or her head. Unfortunately, the individual physician may be most impressed by observations made in his or her individual practice. This source of evidence is notoriously vulnerable to bias and error. What a physician sees and remembers is biased by the types of patients who come in; by the decisions of the patients to accept a treatment and return for follow-up; by a natural desire to see good things; and by a whole series of emotions that charge one's memory. On top of these biases, the observations are vulnerable to large statistical errors because of the small number of patients a physician sees in a personal practice. . . .

Now assume that a physician can know the outcomes of recommending a particular procedure for a particular patient. Is it possible to declare whether those outcomes are good or bad? Unfortunately, no. The basic problem is that any procedure has multiple outcomes, some good and some bad. The expected reduction in chest pain that some people will get from coronary artery bypass surgery is accompanied by a splitting of the chest, a chance of an operative mortality, days in the hospital, pain, anxiety, and financial expense. Because the outcomes are multiple and move in different directions, tradeoffs have to be made. And making tradeoffs involves values. . . . Imagine the variation in how different people value pain, disability, operative mortality, life expectancy, a day in a hospital, and who is going to feed the dogs. . . .

PUTTING IT ALL TOGETHER

The final decision about how to manage a patient requires synthesizing all the information about a disease, the patient, signs and symptoms, the effectiveness of dozens of tests and treatments, outcomes and values. All of this must be done without knowing precisely what the patient has, with uncertainty about signs and symptoms, with imperfect knowledge of the sensitivity and specificity of tests, with no training in manipulating probabilities, with incomplete and biased information about outcomes, and with no language for communicating or assessing values. If each piece of this puzzle is difficult, it is even more difficult for anyone to synthesize all the information and be certain of the answer. It would be an extremely hard task for a research team; there is no hope that it could occur with any precision in the head of a busy clinician. Hence the wide variability in the estimates physicians place on the values of procedures.

[A] final example document[s] how difficult it is to combine information from many sources to estimate the value of a particular procedure. . . . A survey of 1,000 11-year-old schoolchildren in New York City found that 65 percent had undergone tonsillectomy. The remaining children were sent for examinations to a group of physicians and 45 percent were selected for tonsillectomy. Those rejected were examined by another group of physicians and 46 percent were selected for surgery. When the remaining children were examined again by another group of physicians, a similar percent were recommended for tonsillectomy, leaving only 65 students. At that point, the study was halted for lack of physicians.

CONSEQUENCES

The view of anyone who wants a close look at the consequences of different medical procedures is, at best, smoky. Some procedures may present a clear picture, and their value, or lack of it, may be obvious; putting a finger on a bleeding carotid artery is an extreme example. But for many, if not most medical procedures, we can only see shadows and gross movements. . . . We certainly do not know how a particular individual will respond. Words like "rare," "common," and "a lot" must be used instead of "one out of 1,000," or "seven on a scale of one to ten." . . .

In the end, given all the uncertainties, incentives, and heuristics, a physician will have to do what is comfortable. If it is admitted that the uncertainty surrounding the use of a procedure is great, and that there is no way to identify for certain what is best, or to prove that any particular action is right or wrong, the safest and most comfortable position is to do what others are doing. The applicable maxim is "safety in numbers." A physician who follows the practices of his or her colleagues is safe from criticism, free from having to explain his or her actions, and defended by the concurrence of colleagues.

■COMPLICATIONS: A SURGEON'S NOTES ON AN IMPERFECT SCIENCE
Atul Gawande*
2002

THE CASE OF THE RED LEG

Seeing patients with one of the surgery professors in his clinic one afternoon, I was struck by how often he had to answer his patients' questions, "I do not know." These are four little words a doctor tends to be reluctant to utter. We're supposed to have the answers. We want to have the answers. But there was not a single person he did not have to say those four little words to that day. . . . The core predicament of medicine—the thing that makes being a patient so wrenching, being a doctor so difficult, and being a part of a society that pays the bills they run up so vexing—is uncertainty. With all that we know nowadays about people and diseases and how to diagnose and treat them, it can be hard to see this, hard to grasp how deeply the uncertainty runs. As a doctor, you come to find, however, that the struggle in caring for people is more often with what you do not know than what you do. Medicine's ground state is uncertainty. And wisdom—for both patients and doctors—is defined by how one copes with it.

This is the story of one decision under uncertainty.

It was two o'clock on a Tuesday afternoon in June. . . . I had just finished admitting someone with a gallbladder infection and was attempting to sneak out for a bite to eat when one of the emergency room physicians stopped me with yet another patient to see: a twenty-three-year-old, Eleanor Bratton, with a red and swollen leg. . . . "It's probably only a cellulitis" [he said]—a simple skin infection. . . . But he wanted me to make sure there wasn't anything "surgical" going on—an abscess that needed draining or some such. "Would you mind taking a quick look?" Groan. No. Of course not. . . .

She looked fit, athletic, and almost teenage, with blond hair tight in a ponytail, nails painted gold, and her eyes fixed on a television. There did not seem anything seriously ill about her. . . . That weekend she had gone back home to Hartford, Connecticut, to attend a wedding . . . and she had kicked off her shoes and danced the whole night. The morning after, however, she woke up with her left foot feeling sore. She had a week-old blister on the top of her foot from some cruddy sandals she had worn, and now the skin surrounding the blister was red and puffy. . . . The redness spread, and during the night she got chills and sweats and a fever of one hundred and three degrees. . . . I asked Eleanor if she had had any pus or drainage from her leg.

No. Any ulcers open up in her skin? No. A foul smell or blackening of her skin? No. Any more fevers? Not in the last two days. I let the data roll around in my head. . . . Objectively, the rash had the exact appearance of a cellulitis, something

---

*Excerpted with permission, Henry Holt and Company. The author is a physician on the faculty of Harvard's Schools of Medicine and of Public Health. This true story uses fictionalized names.

antibiotics would take care of. But another possibility lodged in my mind now, one that scared the hell out of me. . . .

Decisions in medicine are supposed to rest on concrete observations and hard evidence. But just a few weeks before, I had taken care of a patient I could not erase from my mind. . . . He was found to have a small and very ordinary skin rash on his chest and was sent home with antibiotic pills for cellulitis. That night the rash spread eight inches. The following morning he spiked a fever of one hundred and two degrees. By the time he returned to the emergency room, the skin involved had become numb and widely blistered. Shortly after, he went into shock. He was transferred to my hospital and we quickly took him to the OR.

He didn't have a cellulitis but instead an extremely rare and horrendously lethal type of infection known as necrotizing fasciitis (fah-shee-EYE-tiss). The tabloids have called it a disease of "flesh-eating bacteria" and the term is not an exaggeration. Opening the skin, we found a massive infection, far worse than what appeared from the outside. All the muscles of the left side of his chest, going around to his back, up to his shoulder, and down to his abdomen, had turned gray and soft and foul with invading bacteria and had to be removed. . . . The next day we had to remove his arm. For a while, we actually thought we had saved him. . . . One by one, however, his kidneys, lungs, liver, and heart went into failure, and then he died. It was among the most awful cases I have ever been involved in.

What we know about necrotizing fasciitis is this: it is highly aggressive and rapidly invasive. It kills up to 70 percent of the people who get it. No known antibiotic will stop it. . . . It is an organism that usually causes little more than a strep throat, but in certain strains it has evolved the ability to do far worse. No one knows where these strains come from. As with a cellulitis, they are understood to enter through breaks in the skin. The break can be as large as a surgical incision or as slight as an abrasion. . . . Survival is possible only with early and radical excisional surgery, often requiring amputation. To succeed, however, it must be done early. By the time signs of deep invasion are obvious—such as shock, loss of sensation, widespread blistering of the skin—the person is usually unsalvageable.

Standing at Eleanor's bedside, bent over examining her leg, I felt a little foolish considering the diagnosis. . . . True, in the early stages, a necrotizing fasciitis can look just like a cellulitis, presenting with the same redness, swelling, fever, and high white blood cell count. But . . . [o]nly about a thousand cases of necrotizing fasciitis occur in the entire United States each year, mainly in the elderly and chronically ill—and well over *three million* cases of cellulitis.

What's more, Eleanor's fever had gone away; she didn't look unusually ill; and I knew I was letting myself be swayed by a single, recent, anecdotal case. If there were a simple test to tell the two diagnoses apart, that would have been one thing. But there is none. The only way is to go to the operating room, open the skin, and look—not something you want to propose arbitrarily. . . .

Eleanor and her father looked on with new dread when [the general surgeon, Dr.] Studdert arrived in his scrubs and operating hat to see her. He had her tell her story again and then uncovered her leg to examine it. He didn't seem too impressed. Talking by ourselves, he told me that the rash looked to him only "like a bad cellulitis." But could he say for sure that it was not necrotizing fasciitis? He could not. It is a reality of medicine that choosing to *not* do something—to not order a test, to not give an antibiotic, to not take a patient to the operating room—is far harder than choosing to do it. . . .

Studdert sat down on the edge of her bed . . . and, in a quiet and gentle voice, he went on to explain the unquiet and ungentle effects of necrotizing fasciitis. . . . "I think it is unlikely you have it," he told Eleanor. "I'd put the chances"—he was guessing here—"at well under five percent." But, he went on, "without a biopsy, we cannot rule it out." He paused for a moment to let her and her father absorb this. Then he started to explain what the procedure involved. . . .

Eleanor went rigid. "This is crazy," she said. "This doesn't make any sense." She looked frantic, like someone drowning. "Why don't we just wait and see how the antibiotics go?" Studdert explained that this was a disease that you cannot sit on, that you had to catch it early to have any chance of treating it. Eleanor just shook her head and looked down at her covers.

Studdert and I both turned to her father to see what he might have to say. He . . . asked what would happen if the biopsy were positive for the disease. Studdert . . . hesitated before going on. "This can mean an amputation," he said. Eleanor began to cry. "I don't want to do this, Dad." Mr. Bratton swallowed hard, his gaze fixed somewhere miles beyond us.

In recent years, we in medicine have discovered how discouragingly often . . . medicine still lacks the basic organization and commitment to make sure we do what we know to do. But spend almost any amount of time with doctors and patients, and you will find that the larger, starker, and more painful difficulty is the still abundant uncertainty that exists over what should be done in many situations. The gray zones in medicine are considerable, and every day we confront situations like Eleanor's—ones in which clear scientific evidence of what to do is missing and yet choices must be made.

Exactly which patients with pneumonia, for example, should be hospitalized and which ones sent home? Which back pains treated by surgery and which by conservative measures alone? Which patients with a rash taken to surgery and which just observed on antibiotics? For many cases, the answers can be obvious. But for many others, we simply do not know. . . . In the absence of algorithms and evidence about what to do, you learn in medicine to make decisions by feel. You count on experience and judgment. And it is hard not to be troubled by this. . . . But in the face of uncertainty, what other than judgment does a physician have—or a patient have, for that matter? . . .

Eleanor and her dad now agreed to go ahead. "Let's get it over with," she said. But then I brought her the surgical consent form to sign. On it, I had written not only that the procedure was a "biopsy of the left lower extremity" but also that the risks included a "possible need for amputation." She cried out when she saw the words. It took her several minutes alone with her father before she could sign. . . .

There is, in fact, another approach to decision making, one advocated by a small and struggling coterie in medicine. The strategy, long used in business and the military, is called decision analysis, and the principles are straightforward. On a piece of paper (or a computer), you lay out all your options, and all the possible outcomes of those options, in a decision tree. You make a numeric estimate of the probability of each outcome, using hard data when you have it and a rough prediction when you don't. You weigh each outcome according to its relative desirability (or "utility") to the patient. Then you multiply out the numbers for each option and choose the one with the highest calculated "expected utility." The goal is to use explicit, logical, statistical thinking instead of just your gut. The decision to recommend annual mammograms for all women over age fifty was made this way and so was the U.S. decision to bail out Mexico when its economy tanked. Why not, the advocates ask, individual patient decisions?

Recently, I tried "treeing out" (as the decision buffs put it) the choice Eleanor faced. The options were simple: to biopsy or not biopsy. The outcomes quickly got complicated, however. There was: not being biopsied and doing fine; not being biopsied, getting diagnosed late, going through surgery, and surviving anyway; not being biopsied and dying; being biopsied and getting only a scar; being biopsied and getting a scar plus bleeding from it; being biopsied, having the disease and an amputation, but dying anyway; and so on. When all the possibilities and consequences were penciled out, my decision tree looked more like a bush. Assigning the probabilities for each potential twist of fate seemed iffy. I found what data I could from the medical literature and then had to extrapolate a good deal. And determining the relative desirability of the outcomes seemed impossible after talking to Eleanor about them. Is dying a hundred times worse than doing fine, a thousand times worse, a million? Where does a scar with bleeding fit in? Nonetheless, these are the crucial considerations, the decision experts argue, and when we decide by instinct, they say, we are only papering this reality over.

Producing a formal analysis in any practical time frame proved to be out of the question, though. It took a couple of days—not the minutes that we had actually had—and a lot of back and forths with two decision experts. But it did provide an answer. According to the final decision tree, we should *not* have gone to the OR for a biopsy. The likelihood of my initial hunch being right was too low, and the likelihood that catching the disease early would make no difference anyway was too high. Biopsy could not be justified, the logic said. I don't know what we would have made of this information at the time. We didn't have the decision tree, however. And we went to the OR. . . .

At first glance beneath her skin, there was nothing apparent to alarm us. . . . When we probed with the tip of a clamp inside the calf incision, however, it slid unnaturally easily along the muscle, as if bacteria had paved a path. This is not a definitive finding, but enough of one that Studdert let out a sudden, disbelieving, "Oh shit." . . . The features he saw were "consistent with necrotizing fasciitis[.]" . . . "She's got it," he finally announced grimly. . . .

Decisions compound themselves, in medicine like in anything else. No sooner have you taken one fork in the road than another and another come upon you. The critical question now was what to do. . . . "I thought about a BKA," a below-knee amputation, Studdert says, "even an AKA," an above-knee amputation. No one would have faulted him for doing either. But he found himself balking. "She was such a young girl," he explains. "It may seem harsh to say, but if it was a sixty-year-old man I would've taken the leg without question." This was partly, I think, a purely emotional unwillingness to cut off the limb of a pretty twenty-three-year-old—the kind of sentimentalism that can get you in trouble. But it was also partly instinct again, an instinct that her youth and fundamentally good health might allow him to get by with just removing the most infested tissue (a "debridement") and washing out her foot and leg. Was this a good risk to take, with one of the deadliest bacteria known to man loose in her leg? Who knows? But take it he did. . . . We ended up operating on her leg four times in four days. . . . Only then was Studdert confident that not only had Eleanor survived, but her foot and leg had, too. . . .

For close to thirty years, Dartmouth physician Jack Wennberg has studied decision making in medicine, . . . [a]nd what he has found is a stubborn, overwhelming, and embarrassing degree of inconsistency in what we do. His research has shown, for example, that the likelihood of a doctor sending you for a gallbladder-removal operation varies 270 percent depending on what city you live in; for a hip replacement, 450 percent; for care in an intensive care unit during the last six months of your life, 880 percent. A patient in Santa Barbara, California, is five times more likely to be recommended back surgery for a back pain than one in Bronx, New York. This is, in the main, uncertainty at work, with the varying experience, habits, and intuitions of individual doctors leading to massively different care for people.

How can this be justified? The people who pay for the care certainly do not see how. (That is why insurers bug doctors so constantly to explain our decisions.) Nor might the people who receive it. Eleanor Bratton, without question, would have been treated completely differently depending on where she went, who she saw, or even just when she saw me (before or after that previous necrotizing fasciitis case I'd seen; at 2 A.M. or 2 P.M.; on a quiet or a busy shift). She'd have gotten merely antibiotics at one place, an amputation at another, a debridement at a third. This result seems unconscionable.

People have proposed two strategies for change. One is to shrink the amount of uncertainty in medicine—with research, not on new drugs or operations (which already attracts massive amounts of funding) but on the small but critical everyday decisions that patients and doctors make (which gets shockingly little funding). Everyone understands, though, that a great deal of uncertainty about what to do for people will always remain. (Human disease and lives are too complicated for reality to be otherwise.) So it has also been argued, not unreasonably, that doctors must agree in advance on what should be done in the uncertain situations that arise—spell out our actions ahead of time to take the guesswork out and get some advantage of group decision. This last goes almost nowhere, though. For it runs counter to everything we doctors believe about ourselves as individuals, about our personal ability to reason out with patients what the best course of action for them is. . . .

The possibilities and probabilities are all we have to work with in medicine, though. What we are drawn to in this imperfect science, what we in fact covet in our way, is the alterable moment—the fragile but crystalline opportunity for one's know-how, ability, or just gut instinct to change the course of another's life for the better. In the actual situations that present themselves, however—a despondent woman arrives to see you about a newly diagnosed cancer, a victim bleeding from a terrible injury is brought pale and short of breath from the scene, a fellow physician asks for your opinion about a twenty-three-year-old with a red leg—we can never be sure whether we have such a moment or not. Even less clear is whether the actions we choose will prove either wise or helpful. That our efforts succeed at all is still sometimes a shock to me. But they do. . . .

Notes: Medical Decisionmaking

1. *The Nature of Medical Judgment.* Medical decisionmaking is best appreciated by examining a range of particular medical cases. One example of a full-length case discussion, which illustrates many of the dimensions of uncertainty of judgment

described by Doctors Gawande and Eddy is linked on the Web site for this book, www.health-law.org. For additional readings on the nature of medical judgment, see Kathryn Montgomery, How Doctors Think (2006); Jerome Groopman, How Doctors Think (2007); Kathryn Hunter, Doctors' Stories: The Narrative Structure of Medical Knowledge (1991).

Dr. Gawande mentions the work of Dartmouth researchers documenting dramatic variations in physicians' practice styles in different communities. Dr. Gawande brought this research to widespread attention in The Cost Conundrum: What a Texas Town Can Teach Us About Health Care, The New Yorker, June 1, 2009. Efforts to standardize medical practice and reduce variations in practice are discussed in Chapter 4.A. For additional discussion of treatment variation, see Institute of Medicine, Variation in Health Care Spending (2013). For discussion of differential treatment based on race, see Chapter 2.A.2.

2. *Medical Terminology.* Early editions of this book contained information about medical terminology, medical science, and anatomy. Lawyers who practice in this field must eventually acquire a fair amount of medical knowledge, and many law students enjoy learning something about a different profession's specialized vocabulary. Others see medical terminology as an obstacle to understanding what's really happening in these cases. We have chosen to cater to the latter group; our feeling is that if you end up working in this field, you will have plenty of opportunity to learn the terminology later. Here, when cases contain uncommon medical terms, we will define them for you. If we fail to do so, most terms used in this book are contained in better-quality general dictionaries. For those who want more specialized information, here is a sampling of various medical texts and treatises, some written especially for lawyers and others for medical professionals or for the lay public. **Medical Dictionaries:** Dorland's Illustrated Medical Dictionary; Stedman's Medical Dictionary; Taber's Cyclopedic Medical Dictionary. Links to the online versions of these can be found on this casebook's Web site, www.health-law.org. A comprehensive guide to medical research for legal purposes is Caroline Young, Medico-Legal Research Using Evidence-Based Medicine, 102 L. Libr. J. 449 (2010).

B. THE HEALTH CARE FINANCING AND DELIVERY SYSTEM

1. The "Crisis" in Access, Cost, and Quality

◼ HEALTH AND MEDICAL CARE REFORM IN THE UNITED STATES: ETHICAL QUESTIONS AND CONCERNS

Thomas W. Merrill, David G. Miller, Joseph A. Raho & Ginger Gruters
President's Council on Bioethics, Staff Background Paper
2008

The reform of health and medical care in the United States has been a topic on our national agenda for decades now. . . . [A]t present, we seem to be witnessing a remarkable coalescence — of the public, health professionals and organizations, and policymakers — around the conclusion that the American "system" of health and medical care is ailing. Three problems—of access and coverage, of quality, and of cost—are usually cited as the signs and symptoms of this increasingly worrisome state. . . . [W]e offer a purely descriptive account of the problems of access, quality, and cost, in order to illustrate their complexity and to draw out their implications for ethical questioning. . . .

I. THE PROBLEM OF ACCESS TO HEALTH AND MEDICAL CARE

In [2010], according to the Current Population Survey of the U.S. Census Bureau, [50] million Americans were uninsured. This statistic is often cited in ways that suggest that it—and it alone—constitutes the whole of the problem of access to health and medical care in the United States. . . . There are other dimensions to the problem of access. The underinsured, who have some coverage but are inadequately protected against high out-of-pocket costs, are the subjects of a growing literature. Difficulties with the supply and geographical distribution of health care professionals, along with some types of health care facilities (for example, emergency rooms), are also constituents of the problem of access. Our focus here, however, is on the uninsured. . . .

According to one estimate, some 18,000 premature deaths per year in the United States (as well as a number of other serious health conditions) could have been prevented by better access to health care.[3] To be sure, the uninsured do have access to emergency room care . . . , but care through this source tends to be less than optimal. Conditions are often treated only when they have become very serious. Moreover, the use of emergency care by the uninsured exacerbates the burdens placed on often strained emergency rooms and centers. . . . Those hospitals and professionals incur costs that eventually lead to higher charges for the insured or to increasing outlays of federal and state funds for uncompensated care. . . .

The preceding review of statistical data underscore[s] one conclusion: the situation of the uninsured in the United States is a complicated one, far more so than the oft-cited figure of [50] million reveals. As this review has shown, that number does not capture how long the uninsured lack this essential component of access to care, nor does it provide important information on who the uninsured are. The number of individuals who lack insurance for a year or more is lower than [50] million—probably somewhere between 30 and 40 million. Nor is it the case that the uninsured are all poor and thus unable to purchase insurance. More than one-third have household incomes above the median national income. Moreover, about a fifth are not citizens. . . . It is also noteworthy that the rates of uninsurance are higher among the poor and among African-American and Hispanic communities. . . .

II. THE PROBLEM OF HEALTH CARE COSTS AND FINANCING

Just as few, if any, would dispute the fact that there are many millions of uninsured Americans, so too would few take issue with the claims that health care costs

---

3. See the Institute of Medicine report *Hidden Costs, Value Lost: Uninsurance in America* (2003). Other scholars point out, however, that it is difficult to establish clear evidence of causation (as opposed to correlation) between insurance status and health status. . . .

in the United States are high compared to other industrialized nations and that these costs are increasing in seemingly unconstrained ways. These facts are cause for concern on a number of fronts. Such broad measures of population health as infant mortality and life expectancy, for example, indicate that the U.S. does no better, and in some cases does far worse, than similar countries that spend less on health care: we may not be getting good value for our money. . . . [T]he current situation is made more worrying still by the historical trends in the growth of health care spending. . . . According to some estimates made by the Congressional Budget Office, if current trends continue, health care spending could rise to almost 50 percent of total Gross Domestic Product (GDP) by 2082. . . .

There is much controversy, of course, over the causes of those increases and the ways we might address those causes. Here, we simply lay out some well-known facts about health care spending in the United States: as a portion of GDP and per capita; as it affects employees and employers; and as it affects federal and state budgets.

Today [as of 2016], the United States spends about [$3.3] trillion per year on health care, which amounts to [18] percent of GDP and about [$10,000] per person. Of course, compared with the poorer nations of the world, all of the wealthier nations spend a greater proportion of their income on health care. The United States, however, spends more on health care—both on a per capita basis and as a percentage of its GDP—than *any* other nation in the world. . . . National spending on health care as a share of GDP increased from about 5 percent in 1960 to our current level of [18] percent today and is projected to continue to grow. . . . The cumulative effect of those growth rates is this: The United States has experienced a *twenty-fold increase* in health care expenditures—a four-fold increase over the consumer price index over the same period. . . .

Of course, the rising share of health care as a portion of GDP may not necessarily be cause for concern. As mentioned above, as countries become wealthier, their citizens tend to spend more money on health care, and there is no way to determine *a priori* what the "appropriate" level of spending on health care may be. Moreover, the percentage of GDP representing health care also depends on the size and character of what happens in other sectors of the economy. Above all, the costs by themselves do not tell us anything about the quality or value of the care being provided. . . . Nevertheless, as the cost of health care rises so quickly relative to growth in GDP, it cannot fail to strain private and public budgets and to make it ever more difficult to solve or ameliorate other problems. . . .

For individuals, rising health care costs lead to increased premiums and to insurance plans that attempt to restrain *their* costs by using higher deductibles, co-pays, and the like. Because individuals and families in the United States tend to get their insurance through their employers, who choose and purchase coverage from an insurer, those employers are often in the middle between the insurance companies and their employees who actually use the insurance. For this reason, employers are often the parties that complain most loudly about rising costs. They also tend to look to devices for holding down costs through cost sharing and the like. In [2017] the average cost of [group] insurance (including both the part of the premium paid by the employer and the employee) was [over $6,000] per year for an individual and [over $18,000] per year for a family. . . .

Most economists argue that, despite appearances, employers are not really paying the insurance premiums of their employees. Rather, the insurance premium is simply part of the total compensation package for the employee. Because of the tax exemption for health insurance, it makes sense for an employee to take part of their compensation as (untaxed) health benefits. For most Americans, our employer picks the insurance company, chooses the plan, and sends in the check, but the employer does not bear the final cost of the insurance premiums. That comes out of whatever the total amount of compensation the employer is willing to pay to the employee. In times of rising health care costs, that means that more of the total compensation has to go to insurance and less can go to increased wages. . . . Rather than coming out of corporate profits, the increasing cost of health care has resulted in relatively flat real wages for 30 years. That is the real health care cost-wage trade-off. . . .

Increased health care costs also put a burden on federal and state governments, primarily through Medicare and Medicaid. . . . [P]ublic funds, including Medicare, Medicaid, Veterans health care, and other programs account for about 45 percent of total health spending in any given year. For the governments that pay for these programs, rising health care costs mean some hard choices: reducing benefits, restricting eligibility, cutting other public programs, raising taxes.

For the states, health care costs are already the single largest part of state budgets. . . . Not surprisingly, states have tended to respond by cutting other programs, most commonly funding for public higher education. . . . For the federal government, rising health care costs . . . could threaten to swamp the budget. . . .

III. THE PROBLEM OF HEALTH CARE QUALITY

In light of the fact that the United States spends much more on health care than other countries, it is reasonable to ask: Are we getting good value for the money? But with respect to the question of the quality of our health care, we find significant division between, on the one hand, those who cite the technological marvels produced in America and the outcomes in the treatment of complex diseases and, on the other hand, those who look to various aggregate measures of population health and find significant defects. . . . Of course, these seemingly opposed arguments are not mutually incompatible: America could produce the world's best technologies while also failing to provide the right care in many routine instances, not to mention the problems of the uninsured. And so we ask: What do we know about the quality of American health care?

On the one hand, it is true that by many measures of population health, the United States does quite poorly: infant mortality rates are higher in the United States than in many other comparable nations, and life expectancy rates are also low compared to other industrialized nations. A study by the World Health Organization (WHO) found that the United States ranked 37th . . . behind many other industrialized nations, all of which, as we have seen, spend far less per capita on health care than the U.S. does. . . .

Yet there is controversy over these facts. Some scholars argue, for example, that the cross-national comparisons fail to take into account differences in the underlying populations in different countries. They suggest that if we control for factors like homicide rates and car accidents—both of which are higher in the United States than in other countries—the measures of population health begin to look more similar to other nations. They also point out that rates of survival after the diagnosis of various serious ailments like cancer tend to be higher in the U.S. than elsewhere. Moreover, defenders of health care in United States point to the medical technologies and innovations developed here: The United States has produced more winners of the Nobel Prize in medicine than any other country. . . . Additionally, the U.S. spends far more of its public and private monies on biomedical research and development than does the European Union. Thus, defenders of U.S. health care argue that we cannot evaluate the level of quality of health care in the United States without keeping in mind the increased quality of the technologies used in health care.

As is often noted, Americans tend to be strongly attached to medical innovation and new medical technologies, more so than citizens of other countries. And there is a respectable body of literature which argues that the benefits of new technologies far outweigh their costs (as heavy as the latter may be). The [Harvard] economist David Cutler . . . and colleagues find that the cost of treating a heart attack has increased by some $10,000 in the 1990s, but that life expectancy after heart attack also rose by about one year. The treatment for low-birth weight infants presents a similarly positive picture. Cutler and colleagues conclude that "technological changes have proved to be worth far more than their costs."[35] . . .

Of course, . . . even the best technology cannot help very much if a particular patient does not have access to it—or does not have *timely* access. [Moreover], with respect to three different indicators—patient safety, receipt of recommended care, and variations in the intensity and outcomes of treatment—evidence suggests troublesome inadequacies in the quality of health care in America.

Patient Safety: Marked and seemingly widespread deficiencies in patient safety were the focus of the Institute of Medicine's *To Err Is Human*, a report published in 2000. According to the IOM, as many as 98,000 deaths are the result of medical error each year in the United States. That is more deaths from medical error than from motor vehicle accidents (around 45,000 deaths annually), from breast cancer (also around 45,000 deaths annually), or from AIDS (around 16,000 deaths annually). . . .

Receipt of Recommended Care: In the last few decades, professional societies along with such government agencies as the Agency for Healthcare Research and Quality have sought to develop and promulgate clinical practice guidelines and clinical pathways that stipulate the evidence-based recommendations for the most effective diagnosis and treatment of a wide range of diseases and disorders, from childhood asthma to adult hypertension. Nonetheless, [the] first national, comprehensive study on quality of care for adults in the U.S. . . . found that patients

35. David Cutler, *Your Money or Your Life: Strong Medicine for America's Healthcare System* (New York: Oxford University Press, 2004).

received the recommended care only 54.9 percent of the time.[41] . . . As [the author] testified before the U.S. Senate, "We spend nearly $2 trillion annually on health care and we get it right about half the time. That may be the best in the world, but I think you would agree that we can and should do better."

Variations in Intensity and Outcomes of Treatment: A substantial body of evidence also supports the finding of wide variations of the amount of money spent and of treatments performed between different areas of the country, but without any corresponding variations in health outcomes. In fact, the evidence seems to suggest that geographical areas that spend more actually have lower levels of quality of care. Researchers at Dartmouth led by Jack Wennberg and Elliott Fisher have shown, for example, that the amount of money spent per capita on Medicare recipients varies widely between different areas of the country, by almost as much as a threefold difference, even after controlling for differences in age, race, and sex. But, . . . the correlation with quality is low.

Many researchers have concluded that increased spending does not translate into better outcomes—in fact it may translate into worse outcomes. Wennberg and Fisher contend that much of the health care spending in Medicare, perhaps as much as 20 percent to 30 percent, does not bring added health benefits and that there may well be a similar proportion of private spending on health care that does not bring better outcomes. Economists suggest that in many cases Americans may be at the "flat of the curve," that is, at that place in a cost-benefit analysis when further resources may not only bring added benefit but may, in fact, bring less benefit. . . . Peter Orszag, director of the Congressional Budget Office, has recently written: "With health care spending currently representing 16 percent of gross domestic product (GDP), [Wennberg and Fisher's results] would suggest that nearly 5 percent of GDP—or roughly $700 billion each year—goes to health care spending that can't be shown to improve health outcomes." Of course, as Orszag observes, trying to figure out how to reduce inappropriate or unnecessary care is no easy task. . . .

Leaving aside the difficult problems of designing the right policies to make American health care more efficient, however, there is a more fundamental question about what we—as patients and as citizens—expect from modern medical technology. Do we have extravagant expectations from medical science? Are we so accustomed to having someone else pay the bill that we no longer question whether a particular intervention is worth its cost? While evaluating the cost-effectiveness of various interventions or organizing the health care system to be more cost effective will not solve all of our health care problems, it may be a necessary condition of a more sustainable system that we come to see that more is not always better.

A variety of problems—access, cost, and quality—make health care in the United States an unavoidably complicated affair, and this is not the place to elaborate specific policy proposals. But we should remember that the health care system is one in which each of us will find ourselves in various capacities at various points in our lives, and the decisions we make about the various aspects of health care reflect our identity as a nation and the type of social union we wish to create and advance. . . .

41. McGlynn, Asch, Adams, et al., "The Quality of Health Care Delivered to Adults in the United States," *New England Journal of Medicine*, vol. 328: 2635-2645, June 26, 2003.

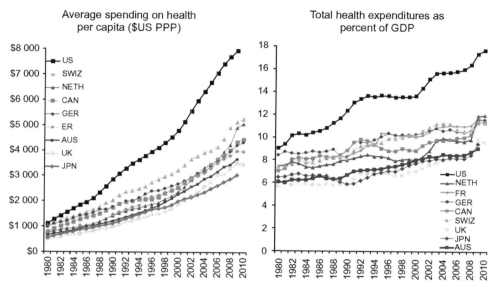

International Comparison of Spending on Health, 1980–2010

Notes: PPP = purchasing power parity; GDP = gross domestic product.
Source: Commonweath Fund, based on OECD Health Data 2012.

Notes: The Crisis in American Medicine

1. *The Perpetual Crisis.* American medicine has been declared to be in a "crisis" since at least the early 1960s. See Marion Sanders, The Crisis in American Medicine (1961). Can things really be all that bad if they've been like this so long? Note the competing viewpoint of Harvard economist David Cutler, cited above, that major increases in medical spending can be traced to substantial gains in health that, at least in certain areas, are clearly worth their costs.

Even if there is not a "crisis," there is still clearly a serious problem in American medicine. In case you're still not convinced, consider the following additional facts, opinions, and anecdotes.

> Medicine, like many other American institutions, suffered a stunning loss of confidence in the 1970s. Previously, two premises had guided government health policy: first, that Americans needed more medical care—more than the market alone would provide; and second, that medical professionals and private voluntary institutions were best equipped to decide how to organize those services. . . . In the 1970s this mandate ran out. The economic and moral problems of medicine displaced scientific progress at the center of public attention. Enormous increases in cost seemed ever more certain; corresponding improvements in health ever more doubtful. The prevailing assumptions about the need to expand medical care were reversed: The need now was to curb its apparently insatiable appetite for resources. In a short time, American medicine seemed to pass from stubborn shortages to irrepressible excess, without ever having passed through happy sufficiency. [Paul Starr, The Social Transformation of American Medicine 379 (1982).]

How much does an overnight stay at a Virginia hospital cost? . . . A year ago, Mr. Shipman, a 43-year-old former furniture salesman from Herndon, Va., experienced severe chest pains during the night. . . . Suspecting a heart attack, doctors first performed a cardiac catheterization to examine and unblock the coronary arteries. Then, they inserted a stent, a small metal device that props open a blocked artery so the blood flows better to the heart. Lacking health insurance, Mr. Shipman . . . checked himself out of the hospital against medical advice. Since then, Mr. Shipman and his wife, Alina, have received hospital bills totaling $29,500. . . . In addition, there were other bills: some $1,000 for the ambulance trip, $6,800 from the cardiologist who performed the stent procedure, and several thousand dollars for the local emergency-room visit. In all, the two-day health crisis left the Shipmans saddled with medical bills totaling nearly $40,000. Once solidly middle class, the couple says the debt triggered a gradual unraveling of their lives. "Middle class or not, when you have a bill of $37,000 hanging over your head, that's all you think about," says Ms. Shipman. . . . "You eat, sleep and breathe that bill." [Lucette Lagnado, Anatomy of a Hospital Bill, Wall St. J., Sept. 21, 2004, at B1.]

In its technical brilliance, American health care is unsurpassed. Its best care would have seemed miraculous just a few years ago. But the bad side of American health care is very bad, and there is reason to think that it will get worse before it gets better. For one thing, the coming years will see a further increase in both the number of the elderly in the population and their percentage of the population. The growth will be particularly great among those over 85, the people most likely to make heavy use of the medical system. New technology, for which one can almost always read "expensive" new technology, continues to invade medicine. [Henry T. Greely, The Future of the American Health Care System, 3 Stan. L. & Pol'y Rev. 16 (1991).]

There are few other areas of the U.S. economy where waste is so apparent and the possibility of savings is so tangible. . . . Perhaps the most troubling . . . [fact] is the amount spent on administration. For every office-based physician in the United States, there are 2.2 administrative workers. That exceeds the number of nurses, clinical assistants, and technical staff put together. One large physician group in the United States estimates that it spends 12 percent of revenue just collecting revenue. . . . The situation is no better in hospitals. . . . Duke University Hospital, for example, has 900 hospital beds and 1,300 billing clerks. On top of this are the administrative workers in health insurance. [David Cutler & Dan P. Ly, The (Paper) Work of Medicine, 25 J. Econ. Perspect. 3 (2011).]

There is no U.S. health care system. What we call our health care system is, in daily practice, a hodgepodge of historic legacies, philosophical conflicts, and competing economic schemes. Health care in America combines the tortured, politicized complexity of the U.S. tax code with a cacophony of intractable political, cultural, and religious debates about personal rights and responsibilities. Every time policymakers, corporate health benefits purchasers, or entrepreneurs try to fix something in our health care system, they run smack into its central reality: the primary producers and consumers of medical care are uniquely, stubbornly self-serving as they chew through vast sums of other people's money. Doctors and hospitals stumble their way through irresolvable conflicts between personal gain and ethical responsibilities; patients struggle with the acrimony and anguish that accompany life-and-death medical decisions; consumers, paying for the most part with everybody's money but their own, demand that the system serve them with the immediacy and flexibility of other industries; and health insurers are trapped in the middle, trying to keep everybody happy. A group of highly imaginative, energetic people armed with the world's largest Mark-n-Wipe board could not purposefully design a more complex, dysfunctional system if they tried. It is a $1.3 trillion per year fiasco narrated with moral shrillness and played out one competing anecdote after another. [J. D. Kleinke, Oxymorons: The Myth of a U.S. Health Care System 1 (2001).]

2. *International Comparisons and Medical Tourism.* According to one analysis, the poor U.S. performance on aggregate health statistics noted above (life expectancy, infant death rate) is not due to major differences in health habits or lifestyles, since the United States is similar in many ways to the comparison European countries. Instead, this author argues that the lower U.S. rankings are due in large part to the relatively inadequate system of primary care physicians and the overuse of high-risk procedures. Barbara Starfield, Is U.S. Health Really the Best in the World?, 284 JAMA 483 (2000). Another prominent study found that the British are much healthier than Americans in all major disease areas, such as diabetes, heart disease, stroke, lung disease, and cancer, even after controlling for all relevant sociodemographic factors. J. Banks, M. Marmot et al., Disease and Disadvantage in the United States and England, 295 JAMA 2037 (2006). Consider also, the following, from a health policy expert at Harvard:

Finally, if you take a big step back and look at the data, Americans do better than average in timely access [to care], especially to specialty services and "elective" surgery (which is often not that elective). They tend to be among the [world] leaders in acute care quality, when healthcare means the difference between life and death, although the quality of primary care could surely be better. And America is the innovation engine of the world, pumping out new drugs and treatments that benefit the whole world. . . . [O]verall, while the U.S. healthcare system has a lot of work ahead, we should not overlook its strengths – and they are sizeable.

Ashish Jha, Judging Health Systems: Focusing on What Matters (Sept. 2017).

One sign of better medical value elsewhere is the extent to which Americans who are footing the bill are willing to receive care in other countries, even lesser-developed ones such as India, Mexico, or the Caribbean. See note 3 for readings on this growing phenomenon of "medical tourism" and its host of legal issues.

3. *More Facts, Figures, and Opinions.* There is seemingly an endless appetite for **facts and figures** about the U.S. health care delivery system. Those who wish for more, or more recent numbers, can find them in the annual reports of the Medicare Payment Advisory Commission (MedPac), in periodic issues of Health Affairs, and on the Web pages for the U.S. Census Bureau and the Centers for Medicare and Medicaid Services (CMS), which are linked to the Web page for this book, www. health-law.org.

For more discussion of **what's right or wrong with the U.S. health care system (note 1),** see Elisabeth Rosenthal, An American Sickness (2017); Jonathan Cohn, Sick: The Untold Story of America's Health Care Crisis (2007); Shannon Brownlee, Overtreated: Why Too Much Medicine Is Making Us Sicker and Poorer (2007); David Goldhill, How American Health Care Killed My Father, The Atlantic, Sept. 2009; Tom Daschle, Critical: What We Can Do About the Health-Care Crisis (2008); Einer Elhauge ed., The Fragmentation of U.S. Health Care (2010); Julius B. Richmond & Rashi Fein, The Health Care Mess: How We Got into It and What It Will Take to

Get Out (2005); Paul Krugman & Robin Wells, The Health Care Crisis and What to Do About It, 53 N.Y. Review of Books No. 5 (Mar. 23, 2006); Jonathan Gruber & Helen Levy, The Evolution of Medical Spending Risk, 23 J. Econ. Perspec. 25 (2009); Robert E. Hall & Charles I. Jones, The Value of Life and the Rise in Health Spending, 122 Q. J. Econ. 39 (2007); Kevin Murphy & Robert Topel eds., Measuring the Gains from Medical Research (2003); Elliott S. Fisher, Medical Care: Is More Always Better?, 349 New Eng. J. Med. 1665 (2003); Nortin M. Hadler, The Last Well Person (2004); Henry Aaron & Paul Ginsburg, Is Health Spending Excessive? If So, What Can We Do About It?, 28(5) Health Aff. 1260 (Oct. 2009); Symposium, 39 J.L. Med. & Ethics 111 (2011); President's Council of Economic Advisors, The Economic Case for Health Care Reform (2009); Thomas Bodenheimer, High and Rising Health Care Costs, 142 Annals Intern. Med. 847, 932 (2005); Symposium, 28 Health Aff. 1250 (Oct. 2009); Symposium, 362 New Eng. J. Med. 1 (2010); Symposium, 22(1) Health Aff. 1 (Jan. 2003).

On **international comparisons (note 2)**, see Cathy Schoen et al., U.S. Health System Performance: A National Scorecard, 25 Health Aff. w457 (Sept. 2006); David Squires, Explaining High Health Care Spending in the United States: An International Comparison (Commonwealth Fund 2012); S. H. Woolf, U.S. Health in International Perspective: Shorter Lives, Poorer Health (Institute of Medicine, 2013).

On **medical tourism (note 2)**, see Glenn Cohen & Holly Lynch, Patients with Passports: Medical Tourism, Law and Ethics (2013); Glenn Cohen, Protecting Patients with Passports: Medical Tourism and the Patient Protective Argument, 95 Iowa L. Rev. 1467 (2010); Nathan Cortez, Cross-Border Health Care and the Hydraulics of Health Reform (2012); Nathan Cortez, Recalibrating the Legal Risks of Cross-Border Health Care, 10 Yale J. Health Pol'y L. & Ethics 1 (Winter 2010); Nicolas P. Terry, Under-Regulated Health Care Phenomena in a Flat World: Medical Tourism and Outsourcing, 29 W. New Eng. L. Rev. 421 (2007); Kerrie S. Howze, Medical Tourism: Symptom or Cure?, 41 Ga. L. Rev. 1013 (2007); Thomas R. McLean, The Offshoring of American Medicine, 14 Annals Health L. 205 (2005); Note, 18 Kennedy Inst. Ethics J. 193 (2008) (bibliography); Symposium, 26 Wis. Int'l L.J. 591-964 (2008).

2. History and Structure of Financing and Delivery Systems

■ THE MARKET STRUCTURE OF THE HEALTH INSURANCE INDUSTRY
D. Andrew Austin & Thomas L. Hungerford, *Congressional Research Service, 2009*

The market structure of the modern U.S. health insurance industry not only reflects the complexities and uncertainties of health care, but also its origins in the 1930s and its evolution in succeeding decades. . . . As population shifted from rural agricultural regions to industrialized urban centers, . . . [m]any workers obtained accident or sickness policies through fraternal organizations, labor unions, or private insurers. These policies were usually indemnity plans, that would pay a set cash amount in the event of a serious accident or health emergency. . . .

How The "Blues" Began

The modern health insurance industry in the United States was spurred by the onset of the Great Depression. In 1929, the Baylor University Hospital in Dallas created a pre-paid hospitalization benefit plan for school teachers after a hospital executive discovered that unpaid bills accumulated by local educators were a large burden on hospital finances as well as on the teachers themselves. Unlike earlier health insurance policies, subscribers were entitled to hospital care and services rather than a cash indemnity. . . . Other hospitals in Dallas quickly followed suit with their own group hospitalization plans as a means of ensuring a steady revenue source in difficult economic times.[11] . . . Community-based plans in St. Paul, Minnesota, Washington, D.C., and Cleveland were created soon afterwards. The Blue Cross emblem, first used by the St. Paul plan, was widely adopted by other prepaid hospital benefit plans adhering to American Hospital Association (AHA) guidelines. . . .

The health insurance market in the United States, according to many historians, was originally structured to avoid competition among providers.[15] . . . Hospital and professional groups . . . soon pushed for joint plans that required "free choice of physicians and hospital," rather than plans offered by individual hospitals. Joint plans dampened incentives for local hospitals to compete on the basis of price or generosity of plan benefits. The American Hospital Association strongly favored joint plans that allowed a subscriber to obtain care from any licensed local hospital and viewed single-hospital plans as a threat to the economic stability of community hospitals. . . .

Insurance coverage of physician services lagged behind the growth of Blue Cross hospital plans due to opposition from the American Medical Association (AMA) and restrictive state laws.[19] In several states, however, medical societies set up prepaid service plans to preempt proposed state or federal plans, which evolved into Blue Shield plans. . . . Blue Cross plans accelerated their growth during World War II and extended to almost all states by 1946. Wartime wage and price controls authorized in October 1942 excluded "reasonable" insurance and pension benefits. As industries struggled to expand war production, many employers used health insurance and other fringe benefits to attract new workers. In the late 1940s, the National Labor Relations Board (NLRB) successfully sued employers that refused to bargain collectively over fringe benefits, opening the way for unions to negotiate with employers over health insurance, which further helped boost enrollments in health insurance plans. . . .

[Today, most] private health insurance is offered through employers. With employer-sponsored plans, employers may simply offer health benefit plans through an insurance company for a negotiated price and bear no insurance risk. At the

---

11. Robert Cunningham III and Robert M. Cunningham Jr., *The Blues: A History of the Blue Cross and Blue Shield System* (Dekalb, IL: Northern Illinois University Press, 1997).

15. Rosemary Stevens, *In Sickness and In Wealth: American Hospitals in the 20th Century* (New York: Basic Books, 1989), p. 156.

19. Paul Starr, *The Social Transformation of American Medicine* (New York: Basic Books, 1983), pp. 296-297.

other extreme, the employer may self-insure and handle the plan itself, thus bearing all of the insurance risk and the administrative burden of the plan. Often, the extent of employer involvement depends on the number of employees. Research has found that 80% of large employers (500 or more employees) choose to self-insure rather than purchase coverage from a health insurer. . . .

TAX ADVANTAGES FOR EMPLOYER-PROVIDED HEALTH INSURANCE BENEFITS

. . . Health insurance is subsidized through the tax system in several ways. First, . . . [the] Internal Revenue Code of 1954 included section 106, which explicitly allowed the exclusion of employer contributions for health insurance. . . . The Joint Committee on Taxation (JCT) estimates that the federal government forgoes [over $250 billion] annually in tax revenue because of this exclusion. . . . The tax exemption for employer-provided health care made health insurance cheaper than non-exempt forms of consumption for individuals. One study found that health insurance coverage following the 1954 tax changes expanded more rapidly among employees with higher incomes, who generally had marginal tax rates, which could indicate that the tax exclusion led workers to demand more extensive or generous plans. Other factors, such as rising income levels, competition for workers, and rising medical costs, also spurred growth in employer-provided health benefits. . . .

COMMERCIAL INSURERS ENTER

Before World War II, many commercial insurers doubted that hospital or medical costs were an insurable risk. Insurers traditionally considered a risk insurable only if the potential losses were definite, measurable and not subject to control by the insured. The financial risks linked to illness or injury, however, could vary depending on the judgment of medical personnel, and behavior of the insured could affect the probability of ill health in many ways. After the rapid spread of Blue Cross plans in the mid-1930s, however, several commercial insurers began to offer similar health coverage. By the 1950s, commercial health insurers had become potent competitors and began to cut into Blue Cross's market share in many parts of the country. The large-scale entry of commercial insurers into the health insurance market changed the competitive environment. . . .

[T]he commercial health insurers were not bound to set premiums using the Blue Cross community rating principle, which linked premiums to average claims costs across a geographic area rather than to the claims experience of particular groups or individuals. Therefore, commercial insurers using an "experience rating" approach were able to underbid Blue Cross for firms that employed healthier-than-average individuals, which on average were cheaper to insure.

The loss of healthier groups then raised average costs among remaining groups, which . . . compelled Blue Cross to adopt experience rating. . . . The shift toward experience rating changed the nature of competition in the health insurance market. Insurers could cut costs by shifting risks to others, by recruiting firms whose employees and their families were healthier than average, rather than finding more efficient ways of managing risks for a given pool of subscribers. . . .

By the 1980s, health researchers and policymakers had begun to view the differences between Blue Cross/Blue Shield insurers, which were organized as non-profit organizations, and for-profit commercial health insurers as having narrowed. . . . In 1994, Blue Cross/Blue Shield guidelines were amended to let affiliates reorganize as for-profit insurers, leading the way for more than a dozen Blue Cross/Blue Shield affiliates to convert to for-profit status. Other Blue Cross/Blue Shield insurers bought other insurers, merged, or restructured in other ways. At the same time, private insurers acquired HMOs and other managed care organizations. Consolidations reduced both the number of commercial and Blue Cross/Blue Shield organizations, leading to the emergence of a small number of very large insurers with strong market positions across the country. . . .

INTRODUCTION OF MEDICARE AND MEDICAID

. . . While Blue Cross/Blue Shield and commercial insurance plans covered a large portion of employees and their dependents at the end of the 1950s, many low-income and elderly people had trouble obtaining affordable health insurance or paying for health care. . . . Social Security was extended to pay providers to cover certain medical costs incurred by aged, blind, and disabled beneficiaries starting in 1950. . . . State governments, subject to certain federal requirements, retained substantial discretion over benefit levels and income limits, which were typically linked to welfare assistance programs. . . .

In 1965, the Johnson Administration worked with Ways and Means Committee Chairman Wilbur Mills to create the Medicare program, which provided health insurance for nearly all Americans over age 65. Medicare combined a compulsory hospital insurance program (Part A) with a voluntary physician services plan (Part B). While some had worried that Medicare would displace private insurers, Blue Cross organizations became fiscal intermediaries for Medicare, responsible for issuing payments to providers and other back office operations. Medicaid, created in the same 1965 act, is a means-tested program financed by federal and state funds. Each state designs and administers its own program under federal rules. Over time, Medicaid eligibility standards and federal requirements have become more complex. . . .

THE RISE OF MANAGED CARE [AND "CONSUMER-DIRECTED" CARE]

In some parts of the country, plans combining insurance with the direct provision of health care evolved into important players in local markets despite the strong opposition of the AHA and AMA. A health plan designed for southern California construction workers in the mid-1930s eventually became the Kaiser Health Plan. . . . While some of these plans prospered locally or regionally, they did not achieve national reach until the 1970s.

In 1971, President Nixon announced a program to encourage prepaid group plans that joined insurance and care functions as a way to constrain the growth of medical care costs, which had risen sharply in the years following the startup of the Medicare and Medicaid programs, and to enhance competition in the health insurance market. Advocates claimed that health maintenance organizations (HMOs), which integrate health care and health insurance functions, would have a financial motive to promote wellness and would lack incentives to overprovide care. . . .

While this ambitious goal was not reached in the 1970s, by the late 1980s policymakers and businesses began to view greater use of managed care organizations such as HMOs and similar organizations as a key strategy for controlling health care costs. In the mid-1990s, the broader use of more restrictive forms of managed care (such as stringent gatekeeper, second medical opinion, and pre-approval requirements) sparked strong consumer resistance, which forced an industry retreat from some of those strategies. Networks of providers, known as preferred provider organizations (PPOs), grew rapidly in the late 1980s and early 1990s. PPOs, often owned by hospital systems and other providers, typically contract with insurers or self-insured firms and offer discounted fee-for-service (FFS) rates. PPO enrollees who receive care outside of the network typically must obtain plan approval or pay more. Thus, PPO plans provided patients with more flexibility than staff-model HMOs, which generally did not cover care provided outside of the HMO. As various types of managed care plans such as HMOs and PPOs became widespread, more employers offered choices among competing health plans to let workers willing to pay higher premiums avoid restrictive plans. . . .

The predominant type of health insurance plan has changed dramatically over the past 25 years. Over 90% of the privately insured were covered by an indemnity or traditional "unmanaged" health insurance plan in 1980; now the share is less than 10%. Today, most people covered by private insurance are covered by some kind of managed care plan ranging from a managed indemnity plan (e.g., PPOs, where the insurers negotiate fees with providers) to a staff HMO (the insurer and the provider are the same, and patients see physicians who are on salary). . . .

In the 1990s, proponents of "consumer-directed" health care proposed measures intended to make consumers more sensitive to medical care costs. In . . . 2003 . . . Congress passed legislation to allow consumers with high-deductible health insurance plans to set up Health Savings Accounts (HSAs) that allow people to pay for out-of-pocket expenses through a tax-advantaged medical savings account. . . .

DESCRIPTION OF THE HEALTH INSURANCE MARKET

Individuals and families typically buy insurance to avoid risks by paying a known premium in order to receive benefits if an adverse event were to occur during the insurance policy's term. Most individuals are willing to pay an insurer to assume the bulk of financial risks associated with unpredictable health outcomes of uncertain severity. . . . Some insured people will become sick or injured and incur significant medical expenses. Most people, however, will remain relatively healthy, thus incurring little or no medical expenses.[54] . . . In essence, money is shifted from those who remain healthy to those who become sick or injured.

The health insurance market is tightly interrelated with other parts of the health care system. . . . Health insurers not only reimburse providers, but also typically have some control over the number and types of services covered and negotiate contracts with providers on the payments for health services. . . .

The health insurance market has many features that push it far from the economic benchmark of perfect competition. . . . How insurers design health care

---

54. A analysis of 2002 Medical Expenditure Panel Survey data found that "[h]alf of the population spends little or nothing on health care, while 5 percent of the population spends almost half of the total amount." . . . [See also National Institute for Health Care Management, The Concentration of Health Care Spending (2012).]

networks influences how consumers use health care. Consumers typically choose a primary physician who selects tests and treatments and makes referrals to medical specialists. Employers negotiate with insurers on behalf of their workers, and labor unions negotiate with employers over health benefits on behalf of their members. Health insurers, in turn, negotiate contracts with providers and handle payments for individual services. A primary physician's admitting privileges typically determine where his patient goes for non-emergency hospital care. Patients must go through a physician to obtain most medical tests and pharmaceuticals. Health care consumers typically rely on these intermediaries instead of interacting directly with other parts of the health care system. This heavy reliance on intermediaries is a key characteristic of the current health care market. . . .

Using intermediaries such as health insurers protects consumers from financial risks linked to serious medical problems, but it also insulates consumers from information about costs and prices for specific health care goods and services. When a third-party, such as a private insurer or a government, pays for the bulk of health care costs, consumers may demand more care and providers may wish to supply more care. Links among intermediaries and providers can also limit consumers' choices. For example, a person's job may limit her health insurance choices, and another person's choice of physician may limit choices among hospitals. Some families and individuals lacking these intermediaries must navigate the health insurance and health care system themselves, which may be a serious challenge. . . .

Finally, how intermediaries interact has important consequences in the health care market. For instance, employers and health insurers, which both intermediate on behalf of individuals, interact through negotiations over insurance benefits packages. Politicians can also act as intermediaries for their constituents by helping to determine reimbursement rates for public insurance programs and by changing the regulatory environment facing health insurers. . . .

MORAL HAZARD

Moral hazard, which occurs when insurance status changes behavior, is another problem in the health insurance market. Moral hazard occurs if an insured individual consumes more medical services than she would have had she been uninsured. For example, having health insurance could induce someone to seek medical care for minor conditions (e.g., a sore throat), choose a high-amenity health care setting (e.g., a more hotel-like hospital), or neglect his health (e.g., by eating fatty foods). Consequently, moral hazard leads the insurer to pay providers more for an insured person's medical services than that person would have paid out of his own pocket had he not been insured. Of course, non-monetary costs, such as the pain and inconvenience of obtaining unnecessary medical care, may help limit moral hazard among patients.

Insurers typically react to moral hazard by raising premiums to cover the costs of additional services and by limiting care, either directly (e.g., through prior approval requirements) or through cost-sharing measures such as copayments and deductibles. . . . The lack of transparency in the pricing of medical services contributes to this problem—most people do not know the cost of medical services (both what the provider normally charges and what the insurance company reimburses the provider).

THE PRINCIPAL-AGENT PROBLEM

A patient (here, a *principal*), as noted above, typically relies on a physician (an *agent*) for care and advice. The physician, or other intermediary, might face incentives to act to further their own interests, rather than those of the patient, by providing a higher quantity or lower quality of care than would be appropriate for a patient. . . . [P]ayment and incentive systems may mitigate conflicts of interests. Professional standards and professional organizations may also help mitigate those conflicts. . . .

While that arrangement may avoid some problems, it may not solve others. In fee-for-service (FFS) arrangements, physicians and other providers may face financial incentives to provide more care than would best suit the patient's interests. When insurance pays most of the costs associated with health care, providers have little financial incentive to control costs and may overprovide health care services. One study randomly selected doctors into a salary group and a fee-for-service group during a nine-month study. The results showed that doctors in the fee-for-service group scheduled more office visits than salaried doctors, and almost all of the difference was due to the fee-for-service doctors seeing well patients rather than sick patients. Defensive medicine, in which physicians or other providers order tests that may reduce the probability of medical malpractice litigation, but which provide limited therapeutic benefits to the patient, presents a similar problem. . . .

Responses to . . . moral hazard and principal-agent problems affect the structure of the health financing system. Health insurers, as noted above, use coinsurance and pre-approval requirements to limit potential moral hazard among patients. Health insurers concerned about moral hazard and principal-agent problems among providers design incentive systems to limit overprovision of care. For example, the rapid transition to managed care in the 1990s might be seen as an attempt to control costs due to moral hazard. In addition, research and development (R&D) decisions made by medical technology and pharmaceutical firms may be indirectly guided by how health insurance coverage affects choices of providers and patients. Reforms that change the health financing system without taking into account potential moral hazards that previous structures and practices were designed to mitigate could encounter unanticipated problems. . . .

■ MEDICARE AND THE AMERICAN HEALTH CARE SYSTEM: 1996 REPORT TO CONGRESS
Prospective Payment Assessment Commission

The most common managed care models are health maintenance organizations (HMOs), preferred provider organizations (PPOs), and point-of-service (POS) plans. In a traditional HMO plan, subscribers must receive their care from a limited group of providers. PPO and POS subscribers may not be subject to the same level of plan oversight as in HMOs: Generally they may go to any provider, but their out-of-pocket payments are lower if they choose participating providers that give the insurer discounted rates. . . .

Managed care plans use a variety of techniques to control their costs. First, they actively seek providers with lower-cost practice patterns and offer them a defined patient base in exchange for favorable payment rates. By limiting the number of providers or by creating strong financial incentives to choose certain ones, managed care plans influence which providers subscribers will use. Through this selective contracting, managed care plans can substantially affect providers' revenues. Plans' bargaining positions are strongest in areas with excess provider capacity. Providers that choose not to participate or that are not selected by the managed care plan may experience a decline in their patient volume.

In addition, managed care plans often use discounted fee-for-service rates to control their costs. They also use per case, per day, or per person payments to shift some of the financial risk of treating patients to providers. Per case or per day payments are generally made to hospitals, whereas per person payments are more often made to physicians, predominately primary care practitioners. These payment methods reward providers for delivering care efficiently, discouraging unnecessary service use.

A per person, or capitation, payment system is the most comprehensive way to shift financial risk to providers. Under capitation, providers receive a prepaid sum to furnish a defined set of services to a plan's enrollees. This creates a monetary incentive for physicians to limit patients' use of services (or encourage preventive services) because the physician receives the same payment regardless of the volume or intensity of care, or even if no care is provided at all. Many managed care plans also require primary care physicians to act as "gatekeepers" to specialty care or hospital services. Under these arrangements, the primary care physician must pre-authorize any services a patient receives. While these physicians usually do not bear the full financial risk for the additional services, delegating the gatekeeping function enables managed care plans to use financial incentives to limit referrals. . . .

Hospitals [and Physicians]

. . . The long-term effects of the changing environment on hospitals are still unclear. . . . Hospitals traditionally have been viewed as the hub of the health care system and often have the capital reserves necessary to finance collaborations with other providers. Those that aggressively pursue such arrangements not only can improve their chances of being the hospital of choice for inpatient services, but also can exert more influence over medical practice decisions. In areas where managed care systems exert more control, however, hospitals may be viewed as cost centers with little input into delivery decisions.

Historically, physicians determined not only which services would be provided, but where those services would be delivered. These decisions generally were made with little accountability for costs. Managed care is changing this. . . . One indication of the level of financial pressure physicians are facing is the [reduced growth] in physician income. . . . Some physicians are responding to the intensified pressures by selling their practices to hospitals or managed care organizations, and becoming employees of those entities. . . . [On the other hand,] [b]ecause physicians generate the demand for hospital services, they have leverage to assume a leadership role in arrangements with other providers. . . .

■ TRANSCRIPT OF INTERVIEW WITH
JAMIE ROBINSON, Ph.D.*
Lehman Brothers Industry Expert Conference Call Series *May 17, 2002*

As we go into the new decade, the insurance industry is reevaluating whether it wants to be America's method of health care cost control. It's found that this is a very difficult and very unappreciated job. It appears to the public that there is a tradeoff between corporate profits and individual health care, which is a very, very bad image for the industry. The insurers now want to have a completely different image, which is helping the consumer make health care choices. . . .

I think the battle is over and the providers won. The health plans don't really want to get in there and second-guess doctor decision-making. That just proved to be a turf where the providers were very strong, and had the support of the patients and the regulators. . . . There is a lot of lousy medicine being practiced out there that the insurance companies could detect, and could clean up, but they could never convince anybody that they're doing it for the right reasons rather than simply for their own profits.

They've essentially abandoned that role. Increasingly they want to see themselves as a financial services company, like a Fidelity, [which manages investment funds for retirement accounts]. . . . Fidelity offer[s] a stock fund and a bond fund and a mixed fund and employees can allocate their savings across these however they want [with the help of] some decision support tools. . . . The health plans want to do that on the health plan side. "We have our PPO product and our HMO product and our Medical Savings Account product and we're not going to try to force people to pick one or the other. We're going to give them choices. We're going to give them information about the different products, about their prices, about access and about quality. We're going to give them Internet based decision support and tools, and we're going to let them choose. After that, what happens is between the patient and their doctor and their hospital. We, the insurance company, are not going to be responsible for that." . . .

One of the reasons that the insurance industry wants to get out of managed care and go back to being like the financial services industry is that it wants to stop being continually compared to the tobacco industry. It doesn't want to be the second most hated industry in America. The industry needs to re-brand itself as a consumer friendly decision support and information industry rather than something that's trying to save money for corporations.

Notes: Managed Care vs. Consumer-Driven Care

1. *Managed Care Is Here to Stay.* Despite fierce resistance by many doctors and some patients, managed care remains the dominant form of insurance. However, enrollment has shifted rather dramatically in recent years from tightly managed HMO plans to PPO and other open network plans that give patients more options. Regardless of the form managed care takes, it raises a host of legal, ethical, and

---

*Reprinted with the permission of Prof. Robinson and the former Lehman Brothers.

regulatory issues. For now, consider these broad inquiries: Are you concerned that insurers are interfering with medical judgment by deciding what treatments to pay for? Would you be more comfortable with a regime that let physicians and patients decide for themselves, but rewarded physicians for saving money or punished them for being excessive? Or is the answer to make patients pay much more out of pocket so that they regulate their own spending decisions?

2. *Accountable Care Organizations.* The latest trend (and newest buzz term) in health care organization and finance are accountable care organizations (or ACOs). ACOs are a loosely defined concept that consists of doctors and hospitals organizing themselves in a fashion that receives and distributes bundled payment for a broader range of services and that claims some joint responsibility for the quality of care across an array of treatment settings. Many skeptics question how this idea differs from the mostly failed attempt in the 1990s to form provider-led HMOs. The typical response is that we've learned from those mistakes and that we'll do it differently this time.

3. *The "Consumer-Directed" Movement.* Patients can be sensitized to the costs of treatment options in a variety of ways, loosely referred to as "consumer-directed" health care. One approach is simply to increase substantially the co-payment and deductible amounts, producing what is known as "catastrophic" insurance. "Catastrophic" refers to insurance that kicks in only after a patient has incurred a very large expense; for instance, after paying out of pocket the first $5,000 in a year.

Although there is no crisp definition of what counts as "catastrophic" coverage, health plans with very high deductibles have proliferated over the past decade. In 2006, just 4 percent of employees were enrolled in a plan with a deductible of at least $1,000 for an individual or $2,000 for a family. By 2016, that figure stood at 29 percent. See Kaiser Family Foundation, 2016 Employer Health Benefits Annual Survey, Fig. 8.5. Notwithstanding consumer dissatisfaction, the trend toward greater cost-sharing persists. A few states are even experimenting with limited cost-sharing in their Medicaid programs. See John Z. Ayanian, Michigan's Approach to Medicaid Expansion and Reform, 369 New Eng. J. Med. 1773 (2013).

4. *The Onslaught of Acronyms.* Regrettably, the health care field is overrun with acronyms. Since 1970 or so, no new institution or phenomenon seemingly can exist in medicine without being known primarily by its three-to-five-letter abbreviation. Most of the specialized organizational terms and acronyms you will encounter in these readings are collected and defined in the glossary at page 363 for convenient reference through the semester.

2

▪

The Treatment Relationship: Formation and Termination

This book explores the legal issues that lie at the core of the provider-patient relationship. By provider, we mean doctors, hospitals, and other people and institutions that deliver health care services. Chapter 2 examines the basic structure of the treatment relationship, including topics such as the duty to treat and the formation and termination of the treatment relationship. Chapter 3 considers the fiduciary nature of the treatment relationship, with coverage including confidentiality, informed consent, and conflicts of interest. Chapter 4 is devoted to medical malpractice liability. These patient care issues all spring directly from how providers and patients interact at the point of treatment. Although these interactions are certainly influenced by institutional, financial, and regulatory forces, this external environment is not explored in depth in this book.

The provider-patient relationship is governed primarily by contract, tort, and fiduciary law—all aspects of private rather than public law. The treatment relationship starts and ends in contract law. Contract principles determine whether there is a duty to accept a patient and whether treatment can be terminated. But, between these defining points, the *content* of the treatment relationship is determined primarily by tort and fiduciary law, not by contract. That is because the treatment encounter creates what is known as a "relational contract," one that governs a complex relationship by incorporating external social norms rather than by specifying detailed performance requirements and standards. Cf. Maureen Armour, A Nursing Home's Good Faith Duty "to" Care: Redefining a Fragile Relationship Using the Law of Contract, 39 St. Louis U. L.J. 217 (1994). Tort and fiduciary law are richer sources for social and professional norms relating to medicine than the law generated by commercial sales. Ultimately, however, medical relationships are constrained by government regulations that determine who is allowed to practice one of the healing arts and whether any particular treatments are unsafe or ineffective.

To better understand this interconnected web of legal doctrine, we begin with a chapter on the basic structure and regulation of the treatment relationship: how it is formed, how it is terminated, and the extent to which it can be altered and defined by private agreement or constrained by government regulation. In the following two chapters, we look more at the content of treatment relationships, starting first with the fiduciary duties of confidentiality, candor, and loyalty, and then in the next chapter considering the full extent of malpractice liability.

While the focus of the following three chapters is, respectively, contract, fiduciary, and tort law, the divisions among these bodies of law are not so neatly confined. Each set of private law concepts can be felt throughout this book. Thus, there is a broad inquiry that connects all of these chapters: To what extent should the structure and content of medical relationships be defined by the parties themselves, by legal norms based in conventional common law doctrine, or by explicit legislative oversight tailored specifically to the medical context?

Ordinarily, the patient-provider relationship is a consensual one to which both parties must agree. Therefore, an individual physician may, generally speaking, refuse to accept patients for any reason or for no reason. The same is true to a lesser extent for hospitals and other institutions. But this general freedom of contract is limited in several important ways. Hospitals may not turn patients away in emergencies until they have at least stabilized the patient's condition. Neither may doctors or hospitals refuse patients for certain discriminatory reasons, such as the patient's race, sex, or HIV status. Once treatment has begun, it may not be ceased without proper arrangements being made. And providers may not impose unreasonable conditions on their agreement to treat. While historically a physician's freedom to turn away patients found its limitations primarily in the law, the growth of formal arrangements between managed care health plans and physicians means that a provider's obligation to treat is being increasingly defined by the private agreements among the patient, insurance plan, and provider. The following materials explore the origins of, and limits on, this freedom of contract between providers and patients.

A. THE DUTY TO TREAT

1. *The Duty to Accept Patients*

■ HURLEY v. EDDINGFIELD
   59 N.E. 1058 (Ind. 1901)

Baker, Justice.

The appellant sued appellee for $10,000 damages for wrongfully causing the death of his intestate. The court sustained appellee's demurrer to the complaint, and this ruling is assigned as error.

The material facts may be summarized thus: At and for years before decedent's death appellee was a practicing physician at Mace, in Montgomery county, duly licensed under the laws of the state. He held himself out to the public as a general practitioner of medicine. He had been decedent's family physician. Decedent became dangerously ill, and sent for appellee. The messenger informed appellee of decedent's violent sickness, tendered him his fee for his services, and stated to him that no other physician was procurable in time, and that decedent relied on him for attention. No other physician was procurable in time to be of any use, and decedent did rely on appellee for medical assistance. Without any reasons whatever, appellee refused to render aid to decedent. No other patients were requiring appellee's immediate service, and he could have gone to the relief of decedent if he had been willing to do so. Death ensued, without decedent's fault, and wholly from appellee's wrongful act. The alleged wrongful act was appellee's refusal to enter into a contract of employment. Counsel do not contend that, before the enactment of the law regulating the practice of medicine, physicians were bound to render professional service to everyone who applied. The act regulating the practice of medicine provides for a board of examiners, standards of qualification, examinations, licenses to those found qualified, and penalties for practicing without license. The act is a preventive, not a compulsive, measure. In obtaining the state's license (permission) to practice medicine, the state does not require, and the licensee does not engage, that he will practice at all or on other terms than he may choose to accept. Counsel's analogies, drawn from the obligations to the public on the part of innkeepers, common carriers, and the like, are beside the mark. Judgment affirmed.

■WILMINGTON GENERAL HOSPITAL v. MANLOVE
174 A.2d 135 (Del. 1961)

SOUTHERLAND, Chief Justice.

This case concerns the liability of a private hospital for the death of an infant who was refused treatment at the emergency ward of the hospital. The facts are these:

On January 4, 1959, Darien E. Manlove, the deceased infant, then four months old, developed diarrhea. The next morning his parents consulted Dr. Hershon. They asked whether the medicine they had for him was all right and the doctor said that it was. In the evening of the same day Mrs. Manlove took the baby's temperature. It was higher than normal. They called Dr. Hershon, and he prescribed additional medication (streptomycin), which he ordered delivered by a pharmacy.

Mrs. Manlove stayed up with the child that night. He did not sleep. On the morning of January 6th, the parents took the infant to Dr. Hershon's office. Dr. Thomas examined the child and treated him for sore throat and diarrhea. He prescribed a liquid diet and some medicine. . . .

On the morning of January 7th (a Wednesday) [the infant's] temperature was still above normal—102. Mr. and Mrs. Manlove determined to seek additional medical assistance. They knew that Dr. Hershon and Dr. Thomas were not in their offices on Wednesdays, and they took their infant to the emergency ward of the Wilmington General Hospital.

There is no real conflict of fact as to what occurred at the hospital. The parents took the infant into the reception room of the Emergency Ward. A nurse was on duty. They explained to the nurse what was wrong with the child, that is, that he had not slept for two nights, had a continuously high temperature, and that he had diarrhea. Mr. Manlove told the nurse that the child was under the care of Dr. Hershon and Dr. Thomas, and showed the nurse the medicines prescribed. The nurse explained to the parents that the hospital could not give treatment because the child was under the care of a physician and there would be danger that the medication of the hospital might conflict with that of the attending physician. The nurse did not examine the child, take his temperature, feel his forehead, or look down his throat. The child was not in convulsions, and was not coughing or crying. There was no particular area of body tenderness.

The nurse tried to get in touch with Dr. Hershon or Dr. Thomas in the hospital and at their offices, but was unable to do so. She suggested that the parents bring the baby Thursday morning to the pediatric clinic.

Mr. and Mrs. Manlove returned home. Mrs. Manlove made an appointment by telephone to see Dr. Hershon or Dr. Thomas that night at eight o'clock. At eight minutes past three o'clock in the afternoon the baby died of bronchial pneumonia. . . .

It was assumed by both parties below that the hospital was a private hospital and not a public one — that is, an institution founded and controlled by private persons and not by public authority. The trial court disagreed, finding a quasi-public status in the receipt of grants of public money and tax exemptions. . . . Hence, the court concluded, liability may be imposed on the defendant in an emergency case.

We are compelled to disagree with the view that the defendant has become a public (or quasi-public) hospital. It is admitted (although the record does not show it) that it is privately owned and operated. We find no dissent from the rule that such a hospital is a private hospital, and may, at least in the absence of control by the legislature, conduct its business largely as it sees fit. . . .

Moreover, the holding that the receipt of grants of public money requires the hospital to care for emergency cases, as distinguished from others, is not logical. Why emergency cases? If the holding is sound it must apply to all the hospital services, and that conclusion, as we shall see, is clearly unsound. . . .

We are of opinion that the defendant is a private and not a public hospital, in so far as concerns the right of a member of the public to demand admission or treatment. What, then, is the liability of a private hospital in this respect?

Since such an institution as the defendant is privately owned and operated, it would follow logically that its trustees or governing board alone have the right to determine who shall be admitted to it as patients. No other rule would be sensible or workable. Such authority as we have found supports this rule. "A private hospital owes the public no duty to accept any patient not desired by it, and it is not necessary to assign any reason for its refusal to accept a patient for hospital service." 41 C. J. S. Hospitals §8, p.345. . . .

. . . Does that rule apply to the fullest extent to patients applying for treatment at an emergency ward? . . .

It may be conceded that a private hospital is under no legal obligation to the public to maintain an emergency ward, or, for that matter, a public clinic. But the maintenance of such a ward to render first-aid to injured persons has become a well-established adjunct to the main business of a hospital. If a person, seriously hurt, applies for such aid at an emergency ward, relying on the established custom to render it, is it still the right of the hospital to turn him away without any reason?

In such a case, it seems to us, such a refusal might well result in worsening the condition of the injured person, because of the time lost in a useless attempt to obtain medical aid. Such a set of circumstances is analogous to the case of the negligent termination of gratuitous services, which creates a tort liability. Restatement, Law of Torts, "Negligence," §323. . . .

As above indicated, we are of opinion that liability on the part of a hospital may be predicated on the refusal of service to a patient in case of an unmistakable emergency, if the patient has relied upon a well-established custom of the hospital to render aid in such a case. . . .

Applying this rule here, we inquire, was there an unmistakable emergency? Certainly, the record does not support the view that the infant's condition was so desperate that a layman could reasonably say that he was in immediate danger. The learned judge indicated that the fact that death followed in a few hours showed an emergency; but with this we cannot agree. It is hindsight. And it is to be noted that the attending physician, after prescribing for the child one morning before, did not think another examination that night or the next morning was required. If this case had gone to the jury on the record here made, we would have been required to hold that it was insufficient to establish liability. We cannot agree that the mere recitation of the infant's symptoms was, in itself, evidence of an emergency sufficient to present a question for the jury. Before such an issue could arise there would have to be evidence that an experienced nurse should have known that such symptoms constituted unmistakable evidence of an emergency. . . .

The possibility that the case might turn on additional evidence respecting the matters we have touched upon was not considered either by the court or counsel. In these circumstances, we think the case should go back for further proceedings. We should add, however, that if plaintiff cannot adduce evidence showing some incompetency of the nurse, or some breach of duty or some negligence, his case must fail. Like the learned judge below, we sympathize with the parents in their loss of a child; but this natural feeling does not permit us to find liability in the absence of satisfactory evidence.

For the reasons above set forth the order denying summary judgment is affirmed, without approving the reasons therefor set forth in the court's opinion.

■ WIDEMAN v. SHALLOWFORD COMMUNITY HOSPITAL
826 F.2d 1030 (11th Cir. 1987)

HILL, Circuit Judge.

This case presents the novel question of whether a county government's alleged practice of using its emergency medical vehicles only to transport patients to certain county hospitals which guarantee the payment of the county's medical bills violates a right protected by the federal constitution. We hold that such a practice, even if proved, would not violate any established constitutional right. . . .

I. BACKGROUND

The facts underlying this case are undeniably tragic. On April 12, 1984, Toni Wideman, who at the time was four months pregnant, began experiencing abdominal pain. She called her obstetrician, Dr. John Ramsey, who instructed her to come immediately to Piedmont Hospital. Ms. Wideman called the 911 emergency telephone number in DeKalb County and requested an ambulance to take her to Piedmont. Three employees of the DeKalb County Emergency Medical Service (EMS) responded to this call. Ms. Wideman claims that she again informed the EMS employees to take her to Piedmont where her doctor was waiting, but they refused and, instead, took her against her wishes to Shallowford Community Hospital. After a substantial delay, during which the attending physician at Shallowford spoke by phone with Dr. Ramsey, Ms. Wideman was transferred to Piedmont. At that point, however, Dr. Ramsey was unable to stop her labor, and Ms. Wideman gave birth to a premature baby, named Ebony Laslun Wideman, who survived for only four hours. . . .

. . . It seems that both parties, as well as the district court, have assumed that the alleged policy violates a cognizable constitutional right, which the plaintiffs characterize as their right to the provision of essential medical treatment and services by the county.[1] However, . . . the proper resolution of this case requires us first to determine whether the Constitution grants a right to medical care and treatment in these circumstances. . . .

III. A. EXISTENCE OF A CONSTITUTIONAL RIGHT TO ESSENTIAL MEDICAL CARE

Beginning from the broadest prospective, we can discern no general right, based upon either the Constitution or federal statutes, to the provision of medical treatment and services by a state or municipality. If such a right exists at all, it must derive from the Fourteenth Amendment's due process clause, which forbids a state to deprive anyone of life, liberty or property without due process of law. The due process clause, however, has traditionally been interpreted as protecting certain "negative liberties," i.e., an individual's right to be free from arbitrary or discriminatory action taken by a state or municipality. This circuit has recognized the "well established notion that the Constitution limits the actions the states can take rather than mandating specific obligations." Bradberry v. Pinellas County, 789 F.2d 1513, 1517 (11th Cir. 1986). . . .

Two Supreme Court decisions dealing with access to abortions also support our conclusion that there is no general right to medical care or treatment provided by the state. In Maher v. Roe, 432 U.S. 464 (1977), two indigent women brought suit challenging a Connecticut regulation prohibiting the funding of abortions that were not medically necessary. The plaintiffs argued under the Fourteenth Amendment that the state regulation impinged on their constitutional right to an abortion, as recognized in Roe v. Wade, 410 U.S. 113 (1973). The Court upheld the state regulation, concluding that *Roe* did not declare an unqualified constitutional right to an abortion; rather, that case declared a woman's right to be protected from

1. The constitutional right alleged by the plaintiffs arguably may be characterized as the much more specific right to the medical care and services of their choice. Ms. Wideman was provided with medical care in this case; indeed, she was rushed to a hospital in an ambulance provided by the county. Her claim appears to be that she should have been able to direct the ambulance wherever she wanted to go. For purposes of our analysis, however, we shall consider the plaintiffs' alleged constitutional right as they have characterized it.

unduly burdensome interference with her freedom to decide whether to terminate her pregnancy. Significantly, in reaching this result, the Court noted that "the Constitution imposes no obligation on the states to pay the pregnancy-related medical expenses of indigent women, or indeed to pay any of the medical expenses of indigents." *Maher*, 432 U.S. at 469 (footnote omitted).

The Court's subsequent decision in Harris v. McRae, 448 U.S. 297 (1980), reinforced the constitutional distinction between requiring the state to provide medical services and prohibiting the state from impeding access to such services. The plaintiffs in *Harris* challenged the constitutionality of the Hyde amendment, which denied public funding for certain medically necessary abortions, as violating their due process liberty interest in deciding whether to terminate a pregnancy. The Supreme Court held that although the liberty protected by the due process clause prohibits unwarranted government interference with freedom of choice in the context of certain personal decisions, "it does not confer an entitlement to such funds as may be necessary to realize all the advantages of that freedom." . . . More recently, the Court has interpreted *Maher* and *Harris* as standing for the proposition that, "as a general matter, the state is under no constitutional duty to provide substantive services for those within its border." Youngberg v. Romeo, 457 U.S. 307, 317 (1982).

Several courts of appeals decisions have addressed the issue of whether a state or municipality has a duty under the Fourteenth Amendment to provide various protective services to its citizens. Almost without exception, these courts have concluded that governments are under no constitutional duty to provide police, fire, or other public safety services. . . .

B

That there exists no such general right to the provision of medical care and services by the state, however, does not end our inquiry. Both the Supreme Court and various circuit courts have indicated that the existence of a "special custodial or other relationship" between an individual and the state may trigger a constitutional duty on the part of the state to provide certain medical or other services. In these special circumstances, the state's failure to provide such services might implicate constitutionally protected rights.

For example, the Supreme Court has held that the Eighth Amendment prohibition against cruel and unusual punishments, applicable to the states via the Fourteenth Amendment, requires states to provide medical care for those whom it is punishing by incarceration. . . . Similarly, the Court has held that an involuntarily committed mental patient retains . . . a clear Fourteenth Amendment right "to adequate food, shelter, clothing, and medical care." *Youngberg*, 457 U.S. at 315. . . .

Following this rationale, a constitutional duty can arise only when a state or municipality, by exercising a significant degree of custody or control over an individual, places that person in a worse situation than he would have been had the government not acted at all. Such a situation could arise by virtue of the state affirmatively placing an individual in a position of danger, effectively stripping a person of her ability to defend herself, or cutting off potential sources of private aid. The key concept is the exercise of coercion, dominion, or restraint by the state. . . .

In the present case, we conclude that DeKalb County did not exercise a degree of coercion, dominion, or restraint over Ms. Wideman sufficient to create a "special relationship." . . . The county did not force or otherwise coerce her into its ambulance; it merely made the ambulance available to her, and she entered it voluntarily. Ms. Wideman's physical condition at the time might have required her to seek immediate medical help, and that need might have induced her to make use of the service provided by the county, hoping that she could convince the EMS employees to take her where she wanted to go. Her physical condition, however, cannot be attributed to the county. . . . Therefore, the county was under no affirmative constitutional duty to provide any particular type of emergency medical service for her. . . .

. . . Because the Constitution does not require municipalities to provide any emergency medical services at all, it would be anomalous indeed to hold them liable for providing limited services which happen to be less extensive than a particular citizen may desire. . . .

Notes: The Differing Obligations of Physicians and Hospitals; Hospitals as Quasi-Public Facilities

1. *The "No Duty" Rule.* The complaint and brief in Hurley v. Eddingfield reveal that the deceased patient was in distress during childbirth, yet, as the *Hurley* court suggests, physicians are not obligated to provide care to a particular patient unless they have agreed to do so. A standard characterization of this principle appears in Oliver v. Brock, 342 So. 2d 1, 3 (Ala. 1976):

> A physician is under no obligation to engage in practice or to accept professional employment, but when the professional services of a physician are accepted by another person for the purposes of medical or surgical treatment, the relation of physician and patient is created. The relation is a consensual one wherein the patient knowingly seeks the assistance of a physician and the physician knowingly accepts him as patient. The relationship between a physician and patient may result from an express or implied contract, either general or special, and the rights and liabilities of the parties thereto are governed by the general law of contract. . . . 61 Am. Jur. 2d, Physicians, Surgeons, and Other Healers, §96.

This "no duty" rule is consistent with tort law's normal "Good Samaritan" doctrine, which does not require individuals, even professionals, to come to the aid of strangers in distress. A physician's *ethical*, as opposed to legal, duty is somewhat more demanding, however. The American Medical Association's Principles of Medical Ethics state that a "physician shall, in the provision of appropriate patient care, except in emergencies, be free to choose whom to serve. . . ." (Principle VI). Why couldn't this ethical pledge to provide emergency care be converted into an implied promise that physicians make to the public at large? See William E. May, Medical Ethics: Code and Covenant or Philanthropy and Contract? 5(6) Hastings Ctr. Rep. 29 (1975). Doesn't the public rely on physicians as much as they do on hospital emergency departments? Consider especially Dr. Eddingfield's status as the plaintiff's family physician. Despite these qualms, *Hurley* is still thought to state the prevailing law for physicians.

2. *Triggering a Treatment Relationship.* A physician's complete freedom to refuse treatment exists only if a treatment relationship has not been initiated. We discuss below what actions constitute the initiation of treatment; but here, the fact that

Dr. Eddingfield may have treated the *Hurley* patient in the past did not suffice, because the law considers treatment relationships to coincide with "spells of illness." Thus, once a patient recovers from an illness or stops seeking treatment, a new treatment relationship must be formed in order to invoke a duty of continuing treatment. See, e.g., Grubbs v. Rawls, 369 S.E.2d 683, 685-686 (Va. 1988).

Consider how this issue might come out differently when the patient receives medical care from a health maintenance organization (HMO). In this regard, see Hand v. Tavera, 864 S.W.2d 678 (Tex. Ct. App. 1993) (holding that "when the health-care plan's insured shows up at a participating hospital emergency department, and the plan's doctor on call is consulted about treatment or admission, there is a physician-patient relationship between the doctor and the insured").

3. *The Hospital's Duty.* Despite the reluctance of the *Manlove* court to find a duty to treat, it is considered a groundbreaking case in that it paved the way for other courts to make more definitive findings of hospital liability for the refusal of emergency care. See, e.g., Stanturf v. Sipes, 447 S.W.2d 558 (Mo. 1969) (hospital may be liable for refusing to treat frostbite victim who could not post $25 deposit); Mercy Medical Center v. Winnebago County, 206 N.W.2d 198 (Wis. 1973) ("It would shock the public conscience if a person in need of medical emergency aid would be turned down at the door of a hospital."); but see Campbell v. Mincey, 413 F. Supp. 16 (N.D. Miss. 1975) (no obligation of hospital emergency department to care for pregnant woman in labor). Many states impose a requirement of open emergency departments by statute or regulation. See generally Karen Rothenberg, Who Cares? The Evolution of the Legal Duty to Provide Emergency Care, 26 Hous. L. Rev. 21 (1989).

How do you explain the fact that hospitals have a duty to provide emergency care to all who seek it while physicians are under no such obligation? Arguably, it does not make sense to expect physicians to be available at all times, while hospitals can reasonably be expected to always have someone staffing their emergency departments. But what about just expecting physicians to be available during their regular office hours for emergencies? Can't doctors factor into their scheduling the possibility of emergencies? Don't they in fact already do that? Is part of the issue that physicians may not necessarily have the expertise for any emergency patient that comes through the door? Suppose the physician is a dermatologist and is confronted with a cardiac emergency. Is there anything the doctor reasonably could do besides call 911? How might it actually not serve patients' interests in less populated areas if physicians have a duty to provide care to those in need?

Hospitals, too, may be able to limit their obligation according to their capacity or expertise. Suppose a hospital has no emergency department because it specializes in elective surgeries. Or suppose the emergency department is full. When this happens, hospital emergency departments often place themselves on "drive-by" status, which means they alert ambulances not to stop there. One court held this was permissible in the case of a child who consequently suffered brain damage, even though the hospital had treated the child many times in the past and had encouraged his parents to pass up other closer hospitals and come there if he had serious problems. Davis v. Johns Hopkins Hospital, 622 A.2d 128 (Md. 1993). Regulations under the Emergency Medical Treatment and Active Labor Act (EMTALA) come to the same conclusion. 42 C.F.R. §489.24(b)(4).

4. *The Meaning of Reliance.* Why is the *Manlove* reliance theory limited to just emergency care? Observe the court's reasoning that "such a refusal [of treatment]

might well result in worsening the condition of the injured person, because of the time lost in a useless attempt to obtain medical aid." Presumably, this is true only in a very serious or "unmistakable" emergency. It might be possible, however, to argue for other types of reliance. Suppose, for instance, that a prospective patient chose to live in the community because of the presence of a hospital, and it would thereby frustrate his or her reliance if the hospital could deny care in nonemergencies as well as emergencies. On the other hand, while such patients may have a psychological reliance, they would not suffer a *detrimental* reliance in the sense of a material change in one's position for the worse.

Where reliance is detrimental, should the patient have to demonstrate actual reliance in the particular case, rather than reliance being assumed? The *Manlove* court appeared to treat only the detriment part as requiring proof, not the psychological expectation. Should we presume that patients always legitimately expect emergency departments to be open to them? Consider, for instance, Guerrero v. Copper Queen Hospital, 537 P.2d 1329 (Ariz. 1975), which found that a hospital in a border town owned by a local mining company had a duty to render emergency aid to two severely burned Mexican children who were injured in their home across the border.

5. *Physicians "On Call."* *Hurley* and *Manlove* appear consistent because one is about doctors and the other is about hospitals. But does it make sense for hospitals to have a duty to accept emergency patients if the doctors who work there are free to refuse treatment? Courts generally have resolved this problem by holding that a doctor who is "on call" for a hospital emergency department voluntarily undertakes the hospital's greater duty of care. The leading decision is Hiser v. Randolph, 617 P.2d 774 (Ariz. 1980). At 11:45 P.M. one night, Bonita Hiser came to the emergency department at Mojave County General Hospital in a semi-comatose condition arising out of an exacerbation of her juvenile onset diabetes. Along with the seven other doctors in the area, Dr. Randolph took turns as the on-call physician for the emergency department, a duty for which he was paid $100 per 12-hour shift, and he was on call when Mrs. Hiser came to the hospital. When the emergency department nurse called Dr. Randolph, he refused to come in. He claimed this was because he lacked the expertise to treat diabetes, but there was also evidence that his refusal was based on personal animosity toward Mrs. Hiser or the fact that Mrs. Hiser's husband was a lawyer. Mrs. Hiser died because of the delay in treatment. The court found that Dr. Randolph breached his duty of care arising from his status as an on-call physician. According to the court,

> the obviously intended effect of the [hospital's] bylaws and rules and regulations was to obligate the emergency room doctor "on call" to provide emergency treatment to the best of the doctor's ability to any emergency patient of the hospital. Under these circumstances, the lack of a consensual physician-patient relationship before a duty to treat can arise has been waived by the signatory doctors.

But see Childs v. Weis, 440 S.W.2d 104 (Tex. Ct. App. 1969) (physicians on emergency call were under no specific duty to see all patients who presented themselves to the emergency department).

A similar analysis is possible for HMO physicians. See St. Charles v. Kender, 646 N.E.2d 411 (Mass. Ct. App. 1995) (HMO subscriber is a third-party beneficiary of an HMO's contracts with its physicians; contract was breached when physician failed to return patient's calls for an appointment). In Hand v. Tavera, 864 S.W.2d 678 (Tex. Ct. App. 1993), Lewis Hand went to the Humana Hospital (Village Oaks) emergency department because of a three-day headache. He also had high blood pressure, and his medical history revealed that his father had died of an aneurysm. The emergency department physician was able to control Mr. Hand's blood pressure and headache temporarily with medication but ultimately concluded that Mr. Hand should be admitted to the hospital. Hospital admissions required the approval of another physician under the Humana Health Care Plan, so the emergency department physician called Dr. Robert Tavera, the physician responsible that evening for authorizing admissions of Humana patients. Dr. Tavera decided that Mr. Hand should be treated as an outpatient. A few hours after returning home, Mr. Hand suffered a stroke. The trial court granted Dr. Tavera summary judgment on the ground that no patient-physician relationship had been formed, but the appellate court held that a patient-physician relationship existed by virtue of Mr. Hand's membership in the Humana Health Care Plan and Dr. Tavera's designation "as the doctor acting for the Humana plan that night." As the court observed, "Hand paid premiums to Humana to purchase medical care in advance of need . . . and Tavera's medical group agreed to treat Humana enrollees in exchange for the fees received from Humana. In effect, Hand had paid in advance for the services of the Humana plan doctor on duty that night, who happened to be Tavera, and the physician-patient relationship existed." Which actions constitute the formation of a doctor-patient relationship is discussed further in Chapter 2.B.1. As discussed there, when physicians serve as on-call *consultants* to the emergency department, courts generally require some involvement in the patient's care before finding a duty to treat.

6. *The Quasi-Public Status of Hospitals.* Another basis for imposing a duty to treat, distinct from the reliance theory, is the assertion that physicians or hospitals owe duties to the public at large simply by virtue of their having chosen to become licensed health care providers. It is a version of this argument that the *Hurley* court rejects with the cryptic comment that "analogies, drawn from the obligations to the public on the part of innkeepers, common carriers, and the like, are beside the mark."

In ancient common law, certain occupations and businesses were considered to be "common callings," meaning that they could not turn away customers without a good reason. Innkeepers and public transport ("common carriers") were the classic examples. The reasons for these heightened public service duties were the importance of the service, the monopoly status of the business, and the support it received from the government. See Charles Burdick, The Origin of the Peculiar Duties of Public Service Companies, 11 Colum. L. Rev. 514, 616, 742 (1911); O. W. Holmes, Jr., Common Carriers and the Common Law, 13 Am. L. Rev. 40 (1879).

In modern times, these "businesses affected with a public interest" are the public utilities (electric, phone, trains, etc.), and common-law duties of public service have been supplanted by overt government regulation. This body of common law has therefore become somewhat archaic, but it is still sometimes invoked against trade associations or labor unions that refuse membership. See generally Comment, 49 U. Chi. L. Rev. 840 (1982); Note, 102 Harv. L. Rev. 1993 (1989).

This body of law has been used to characterize hospitals as "quasi-public" facilities for purposes of giving *physicians* rights of access to their medical staffs. Considering that patients are the ultimate customers for whom public benefit is intended, shouldn't this analogy have even more application to them? It would be ironic indeed to insist on physician access but deny patient access. Nevertheless, the *Manlove* court rejected this view. In other states, later decisions have been more receptive to the quasi-public characterization. For instance, in Thompson v. Sun City Community Hospital, 688 P.2d 605 (Ariz. 1984), the court found that a cause of action exists against a hospital that stabilized a patient with a severed artery and then transferred him for financial reasons. The court based the duty to treat on the general public policy embodied in hospital licensing regulations and private accreditation standards. Also, in Payton v. Weaver, considered at page 117, the court suggested in dictum that this public service theory could be used to impose a community-wide obligation on kidney dialysis centers to share the burden of treating an unwanted disruptive patient. Cf. A. J. G. Priest, Possible Adaptation of Public Utility Concepts in the Health Care Field, 35 Law & Contemp. Probs. 839 (1970).

7. *The Private Status of Physicians.* Reconsider the situation of physicians. Why shouldn't medical practice by physicians be considered a "common calling" or a quasi-public service? Indeed, it turns out that, in fifteenth-century English law, physicians were included on the list of common callings along with blacksmiths and other important professions. Perhaps today, the missing ingredient is that a physician rarely has a local monopoly; usually there are several in town. But not always. One court found a common-law duty to treat where the sole physician practice group in town refused to accept a patient who had filed a complaint against one of the doctors in the group. Leach v. Drummond Medical Group, 192 Cal. Rptr. 650 (Cal. Ct. App. 1983).

There is an alternative explanation for the law no longer treating physicians as being engaged in a common calling. Consider this perspective:

Although the law was ambiguous, there is a substantial argument that the duty to serve the public extended to all businesses that held themselves out as open to the public. Only around the time of the Civil War did this rule begin formally to narrow, and only after the Civil War, when civil rights were extended to African-Americans for the first time, did the courts clearly state for the first time that most businesses had no common-law duties to serve the public. The rule achieved its present form only when the issue became enmeshed in the problem of race relations. This change in the law had the effect – and without doubt the purpose – of enabling businesses to continue to serve white customers while choosing to exclude black customers. [Joseph W. Singer, No Right to Exclude: Public Accommodations and Private Property, 90 Nw. U. L. Rev. 1283, 1294-1295 (1996).]

In a few state statutes, regulatory law imposes some limited duties on physicians to provide care for patients. In Massachusetts, for instance, physicians, as a condition of being licensed, must agree to charge Medicare patients no more than Medicare's "reasonable charge." This has been held not to violate the constitutional rights of physicians. Dukakis v. Massachusetts Medical Society, 815 F.2d 790 (1st Cir. 1987).

8. *Paying vs. Indigent Patients.* Perhaps this body of law is not more developed because doctors and hospitals rarely turn away patients who can pay. For patients who cannot pay, the public service theory is usually no help, since the common law never required common callings to serve people for free. Only the reliance theory reaches this result, but it is restricted to serious emergencies, those in which the patient is worse off for having made a futile attempt to secure service. Only in

Arizona have courts used a public service theory to impose a duty to treat patients who cannot pay, and there too the duty is limited to emergency care. (Should it be?) For the view that physicians, hospitals, and other providers should be regulated as a public utility, both to promote access and contain costs, see Nicholas Bagley, Medicine as a Public Calling, 114 Mich. L. Rev. 57 (2015).

9. *Enforcement of Public Rights.* For patients who cannot pay, regulatory law may place hospitals under somewhat greater duties than the common law to treat both emergency and nonemergency patients, but these public law duties have been limited and are not enforceable by individual patients.

Consider, for example, tax law. Nonprofit hospitals are considered to be "charities" that are exempt from property and income tax. Part of this charitable status includes an obligation to treat some patients for free. Federal law restricts this free-care obligation to emergency patients, as do most states, but a few states are beginning to require hospitals to devote a certain percentage of their overall services to patients who cannot pay. Once again, however, this is a community service obligation owed to the public at large, not to individual patients, and so it cannot be enforced very easily by private action. Finally, the Joint Commission on Accreditation of Healthcare Organizations (JCAHO) private accreditation standards require hospitals to accept patients without regard to "source of payment," but this is interpreted to mean accepting all patients with some source of payment (e.g., not turning away Medicaid patients) rather than a duty to accept patients who cannot pay.

This leaves us with the following patchwork of laws: for physicians, no common-law duty to treat, even in emergencies. For hospitals: (1) a common-law duty to treat emergency patients regardless of payment, but only in serious emergencies; (2) common law and regulatory duties to treat all patients who can pay; but (3) no enforceable duty to treat nonemergency or mild emergency patients who cannot pay. This set the stage for enactment of a new federal statute, the Emergency Medical Treatment and Active Labor Act (EMTALA), discussed in the *Burditt* case at page 69.

Notes: Moral and Constitutional Rights to Health Care

1. *Moral Rights to Treatment.* The discussion of legal rights to treatment surely must be informed by how our society views moral rights to health care. What message does society send when the law limits the right to treatment so narrowly as to encompass only serious emergencies? Does the emergency care limitation suggest that we are trying to limit care to the most compelling needs and to avoid people demanding too much care (emergencies being thought of as unpredictable)? This might be seen as a partial embodiment of the "rescue principle," which declares that the strongest ethical demand in medicine is to help those in greatest need. In this regard, the moral dimension of medicine is stronger than in any other commercial arena, because there is no equivalent requirement that grocers, restaurants, or hotels provide their services for free to people in dire straits. What justifies this distinction? Is it that if food and housing were available on demand, it would be too easy to abuse the privilege? But what kinds of incentives for patients does a right only to emergency care generate? Is the reluctance of the courts to find even broader rights to health care a reflection of the difficulty in deciding who to hold

responsible for vindicating these rights? Or perhaps it reflects the difficulty in defining what a right to health care would include. Consider in this regard the difference between defining a right to food or housing and a right to health care.

The moral issue can also be debated from a broader, social perspective. So far, we have thought only about whether patients have a right to demand treatment from particular doctors and hospitals. Even where they do not have these private rights, perhaps they have a claim to a more public right, one that society as a whole owes to provide minimally decent health care to all. For some time, we have recognized this claim to basic social support for education and to a more limited extent for food and housing. But for health care, there was no national safety net until the enactment of the Patient Protection and Affordable Care Act in 2010. Importantly, the Act expands Medicaid coverage to all persons whose family income is no more than 138 percent of the federal poverty level. Still, even with the Act's implementation, more than 25 million Americans (many of them undocumented immigrants) lack health insurance of any kind. Perhaps it was politically and morally sustainable to deny coverage to so many people before enactment of the Affordable Care Act—and to continue denying coverage to millions of Americans—only because private hospital emergency departments exist as a last resort for those without insurance. Could it be, then, that the heightened private law duties of hospitals weakened our nation's public law commitment to health care access? See Mark A. Hall, The Unlikely Case in Favor of Patient Dumping, 28 Jurimetrics 389 (1988). For an argument that private law duties tend to undermine voluntary charity, see Richard Epstein, Mortal Peril: Our Inalienable Right to Health Care? (1997). For responses to Epstein, see Symposium: Is America's Health Care System in Mortal Peril?, 1998 U. Ill. L. Rev. 683.

2. *Positive vs. Negative Liberty.* If there is a moral right to health care generally, it is clearly not vindicated as a substantive due process right by the U.S. Constitution. *Wideman* is a classic statement of the principle that the Bill of Rights embodies primarily negative, not positive, liberties, that is, it is concerned mainly with freedoms from government imposition, not rights to government assistance. Thus, the Constitution becomes relevant to health care when the government bans treatment choices or forces treatment, but not when it simply declines to assist in obtaining treatment. In this regard, the U.S. Constitution differs markedly from constitutional models in Europe. B. Jessie Hill, What Is the Meaning of Health? Constitutional Implications of Defining "Medical Necessity" and "Essential Health Benefits" Under the Affordable Care Act, 38 Am. J.L. & Med. 445 (2012); John A. Robertson, Controversial Medical Treatment and the Right to Health Care, 36(6) Hastings Center Rep. 15 (2006).

Wideman was followed by an important Supreme Court opinion confirming its general analysis in this regard. In DeShaney v. Winnebago County Department of Social Services, 489 U.S. 189 (1989), the Court held that no constitutional violation occurred in a case where a child was left with permanent brain damage when a state social services agency failed to intervene aggressively enough to prevent child abuse. The state had received several reports of severe beatings by the father. The Court reaffirmed "that the due process clauses generally confer no affirmative right to governmental aid," and it reasoned that the state agency had not assumed a "special relationship" with the child by virtue of having made some ineffectual efforts to protect him since the agency did nothing to make him more vulnerable to the danger. See also Archie v. Racine, 847 F.2d 1211 (7th Cir. 1988) (en banc) (§1983 action not maintainable for city rescue service's negligent failure to dispatch ambulance; no constitutional right to treatment exists).

As *Wideman* indicates, government will assume duties to provide health care when it confines individuals in psychiatric hospitals, prisons, or other facilities. Before the enactment of the Affordable Care Act, occasional press reports described cases of uninsured people committing crimes so they would have access to health care while incarcerated. Katie Moisse & James Verone, The Medical Motive for His $1 Bank Robbery, ABC News, June 23, 2011.

3. *Equal Protection.* In Maher v. Roe, 432 U.S. 464, 469-470 (1977), discussed in *Wideman,* the Court identified another possible source of a constitutional duty to treat: "The Constitution imposes no obligation on the states to pay . . . any of the medical expenses of indigents. But when a state decides to alleviate some of the hardships of poverty by providing medical care, the manner in which it dispenses benefits is subject to constitutional limitations." For example, in Memorial Hospital v. Maricopa County, 415 U.S. 250 (1974), the Court struck down Arizona's requirement of a year's residence in a county as a condition of receiving nonemergency medical care at county expense as infringing on the right to travel. Might a state be subject to an equal protection attack for funding some procedures but not others? See Doe v. Colautti, 592 F.2d 704 (3d Cir. 1978) (finding no violation of the equal protection clause when Pennsylvania's medical assistance program provided less generous benefits for psychiatric care than for general medical care).

4. *Legislative Mandates.* In Harris v. McRae, 448 U.S. 297 (1980), another abortion funding case discussed in *Wideman,* the Court addressed a nonconstitutional theory for compelling government funding of health care. States that participate in Medicaid are, generally speaking, required to fund most medically necessary forms of treatment. Beal v. Doe, 432 U.S. 438, 444 (1977). Although *McRae* found this statutory requirement to be inapplicable to abortions, in other cases the medical necessity mandate has proved to be an effective tool for obtaining Medicaid coverage. Pittman v. Secretary, Florida Dept. Health & Rehab. Services; 998 F.2d 887 (11th Cir. 1993) (requiring coverage of a liver-intestine transplant for a child); Rush v. Parham, 625 F.2d 1150 (5th Cir. 1980) (requiring funding for sex change operations in certain circumstances). However, there is no statutory requirement that Medicaid be funded at a level sufficient to cover all people who need it.

■BURDITT v. U.S. DEPARTMENT OF HEALTH AND HUMAN SERVICES
934 F.2d 1362 (5th Cir. 1991)

REAVLEY, Circuit Judge.

Hospitals that execute Medicare provider agreements with the federal government pursuant to 42 U.S.C. §1395cc must treat all human beings who enter their emergency departments in accordance with the Emergency Medical Treatment and Active Labor Act (EMTALA), 42 U.S.C. §1395dd. Hospitals and responsible physicians found to have violated EMTALA's requirements are subject to civil money penalties. [This case is an appeal by Dr. Burditt of a $20,000 fine assessed against him by the Department of Health and Human Services. EMTALA also provides for a private cause of action, with prevailing plaintiffs entitled to monetary damages from the offending hospital and appropriate equitable relief. Damages may not be recovered from physicians in a private cause of action, however.]

I.A. FACTS

Mrs. Rosa Rivera arrived in the emergency room of DeTar Hospital in Victoria, Texas at approximately 4:00 P.M. on December 5, 1986. At or near term with her sixth child, she was experiencing one-minute, moderate contractions every three minutes and her membranes had ruptured. Two obstetrical nurses, Tammy Kotsur and Donna Keining, examined her and found indicia of labor and dangerously high blood pressure. Because Rivera had received no prenatal care, and had neither a regular doctor nor means of payment, Kotsur telephoned Burditt, who was next on DeTar's rotating call-list of physicians responsible for such "unaligned" obstetrics patients. Upon hearing Rivera's history and condition, Burditt told Kotsur that he "didn't want to take care of this lady" and asked her to prepare Rivera for transfer to John Sealy Hospital in Galveston, Texas, 170 miles away. Burditt agreed to call back in five to ten minutes.

Kotsur and Keining told the nursing supervisor, Jean Herman, and DeTar's administrator, Charles Sexton, of their belief that it would be unsafe to transfer Rivera. When Burditt called back, Keining told him that, according to Sexton's understanding of hospital regulations and federal law, Burditt would have to examine Rivera and personally arrange for John Sealy to receive her before he could legally transfer her. Keining asked Burditt for permission to start an intravenous push of magnesium sulfate as a precaution against convulsive seizures. Burditt told Keining to begin administering this medication only if Rivera could be transported by ambulance. . . .

Burditt arrived at approximately 4:50 to examine Rivera. He confirmed her blood pressure to be the highest he had ever seen, 210/130, and he assumed that she had been hypertensive throughout her pregnancy. As the experienced head of DeTar's obstetrics and gynecology department, Burditt knew that there was a strong possibility that Rivera's hypertension would precipitate complications which might kill both Rivera and her baby. He also knew that the infants of hypertensive mothers are at higher-than-normal risk of intrauterine growth retardation. He estimated that Rivera's baby was six pounds—less than normal weight—and arranged her transfer to John Sealy, a perinatal facility better equipped than DeTar to care for underweight infants. . . .

At approximately 5:00, Herman showed Burditt DeTar's guidelines regarding EMTALA, but he refused to read them. Burditt told Herman that Rivera represented more risk than he was willing to accept from a malpractice standpoint. Herman explained that Rivera could not be transferred unless Burditt signed a DeTar form entitled "Physician's Certificate Authorizing Transfer." Burditt asked for "that dang piece of paper" and signed his name under the following:

> I have examined the patient, _____, and have determined that, based upon the information available to me at this time, the medical benefits reasonably expected from the provision of appropriate medical treatment at another medical facility outweigh the increased risks to the patient's medical condition from effecting [the] transfer. The basis for my conclusion is as follows: _____

Burditt listed no basis for his conclusion and remarked to Herman that "until DeTar Hospital pays my malpractice insurance, I will pick and choose those patients that I want to treat."

Burditt then went to care for another unaligned patient, Sylvia Ramirez, while the nurses arranged Rivera's transfer. They found another obstetrical nurse, Anita Nichols, to accompany Rivera to John Sealy. Burditt returned to the nurses' station and stayed there from 5:30 to 6:18. He never again examined Rivera or asked about her medical condition, though he inquired several times about the status of her transfer. Burditt delivered the Ramirez baby at 6:22. Afterward, Nichols told him the results of her examination of Rivera and informed him that the ambulance had arrived. Based exclusively on Nichols' statements, Burditt concluded that Rivera's condition had not changed since his examination two hours before. Burditt did not reexamine Rivera though he saw her being wheeled to the ambulance. He did not order any medication or life support equipment for Rivera during her transfer.

Nichols delivered Rivera's healthy baby in the ambulance approximately 40 miles into the 170-mile trip to John Sealy. She directed the driver to nearby Ganado Hospital to get a drug called pitocin to staunch Rivera's bleeding. While there, Nichols telephoned Burditt, who ordered her to continue to John Sealy despite the birth. Instead, per Rivera's wishes, Nichols returned Rivera to DeTar, where Burditt refused to see her because she failed to proceed to John Sealy in accordance with his instructions. Burditt directed that Rivera be discharged if she was stable and not bleeding excessively. A DeTar official pressed Burditt to allow Dr. Shirley Pigott to examine Rivera. Rivera stayed at DeTar under Pigott's care for three days and left in good health. . . .

II.A.1. SCREENING

Because Rivera presented herself to DeTar's emergency department and a request was made on her behalf for care, EMTALA required DeTar to

> provide for an *appropriate* medical screening examination *within the capability of the hospital's emergency department* to determine whether or not an emergency medical condition . . . exists or to determine if the individual is in active labor. . . .

42 U.S.C. §1395dd(a) (emphasis added). The parties agree that DeTar appropriately screened Rivera and discovered that she had an "emergency medical condition"—severe hypertension—within the meaning of 42 U.S.C. §1395dd(e)(1).[2]

---

2. EMTALA defines "emergency medical condition" as
a medical condition manifesting itself by acute symptoms of sufficient severity (including severe pain) such that the absence of immediate medical attention could reasonably be expected to result in—
    (A) placing the patient's health in serious jeopardy,
    (B) serious impairment to bodily functions, or
    (C) serious dysfunction of any bodily organ or part.
42 U.S.C. §1395dd(e)(1) (Supp. IV 1987).

II.A.2. EMERGENCY MEDICAL CONDITION AND ACTIVE LABOR

Patients diagnosed with an "emergency medical condition" or "active labor" must either be treated or be transferred in accordance with EMTALA. Burditt claims that Rivera received all of the care that she was due under EMTALA because he stabilized her hypertension sufficiently for transfer and she was not in active labor when she left DeTar for John Sealy.

II.A.2.a. Unstable Emergency Medical Condition

Rivera's blood pressure was 210/130 at 4:00 and 5:00. This was the last reading known to Burditt before he facilitated her transfer. Nurses also measured her blood pressure as 173/105 at 5:30, 178/103 at 5:45, 186/107 at 6:00, and 190/110 at 6:50. Experts testified that Rivera's hypertension put her at high risk of suffering serious complications, including seizures, heart failure, kidney dysfunction, tubular necrosis, stroke, intracranial bleeding, placental abruption, and fetal hypoxia. This is substantial, if not conclusive evidence that Rivera entered and exited DeTar with an emergency medical condition.

Burditt argues that he fulfilled EMTALA's requirements with respect to Rivera's hypertension by "stabilizing" it, or

> provid[ing] such medical treatment of the condition as may be necessary to assure, within reasonable medical probability, that no material deterioration of the condition is likely to result from [a] transfer. . . .

42 U.S.C. §1395dd(e)(4)(A). He claims that the magnesium sulfate that he ordered for Rivera has an antihypertensive effect that complements its primary anticonvulsive purpose.

Development of any of the possible complications could have killed or seriously injured Rivera, her baby, or both, and thus would constitute a "material deterioration" under 42 U.S.C. §1395dd(e)(4)(A). Any deterioration would "result" from transfer in that Rivera would have received better care for any complication at DeTar than in the ambulance. Thus, Burditt could not have stabilized Rivera unless he provided treatment that medical experts agree would prevent the threatening and severe consequences of Rivera's hypertension while she was in transit. [The HHS appeals board] could properly disregard Burditt's testimony and accept that of all other testifying experts in holding that Burditt provided no such treatment, and thus did not stabilize Rivera's emergency medical condition. . . .

II.A.2.b. Active Labor

EMTALA defines "active labor" as labor at a time when

> (B) there is inadequate time to effect safe transfer to another hospital prior to delivery, or
> (C) a transfer may pose a threat [to] the health and safety of the patient or the unborn child.

42 U.S.C. §1395dd(e)(2)(B)-(C). This statutory definition renders irrelevant any medical definition of active labor. . . .

Burditt challenges the ALJ's finding that, at approximately 5:00, there was inadequate time to safely transfer Rivera to John Sealy before she delivered her baby. Dr. Warren Crosby testified that, based on Burditt's own examination results, Rivera would, more likely than not, deliver within three hours after Burditt [made the decision to transfer her to] John Sealy. . . . Burditt does not challenge [the] conclusion that the ambulance trip from DeTar to John Sealy takes approximately three hours. We therefore hold that [the HHS appeals board] properly concluded that Rivera was in active labor under 42 U.S.C. §1395dd(e)(2)(B).

The ALJ also found that Rivera was in active labor under clause C at the time Burditt examined her. There is always some risk of a vehicular accident in transit, so transfer always "may" pose a threat to the health and safety of the patient or fetus. . . . We believe that Congress intended clause C to extend EMTALA's . . . protection to women in labor who have any complication with their pregnancies regardless of delivery imminency. Because better medical care is available in a hospital than in an ambulance, whether a transfer "may pose a threat" under 42 U.S.C. §1395dd(e)(2)(C) depends on whether the woman in labor has any medical condition that could interfere with the normal, natural delivery of her healthy child. Under the statutory language, a woman in labor is entitled to EMTALA's . . . protections upon a showing of possible threat; it does not require proof of a reasonable medical probability that any threat will come to fruition. . . .

The record overwhelmingly confirms that Rivera's hypertension could have interfered with a normal delivery, and she was thus in active labor under 42 U.S.C. §1395dd(e)(2)(C). . . .

II.A.3. TREAT OR TRANSFER

Upon discovery of active labor or an emergency medical condition, EMTALA usually requires hospitals to treat the discovered condition. Under certain circumstances, however, EMTALA allows hospitals to transfer patients instead of treating them. 42 U.S.C. §1395dd(b)(1)(B). . . . [The court went on to find that Burditt had not satisfied the requirements under EMTALA for a transfer before stabilization. Under EMTALA, transfer is permitted if the patient requests transfer *or* the physician has certified in writing that the medical benefits of transfer outweigh the increased risks to the patient. In addition, the receiving hospital must be capable of providing the needed treatment and must have agreed to accept the transfer. Finally, the transfer must occur with appropriate personnel and transportation, including appropriate life support measures. While Burditt had obtained consent from John Sealy before the transfer, he had not reasonably concluded that the benefits of transfer outweighed the risks nor had he arranged for the transfer with appropriate personnel and transportation.]

II.C. EMTALA'S CONSTITUTIONALITY

As his final attempt to escape [liability], Burditt claims that EMTALA effects a public taking of his services without just compensation in contravention of the Constitution's Fifth Amendment.

Assuming *arguendo* that professional services constitute property protected by the takings clause, Burditt has not shown that EMTALA effects a taking. EMTALA imposes no responsibilities directly on physicians; it unambiguously requires hospitals to examine and stabilize, treat, or appropriately transfer all who arrive requesting treatment. Its provision for sanctions against physicians who knowingly violate its requirements is merely an enforcement mechanism that does not alter its explicit assignment of duties.

Governmental regulation that affects a group's property interests "does not constitute a taking of property where the regulated group is not required to participate in the regulated industry." Whitney v. Heckler, 780 F.2d 963, 972 (11th Cir.), *cert. denied*, 479 U.S. 813 (1986).

Two levels of voluntariness undermine Burditt's taking assertion. Only hospitals that voluntarily participate in the federal government's Medicare program must comply with EMTALA. Hospitals must consider the cost of complying with EMTALA's requirements in deciding whether to continue to participate in the Medicare program.

Second, Burditt is free to negotiate with DeTar or another hospital regarding his responsibility to facilitate a hospital's compliance with EMTALA. Thus, physicians only voluntarily accept responsibilities under EMTALA if they consider it in their best interest to do so. Accordingly, Burditt's claim under the takings clause is without merit. . . .

Notes: The Federal Patient Dumping Statute

1. *Historical Background.* Congress passed the Emergency Medical Treatment and Active Labor Act (EMTALA) as part of the Consolidated Omnibus Reconciliation Act of 1986 (COBRA), in response to the perception that state law was too weak to prevent widespread patient dumping. While EMTALA, or COBRA, has worked better than previous legal efforts, in part because of the private right of action, there are still concerns that patient dumping persists at unacceptable levels. One scholar argues, however, that

> EMTALA is a virtual catalogue of how to get a statute wrong. First, generalize from unrepresentative anecdotal evidence in identifying the problem. Draft the statute sloppily, and leave the most important words undefined or defined too broadly. Finance the resulting open-ended entitlement with an unfunded mandate imposed on private parties. . . . [Design the enforcement system] to reward the wrong people. Finally, apply the statute even after the world on which it depended has vanished. Any one of these problems would be bad enough in isolation, but their combined effect is devastating to the interests EMTALA was intended to protect.

David A. Hyman, Dumping EMTALA: When Bad Laws Happen to Good People (1998) (unpublished). As you read the following notes, see if you can determine why someone might reach such a conclusion. Nevertheless, Prof. Hyman acknowledges that

> the statute is wildly popular across the entirety of the political spectrum and among such disparate interest groups as physicians, advocates for the poor, [academics,] and consumer groups. Unlike many reforms, EMTALA does not create a new administrative bureaucracy; it does not favor the interests of the well-connected against the less fortunate; its on-budget costs are modest; and it seems to be no more intrusive than is absolutely necessary to accomplish its objectives.

David A. Hyman, Patient Dumping and EMTALA: Past Imperfect/Future Shock, 8 Health Matrix 29, 29 (1998).

As the *Burditt* court indicated, courts have not thought EMTALA poses constitutional problems. But not everyone agrees. E. Haavi Morreim, EMTALA: Medicare's Unconstitutional Condition on Hospitals, 43 Hastings Const. L.Q. 61 (2015).

Dr. Michael Burditt was the first physician fined for an EMTALA violation, and his actions were vigorously defended by the Texas Medical Association. For a critical view of the Fifth Circuit's decision in the *Burditt* case, see David Hyman, Lies, Damned Lies, and Narrative, 73 Ind. L.J. 797, 824-832 (1998). As a general matter, the government rarely penalizes individual physicians under EMTALA, levying most of its fines on hospitals. Sophie Terp et al., Individual Physician Penalties Resulting from Violation of Emergency Medical Treatment and Labor Act, 24 Academic Emergency Med. 442 (2017).

2. *Screening and Stabilizing.* EMTALA creates two distinct duties. First, the duty to screen patients is triggered by their arrival at the hospital, and it ceases if it is determined they are not in what the statute defines as an "emergency" condition. Second, if patients are in an emergency condition, then the hospital must stabilize them. (The statutory requirements are similar for patients in active labor.) Most litigation has arisen at the first stage, in cases where patients claim the hospital failed entirely to evaluate or recognize their emergency condition.

But that is not our main concern in this note. Our concern is, if there clearly is an emergency, how far does the duty to treat extend? Do hospitals have to perform bypass surgery after they halt a heart attack? Although *Burditt* found that "stabilizing" care was not rendered in that case, what about other typical situations? Consider whether the outcome would be any different under EMTALA than it was under this state law decision: Joyner v. Alton Ochsner Medical Foundation, 230 So. 2d 913 (La. Ct. App. 1970) (auto accident victim did not "require immediate admission" after stabilizing care was rendered, despite "multiple deep facial lacerations, a possible head injury, traumatic damage to the teeth and multiple bruises and contusions of the body, resulting in considerable loss of blood"). Consider whether the duty to treat under EMTALA is as strong as it is under this state law decision: Thompson v. Sun City Community Hospital, 688 P.2d 605 (Ariz. 1984) (a cause of action exists against a hospital that stabilized a patient with a severed artery and then transferred him for financial reasons). Is the federal statute any more demanding than the *Manlove* reliance theory?

Moreover, courts have applied the stabilization requirement of EMTALA only when a hospital discharges a patient or transfers the patient to another hospital, and not when the hospital provides care. Harry v. Marchant, 291 F.3d 767, 770-772 (11th Cir. 2002) (en banc) (observing that the stabilization requirement of EMTALA is defined in terms of transfer or discharge). See also Alvarez-Torres v. Ryder Memorial Hospital, Inc., 582 F.3d 47, 51-52 (1st Cir. 2009); Bryan v. Rectors and Visitors of the University of Virginia, 95 F.3d 349, 352 (4th Cir. 1996).

For a view that EMTALA has blocked blatantly discriminatory practices without actually improving the quality of health care received by disadvantaged populations, see Karin V. Rhodes & Kristofer L. Smith, Short-term Care with Long-term Costs, 69 Annals Emergency Med. 163 (2017). For proposals to make EMTALA work more effectively, see Katharine Van Tassel, Modernizing the Emergency Medical Treatment & Labor Act to Harmonize with the Affordable Care Act to Improve

Equality, Quality and Cost of Emergency Care, 15 Hous. J. Health L. & Pol'y 131 (2015).

There are other consequences of an obligation only to stabilize. For example, hospitals may send undocumented immigrants back to their home countries, and many of these patients die because of their inability to access follow-up care upon their return.

Although EMTALA only requires stabilization, other federal rules may extend the duty to provide care. Medicare's conditions for participation require safe discharge planning for hospitalized patients, and it may not be safe to discharge a patient who has only been stabilized. Jennifer L. Herbst, Permanent Patients, 47(1) Hastings Center Rep. 6 (2017).

In its requirement to stabilize emergency patients, EMTALA does not require the impossible. If a hospital does not have the facilities or personnel necessary to fully stabilize a patient, and the patient must be transferred to a more sophisticated hospital to receive needed care, the first hospital can transfer the patient to the more sophisticated hospital without violating EMTALA. The transferring hospital must do all it can to stabilize the patient's condition, but it need not do what it cannot do. Cherukuri v. Shalala, 175 F.3d 446 (6th Cir. 1999) (absolving physician at small rural hospital after the physician transferred two patients who needed surgery to stop internal bleeding from an automobile accident).

And to ensure that potential receiving hospitals do not undermine patient protections, EMTALA imposes on those hospitals a duty to accept appropriate transfers (no "reverse dumping"). St. Anthony Hospital v. U.S. Dept. HHS, 309 F.3d 680 (10th Cir. 2002).

3. *The Patient's Indigency.* While the passage of EMTALA was motivated by concerns about private hospitals "dumping" indigent or uninsured patients on public hospitals, the statutory language imposes no requirement that patients show that they were denied emergency services because of indigency or lack of insurance. See 42 U.S.C. §1395dd(a) ("if any individual . . . comes to the emergency department . . . , the hospital must provide for an appropriate medical screening examination within the capability of the hospital's emergency department").

Accordingly, courts have generally held that it is irrelevant why a person did not receive an appropriate screening exam or, if an emergency was identified, why a person did not receive stabilizing care before discharge or transfer. As one court observed, "[EMTALA] applies to any and all patients, not just to patients with insufficient resources." Brooker v. Desert Hospital Corp., 947 F.2d 412, 415 (9th Cir. 1991). Accord Summers v. Baptist Medical Center, 91 F.3d 1132 (8th Cir. 1996); Gatewood v. Washington Healthcare Corp., 933 F.2d 1037, 1040 (D.C. Cir. 1991).

The Supreme Court addressed the motive question in the context of EMTALA's stabilization requirement and rejected any need to show an improper motive. Roberts v. Galen of Virginia, Inc., 525 U.S. 249 (1999). The Court "express[ed] no opinion" on the need to show an improper motive for a claim of inappropriate medical screening.

Perhaps the most controversial extension of EMTALA beyond economic discrimination occurred in the *Baby K* case, which involved a baby with anencephaly—a baby missing the major part of the brain that is necessary for conscious thought. In In re Baby K, 16 F.3d 590 (4th Cir. 1994), parents of an anencephalic child sought ventilatory treatment of their child during periodic bouts of respiratory distress.

After the second of three such episodes, the hospital sought judicial permission to withhold the ventilator when the child next came to the emergency department. In the view of the hospital, it was medically and ethically inappropriate to ventilate the child given her limited life expectancy, her total absence of consciousness, and the futility of treatment at improving her condition. According to the hospital, the only appropriate treatment for the child was the treatment "it would provide other anencephalic infants—supportive care in the form of warmth, nutrition, and hydration." The court rejected the hospital's argument. It observed that EMTALA requires stabilizing treatment in the event of a medical emergency, and the child's respiratory distress met EMTALA's definition of a medical emergency. If there was to be an exception for "futile" care under EMTALA, Congress would have to write that exception into the statute.

The *Baby K* decision raises serious questions about the ability of society to contain health care costs. If the hospital in the case could not deny a ventilator to an anencephalic child, how could any emergency medical care be withheld on the ground that its high costs were not justified by its minimal benefit? Is there a distinction between the economic or other discrimination prohibited by EMTALA and the denial of care that results when a hospital is concerned about the limits of society's resources?

Perhaps in recognition of these concerns, the Fourth Circuit limited the impact of *Baby K* two years later. In Bryan v. Rectors and Visitors of the University of Virginia, 95 F.3d 349 (4th Cir. 1996), an EMTALA claim was brought on behalf of a patient who died of a heart attack after her physicians decided that "no further efforts to prevent her death should be made." Twenty days before the heart attack, the patient had been admitted to the hospital in respiratory distress. Eight days before the heart attack, apparently because of the hopelessness of the patient's condition, her physicians decided to withhold further life-sustaining treatment, including cardiopulmonary resuscitation, in the event of a cardiac arrest. When she suffered her heart attack, no efforts were made to prevent her death. According to the court, there was no EMTALA violation because EMTALA "was intended to regulate the hospital's care of the patient only in the immediate aftermath of the act of admitting her for emergency treatment and while it considered whether it would undertake longer-term full treatment or instead transfer the patient to a hospital that could and would undertake that treatment." Id. at 352.

4. *Preventive Dumping.* There has been concern that hospitals would try to evade their EMTALA obligations by dumping patients before they reach the emergency department. For example, when called by a paramedic or emergency medical technician who is transporting a patient by ambulance, the emergency department staff might direct the ambulance to another hospital. Early cases suggested that hospitals would have considerable freedom to prevent patients from reaching the emergency department. See Miller v. Medical Center of Southwest Louisiana, 22 F.3d 626 (5th Cir. 1994) (hospital not liable under EMTALA for refusing to accept the transfer of a patient who needed specialized emergency care beyond the capabilities of the transferring hospital); Johnson v. University of Chicago Hospitals, 982 F.2d 230 (7th Cir. 1992) (hospital not liable for diverting an ambulance to another hospital).

Subsequent amendment of the EMTALA regulations and case law interpreting the amendment have limited the ability of hospitals to engage in preventive dumping. Under one regulation, patients have come to the hospital's emergency department for purposes of EMTALA once they have reached any part of the hospital's property, including a hospital-owned ambulance service. 42 C.F.R. §489.24(b) (2011) (applied in Hernandez v. Starr County Hospital District, 30 F. Supp. 2d 970 (S.D. Tex. 1999); Preston v. Meriter Hospital, Inc., 700 N.W.2d 158 (Wis. 2005)). The same regulation permits hospitals to divert non-hospital-owned ambulance services if the emergency department "does not have the staff or facilities to accept any additional emergency patients." 42 C.F.R. §489.24(b)(4). The Ninth Circuit has interpreted this provision to mean that a hospital violates EMTALA when it diverts a non-hospital-owned ambulance in the absence of an inability to provide treatment for the patient. Arrington v. Wong, 237 F.3d 1066 (9th Cir. 2001); see also Morales v. Sociedad Espanola de Auxilo Mutuo y Beneficencia, 524 F.3d 54 (1st Cir. 2008). See Caroline J. Stalker, Comment, How Far Is Too Far?: EMTALA Moves from the Emergency Room to Off-Campus Entities, 36 Wake Forest L. Rev. 823 (2001).

Note that there is some ambiguity to §489.24(b). Although the regulation seems to limit the ability of hospitals to divert non-hospital-owned ambulances, it also states that "[a]n individual in a non-hospital-owned ambulance off hospital property is not considered to have come to the hospital's emergency department even if a member of the ambulance staff contacts the hospital by telephone or telemetry communications and informs the hospital that they want to transport the individual to the hospital for examination and treatment."

As indicated, under 42 C.F.R. §489.24(b), EMTALA is triggered when an individual comes to areas of the hospital other than the emergency department. Thus, a First Circuit decision emphasizes the point that a hospital's duty to stabilize before transfer applies to any patient in the hospital, "regardless of how that person enters the institution or where within the walls he may be when the hospital identifies the problem." Lopez-Soto v. Hawayek, 175 F.3d 170, 173 (1st Cir. 1999) (observing that the stabilization requirement of EMTALA applies to an individual who "comes to a hospital" and holding that EMTALA applies when a pregnant woman is admitted to the maternity ward and taken to the operating room for a cesarean section, and her infant is born with respiratory distress and needs emergency care).

5. *Dumping After Admission to the Hospital.* Courts disagree as to whether EMTALA's stabilization requirement continues to apply once the patient has been admitted to the hospital. Cases have arisen in which patients were admitted to the hospital for treatment and, after a few or more days of treatment, been transferred to another hospital or discharged before their illness was fully treated. Or as in *Lopez-Soto, supra* note 4, the emergency condition may develop after the individual has become an inpatient or outpatient at the hospital.

Some courts have concluded that the obligation to stabilize exists throughout the patient's visit to the hospital. In addition to *Lopez-Soto*, see Thornton v. Southwest Detroit Hospital, 895 F.2d 1131 (6th Cir. 1990).

Other courts have concluded that the stabilization requirement ceases upon the patient's admission to the regular hospital. Bryan v. Rectors and Visitors of the University of Virginia, 95 F.3d 349, 352 (4th Cir. 1996); James v. Sunrise Hospital, 86 F.3d 885 (9th Cir. 1996); Bryant v. Adventist Health Systems/West, 289 F.3d 1162 (9th Cir. 2002). Note that in *Bryan* and *Bryant*, the courts were deciding about the stabilization requirement for care rendered during the patient's hospital stay and not in the context of a transfer or discharge. Hence, it is not surprising that the courts were especially concerned about converting state malpractice claims into federal EMTALA claims. See note 6, infra. In *Bryant*, the Court observed that the stabilization requirement would not cease upon the patient's admission to the hospital "if a patient demonstrates in a particular case that inpatient admission was a ruse to avoid EMTALA's requirements." 289 F.3d at 1169. A federal district court invoked that point in a case in which a patient was sent home after admission but before his injuries had been stabilized. Morgan v. North Mississippi Medical Center, Inc., 403 F. Supp. 2d 1115, 1130 (S.D. Ala. 2005). Although the court denied the hospital's motion to dismiss the EMTALA claim, it ultimately concluded on summary judgment that the hospital had not engaged in a ruse to avoid EMTALA's requirements when it admitted the patient. Morgan v. North Mississippi Medical Center, Inc., 458 F. Supp. 2d 1341 (S.D. Ala. 2006).

In a final rule that took effect in 2003, the Centers for Medicare & Medicaid Services took the position that EMTALA does not apply to individuals who are inpatients or outpatients at a hospital. 42 C.F.R. §489.24(b), (d)(2). The Sixth Circuit, which concluded in the *Thornton* case, supra, that the obligation to stabilize persists through the patient's hospitalization, has rejected the regulation. Moses v. Providence Hospital & Medical Centers, Inc., 561 F.3d 573, 583 (6th Cir. 2009). The Third Circuit, on the other hand, has upheld the regulation. Torretti v. Main Line Hospitals, Inc., 580 F.3d 168, 174-176 (3d Cir. 2009) (interpreting 42 C.F.R. §489.24(b) when an EMTALA claim was brought by an outpatient). So too have many district courts. Thornhill v. Jackson Parish Hospital, 184 F. Supp. 3d 392, 399-400 (W.D. La. 2016) (citing cases).

6. *Appropriate Medical Screening.* In interpreting EMTALA's requirement of an "appropriate medical screening examination," courts have recognized an important tension between ensuring access to emergency care for all persons and creating a federal cause of action for charges of malpractice in the emergency department. If a person is sent home from the emergency department after a physician wrongly concludes that there is no serious health problem, the mistaken diagnosis may reflect either the negligent provision of care or the purposeful denial of care. A hospital trying to evade its EMTALA obligations might do so by giving undesired patients short shrift when screening them. At the same time, patients who have been injured by malpractice may try to bring their claim under both state tort law and federal EMTALA law, thereby increasing their potential recovery, gaining access to a federal forum and its quicker judgments, and increasing their bargaining power with the hospitals by virtue of the latter's possible loss of its participation in Medicare. EMTALA claims are often appended to state tort claims when people sue for injuries allegedly caused by inadequate emergency care. Singer, supra note 1; 33 Hous. L. Rev. at 118 & n.22.

Courts have consistently stated that EMTALA cannot be used to bring claims for medical malpractice, and they have tried to distinguish between a denial of care and the negligent provision of care by looking at whether the hospital screened the patient in the same way it screens similarly situated patients. As the D.C. Circuit explained, the issue is whether the hospital "conform[ed] its treatment of a particular patient to its standard screening procedures. . . . [A]ny departure from standard screening procedures constitutes inappropriate screening." Gatewood v. Washington Healthcare Corp., 933 F.2d 1037, 1041 (D.C. Cir. 1991). Similarly, the Fourth Circuit has stated that EMTALA's screening requirement is designed to prevent "disparate treatment." Vickers v. Nash General Hospital, Inc., 78 F.3d 139, 143 (4th Cir. 1996). Hospitals are obligated only to "apply uniform screening procedures to all individuals coming to the emergency room." In re Baby K, 16 F.3d 590, 595 (4th Cir. 1994). Accord Correa v. Hospital San Francisco, 69 F.3d 1184 (1st Cir. 1995); Summers v. Baptist Medical Center, 91 F.3d 1132, 1138 (8th Cir. 1996); Repp v. Anadarko Municipal Hospital, 43 F.3d 519, 522 (10th Cir. 1994); Holcomb v. Monahan, 30 F.3d 116, 117 (11th Cir. 1994).

The Sixth Circuit has adopted a similar standard, although it has indicated that the departure from the hospital's standard screening procedures must have resulted from some invidious motive like bias against the patient on the basis of "race, sex, politics, occupation, education, personal prejudice, drunkenness, spite . . . distaste for the patient's condition (e.g., AIDS patients). . . ." Cleland v. Bronson Health Care Group, Inc., 917 F.2d 266, 271-272 (6th Cir. 1990); Roberts v. Galen of Virginia, 111 F.3d 405, 408-409 (6th Cir. 1997), rev'd in part, 525 U.S. 249 (1999). Even if the Sixth Circuit requires some invidious motive, would it ever be difficult to find a bias lurking that would be unacceptable under the *Cleland* standard? Perhaps not often, but see Garrett v. Detroit Medical Center, 2007 U.S. Dist. LEXIS 17584 (E.D. Mich. Mar. 14, 2007) (dismissing patient's EMTALA claim on grounds that the defendant hospital transferred the patient to a hospital so he could be treated at a hospital that was "in-network" for his insurance).

Since EMTALA requires hospitals to apply their standard screening procedures, cases can turn on whether the defendant hospital had established standard screening guidelines and whether the defendant physician had followed those guidelines. See, e.g., Delibertis v. Pottstown General Hospital, 152 F. Supp. 3d 394, 399-400 (E.D. Pa. 2016) (rejecting summary judgment since hospital presented evidence that treating physician followed his own standard practices rather than the hospital's standard practices).

For an argument that trial courts are too quick to grant summary judgment for hospitals on the question of whether patients received an appropriate screening, see Note, 87 N.Y.U. L. Rev. 591 (2012).

Despite the courts' admonition that EMTALA does not create a federal malpractice cause of action, there inevitably will be some overlap between EMTALA claims and malpractice claims. Do you see how a requirement that hospitals provide all patients with their standard screening procedures amounts to requiring that the hospitals provide nonnegligent care? See Demetrios G. Metropoulos, Note, Son of COBRA: The Evolution of a Federal Malpractice Law, 45 Stan. L. Rev. 263 (1992).

As the preceding discussion indicates, courts have interpreted the requirement of an appropriate screening examination as an equal treatment right rather than an entitlement right. But isn't EMTALA a statute that grants an entitlement rather than a right of equal treatment? Is there a way to define appropriate screening examination as an entitlement without turning it even more clearly into the equivalent of nonnegligent care?

7. *Further Reading.* On EMTALA and its **role in the health care system** (note 1), see Russell Korobkin, Determining Health Care Rights from Behind a Veil of Ignorance, 1998 U. Ill. L. Rev. 801; Paul T. Menzel, Justice and Fairness, 40 J.L. Med. & Ethics 582 (2012); Sara Rosenbaum, The Enduring Role of the Emergency Medical Treatment and Active Labor Act, 32 Health Aff. 2075 (2013); Sara Rosenbaum et al., EMTALA and Hospital "Community Engagement," 53 Buff. L. Rev. 499 (2005); Karen Rothenberg, Who Cares? The Evolution of the Legal Duty to Provide Emergency Care, 26 Hous. L. Rev. 21 (1989); Dana E. Schaffner, Note, EMTALA: All Bark and No Bite, 2005 U. Ill. L. Rev. 1021; Lawrence E. Singer, Look What They've Done to

My Law, Ma: COBRA's Implosion, 33 Hous. L. Rev. 113 (1996); Annot., 104 A.L.R. Fed. 166.

On the **duty to stabilize** (note 2), see Mark A. Hall, The Unlikely Case in Favor of Patient Dumping, 28 Jurimetrics J. 389 (1990) ("In the great majority of cases, the federal standard will do nothing to prevent patient dumping. . . . Even for those patients who do require stabilization prior to transfer, the federal law will result only in a delay in the transfer."); Kenneth R. Wing & John R. Campbell, The Emergency Room Admission: How Far Does the "Open Door" Go?, 63 U. Det. L. Rev. 119 (1985); Will Jay Pirkey, Shameful Practice, 39 L.A. Law. 20 (July/Aug. 2016).

On the ethical and financial concerns with **undocumented immigrants** (note 2), see Maya Babu & Joseph Wolpin, Undocumented Immigrants, Healthcare Access and Medical Repatriation Following Serious Medical Illness, 3 J. Health & Life Sci. L. 83 (2009); Janet L. Dolgin & Katherine R. Dieterich, When Others Get Too Close, 19 Cornell J.L. & Pub. Pol'y 283 (2010); Svetlana Lebedinski, EMTALA: Treatment of Undocumented Aliens and the Financial Burden It Places on Hospitals, 7 J.L. Soc'y 146 (2005-2006); Jennifer M. Smith, Screen, Stabilize, and Ship: EMTALA, U.S. Hospitals, and Undocumented Immigrants, 10 Hous. J. Health L. & Pol'y 309 (2010); Michael J. Young & Lisa Soleymani Lehmann, Undocumented Injustice, 370 New Eng. J. Med. 669 (2014).

2. Wrongful Reasons to Reject Patients

While physicians or hospitals may, for most patients, refuse to treat for "good" reasons (such as inability to pay), or even for no particular reason, they may not deny care for the wrong reasons. For example, Title VI of the Civil Rights Acts of 1964 makes it unlawful for hospitals that receive federal money (such as Medicare and Medicaid) to discriminate on the basis of a patient's race, color, or national origin. On the other hand, without a statute that specifically prohibits the particular reason for discrimination, morally problematic denials of care are generally permissible, as the first case demonstrates.

■ WALKER v. PIERCE
560 F.2d 609 (4th Cir. 1977)

BRYAN, Senior Circuit Judge.

Violation of their civil rights was laid in this action for damages and declaratory and injunctive relief by Virgil Walker and Shirley Brown, black females, to Clovis H. Pierce, the attending obstetrician at the Aiken County Hospital in South Carolina for sterilizing them, or threatening to do so, solely on account of their race and number of their children, while they were receiving medical assistance under the [state's] Medicaid program. . . .

Centering the controversy is the policy previously announced and constantly pursued in practice by the doctor, testified to by him as follows:

> My policy was with people who were unable to financially support themselves, whether they be on Medicaid or just unable to pay their own bills, if they were having a third child, to request they voluntarily submit to sterilization following the

delivery of the third child. If they did not wish this as a condition for my care, then I requested that they seek another physician other than myself.

There is no question of his professional qualifications or experience.

As drawn by the plaintiffs, he is the arch-offender. The accusation is incursion upon their constitutional rights of privacy, due process of law, and equal protection of the law as well as of their statutory privileges against discrimination on account of their race and color, all by subjecting or threatening the plaintiffs as citizens of the United States with involuntary sterilization. . . .

Virgil Walker had completed the seventh grade, was separated from her husband, and was receiving Aid to Families with Dependent Children and Medicaid benefits. Expecting her fourth child, she first went to Pierce on January 7, 1972. During this consultation, he discussed family planning and his sterilization policy. Walker refused to consent. The issue again came up at the second visit and she again declined. Walker testified that Pierce threatened to have her state assistance terminated unless she cooperated. She called another doctor, but he was not taking new patients.

On February 4, 1972, Spears, a Department of Social Services caseworker assigned to Walker, received a note from Pierce's office asking that he talk with Walker about sterilization. Thereupon, Spears, according to his testimony, spoke with her on February 17th, offering to get her a second doctor. On the other hand, Walker stated that Spears had said there was nothing he could do. Then she returned to Pierce and subsequently signed a consent form for sterilization.

Her fourth child was delivered at the Aiken County Hospital April 16, 1972 by Dr. Billy Burke, an obstetrician who substituted for Pierce on occasion. Burke discussed tubal ligation with Walker. Her response was that she did not want additional children and understood that it would be a permanent sterilization. Two more consent forms were then signed. Pierce performed the operation April 17, 1972. She protested no further because, she said, it would have been futile.

Walker's hospital bills and doctor's fees were paid by Medicaid. Under the South Carolina plan operated by the Department of Social Services, the patient-physician relationship is one of free choice for both parties. The physician, under no contract with the state, simply submits his bill when treatment is concluded to the Medicaid insurance carrier instead of the patient. . . .

We perceive no reason why Dr. Pierce could not establish and pursue the policy he has publicly and freely announced. Nor are we cited to judicial precedent or statute inhibiting this personal economic philosophy. Particularly is this so when all persons coming to him as patients are seasonably made fully aware of his professional attitude toward the increase in offspring and his determination to see it prevail. At no time is he shown to have forced his view upon any mother. Indeed, quite the opposite appears. In the single occasion in this case of a sterilization by this doctor, not just one but three formal written consents were obtained—the first before delivery of the fourth child and two afterwards. . . .

[The court also held that Dr. Pierce was not a state actor and therefore could not be found to have violated his patients' constitutional rights. Also, as an aside (not addressed by the court), recognize that, although hospitals were subject to Title VI of the federal Civil Rights Act, at the time physicians were not, due to political obstacles and administrative complexities that prompted a strained reading of

Title VI's application to payments to physicians. David Barton Smith, Health Care Divided: Race and Healing a Nation 161-164, 227-278 (1999).]

Notes: Discriminatory Denials of Care

1. *Racial Discrimination in Health Care.* As with other parts of society, the health care system has suffered from a long history of discrimination on the basis of race. At one time, it was commonplace, especially in the South, for hospitals to refuse admission to blacks. These and other forms of overt discrimination have now largely disappeared as the result of various prohibitions contained in federal and state regulatory law, as well as in the hospital industry's own private accreditation code. See generally Sara Rosenbaum et al., U.S. Civil Rights Policy and Access to Health Care by Minority Americans, 57 Med. Care Res. & Rev. 226 (2000); Symposium, 42(5) J. Health Pol. Pol'y L. 739 (Oct. 2017).

Serious concerns remain, however, over more subtle forms of racial bias in the delivery of health care services. One form occurs in the location of health care facilities, which in inner cities are sometimes older, less accessible, or not as well equipped. See Sara J. Rosenbaum & Sara Schmucker, Viewing Health Equity Through a Legal Lens, 42 J. Health Pol. Pol'y L. 771 (2017).

Discrimination can also arise in individual treatment decisions. Numerous studies have documented that physicians treat blacks, and sometimes women, differently for the same medical conditions. For instance, blacks are less likely than whites to receive a kidney transplant, coronary artery bypass surgery, or other major surgical procedures. See Dayna Bowen Matthew, Just Medicine: A Cure for Racial Inequality in American Health Care (2015); R. Yearby, Breaking the Cycle of Unequal Treatment with Health Care Reform, 44 U. Conn. L. Rev. 1281 (2010); Symposium, 42 (5) J. Health Pol. Pol'y L. (2017); Symposium, 25 Health Matrix 1 (2015); Symposium, 55 How. L.J. 679 (2012).

2. *Race-Based Medicine.* Some analysts respond that the studies just cited are not as conclusive as they may appear because of real or possible differences among racial groups in income, medical considerations, biological factors, and patient preferences. Jonathan Klick & Sally Satel, The Health Disparities Myth (2006); Kimani Paul-Emile, Patient Racial Preferences and the Medical Culture of Accommodation, 60 UCLA L. Rev. 462 (2012). See also Nancy Kressin & Peter Groeneveld, Race/Ethnicity and Overuse of Care, 93 Milbank Q. 112 (2015) (reporting that whites are more *over*treated than others).

Is it *ever* legitimate for doctors to take race into account as relevant in deciding how best to treat patients? Critics argue that skin color is an imperfect proxy for genetic or environmental factors that are relevant to choosing the best treatment for each patient. Defenders of "race-based medicine" say that ethnic heritage is a reasonably accurate indicator of a variety of medical risk factors that physicians should and do take into account.

For policy and legal analysis race-based medicine, see Michael J. Malinowski, Dealing with the Realities of Race and Ethnicity, 45 Hous. L. Rev. 1415 (2009); D. Wasserman, The Justifiability of Racial Classification and Generalizations in Contemporary Clinical and Research Practice, 9 Law, Probability & Risk 215 (2010); Erik Lillquist & Charles A. Sullivan, The Law and Genetics of Racial Profiling in Medicine, 39 Harv. C.R.-C.L. L. Rev. 393 (2004); Sharona Hoffman, "Racially-Tailored"

Medicine Unraveled, 55 Am. U. L. Rev. 395-456 (2005) ("'race-based' medicine might violate numerous anti-discrimination provisions contained in federal law, state law, and federal research regulations and guidelines"); Symposium, 34 J.L. Med. & Ethics 483 (2006); Symposium, 36 J.L. Med. & Ethics 443 (2008); and articles by Jonathan Kahn in 4 Yale J. Health Pol'y L. & Ethics 1 (2004); and 92 Iowa L. Rev. 353 (2007).

3. *Filling the legal void.* No cases have yet arisen that attack differential treatment patterns by physicians as forms of racial discrimination. In part, that is because, prior to now, Title VI of the Civil Rights Act, which applies to federallyfunded services, has been interpreted as not applying to physicians, supra page 82. And no federal statute prohibited discrimination on the basis of sex in health care services. The Affordable Care Act closes these gaps by broadening the definition of federally funded activities and the kinds of discrimination that are prohibited. Sandra H. Johnson, The ACA's Provision on Nondiscrimination Takes Shape, 46(5) Hastings Center Rep. 5 (2016); Symposium, 42(5) J. Health Pol. Pol'y L. (2017).

4. *Conscience Defense to Discrimination.* When a patient is protected from discrimination by a civil rights statute, may a physician nevertheless refuse to treat on grounds of religious belief? The California Supreme Court answered that question for a patient denied fertility services, allegedly on the basis of her sexual orientation. The Court held that a physician may not refuse treatment if it is on a basis protected from discrimination by statute. However, the Court left open the possibility for denying treatment based on an unprotected status (e.g., unmarried status of parents). North Coast Women's Care Medical Group, Inc. v. Superior Court, 189 P.3d 959 (Cal. 2008). For further discussion, see Symposium: The Future of Rights of Conscience in Health Care: Legal and Ethical Perspectives, 9(1) Ave Maria Law Rev. (2010).

5. *Discrimination on the Basis of Disability.* While Congress waited until 2010 to close the gaps in Title VI's protection against treatment that discriminates on the basis of race or sex, Congress enacted protections against discrimination on the basis of disability in two important statutes much earlier, the Rehabilitation Act of 1973 and the Americans with Disabilities Act of 1990.

The analysis of discrimination under disability statutes is inherently complicated. Often a person's disability is relevant in deciding whether the person is a candidate for treatment. For example, it would not make much sense to transplant a kidney or liver into a patient dying of cancer. Accordingly, while physicians or hospitals rarely would acknowledge that they discriminate on the basis of race or sex, they often will be comfortable citing a patient's disability as a reason for denying care. As we will see, unlawful denials of care can occur both from a refusal to treat at all or a refusal to provide certain kinds of care after the patient-physician relationship is formed.

■ UNITED STATES v. UNIVERSITY HOSPITAL
729 F.2d 144 (2d Cir. 1984)

PRATT, Circuit Judge.

. . . Baby Jane Doe was born on October 11, 1983 at St. Charles Hospital in Port Jefferson, New York. She was suffering from multiple birth defects, the most serious of which were myelomeningocele, commonly known as spina bifida, a condition in which the spinal cord and membranes that envelop it are exposed; microcephaly, an abnormally small head; and hydrocephalus, a condition characterized by an accumulation of fluid in the cranial vault. In addition, she exhibited a "weak face," which prevents the infant from closing her eyes or making a full suck with her tongue; a malformed brain stem; upper extremity spasticity; and a thumb entirely within her fist.

As a result of the spina bifida, the baby's rectal, bladder, leg, and sensory functions were impaired. Due to the combination of microcephaly and hydrocephalus, there was an extremely high risk that the child would be so severely retarded that she could never interact with her environment or with other people.

At the direction of the first pediatric neurosurgeon to examine her, the baby was immediately transferred to University Hospital for dual surgery to correct her spina bifida and hydrocephalus. Essentially, this would entail excising a sac of fluid and nerve endings on the spine and closing the opening, and implanting a shunt to relieve pressure caused by fluid build-up in the cranial cavity. The record indicates that these dual, corrective surgical procedures were likely to prolong the infant's life, but would not improve many of her handicapping conditions, including her anticipated mental retardation.

After consulting with several physicians, nurses, religious advisors, a social worker, and members of their family, the parents of the baby decided to forego the corrective surgery. Instead, they opted for a "conservative" medical treatment consisting of good nutrition, the administration of antibiotics, and the dressing of the baby's exposed spinal sac.

Litigation surrounding Baby Jane Doe began on October 16, when A. Lawrence Washburn, Jr., a Vermont attorney unrelated to the child and her family, commenced a proceeding in New York State Supreme Court seeking appointment of a guardian ad litem for the child and an order directing University Hospital to perform the corrective surgery, [contending that failure to do so would violate Section 504 of the Rehabilitation Act of 1973, 29 U.S.C. §794] . . .

. . . The Appellate Division found that the "concededly concerned and loving parents have made an informed, intelligent, and reasonable determination based upon and supported by responsible medical authority." As the court elaborated:

> The record confirms that the failure to perform the surgery will not place the infant in imminent danger of death, although surgery might significantly reduce the risk of infection. On the other hand, successful results could also be achieved with antibiotic therapy. Further, while the mortality rate is higher where conservative medical treatment is used, in this particular case the surgical procedures also involved a great risk of depriving the infant of what little function remains in her legs, and would also result in recurring urinary tract and possibly kidney infections, skin infections and edemas of the limbs.

Thus, the Appellate Division determined that the parents' decision was in the best interest of the infant and that there was, therefore, no basis for judicial intervention. . . . [The Appellate Division's decision was affirmed by the New York Court of Appeals, but on the ground that the trial court had abused its discretion in permitting the case to go forward. The Court of Appeals observed that (a) Mr. Washburn (the petitioner) had no direct interest in the case, (b) Mr. Washburn had not contacted the State Department of Social Services, which had primary responsibility under state law for initiating child abuse proceedings, and (c) the trial court had failed to seek the Department of Social Service's assistance.]

[Meanwhile, as the state court proceedings were unfolding, HHS received a complaint that Baby Jane Doe was being denied medical treatment because of her handicap. In response to the complaint, HHS obtained the record of the state court proceedings and, after personal review by the Surgeon General, requested the infant's medical records from the hospital. When the hospital refused to provide the records, HHS brought its case in federal court, alleging that the hospital was violating Section 504 of the Rehabilitation Act. The federal district court granted summary judgment for the hospital on two grounds: first, the hospital refused to operate on Baby Jane Doe, not because of her handicap, but because her parents did not consent to the procedures; and second, the parents' refusal of treatment was reasonable given the medical options. The federal government appealed, resulting in this opinion.]

To focus more sharply on this central issue, it is first necessary to examine the theory upon which the government predicates its [claim]. The theory rests on two premises. First, the government draws a distinction between decisionmaking based on a "bona fide medical judgment," which without definition it concedes to be beyond the reach of §504, and decisionmaking based solely on an individual's handicap, which it argues is covered by §504. Second, the government identifies Baby Jane Doe's microcephaly, which the record indicates will result in severe mental retardation, as the handicapping condition. From these premises, the government reasons that if a newborn infant suffering from spina bifida and hydrocephalus, but not microcephaly, would receive treatment or services that differ from those provided to an infant suffering from all three defects, or alternatively, if the hospital would seek a state court order compelling surgery in the former case, but not in the latter, then a violation of §504 would have been established. . . .

With this unsettled regulatory background in mind, we turn to the statutory language, which is fundamental to any issue of statutory construction. Section 504 provides in pertinent part as follows:

> No otherwise qualified handicapped individual in the United States, as defined in section 706(7) of this title, shall, solely by reason of his handicap, be excluded from the participation in, be denied the benefits of, or be subjected to discrimination under any program or activity receiving federal financial assistance.

Under 29 U.S.C. §706(7)(B), "the term 'handicapped individual' means . . . any person who (i) has a physical or mental impairment which substantially limits one or more of such person's major life activities, (ii) has a record of such an impairment, or (iii) is regarded as having such an impairment." . . .

[We] next consider whether [Baby Jane Doe] possibly can be considered an "otherwise qualified" handicapped individual or to have been "subjected to discrimination" under §504. These two issues are intertwined.

The leading cases construing the "otherwise qualified" criterion of §504 have involved allegedly discriminatory denials of admission to certain educational programs. Southeastern Community College v. Davis, 442 U.S. 397 (1979); Doe v. New York University, 666 F.2d 761 (2d Cir. 1981). In that context, this court in Doe v. New York University recognized that

> it is now clear that [the phrase "otherwise qualified handicapped individual"] refers to a person who is qualified *in spite of* her handicap and that an institution is not required to disregard the disabilities of a handicapped applicant, provided the handicap is relevant to reasonable qualifications for acceptance, or to make substantial modifications in its reasonable standards or program to accommodate handicapped individuals but may take an applicant's handicap into consideration, along with all other relevant factors, in determining whether she is qualified for admission. [Id. at 775 (emphasis in original).]

Doe establishes that §504 prohibits discrimination against a handicapped individual only where the individual's handicap is unrelated to, and thus improper to consideration of, the services in question. As defendants here point out, however, where medical treatment is at issue, it is typically the handicap itself that gives rise to, or at least contributes to, the need for services. Defendants thus argue, and with some force, that the "otherwise qualified" criterion of §504 cannot be meaningfully applied to a medical treatment decision. Similarly, defendants argue that it would be pointless to inquire whether a patient who was affected by a medical treatment decision was, "solely by reason of his handicap, . . . subjected to discrimination."

The government's answer to both these arguments is that Baby Jane Doe can be viewed as suffering from not one, but multiple handicaps. Indeed, the crux of the government's case is that her microcephaly is the operative handicap, and that the requested records are necessary to determine whether she has been discriminated against solely for that reason.

Despite its superficial logic, the government's theory is flawed in at least two respects. First, the government's view of "otherwise qualified" is divorced from the statutory language. As the mainstream of cases under §504 exemplifies, the phrase "otherwise qualified" is geared toward relatively static programs or activities such as education, employment, and transportation systems. As a result, the phrase cannot be applied in the comparatively fluid context of medical treatment decisions without distorting its plain meaning. In common parlance, one would not ordinarily think of a newborn infant suffering from multiple birth defects as being "otherwise qualified" to have corrective surgery performed or to have a hospital initiate litigation seeking to override a decision against surgery by the infant's parents. If Congress intended §504 to apply in this manner, it chose strange language indeed.

Second, in arguing that Baby Jane may have been "subjected to discrimination" the government has taken an oversimplified view of the medical decision-making process. Where the handicapping condition is related to the (conditions) to be treated, it will rarely, if ever, be possible to say with certainty that a particular decision was "discriminatory." It is at this point that the analogy to race, relied on so heavily by the dissent, breaks down. Beyond the fact that no two cases are likely to be the same, it would invariably require lengthy litigation primarily involving conflicting expert testimony to determine whether a decision to treat, or not to treat, or to litigate or not to litigate, was based on a "bona fide medical judgment," however that phrase might be defined. Before ruling that congress intended to spawn this type of litigation under §504, we would want more proof than is apparent from the face of the statute.

The legislative history, moreover, indicates that congress never contemplated that §504 would apply to treatment decisions of this nature. . . . [According to t]he Senate Report accompanying the 1974 amendments:

... Section 504 was enacted to prevent discrimination against all handicapped individuals . . . in relation to federal assistance in employment, housing, transportation, education, health services, or any other federally-aided programs. Examples of handicapped individuals who may suffer discrimination in receipt of federally-assisted services . . . are as follows: physically or mentally handicapped children who may be denied admission to federally-supported school systems on the basis of their handicap; handicapped persons who may be denied admission to federally-assisted nursing homes on the basis of their handicap; those persons whose handicap is so severe that employment is not feasible but who may be denied the benefits of a wide range of federal programs. . . .

S. Rep. No. 1297, supra at 6388-6389.

This passage provides the best clue to congressional intent regarding §504's coverage of "health services." As Judge Gesell noted in American Academy of Pediatrics v. Heckler, 561 F. Supp. at 401:

The legislative history . . . [on this subject] focuses on discrimination against adults and older children and denial of access to federal programs. As far as can be determined, no congressional committee or member of the House or Senate ever even suggested that section 504 would be used to monitor medical treatment of defective newborn infants or establish standards for preserving a particular quality of life. No medical group appeared alert to the intrusion into medical practice which some doctors apprehend from such an undertaking, nor were representatives of parents or spokesmen for religious beliefs that would be affected heard. . . .

We are aware, of course, that "where the words and purpose of a statute plainly apply to a particular situation, . . . the fact that the specific application of the statute never occurred to Congress does not bar us from holding that the situation falls within the statute's coverage." United States v. Jones, 607 F.2d 269, 273 (9th Cir. 1979), cert. denied, 444 U.S. 1085 (1980). Here, however, the government's theory not only strains the statutory language but also goes well beyond Congress's overriding concern with guaranteeing handicapped individuals access to programs or activities receiving federal financial assistance. Further, the situation in question is dramatically different in kind, not just in degree, from the applications of §504 discussed in the legislative history. . . .

This void in the legislative history is conspicuous for another reason. Prior to the enactment of the Rehabilitation Act, congress had passed a number of measures limiting federal involvement in medical treatment decisions. For example, the very first section of the Medicare law, . . . codified at 42 U.S.C. §1395, . . . provides that "nothing in this subchapter shall be construed to authorize any federal officer or employee to exercise any supervision or control over the practice of medicine or the manner in which medical services are provided." . . .

In view of this consistent congressional policy against the involvement of federal personnel in medical treatment decisions, we cannot presume that Congress intended to repeal its earlier announcements in the absence of clear evidence of congressional intent to do so. . . .

In the present case, Baby Jane Doe has been treated in an evenhanded manner at least to the extent that the hospital has always been and remains willing to perform the dual, corrective surgeries if her parents would consent. Requiring the hospital either to undertake surgery notwithstanding the parents' decision or alternatively, to petition the state court to override the parents' decision, would impose a particularly onerous affirmative action burden upon the hospital. . . .

WINTER, Circuit Judge, dissenting.

Since I believe that §504 applies to the provision of medical services to handicapped infants, I respectfully dissent. . . . Section 504 . . . states with as much clarity as is reasonably possible that in some circumstances recipients of federal financial assistance may not differentiate between individuals on grounds that one or more is handicapped. . . . Although modern courts frequently rely upon legislative history to reach results at odds with the seemingly plain language of a statute, only the most compelling reasons should induce a court to override statutory language because the legislative history is silent on a particular point. Such compelling circumstances might exist in the present case if Congress had no reason to address the questions at hand when it enacted §504. It hardly needs stating that the underlying issues brim with political and moral controversy and portend to extend the hand of the federal government into matters traditionally governed by an interaction of parental judgment and state authority. Were I able to conclude that Congress had no reason to address these issues in its consideration of §504, I would concur with the majority on the grounds that specific consideration by the Congress of this political and moral minefield would be appropriate before applying the statute as written.

However, such a conclusion is untenable since §504 is no first step into a hitherto uncharted legal wilderness. As the Senate Report stated:

> Section 504 was patterned after, and is almost identical to, the antidiscrimination language of section 601 of the Civil Rights Act of 1964, 42 U.S.C. 2000d-1 (relating to race, color, or national origin), and section 901 of the Education Amendments of 1972, 42 U.S.C. 1683 (relating to sex). The section therefore constitutes the establishment of a broad government policy that programs receiving federal financial assistance shall be operated without discrimination on the basis of handicap.

S. Rep. No. 1297, 93d Cong., 2d Sess., *reprinted* in 1974 U.S. Code Cong. & Ad. News 6373, 6390. Section 504 was thus enacted against a background of well understood law which was explicitly designated as a guide to interpretation. Congress was persuaded that a handicapped condition is analogous to race and that, so far as the administration of federal financial assistance is concerned, discrimination on the basis of a handicap should be on statutory par with discrimination on the basis of race.

Once §504's legislative heritage is acknowledged, the "void" in the legislative history is eliminated and the many issues raised by defendants with regard to medical decisions, parental judgments and state authority simply evaporate. The government has never taken the position that it is entitled to override a medical judgment. Its position rather is that it is entitled under §504 to inquire whether a judgment in question is a bona fide medical judgment. While the majority professes uncertainty as to what that means, application of the analogy to race eliminates all doubt. A judgment not to perform certain surgery because a person is black is not a bona fide medical judgment. So too, a decision not to correct a life threatening digestive problem because an infant has Down's Syndrome is not a bona fide medical judgment. The issue of parental authority is also quickly disposed of. A denial of medical treatment to an infant because the infant is black is not legitimated by parental consent. Finally, once the legislative analogy to race is acknowledged, the intrusion on state authority becomes insignificant. . . .

Bragdon v. Abbott, 524 U.S. 624 (1998). Invoking the Americans with Disabilities Act's (ADA's) protection from discrimination based on disability, a woman with HIV infection challenged her dentist's refusal to fill her cavity unless he performed the procedure in a hospital. (The woman, Sidney Abbott, would have been responsible for the cost of using the hospital's facilities.) Important issues in the case were whether HIV infection constitutes a disability for purposes of the ADA and whether the dentist could nevertheless justify denying treatment in his office to protect himself from becoming infected with HIV during the procedure. (The ADA generally tracks the framework of the Rehabilitation Act's protection against discrimination based on disability but expands to more people the protection of the Rehabilitation Act.)

The Court concluded that Ms. Abbott's HIV infection constituted a disability under the ADA on the ground that HIV infection is a "physical . . . impairment that substantially limits one or more . . . major life activities." 42 U.S.C. §12102(2)(A). According to the Court, HIV infection is a physical impairment from the moment of infection because the virus immediately begins to damage an infected person's white blood cells and because of the severity of the disease. As to whether HIV infection substantially limits a major life activity, the Court observed that it might have identified many major life activities substantially limited by HIV infection. Since Ms. Abbott claimed that HIV infection substantially limited her ability to have children, the Court restricted its inquiry to that life activity. As an activity "central to the life process itself," reproduction constitutes a major life activity, wrote the Court. Moreover, HIV infection substantially limits reproduction in two ways: "First, a woman infected with HIV who tries to conceive a child imposes on the man a significant risk of becoming infected. . . . Second, an infected woman risks infecting her child during gestation and childbirth. . . ." The Court also noted that, even though the risk of transmission of HIV from mother to infant could be reduced by treatment to 8 percent, such a risk of transmitting a fatal disease rose to the level of a substantial limitation.

As to whether the dentist could defend his insistence on treatment at a hospital, he would have to show that Ms. Abbott "pose[d] a direct threat to [his] health or safety. . . ." 42 U.S.C. §12182(b)(3), with direct threat defined as "a significant risk to the health or safety of others that cannot be eliminated by a modification of policies, practices, or procedures or by the provision of auxiliary aids or services." Id. In assessing whether the dentist's fear of HIV transmission was objectively reasonable, "the views of public health authorities, such as the U.S. Public Health Service, CDC, and the National Institutes of Health, are of special weight and authority. The views of these organizations are not conclusive, however. A health care professional who disagrees with the prevailing medical consensus may refute it by citing a credible scientific basis for deviating from the accepted norm." The Court remanded the case for consideration of the dentist's defense of a direct threat to his health if he were to fill Ms. Abbott's cavity in his office instead of a hospital.

On remand, the First Circuit found in favor of Ms. Abbott. The court concluded that, because of the availability of universal precautions to prevent transmission of HIV infection from patient to dentist, the dentist could not justify his denial of treatment in terms of the need to protect himself from becoming infected with HIV. Abbott v. Bragdon, 163 F.3d 87 (1st Cir. 1998), *cert. denied*, 526 U.S. 1131 (1999). (Universal precautions are measures that health care providers are supposed to take with every patient to prevent the spread of infectious diseases like HIV and hepatitis. Examples of universal precautions are the wearing of gloves and other protective attire by health care providers, the use of special wastebaskets to dispose of used needles, and sterilization of medical instruments after each use.) The First Circuit decided that once physicians take universal precautions, no significant risk of HIV transmission remains.

■ GLANZ v. VERNICK
756 F. Supp. 632 (D. Mass. 1991)

MAZZONE, Judge.

In April, 1989, plaintiff's decedent, Raymond Vadnais, brought this suit alleging discrimination in violation of §504 of the Rehabilitation Act of 1973 (the "Act"), 29 U.S.C. §794. . . . The case is now before [this court] on the [defendants' motions for] summary judgment.

The allegations in the complaint can be briefly summarized as follows. In December, 1986, defendant Dr. Vernick saw Mr. Vadnais at the Ear, Nose, and Throat Clinic (the "ENT Clinic") at Beth Israel Hospital and treated him for severe pain in the right ear, at first by prescribing antibiotics and ear drops. In January, 1987, Dr. Vernick diagnosed a perforation in Mr. Vadnais's right ear and, at Mr. Vadnais's third visit, recommended surgery to repair the perforation. After Mr. Vadnais agreed to undergo surgery, Dr. Vernick learned that Mr. Vadnais was infected with HIV and in March, 1987, informed Mr. Vadnais that he would not perform the operation. The ear condition persisted, causing severe pain and discomfort, while Mr. Vadnais continued the ineffective use of antibiotics and ear drops.

In August, 1988, Dr. Yale Berry, unaware of Mr. Vadnais's HIV status, performed the surgery, curing Mr. Vadnais's ear problem. Subsequently, Mr. Vadnais brought this lawsuit seeking . . . compensatory damages for the pain and suffering and emotional distress caused by the delay in receiving corrective surgery, along with punitive damages and attorney's fees. . . .

Count I of the complaint charges that Dr. Vernick, . . . by refusing to perform surgery, unlawfully discriminated against Mr. Vadnais because of his handicap, HIV seropositivity, in violation of §504 of the Rehabilitation Act. . . .

Section 504 states in pertinent part that "no otherwise qualified handicapped individual in the United States . . . shall, solely by reason of his handicap, be excluded from the participation in, be denied the benefits of, or be subjected to discrimination under any program or activity receiving federal financial assistance. . . ." 29 U.S.C. §794.

The defendants argue that summary judgment is appropriate for several . . . reasons . . . [including] the ground that Mr. Vadnais was not "otherwise qualified" for elective ear surgery. They argue that it is proper for a doctor to consider a patient's handicap in determining whether a patient is qualified for surgery. On the basis of this argument, they conclude that Mr. Vadnais was not "otherwise qualified" for surgery because his HIV disease increased his risk of infection, and, furthermore, that the court should defer to the doctor's determination that it was in his patient's best interest to postpone surgery. . . .

As the Court made clear in *Arline*, the "otherwise qualified" determination requires an individualized inquiry and appropriate findings of fact. With respect to the defendants' assertions about the risks of surgery, the facts are in dispute. The defendants contend that surgery was postponed because Dr. Vernick thought that Mr. Vadnais was "AIDS positive," because the proposed ear surgery was elective, and because it would pose significant risks to the patient. In addition, they offer Dr. Berry's statement in his deposition that he would not have performed the surgery had he known that Mr. Vadnais had AIDS. The plaintiff offers the contradicting evidence that Mr. Vadnais was HIV-positive and had not yet been diagnosed as having AIDS when surgery was refused. Moreover, Dr. Vernick in answers to interrogatories and Dr. Berry in his deposition stated that they do not consider HIV seropositivity alone as a disqualifying factor for surgery. Based on the evidence that the plaintiff has produced, facts are certainly available to warrant the conclusion that Mr. Vadnais was "otherwise qualified" for surgery. Moreover, the defendants have not produced any evidence that reasonable accommodations could not have been made.

There is some merit to the argument that the court should defer to a doctor's medical judgment. Cf. *Arline*, 480 U.S. at 288 ("courts normally should defer to the reasonable medical judgments of public health officials" when conducting "otherwise qualified" inquiry). Accepting this argument at face value, however, would completely eviscerate §504's function of preventing discrimination against the disabled in the healthcare context. A strict rule of deference would enable doctors to offer merely pretextual medical opinions to cover up discriminatory decisions. The evidentiary approach to §504 cases discussed in Pushkin v. Regents of the Univ. of Colo., 658 F.2d 1372 (10th Cir. 1981), properly balances deference to sound medical opinions with the need to detect discriminatory motives. The plaintiff must first make out a prima facie case that he was otherwise qualified for surgery, and only then does the burden shift to the defendant to show that the plaintiff's handicap made him unqualified. The plaintiff, however, must still be given an opportunity "to prove either that the reason given by defendants is a pretext or that the reason . . . 'encompasses *unjustified* consideration of the handicap itself.'" *Leckelt*, 714 F. Supp. at 1385 (citing *Pushkin*, 658 F.2d at 1387) (emphasis added).

In sum, because . . . there are genuine issues of material fact surrounding the "otherwise qualified" inquiry, summary judgment on the §504 claim is inappropriate.

Notes: Denials of Care Because of Disability

1. *Subsequent Developments.* In the end, the parents in *University Hospital* agreed to have a shunt implanted to drain the fluid in their daughter's brain, although the surgery was delayed because of an infection that was likely related to the opening in her spine. The child, Keri-Lynn, has done much better than predicted. Although she is confined to a wheelchair and developmentally disabled, she can talk, and by

age 30 in 2013, she was living in a group home Monday through Friday, taking academic classes, and receiving physical therapy. It is not clear whether surgery to close Keri-Lynn's spine would have improved her outcome.

2. *The Americans with Disabilities Act. University Hospital* and *Glanz* were decided under the Rehabilitation Act, which applies only to federally funded programs or services and federal executive agencies. Since those cases, the Americans with Disabilities Act (ADA) has gone into effect, and its provisions apply to all nonfederal providers of health care services, public or private. The statutory language of the ADA was designed to track the Rehabilitation Act and court decisions interpreting that Act.

For further discussion of the ADA and denials of health care, see Carl H. Coleman, Conceiving Harm: Disability Discrimination in Assisted Reproductive Technologies, 50 UCLA L. Rev. 17 (2002); Mary A. Crossley, Of Diagnoses and Discrimination: Discriminatory Nontreatment of Infants with HIV Infection, 93 Colum. L. Rev. 1581 (1993); Wendy F. Hensel & Leslie E. Wolf, Playing God: The Legality of Plans Denying Scarce Resources to People with Disabilities in Public Health Emergencies, 63 Fla. L. Rev. 719 (2011); Kimberly M. Mutcherson, Disabling Dreams of Parenthood, 27 Law & Ineq. 311 (2009); David Orentlicher, Destructuring Disability: Rationing of Health Care and Unfair Discrimination Against the Sick, 31 Harv. C.R.-C.L. L. Rev. 49 (1996); Philip G. Peters, Jr., When Physicians Balk at Futile Care, 91 Nw. U. L. Rev. 798 (1997); and Philip G. Peters, Jr., Health Care Rationing and Disability Rights, 70 Ind. L.J. 491 (1995).

3. *Definition of Disability.* As indicated by the Supreme Court in *Bragdon*, one has to determine whether a person is in fact disabled under the ADA or Rehabilitation Act before deciding whether there has been unlawful discrimination on account of disability. Until 1999, it did not seem to be very difficult for plaintiffs to prove that they were disabled under the ADA. Disability can be shown not only by the presence of a disabling condition but also by a history of a disabling condition or by showing that one is regarded by others as having a disabling condition. 42 U.S.C. §12102(2). Moreover, the legislative history indicated that the judgment whether a patient is disabled should be made assuming that no treatment is provided. Thus, even if a patient's disabling symptoms could be alleviated with medication, the patient would still be considered disabled under the ADA.

In 1999, the Supreme Court raised the bar on the definition of disability by holding that a person is not actually disabled if medications or medical devices can alleviate the disabling symptoms. Moreover, the Court established a relatively high threshold for showing that one is disabled because of being "regarded as having" a disabling condition. Sutton v. United Air Lines, 527 U.S. 471 (1999). The ADA Amendments Act of 2008 overrode *Sutton* and other narrowing decisions by the Supreme Court. As a result, the definition of disability is consistent again with the legislative history of the ADA. For a discussion of the 2008 Act, see Jeannette Cox, Crossroads and Signposts: The ADA Amendments Act of 2008, 85 Ind. L.J. 187 (2010). For a very helpful discussion about defining disability, see Mary Crossley, The Disability Kaleidoscope, 74 Notre Dame L. Rev. 621 (1999).

4. *When Denial of Treatment Is Discriminatory.* What standard does the *Glanz* court suggest for deciding whether a denial of care constitutes unlawful discrimination on the basis of disability? What theories does the *University Hospital* court use to find no unlawful discrimination when medical care is withheld from a severely disabled newborn? Which of the different approaches do you think makes the most sense?

Note that, while the court's decision in *University Hospital* rested in part on the fact that Baby Jane Doe's parents agreed to the withholding of care, there is much more to the opinion. In addition, another court reached the same result as *University Hospital* in a case in which the parents charged that the physicians' treatment recommendations were biased by the presence of the child's severe disability and that the physicians failed to disclose their bias when obtaining the parents' consent to withhold care. Johnson v. Thompson, 971 F.2d 1487, 1493-1494 (10th Cir. 1992) (citing *University Hospital* for the proposition that, "[w]here the handicapping condition is related to the condition(s) to be treated, it will rarely, if ever, be possible to say . . . that a particular decision was 'discriminatory'"). There are other reasons to discount parental agreement. As Judge Winter observed in his *University Hospital* dissent, parental agreement does not necessarily vitiate a discrimination claim. The parents may not be adequately representing the child's interests.

Both *Glanz* and *University Hospital* take the view that a person's disability can be a relevant consideration in the person's access to health care. If a disability affects the benefit that the patient can receive from health care, then the disability can be a factor in deciding how to treat the patient. But that leaves most disabled persons subject to denials of health care. The immune system compromise of an HIV-infected person, for example, will have wide-ranging effects on that person's response to medical or surgical therapy. Crossley, supra note 2, at 1650. Indeed, the argument in *Glanz* that Mr. Glanz's HIV infection would predispose him to infection would apply to any HIV-infected patient undergoing surgery. How do we consider the effects of a person's disability without discriminating unfairly against that person? What if it is true that a disabled person would not gain as much benefit from treatment as a nondisabled person? Is an appropriate analogy the educational services that states are required to provide in the primary public schools for children with disabilities? See New Mexico Association for Retarded Citizens v. New Mexico, 678 F.2d 847, 854-855 (10th Cir. 1982) (requiring special education to ensure that children with disabilities receive an education appropriate to their needs).

To what extent are the costs of care relevant to the analysis? If Baby Jane Doe's care cost thousands instead of hundreds of thousands of dollars, should that make a difference in deciding whether disability discrimination occurred? If you think social costs are relevant, then why does the denial of care by Dr. Pierce seem more troubling than the withholding of care from Baby Jane Doe? Wasn't he also concerned primarily about social costs? Is his decision worse because it was directed toward only the poor, or because welfare status is correlated with race? Or is it that sterilization is reminiscent of discredited eugenic social policies of the past?

Rather than avoiding the care of certain patients by claiming that the patient is not a candidate for care (as in *University Hospital* or *Glanz*), physicians might claim that the patient needs to be referred for more specialized care. In Lesley v. Chie, 250 F.3d 47 (1st Cir. 2001), the U.S. Court of Appeals for the First Circuit addressed a disability discrimination claim in the context of a physician's referral of the patient to a more specialized colleague. In *Leslie*, the court considered "the extent to which a court should defer to a physician's claim that he lacks the experience, knowledge, or other prerequisites necessary to address the medical conditions that allegedly prompted his referral of a patient to another physician." The case arose after an obstetrician referred an HIV-infected, pregnant woman to another hospital for drug therapy designed to prevent transmission of HIV to the woman's child. The other hospital had a special Women and Infants HIV Program. The court found no Rehabilitation Act violation, writing,

> Under the Rehabilitation Act, a patient may challenge her doctor's decision to refer her elsewhere by showing the decision to be devoid of any reasonable medical support. This is not to say, however, that the Rehabilitation Act prohibits unreasonable medical decisions as such. Rather, the point of considering a medical decision's reasonableness in this context is to determine whether the decision was unreasonable in a way that reveals it to be discriminatory. In other words, a plaintiff's showing of medical unreasonableness must be framed within some larger theory of disability discrimination. For example, a plaintiff may argue that her physician's decision was so unreasonable—in the sense of being arbitrary and capricious—as to imply that it was pretext for some discriminatory motive, such as animus, fear, or "apathetic attitudes." See, e.g., Howe v. Hull, 874 F. Supp. 779, 788-89 (N.D. Ohio 1994) (under ADA, jury could find doctor's diagnosis that plaintiff had extremely rare disorder requiring transfer was pretextual, where patient only had an allergic drug reaction, and doctor did not mention the rare disorder in requesting the transfer but only mentioned plaintiff's HIV-status). Or, instead of arguing pretext, a plaintiff may argue that her physician's decision was discriminatory on its face, because it rested on stereotypes of the disabled rather than an individualized inquiry into the patient's condition—and hence was "unreasonable" in that sense. [Id. at 55.]

5. *Infectious Patients.* As *Bragdon* indicates, an outright denial of care on account of the person's HIV status is unlawful disability discrimination. However, *Bragdon* also indicates that in deciding whether to provide care, physicians may take into account the risk to the physician of becoming infected from the patient. How should the risk be taken into account? What if an orthopedic surgeon refuses to operate on an HIV-infected (or hepatitis-infected) patient on the grounds that orthopedic surgery is "bloody" and involves exposure to sharp edges of bone as well as to sharp surgical instruments? What if the surgeon already provides care to a significant number of HIV-infected patients and the surgeon is trying to have a child? Should it matter whether the denial of care is for elective rather than essential surgical procedures? Consider a dermatologist who refuses to perform a hair transplant on an HIV-infected person on the ground that the procedure invariably causes significant bleeding from the patient's scalp. It is important to note that the circuit courts disagree on exactly when a risk is serious enough to be "significant." For a discussion of the different standards, see Onishea v. Hopper, 171 F.3d 1289, 1296-1299 (11th Cir. 1999) (interpreting "significant risk" in the context of a Rehabilitation Act case).

Concerns about discrimination against HIV-infected physicians are discussed at pages 247-248.

B. THE STRUCTURE OF THE TREATMENT RELATIONSHIP

1. Forming a Patient-Physician Relationship

In general, it is clear when a patient-physician relationship has been created. A patient seeks care, and the physician provides the care. In many situations, however, it is not so clear whether a relationship was formed. There may have been some inter-action between the patient and the physician, for example, a telephone call or con-versation, but not enough interaction to create a professional relationship. Or the patient's physician may have consulted another physician, and the question is whether the second physician's participation creates a professional relationship between that physician and the patient. In some cases, as we saw in *Hiser*, page 64, when physi-cians refuse to see patients, the patients will claim that the physicians had previously bound themselves to provide care. There will also be cases when the physician actu-ally examines the patient, but the examination is arranged on behalf of an employer or insurer. Then the issue arises whether the physician's primary obligation is to the patient or to the company that retains him. Finally, when a physician clearly has obli-gations to a patient, issues arise over whether those obligations extend to third parties who might also be harmed by the physician's professional decisions. The following materials explore each of these issues in varying depth.

■ ADAMS v. VIA CHRISTI REGIONAL MEDICAL CENTER
19 P.3d 132 (Kan. 2001)

ALLEGRUCCI, Justice.

This is a personal injury and wrongful death action filed by Albert and Forestean Adams, the parents of Nichelle Adams, who died as a result of a ruptured ectopic pregnancy. [After settling with Via Christi, the plaintiffs proceeded to trial against their daughter's physician, Dr. Louis Ohaebosim.] The jury returned a ver-dict in favor of the parents. . . .

In July 1992, Nichelle Adams was 22 years old and was living with her parents and her younger sister. On July 22, Mrs. Adams got home from work at approxi-mately 8:40 P.M. to find that Nichelle had been complaining about her stomach and had gone to bed. Mrs. Adams was concerned because Nichelle generally was a very active person.

Dr. Ohaebosim, an osteopath, who had been a family practitioner for 22 years, had been the family physician for Mr. and Mrs. Adams and their three children for several years. He had a patient file on Nichelle, but he had not seen her in his office since 1988. On July 6, Nichelle completed a form for Planned Parenthood in which she answered "no" to the question "Do you have a family physician?" Dr. Ohaebosim continued to provide medical care to other members of the family. Mrs. Adams had gotten medical advice from Dr. Ohaebosim over the telephone on a number of occasions.

Until 1990, Dr. Ohaebosim included as part of his family practice the treat-ment of women through pregnancy, labor, and delivery. He delivered over a thousand babies. After 1990, he continued to treat pregnant women for nonpregnancy-related conditions and to make the determination for women that they were pregnant, but he referred women to other practitioners for prenatal care, labor, and delivery. Dr. Ohaebosim testified about sending a letter to his patients to advise them that he would no longer be providing obstetrical care. He also testified that he advised all the hospitals, "I don't deliver babies anymore." He further stated, "This is my notice writ-ten. I'm writing to inform you that I would cease delivering babies on January, 1990, on the 1st of January, 1990." Mrs. Adams testified that she did not receive a letter from the doctor advising that he no longer offered obstetrical care. She was unaware that Dr. Ohaebosim had eliminated obstetrical care from his practice.

At approximately 9 P.M. on July 22, Mrs. Adams called Dr. Ohaebosim. She got his answering service, and then the doctor called Mrs. Adams right back. She told Dr. Ohaebosim that Nichelle was 5 to 8 weeks pregnant and was experiencing abdominal pain. Mrs. Adams later told a doctor at the hospital that she mentioned shortness of breath to Dr. Ohaebosim in the telephone conversation, but Dr. Ohaebosim later denied it, and at the time of trial Mrs. Adams could not remember telling him anything other than Nichelle was pregnant and had abdominal pain.

Dr. Ohaebosim testified that 8 weeks is the typical time when an ectopic pregnancy becomes symptomatic because the fetus becomes too large for the fallopian tube. When Mrs. Adams told Dr. Ohaebosim of Nichelle's condition, he did not suspect that Nichelle might have an ectopic pregnancy. . . .

Dr. Ohaebosim testified that he told Mrs. Adams that abdominal pain is not abnormal during pregnancy but to take Nichelle to the emergency room if she got any worse. He also told her to have Nichelle see a doctor the next day. Mrs. Adams testified that Dr. Ohaebosim did not mention taking Nichelle to the emergency room, but that he did say to bring her into his office the next day. Dr. Ohaebosim and Mrs. Adams agreed that he did not ask her any questions about Nichelle's condition.

At approximately midnight, Mrs. Adams drove Nichelle to the hospital, where she was admitted into the emergency room at 12:25 A.M. on July 23. By the time Nichelle was taken into an examining room, she was agitated and thrashing around. While Mrs. Adams was alone with Nichelle in the examination room, Nichelle vomited. Mrs. Adams called for help, and, when hospital personnel took over Nichelle's care, Mrs. Adams was taken to a nursing station to call her husband. . . . Before her husband arrived at the hospital, Mrs. Adams was told that Nichelle had gone into cardiac arrest. Later she was told that Nichelle was being taken to surgery.

Dr. Ohaebosim was not contacted with regard to Nichelle until approximately 4 P.M. on July 23. He immediately went to the hospital. Nichelle was on life support systems and nonreactive to the light Dr. Ohaebosim shined in her eyes. He discussed Nichelle's condition with her family, and at approximately 6:30 P.M. she died after being removed from the support systems pursuant to her family's decision. There was evidence that Nichelle might have lived if she had received medical care at 9 or 9:30 P.M. on July 22, instead of after midnight.

Mr. and Mrs. Adams, individually and as administrators of the estate of Nichelle Adams, sued St. Francis Regional Medical Center and Dr. Ohaebosim. . . .

Dr. Ohaebosim contends that there was no physician-patient relationship between him and Nichelle Adams on July 22, 1992, and that in the absence of a physician-patient relationship, no duty arose. . . .

The factors Dr. Ohaebosim advances in support of his position that no physician-patient relationship existed on July 22, 1992, between him and Nichelle Adams are the following:

1. A physician-patient relationship did exist on that date between him and Mrs. Adams.

2. He had not seen, talked to, or treated Nichelle for approximately four years prior to July 22.
3. He did not speak to Nichelle on July 22.
4. His only knowledge of Nichelle's obstetric history was the information provided by Mrs. Adams during the telephone conversation.
5. He no longer provided obstetrical care.
6. He "took no action other than discussing, in very general terms," Nichelle's condition with Mrs. Adams.
7. He did not consider Nichelle to be his patient, and Nichelle did not consider him to be her doctor.

Of these factors, the key to resolving this issue is Dr. Ohaebosim's own statement that he discussed Nichelle's condition with Mrs. Adams. In doing so, he consented to give medical advice about Nichelle's condition and he gave it. It is immaterial that he had not seen Nichelle for several years. It is immaterial that he did not speak directly to Nichelle on July 22. It is not significant in the circumstances that he states that he did not consider Nichelle to be his patient and that Nichelle did not consider him to be her doctor. He did consider Mrs. Adams to be his patient. He was a family physician, and in years past he had treated her daughter, Nichelle. When Mrs. Adams spoke to him by telephone on July 22 and told him that Nichelle was 5-8 weeks pregnant and experiencing abdominal pain, Dr. Ohaebosim did not say that he did not consider Nichelle to be his patient. He did not say that he no longer provided obstetrical care. Rather than suggesting to Mrs. Adams that she contact another doctor at that time, he listened to what Mrs. Adams told him about Nichelle and gave her his medical opinion in response. Dr. Ohaebosim's undertaking to render medical advice as to Nichelle's condition gave rise to a physician-patient relationship. Thus, even if the earlier physician-patient relationship between Dr. Ohaebosim and Nichelle had lapsed or been extinguished, it was renewed.

The essential difference between the facts of this case and those cited by Dr. Ohaebosim is his taking some action to give medical assistance. Typical of the cases he cites is *Ortiz v. Shah, 905 S.W.2d 609 (Tex. App. 1995)*. Ortiz was taken to the emergency room with a gunshot wound. The emergency room nurse paged Dr. Shah, who was the "on call" surgeon. Before Dr. Shah reached the hospital, Ortiz had been treated in the emergency room and taken to surgery, where he died. Dr. Shah had no prior relationship with Ortiz. Dr. Shah never saw the patient Ortiz. He never talked to him, and he never gave any advice to anyone about Ortiz's care. He simply told the nurse who contacted him that he was on his way to the hospital. Dr. Shah had taken no action that affected the medical treatment received by Ortiz. Dr. Ohaebosim, in contrast, gave his medical opinion about Nichelle Adams' condition. His opinion was that she was experiencing nothing unusual, which served to reassure Mrs. Adams about her daughter's condition and dissuade her from promptly seeking medical attention for Nichelle.

Dr. Ohaebosim contends that he declined to treat Nichelle. He did not decline to express his medical opinion about her condition. Thus, he cannot be said to have declined to treat her. A physician-patient relationship existed between Dr. Ohaebosim and Nichelle, and a duty of care was owed by Dr. Ohaebosim to Nichelle. . . .

■ESTATE OF KUNDERT v. ILLINOIS VALLEY COMMUNITY HOSPITAL
964 N.E.2d 670 (Ill. App. 2012)

SCHMIDT, Justice

Plaintiffs, Dustin Kundert and Krista Grady, brought this medical malpractice suit on behalf of their deceased child, Kameryn Kundert, and his estate against defendant, Illinois Valley Community Hospital (Illinois Valley). The circuit court . . . dismissed the action. . . . Plaintiffs appeal, claiming the court erred when holding, as a matter of law, no relationship existed between the decedent, or his parents, and defendant sufficient to create a legal duty of care. We affirm.

FACTS

Given the procedural history of this case, the facts we recite are derived from plaintiffs' second amended complaint. On April 18, 2007, Krista Grady gave birth to Kameryn Kundert. . . . On May 31, 2007, Kameryn exhibited signs and symptoms of a serious illness. Unable to reach [Kameryn's pediatrician] Dr. Fess . . . Krista called Illinois Valley at 7:29 P.M. that night. She informed the operator that she needed to speak to a medical professional for advice about Kameryn's symptoms.

The operator transferred the call to an individual in the emergency room. Krista told this unknown individual that Dr. Fess . . . could not be reached. Krista then described Kameryn as a six-week-old newborn with a high temperature who was very fussy, unable to sleep and refusing to eat. The individual informed Krista that she was overreacting, which was typical for new mothers, to administer Tylenol and give Kameryn tepid baths. The individual was unsure of the proper dosage of Tylenol and, as such, instructed Krista to contact a pharmacy. The individual noted that the symptoms described did not require immediate medical attention and to follow up with Dr. Fess in the morning. Finally, "the individual on the telephone advised [Krista] that Illinois Valley did not have the equipment or medical personnel to provide medical services to infants." Krista called a pharmacy to determine the proper amount of Tylenol to give Kameryn.

Relying on the information received during the phone call, Krista postponed seeking medical treatment for Kameryn until Dr. Fess's office opened at 8 A.M. on June 1, 2007. Following an examination in Dr. Fess's office, Dr. Fess arranged for Kameryn to be transported via ambulance to Illinois Valley's emergency room. Dr. Fess advised the emergency room personnel that a septic six-week-old would be arriving. Once there, medical personnel performed a lumbar puncture, took a chest X-ray and administered intravenous fluids and oxygen. Within an hour of arriving, Kameryn was transferred to St. Francis Medical Center to receive a "higher level of specialized medical treatment not available at Illinois Valley." At St. Francis, Kameryn was treated for bacterial meningitis. He died on June 15, 2007. . . .

ANALYSIS

. . . Plaintiffs argue that their complaint unequivocally establishes: (1) "a direct connection" between Krista and defendant; (2) the fact that Krista knowingly sought medical advice from defendant; (3) that defendant's agent "consented to render medical advice," which equated to "accept[ing] Kameryn as a patient"; and (4) Krista "relied on that advice."

. . . [T]he "relationship of physician and patient is a consensual relationship in which the patient knowingly seeks the physician's assistance and the physician knowingly accepts the person as a patient." . . . Plaintiffs' second amended complaint specifically states that "the individual on the telephone advised [Krista] that Illinois Valley did not have the equipment or medical personnel to provide medical services to infants." We fail to see how the actions of the person on phone, even while viewing all the allegations of the complaint in the light most favorable to the plaintiffs, evince a "knowing acceptance" of Kameryn as a patient. Plaintiffs acknowledge that the person who took the phone call informed Krista that Illinois Valley did not have the equipment or personnel to treat Kameryn that evening.

Plaintiff argues that the act of recommending Tylenol and tepid baths is constructive acceptance of the patient. . . . Plaintiffs would have us hold that a physician-patient relationship is created anytime a physician dispenses advice. That is, the singular act of dispensing any quantum of advice equates to knowing or at least constructive acceptance of a patient. Case law does not support such a holding. [The court described previous cases in which the dispensation of medical advice] was insufficient to create a physician-patient relationship.

The unidentified person with whom Krista spoke was not asked to perform any tests, interpret any results or examine Kameryn. The circumstances surrounding the inquiry and response indicate that the person merely gave an informal opinion based upon rather common symptoms: those being a temperature, fussiness and refusal to eat or sleep.

. . . [The] "consequence" of finding that [a patient's inquiry coupled with an] informal opinion . . . creates a [treatment] relationship "would have a chilling effect upon the practice of medicine. It would stifle communication . . . to the detriment of the patient." . . . It is, we think, not unreasonable to expect medical providers would attempt to limit their tort exposure. We would expect that the result of finding that this phone call created a physician-patient relationship would be that anytime a parent called and reported a child with a fever, the response would be the same: "Hang up and call 911 or drive your child to an emergency room." We believe that this would benefit neither the providers nor consumers of medical care. We find public policy supports the trial court's decision.

. . . We can think of no other way to categorize the statement made to Krista that Illinois Valley "did not have the equipment or medical personnel to provide medical services to infants" than a refusal to provide services. . . . At a minimum, that allegation made by plaintiffs defeats any notion that Illinois Valley "knowingly accepted" Kameryn as a patient on the night in question. As such, we hold plaintiffs' second amended complaint fails to properly allege the existence of a hospital-patient relationship and as such no duty existed as a matter of law. Therefore, the trial court did not err in granting defendant's motion to dismiss.

Finally, citing to [two earlier Illinois cases] and *Adams v. Via Christi Regional Medical Center*, plaintiffs assert that the "common thread amongst cases imposing a duty of care is whether the patient sought and received medical advice during the telephone call." We disagree. The common thread running through these cases is whether a patient knowingly sought a physician's service and the physician knowingly accepted the patient. As detailed above, . . . the singular act of dispensing advice does not equate to knowing acceptance of a patient. A review and analysis of *Adams* does not change our opinion that no hospital-patient relationship was created in this case. . . .

While noting the question of whether a duty exists is a question of law, the *Adams* court found it proper to submit a question to the jury for it to determine whether the phone call from the mother to the doctor created a physician-patient relationship. The jury found it did. The *Adams* court found that the doctor "did not decline to express his medical opinion about her condition. Thus, he cannot be said to have declined to treat her." As such, the *Adams* court found a physician-patient relationship existed sufficient to create a duty of care.

. . . Even if we were bound by *Adams*, we see two major distinctions. First, as this matter comes to us following the granting of a motion to dismiss, there can be no question of fact; we must consider all well-pled facts as true. Secondly, and maybe most importantly for our analysis, that forces us to accept as true plaintiffs' contention that the person at the hospital "advised [Krista] that Illinois Valley did not have the equipment or medical personnel to provide medical services to infants." We see no way to interpret this language other than as declining to treat Kameryn.

■ REYNOLDS v. DECATUR MEMORIAL HOSPITAL
660 N.E.2d 235 (Ill. App. 1996)

McCULLOUGH, Judge.

. . . The only issue is whether, as a matter of law, a telephone conference between treating pediatrician Dr. Sharon Bonds and [Dr. Thomas] Fulbright concerning Kevin [Reynolds]'s condition created a physician-patient relationship between Kevin and Fulbright. . . . The trial court found there was no physician-patient relationship and, therefore, no duty was owed by Fulbright to plaintiffs. We affirm. . . .

At about 10:45 P.M. on November 29, 1990, Kevin was seen in the emergency room of Decatur Memorial Hospital by Dr. Terry Balagna. The history given indicated he was injured at 8:30 or 9 P.M. by falling while jumping on the couch in the family living room. Upon examination, an abnormal breathing pattern was observed. Tests were conducted to discover the possibility of an infection or an electrolyte or metabolic problem. Cervical spine X-rays were taken at about 1:05 A.M. which appeared normal. Nevertheless, Kevin was admitted to the hospital. Balagna called Bonds, a pediatrician, to examine him.

Bonds arrived at the hospital at about 1:45 A.M. on November 30, 1990. At that time, Kevin's temperature was 102 degrees Fahrenheit. Bonds made a quick assessment of plaintiff and took a history from Barbara [Reynolds, Kevin's mother], which indicated Kevin had jumped off the couch, landed on his arm, walked to his mother, and gradually become limp after that. Bond noticed the child's breathing difficulties and that he was flaccid. She reviewed the emergency room records and X-ray reports, conducted reflex tests, and noticed he was moving his head. His neck was not tender. Among the possible reasons for his condition which Bonds considered were neurologic, traumatic, metabolic, infectious, or post-infectious problem. Because of the fever, she was leaning toward the infectious process diagnosis, and she did not consider a spinal cord injury. A history of a two-foot fall with a normal

2-½-year-old child did not indicate to her the existence of a cervical cord injury from trauma.

At 2:05 A.M., Bonds telephoned Fulbright[, a neurologist,] at his home. She advised Fulbright that Kevin walked following the fall, he had an elevated temperature and was flaccid and responsive, and the cervical spine X-rays were negative. She probably told him the child was flaccid from the neck down, including all four extremities. Fulbright inquired if the child had a stiff neck. Bonds said she did not know, went to check Kevin's neck, and returned to inform Fulbright that his neck was stiff. At the end of the conversation, Fulbright suggested a spinal tap to determine whether meningitis, encephalitis, or something similar was involved. Bonds did not ask Fulbright to treat Kevin, nor did Fulbright commit himself to further involvement with Kevin. Bonds was under the impression that Fulbright would see Kevin if she contacted him and requested that he treat Kevin.

Fulbright's recollection of his telephone conversation was as follows:

> Dr. Bonds called me regarding Kevin Reynolds. She related to me that the patient had presented with a history of a fall, I believe from a couch. The height estimated to be less than two feet. She related that the child was listless, and that the child was febrile with a fever of—on the order of 102 degrees Fahrenheit. I questioned Dr. Bonds regarding the history. My first concern was the veracity of the history. My major concern here was the question of child abuse. There was some report on her part that the history had been somewhat inconsistent. That in itself is a hallmark of abuse. I questioned her specifically as to whether or not she felt abuse was operative in this case. She stated relatively emphatically that she did not think that it was. She did not think that the fall was overly significant because of its apparently benign nature, that is, a fall from a low height of a young child as happens to every young child. The question of the cause of the fever and the possible neurological causes of the fever was raised. The question of meningitis was discussed. The question of an ascending neuritis was discussed. The performance of a lumbar puncture was discussed. The conclusion was that Dr. Bonds would perform the lumbar puncture and let me know if she wanted me to see the child thereafter. I offered to make myself physically available if she wished. We elected to proceed with the plan of her performing the lumbar puncture and letting me know if she needed me there.

Fulbright often received informal inquiries from other doctors asking questions and seeking suggestions. These inquiries do not include a request to see a patient, review a patient, or render an opinion, but only to discuss the case. He considered this a courtesy service for which he did not bill. He offered to make himself available because the other physician may be inhibited about asking him to see the patient due to the late hour or the marginal neurosurgical nature of the case.

. . . Fulbright stated he did not receive another call from Bonds or anyone else at the hospital with regard to Kevin's condition or treatment. Kevin's family never asked Fulbright to treat Kevin, and he never saw, examined, or came to a diagnosis as to Kevin's condition. Fulbright did not bill for any services to Kevin. . . .

[Bonds concluded that Kevin had an infectious cause for his symptoms. In fact, he had suffered a spinal cord injury that left him with quadriplegia.]

In a negligence action for medical malpractice, there must be a duty owed by defendant to the plaintiff, a breach of duty, an injury proximately caused by the breach, and resultant damages. The determination of whether the parties stood in such a relationship to one another that the law would impose on defendant a duty of reasonable conduct for the benefit of the plaintiff is a question of law. That policy determination is based on consideration of the likelihood of injury, the magnitude of the burden of guarding against it, and the consequences of placing that burden on the defendant. . . .

The relationship of physician and patient is . . . a consensual relationship in which the patient knowingly seeks the physician's assistance and the physician knowingly accepts the person as a patient. A consensual relationship can exist where other persons contact the physician on behalf of the patient, but this is not a case in which Fulbright was asked to provide a service for Kevin, conduct laboratory tests, or review test results. Fulbright did nothing more than answer an inquiry from a colleague. He was not contacted again and he charged no fee. A doctor who gives an informal opinion at the request of a treating physician does not owe a duty of care to the patient whose case was discussed. . . .

Plaintiffs suggest that what needs to be done is to find a physician-patient relationship to result from every such conversation. The consequence of such a rule would be significant. It would have a chilling effect upon [the] practice of medicine. It would stifle communication, education and professional association, all to the detriment of the patient. The likely effect in adopting plaintiffs' argument also would be that such informal conferences would no longer occur. . . .

■ LYONS v. GRETHER
239 S.E.2d 103 (Va. 1977)

POFF, Justice.

. . . Plaintiff, a blind person, accompanied by her four-year-old son and her guide dog, arrived at defendant's "medical office" on the morning of October 18, 1975, a Saturday, to keep an appointment "for treatment of a vaginal infection." She was told that defendant would not treat her unless the dog was removed from the waiting room. She insisted that the dog remain because she "was not informed of any steps which would be taken to assure the safety of the guide dog, its care, or availability to her after treatment." Defendant "evicted" plaintiff, her son, and her dog, refused to treat her condition, and failed to assist her in finding other medical attention. By reason of defendant's "wrongful conduct," plaintiff was "humiliated" in the presence of other patients and her young son, and "for another two days while she sought medical assistance from other sources," her infection became "aggravated" and she endured "great pain and suffering." . . . [P]laintiff demanded damages resulting from "breach of his duty to treat." [The trial court dismissed the case.] . . .

Although there is some conflict of authority, the courts are in substantial accord upon the rules concerning the creation of a physician-patient relationship and the rights and obligations arising therefrom. In the absence of a statute, a physician has no legal obligation to accept as a patient everyone who seeks his services. A physician's duty arises only upon the creation of a physician-patient relationship; that relationship springs from a consensual transaction, a contract, express or implied, general or special, and a patient is entitled to damages resulting from a breach of a physician's duty. Whether a physician-patient relationship is created is a question of fact, turning upon a determination whether the patient entrusted his treatment to the physician and the physician accepted the case.

We consider first whether the facts stated in the motion for judgment, and the reasonable inferences deducible therefrom, were sufficient to allege the creation of a physician-patient relationship and a duty to treat. Standing alone, plaintiff's allegation that she "had an appointment with defendant" would be insufficient, for it connotes nothing more than that defendant had agreed to see her. But plaintiff alleged further that the appointment she had been given was "for treatment of a vaginal infection." The unmistakable implication is that plaintiff had sought and defendant had granted an appointment at a designated time and place for the performance of a specific medical service, one within defendant's professional competence, viz., *treatment* of a particular ailment. It is immaterial that this factual allegation might have been contradicted by evidence at trial. Upon demurrer, the test of the sufficiency of a motion for judgment is whether it states the essential elements of a cause of action, not whether evidence might be adduced to defeat it. . . . [The court went on to observe that, on remand, there was also a factual question as to whether Dr. Grether's refusal to treat Ms. Lyons amounted to a lawful termination of their professional relationship.]

Notes: Creating the Patient-Physician Relationship

1. *Telephone Calls by a Prospective Patient.* Are *Adams* and *Kundert* consistent with each other? In what way was the argument for the existence of a patient-physician relationship stronger in *Kundert* than in *Adams*? Is there another way to interpret the *Kundert* court's statement that the hospital "did not have the equipment or medical personnel to provide medical services to infants," other than as a refusal to provide care? Is it appropriate to read *Lyons* as holding that scheduling a specific appointment creates a professional relationship, or was this case driven by the physician's reason for cancelling the appointment? Compare Weaver v. University of Michigan Board of Regents, 506 N.W.2d 264, 266 (Mich. App. 1993) (merely scheduling an appointment does not by itself establish a patient-physician relationship).

The ease with which a treatment relationship can be formed perhaps explains why hospital emergency department staff have been accused of engaging in what is known as a "wallet biopsy"—asking the patient or family more detailed questions about insurance and financial responsibility when they first come in than they do about the patient's condition, in order to be sure they can refuse treatment if the patient cannot pay and is not in a serious condition. For additional examples and discussion from the case law, see Annot., What Constitutes Physician-Patient Relationship for Malpractice Purposes, 17 A.L.R. 4th 132 (1982).

2. *Consultations by a Patient's Physician.* As the *Reynolds* court concluded, when a colleague of a patient's physician is informally consulted for advice rather than being asked to see the patient, conduct laboratory tests, or render a formal opinion, the "curbside" consultation does not create a patient-physician relationship between the patient and the colleague. In one case, which is probably at the extreme, the court so held even though the treating physician consulted a colleague in response to concerns expressed by the patient's mother about the appropriateness of care being provided her daughter. In that case, the treating physician reassured the

mother on the basis of the consultation and also mentioned the consultation on his discharge summary. Oliver v. Brock, 342 So. 2d 1 (Ala. 1976). See also Irvin v. Smith, 31 P.3d 934 (Kan. 2001); Jennings v. Badgett, 230 P.3d 861 (Okla. 2010).

However, if a physician assumes some responsibility for diagnostic or treatment decisions, then a patient-physician relationship may be created. See Crisp Regional Hospital v. Oliver, 621 S.E.2d 554, 560-561 (Ga. App. 2005) (jury could conclude that a patient-physician relationship was formed when the physician wrote an order for an MRI scan before patient's first appointment with the physician). Or if a physician sees a patient as part of a formal consultation, supplies a diagnostic impression, and recommends a treatment plan, a limited doctor-patient relationship may be created, which carries with it some duties of care, even though the physician has no further involvement in the patient's care. White v. Harris, 36 A.3d 203 (Vt. 2011) (psychiatrist met with patient via a 90-minute video conference and in so doing "assumed a duty to act in a manner consistent with the applicable standard of care so as not to harm decedent through the consultation services provided"). But a simple, formal consultation without any further involvement by the physician need not trigger a patient-physician relationship. Gilbert v. Miodovnik, 990 A.2d 983 (D.C. 2010) (no relationship for an obstetrician who conducted a routine "chart review" of a case and wrote notes with his advice on a form inserted into the patient's medical record). A recent case from Georgia sets some useful parameters: while recognizing that a doctor "does not have to physically examine a patient in order for the doctor-patient relationship to arise," and "[m]erely listening to another physician's description of a patient's problem and offering a professional opinion regarding the course of treatment is not enough," a relationship is formed when the doctor "essentially directs the course of that patient's treatment." Smith v. Rodillo, 765 S.E.2d 432 (Ga. App. 2015).

For a sense of the distinction between informal, curbside consultations and more formal consultations, see Farrin A. Manian & David A. Janssen, Curbside Consultations: A Closer Look at a Common Practice, 275 JAMA 145 (1996).

Do you agree with the policy reasons given by the *Reynolds* court for its holding? Given the principle that a patient-physician relationship is not created by a consultation, does this effectively mean that patients receive the benefit of free consultations but they "pay" for the consultations by "waiving" their right to sue the consulted physician? If that is what is going on here, does it follow that patients should be able to waive their right to sue their treating physician in exchange for a lower fee for their care? See discussion of Tunkl v. Regents of the University of California and related cases at page 110.

Phone consultations with a medical specialist are much more likely to lead to the formation of a patient-physician relationship when the physician is serving as an "on-call" physician to the hospital's emergency department, as illustrated by two Missouri cases. In Corbet v. McKinney, 980 S.W.2d 166 (Mo. App. 1998), a patient sued an emergency department physician for misdiagnosis of an ear problem and also sued an ear, nose, and throat specialist who had been telephoned by the emergency department physician. Since the specialist had not seen or billed the patient and was not under any contractual obligation to participate in the patient's care, the court held that no patient-physician relationship had been created. In contrast, in Millard v. Corrado, 14 S.W.3d 42 (Mo. App. 1999), the court found a patient-physician relationship between a patient and an on-call physician who never saw the patient and who allegedly failed to respond quickly enough to his pages, on the ground that the hospital bylaws required on-call physicians to respond to calls within a reasonable amount of time.

While the Missouri court in *Millard* found a duty to treat for the on-call consultant based solely on the physician's preexisting contractual obligation, courts in Georgia and Michigan have followed an Ohio decision, McKinney v. Schlatter, 692 N.E.2d 1045 (Ohio App. 1997), in requiring some involvement by the physician in the patient's care. See Anderson v. Houser, 523 S.E.2d 342 (Ga. App. 1999); Oja v. Kin, 581 N.W.2d 739 (Mich. App. 1998). (Note that the Ohio Supreme Court rejected the *McKinney* test in a later case, *Lownsbury*, mentioned below.)

Kundert is not the only example of how Illinois courts have extended the principle in *Reynolds* from a conversation between two doctors to apply as well to a conversation between a patient and a doctor. In Siwa v. Koch, the court of appeals also held that the mere dispensation of advice does not create a treatment relationship even when a physician gives advice directly to the patient in person. According to the *Siwa* court, plaintiffs must show additional evidence demonstrating that the health care provider chose to enter into a patient-provider relationship. 902 N.E.2d 1173 (Ill. App. 2009) (no relationship when a hospital employee volunteered to undergo a CT scan so the hospital and radiologist could test out new computer software for the scanner).

Some courts avoid the entire debate over whether a full-scale doctor-patient relationship has been triggered and hold simply that the physician owes a duty of care to the extent of his or her involvement, whatever that is. Diggs v. Arizona Cardiologists, 8 P.3d 386 (Ariz. App. 2000). For instance, in Mozingo v. Pitt County Memorial Hospital, 415 S.E.2d 341 (N.C. 1992), the court allowed suit against a physician who merely supervised the obstetrical residents who made an error. The supervising physician was at home "on call" when the difficulty arose and responded immediately when asked to come to the hospital. By the time he arrived, the delivery had been completed. The court accepted the plaintiff's allegations that supervising physicians have a duty to check in periodically when they know that a difficult case is in the hospital. Thus, duty was imposed by virtue of the physician's supervising status even though he never saw the patient until it was too late. Accord Lownsbury v. Van Buren, 762 N.E.2d 354 (Ohio 2001). But see Prosise v. Foster 544 S.E.2d 331 (Va. 2001) (no patient-physician relationship solely on account of on-call physician's obligation to supervise medical residents in the emergency department).

3. *Employment or Insurance Physicals.* Patients are often examined by physicians in situations in which the physician is retained by a third party. For example, a company may require a preemployment examination, or an insurer may require an examination before issuing a policy or paying benefits. In general, no patient-physician relationship is created when the physician examines a patient at the request and for the benefit of a third party, and the patient therefore has no cause of action if the physician fails to diagnose a disease or disclose abnormal findings. Smith v. Radecki, 238 P.3d 111, 115 (Alaska 2010) (rejecting malpractice claim when independent medical exam after a workplace accident failed to detect abnormalities); Payne v. Sherrer, 458 S.E.2d 916 (Ga. App. 1995) (no cause of action for breach of confidentiality against a physician who examined employee on behalf of employer); Murphy v. Blum, 554 N.Y.S.2d 640 (App. Div. 1990) (no cause of action

for basketball referee who was not told of abnormal EKG findings by physician who performed yearly physical examinations for the NBA).

However, there are important exceptions to this general principle. For example, the physician may have a duty "to take reasonable steps to make information available timely to the examinee of any findings that pose an imminent danger to the examinee's physical or mental well-being." Green v. Walker, 910 F.2d 291, 296 (5th Cir. 1991) (interpreting Louisiana law in case in which a physician allegedly failed to diagnose lung cancer during an annual employment examination). Accord Stanley v. McCarver, 92 P.3d 849 (Ariz. 2004); Reed v. Bojarski, 764 A.2d 433 (N.J. 2001) (both imposing a duty of care on physicians who find evidence of serious illness); Daly v. United States, 946 F.2d 1467 (9th Cir. 1991) (interpreting Washington state law in a case in which a job applicant had undergone a preemployment examination, and the radiologist failed to inform the applicant of an abnormal X-ray). A patient-physician relationship may also be found if the physician "affirmatively" advises the patient on "how to be treated." Hickey v. Travelers Insurance Co., 558 N.Y.S.2d 554 (App. Div. 1990) (workers' compensation physician mistakenly advised employee that surgery was not necessary to treat work-related injuries). See also Webb v. T.D., 951 P.2d 1008 (Mont. 1997) (liability when physician negligently diagnoses a patient's condition and communicates the misdiagnosis directly to the patient). Such advice need not be extensive. See Dugan v. Mobile Medical Testing Services, 830 A.2d 752 (Conn. 2003) (denying the defendant summary judgment when an employee, during his employment physical, asked "about the results of his EKG" and the defendant's employee said, "Everything looks fine. We only found one irregular heartbeat.").

While the physician may not have an affirmative duty to the patient, the physician does have a duty not to harm the patient. Greenberg v. Perkins, 845 P.2d 530 (Colo. 1993) (physician referred patient for an evaluation that aggravated an old back injury); Dyer v. Trachtman, 679 N.W.2d 311 (Mich. 2004) (physician allegedly tore shoulder cartilage that had been recently repaired surgically by another physician).

A few states permit malpractice claims to be brought in the absence of a patient-physician relationship. Ritchie v. Krasner, 211 P.2d 1272 (Ariz. 2009) (permitting negligence claim against physician who performed an independent medical examination after a workplace injury on ground that the physician did not adequately "investigate the symptoms of a cervical spine injury"); Berry v. National Medical Services, Inc., 205 P.3d 745 (Kan. Ct. App. 2009) (allowing claim of employee who lost job after enrolling in alcohol treatment program and failing test administered by third party for its negligence in test administration). Finally, even where the examining physician has no duty to the patient, the third party that requires the exam and chooses the physician may have a duty of care. Dornak v. Lafayette General Hospital, 399 So. 2d 168 (La. 1981) (employer liable for failing to disclose tuberculosis diagnosed during preemployment examination).

For further discussion, see Patrick D. Blake, Note, Redefining Physicians' Duties: An Argument for Eliminating the Physician-Patient Relationship Requirement in Actions for Medical Malpractice, 40 Ga. L. Rev. 573 (2006).

4. *Telemedicine.* In telemedicine, the patient and physician are in separate places (indeed in some instances in separate states or countries) and care is provided over the telephone or the Web. The level of interaction and technology can

vary greatly from the relatively low-tech (such as telepsychiatry) to the high-tech (telerobotics for surgery) to something in between (teleradiology). Because telemedicine necessarily deviates from the traditional context of a physician-patient relationship, even seemingly straightforward telemedicine interactions can add ambiguity to the formation of a legal relationship. According to the Federation of State Medical Boards' Model Policy for the Appropriate Use of Telemedicine Technologies in the Practice of Medicine, the physician-patient relationship "tends to begin when an individual with a health-related matter seeks assistance from a physician who may provide assistance. However, the relationship is clearly established when the physician agrees to undertake diagnosis and treatment of the patient, and the patient agrees to be treated, whether or not there has been an encounter in person between the physician (or other appropriately supervised health care practitioner) and patient." Federation of State Medical Boards, Model Policy for the Appropriate Use of Telemedicine Technologies in the Practice of Medicine, Apr. 2014. For further discussion see John D. Blum, Internet Medicine and the Evolving Legal Status of the Physician-Patient Relationship, 24 J. Legal Med. 413 (2003); Paul Spradley, Comment, Telemedicine: The Law Is the Limit, 14 TuL.J. Tech. & Intell. Prop. 307 (2011).

5. *Retail Clinics.* Increasingly, Americans receive health care through retail health clinics in drug stores, grocery stores, or big-box retailers like Wal-Mart. These clinics typically offer on-demand primary care from nurse practitioners (NPs) or physician assistants (PAs) at a lower cost than a typical physician visit. Visits to retail clinics have eclipsed 10 million annually and make up about 2 percent of all primary care visits in the United States. Bachrach et al., Building a Culture of Health: The Value Proposition of Retail Clinics, RWJF, Apr. 2015. The inherent nature of these clinics, however, featuring the use of non-physicians in administering care, raises questions as to the type of treatment relationship created and the required standard of care. If no physician is involved, no physician-patient relationship is created. Is the correct standard of care in a malpractice action that of a reasonable PA? See Annie Hsu, Legal Issues Concerning Retail Clinics, 20 Health Law 13 (2008). Most retail clinic practitioners communicate frequently with a consulting physician. Indeed, many states require physicians to supervise and/or collaborate with NPs and PAs. Traditionally, when physicians are supervising the work of NPs and PAs, physicians can be liable for inadequate supervision, or under *respondeat superior*, negligent acts performed by the NP or PA. Should a collaborative relationship between a physician and NP in the retail clinic setting establish the requisite control for vicarious liability? See Lauren E. Battaglia, Supervision and Collaboration Requirements: The Vulnerability of Nurse Practitioners and Its Implications for Retail Health, 87 Wash. U. L. Rev. 1127 (2010); Kristen E. Schleiter, Retail Medical Clinics: Increasing Access to Low Cost Medical Care Amongst a Developing Legal Environment, 19 Annals of Health Law 527 (2010).

6. *Duties to Third Parties.* Similar issues arise when physicians have a clear treatment relationship with a patient but their treatment decisions affect third parties. The question then is whether physicians owe a duty of care to someone who is not their patient and who may be a complete stranger. For example, if a physician negligently stops prescribing a drug to control a patient's seizures, and the patient injures a third party because of a seizure while driving an automobile, does the third party have a malpractice cause of action against the physician?

The issue here is similar to the question of a physician's duty to warn third parties who might be injured by the physician's patient (because the patient may act on a psychotic delusion, for example), or who share a health risk with the patient (either because the patient carries an infectious disease, or because the patient and third party share a genetic risk of disease). That issue is taken up in Chapter 3. In both kinds of cases, there is a common issue as to whether the physician owes a duty of care to the third party. The two kinds of cases differ in that here the issue is whether a physician owes a duty of nonnegligence to third parties, while in the other cases the issue is whether the physician has a duty to warn third parties of their risk.

While courts generally recognize some duty of nonnegligence to third parties, they differ on the extent of that duty. In Welke v. Kuzilla, 375 N.W.2d 403 (Mich. App. 1985), the court found liability simply because the injury to the third party was reasonably foreseeable. In that case, a woman driving her car was killed in an automobile collision that was allegedly precipitated by medication given by the physician to the driver of the other car. See also Hardee v. Biomedical Applications of South Carolina, 636 S.E.2d 629 (S.C. 2006). Other states find a duty only when there is a "special relationship" between the third party and either the patient or the physician. Thus, in Renslow v. Mennonite Hospital, 367 N.E.2d 1250 (Ill. 1977), the court held a hospital and physician liable for prenatal injuries to a child from blood transfusions that nine years earlier had caused Rh-sensitization in the child's mother. However, the same court rejected liability when a passenger was injured in an automobile accident allegedly caused because the car's driver was impaired by medications that the physician negligently prescribed, observing that the relationship between driver and passenger does not have the intimacy of mother and fetus. Kirk v. Michael Reese Hospital, 513 N.E.2d 387, 399 (Ill. 1987).

A New York court has required the additional showing that the physician had "sufficient ability and authority to control the conduct" of the patient before finding a duty of care to third parties. The court found no duty of care to the children of a driver who crashed into a bridge abutment after losing consciousness, allegedly because of negligently prescribed medication, on the ground that the driver "was free to accept or reject defendant's diagnosis and advice and she was at liberty to seek a second opinion. . . . [S]he had the right to decide what treatment and advice she would accept or reject." Conboy v. Mogeloff, 567 N.Y.S.2d 960, 961-962 (App. Div. 1991). Is this a fair characterization of the way patients respond when physicians prescribe medication for them?

In an interesting twist on the third-party question, courts have considered whether a kidney donor can sue a physician on the ground that the physician's negligence caused the recipient's need for the kidney transplant. The courts generally have rejected such claims on the ground that no patient-physician relationship existed between the donor and the recipient's physician. See, e.g., Dabdoub v. Ochsner Clinic, 802 So. 2d 651 (La. App. 2000); Moore v. Shah, 458 N.Y.S.2d 33 (N.Y. App. Div. 1982). However, a Massachusetts court allowed a donor to claim that a physician wrongly concluded that a transplant was needed by the recipient when the donor had established his own patient-physician relationship with the physician. Montalto v. Stoff, 2007 Mass. Super LEXIS 404 (Super. Ct. 2007). In an Ohio case, the donor was able to sue the hospital when the recipient of a kidney donation died from negligence shortly after the transplant was performed. Siebe v. Univ. of Cincinnati, 766 N.E.2d 1070 (Ohio Ct. Cl. 2001).

2. *Limiting the Scope of the Treatment Relationship*

In contrast with finding that a provider has no obligation to a third party or ostensible patient, it might be conceded that a treatment relationship exists but that the provider's obligation is limited in some important respects. The section considers both limitations on the standard of care that determines liability and limitations on other obligations such as the scope of practice.

■ TUNKL v. REGENTS OF THE UNIVERSITY OF CALIFORNIA
383 P.2d 441 (Cal. 1963)

TOBRINER, Justice.

. . . Hugo Tunkl brought this action to recover damages for personal injuries alleged to have resulted from the negligence of two physicians in the employ of the University of California Los Angeles Medical Center, a hospital operated and maintained by the Regents of the University of California as a nonprofit charitable institution . . . for the primary purpose of aiding and developing a program of research and education in the field of medicine. . . . Upon his entry to the hospital, Tunkl signed a document setting forth certain "Conditions of Admission." The crucial condition number six reads as follows:

> RELEASE: The hospital is a nonprofit, charitable institution. In consideration of the hospital and allied services to be rendered and the rates charged therefor, the patient or his legal representative agrees to and hereby releases The Regents of the University of California, and the hospital from any and all liability for the negligent or wrongful acts or omissions of its employees, if the hospital has used due care in selecting its employees. . . .

Plaintiff at the time of signing the release was in great pain, under sedation, and probably unable to read. At trial plaintiff contended that the release was invalid, asserting that a release does not bind the releasor if at the time of its execution he suffered from so weak a mental condition that he was unable to comprehend the effect of his act. The jury, however, found against plaintiff on this issue. Since the verdict of the jury established that plaintiff either knew or should have known the significance of the release, this appeal raises the sole question of whether the release can stand as a matter of law. . . .

We begin with the dictate of the relevant Civil Code §1668. The section states: "All contracts which have for their object, directly or indirectly, to exempt anyone from responsibility for his own fraud, or willful injury to the person or property of another, or violation of law, whether willful or negligent, are against the policy of the law."

The course of §1668, however, has been a troubled one. . . . Some of the cases have applied the statute strictly, invalidating any contract for exemption from liability for negligence. . . . Other cases hold that the statute prohibits the exculpation of gross negligence only; still another case states that the section forbids exemption from active as contrasted with passive negligence. In one respect, as we have said, the decisions are uniform. The cases have consistently held that the exculpatory provision may stand only if it does not involve "the public interest."[3] . . . [C]ourts [have] struck down exculpatory clauses as contrary to public policy in the case of a contract to transmit a telegraph message and in the instance of a contract of bailment. . . .

If, then, the exculpatory clause which affects the public interest cannot stand, we must ascertain those factors or characteristics which constitute the public interest. The social forces that have led to such characterization are volatile and dynamic. No definition of the concept of public interest can be contained within the four corners of a formula. The concept, always the subject of great debate, has ranged over the whole course of the common law. . . .

In placing particular contracts within or without the category of those affected with a public interest, the courts have revealed a rough outline of that type of transaction in which exculpatory provisions will be held invalid. Thus, the attempted but invalid exemption involves a transaction which exhibits some or all of the following characteristics. It concerns a business of a type generally thought suitable for public regulation. The party seeking exculpation is engaged in performing a service of great importance to the public, which is often a matter of practical necessity for some members of the public. The party holds himself out as willing to perform this service for any member of the public who seeks it, or at least for any member coming within certain established standards.[4] As a result of the essential nature of the service, in the economic setting of the transaction, the party invoking exculpation possesses a decisive advantage of bargaining strength against any member of the public who seeks his services. In exercising a superior bargaining power the party confronts the public with a standardized adhesion contract of exculpation, and makes no provision whereby a purchaser may pay additional reasonable fees and obtain protection against negligence. Finally, as a result of the transaction, the person or property of the purchaser is placed under the control of the seller, subject to the risk of carelessness by the seller or his agents. . . .

In the light of the decisions, we think that the hospital-patient contract clearly falls within the category of agreements affecting the public interest. To meet that test, the agreement need only fulfill some of the characteristics above outlined; here, the relationship fulfills all of them. . . . The would-be patient is in no position to reject the proffered agreement, to bargain with the hospital, or in lieu of agreement to find another hospital. The admission room of a hospital contains no bargaining table where, as in a private business transaction, the parties can debate the terms of their contract. As a result, we cannot but conclude that the instant agreement manifested the characteristics of the so-called adhesion contract. . . .

Defendant [next] contends that while the public interest may possibly invalidate the exculpatory provision as to the paying patient, it certainly cannot do so as to the charitable one. . . . [W]e see no distinction in the hospital's duty of due care

---

3. The view that the exculpatory contract is valid only if the public interest is not involved represents the majority holding in the United States. . . .

4. . . . There is a close historical relationship between the duty of common carriers, public warehousemen, innkeepers, etc. to give reasonable service to all persons who apply, and the refusal of courts to permit such businesses to obtain exemption from liability for negligence. . . .

between the paying and nonpaying patient. The duty, emanating not merely from contract but also tort, imports no discrimination based upon economic status. . . . To immunize the hospital from negligence as to the charitable patient because he does not pay would be as abhorrent to medical ethics as it is to legal principle. . . .

In substance defendant here asks us to modify our decision in Malloy v. Fong, 37 Cal. 2d 356, 232 P.2d 241 (1951), which removed the charitable immunity; defendant urges that otherwise the funds of the research hospital may be deflected from the real objective of the extension of medical knowledge to the payment of claims for alleged negligence. Since a research hospital necessarily entails surgery and treatment in which fixed standards of care may not yet be evolved, defendant says the hospital should in this situation be excused from such care. But the answer lies in the fact that possible plaintiffs must prove negligence; the standards of care will themselves reflect the research nature of the treatment; the hospital will not become an insurer or guarantor of the patient's recovery. To exempt the hospital completely from any standard of due care is to grant it immunity by the side-door method of a contractual clause exacted of the patient. We cannot reconcile that technique with the teaching of *Malloy*. . . .

The judgment is reversed.

Notes: Limiting the Standard of Care and Scope of Practice

1. *Limiting Liability.* Other courts that have disallowed contractual provisions that would relieve doctors of malpractice liability include Emory University v. Porubiansky, 282 S.E.2d 903 (Ga. 1981) (university dental clinic's liability release was void as against public policy even though the clinic was used for training purposes as part of the dental school); Meiman v. Rehabilitation Center, Inc., 444 S.W.2d 78 (Ky. 1969) (rehabilitation facility's liability release was invalid as being against public policy); Olson v. Molzen, 558 S.W.2d 429 (Tenn. 1977) (physician's liability release for an abortion patient was invalid as contrary to public policy).

Nevertheless, partial waivers may be allowed in some situations. The leading example is Madden v. Kaiser Foundation Hospitals, 552 P.2d 1178 (Cal. 1976), excerpted and discussed at page 453, which upheld a provision in an HMO contract that required malpractice claims to be decided by arbitration. Unlike in *Tunkl*, arbitration does not alter the standard of care, only the process of dispute resolution; the limitation was imposed on healthy employees as part of their health insurance, not on a sick patient coming to the hospital; and the limitation was part of a contract negotiated by a very large employer on behalf of its workers in a situation where the employees had a choice of other health insurance that did not contain this limitation.

Waivers or limitations of liability are also commonly enforced when, for good reason, physicians depart from standard medical practice. This might occur, for instance, if a patient insists on leaving the hospital "against medical advice" (a so-called discharge A.M.A.). Such patients are asked to sign a waiver or release from liability for harm resulting from refusing recommended treatment. Consider also a patient, who for religious or other reasons, insists on a type of treatment that is not medically recommended, or one who agrees to participate in a medical experiment. See, e.g., Colton v. New York Hospital, 414 N.Y.S.2d 866 (Sup. Ct.

1979) (permitting release from liability for injury resulting from nonnegligent care when the treatment—a kidney transplant—was experimental); Shorter v. Drury, 695 P.2d 116 (Wash. 1985) (permitting a hospital to require a Jehovah's Witness patient who refused blood transfusions to release the hospital, its personnel, and the patient's physician from liability for any injury resulting from the refusal); see generally 6 A.L.R.3d 704.

Separate from contractual waiver, there are also cases of de facto waiver. One example comes from so-called "medical tourism," where a patient might travel from Milwaukee to Bangkok to receive a cardiac bypass. Given civil procedural difficulties in suing in U.S. courts (personal jurisdiction, forum non conveniens, choice of law, enforcement of judgments) and the difficulty in bringing suit abroad, many patients will not recover. How should our public policy differentiate between these de facto waivers and contractual ones? For a discussion see I. Glenn Cohen, Protecting Patients with Passports: Medical Tourism and the Patient Protective-Argument, 95 Iowa L. Rev. 1467 (2010).

2. *Scope of Practice; Futility.* The remainder of these notes explore other types of limitations on a physician's or hospital's treatment obligation. One such limitation concerns the scope of practice. Physicians are entitled to limit their practice to a particular specialty and geographic area. See, e.g., McNamara v. Emmons, 97 P.2d 503 (Cal. 1939) (physician absolved of responsibility for follow-up care when patient had gone to stay 20 miles out-of-town, and the physician arranged for care with another physician where the patient was staying); Thaddeus Mason-Pope, Medical Futility Statutes: No Safe Harbor to Unilaterally Refuse Treatment, 75 Tenn. L. Rev. 1 (2007).

Also, physicians are not obligated to provide care that offers no medical benefit. However, there is considerable disagreement as to when medical treatment becomes futile.

3. *Conscientious Objection.* In some situations, physicians or other medical workers may have a conscientious objection to providing care. For example, obstetrician-gynecologists often are unwilling to perform abortions. Congress and many state legislatures have enacted so-called conscience clause statutes that protect medical personnel from retaliatory measures for refusing to participate in abortions. See 42 U.S.C. §300a-7 (2011) (known as the "Church Amendment"); Lara Cartwright-Smith, HHS Provider Conscience Regulation, Health Reform GPS (Apr. 12, 2011). Because only a minority of obstetrician-gynecologists perform abortions, abortions are not available in many parts of the country. Should a state respond to the poor access of its residents to abortion by requiring that, as a condition of licensure, obstetrician-gynecologists must be willing to perform abortions?

A physician who is morally opposed to abortion may be not only unwilling to perform abortions but also unwilling to facilitate abortions by referring patients to an abortion provider or informing them of the option to have an abortion. Would a refusal to discuss abortion violate the patient's right to informed consent? See Rust v. Sullivan, 500 U.S. 173, 195 (1991) (permitting the federal government to refuse family planning funds to organizations that counsel or refer for abortions where there is no medical need).

In recent years, many states have enacted or considered legislation dealing with pharmacists' objections to filling prescriptions for birth control pills, emergency contraception, or other drugs. The majority of the laws permit pharmacists to exercise their conscience and not fill a prescription, but some states require pharmacists or emergency departments to fill the prescriptions. National Conference of State Legislatures, Pharmacist Conscience Clauses: Laws and Information (updated May 2012).

Professor Sepper explains how conscience clause legislation modifies the common law and the current lay of the land:

> [T]he legislation shifts the burden of any harm caused by refusal onto specific patients and the general public by immunizing refusing institutions and individuals from civil and criminal liability or professional discipline. Patients harmed by refusal have no recourse to courts or state medical boards. Under all but a few conscience clauses, patients may be refused care even in emergencies. For example . . . delaying an abortion procedure for a woman who is miscarrying—as Catholic hospitals often require—may contravene the standard of care; yet, under conscience legislation, the patient's injuries—from, for example, going septic—go unremedied. In recent years, legislatures across the United States have expanded the reach of conscience laws substantially. More procedures have been specified as appropriate subjects of conscientious objection. Several states have moved from abortion to sterilization to contraception. The broadest legislation—in Mississippi, Illinois, and Washington—permits conscientious objections to any medical treatment at all. In these states, Jehovah's Witnesses could refuse to transfuse patients. A vegan could withhold vaccines that contain egg proteins on the ground that the use of animal products is morally wrong. Under some statutes, healthcare providers may withhold information, refuse to refer for treatment, and deny patients care distant from the contested procedure. With the country's broadest conscience legislation, Mississippi permits refusal to participate in "patient referral, counseling, therapy, testing, diagnosis or prognosis" for any medical procedure. . . A clinic could withhold information about HIV testing. A doctor could fail to tell a patient about the terminal nature of his cancer in order to ensure aggressive treatment, instead of hospice care. Under such broad conscience laws, these actions could generate no tort liability, professional discipline, or adverse employment action. Finally, a growing number of individuals and entities can claim rights to accommodation. In addition to direct providers like doctors and nurses, the new generation of conscience legislation covers pharmacists, medical secretaries, orderlies, billing clerks, and the like. The category of entities covered has also widened from hospitals to other healthcare facilities and even to insurance companies.

Elizabeth Sepper, Conscientious Refusals of Care, in The Oxford Handbook of U.S. Healthcare Law (I. Glenn Cohen, Allison K. Hoffman, William M. Sage eds. 2015).

For further discussion of these issues, see Alta Charo, The Celestial Fire of Conscience—Refusing to Deliver Medical Care, 352 New Eng. J. Med. 2471 (2005); Farr A. Curlin et al., Religion, Conscience, and Controversial Clinical Practices, 356 New Eng. J. Med. 593 (2007); Kent Greenawalt, Refusals of Conscience, What Are They and When Should They Be Accommodated, 9 Ave Maria L. Rev. 47 (2010); David Orentlicher, Law, Religion, and Health Care, 8 UC Irvine L. Rev. (2018). Joanna K. Sax, Access to Prescription Drugs: A Normative Economic Approach to Pharmacist Conscience Clause Legislation, 63 Me. L. Rev. 89 (2010); Martha S. Swartz, "Conscience Clauses" or "Unconscionable Clauses," 6 Yale J. Health Pol'y L. & Ethics 269 (2006); Lynn D. Wardle, Protection of Health-Care Providers' Rights of Conscience in American Law, 9 Ave Maria L. Rev. 1 (2010); Pamela H. Del Negro and Stephen W. Aronson, Religious Accommodations for Employees in the Health Care Workplace, 8 J. Health & Life Sci. L. 72 (2015).

Issues about conscientious objection also arise when patients request that life-sustaining treatment be withdrawn, and may arise in other circumstances as well. For a thorough analysis of different contexts and legal implications, see Anne Dellinger & Anne Vickery, When Staff Object to Participating in Care, 28 J. Health & Hosp. L. 269 (1995).

3. *Terminating the Treatment Relationship*

■ RICKS v. BUDGE
64 P.2d 208 (Utah 1937)

HANSON, Justice.

This is an action for malpractice against the defendants who are physicians and surgeons at Logan, Utah, and are copartners doing business under the name and style of the "Budge Clinic." . . . [P]laintiff alleges that he was suffering from an infected right hand and was in immediate need of medical and surgical care and treatment, and there was danger of his dying unless he received such treatment; that defendants for the purpose of treating plaintiff sent him to the Budge Memorial Hospital at Logan, Utah; that while at the hospital and while he was in need of medical and surgical treatment, defendants refused to treat or care for plaintiff and abandoned his case. . . .

The evidence shows that on or about March 8, 1935, plaintiff caught the middle finger of his right hand on a barbed wire. Soon thereafter the finger and hand began to swell and became reddened. In the early morning of March 11th, plaintiff went to the Budge Memorial Hospital to seek treatment from the defendants. Dr. S. M. Budge . . . made two lateral incisions in the finger, waited a few hours to see the result, and then later the same morning deepened the incisions in order to reach the pus, which he believed had developed. . . .

The plaintiff remained in the hospital from March 11th until March 15th, during which time he was under the care of Dr. S. M. Budge. . . . On the morning of March 15th, plaintiff told the nurse and Dr. Budge that he intended leaving the hospital that morning. Dr. Budge advised plaintiff against leaving, but notwithstanding the protests of Dr. Budge, plaintiff left the hospital after paying the amount that was due at that time. . . .

[T]he evidence shows that when plaintiff left the hospital on March 15th, Dr. Budge advised him to continue the same treatment that had been given him at the hospital, and that if the finger showed any signs of getting worse at any time, plaintiff was to return at once to Dr. Budge for further treatment; that on the morning of March 17th, plaintiff telephoned Dr. Budge, and explained the condition of his hand; that he was told by the doctor to come to his office. . . . Dr. Budge again examined the hand[,] told plaintiff the hand was worse and . . . said to plaintiff: "You have got to go back to the hospital." . . . Plaintiff left immediately for the hospital. . . . Within a short time after the arrival of plaintiff, Dr. [Budge] arrived at the hospital. Plaintiff testified: "He [meaning Dr. S. M. Budge] came into my room and said, 'You are owing us. I am not going to touch you until that account is taken care of.'" (The account referred to was, according to plaintiff, of some years' standing and did not relate to any charge for services being then rendered.) Plaintiff testified that he did not know what to say to the doctor, but that he finally asked the doctor if he was going to take care of him, and the doctor replied: "No, I am not going to take care of you. I would not take you to the operating table and operate on you and keep you here 30 days, and then there is another $30.00 at the office, until your account is taken care of." Plaintiff replied: "If that is the idea, if you will furnish me a little help, I will try to move."

Plaintiff testified that this help was furnished, and that after being dressed, he left the Budge Memorial Hospital to seek other treatment. . . . He walked to the Cache Valley Hospital, a few blocks away, and there met Dr. Randall, who examined the hand. Dr. Randall testified that when the plaintiff arrived at the Cache Valley Hospital, the hand was swollen with considerable fluid oozing from it; that the lower two-thirds of the forearm was red and swollen from the infection which extended up in the arm, . . . and that plaintiff required immediate surgical attention. . . . Plaintiff remained under the care of Dr. Randall for approximately a month. About two weeks after the plaintiff entered the Cache Valley Hospital, it became necessary to amputate the middle finger and remove about an inch of the metacarpal bone.

Dr. S. M. Budge testified that at the time he sent the plaintiff to the Budge Memorial Hospital on March 17th, plaintiff was in a dangerous condition and needed immediate surgical and medical attention; that the reason for sending him to that hospital was in order to give him the necessary immediate surgical and medical attention. . . . There can be no question from the evidence that it was the intention of Dr. S. M. Budge to operate at once on plaintiff's hand.

Defendants contend: (1) That there was no contract of employment between plaintiff and defendants and that defendants in the absence of a valid contract were not obligated to proceed with any treatment. . . . We cannot agree. . . . The evidence shows that plaintiff had been under the care and treatment of the defendants at the Budge Memorial Hospital from March 11th to March 15th; that when he left that hospital on March 15th, Dr. S. M. Budge said to him: "If you are going home, you had better follow out the treatment at home just as near as you can the same as you were doing here. Here is another thing I want to tell you, if you see any signs of that finger getting worse at any time, you come in and see me immediately." On March 17th, plaintiff, realizing that his condition was getting worse, telephoned Dr. S. M. Budge and was told by that doctor to come to the doctor's office, which plaintiff did; that there both Dr. S. M. Budge and Dr. D. C. Budge examined the hand; that Dr. D. C. Budge indicated on it where it should be opened; and that under the instructions of these doctors, plaintiff was returned to the hospital for no other purpose than having his hand operated upon at once.

Under this evidence, it cannot be said that the relation of physician and patient did not exist on March 17th. It had not been terminated after its commencement on March 11th. When the plaintiff left the hospital on March 15th, he understood that he was to report to Dr. S. M. Budge if the occasion required and was so requested by the doctor. Plaintiff's return to the doctor's office was on the advice of the doctor. While at the doctor's office, both Dr. S. M. Budge and Dr. D. C. Budge examined plaintiff's hand and they ordered that he go at once to the hospital for further medical attention. That plaintiff was told by the doctor to come to the doctor's office and was there examined by him and directed to go to the hospital for further treatment would create the relationship of physician and patient. That the relationship existed at the time the plaintiff was sent to the hospital on March 17th cannot be seriously questioned.

We believe the law is well settled that a physician or surgeon, upon undertaking an operation or other case, is under the duty, in the absence of an agreement limiting the service, of continuing his attention, after the first operation or first treatment, so long as the case requires attention. The obligation of continuing attention can be terminated only by the cessation of the necessity which gave rise to the relationship, or by the discharge of the physician by the patient, or by the withdrawal from the case by the physician after giving the patient reasonable notice so as to enable the patient to secure other medical attention. A physician has the right to withdraw from a case, but if the case is such as to still require further medical or surgical attention, he must, before withdrawing from the case, give the patient sufficient notice so the patient can procure other medical attention if he desires. . . .

[The court remanded the case for consideration of whether Mr. Ricks suffered any physical and mental suffering by virtue of having to go to Cache Valley Hospital for care. The outcome on remand was not reported.]

■ PAYTON v. WEAVER
182 Cal. Rptr. 225 (Cal. Ct. App. 1982)

GRODIN, Judge.

Occasionally a case will challenge the ability of the law, and society, to cope effectively and sensitively with fundamental problems of human existence. This is such a case. Appellant, Brenda Payton, is a 35-year-old black woman who suffers from a permanent and irreversible loss of kidney function, a condition known as chronic end stage renal disease. To stay alive, she must subject herself two or three times a week to hemodialysis (dialysis), a process in which the patient's circulatory system is connected to a machine through which the blood is passed . . . [and] artificial kidneys . . . drain the blood of excess liquids and accumulated impurities. Without such treatment, . . . liquid will begin to fill the lungs, making breathing difficult and possibly leading to heart failure. The resulting toxic waste buildup and chemical imbalances can also threaten the function of the heart and other organs.

Brenda has other difficulties. Unable to care for her children, she lives alone in a low-income housing project in West Oakland, subsisting on a $356 per month Social Security check. She has no family support; one brother is in prison and another is a mental patient. She confesses that she is a drug addict, having been addicted to heroin and barbiturates for over 15 years. She has alcohol problems, weight problems and, not surprisingly, emotional problems as well.

Despite these difficulties, Brenda appears from the record to be a marvelously sympathetic and articulate individual who in her lucid moments possesses a great sense of dignity and is intent upon preserving her independence and her integrity as a human being. At times, however, her behavior is such as to make extremely difficult the provision of medical care which she so desperately requires.

The other principal figure in this case is respondent John C. Weaver, Jr., a physician specializing in kidney problems. He conducts his practice through respondent

Biomedical Application of Oakland, Inc. (BMA), which operates an outpatient dialysis treatment unit on the premises of respondent Providence Hospital.

Dr. Weaver began treating Brenda in 1975 when, after the birth of Brenda's twin daughters, her system rejected a transplanted kidney. . . . On December 12, 1978, Dr. Weaver sent Brenda a letter stating he would no longer permit her to be treated at BMA because of her "persistent uncooperative and antisocial behavior over . . . more than . . . three years . . . her persistent refusal to adhere to reasonable constraints of hemodialysis, the dietary schedules and medical prescriptions . . . the use of barbiturates and other illicit drugs and because all this resulted in disruption of our program at BMA."

In the latter part of 1978, Brenda applied for admission to the regular dialysis treatment programs operated by respondents Alta Bates and Herrick Hospitals, and was refused.

For several months, Dr. Weaver continued to provide Brenda with necessary dialysis on an emergency basis, through Providence. On April 23, 1979, he again notified her by letter that he would no longer treat her on an outpatient basis. This letter led to Brenda's filing of a petition for mandate to compel Dr. Weaver, BMA, and Providence to continue to provide her with outpatient dialysis services. That litigation was settled by a stipulated order which called for continued treatment provided Brenda met certain conditions: that she keep all appointments at their scheduled time; that she refrain from use of alcohol and drugs; that she maintain prescribed dietary habits; and that she "in all respects cooperate with those providing her care and abide by her physician's prescribed medical regimen." Later, a sixth stipulation was added: that Brenda would "enter into and participate in good faith in a program of regular psychotherapy and/or counselling."

Dr. Weaver and BMA continued treatment of Brenda as an outpatient pursuant to the stipulation, but on March 3, 1980, Dr. Weaver, contending that Brenda had failed to fulfill any part of the bargain, again notified her that treatment would be terminated. He provided her with a list of dialysis providers in San Francisco and the East Bay, and volunteered to work with her counsel to find alternative care.

Brenda then instituted a second proceeding, . . , this time naming Herrick and Alta Bates Hospitals as respondents, along with Dr. Weaver, BMA and Providence. . . .

The trial court, after a lengthy evidentiary hearing, found that Brenda had violated each and every condition which she had accepted as part of the stipulated order providing for continued treatment, and that finding is basically undisputed. There was evidence that Brenda continued [to abuse alcohol and drugs, not adhere to dietary restrictions or her counseling program, miss numerous dialysis appointments thereby triggering 30 emergencies requiring hospitalization in the 11 months preceding trial, and in general display] "gross non-cooperation with her treating physician, BMA of Oakland and Providence Hospital." The trial court found that her behavior in these respects was "knowing and intentional."

Brenda's behavior was found to affect not only Dr. Weaver but the other patients and the treating staff as well. Dialysis treatment is typically provided to several patients at a time, all of them connected to a single dialysis machine. There was evidence that Brenda would frequently appear for treatment late or at unscheduled times in a drugged or alcoholic condition, that she used profane and vulgar language, and that she had on occasion engaged in disruptive behavior, such as bothering other patients, cursing staff members with obscenities, screaming and demanding that the dialysis be turned off and that she be disconnected before her treatment was finished, pulling the dialysis needle from the connecting shunt in her leg causing blood to spew, and exposing her genitals in a lewd manner. . . .

DISCUSSION

We begin our analysis by considering the trial court's conclusion that Dr. Weaver and the clinic with which he is associated have no present legal obligation to continue providing Brenda with dialysis treatment. . . . Brenda relies upon the general proposition that a physician who abandons a patient may do so "only . . . after due notice, and an ample opportunity afforded to secure the presence of other medical attendance." Lathrope v. Flood, 63 P. 1007, 1008 (1901). The trial court found, however, that Dr. Weaver gave sufficient notice to Brenda, and discharged all his obligations in that regard, and that finding, also, is amply supported. Dr. Weaver supplied Brenda with a list of the names and telephone numbers of all dialysis providers in San Francisco and the East Bay, and it is apparent from the record that nothing would have pleased him more than to find an alternative facility for her, but there is no evidence that there is anything further he could have done to achieve that goal under the circumstances.

During the proceedings, the trial court observed that Dr. Weaver "is one of the most sensitive and honest physicians that I have been exposed to either in a courtroom or out of a courtroom," that he was "in fact sensitive to [Brenda's] needs, that he has attempted to assist her to the best of his medical abilities, that he continues to have concern for her as a person and has continued to serve her medical needs," and that "[the] man has the patience of Job." It appears that Dr. Weaver has behaved according to the highest standards of the medical profession, and that there exists no basis in law or in equity to saddle him with a continuing sole obligation for Brenda's welfare. The same is true of the clinic, the BMA.

We turn now to Brenda's contention that Herrick and Alta Bates Hospitals violated their obligations under Health and Safety Code §1317 [to provide emergency care] by denying her admission to their regular outpatient dialysis programs in late 1978. The trial court found that at the time Brenda applied for admission to these programs she was not in an "emergency condition," by which the court obviously meant that she was in no imminent physical danger on the day she applied. Brenda contends, however, that her illness is itself "a chronic/acute emergency which requires that she receive medical treatment every third day to avoid death," and that such a condition qualifies for mandated service under §1317. . . .

. . . While end stage renal disease is an extremely serious and dangerous disease, which can create imminent danger of loss of life if not properly treated, the need for continuous treatment as such cannot reasonably be said to fall within the scope of §1317. There are any number of diseases or conditions which could be fatal to the patient if not treated on a continuing basis. If a patient suffering from such a disease or condition were to appear in the emergency room of a hospital in need of immediate life-saving treatment, §1317 would presumably require that such treatment be provided. But it is unlikely that the legislature intended to impose upon whatever health care facility such a patient chooses the unqualified obligation to provide continuing preventive care for the patient's lifetime.

It does not necessarily follow that a hospital, or other health care facility, is without obligation to patients in need of continuing medical services for their survival. While it has been said that "[a] private hospital owes the public no duty to accept any patient not desired by it, and it is not necessary to assign any reason for its refusal to accept a patient for hospital service" (41 C.J.S. Hospitals, §8, p.345), it is questionable whether a hospital which receives public funding under the Hill-Burton Act (42 U.S.C. §291), and perhaps from other sources, can reasonably be said to be "private" in that sense. Rather, where such a hospital contains a unique, or scarce, medical resource needed to preserve life, it is arguably in the nature of a "public service enterprise," and should not be permitted to withhold its services arbitrarily, or without reasonable cause. And, while disruptive conduct on the part of a patient may constitute good cause for an individual hospital to refuse continued treatment, since it would be unfair to impose serious inconvenience upon a hospital simply because such a patient selected it, it may be that there exists a *collective* responsibility on the part of the providers of scarce health resources in a community, enforceable through equity, to *share* the burden of difficult patients over time, through an appropriately devised contingency plan.

This argument was not presented to the trial court, however, and the record is not adequate to support relief on that ground as a matter of law. . . . Whatever collective responsibility may exist, it is clearly not absolute, or independent of the patient's own responsibility.

Notes: Abandonment Liability

1. *The* Payton *Case.* After the court decided the *Payton* case, dialysis providers in the area did arrange to share the responsibility for treating Ms. Payton. The court's suggestion of a public service obligation is mentioned at the end of its opinion. For additional discussion, see Stella Smetanka, Who Will Protect the "Disruptive" Dialysis Patient?, 32 Am. J.L. & Med. 53 (2006).

How might Ms. Payton have challenged Dr. Weaver's decision to discontinue care under the Americans with Disabilities Act? See David Orentlicher, Denying Treatment to the Noncompliant Patient, 265 JAMA 1579 (1991). Is it so clear that noncompliance is a legitimate basis for a physician to stop treating a patient? Why might a patient not follow the physician's recommendations? If noncompliance is an accepted justification for terminating the patient-physician relationship, what implications does that have for the patient's right to refuse medical treatment?

What do you think about the fact that the court decided to mention the plaintiff's race? Is her race relevant to a full assessment of the case? For a critical view of the court's discussion of Ms. Payton and Dr. Weaver, see Lois Shepherd & Margaret Mohrmann, Welcome, Healing, and Ethics, 50 Wake Forest L. Rev. 259 (2015).

For a discussion of termination of care on grounds of conscience, see John K. Davis, Conscientious Refusal and a Doctor's Right to Quit, 29 J. Med. Philos. 75 (2004) (arguing that a physician can terminate care only if "the doctor's refusal does not make the patient worse off than she would have been had she gone to another doctor in the first place").

2. *Ricks v. Budge.* What are the critical factors that resulted in the courts coming to different conclusions in *Ricks* and *Payton* as to the physician's liability? Was it fair to hold the Drs. Budge responsible for Mr. Ricks's difficulties when he originally left the hospital against their advice? Why not conclude that the patient-physician relationship ended when Mr. Ricks left the hospital and that the Drs. Budge refused to renew the relationship when they found that Mr. Ricks had an unpaid bill?

3. *Abandonment Liability.* Once a patient-physician relationship is formed, it is implicit that the relationship continues as long as the patient needs treatment for the condition that brought the patient to the physician. Once the need is satisfied, the relationship ends. The professional relationship can also be ended explicitly if the patient unilaterally chooses to dispense with the physician's services or if both parties agree to the termination of the relationship. Finally, as the *Payton* case demonstrates, physicians can terminate the patient-physician relationship as long as they give notice to the patient such that the patient has sufficient opportunity to secure care from another physician. Failure to adhere to the required notice can result in abandonment liability if the patient is injured as a result.

Strictly speaking, abandonment liability results from purposefully ceasing treatment for primarily nonmedical reasons, not from mistakenly ceasing treatment due to medical error. In other words, it is more akin to breach of contract than to medical malpractice. Nevertheless, courts and lawyers often confuse the two theories when patients are injured by failure to treat. See generally Comment, The Action of Abandonment in Medical Malpractice Litigation, 36 Tulane L. Rev. 834 (1962); Annot., Liability of Physician Who Abandons Care, 57 A.L.R.2d 432 (1958).

4. *Lack of Payment.* As the *Ricks* case indicates, failure of a patient to pay does not permit the physician to discontinue care before satisfying the usual requirements for terminating the patient-physician relationship. This principle contrasts with the physician's freedom to take a patient's ability to pay into account when deciding whether to commence a professional relationship. As one court observed in a case in which a physician treated a patient for a miscarriage but suspended his care before the end of her need for treatment,

> Whether the patient be a pauper or a millionaire, whether he be treated gratuitously or for reward, the physician owes him precisely the same measure of duty, and the same degree of skill and care. He may decline to respond to the call of a patient unable to compensate him; but if he undertakes the treatment of such a patient, he cannot defeat a suit for malpractice, nor mitigate a recovery against him, upon the principle that the skill and care required of a physician are proportioned to his expectation of pecuniary recompense.

Becker v. Janinski, 15 N.Y.S. 675, 677 (Civ. Ct. 1891). For further discussion of the effects of cost containment on the standard of care, see pages 350-356.

While a physician may not simply discontinue care because of nonpayment, nonpayment is an acceptable basis for a physician to terminate the patient-physician relationship so long as the termination is accomplished properly. See, e.g., Surgical Consultants, P.C. v. Ball, 447 N.W.2d 676, 682 (Iowa App. 1989) (terminating care for nonpayment is permissible because there is no "evidence that the physician has terminated the relationship at a critical stage of the patient's treatment [or] that the termination was done without reason or sufficient notice to enable the patient to procure another physician"). The critical issue is whether proper termination entails only notice or also requires that the patient actually secure another physician. The usual practice is for physicians to find a substitute and arrange the transfer themselves if, for instance, they are retiring from practice or going on vacation. This avoids any question of liability. There is little legal guidance where another willing physician cannot be located but a patient who cannot pay still receives ample notice. What does *Payton* suggest as the answer? See Mark A. Hall, A Theory of Economic Informed Consent, 31 Ga. L. Rev. 511, 527-533 (1997); Mark A. Hall & Carl E. Schneider, When Patients Say No (to Save Money): An Essay on the Tectonics of Health Law, 41 Conn. L. Rev. 743 (2009).

C. REGULATING THE TREATMENT RELATIONSHIP

1. *Professional Licensure*

During the nineteenth century, snake oil salesmen and other quacks roamed the countryside preying on the gullible public with unfounded promises of miracle cures. To eliminate such practices, around the turn of the twentieth century every state began to license medical practitioners. The typical Medical Practice Act makes it a criminal offense to practice medicine without a physician's license and establishes the grounds for revocation or suspension of a license. The job of medical licensure and discipline is entrusted to a Board of Medical Examiners, which usually consists predominantly of physicians. Some alternative practitioners, such as osteopaths, chiropractors, and podiatrists, have likewise been successful in petitioning the legislature for recognition and protection through professional licensure and self-regulation. Thus, professional licensure serves a "fencing" function, one that keeps some persons from providing health care services altogether and that separates providers into different categories of professionals with at least somewhat distinct areas of permissible practice. And licensure also serves a policing function that investigates and disciplines allegedly errant providers.

■ STATE v. MILLER
542 N.W.2d 241 (Iowa 1995)

ANDREASEN, Justice.

Albert C. Miller appeals from his convictions for practicing medicine without a license. He urges . . . that the record contains insufficient evidence to support his convictions. We affirm the judgment of the district court.

Miller was charged by a trial information with seven counts of practicing medicine without a license. [This prosecution was brought after Mr. Miller repeatedly violated injunctions to cease treated patients as described below. Most of the offenses charged were Class D felonies.] . . .

Several persons testified at trial describing treatments they received from Miller in his home for various ailments. His usual method of treatment was to put a lock of the person's hair or a photograph of the person into a machine called a radionics device. After recording numerous readings from the device on a chart, he would treat the person by administering mild electric shocks from a "function generator," massaging the person's feet or neck, or placing large magnets next to the person. In addition, he often sold or recommended natural vitamins or nutrients to the people who visited him. Although Miller did not charge for the treatments, he consistently accepted donations of $10 for each treatment. He did not have any license to practice medicine, osteopathy, or surgery.

Dr. John Renner, M.D., Director of the Consumer Health Information Research Institute, testified as an expert witness for the state. He found the various treatments and vitamins given by Miller to his patients, while not necessarily harmful, were generally not medically useful. In his opinion the primary danger was not from the medicine itself, but from the fact it delayed appropriate, potentially beneficial, medical treatment.

On July 14, 1994, the jury returned verdicts finding Miller guilty on all seven counts. He was sentenced to a term of incarceration not to exceed five years on six counts. On the seventh count, he was sentenced to four months in the county jail. All the sentences were suspended and Miller was placed on probation for five years. . . .

We must uphold the jury's verdict unless the record lacks substantial evidence to support the charges. Substantial evidence is evidence which could convince a rational jury the defendant is guilty of the crimes charged beyond a reasonable doubt. . . .

Miller was charged with practicing medicine and osteopathic medicine in violation of Iowa Code §147.2. Two separate instructions were given to the jury defining the practice of medicine and osteopathic medicine. One instruction . . . provided the following definition:

> The practice of medicine and osteopathic medicine means holding one's self out as being able to diagnose, treat, or prescribe for any human disease, pain, injury, deformity, or physical or mental condition and who shall either offer or undertake, by any means or methods, to diagnose, treat, or prescribe for any human disease, pain, injury, deformity or physical or mental condition.

The other instruction provided that the following "persons shall be deemed to be engaged in the practice of medicine and osteopathic medicine":

1. Persons who publicly profess to be physicians or who publicly profess to assume the duties incident to the practice of medicine and osteopathic medicine.
2. Persons who prescribe, or prescribe and furnish medicine for human ailments. . . .

Miller argues that he did not publicly profess to be a physician or publicly profess to assume the duties incident to the practice of medicine and osteopathic medicine. He emphasizes that he never advertised nor described himself as a doctor; he would sometimes recommend that his customers consult a licensed physician or chiropractor; and he only met people in his home, not in an office.

We conclude there is sufficient evidence to conclude that Miller publicly professed to assume the duties incident to the practice of medicine and osteopathic medicine. We have defined the "duties incident to the practice of medicine" to include diagnosing patients' ailments and prescribing the proper treatment. Witnesses testified that they were treated by Miller for various ailments including arthritis, rash, infection, headaches, constipation, and neck, shoulder, and back pain. Although he may not have referred to himself as a doctor, he led his customers to believe that he could diagnose and treat their ailments. Even though Miller did not formally advertise his treatments, he gained a large local customer base by means of referral from one customer to another. The fact that Miller would sometimes recommend that his customers consult a licensed physician or chiropractor does not detract from the fact that he would diagnose and treat their physical conditions, at least up to a certain point.

We also conclude there was sufficient evidence that Miller routinely prescribed and furnished medicine. Miller argues that he sold or recommended only natural vitamins or nutrients. His defense, through the testimony of a witness, was that vitamins and nutrients were not medicines, but food.

We have broadly construed the statutory words "prescribe and furnish medicine" to include administering any substance or remedy in the treatment of an ailment or disease. The fact that a substance may also have value as a food "will not deprive of its character as a medicine if it be administered and employed for that purpose." State v. Bresee, 114 N.W. 45, 47 (1907).

> It is evident [the defendant] was catering to patronage of the sick who were asking relief from their ills, and, if [he] listened to their statements, assured them of [his] ability to help them out, and supplied them with [his] alleged appropriate remedies giving instructions for their application or use, this would seem to come . . . within the ordinary and usual signification attached to the words "prescribing" or "prescribing and furnishing medicines," as they are commonly used and understood. Id.

We believe Miller's actions of selling or recommending natural vitamins to his customers constitutes furnishing a substance or remedy for treating their ailments.

We conclude there is sufficient evidence to convince a rational jury beyond a reasonable doubt that Miller was guilty of practicing medicine and osteopathic medicine without a license.

[On an ironic note, the court also rejected Miller's appellate lawyers' claim that the district court had erred in permitting him to represent himself at trial. Miller had initially sought to appoint "unlicensed" counsel to represent him at trial and chose to represent himself when his request was rejected. The court held that Miller knowingly and intelligently waived his right to licensed representation.]

■ CHARACTER, COMPETENCE, AND THE PRINCIPLES OF MEDICAL DISCIPLINE
Nadia N. Sawicki
13 J. Health Care L. & Pol'y 285 (2010)

As the state agencies responsible for the licensure and discipline of physicians, medical boards serve as the gatekeepers of the medical profession. However, critics frequently question whether boards have, in fact, been living up to their potential in this regard, particularly in the context of professional discipline. Since the 1970s, state medical boards have faced criticism from a variety of sources for inappropriately screening applicants for medical licensure,[3] failing to discipline dangerous

---

3. *See* Marc T. Law & Zeynep K. Hansen, *Medical Licensing Board Characteristics and Physician Discipline: An Empirical Analysis*, 35 J. HEALTH POL. POL'Y & L. 63, 66 (2010).

physicians, and generally being lax in their oversight duties at the expense of a vulnerable public.[7] . . .

[A] common explanation for medical boards' lax approach to professional discipline is that the boards are "captured" by professional interests or otherwise lack meaningful public oversight. Indeed, one of the most prominent criticisms of the medical profession in the 20th century has been that it is self-protective, monopolistic, and more attuned to the economic security of its members than to the welfare of the public at large. . . .

While there is likely some element of truth to the argument that medical boards discipline physicians too infrequently, this Article identifies a more substantive problem—namely, that when boards do choose to exercise their disciplinary discretion, they often focus on character-related misconduct, including criminal misconduct, that bears only a tangential relation to clinical quality and patient care. . . . In recent years, medical providers have been disciplined on grounds as varied as tax fraud, failure to facilitate review of child support obligations, soliciting sex in a public restroom, possession of marijuana for personal use, and reckless driving involving alcohol, as well as other conduct allegedly bringing the medical profession into disrepute. While these are not commendable activities by any stretch of the imagination, this Article questions whether, in light of the traditional goals of professional discipline, sanctioning physicians on these grounds (as opposed to grounds more clearly linked to clinical practice) is the most effective or efficient use of medical boards' resources. . . .

A. MEDICAL BOARD AUTHORITY: HISTORY AND PRACTICE

Among the unenumerated powers reserved to each state under the Tenth Amendment is the power to protect the health, safety, and welfare of its citizenry, commonly known as the police power. . . . As explained by the Supreme Court in *Dent v. West Virginia*, 129 U.S. 114 (1889), . . . [i]t is pursuant to their police powers that states are authorized to regulate law, medicine, and other professions, which they typically do by delegating authority to professional licensing boards.

. . . The first state medical boards were created in the late 1800s when private medical associations pushed state legislators to adopt laws regulating the practice of medicine. These efforts were driven by physicians who, fearful of incursions on their territory by "irregulars" and "quacks," were convinced that well-drafted legislation—far from being self-defeating—could serve an important role in protecting their professional interests. Though some historians suggest that professional self-protection, rather than concern for patient safety, was the driving force behind

---

7. Economists, in particular, have long made similar arguments, questioning the value of licensure and self-regulation in highly insulated and self-protective professions, like medicine. These authors and others suggest that medical quality and patient safety could be better safeguarded through market-based solutions that close the information gap between physicians and consumers. *See generally* Walter Gellhorn, *The Abuse of Occupational Licensing*, 44 U. CHI. L. REV. 6, 16-18, 22, 25 (1976) (arguing that occupational licensing impedes access to needed services and serves only to protect those who have already been licensed, rather than protect the public from incompetent professionals); Anthony Ogus, *Rethinking Self-Regulation*, 15 OXFORD J. LEGAL STUD. 97 (1995) (offering general criticism of the self-regulatory model). . . .

these lobbying efforts, the medical practice acts that resulted were, as a matter of law, clearly adopted pursuant to the legislative authority to protect public health and safety.

At a minimum, modern medical practice acts define the practice of medicine, establish the requirements for medical licensure, and set forth procedures for disciplinary action against licensees. . . . Modern medical boards generally include some public members but are dominated by physicians appointed by the governor.

American licensure laws are exclusive in that they grant qualified individuals the right to engage in the lawful practice of medicine and prohibit the practice of medicine by unlicensed persons. The requirements for obtaining a medical license are relatively consistent from state to state—generally, the applicant must be a graduate of an approved medical school, have completed at least one year of an approved graduate medical education program (residency or fellowship), and have passed the United States Medical Licensing Examination (USMLE). Beyond imposing educational and training requirements, many medical practice acts also require that applicants for medical licensure demonstrate good moral character. . . .

Medical boards' ongoing duties include periodic reregistration of licensees, which is typically contingent on completion of specified hours of Continuing Medical Education training. However, medical boards rarely impose additional requirements intended to ensure the quality of care, such as mandatory recertification or random practice audits, upon physicians who have already received their licenses. As a result, the most important of state medical boards' oversight responsibilities with respect to medical quality is the discipline of professional licensees.

The medical disciplinary process is generally reactive, rather than proactive. It begins when a member of the public files a complaint, or, in the case of discipline on the grounds of criminal or civil liability, when a court or law enforcement agency files a report with the medical board. The board screens, and, if appropriate, investigates the complaint; if the board finds the complaint is valid, it may exercise its discretion to pursue disciplinary action against the physician, which can range from oral or written reprimand to license revocation or suspension.

Although the substantive grounds for professional discipline vary from state to state, most state medical practice acts authorize discipline for gross incompetence, physical or mental impairment, alcohol or drug abuse, practicing without a license or aiding the unlicensed practice of medicine, as well as reciprocal discipline against those providers who have been subject to disciplinary action in other states. Moreover, most states authorize discipline under a broad category of "unprofessional conduct," which may include violations of codes of medical ethics, conduct that brings the medical profession into disrepute, or other unspecified forms of "dishonorable conduct," including criminal acts (typically felonies or crimes of "moral turpitude"). . . .

In foundational cases such as *Dent* [*v. West Virginia*] and *Schware v. Board of Bar Examiners*, 353 U.S. 232 (1957), the Supreme Court held that the criteria for licensure and discipline may not be vague, arbitrary, or unattainable, and "must have a rational connection with the applicant's fitness or capacity to practice" his profession. However, because no fundamental rights are implicated in the loss of a professional license, courts review boards' disciplinary determinations under a highly deferential standard. . . .

[T]he medical board's disciplinary authority is aimed at protecting medical consumers from the harms they may incur at the hands of incompetent or dishonest physicians. This is reflected in the sanctions that may be imposed on physicians, which range from alerting the medical board and community of a potential for harm (via a public letter of reprimand) to withdrawing the physician's right to practice (delicensure). Unlike criminal law, which is aimed at punishing wrongdoers, or civil law, which is aimed at victim compensation, professional discipline seeks to protect public welfare by incapacitating or rehabilitating dangerous physicians. . . .

A final, and related, insight . . . is [that] professional licensure and discipline standards are established to ensure a minimal level of competence, rather than to identify aspirational standards of professional conduct. . . . The appropriate view of professional licensure, then, is as a floor beyond which practitioners may not drop, rather than an ideal towards which they must strive. In other words, though we view a medical license as evidence that a physician possesses the basic tools necessary to practice medicine safely, the license does not ensure that he will actually use these tools correctly going forward. Moreover, a medical license does not distinguish the merely competent provider from the excellent provider—that distinction takes place at the marketplace level. . . .

C. QUANTITATIVE AND QUALITATIVE CONCERNS

Despite the fact that the theoretical underpinnings of the American medical disciplinary regime are sound, the system as it is being practically implemented boasts few supporters. . . . The most common criticism that has been traditionally levied against medical boards is that they simply do not discipline physicians often enough to have a substantial impact on patient safety and public health. . . . [E]stimates suggest that less than one-half of one percent of licensed physicians face serious discipline annually. . . .

While there may be some truth to [these] claims, . . . [t]he rate at which medical professionals face serious discipline annually is comparable to the rate of serious professional discipline in other professions, including law. It is also comparable to the rate of felony convictions among the American public. While professional boards and prosecutors certainly could be doing more to pursue those who violate professional standards or break the law, given the parallels between the rates of professional discipline and criminal conviction, the degree of invective levied at medical boards by public advocates seems disproportionate. . . .

Arguably more important in determining whether medical boards are likely to be successful in protecting the public is the qualitative issue of which physicians are being disciplined and on what substantive grounds. That is, if medical boards can pursue only 3,000 serious disciplinary actions against physicians each year, boards . . . ought to ask which is likely to have the greatest impact on patient protection, which [complaints have] the closest link to fitness to practice, and where each [case] falls on the spectrum from minimal competencies to aspirational standards. . . .

[M]edical boards rarely take disciplinary action on the basis of incompetent medical practice or poor quality of care. . . . [F]ewer than 15% of professional disciplinary actions taken between 1999 and 2008 appear to have been taken on grounds clearly related to clinical competence. . . . Although the majority of disciplinary actions are taken on unspecified grounds, the ones that are categorized tend to fall within three broad categories—drug or alcohol abuse, criminal convictions, and unspecified unprofessional conduct. . . . [B]etween 1994 and 2002, unspecified "unprofessional conduct" was the single most frequently cited ground for discipline, appearing in approximately a third of all cases. . . .

Often, when boards take serious disciplinary action on the basis of unprofessional behavior or criminal conduct, the sanctioned physicians challenge their suspensions on due process grounds, arguing that their behavior, while possibly indicative of poor personal judgment or character, is simply not relevant to their fitness to practice medicine. . . .

[D]. AN IMPERFECT FIT WITH THE PRINCIPLES OF PROFESSIONAL DISCIPLINE

The fact that physicians are frequently sanctioned for engaging in character-related or criminal misconduct is troubling in light of the [principle] . . . that boards ought to be primarily concerned with enforcing minimal standards of fitness to practice in an effort to protect consumers of medical services. It hardly seems obvious why . . . boards should be using their scarce resources to discipline physicians for character-related misconduct occurring outside the clinical sphere, particularly where such behavior is already subject to criminal or civil sanctions. . . . [M]ost state court decisions in disciplinary matters simply conclude that moral character broadly defined is a necessary component of fitness to practice without providing adequate support for this assertion. . . . Even *Hawker v. New York*, 170 U.S. 189 (1898), the case that speaks most directly to the issue of character-related criteria for professional licensure and discipline, offers little guidance. In *Hawker*, the Supreme Court upheld a New York state law prohibiting the practice of medicine by those who have been convicted of a felony, but provided little support for its conclusion that personal "[c]haracter is as important a qualification as knowledge" for professional practice and is therefore subject to discipline. In two brief sentences, the Court offered the following meager explanation of its conclusion: "The physician is one whose relations to life and health are of the most intimate character. It is fitting, not merely that he should possess a knowledge of diseases and their remedies, but also that he should be one who may safely be trusted to apply those remedies." . . .

Trust theorists posit that misconduct outside the clinical sphere is a legitimate subject for professional discipline if it is likely to cause public distrust of the medical profession. . . . [But] [p]atients may place faith in their physicians for any number of reasons—their religion, their affiliation with a particular hospital, their personal appearance—and it is by no means clear why a state should facilitate patient decisions that are based on non-clinical, irrelevant, or potentially discriminatory factors that have no clear link with fitness or competency to practice medicine. . . .

Much like criminal law, professional discipline serves an important signaling function for the medical community. It is the rare doctor who, in an effort to understand the boundaries of permissible professional behavior, turns first to the local law library to brush up on recent state legislation and case law. More likely, he receives periodic disciplinary updates from his state medical board, reads about cases of professional discipline in the media, and hears about the experiences of colleagues and friends. Given that some of the most public and visible cases of professional discipline deal with cases of misconduct that bear little connection to the practice of medicine, I argue that modern medical boards that discipline on character-related grounds may not be sending the most constructive signals to physicians trying to conform their behavior to the law. . . .

Notes: Professional Licensure

1. *Criminal Prosecution.* Note that the unlicensed practice of medicine is a criminal offense; persons convicted of the offense can be fined and imprisoned. Suppose that the patient of an unlicensed provider is injured in the course of receiving care. Is the provider liable in tort under a negligence per se theory? See Chapter 4.C.1. Jurisdictions may also criminalize "assisting" in the unlicensed practice of medicine. This criminal offense can have civil law implications as well. Physicians and other licensed health care professionals are subject to professional disciplinary action, such as license revocation or suspension, for assisting in the unlicensed practice of medicine. Annot., 99 A.L.R.2d 654 (1965).

2. *Physician Supply.* Most states require M.D.s to graduate from an AMA-accredited medical school (or, for foreign medical graduates, certification by the Educational Commission for Foreign Medical Graduates (ECFMG) and an internship in an AMA-approved residency program). As a result, medical licensure essentially cedes to the medical profession control of how many doctors can enter practice, since the AMA can control the size of medical school classes through the accreditation process and the ECFMG can control the certification process. Mark A. Peterson, From Trust to Political Power: Interest Groups, Public Choice, and Health Care, 26 J. Health Pol. Pol'y & L. 1145 (2001).

Allowing the medical profession to control entry into its own market creates the anticompetitive risk that the AMA will act out of economic self-interest to maintain artificial shortages. Barriers to entry into service professions tend automatically to drive up prices by creating a supply shortage. Reuben Kessel, Price Discrimination in Medicine, 1 J.L. & Econ. 20 (1959); Reuben Kessel, The A.M.A. and the Supply of Physicians, 35 Law & Contemp. Probs. 267 (Spring 1970).

Concern about physician shortages seems misplaced these days, when we are much more apt to hear about the "glut" of physicians, particularly of specialists. The ratio of physicians to citizens in the United States has been steadily increasing, rising from 146 physicians/100,000 in 1950 to 233/100,000 in 1990, to 277/100,000 in the year 2008. Some experts argue that the ideal ratio lies somewhere between 160 and 200 physicians per 100,000. More important than the total number, however, is their distribution. Policymakers are concerned that there are too few primary care physicians, who are less expensive, and too many specialists, who drive up the cost of care by providing services that could be more cheaply provided by family practitioners or other generalists. Also, the geographic distribution of physicians clearly remains problematic. Many rural areas have found it difficult to attract physicians. A similar problem can be found in some urban centers, where physicians have not been willing to establish practices that serve low-income populations. Tracy Hampton, US Medical School Enrollment Rising, but Residency Programs Too Limited, 299 JAMA 284 (2008).

3. *Defining Medical Practice.* The legislative definition of the "practice of medicine" typically is quite broad, as can be seen by examining the jury instructions in *Miller*. The breadth of the definition is important because persons who engage in the specified activities without an appropriate license are subject to criminal penalties. How far can the definition of medical practice be stretched?

The various exotic and peripheral ministrations successfully attacked under the medical licensure statutes range from the sublime to the ridiculous. Magnetism, mental suggestion, faith healing, color wave therapy, reflexology, massage, hypnotism, tattooing, and electrical hair removal all have been held to constitute the practice of medicine. See, e.g., State v. White, 560 S.E.2d 420 (S.C. 2002) (state statute restricting tattooing to licensed physicians for cosmetic or reconstructive purposes does not violate free speech and is valid exercise of police power.) Even the commonplace practice of offering nutritional advice might subject the advisor to criminal prosecution, as in *Miller*. Courts have found that some activities, such as ear piercing and cosmetic hair removal, lie outside the sometimes seemingly unlimited scope of medical practice.

The very breadth of the typical medical practice act definition suggests a trap for the unwary, who might unexpectedly confront criminal liability for engaging in seemingly innocuous activities. Do the instructions given to the jury in *Miller* provide appropriate guidance for their decision? Defendants have challenged these statutes on vagueness grounds; however, courts have been understandably reluctant to agree and have upheld the statutes by artfully using a number of different techniques of statutory construction. See People v. Rogers, 641 N.W.2d 595 (2001) (statutory definition not facially overbroad or unconstitutionally vague).

4. *Licensure vs. Credentialing.* Thinking about both the broader purposes and criticisms of licensing health care professionals, what benefits does professional licensure have over a system of accreditation or certification? Under the latter, patients would be given clear notice about who does and does not have recognized credentials, but they would be permitted to choose whether to seek care from an unaccredited or uncertified person. Health care payers, such as insurance companies, might be empowered to reject payment claims made by those lacking certification. Licensure schemes are preferred where there is a risk that consumers might not be able to exercise reasoned judgment about the qualifications of their health care providers, perhaps because of lack of knowledge, the decisionmaking deficits created by disease, or financial distress. See Timothy Stoltzfus Jost, Oversight of the Quality of Medical Care: Regulation, Management, or the Market, 37 Ariz. L. Rev. 825 (1995); Randall G. Holcombe, Eliminating Scope of Practice and Licensing Laws to Improve Health Care, 31 J.L. Med. & Ethics 236 (2003).

5. *A Right to Receive Treatment?* Do patients have any constitutionally protected interest in being able to choose to receive health care services of one type or another, from one type of provider or another? The issue was not raised in *Miller* but has been litigated elsewhere. Most courts have found that there is no fundamental right of access to treatment by unlicensed providers. See, e.g., Mitchell v. Clayton, 995 F.2d 772, 775-776 (7th Cir. 1993). The Supreme Court's ruling in the physician-assisted suicide cases suggests that the Constitution does not give patients a protected interest in obtaining particular types of medical treatment. What if, however, a case could be made that the particular treatment is the only one that might work? See Chapter 2.A. for discussion of related constitutional issues.

6. *A Right to Provide Care?* Medical practitioners have been equally unsuccessful in their attempts to claim a constitutional right to provide care. Courts uniformly have upheld state licensing regulations so long as they are rationally related to serving some legitimate state interest. In Williamson v. Lee Optical of Oklahoma, Inc., the plaintiff challenged the constitutional validity of Oklahoma's licensure provisions that made it "unlawful for any person not a licensed optometrist or ophthalmologist to fit lenses to a face or to duplicate or replace into frames lenses or other optical appliances, except upon written prescriptive authority of an Oklahoma

licensed ophthalmologist or optometrist." 348 U.S. 483, 485 (1955). The district court had held a portion of the statute unconstitutional, finding in part that it unreasonably prohibited opticians from making duplicate lenses for persons whose glasses were lost or broken. The Court upheld the statute, using classic rational basis review:

> The Oklahoma law may exact a needless, wasteful requirement in many cases. But it is for the legislature, not the courts, to balance the advantages and disadvantages of the new requirement. It appears that in many cases the optician can easily supply the new frames or new lenses without reference to the old written prescription. . . . But the law need not be in every respect logically consistent with its aims to be constitutional. It is enough that there is an evil at hand for correction, and that it might be thought that the particular legislative measure was a rational way to correct it.
>
> The day is gone when this Court uses the due process clause of the Fourteenth Amendment to strike down state laws, regulatory of business and industrial conditions, because they may be unwise, improvident, or out of harmony with a particular school of thought. . . . Id. at 487-488.

The Court also rejected an equal protection claim, again stating the applicable rational basis test in classic terms:

> The problem of legislative classification is a perennial one, admitting of no doctrinaire definition. Evils in the same field may be of different dimensions and proportions, requiring different remedies. Or so the legislature may think. Or the reform may take one step at a time, addressing itself to the phase of the problem which seems most acute to the legislative mind. The legislature may select one phase of one field and apply a remedy there, neglecting the others. The prohibition of the equal protection clause goes no further than the invidious discrimination. We cannot say that that point has been reached here. . . . Id. at 489.

The rational basis approach adopted in *Lee* has been applied in nearly every case since. See, e.g., National Ass'n for the Advancement of Psychoanalysis v. California Board of Psychology, 228 F.3d 1043 (9th Cir. 2000) (upholding state's mental health licensing scheme under rational basis test); Sherman v. Cryns, 786 N.E.2d 139 (Ill. 2003) (state midwifery licensing statute is rationally related to a legitimate state interest).

States often provide an exception to the normal rules governing the practice of medicine for religious practitioners. See, e.g., Cal. Bus. & Prof. Code §2063 ("Nothing in this chapter shall be construed . . . [to] regulate, prohibit, or apply to any kind of treatment by prayer, nor interfere in any way with the practice of religion."). Is this religious exemption required by the First Amendment? Does an exemption for religious practitioners violate the First Amendment's prohibition of state establishment of religion? Does the exemption for religious practitioners undercut the rationale for general licensure requirements—if the public health is at risk from "unscientific" practitioners, then shouldn't the public be protected from religious practitioners? Most academic attention focuses on the liability of parents for child neglect for the use of religious or spiritual healers. See, e.g., Jessie Hill, Whose Body, Whose Soul?, 32 Cardozo L. Rev. 1857 (2011).

7. *Alternative Healing Techniques.* Why did Miller's patients seek his assistance? Why are alternative practitioners so popular? First, of course, critics of the medical

system note that the appeal can be directly related to the "ills" of traditional medicine. Medical practice is expensive, impersonal, and bureaucratic. Second, alternative therapies apparently work, at least some therapies for some people. The National Institutes of Health (NIH) created the Center for Complementary and Alternative Medicine (CAM) in 1992 to fund research designed to test the efficacy of a wide range of alternative therapies. Even if the alternative therapy is scientifically worthless, a significant percentage of people given a placebo will experience relief from their symptoms and even an improvement in their condition. See Chapter 1.B.3. Given all of this, perhaps licensure requirements keep people from seeking out potentially effective care. Does that mean alternative healers should be exempted from licensure, or should instead petition legislatures for their own licensure schemes? See John Lunstroth, Voluntary Self-Regulation of Complementary and Alternative Medicine Practitioners, 70 Alb. L. Rev. 209 (2006).

8. *Interprofessional Disputes.* Rules prohibiting the unlicensed practice of various professions also serve to establish boundaries between particular classes of health care providers. Persons providing health care services pursuant to statutory authorization are not guilty of the unlicensed practice of medicine. Thus a nurse is not engaging in the unlicensed practice of medicine when she or he makes a nursing diagnosis or provides nursing services to a patient.

Still, interprofessional turf battles are waged, particularly where nonphysician health care providers have attempted to expand their scope of practice. See, e.g., Brown v. Belinfante, 557 S.E.2d 399 (Ga. Ct. App. 2001) (oral surgeon violates dental practice act by performing facelift); Connecticut State Medical Society v. Connecticut Board of Examiners of Podiatry, 546 A.2d 830 (Conn. 1988) (litigation to determine whether podiatrists can treat ankles).

9. *Physician Extenders.* Physicians often delegate functions to other types of health care practitioners, such as nurses or physician assistants. The educational training of these other health care providers can vary widely. Traditionally, nurses have performed a wide range of functions within the health care system, sometimes under the control of physicians and sometimes exercising independent, nursing judgment. Physician assistants, in contrast, have traditionally been characterized as "dependent" practitioners, who perform only tasks delegated by physicians. Many states now certify or otherwise regulate physician assistants to ensure that they are appropriately supervised.

Can physicians delegate tasks to assistants who are not independently licensed, without assisting in the unlicensed practice of medicine? Some legislatures have been extremely active in attempting to mark the bounds of appropriate delegation. Others provide physicians broad discretion to delegate tasks however they want as long as they do so consistent with proper medical standards, they supervise and retain responsibility, and the person doing the tasks does not purport to be practicing medicine. See, e.g., Tex. Occ. Code Ann. §157.001.

Nurse practitioners and physician assistants play a particularly important role in providing medical services in rural and central urban areas, where physicians are rare. Residents of these areas will often not have access to any health care unless they can be treated by "physician extenders." As a consequence, many states permit physicians to delegate more tasks, such as signing certain prescriptions, in "medically underserved" areas of the state.

Physician assistants or nurses performing delegated tasks generally do so pursuant to physician's orders, standing medical orders, standing delegation orders, or written protocols. Courts, administrative agencies, and legislatures have struggled to define when a physician's degree of supervision is inadequate. Some jurisdictions have at least partially defined the degree of required supervision by establishing periodic physician reviews (e.g., daily status reports, once a week on-site direction, etc.) and limiting the number of persons whom the physician can supervise. Should surgeons be permitted to delegate some tasks during surgery to persons not licensed to practice medicine?

10. *Telemedicine and "Mobile" Medicine.* Health care provider licensure is a matter of state law. How should this state-level system respond to the growing nationalization of health care practice, in which physicians in other states may use telemedicine or Internet technology to diagnose and recommend treatment for patients from afar? Many states have amended their licensing statutes or regulations in recent years to respond to this issue, some by tightening rules that prohibit out-of-state physicians from providing regular and ongoing direct care to patients, and others by specifying under which conditions this may be done. See note 13 below.

A related, but potentially even more revolutionary, development is "mobile medicine" in the form of small devices and apps that monitor health, facilitate self-help measures, and connect people with care advisors potentially anywhere in the world, or perhaps only through artificial intelligence. At the federal level, the FDA has indicated its intent to assert its jurisdiction over medical devices. Nathan Cortez, The Mobile Health Revolution?, 47 U.C. Davis L. Rev. 1173 (2014). At the state level, there are potential issues, not yet widely asserted, regarding whether these apps constitute diagnosis or prescription that amounts to the practice of medicine. Fazal Khan, The "Uberization" of Healthcare: The Forthcoming Legal Storm over Mobile Health Technology's Impact on the Medical Profession, 26 Health Matrix 123 (2016).

11. *Grounds for Discipline.* Despite Prof. Sawicki's criticisms, medical boards sometimes do discipline physicians who have delivered substandard, incompetent, or negligent care. When they do, boards are generally not required to prove that any patients were actually harmed. See Annot., 93 A.L.R.2d 1398 (1964); Annot., 28 A.L.R.3d 487 (1969); Annot., 22 A.L.R.4th 668 (1983).

As Prof. Sawicki notes, however, professional discipline often targets purely economic misbehavior. For instance, licensure codes often attempt to restrict the range of permissible advertising or solicitation that practitioners may use. One rationale for these restrictions is that they prevent consumer fraud and abuse. Another is that they insulate the profession from the demands of competition, which might result in price wars and lost income. States generally may not restrict truthful, non-misleading professional advertisements without violating the First Amendment's protection of free speech. See, e.g., Virginia State Board of Pharmacy v. Virginia Citizens Consumer Council, Inc., 425 U.S. 748, 762 (1976) (striking down ban on price advertising by pharmacists); Culpepper v. Arkansas Board of Chiropractic Examiners, 36 S.W.3d 335 (Ark. 2001) (ban on direct contact by chiropractors with potential patients is unconstitutional).

12. *An Administrative Law Primer.* Complaints against medical practitioners are adjudicated initially by "hearing officers," who determine if a violation has occurred and recommend an appropriate sanction. The agency typically has an internal appeals process with the final agency determination rendered by the relevant board itself. The agency's procedures are likely to be established within its enabling legislation and within the state's Administrative Procedure Act. Alleged

flaws in this process are often the main focus of any court challenges, giving rise to constitutional and statutory issues that are studied at length in Administrative Law. For additional discussion, see materials on the Web site for this book, www.health -law.org, and note 13.

13. *Additional Readings.* On the *history of medical licensure,* see Lewis Grossman, The Origins of American Health Libertarianism, Yale J. Health Pol'y L. & Ethics 76 (2013).

On **scope of practice issues** (notes 8 and 9), see Barbara J. Safriet, Closing the Gap Between *Can* and *May* in Health-Care Providers' Scopes of Practice: A Primer for Policymakers, 19 Yale J. on Reg. 301 (2002); Lori B. Andrews, The Shadow Health Care System: Regulation of Alternative Health Care Providers, 32 Hous. L. Rev. 1273, 1275 (1996); Laura Hermer & William Winslade, Access to Health Care in Texas: A Patient-Centered Perspective, 35 Tex. Tech L. Rev. 33 (2004); Joy L. Delman, The Use and Misuse of Physician Extenders, 24 J. Leg. Med. 249 (2003); Symposium, 32(11) Health Aff. 1870 (2013).

On **telemedicine and mobile apps/devices** (note 10), see Roundtable on Legal Impediments to Telemedicine, 14 J. Health Care L. & Pol'y 1-117 (2011); Amar Gupta & Deth Sao, The Constitutionality of Current Legal Barriers to Tele-medicine in the United States, 21 Health Matrix 385 (2011); John Blum, Internet Medicine and the Evolving Legal Status of the Physician-Patient Relationship, 24 J. Leg. Med. 413 (2003); Symposium, 33(30 Health Aff. 194 (2014); Symposium, 14 J. Health Care L. & Pol'y 1 (2011); Symposium, 46 St. Louis U. L.J. 1-110 (2002).

On **First Amendment issues** (note 11), see Jess Alderman, Words to Live By: Public Health, the First Amendment, and Government Speech, 57 Buff. L. Rev. 161 (2009); Paula Berg, Toward a First Amendment Theory of Doctor-Patient Discourse and the Right to Receive Unbiased Medical Advice, 74 B.U. L. Rev. 201, 241-243 (1994).

On **administrative and due process issues** (note 12), see Eleanor Kinney, Administrative Law of Health Care in a Nutshell (2016); J. Bruce Bennet, The Rights of Licensed Professionals to Notice and Hearing in Agency Enforcement Actions, 7 Tex. Tech Admin. L.J. 205 (2006); Annot., 10 A.L.R.5th 1 (1993); Annot., 74 A.L.R.4th 969 (1989).

Problem: Professional Licensure

Dr. Alicia Chuanski lives in an urban area in a state that has many underpopulated, rural areas. She has established a thriving family practice in the city. She is interested in expanding her practice into a rural area about 90 miles from her office. She hopes to set up a satellite office, staffed with a nurse and a physician assistant. Dr. Chuanski plans to supervise the satellite office in several ways:

1. She will establish detailed protocols for the nurse and physician assistant. They both will meet with patients, take patient histories and record patient symptoms, and establish baseline heart rates, blood pressures, and temperatures. The protocols will establish diagnostic or other procedures that should be followed for patients with particular symptoms. The protocols also will establish "opt-out" points: symptoms or complaints that indicate the need to refer patients to the nearest emergency room, which is about

20 miles away. Dr. Chuanski will leave a presigned prescription pad at the satellite for the use of the nurse and physician assistant (pursuant to the protocols); prescriptions will be reviewed on a daily basis.

2. Dr. Chuanski will attempt to establish a backup relationship with a nearby physician, perhaps one who maintains an office near the hospital mentioned above.

3. Dr. Chuanski will be available for phone consultations from 12 to 1:00 P.M. and from 4:30 to 5:30 P.M. every work day. Summary reports on the day's patients will be faxed to her each evening.

4. As the price of technology decreases, Dr. Chuanski will consider establishing a video link to the satellite so that she could "see" and "examine" patients from her office in the city.

5. Dr. Chuanski will visit the satellite once every ten days or so.

Evaluate Dr. Chuanski's plans. Will the nurse and/or physician assistant be engaged in the unlicensed practice of medicine? Is Dr. Chuanski assisting in the unlicensed practice of medicine? Is Dr. Chuanski engaged in unprofessional conduct that could lead to disciplinary action? Where would you look to answer these questions? What additional information might you need to answer the questions? Can you suggest any improvements to Dr. Chuanski's plans?

2. Facility Licensure and Accreditation

■ PATIENT POWER: SOLVING AMERICA'S HEALTH CARE CRISIS
John C. Goodman & Gerald L. Musgrave
(1992)

In terms of rules, restrictions, and bureaucratic requirements, the health care sector is one of the most regulated industries in our economy. Consider Scripps Memorial Hospital, a medium-sized acute care facility in San Diego, California. As [the following] table shows, Scripps must answer to 39 governmental bodies and 7 nongovernmental bodies, and must periodically file 65 different reports, about one report for every four beds.[1] . . . Regulatory requirements intrude in a highly visible

---

1. The hospital association in New York once claimed that its members were subject to 174 regulatory bodies, and another survey found that hospitals have to submit themselves to over 50 different inspections and reports each year, often requiring into similar matters. B. Gray, The Profit Motive and Patient Care 112 (1991). [The American Hospital Association claims that, for every hour of patient care, hospitals engage in 30 to 60 minutes of paperwork. Patients or Paperwork? The Regulatory Burden Facing America's Hospitals (2001). See also John Braithwaite & Valerie Braithwaite, The Politics of Legalism: Rules Versus Standards in Nursing-Home Regulation, 4 Soc. Leg. Stud. 307, 320 (1995) ("the people who inspect U.S. nursing homes are checking compliance with over a thousand regulations"); Christopher J. Conover, Health Care Regulation: A $169 Billion Hidden Tax (Cato Institute, 2004) (finding that health care regulation costs twice as much as its benefits are worth). See generally Robert I. Field, Health Care Regulation in America: Complexity, Confrontation and Compromise (2007).]

way on the activities of the medical staff and affect virtually every aspect of medical practice. Another California hospital, Sequoia Hospital in the San Francisco Bay area, has attempted to calculate how many additional employees are required as a result of government regulations. Sequoia's [administrative and nursing] staff increased by 163.6 percent [from 450 to 736] between 1966 and 1990, even though the average number of patients per day (250) did not change. . . .

Regulatory Agencies Over Scripps Memorial Hospital, 1989

Agency
Government
Occupational Safety and Health Administration
San Diego County Health Department
State Board of Equalization (hazardous waste tax return)
Internal Revenue Service
Franchise Tax Board
Secretary of State
Medicare
State Board of Equalization (sales tax return)
California Hospital Facilities Commission
State Board of Health
Environmental Protection Agency
Department of Transportation
Department of Health Services
Air Resources Board
Office of Emergency Services
Health and Welfare Agency
Air Pollution Control/Air Quality Management District
Regional Water Quality Control Board
Local Sewering Agencies
San Diego Department of Health Services
State Licensing Board
Board of Registered Nursing
Licensed Vocational Nursing Board
U.S. Department of Labor
Industrial Welfare Commission
Fair Employment Practice Commission
National Labor Relations Board
Immigration and Naturalization Service
Employment Development Department
Social Security Administration
Employee Retirement Income Security Requirements
State Board of Pharmacy
Drug Enforcement Agency
Food and Drug Administration
Bureau of Narcotic Enforcement
California Department of Health, Radiologic Health Branch

Agency

Nongovernment
 Joint Commission on Accreditation of Hospitals
 American Hospital Association
 American Conference of Governmental Industrial Hygienists
 California Medical Association
 Radiation Safety Organization (Syncor, Inc.)
 National Association of Social Workers
 American College of Surgeons
 San Diego and Imperial Counties Organization for Cancer Control

Note: Facility Licensing, Accreditation, and Certification

Three terms are commonly used to describe the multilevel process for inspecting and approving health care facilities by state, federal, and private agencies: licensure, accreditation, and certification. Each of these terms has a specific meaning, and each represents a different level of significance for operation within the health care community. The requirements for licensure, accreditation, and certification exert a strong regulatory force on the organization and operation of health care facilities.

Licensure is the mandatory governmental process whereby a health care facility receives the right to operate. In the United States, licensure operates on a state-by-state basis. A health care facility (as that term is defined in the statute) cannot open its doors lawfully without a license from the appropriate state agency. Licensed health care facilities include hospitals, nursing homes, ambulatory surgery centers, freestanding emergency centers, pharmacies, and, in some instances, diagnostic centers. State licensing schemes also exist for various financing systems, both for ordinary health insurance and for innovative delivery systems such as HMOs, PPOs, and utilization review systems.

Accreditation is a private voluntary approval process through which a health care organization is evaluated and can receive a designation of competence and quality. Most private accreditation for health care organizations today is done under the auspices of the Joint Commission for the Accreditation of Healthcare Organizations (called "JCAHO," "Jayco," or "Joint Commission," formerly known as the Joint Commission for the Accreditation of Hospitals). The Joint Commission is governed by the major trade associations, primarily the American Medical Association, the American Hospital Association, the American College of Surgeons, and the American College of Physicians, and its accreditation programs serve all sorts of health care organizations, although its primary participants are hospitals. Although the Joint Commission is private and purely voluntary, historically it has wielded enormous power and influence because virtually no hospital of respectable size risks the business consequences of jeopardizing its accreditation status. However, the Joint Commission's dominance of facility accreditation is starting to wane somewhat in the face of increasing competition from other accrediting bodies for nonhospital facilities.

Certification is a voluntary procedure for health care organizations to meet the qualifications for participation in government funding programs, specifically Medicare and Medicaid. Although certification is voluntary, more often than not

Medicare and Medicaid certification are necessary to the economic survival of a health care organization.

The three functions of licensure, accreditation, and certification are intertwined to a considerable extent. Joint Commission accreditation, for example, frequently satisfies the requirements for both state licensing and Medicare/Medicaid certification. Where this is not the case, Medicare/Medicaid certification surveys are often performed by the same agency and personnel that conduct state licensing surveys. Not only are the three functions intertwined, but there is also a high level of congruence among the various standards and processes employed in each function. Therefore, these materials will examine all three systems interchangeably.

■ ESTATE OF SMITH v. HECKLER
747 F.2d 583 (10th Cir. 1984)

McKay, Circuit Judge.

Plaintiffs . . . brought this class action on behalf of Medicaid recipients residing in nursing homes in Colorado. They alleged that the Secretary of Health and Human Services (Secretary) has a statutory duty . . . to develop and implement a system of nursing home review and enforcement designed to ensure that Medicaid recipients residing in Medicaid certified nursing homes actually receive the optimal medical and psychosocial care that they are entitled to under the Act. The plaintiffs contended that the enforcement system developed by the Secretary is "facility oriented," not "patient oriented" and thereby fails to meet the statutory mandate. . . .

[P]laintiffs instituted the lawsuit in an effort to improve the deplorable conditions at many nursing homes. They presented evidence of the lack of adequate medical care and of the widespread knowledge that care is inadequate. Indeed, the district court concluded that care and life in some nursing homes is so bad that the homes "could be characterized as orphanages for the aged." . . . [Nevertheless] [t]he trial court denied relief. This appeal is from that judgment. . . .

An understanding of the Medicaid Act (the Act) is essential to understand plaintiffs' contentions. The purpose of the Act is to enable the federal government to assist states in providing medical assistance to "aged, blind or disabled individuals, whose income and resources are insufficient to meet the costs of necessary medical services, and . . . rehabilitation and other services to help such . . . individuals to attain or retain capabilities for independence or self care." To receive funding, a state must submit to the Secretary and have approved by the Secretary a plan for medical assistance which meets the requirements of 42 U.S.C. §1396a(a). . . . The plan must include descriptions of the standards and methods the state will use to assure that medical or remedial care services provided to the recipients "are of high quality." . . . The appropriate state agency must determine on an ongoing basis whether participating institutions meet the requirements for continued participation in the Medicaid program. . . . In conducting the review, however, the states must use federal standards, forms, methods and procedures. . . .

Among other things, the regulations provide for the frequency and general content of patients' attending physician evaluations, nursing services with policies "designed to ensure that each patient receives treatments, medications, . . . diet as prescribed . . . rehabilitative nursing care as needed, . . . is kept comfortable, clean, well-groomed, [is] protected from accident, injury, an infection, and [is] encouraged, assisted, and trained in self-care and group activities." The rehabilitative nursing care is to be directed toward each patient achieving an optimal level of self-care and independence. The regulations require a written patient care plan to be developed and maintained for each patient. . . . Finally, the regulations provide for treatment of the social and emotional needs of recipients.

The Secretary has established a procedure for determining whether state plans comply with the standards set out in the regulations. This enforcement mechanism is known as the "survey/certification" inspection system. Under this system, the states conduct reviews of nursing homes. . . . The Secretary then determines, on the basis of the survey results, whether the nursing home surveyed is eligible for certification and, thus, eligible for Medicaid funds. . . .

The plaintiffs do not challenge the substantive medical standards, or "conditions of participation," which have been adopted by the Secretary and which states must satisfy to have their plans approved. Rather, plaintiffs challenge the enforcement mechanism the Secretary has established. The plaintiffs contend that the federal forms . . . which states are required to use, evaluate only the physical facilities and theoretical capability to render quality care. They claim that . . . out of the 541 questions contained in the Secretary's form which must be answered by state survey and certification inspection teams, only 30 are "even marginally related to patient care or might require any patient observation. . . ." Plaintiffs contend that the enforcement mechanism's focus on the facility, rather than on the care actually provided in the facility, results only in "paper compliance" with the substantive standards of the Act. Thus, plaintiffs contend, the Secretary has violated her statutory duty to assure that federal Medicaid monies are paid only to facilities which meet the substantive standards of the Act—facilities which actually provide high quality medical, rehabilitative and psychosocial care to resident Medicaid recipients. . . .

Congress intended the Secretary to be responsible for assuring that federal Medicaid money is given only to those institutions that actually comply with Medicaid requirements. The Act's requirements include providing high quality medical care. . . . Being charged with this function, we must conclude that a failure to promulgate regulations that allow the Secretary to remain informed, on a continuing basis, as to whether facilities receiving federal money are meeting the requirements of the Act, is an abdication of the Secretary's duty. . . .

■ COSPITO v. HECKLER
742 F.2d 72 (3d Cir. 1984)

GARTH, Circuit Judge.

Appellants Douglas Cospito, et al., ("the Patients") are or have been patients at the Trenton Psychiatric Hospital (TPH). In 1975, TPH lost its accreditation from codefendant Joint Commission on Accreditation of [Healthcare Organizations (JCAHO or JCAH)]. As a result, codefendant Secretary of the Department of Health, Education, and Welfare (now the Department of Health and Human Services) terminated various federal benefits which were conditioned upon the beneficiaries being treated at a qualified psychiatric hospital. . . . The Patients brought this action in district court challenging the loss of their federal benefits on several constitutional grounds. . . .

Beginning in 1973, TPH was surveyed under the standards for "psychiatric facilities" recently promulgated under the auspices of JCAH. Following the 1973 survey, major deficiencies were disclosed in several areas, including patient treatment, staffing, environment, and fire safety. TPH was accredited for only one year, and was notified that these deficiencies must be corrected to maintain accreditation. In 1974, however, many of the same deficiencies were found again. A preliminary decision was made by JCAH not to accredit. At TPH's request, a resurvey was conducted in May, 1975, which again resulted in a preliminary decision not to accredit. TPH did not appeal from that decision, and the deaccreditation became final. . . .

JCAH is an Illinois not-for-profit corporation formed in 1951 for the purpose of creating and maintaining professional standards for evaluating hospital performance. The body is governed by a 22-member Board of Commissioners. Its constituent members consist of the American College of Physicians, the American College of Surgeons, the American Dental Association, the American Hospital Association, and the American Medical Association. . . .

The survey itself consists of an on-site visit conducted by a team of surveyors designated by JCAH. The surveyors evaluate the quality of the facility's environment and review its administrative records to determine whether they conform to applicable standards. . . .

JCAH accreditation, however, must be distinguished from certification by the Secretary for eligibility in federal assistance programs. While JCAH accreditation may, depending on the circumstances, be a component of certification, the two are not necessarily coextensive, and at least as a matter of terminology, we will refer to the two separately. . . .

The Patients at TPH had, before decertification by the Secretary, been the beneficiaries of three types of federally funded benefits: (1) Medicare, (2) Medicaid, and (3) Supplemental Social Security Income. . . . When TPH was decertified in 1975, all of the benefits described above were terminated, since TPH was no longer an institution eligible under Medicare and Medicaid. . . . The Patients brought suit in district court alleging that deprivation of their Medicare, Medicaid, and Social Security benefits was unconstitutional. They alleged lack of procedural due process, lack of substantive due process, lack of equal protection, and unconstitutional delegation of authority to JCAH. . . .

Our analysis of the procedural due process aspects of this case is guided by the Supreme Court's decision in O'Bannon v. Town Court Nursing Center, 447 U.S. 773 (1980), which involved facts comparable to those presented here. In *Town Court*, residents of a nursing home claimed a violation of due process when they lost federal benefits as a result of the decertification of their facility. Like the Patients here, they claimed a right to a pretermination hearing.

The Supreme Court found as a threshold matter, however, that the residents of the nursing home had not been deprived of any protectable property interest, and thus, absent this foundation, no due process right was triggered. Writing for the Court, Justice Stevens found that patients did not have a settled interest in receiving benefits at any [particular] facility, including a decertified one, and therefore there had been no deprivation of "property." . . .

[T]he only factor which even arguably distinguishes this case from *Town Court* is the fact that the Patients are unable to transfer out of TPH [because they were involuntarily committed under state mental health law]; [therefore], they are barred from receiving federal benefits at another qualified institution. Thus, they contend that there has been an actual "deprivation" of a protectable interest. Even accepting that contention, however, . . . [b]ecause any loss of benefits to the Patients was only "indirectly" caused by the Secretary's decision to decertify TPH, whatever deprivation which was suffered [by virtue of the state-law psychiatric commitment] was not the result of any [federal] governmental action. The Patients are therefore not in a position to claim any Fifth Amendment due process protection, even if they alleged a "deprivation."[17] . . .

Finally, we turn to the Patients' argument that the Medicare (and thus Medicaid) provisions improperly delegate authority to JCAH, in derogation of Congress' ultimate responsibility to establish federal policy. . . . We need not reach the question of whether delegation of such authority to a private entity breaches the constitutional barrier, since our reading of the Medicare statute, which in turn is applicable to the Medic[aid] and Social Security programs, convinces us that the Secretary retains ultimate authority over decertification decisions, through the ability to engage in a "distinct part" survey. . . .

While JCAH accreditation may, under certain circumstances, independently satisfy the statutory requirements for participation in Medicare, the Secretary is free to prescribe standards which are higher than those of the Commission, in which case JCAH accreditation would not be effective. Moreover, if the Secretary determines that, despite JCAH accreditation, a particular hospital nevertheless has serious deficiencies, he may, after appropriate notice, decertify the institution. On the other hand, if the Secretary chose to promulgate a standard lower than that of JCAH, a general hospital could presumably be certified by meeting only that lesser standard, even if it did not meet the requirements imposed by the Commission.

The Patients argue, however, that in the case of psychiatric hospitals, the statute places JCAH accreditation in a position of ascendancy over approval by the Secretary, thus leading to the question of unconstitutional delegation to a private group. Our reading of the statute leads us to disagree. While Congress did choose to give special attention to JCAH accreditation in the context of psychiatric hospitals,[27] it still provided the "distinct part" survey as a mechanism whereby the Secretary could independently determine whether a particular institution was qualified for participation. Through consecutive or simultaneous distinct part surveys,

---

17. The district court granted summary judgment on the procedural due process claim for the reason that, in its opinion, the procedures used adequately safeguarded the Patients' interests, [a]pplying the tests of Mathews v. Eldridge, 424 U.S. 319 (1976). . . . Without disagreeing with the district court's reasoning, we note that our analysis makes it unnecessary to reach the issues addressed by the court below. . . .

27. The legislative history reveals that Congress intended "to support the efforts of the various professional accrediting organizations sponsored by the medical and hospital associations. . . ."

therefore, it is possible to obtain a de novo evaluation by the Secretary on the adequacy of a hospital's facilities. . . .

Since, in effect, all actions of JCAH are subject to full review by a public official who is responsible and responsive to the political process, we find that there has been no real delegation of authority to JCAH.[29] . . .

BECKER, Circuit Judge, dissented.

Notes: Facility Regulation and Accreditation

1. *Which Facilities Are Covered?* The first question under any licensing scheme is its jurisdiction. Jurisdictional issues arise with increasing frequency as the result of innovative service delivery and ownership arrangements in the medical industry. One common issue is whether a license for a central facility such as a hospital covers satellite facilities such as urgent care centers, or whether they must be separately licensed. Another issue is whether a specialty clinic, say for abortions or for expensive diagnostic scans, can be treated as simply a physician's office, which does not require a facility license. See RIH Medical Foundation v. Nolan, 723 A.2d 1123 (R.I. 1999) (physician-owned corporation that operates physician offices is exempt from health facility licensing); Ex parte Sacred Heart Health System, 155 So. 2d 980 (Ala. 2012) (announcing five-part test to determine when a physician's office is not a regulated facility); Covenant Healthcare System, Inc. v. City of Wauwatosa, 800 N.W.2d 906 (Wis. 2011) (urgent care center is not just an expanded doctor's office, but functions more like a "hospital," for purposes of tax-exempt status). A third issue is whether an existing license covers the buyer or lessor of a health facility, and whether turning the facility's operation over to a management company requires applying for a formal transfer of the license. Often, the same questions apply generally to accreditation and certification. Usually, the only way to know the answer is to simply ask the governing authorities, since statutes and regulations frequently fail to flesh out these details. The consequences for wrongly interpreting licensing jurisdiction can be severe. In one case, the court refused to enforce any of the contracts entered into by an unlicensed nursing agency. U.S. Nursing Corp. v. St. Joseph Medical Center, 39 F.3d 790 (7th Cir. 1994).

2. *Regulation Run Amok?* One possible result of excess regulation may be to spur the increasing trend, known as "medical tourism," of traveling overseas to receive medical care much more cheaply in foreign countries. See page 44 for articles reviewing the legal and public policy implications. On health care regulation generally, see Robert Field, Health Care Regulation in America: Complexity, Confrontation, and Compromise (2007); Symposium, Rethinking Regulation in an Era of Reform, 32 Hamline J. Pub. L. & Pol'y 301 (2011).

---

29. Our resolution of this issue renders somewhat academic the Patients' contention that it was improper for JCAH to "subdelegate" the responsibility for evaluating psychiatric hospitals to the various accreditation councils. Since we have found that no real authority was actually vested in JCAH, it follows that there could be no improper "subdelegation" of authority to divisions of the Commission. . . .

3. *Measuring Quality Through Structure or Outcomes.* The next question under any of these regulatory or quasi-regulatory schemes is their content. A detailed understanding is beyond the scope of this book. However, it is possible to convey the gist of this content in terms of Donabedian's famous distinction among structural, process, and outcome measures of quality, summarized at page 319. State licensing authorities, like the Medicaid nursing home requirements in *Estate of Smith*, do not inquire into the actual outcomes of patient treatment. Instead, facility licensure provisions typically read like a gigantic building code for the industry, specifying a host of architectural, safety, and sanitation minutiae. Similarly, the Joint Commission accreditation standards traditionally have addressed only the organizational and structural aspects of each hospital department—issues such as whether bylaws are properly drafted, whether proper committees are established, and whether administrative structures contain proper monitoring and documentation—rather than attempting any direct assessment of the actual outcomes of medical care in the hospital. This point was articulated in an Internet discussion group by someone who worked as a hospital therapist and department manager for 13 years:

> We never worried about JCAHO until the three months prior and the two days of the inspection. In the three months prior, we backdated all the documentation that we needed to get through the inspection, and in the two days they were there we spent telling them how focused we were on quality, etc. As long as the paperwork is in order, people can be dying in the halls and there could be guppies in the IV fluids; the JCAHO wouldn't notice.

For an extensive critique of the traditional structural and process measures of institutional quality and an argument for adopting outcomes measures, see Troyen Brennan & Donald Berwick, New Rules: Regulation, Markets and the Quality of American Health Care (1996), which also contains an excellent overview and historical account of licensure and accreditation. Assessing regulatory approaches in light of vastly expanded sources of information about quality and costs, see Kristin Madison, Regulating Health Care Quality in an Information Age, 40 U.C. Davis L. Rev. 1577 (2007).

More generally, "new governance" is an important intellectual movement in administrative law, which considers from an empirically informed behavioral perspective a more diverse set of tools to accomplish regulatory goals than traditional "command and control" regulation. For a review of applications to hospital, insurance, and health care regulation, see Nan D. Hunter, Risk Governance and Deliberative Democracy in Health Care, 97 Geo. L.J. 1-60 (2008); John Blum, The Quagmire of Hospital Governance: Finding Mission in a Revised Licensure Model, 31 J. Leg. Med. 35 (2010); Symposium, 2 Regulation & Governance 1 (2008).

4. *Process and Outcomes Measures.* The *Smith* case presaged a move away from purely structural measures of quality. That decision resulted in a statutory amendment (known as OBRA '87) and an extensive set of regulations (updated in 2016) that govern in considerable detail the treatment plans, living environment, legal rights, and human dignity of nursing home patients. 42 C.F.R. §§483 et seq. These regulations are focused primarily on the process of care. In a controversial decision, the Third Circuit ruled that Medicaid's nursing home standards can form the basis for a personal injury suit against the nursing home, by the estate of a deceased

patient. Grammer v. John J. Kane Regional Centers, 570 F.3d 520 (3d Cir. 2009). See generally David Bohm, Striving for Quality Care in America's Nursing Homes, 4 DePaul J. Health Care L. 317 (2001); Jennifer Brady, Long-Term Care Under Fire: A Case for Rational Enforcement, 18 J. Contemp. Health L. & Pol'y 1 (2001); Comment, 73 U. Colo. L. Rev. 1013 (2002); Symposium, 26 J. Leg. Med. 1 (2005).

Reformers have tried to move even further toward evaluating institutions based on the outcomes of treatment. For instance, CMS at one point (in 1997) proposed fundamentally revising the standards for hospital participation in Medicare and Medicaid to focus much more extensively on outcomes of care and systems for continuous quality improvement. The proposed standards would have required each patient to receive a comprehensive assessment of care needs and a coordinated plan of care within 24 hours of admission. However, the final rule (adopted in 2003) falls back on general process requirements of having "data-driven quality assessment and performance improvement" systems that "measure, analyze, and track quality indicators," and then taking unspecified "actions aimed at performance improvement" that "track performance to ensure that improvements are sustained." 42 C.F.R. §482.

The Joint Commission has also attempted to streamline accreditation standards and focus more on patient safety issues. One key feature is a self-assessment and a "sentinel event" policy that requires hospitals to take the following actions whenever there is an unexpected death or serious injury resulting from treatment: inform the patient or family, conduct a "root cause" analysis, and institute a corrective action plan. However, hospitals do not have to report these events to the Joint Commission, since doing so might compromise the hospital's ability to protect the information from discovery in lawsuits. Symposium, 35 J. Health L. 179 (2002). As a result, the Joint Commission's outcomes initiative has become simply another process measure, one that requires institutions to assess internally their bad outcomes rather than enforcing mandatory outcomes standards.

Outcomes measures of quality may find their purest expression in the accreditation of HMOs and other types of integrated delivery systems. The National Committee for Quality Assurance (NCQA) is the leading accreditation organization for these new comprehensive financing and delivery systems. From the start, it has spearheaded a focus on outcomes measures in the form of the quality report cards discussed at page 320. These report cards adopt a standard reporting format about matters such as patient satisfaction, childhood immunization rates, and other broad indicators of health status (not just medical treatment) in the covered population. The aim is to provide this information as a basis on which subscribers and employers can comparison shop based on both price and quality, thereby substituting more market-based forces for regulatory oversight.

5. *Challenging Adverse Decisions.* The third major area of concern under licensure, accreditation, and certification programs is the processes for determining compliance and challenging adverse decisions. Space limitations preclude us from covering these important aspects of public oversight and legal practice. In brief summary, substantial procedural protections are usually built into these regulatory schemes, so challenges for denial of due process usually fail. The most intense disputes arise when licensing inspectors find such glaring safety concerns that the facility is shut down immediately without a chance for correction or rebuttal. These shutdowns have been challenged as unconstitutional, but usually without success

considering the patient protection concerns at stake and the ample procedural rights following a temporary shutdown.

Constitutional challenges depend on the presence of state action, which usually does not exist for private accreditation. McKeesport v. Accreditation Council for Graduate Medical Education, 24 F.3d 519 (3d Cir. 1994). Contra St. Agnes Hospital v. Riddick, 668 F. Supp. 478 (D. Md. 1987) (state action exists where private accreditation affects state licensure). Therefore, suit against accreditation organizations depends on somewhat obscure common-law theories of fairness in business dealings. There are only a few such cases, the leading ones arising in connection with physician accreditation and membership in professional societies. They reason that when membership organizations control important economic and public interests, they must provide rational reasons and a fair process for their exclusion decisions. See Pinsker v. Pacific Coast Society of Orthodontists, 526 P.2d 253 (Cal. 1974); Falcone v. Middlesex County Medical Society, 170 A.2d 791 (N.J. 1961). See generally Robert Trefney, Judicial Intervention in Admissions Decisions of Private Professional Associations, 49 U. Chi. L. Rev. 840 (1992).

6. *The Public Role of Private Accreditation. Cospito* raises the important public policy question of whether public regulatory authorities cede too much control to private accreditation organizations that are controlled by the regulated industry. State licensure of health care facilities, like federal certification, sometimes defers to the Joint Commission, either by using its accreditation as a proxy for licensure or by incorporating many of its standards. Even if this passes constitutional muster, it still deserves critique for whether this essentially self-regulatory approach is good public policy. See generally Symposium, Private Accreditation in the Regulatory State, 57 Law & Contemp. Probs. 4 (Autumn 1994) (exploring this and a number of other important legal and public policy issues concerning accreditation). It is worth observing that, although the Joint Commission arose from the hospital industry, it has long been sufficiently independent that it sometimes receives harsh criticism from hospitals for the expense and intrusiveness of its inspections. At the same time, consumer groups lash out against the Joint Commission for its relationship with the hospital industry.

7. *Occupational Hazards and Medical Wastes.* These are not the only regulatory authorities affecting health care facilities. Because of the size, complexity, and public importance of hospitals, they are subject to numerous specialized regulatory laws and generalized laws that have special importance in the hospital setting. Two prime examples are the laws governing workers' exposure to infectious diseases and the disposal of medical waste. For more detail, see the Web site for this book, www.health-law.org.

Research Exercise: Medicare/Medicaid Certification*

Your client is a hospital that has recently undergone a series of layoffs. A disgruntled former employee, a nurse, has complained to the state health department that the quality of patient care has suffered significantly. The hospital has

---

* The editors are grateful to Prof. Phyllis Bernard for permission to use this problem, which she devised.

had reason to be concerned about high rates of nosocomial infections (infections acquired in a hospital). There is also concern about bedsores and soiled linen. One patient's open wound was infected by maggots. The nurse's call to the state health department triggered a surprise inspection by the unit charged with overseeing certification for participation in the Medicare and Medicaid programs. It appears likely that the state Department of Health will seek summarily to terminate the hospital's status under these programs as a "participating provider" (also known as the "provider agreement"). Consult the Code of Federal Regulations or one or more of the relevant practitioner treatises (e.g., Wolters Kluwer's Medicare and Medicaid Guide or Hospital Law Manual) to determine what this means and what can be done about it.

3. The FDA, Pharmaceutical Regulation, and the Constitution

■ ABIGAIL ALLIANCE FOR BETTER ACCESS TO DEVELOPMENTAL DRUGS v. VON ESCHENBACH
495 F.3d 695 (D.C. Cir. 2007)

GRIFFITH, Circuit Judge:

This case presents the question whether the Constitution provides terminally ill patients a right of access to experimental drugs that have passed limited safety trials but have not been proven safe and effective. The district court held there is no such right. A divided panel of this Court held there is. Because we conclude that there is no fundamental right "deeply rooted in this Nation's history and tradition" of access to experimental drugs for the terminally ill, see Washington v. Glucksberg, 521 U.S. 702, 720-21 (1997), we affirm the judgment of the district court.

I.A.

The Abigail Alliance for Better Access to Developmental Drugs (the "Alliance") is an organization of terminally ill patients and their supporters that seeks expanded access to experimental drugs for the terminally ill. The Food, Drug, and Cosmetic Act ("FDCA" or "Act"), however, generally prohibits access to new drugs unless and until they have been approved by the Food and Drug Administration ("FDA"). See 21 U.S.C. §355(a). Gaining FDA approval can be a long process. First, an experimental drug's sponsor (e.g., a drug company) must submit an application for approval. Because no drug may be approved without a finding of "substantial evidence that the drug will have the effect it purports or is represented to have," an application must contain "full reports of investigations which have been made to show whether or not such drug is safe for use and whether such drug is effective in use," id. §355(b)(1)(A). Such reports rely in large measure on clinical trials with human subjects.

But before a sponsor can even begin human testing, it must submit for the FDA's approval an investigational new drug application ("IND") containing detailed information establishing that human testing is appropriate. Once the application for human testing has been approved, several phases of clinical testing begin. The Alliance's amended complaint alleges that this testing process is an extremely lengthy one, requiring nearly seven years for the average experimental [or "investigational"] drug.

Clinical testing for safety and effectiveness requires three or sometimes four phases. See 21 C.F.R. §312.21. Phase I involves the initial introduction of a new drug into human subjects. A Phase I study usually consists of twenty to eighty subjects and is "designed to determine the metabolism and pharmacologic actions of the [new] drug in humans, the side effects associated with increasing doses, and, if possible, to gain early evidence on effectiveness." Although gathering data on effectiveness may be part of Phase I, its primary focus is to determine whether the drug is safe enough for continued human testing. See id. Phase II studies are "well controlled" and "closely monitored" clinical trials of no more than several hundred subjects, used to evaluate both the "effectiveness of the drug for a particular indication" and its "common short-term side effects and risks." Id. §312.21(b).

Phase III studies are expanded clinical trials of several hundred to several thousand subjects designed to "gather . . . additional information about effectiveness and safety that is needed to evaluate the overall benefit-risk relationship of the drug and to provide an adequate basis for physician labeling." At any time during the clinical trials, a drug sponsor is required to notify the FDA of "[a]ny adverse experience associated with the use of the drug that is both serious and unexpected," and the FDA may order a "clinical hold" halting the trials if it determines that safety concerns so warrant, id. §312.42. To guide the clinical testing process, Congress has directed the FDA to establish "[s]cientific advisory panels" to "provid[e] expert scientific advice and recommendations to the Secretary regarding a clinical investigation of a drug or the approval for marketing of a drug." . . .

Terminally ill patients need not, however, always await the results of the clinical testing process. The FDA and Congress have created several programs designed to provide early access to promising experimental drugs when warranted. For example, under the "treatment IND" program, the FDA may approve use of an investigational drug by patients not part of the clinical trials for the treatment of "serious or immediately life-threatening disease[s]" if there exists "no comparable or satisfactory alternative drug or other therapy." . . .*

B.

Concluding that the FDA's current process for early access to new drugs was inadequate to meet the needs of its terminally ill members, the Alliance submitted its own proposals to the FDA. Those proposals culminated in a "citizen petition" to the FDA, arguing that there is a "different risk-benefit tradeoff facing patients who are terminally ill and who have no other treatment options." . . . Having thus been rejected by the FDA, the Alliance turned to the courts, arguing that the United States Constitution provides a right of access to experimental drugs for its members. In a complaint that mirrored much of its earlier submissions to the FDA, the Alliance argued that the FDA's lengthy clinical trials, combined with the "FDA's restrictions on pre-approval availability[,] amount to a death sentence for these

---

* [The Court cited proposed regulations now codified as amended at 21 C.F.R. §312.300-.320. — Eds.]

[terminally ill] patients." Nor, the Alliance argues, are the FDA's exceptions to the clinical testing process sufficient to provide the terminally ill the access they need because they "are small, when they exist at all," and the ban on profits prevents many drug sponsors from participating.

"Terminally ill patients," in the Alliance's view, "are typically willing to assume risks. . . ." Before the district court, the Alliance argued that the Constitution guarantees them the right to do so. The district court rejected that argument, holding that "there is no constitutional right of access to unapproved drugs." A divided panel of this Court reversed, concluding that "where there are no alternative government-approved treatment options, a terminally ill, mentally competent adult patient's informed access to potentially life-saving investigational new drugs determined by the FDA after Phase I trials to be sufficiently safe for expanded human trials warrants protection under the Due Process Clause." Abigail Alliance for Better Access to Developmental Drugs v. von Eschenbach, 445 F.3d 470, 486 (D.C. Cir. 2006). We vacated that decision and granted rehearing en banc.

As framed by the Alliance, we now consider:

> Whether the liberty protected by the Due Process Clause embraces the right of a terminally ill patient with no remaining approved treatment options to decide, in consultation with his or her own doctor, whether to seek access to investigational medications that the [FDA] concedes are safe and promising enough for substantial human testing.

Appellants' Br. at 1.[5] That is, we must determine whether terminally ill patients have a fundamental right to experimental drugs that have passed Phase I clinical testing. If such a right exists, the Alliance argues that both 21 C.F.R. §312.34(b)(3) (preventing access to experimental drugs for terminally ill patients where there is insufficient evidence of effectiveness or where there is an unreasonable risk of injury) and 21 C.F.R. §312.7 (prohibiting drug manufacturers from profiting on the sale of experimental drugs) must be subjected to strict scrutiny because they interfere

---

5. The dissent has recast the Alliance's proposed right away from the terms used in its briefs and oral argument—a right to access investigational new drugs—into a right "to try to save one's life," which has "its textual anchor in the right to life [expressed in the Fifth Amendment]." Dissent at 714-15. Regardless of how it is described, we must examine the proposed right under *Glucksberg*, which specifically cautions against the type of broad generalization the dissent now employs. See *Glucksberg*, 521 U.S. at 721 (requiring a " 'careful description' of the asserted fundamental liberty interest"). If the asserted right is so broad that it protects a person's efforts to save his life, it might subject to strict scrutiny any government action that would affect the means by which he sought to do so, no matter how remote the chance of success. The Supreme Court rejected a similar attempt to broadly define the right at issue in . . . Reno v. Flores, 507 U.S. 292, 302 (1993). The dissent suffers from the same flaw in arguing that this is about the right to save one's life, because, in the end, this case is about the right to access experimental and unproven drugs in an attempt to save one's life, which we conclude under *Glucksberg* is not deeply rooted in our Nation's history and traditions. By describing too broadly at the outset a proposed right that will cover the Alliance's more narrow claim, the dissent fails *Glucksberg*'s threshold requirement of a carefully described right. We need not pursue the arguments that follow that initial misstep.

with a fundamental constitutional right. We do not address the broader question of whether access to medicine might ever implicate fundamental rights.

II.

The Due Process Clause of the Fifth Amendment provides that "[n]o person shall be . . . deprived of life, liberty, or property, without due process of law." U.S. CONST. amend. V. The Supreme Court has held that the protections of the Amendment "guarantee[ ] more than fair process." *Glucksberg*, 521 U.S. at 719. The Court has stated that "[t]he Clause . . . provides heightened protection against government interference with certain fundamental rights and liberty interests," (citing Planned Parenthood of Se. Pa. v. Casey, 505 U.S. 833, 851 (1992)), including "the rights to marry, to have children, to direct the education and upbringing of one's children, to marital privacy, to use contraception, to bodily integrity, and to abortion," *Glucksberg*, 521 U.S. at 720.

As such rights are not set forth in the language of the Constitution, the Supreme Court has cautioned against expanding the substantive rights protected by the Due Process Clause "because guideposts for responsible decisionmaking in this unchartered area are scarce and open-ended." Collins v. Harker Heights, 503 U.S. 115, 125 (1992). There is an additional and substantial concern that courts must also consider: "By extending constitutional protection to an asserted right or liberty interest, we, to a great extent, place the matter outside the arena of public debate and legislative action." *Glucksberg*, 521 U.S. at 720. Thus, the Supreme Court has directed courts to "exercise the utmost care whenever we are asked to break new ground in this field, lest the liberty protected by the Due Process Clause be subtly transformed into the policy preferences of the [courts' members]." Id. (and citing "history of the *Lochner* era").

In *Glucksberg*, the Supreme Court described its "established method of substantive-due-process analysis" as having "two primary features."

> First, we have regularly observed that the Due Process Clause specially protects those fundamental rights and liberties which are, objectively, deeply rooted in this Nation's history and tradition and implicit in the concept of ordered liberty, such that neither liberty nor justice would exist if they were sacrificed. Second, we have required in substantive-due-process cases a careful description of the asserted fundamental liberty interest.

We will assume arguendo that the Alliance's description of its asserted right would satisfy *Glucksberg*'s "careful description" requirement.[6] Looking to whether the Alliance has demonstrated that its right is deeply rooted in this Nation's history, tradition, and practices, the Alliance's claim for constitutional protection rests on two arguments: (1) that "common law and historical American practices have tradi-

---

6. We nonetheless have serious doubt about whether the Alliance's description of its proposed constitutional right could ever pass constitutional muster. The Alliance's claimed right depends on a regulatory determination that the drug is safe for testing, prompting an obvious question: How can a constitutional right be defined by an administrative regulation that is subject to change?

tionally trusted individual doctors and their patients with almost complete autonomy to evaluate the efficacy of medical treatments"; and (2) that FDA policy is "inconsistent with the way that our legal tradition treats persons in all other life-threatening situations." More specifically, the Alliance argues that the concepts of self-defense, necessity, and interference with rescue are broad enough to demonstrate the existence of the fundamental right they seek—a right for "persons in mortal peril" to "try to save their own lives, even if the chosen means would otherwise be illegal or involve enormous risks."

. . . The Alliance argues that its right can be found in our history and legal traditions because "the government never interfered with the judgment of individual doctors about the medical efficacy of particular drugs until 1962," i.e., when major amendments were made to the Food, Drug, and Cosmetic Act. Appellants' Br. at 44. . . . The Alliance has little to say, however, about our Nation's history of regulating the safety of drugs. The Alliance's effort to focus on efficacy regulation ignores one simple fact: it is unlawful for the Alliance to procure experimental drugs not only because they have not been proven effective, but because they have not been proven safe. Although the Alliance contends that it only wants drugs that "are safe and promising enough for substantial human testing," i.e., drugs that have passed Phase I testing, current law bans access to an experimental drug on safety grounds until it has successfully completed all phases of testing. . . . Thus, to succeed on its claim of a fundamental right of access for the terminally ill to experimental drugs, the Alliance must show not only that there is a tradition of access to drugs that have not yet been proven effective, but also a tradition of access to drugs that have not yet been proven safe.

. . . [W]e conclude that our Nation has long expressed interest in drug regulation, calibrating its response in terms of the capabilities to determine the risks associated with both drug safety and efficacy. Drug regulation in the United States began with the Colonies and States when the Colony of Virginia's legislature passed an act in 1736 that addressed the dispensing of more drugs than was "necessary or useful" because that practice had become "dangerous and intolerable." Edward Kremers, Kremers and Urdang's History of Pharmacy 158 (4th ed. 1976). . . .

Nor were the States the only regulators of access to drugs. Although early federal regulation was not extensive, perhaps because "[n]ot until interstate commerce began its great expansion after the Civil War did the need for Federal rule-making become widely realized," Wallace F. Janssen, Outline of the History of U.S. Drug Regulation and Labeling, 36 Food Drug Cosm. L.J. 420, 425 (1981), there are early examples of federal government intervention. In 1848, the Import Drug Act, ch. 70, 9 Stat. 237 (1848), banned "imported adulterated drugs" after a congressional committee concluded that "this country had become the grand mart and receptacle of all the refuse [drug] merchandise . . . , not only from the European warehouses, but from the whole Eastern world." Wesley J. Heath, America's First Drug Regulation Regime: The Rise and Fall of the Import Drug Act of 1848, 59 Food & Drug L.J. 169, 175 (2004).

The current regime of federal drug regulation began to take shape with the Food, Drug, and Cosmetic Act of 1938, 21 U.S.C. §301 et seq. The Act required that drug manufacturers provide proof that their products were safe before they could be marketed. . . . We end our historical analysis where the Alliance would prefer it begin—with the 1962 Amendments to the FDCA. Undoubtedly, as the Alliance argues at length, Congress amended the FDCA in 1962 to explicitly require that the FDA only approve drugs deemed effective for public use. Thus, the Alliance argues that, prior to 1962, patients were free to make their own decisions whether a drug might be effective. But even assuming arguendo that efficacy regulation began in 1962, the Alliance's argument ignores our Nation's history of drug safety regulation. . . .

Nor can the Alliance override current FDA regulations simply by insisting that drugs which have completed Phase I testing are safe enough for terminally ill patients. Current law bars public access to drugs undergoing clinical testing on safety grounds. The fact that a drug has emerged from Phase I with a determination that it is safe for limited clinical testing in a controlled and closely-monitored environment after detailed scrutiny of each trial participant does not mean that a drug is safe for use beyond supervised trials.[11] FDA regulation of post-Phase I drugs is entirely consistent with our historical tradition of prohibiting the sale of unsafe drugs.

But even setting the safety issue to one side, . . . an arguably limited history of efficacy regulation prior to 1962 does not establish a fundamental right of access to unproven drugs. The amendments made to the FDCA by Congress throughout the twentieth century demonstrate that Congress and the FDA have continually responded to new risks presented by an evolving technology. Recent government efficacy regulation has reflected Congress's exercise of its well-established power to regulate in response to scientific, mathematical, and medical advances [such as the development of clinical trials during and after WW II]. . . . [C]reating constitutional rights to be free from regulation based solely upon a prior lack of regulation would undermine much of the modern administrative state, which, like drug regulation, has increased in scope as changing conditions have warranted. . . .[17]

Although it has not addressed the precise constitutional argument urged by the Alliance, we find it highly significant that the Supreme Court has rejected several similar challenges to the FDCA and related laws brought on statutory grounds. See, e.g., United States v. Rutherford, 442 U.S. 544, 552, (1979) ("we are persuaded by the legislative history and consistent administrative interpretation of the [FDCA] that no implicit exemption for drugs used by the terminally ill is necessary to attain congressional objectives"). And other courts have rejected arguments that the Constitution provides an affirmative right of access to particular medical treatments reasonably prohibited by the Government [citing, e.g., Mitchell v. Clayton, 995 F.2d 772, 775 (7th Cir. 1993) ("most federal courts have held that a patient does not have a constitutional right to obtain a particular type of treatment or to obtain treatment from a particular provider if the government has reasonably prohibited that type of treatment or provider")]. In keeping with those decisions, we conclude that the Alliance has not provided evidence of a right to procure and use experimental

11. In fact, the FDA cites numerous examples in which drugs have been pulled from the market post-Phase I due to safety concerns.

17. . . . The Alliance can, of course, advocate its position vigorously before Congress and the FDA, and convince our Nation's democratic branches that the values the Alliance favors should be protected. In fact, within the last year, the political branches have responded to the concerns of the Alliance and others. The FDA recently issued a notice of proposed rulemaking [which resulted in the expansion of access to investigational new drugs for seriously ill patients outside of formal clinical trials, see 21 C.F.R. §312.300-.320].

drugs that is deeply rooted in our Nation's history and traditions. To the contrary, our Nation's history evidences increasing regulation of drugs as both the ability of government to address these risks has increased and the risks associated with drugs have become apparent. . .[19]

IV.

Because the Alliance's claimed right is not fundamental, the Alliance's claim of a right of access to experimental drugs is subject only to rational basis scrutiny. . . . [W]e cannot say that the government's interest does not bear a rational relation to a legitimate state interest. That conclusion is compelled by the Supreme Court's decision in United States v. Rutherford, 442 U.S. 544 (1979). In that case, terminally ill patients sought to prevent the FDA from prohibiting access to the drug laetrile, even though the drug had not been approved for public use. In rejecting a challenge by terminally ill patients claiming that the FDCA's safety requirement did not apply to them, the Supreme Court held that "[f]or the terminally ill, as for anyone else, a drug is unsafe if its potential for inflicting death or physical injury is not offset by the possibility of therapeutic benefit." See also id. at 558 (noting that history has demonstrated that numerous "resourceful entrepreneurs" might try to take advantage of an unregulated market, which "suggest[s] why Congress could reasonably have determined to protect the terminally ill, no less than other patients, from the vast range of self-styled panaceas that inventive minds can devise").

Although terminally ill patients desperately need curative treatments, as *Rutherford* holds, their deaths can certainly be hastened by the use of a potentially toxic drug with no proven therapeutic benefit. Thus, we must conclude that, prior to distribution of a drug outside of controlled studies, the Government has a rational basis for ensuring that there is a scientifically and medically acceptable level of knowledge about the risks and benefits of such a drug. We therefore hold that the FDA's policy of limiting access to investigational drugs is rationally related to the legitimate state interest of protecting patients, including the terminally ill, from potentially unsafe drugs with unknown therapeutic effects. . . .

Our Nation's history and traditions have consistently demonstrated that the democratic branches are better suited to decide the proper balance between the uncertain risks and benefits of medical technology, and are entitled to deference in doing so. . . . Jacobson v. Massachusetts, 197 U.S. 11, 30 (1905); see also Gonzales v. Carhart, 550 U.S. 124 (2007). Consistent with that precedent, our holding today

---

19. As there exists no deeply rooted right, . . . we need not and do not address all of the Alliance's arguments regarding whether their proposed right is implicit in our Nation's system of ordered liberty, [but] we note a crucial difference between this case and one of the cases relied upon by the Alliance in making that argument, Cruzan v. Director, Mo. Dep't of Health, 497 U.S. 261 (1990). . . . Looking to *Cruzan*, the Alliance argues that "[i]f a patient has a fundamental right to medical self-determination that gives them the right to starve themselves to death, then surely they have a right to choose to fight for their lives even if that means taking a drug that has not yet met the FDA's full approval standards." . . . But a tradition protecting individual freedom from life-saving, but forced, medical treatment does not evidence a constitutional tradition of providing affirmative access to a potentially harmful, and even fatal, commercial good.

ensures that this debate among the Alliance, the FDA, the scientific and medical communities, and the public may continue through the democratic process.

ROGERS, Circuit Judge, with whom Chief Judge GINSBURG joins, dissenting:

Today, the court rejects the claim that terminally ill patients who have exhausted all government-approved treatment options have a fundamental right to access investigational new drugs. The court's opinion reflects a flawed conception of the right claimed by the Abigail Alliance for Better Access to Developmental Drugs and a stunning misunderstanding of the stakes. The court shifts the inquiry required by Washington v. Glucksberg, 521 U.S. 702 (1997), by changing the nature of the right, by conflating the right with the deprivation, and by prematurely advancing countervailing government interests. The court fails to come to grips with the Nation's history and traditions, which reflect deep respect and protection for the right to preserve life, a corollary to the right to life enshrined in the Constitution. The court confuses this liberty interest with the manner in which the Alliance alleges that the liberty has been deprived, namely by denying terminally ill patients access to investigational medications under the narrow conditions described by the Alliance. The court conflates the inquiry as to whether a fundamental right exists at all with whether the government has demonstrated a compelling interest, when strictly scrutinized, rendering its restrictive policy constitutional.

These missteps lead the court to rely upon how rights and liberties have been limited and restricted—addressing regulations to prevent fraud in the sale of mis-branded and adulterated medications or safety restrictions applicable to all medi-cines for any palliative purpose—which says little about the historic importance of the underlying right of a person to save her own life. . . . The common law doctrines [of necessity and self defense] remain good evidence of a history and tradition of protecting life and attempts to preserve life as a deep-seated personal right. That the right may be and has been denied in the face of compelling governmental interests is no reason for conflating the two stages of the analysis and looking only to the results of past cases in order to avoid the analysis prescribed by the Supreme Court in *Glucksberg*. . . .

In the end, it is startling that the oft-limited rights to marry, to fornicate, to have children, to control the education and upbringing of children, to perform varied sexual acts in private, and to control one's own body even if it results in one's own death or the death of a fetus have all been deemed fundamental rights covered, although not always protected, by the Due Process Clause, but the right to try to save one's life is left out in the cold despite its textual anchor in the right to life. This alone is reason the court should pause about refusing to put the FDA to its proof when it denies terminal patients with no alternative therapy the only option they have left, regardless of whether that option may be a long-shot with high risks. The court is on even weaker footing when it relies upon the risks entailed in med-ical procedures to wrest life-and-death decisions that once were vested in patients and their physicians. The court commits a logical error of dramatic consequence by concluding that the investigational drugs are somehow not "necessary." While the potential cures may not prove sufficient to save the life of a terminally ill patient, they are surely necessary if there is to be any possibility of preserving her life. . . .

[T]he history and traditions of this Nation support the right of a terminal patient, and not the government, to make this fundamentally personal choice involving her own life. Because judicial precedents and the historical record require strict scrutiny before upsetting rights of this magnitude, the FDA must demonstrate a compelling governmental interest before its policy restricting access can survive. Accordingly, I would remand the case to the district court to make the initial determination as to whether FDA has met its burden, and I respectfully dissent.

Notes: The Scope and Constitutionality of Pharmaceutical Regulation

1. *Federal and State Regulation of Pharmaceuticals.* The federal government has enacted a complex web of food, drug, and medical device regulations under the federal authority to regulate interstate commerce. The power to regulate interstate commerce includes the power to regulate commerce to protect public health. Federal law preempts many state law claims. See, e.g., Patricia J. Zettler, Pharmaceutical Federalism, 92 Ind. L.J. 845 (2017). The regulation of drugs and medical devices is complex and detailed. See generally David G. Adams et al. eds., Food and Drug Law and Regulation (3d ed. 2015); and FDA in the Twenty-First Century (Holly Fernandez Lynch & I. Glenn Cohen eds., 2015). The Food and Drug Law Institute offers programs and resources at www.fdli.org. The discussion here will focus on the intersection between the regulation of drugs and individual access to therapy.

2. *The Drug Approval Process and Access to Experimental Therapies.* As noted in *Abigail Alliance*, new drugs must go through at least three phases of drug trials to be proven to be "safe" and "effective" in treating a particular condition. 21 U.S.C. §355; 21 C.F.R. §312.21. The fourth phase of drug trials alluded to in the opinion is the post-market surveillance trial, which is used to identify any safety or efficacy issues related to drugs across a broader population sample. See Anna B. Laakman, Collapsing the Distinction Between Experimentation and Treatment in the Regulation of New Drugs, 62 Ala. L. Rev. 305, 337-341 (2011).

Under current federal regulations, patients with serious or life-threatening illnesses may be given access to certain types of investigational new drugs under some circumstances. Regulations designed to enhance access to investigational drugs for treatment purposes, noted by the *Abigail* court, are now codified at 21 C.F.R. §312.300-320. These regulations apply to persons with life-threatening diseases or serious diseases or conditions "associated with morbidity that ha[ve] substantial impact on day-to-day functioning. . . . Whether a disease or condition is serious is . . . based on its impact on such factors as survival, day-to-day functioning, or the likelihood that the disease, if left untreated, will progress from a less severe condition to a more serious one." Id. at §312.300.

Access to investigational drugs under the regulations depends in part on a determination that there are no other treatment options, that the patient benefits outweigh the risks, and that "[p]roviding the investigational drug for the requested use will not interfere with the initiation, conduct, or completion of clinical investigations that could support marketing approval of the expanded access use or otherwise compromise the potential development of the expanded access use." 21 C.F.R. §312.305(a). Is there any constitutional problem with a regulatory regime that explicitly subordinates the needs of individual patients to the "greater good" that can result from the completion of clinical trials? See Jonathan J. Darrow et. al.,

Practical, Legal, and Ethical Issues in Expanded Access to Investigational Drugs, 372 N. Eng. J. Med. 279 (2015) (considering a number of issues, including impact of expanded access on clinical trials). If the *Abigail* plaintiffs had succeeded, would the need to preserve clinical trials have provided the compelling justification required to uphold the regulations in strict scrutiny review? Would this rationale apply to patients who are ineligible for clinical trials, who therefore could not be deterred from participating? See Abigail R. Moncrieff, The Freedom of Health, 159 U. Pa. L. Rev. 2209, 2243-2245 (2011). The FDA reports that 99 percent of applications for access are accepted but patients nonetheless may not be able to secure access to the drug from the manufacturer. Could patients bring claims against drug companies demanding participation in these alternative access schemes? See Cacchillo v. Insmed, 551 Fed. Appx. 592 (2d Cir. 2014) (affirming summary judgment for company).

  3. *Legislative Success for "The Right to Try."* As noted in *Abigail*, the U.S. Supreme Court had not yet directly ruled on whether terminally ill patients had any constitutionally protected right to access unapproved potential therapies. The *Rutherford* decision cited in the opinion is almost solely concerned with the issue of whether the FDA's statutorily granted power to regulate the safety and effectiveness of drugs could be applied to drugs used to treat terminal conditions. On remand from the Supreme Court decision, the Tenth Circuit confronted and rejected the constitutional claim, holding that "the decision by the patient whether to have a treatment or not is a protected right, but his selection of a particular treatment, or at least a medication, is within the area of governmental interest in protecting public health." Rutherford v. United States, 616 F.2d 455, 457 (10th Cir. 1980).

  The issue dramatically reemerged with the D.C. Circuit panel's initial decision in *Abigail Alliance*, 445 F.3d 470 (2006), which the decision above reversed en banc. The initial D.C. Circuit panel decision found that:

> where there are no alternative government-approved treatment options, a terminally ill, mentally competent adult patient's informed access to potentially life-saving investigational new drugs determined by the FDA after Phase I trials to be sufficiently safe for expanded human trials warrants protection under the Due Process Clause. The prerogative asserted by the FDA—to prevent a terminally ill patient from using potentially life-saving medication to which those in Phase II clinical trials have access—thus impinges upon an individual liberty deeply rooted in our Nation's history and tradition of self-preservation. . . . [W]e remand the case . . . to determine whether the FDA's policy . . . is narrowly tailored to serve a compelling governmental interest.

Id. at 486. Is restricting access to potential treatments for terminally ill patients consistent with the jurisprudence governing the termination of life-sustaining treatment? With case law on a woman's right to choose abortion? For more on the right to self-preservation, see Eugene Volokh, Medical Self-Defense, Prohibited Experimental Therapies, and Payment for Organs, 120 Harv. L. Rev. 1813 (2007).

  The fight for access moved to the legislatures. The libertarian Goldwater Institute developed "Right to Try" model legislation authorizing manufacturers to provide terminally ill patients with investigational drugs, biological products, or devices that had completed phase 1 of the clinical trial process. The model legislation requires physician certification of the patient's medical condition and the need for the unproven therapy. Patients are to provide informed consent. Manufacturers may choose whether to provide the therapy and whether to recover any costs. "Right to Try" legislation has now been adopted in 37 states. Richard Cauchi, State Laws and Legislation Related to Biologic Medications and Substitution of Biosimilars, National Conference of State Legislatures, available at: www.ncsl.org (as of September 2017). Do states have authority to legislate in this area? Rebecca Dresser, "Right to Try" Laws: The Gap between Experts and Advocates, 45(3) Hastings Center Report 9 (May–June 2015). Would the patient's informed consent preclude subsequent liability claims against the manufacturer? "Right to Try" legislation passed the U.S. Senate in August of 2017, and it was under consideration in the House as of October 2017. The federal bill includes measures designed to encourage manufacturers to participate. Robert Pear & Sheila Kaplan, Senate Passes F.D.A. Funding and 'Right to Try' Drug Bills, N.Y. Times, Aug. 3, 2017.

4. *The FDA and Drug Development Efforts.* The FDA has been criticized for unnecessary delays in the approval of important drugs. The laetrile dispute in the 1970s paved the way for vigorous protests by HIV/AIDS activists in the 1980s and 1990s. Lewis A. Grossman, AIDS Activists, FDA Regulation, and the Amendment of America's Drug Constitution, 42 Am. J.L. & Med. 687 (2016). Congress sought to speed up the development of new drugs by providing additional incentives to pharmaceutical firms. Under the Orphan Drug Act, Pub. L. No. 97-414, 96 Stat. 2049 (1983), as amended, those companies are encouraged to develop and market drugs for rare illnesses, where the relatively small number of persons affected might otherwise not constitute a sufficient market to sustain the research and development costs of providing treatment. See also 21 C.F.R. §316.1-.40. The court in *Abigail* cites the "Fast Track" program, designed to provide access to "drugs intended to treat life-threatening and severely-debilitating illnesses." Congress has since approved a number of additional programs designed to speed FDA review of various therapies. See e.g., Veronica S. Jae, Simplifying FDASIA: The "Fast Track" to Expedited Drug Approval Efficiency, 66 Admin L. Rev. 173 (2014) (discussing new "Breakthrough Therapies" program); Aaron S. Kesselheim & Jerry Avorn, New "21st Century Cures" Legislation: Speed and Ease vs. Science, 317 JAMA 581 (2017) (expressing concern about new legislation designed to reduce perceived barriers in drug approval process and to spur expedited review for regenerative therapies, such as those using human stem cells).

Any effort to speed up the approval of new drugs inevitably creates the risk that truncated studies and review will result in the release of drugs with unknown hazards and uncertain effectiveness. The ongoing debate focuses on whether the reform of the drug approval process has gone too far or not far enough in providing consumers with access to safe and effective drugs. Data from the FDA's postmarket surveillance process indicates that 32 percent of the "222 novel therapeutics approved by the FDA from 2001 through 2010 . . . were affected by a postmarket safety event." Nicholas S. Downing et al., Postmarket Safety Events Among Novel Therapeutics Approved by the US Food and Drug Administration Between 2001 and 2010, 317 JAMA 1854 (2017). Does this help to resolve the debate, one way or another?

5. *Drug Labeling, "Off-Label Use," and the Learned Intermediary Doctrine.* Under the regulatory policy of the FDA, each prescription drug carries a package-insert label with quite elaborate information on the methods of administering the drug,

conditions for which the drug is recommended, as well as warnings about contraindications for use and about known dangers and side effects. As discussed in Chapter 4, the package inserts have considerable, although not totally controlling, influence over the proper standard of accepted patient care related to the drug. Physicians may, and often do, prescribe drugs for "off-label" uses, although there has been controversy in recent years about physician discretion in this area. See, e.g., Wendy Teo, FDA and the Practice of Medicine: Looking at Off-Label Drugs, 41 Seton Hall Legis. J. 305 (2017) (discussing the FDA's deferential approach).

Should drug manufacturers be permitted to disseminate information about off-label uses to physicians? The FDA initially took the view that these communications should be severely restricted to prevent circumvention of the labeling process. Drug company off-label marketing practices generated significant litigation and very significant judgments moving into the early 2010s. For a sampling of parties and theories, see, e.g., Gardiner Harris, Pfizer Pays $2.3 Billion to Settle Marketing Case, N.Y. Times, Sept. 3, 2009; Krumplebeck v. Breg, Inc., 2012 WL 3241587 (6th Cir.) (analyzing possible liability claims related to off-label marketing in context of medical device); Thomas M. Greene, A New Weapon in Pharma Cases, Trial 40 (Nov. 2011) (RICO).

The FDA's rules restrict the freedom of drug companies to express their views. The Supreme Court historically applied low-level scrutiny to governmental regulation of commercial speech. However, in Sorrell v. IMS Health, 564 U.S. 552 (2011), the Court invalidated Vermont legislation restricting sale and disclosure of physician prescribing behavior under the First Amendment. The decision suggested that the Court might apply some form of heightened scrutiny to regulations restricting commercial speech, including the flow of information to physicians and to patients. See Symposium, Marketing Health: The Growing Role of Commercial Speech Doctrine in FDA Regulation, 37 Am. J.L. & Med. 203-421 (2011); Symposium, Commercial Speech and Public Health, 21 Health Matrix 1-230 (2011). In U.S. v. Caronia, a pharmaceutical sales consultant had been recorded speaking with physician-customers about off-label uses of a drug. He was convicted of conspiracy to introduce a misbranded drug into interstate commerce. The conviction was overturned by the Second Circuit, which held that "the FDA cannot prosecute pharmaceutical manufacturers and their representatives under the FDCA [Food, Drug, and Cosmetic Act] for speech promoting the lawful, off-label use of an FDA-approved drug." 703 F.3d 149, 168-169 (2d Cir. 2012). A New York district court subsequently held in another case that the "FDA could not prevent promotion of a drug for an unapproved use if a manufacturer's promotional statements are 'truthful.'" Jerry Avorn, Ameet Sarpatwari & Aaron S. Kesselheim, Forbidden and Permitted Statements about Medications—Loosening the Rules, 373 N. Eng. J. Med. 967 (2015) (discussing Amarin case, conflicting precedents and more permissive FDA policies). Could the FDA justify a restriction on truthful speech between manufacturers and physicians? Christopher Robertson & Aaron Kesselheim, Regulating Off-Label Promotion—A Critical Test, 375 N. Eng. J. Med. 2313 (2016) (arguing that Caronia approach should be rejected by courts and the FDA). If truthfulness is the standard, who should have the burden of proof?

6. *Direct to Consumer (DTC) Advertising.* In the prescription drug field, the courts have quite uniformly accepted the package-insert warnings to physicians as meeting the drug manufacturers' legal obligation. As discussed in Chapter 4, the

physician is expected to be a "learned intermediary" between the company and the patient in protecting the patient and in providing direct information about the drug to the patient. The retail pharmacist is also a source of advice for drug consumers. These assumptions have been shaken somewhat by the expansion of direct-to-consumer (DTC) advertising by pharmaceutical companies. See Prescription-Drug Advertisements, 21 C.F.R. §202.1; and Christopher T. Robertson, New DTCA Guidance—Enough to Empower Consumers?, 373 N. Eng. J. Med. 1085 (2015). The potential for state law claims, using tort or other theories, is limited by the ability of defendants to argue that state claims are preempted by federal law. Compare Pliva v. Mensing, 565 U.S. 604 (2011) (state warning claim preempted by federal law governing generic drugs when impossible for manufacturer to comply with both state and federal warning requirements), with Wyeth v. Levine, 555 U.S. 555 (2009) (state failure to warn claim not preempted by FDA labeling rule for non-generic drug where manufacturer could comply with both). Could greater public access to drug trial data benefit consumers? Aaron S. Kesselheim & Michelle M. Mello, Confidentiality Laws and Secrecy in Medical Research: Improving Public Access to Data on Drug Safety, 26 Health Aff. 483 (2007); and Kevin Outterson, Clinical Trial Transparency—Antidote to Weaker Off-Label-Promotion Rules?, 371 N. Eng. J. Med. 1 (2014)

a. *The FDA and New Regulatory Challenges: From Tobacco to Medical Apps.* The FDA's regulatory activities frequently generate controversy. Some critics lambaste the agency for its ties to industry and alleged failure to safeguard citizens, while others lament the agency's aggressive regulatory stance and its alleged stifling of innovation. The debate can be seen in the FDA's approach to tobacco, nutritional supplements, genetic tests, and medical apps.

a) *Tobacco.* One major controversy, involving the agency's attempt to regulate tobacco, resulted in legislation in 2009 giving the FDA the power to regulate tobacco products. See Lawrence Deyton et al., Tobacco Product Regulation—A Public Health Approach, 362 New Eng. J. Med. 1753 (2010) (Family Smoking Prevention and Tobacco Control Act, 21 U.S.C. §§387-387u). There was a setback when one early initiative under the Act—an effort to require graphic warnings on cigarette packages—was found to violate the First Amendment. Eric N. Lindblom, Micah L. Berman & James F. Thrasher, FDA-Required Tobacco Product Inserts & Onserts—And the First Amendment, 72 Food & Drug L.J. 1 (2017) (discussing caselaw and making recommendations for additional action). Researchers have expressed concerns that e-cigarettes could fuel continuing and perhaps even expanding addiction to nicotine. See, Amy L. Fairchild, Ronald Bayer & James Colgove, The Renormalization of Smoking? E-Cigarettes and the Tobacco "Endgame," 370 N. Eng. J. Med. 293 (2014). The FDA moved to exert regulatory authority over all tobacco products, issuing a final rule that extended authority to e-cigarettes and other products in 2016. FDA, Deeming Tobacco Products to Be Subject to the Federal Food, Drug and Cosmetic Act, 81 Fed Reg. 28974-01 (May 10, 2016). This initiative was followed in 2017 by a new plan that would reduce the level of nicotine in cigarettes to levels that would no longer sustain addiction while encouraging development of alternative, safer products to deliver nicotine to consumers. Kenneth E. Warner & Steven A. Schroeder, FDA's Innovative Plan to Address the Enormous Toll of Smoking, 318 JAMA 1755 (2017). What are the benefits and risks of the plan to reduce nicotine in cigarettes?

b. *Dietary Supplements.* The regulation of dietary supplements has been controversial, in part because of industry claims that the supplements are more like food than they are like classic pharmaceuticals. The FDA's suggestion that it might regulate supplements as though they were drugs drew congressional action in the form of the Dietary Supplement Health and Education Act of 1994 (DSHEA). The DSHEA gives the FDA the authority to "regulate[] vitamins, minerals, herbs, amino acids, and other dietary substances. Dietary supplements are generally regulated in a manner similar to food and the FDA is authorized to prevent adulterated products from entering the market." Nutraceutical v. von Eschenbach, 459 F.3d 1033, 1035 (2006) (interpreting DSHEA; upholding FDA ban on ephedrine-alkaloid dietary supplements). A dietary supplement is adulterated if it "presents a significant or unreasonable risk of illness or injury" under suggested or ordinary use. 21 U.S.C. §342(f)(1). Nutritional supplements are also subject to adverse event reporting requirements. 21 U.S.C. §379aa-1. See generally GAO, Dietary Supplements: FDA Should Take Further Actions to Improve Oversight and Consumer Understanding (2009); Ranjani R. Starr, Too Little, Too Late: Ineffective Regulation of Dietary Supplements in the United States, 105 Amer. J. Public Health 478 (2015). As research continues to reveal the importance of the microbiome to health, should "probiotics" be regulated as food, drugs, dietary supplements, or within a different framework? See Diane E. Hoffmann et al., Probiotics: Achieving a Better Regulatory Fit, 69 Food & Drug L.J. 237 (2014).

c. *Genetic Tests.* The regulation of genetic tests is another area of controversy. The advances in genetics that made it possible to develop associations between certain genetic variants and potential health conditions raised a number of concerns for experts and policymakers. Was the information meaningful? Would efforts to market genetic testing and reporting confuse consumers about the utility of the results or would consumers be able to understand the serious limits to the information? Is it appropriate to offer consumers information about possible increased risk for serious conditions for which there is no treatment? Should the "consumers" be considered to be "patients" who required personalized counseling before and after the testing process? Should genetic tests be regulated as medical devices? Laboratory procedures and standards? Clinical practice? Ordinary consumer products? Consumer education? See GAO, Direct-to-Consumer Genetic Tests: Misleading Test Results Are Further Complicated by Deceptive Marketing and Other Questionable Practices (2010).

Genetic testing companies began marketing DTC genetic testing in the 2000s. The FDA announced in 2010 that it considered the DTC genetic tests to be medical devices and the genetic testing services to be medical interventions. Andrew Pollack, F.D.A. Faults Companies on Unapproved Genetic Tests, N.Y. Times, June 11, 2010. After failing to come to an agreement with the company, the FDA ordered 23andMe to discontinue offering its genetic analyses to consumers for a period of time. Andrew Pollack, FDA Orders Genetic Testing Firm to Stop Selling DNA Analysis Service, N.Y. Times, Nov. 25, 2013; Andrew Pollack, 23andMe Will Resume Giving Users Health Data, Oct. 21, 2015 (authorizing limited genetic testing for carrier status). The FDA authorized a broader range of genetic testing services in April 2017. Gina Kolata, F.D.A. Will Allow 23andMe to Sell Genetic Tests for Disease Risk to Consumers, N.Y. Times, Apr. 6, 2017 (authorizing testing that includes 10 disease risks for consumers). The FDA approval did not extend to "diagnostic" genetic testing: tests that are used to make clinical decisions, such as testing for BRCA. FDA, FDA Allows Marketing of First Direct-to-Consumer Tests That Provide Genetic Risk Information for Certain Conditions, April 6, 2017, available at: www.fda.gov (noting as well the specific regulatory pathways used to consider and approve the DTC genetic tests).

Take a few moments to look online for a genetic testing company. How does the company provide information about the nature of its genetic tests, the meaning of test results, the risks to individuals who may discover that they have a heightened risk for a serious, but currently untreatable, condition? Companies may use the information they collect to carry out additional research. Are consumers being given sufficient information about the commercial use of their health data? See Jennifer Abbasi, 23andMe, Big Data, and the Genetics of Depression, 317 JAMA 14 (2017); J. Scott Roberts et al., Direct-to-Consumer Genetic Testing, 20 Public Health Genomics 36 (2017) (2 percent of surveyed DTC genetic testing consumers reported regret about seeking testing; 1 percent reported harm from results).

d. *Medical "Apps."* How should the FDA respond to the plethora of health-related applications for mobile phones and the development of fitness-related wearables from watches to clothing? These developments—sometimes called "mobile health" or "mhealth"—can provide greater access to health-related information and personal data for billions of people. The FDA issued guidance to industry in 2013, indicating that it would regulate these developments as medical devices but that it would focus its regulatory attention on "apps that present greater risk to patients if they don't work as intended and on apps that cause smartphones or other mobile platforms to impact the functionality or performance of traditional medical devices." FDA, Mobile Medical Applications, available at www.fda.gov/. The regulatory structure is in flux, with multiple studies, legislative, and regulatory proposals, many of which have been focused more on loosening regulatory oversight than on "creating a regulatory framework that encourages high-value innovation while also preventing the market from being overcome with products that are ineffective or unsafe." Nathan G. Cortez, I. Glenn Cohen & Aaron S. Kesselheim, FDA Regulation of Mobile Health Technologies, 371 N. Eng. J. Med. 372, 376 (2014) (comprehensive analysis of range of mhealth products, benefits and risks, and the regulatory response). See also, Sarah Duranske, This Article Makes You Smarter! (Or, Regulating Health and Wellness Claims), 43 Amer. J.L. & Med. 7 (2017) (noting importance of Federal Trade Commission (FTC) role in addressing false claims of health products). This is a rapidly evolving area that may transform aspects of our health care system in the years ahead.

8. *Additional Commentaries.* As noted above, there are numerous treatises, looseleaf services, journals, and commentaries focused on the **regulation of food, drugs, medical devices, biologics,** and so on (note 1). Some helpful sources include: Audrey L. Gassman, Christine P. Nguyen & Hylton V. Joffe, FDA Regulation of Prescription Drugs, 376 N. Eng. J. Med. 674 (2017); Kenneth R. Piña & Wayne L. Pines eds., A Practical Guide to Food and Drug Law and Regulation (5th ed. 2014). For more on the **drug approval process and access to experimental therapies** (note 2), see George Annas, Cancer and the Constitution, 357 New Eng. J. Med. 4 (2007); Richard Epstein, The Erosion of Individual Autonomy in Medical Decisionmaking: Of the FDA and IRBs, 96 Geo. L.J. 559 (2008); William M. Janssen, A "Duty" to Continue Selling Medicines, 40 Am. J.L. & Med. 330 (2014); Elizabeth Weeks Leonard,

Right to Experimental Treatment: FDA New Drug Approval, Constitutional Rights, and the Public's Health, 37 J.L. Med. & Ethics 269 (2009). For more on the **"right to try" and constitutional aspects** of pharmaceutical choice (note 3), see, e.g., Daniel Carpenter et al., Drug-Review Deadlines and Safety Problems, 358 New Eng. J. Med. 1354 (2008); Jennifer Couzin-Frankel & Yasmin Ogale, Once on "Fast Track," Avastin Now Derailed, 333 Science 143 (2011); Anna B. Laakman, Collapsing the Distinction Between Experimentation and Treatment in the Regulation of New Drugs, 62 Ala. L. Rev. 305, 337-341 (2011); and Special Section on "Right to Try," 51 Therapeutic Innovation and Regulatory Science 142-179 (2017). For more on the **FDA and the drug development** process (note 4), see FDA, The FDA's Drug Review Process, available at: www.fda.gov/Drugs/ResourcesForYou/Consumers/ucm143534.htm; and FDA, Fast Track, Breakthrough Therapy, Accelerated Approval, Priority Review www.fda.gov/forpatients/approvals/fast/default.htm. **Drug labeling, off-label use, and the learned intermediary doctrine** (note 5) are discussed in Chapter 4. For some additional resources about some of the risks of marketing, see Symposium, Institutional Corruption and the Pharmaceutical Industry, 41 J.L. Med. & Ethics 544-687 (2013). For more on the **Direct to Consumer** advertising (note 6), see FDA, Advertising Guidances, available at: https://www.fda.gov/Drugs/GuidanceCompliance-RegulatoryInformation/Guidances/ucm064956.htm; Jeremy A. Greene & David Herzberg, Hidden in Plain Sight: Marketing Prescription Drugs to Consumers in the Twentieth Century, 100 Am. J. Public Health 793 (2010) (tracing history of DTC advertising). There are a number of commentaries focused on the FDA's efforts relating to tobacco, dietary supplements, genetic tests, and medical applications: George J. Annas, 23andMe and the FDA, 370 N. Eng. J. Med. 985 (2014); Barbara J. Evans, The FDA and Genomic Tests—Getting Regulation Right, 372 N. Eng. J. Med. 2258 (2015); Scott Gottlieb & Mitchell Zeller, A Nicotine-Focused Framework for Public Health, 377 N. Eng. J. Med. 1111 (2017) (announcing initiative); Institute of Medicine, Dietary Supplements: A Framework for Evaluating Safety (2005); NIH, Regulation of Genetic Tests, available at: https://www.genome.gov/10002335/regulation-of-genetic-tests/ (providing overview of regulatory environment and initiatives through 2016); Lars Noah & Barbara Noah, A Drug by Any Other Name . . . ? Paradoxes in Dietary Supplement Risk Regulation, 17 Stan. L. & Pol'y Rev. 165 (2006); N. Sawicki, Compelling Images: The Constitutionality of Emotionally Persuasive Health Campaigns, 73 Md. L. Rev. 458 (2014); Kayte Spector-Bagdady, Reconceptualizing Consent for Direct-to-Consumer Health Services, 41 Amer. J. of L. & Med. 568 (2015); Symposium, 39 Amer. J.L. & Med. 199-489 (2013).

3

■

The Treatment Relationship: Confidentiality, Consent, and Conflicts of Interest

A. THE FIDUCIARY NATURE OF THE TREATMENT RELATIONSHIP

The interactions between healers and those hoping to be healed are complex. Science, sociology, and psychology all provide important perspectives on the rich character of these important relationships. As noted in Chapter 1.A.2 and the Somers & Somers excerpt at page 8, the experience of illness may include anxiety and physical distress that, combined with the patient's relative lack of knowledge, create a substantial power imbalance between the patient and her caregiver. Moreover, many aspects of the treatment relationship involve sensitive personal matters, ranging from one's weight to one's sexual history and mental health needs. This chapter initially explores the implications of these special vulnerabilities for the laws governing confidentiality of medical information, informed consent, and conflicts of interest. The final section of the chapter explores the implications of this power imbalance for the rules governing research on human subjects, where risks to participants may eventually result in advances in treatment.

Traditional contract and tort norms have been radically altered in many of these areas through the interventions of courts, legislatures, and administrative agencies. Courts have found protections for patients in the implied or expressed belief that the treatment relationship is a fiduciary one, in which physicians in particular, but perhaps some other providers as well, owe heightened duties to protect

163

the vulnerable patient's interests. This chapter explores the extent to which physicians have fiduciary obligations to their patients as well as the implications of those obligations. The chapter also examines when and how special protections for patients have been extended—often by legislation or regulation—beyond the physician-patient relationship to other health care providers and institutional actors.

Fiduciary law is not usually a topic of thorough study in the law school curriculum and it is worth considering its key elements before turning to legislative, regulatory, and judicial approaches to protecting patients' interests. As a common law doctrine, fiduciary law can be thought of as a separate source of distinct legal duties or as a legal status that heightens or alters ordinary contract and tort law duties. Fiduciary principles impose a special measure of loyalty and devotion on several classes of professionals (lawyers, trustees, and general agents) by virtue of their control over an important subject matter, the vulnerability of their clients and the resulting potential for abuse. The materials in Chapter 1.A.2 explain why some courts have found that "the relationship of patients and physicians is a fiduciary one of the highest degree. It involves every element of trust, confidence and good faith."[1] Doctors have a complex body of knowledge and skills that are critical to preserving the life and restoring the health of their patients. Doctors control their patients' welfare in the most vital aspects imaginable. Sick patients, by virtue of their debilitated and vulnerable state, are dependent on their physicians' judgments and actions. Accurate diagnosis requires patients to reveal the most personal details of their lives, and effective treatment often entails invasion of the most essential aspects of bodily intimacy, invading the very blood and guts of our integrated sense of self. Thus many legal decisions and commentators have recognized doctors' fiduciary status.[2] For a sampling of the literature, see Robert Gatter, Faith, Confidence, and Health Care: Fostering Trust in Medicine Through Law, 39 Wake Forest L. Rev. 395, 396 (2004); Thomas L. Hafemeister & Sarah P. Bryan, Beware Those Bearing Gifts: Physicians' Fiduciary Duty to Avoid Pharmaceutical Marketing, 57 U. Kan. L. Rev. 491 (2009); Mark A. Hall, Law, Medicine, and Trust, 55 Stan. L. Rev. 463 (2002); Dayna Bowen Matthew, Implementing American Health Care Reform: The Fiduciary Imperative, 59 Buff. L. Rev. 715 (2011); Maxwell J. Mehlman, Why Physicians Are Fiduciaries for Their Patients, 12 Ind. Health L.J. 1 (2015); and Marc A. Rodwin, Medicine, Money & Morals: Physicians' Conflicts of Interest (1993).

Classifying physicians as fiduciaries might appear to be a simple matter; it is much more difficult, however, to say precisely what obligations result. Fiduciary law is far from a seamless web. There is no integrated body of principles or precise doctrine that applies uniformly to all forms of fiduciary relationships.[3] Nonetheless,

---

1. Lockett v. Goodill, 430 P.2d 589, 591 (Wash. 1967).

2. Some authorities, however, distinguish confidential relations from fiduciary relations and declare that physicians are subject only to the former. See, e.g., Restatement (Third) of Trusts §2 *cmt b(1)* (2003); 1 Austin W. Scott & William F. Fratcher, The Law of Trusts §2.5, at 43 (4th ed. 1987). The primary thrust of the distinction, however, is one of burden of proof, not scope of obligation. The law does not assume that a position of trust exists in a confidential relation as quickly as it does in a fiduciary one, but where such trust exists, the duties are essentially the same.

3. See L. S. Sealy, Fiduciary Relationships, 1962 Cambridge L.J. 69, 73 (observing that labelling a relationship fiduciary "does not warrant the inference that any particular fiduciary

there are basic principles of fiduciary obligation that share a broad, familial resemblance across many categories of relationships. One of the common themes is a modification of the ordinary rules of contract. In a classic contractual relationship, neither party has a duty to maintain the secrecy of information provided by the other party, nor a duty to disclose information to the other about the qualities of the product or service sold or the particular needs of the purchaser. *Caveat emptor,* let the buyer beware, is the most common rule associated with classic contract law. Parties to the contract can impose additional obligations on each other only by bargaining for specific contract terms.

As noted in Chapter 2, courts have modified the ordinary contract regime by limiting the ability to alter or waive the basic standard of care or by limiting the ability to terminate the relationship. This chapter explains that courts have modified these pure contract principles to provide additional special protections for patients. Courts have used ordinary tort law as well as fiduciary law to achieve these protections, holding, for example, that physicians can be sued for damages if they fail to maintain patient confidences or to disclose important information about any proposed treatment. State and federal regulators also have responded to the special characteristics of the treatment relationship and the concomitant special duties of health care providers by enacting a wide range of statutes and regulations designed to protect patient confidentiality and to control conflicts of interest.

As you read the following materials, consider how well courts and legislatures have responded to the unique attributes and requirements of the doctor-patient relationship. Are the protections sufficient? Are they excessive or dysfunctional? Should federal or state law be used to address these concerns? When and how should similar obligations be imposed on other types of health care providers? Should similar rules be applied to facilities and institutions such as hospitals and HMOs?

B. CONFIDENTIALITY OF MEDICAL INFORMATION

Both patients and health care providers have long believed that the health care relationship creates a special duty on the part of the provider to protect the patient's interests. One example is the duty to protect the confidentiality of patient information, which was thought necessary to encourage patients to seek treatment and to disclose personal information fully and truthfully. The common belief that there was such a duty obscured a significant number of important legal questions. What is the source of the obligation? On whom is the duty imposed? What are the limits of the duty? What remedies are available for breaches of confidentiality? Does the system of legal protections effectively balance patient rights, provider duties, and social interests? Historically state courts and legislatures attempted to protect

---

principle or remedy can be applied"). For other works that address fiduciary principles at this more general level, see Paul D. Finn, Fiduciary Obligations 15-76 (1977); Tamar Frankel, Fiduciary Law, 71 Cal. L. Rev. 795, 808-816 (1983); Tamar Frankel, Fiduciary Duties as Default Rules, 74 Or. L. Rev. 1209 (1995); Philosophical Foundations of Fiduciary Law (Andrew S. Gold and Paul B. Miller eds. 2014); Marc Rodwin, Medicine, Money & Morals 179-211 (1993); Symposium, The Role of Fiduciary Law and Trust in the Twenty-First Century: A Conference Inspired by the Work of Tamar Frankel, 91 Boston U. L. Rev. 833-1299 (2011).

patients' interests in medical privacy by imposing duties to maintain confidentiality on individual health care providers, primarily physicians. There has been a sea change in the last 15 years, as the federal government has flooded the health care system with detailed regulations designed to protect patients' interests in controlling disclosure and use of their medical information. Yet federal regulations—even of the intense sort that will begin this chapter—have not totally displaced the importance of state laws, which in many cases still provide the best avenue for aggrieved patients to challenge breaches of confidentiality.

1. The Federal Duty to Maintain Medical Privacy: Federal Privacy Regulations (HIPAA)

The confidentiality of health information was protected in varying ways by a patchwork of state common law and regulatory approaches for many decades. Critics and patients' rights advocates contended that the framework was seriously deficient because protections varied from place to place and because the narrow focus on physician obligations left vast swaths of the health care system without effective constraints on the disclosure of medical information. At the same time as the complexity and range of participants in the health care system were expanding, technological advances were moving health care records from often illegible paper notes and files found in a single physician's office to comprehensive electronic health records (EHRs) stored in databases that could be accessed by many individuals and institutional participants in health care.

The Health Insurance Portability and Accountability Act of 1996 (HIPAA) was concerned mainly with improving how health insurance is designed and sold—but it also included a set of provisions facilitating the electronic processing of insurance claims and other types of medical information. In order to ensure that greater use of electronic health information would not compromise privacy, the HIPAA statute also required the Secretary of Health and Human Services to issue rules improving privacy protections. The key privacy regulations, which were first issued in 2006 and substantially revised in 2013, are found at 45 C.F.R. §160 et seq.

In general, the federal privacy regulations (the "Privacy Rule") require certain "covered entities" to maintain the confidentiality of defined types of "protected health information" (PHI). Covered entities include health insurers, claims-processing clearinghouses, and health care providers. 45 C.F.R. §160.102(a). These entities must (1) adopt internal procedures to protect the privacy of protected health information; (2) train employees regarding privacy procedures; (3) designate a privacy officer; (4) secure patient records that contain protected information; and (5) establish and enforce agreements with certain third parties (called "business associates") that ensure that they maintain privacy protection for information they have access to. The HITECH Act of 2009 expanded the reach of the Act by imposing many of the Privacy Rule's requirements to business associates. 45 C.F.R. §160.102(b). A "business associate" is "a person [defined to include various organizations and businesses] who" is not an employee of a covered entity but "creates, receives, maintains, or transmits protected health information for a function or activity . . . including claims processing or administration . . . or . . . provides" services such as legal, accounting, or management services. 45 C.F.R. §160.103. The current version of the rule makes clear that a "subcontractor that creates, receives, maintains, or transmits protected health information on behalf of the business associate" also qualifies as a business associate. Id.

The definition of "health information" is comprehensive. The term means:

> any information, including genetic information, whether oral or recorded in any form or medium, that
>   (1) Is created or received by a health care provider . . . [or a broad range of other entities]; and
>   (2) Relates to the past, present, or future physical or mental health or condition of an individual; the provision of health care to an individual; or the past, present, or future payment for the provision of health care to an individual.

45 C.F.R. §160.103. The Privacy Rule focuses on the protection of a particular subset of health information, called "protected health information," defined as "individually identifiable health information" held or transmitted in electronic media or "transmitted or maintained in any other form or medium." Id. (noting specific exceptions).

The central requirements for using or disclosing PHI are found in a single section, 45 C.F.R. §164.502, but this provision links to and incorporates definitions, standards, and exceptions found in more than 25 other sections or subsections in the Privacy Rule. The Rule thus has gained a reputation for complexity; handbooks, seminars, and training sessions have sprung up to help those working with health care information to master the technical details. A broad summary of the disclosure aspects of the Rule is nonetheless possible.

The standard for the use and disclosure of PHI by covered entities establishes a strict baseline rule of confidentiality, essentially prohibiting *any* use or disclosure of patient medical information, unless a specific regulatory exception applies. The standard provides seven general avenues for disclosure:

1. PHI can be disclosed to the individual or the individual's personal representative (with special rules if there are concerns about abuse or neglect).
2. The information can be used for "treatment, payment, or health care operations" with the patient's general consent (called "TPO" in the increasingly common HIPAA lingo of health lawyers and consultants).
3. The information can be disclosed where the entity receives a more specific "valid authorization," typically via a written and signed document, the nature of which may vary depending on whether the general authorization rule or special rules governing psychotherapy notes, marketing, or sale of PHI apply.
4. A specified subset of PHI can be disclosed without written authorization in certain defined situations after giving the patient an opportunity to object. For example, basic information about an individual's identity and condition can be added to the hospital directory and made available to callers based on an oral agreement after the individual has been given an opportunity to object and can even be provided in emergency circumstances when the individual is unable to communicate approval or disapproval if this

would be consistent with any known patient preferences and in the best interests of the patient.

5. An individual's PHI can be disclosed without his or her authorization or agreement in roughly a dozen categories of special circumstances, e.g., where the disclosure is required by law.

6. A "limited data set" that excludes most identifying information can be disclosed for use in public health, research, and operations. Limited types of PHI may also be disclosed in carefully circumscribed circumstances for institutional fundraising and by health plans involved in underwriting decisions.

7. Covered entities are also permitted to disclose PHI "incident to use[s] or disclosures otherwise permitted or required" so long as the covered entity has followed the standards governing the minimum necessary disclosure of information and has put in place proper administrative, physical, and technical safeguards.

45 C.F.R. §164.502. The complex regulatory framework addresses a host of other issues, ranging from the rules governing the creation of de-identified health information that can be used without consent, to the use of health information in research, to the responsibility of the covered entities to ensure that business associates comply with privacy requirements.

Any use or transfer of medical information that does not comply with these detailed rules violates the law, even if completely inadvert and resulting in no actual harm to the patient, but many such technical violations went unpunished. Thus, enforcement of the Privacy Rule initially appeared lax to some critics, until passage of the HITECH Act in 2009 required the imposition of penalties for all violations. The new regulations issued under the HITECH Act provide that DHHS "will impose a civil money penalty upon a covered entity or business associate" for violations. 45 C.F.R. §160.402(a). The civil penalties begin at a minimum of $100 for inadvertent breaches but rise to a minimum of $50,000 for offenses committed with a higher level of culpability. 45 C.F.R. §160.404. The Rule establishes factors for the Secretary to consider in setting the penalty between the established minimums and maximums. These civil penalty provisions create significant financial exposure for covered entities, even at the lowest dollar level. For example, continuing violations generate a separate violation each day, 45 C.F.R. 160.406. The risk is lessened somewhat by a cap of $1,500,000 placed on the total penalty for identical violations in a calendar year.

Knowing violations of the privacy rules that involve using unique health identifiers or obtaining or disclosing identifiable health information can result in fines and imprisonment. 42 U.S.C. §1320d-6. Notably, the most severe penalties (fines up to $250,000 and ten years imprisonment) are reserved for persons who commit the offense with the "intent to sell, transfer or use individually identifiable health information for commercial advantage, personal gain, or malicious harm . . . ." Id.

The Privacy Rule does not explicitly create a private cause of action or remedy and courts have been unwilling to find an implied right of action for individuals harmed by disclosures. Acara v. Banks, 470 F.3d 569 (5th Cir. 2006); Bonney v. Stephens Memorial Hospital, 17 A.3d 123 (Me. 2011); Espinoza v. Gold Cross Services, 234 P.3d 156 (Utah 2010).

The Privacy Rule includes important preemption rules that ultimately rein-force the role of states in establishing and enforcing strict privacy protections. First, HIPAA preemption applies only to state laws that provide weaker protections of privacy; states remain free to adopt and to enforce more protective regimes. 45 C.F.R. §160.201-.205. Second, the Privacy Rule provides that in cases involving civil penalties, the federal penalty "is in addition to any other penalty prescribed by law," 45 C.F.R. §160.418. Plaintiffs are therefore free to pursue whatever damage claims might otherwise be available under state law. This is particularly important given that the federal Privacy Rule does not provide a direct cause of action for individuals injured by improper disclosures. Courts have begun to wrestle with the potential impact of the Privacy Rule on a wide range of state provisions and practices.

▮IN THE MATTER OF MIGUEL M. v. BARRON
950 N.E.2d 107 (N.Y. 2011)

SMITH, J.

We hold that the Privacy Rule adopted by the federal government pursuant to the Health Insurance Portability and Accountability Act (HIPAA) prohibits the disclosure of a patient's medical records to a state agency that requests them for use in a proceeding to compel the patient to accept mental health treatment, where the patient has neither authorized the disclosure nor received notice of the agency's request for the records. . . .

Dr. Charles Barron, as designee of the New York City Department of Health and Mental Hygiene, applied for an order under Mental Hygiene Law §9.60 requir-ing "assisted outpatient treatment" (AOT) for Miguel M. The petition alleged that Miguel was suffering from a mental illness; that he was unlikely to survive safely in the community without supervision; that he had a history of failing to comply with treatment; that he was unlikely to participate in necessary treatment voluntarily; and that he needed, and would benefit from, AOT to prevent a relapse or deterio-ration of his mental status, which would be likely to result in serious harm to Miguel or to others.

At the hearing on the petition, Barron offered in evidence records from two hospitals relating to three occasions on which Miguel was hospitalized. A witness called by Barron testified that the hospitals had furnished the records in response to a request—a request made, it is clear from the record, without notice to Miguel. The witness acknowledged that Miguel had not authorized the release of the records, and that no court order for their disclosure had been sought or obtained.

The records were received in evidence over Miguel's objection and Barron's witness described their contents. After the hearing, [the] Supreme Court directed that Miguel "receive and accept assisted outpatient treatment" for a period of six months. The Appellate Division affirmed. We granted leave to appeal, and now reverse. . . .

Mental Hygiene Law §9.60, known as "Kendra's Law," was enacted in 1999. It is named for Kendra Webdale, who was killed by a mentally ill man who pushed her off a subway platform. It says that, on a proper showing, a mentally ill person whose lack of compliance with treatment has, twice within the last 36 months, caused him or her to be hospitalized may be the subject of AOT pursuant to a plan stated in a court order. Public officials identified as "directors of community services" are given the duty of enforcing Kendra's Law, and a petition to require AOT may be filed by a director of community services or his or her designee. [The] Mental Hygiene Law permits disclosure of medical records to a director of community services who requests it in the exercise of his or her duties. Thus, the disclosure of a patient's medical records for purposes of an AOT proceeding is permitted by state law, unless the applicable state law is preempted. Miguel argues that it is.

Miguel says that preemption is found in HIPAA and the Privacy Rule. The Privacy Rule prohibits disclosure of an identifiable patient's health information without the patient's authorization, subject to certain exceptions (45 CFR 164.508[a] [1]). HIPAA . . . and the Privacy Rule say that contrary state laws are preempted unless they offer privacy protections that are "more stringent" than those of the federal law; New York does not offer any more stringent protection that is relevant here. The preemption issue thus comes down to whether the disclosure of Miguel's medical records was permitted by one of the exceptions to the Privacy Rule.

Barron relies on two exceptions, those permitting disclosure for purposes of "public health" and "treatment." It is possible to read the language of both exceptions as covering the disclosure now at issue, but in both cases the reading is strained. Considering the apparent purposes of these two exceptions, we conclude that neither fits these facts.

The public health exception permits disclosure of protected information to:

> [a] public health authority that is authorized by law to collect or receive such information for the purpose of preventing or controlling disease, injury, or disability, including, but not limited to, the reporting of disease, injury, vital events such as birth or death, and the conduct of public health surveillance, public health investigations, and public health interventions.

Barron reasons that disclosure of a mentally ill person's hospital records for purposes of requiring that person to accept AOT protects the public health, because mentally ill people might kill or injure other people—like Kendra Webdale—who, of course, are members of the public. Thus Barron, a person designated to enforce Kendra's Law, would be a "public health authority," collecting information for the "purpose of preventing . . . injury," and his action to require AOT in Miguel's case could be called a public health intervention. We are not convinced, however, that the authors of the Privacy Rule meant "public health" in this literal, but counterintuitive, sense.

The apparent purpose of the public health exception is to facilitate government activities that protect large numbers of people from epidemics, environmental hazards, and the like, or that advance public health by accumulating valuable statistical information. To disclose private information about particular people, for the purpose of preventing those people from harming themselves or others, effects a very substantial invasion of privacy without the sort of generalized public benefit that would come from, for example, tracing the course of an infectious disease. The disclosure to Barron of Miguel's hospital records was not within the scope of the public health exception.

The treatment exception permits disclosure of protected health information "for treatment activities of a health care provider." "Treatment" is defined as:

the provision, coordination, or management of health care and related services by
one or more health care providers, including the coordination or management of
health care by a health care provider with a third party; consultation between health
care providers relating to a patient; or the referral of a patient for health care from
one health care provider to another.

Again, Barron's argument is literalistic: AOT—assisted outpatient treatment—
is literally "treatment"—"the provision . . . of health care . . . by one or more health
care providers." But the thrust of the treatment exception is to facilitate the sharing
of information among health care providers working together. We see no indication
that the authors of the regulation meant to facilitate "treatment" administered by
a volunteer "provider" over the patient's objection. Disclosure for that purpose is
a more serious invasion of privacy than, for example, the transmission of medical
records from a patient's primary care physician to a specialist—the sort of activity
for which the treatment exception seems primarily designed. The treatment exception is inapplicable here.

We find support for our conclusion that the two exceptions Barron relies on
are inapposite in the existence of other exceptions that Barron might have invoked
but did not. The Privacy Rule authorizes disclosure of health information, subject
to certain conditions, "in the course of any judicial or administrative proceeding," in response to either "an order of a court or administrative tribunal" or "a
subpoena, discovery request, or other lawful process" (45 CFR 164.512[e]). Thus,
Barron could have pursued Miguel's records either by seeking a court order or by
serving a subpoena. To do so in compliance with the Privacy Rule, however, Barron
would have had to give notice to Miguel of his request for the records. He could
not, absent extraordinary circumstances, have obtained a court order requiring disclosure without giving such notice. And the Privacy Rule's exception for subpoenas
and the like is conditioned on "satisfactory assurance" from the person seeking
the information to the entity providing it either "that reasonable efforts have been
made . . . to ensure that the individual who is the subject of the protected health
information . . . has been given notice of the request," or that an order protecting
the confidentiality of the information has been sought. In a case, like this one, to
which the patient is a party, a request for a protective order would require notice
to the patient.

We can see no reason, and Barron has suggested none, why notice should not
have been given here. It may well be, in this case as in many others, that no valid
ground for withholding the records exists; courts ruling on disclosure issues will
surely be conscious, as we are, of the strong public interest in seeing that mentally
ill people who might otherwise be dangerous receive necessary treatment. But it
seems only fair, and no great burden on the public agencies charged with enforcing
Kendra's Law, to give patients a chance to object before the records are delivered.

We emphasize that it is far from our purpose to make the enforcement of
Kendra's Law difficult. It may often be possible to avoid all disclosure problems by
getting the patient to authorize the disclosure in advance; surely many mentally
ill people will, while they are under proper care, recognize that disclosure is very
much in their own interest. When there is no advance authorization, patients who
are given notice that their records are being sought often may not object; when they
do object, their objections may often be overruled. We hold only that unauthorized

disclosure without notice is, under circumstances like those present here, inconsistent with the Privacy Rule. . . .

Barron argues in the alternative that, even if the disclosure of the records to him was unlawful—as we have held it was—the Supreme Court did not err by admitting the records into evidence at the AOT hearing. HIPAA, as Barron points out, contains its own remedies for violations: civil penalties and, for the knowing and wrongful disclosure of individually identifiable health information, fines and imprisonment. Neither exclusion of the records from evidence nor suppression of evidence obtained by use of the records is among the remedies listed. Barron cites decisions from other states holding that evidence obtained as a result of a HIPAA violation need not be suppressed in a criminal case. . . .

We assume it is correct that, in a criminal case, a HIPAA or Privacy Rule violation does not always require the suppression of evidence. . . . But this case is different. It is one thing to allow the use of evidence resulting from an improper disclosure of information in medical records to prove that a patient has committed a crime; it is another to use the records themselves, or their contents, in a proceeding to subject to unwanted medical treatment a patient who is not accused of any wrongdoing. Using the records in that way directly impairs, without adequate justification, the interest protected by HIPAA and the Privacy Rule: the interest in keeping one's own medical condition private. We therefore hold that medical records obtained in violation of HIPAA or the Privacy Rule, and the information contained in those records, are not admissible in a proceeding to compel AOT.

Accordingly, the order of the Appellate Division should be reversed, with costs, and the case remitted to Supreme Court for further proceedings in accordance with this opinion.

Notes: HIPAA Privacy Protections

1. *Preempting Patient Access?* Should the preemption analysis of *Miguel M.* turn on who is seeking the records? In Marabello ex rel Marabello v. State of New York, 964 N.Y.S.2d 863 (N.Y. Ct. Cl. 2013), a New York claims court case read *Miguel M.* narrowly as applying to patients seeking to shield disclosure of health records to *third parties* without notice. The *Marabello* court denied plaintiff's request to access incident reports and other records related to his stay in a group home operated by New York State. Plaintiff argued that a state education law, which allowed institutions not to disclose health information collected solely for internal quality assurance purposes, was preempted by the HIPAA Privacy Rule. Id, at 239. The court disagreed, holding that although under *Miguel M.,* HIPAA preempted state law as to disclosure of health information to third parties, it did not similarly preempt state law as to patient access, particularly when the information was not relevant to making medical decisions concerning the patient.

2. *Challenges to HIPAA.* Efforts to challenge HIPAA on constitutional or statutory grounds have failed. In South Carolina Med. Assn. v. Thompson, 327 F.3d 346 (4th Cir. 2003), the court rejected the plaintiffs' claims that the HIPAA regulations constituted an unconstitutionally vague and improper, standardless delegation of legislative authority. See also Citizens for Health v. Leavitt, Secretary U.S. Department Health and Human Services, 428 F.3d 167 (3d Cir. 2005). For a summary of litigation under HIPAA, see Annot., 194 A.L.R. Fed. 133 (2004).

3. *The Special Nature of Medical Information and EHRs.* The HIPAA privacy standard and related provisions regulating the security of electronic health records (EHRs) represent a very significant investment of public and private resources into the privacy of health care information. The Privacy Rule protects a broad range of information created and held by individual health care providers, practice groups, hospitals, HMOs, and other entities. HIPAA compliance efforts undoubtedly impose hundreds of millions of dollars in costs across the health care system. In theory, our willingness to bear these costs is based on the special character of medical information as distinct from other types of personal information and the nature of the health care provider-patient relationship. See, e.g., Mark A. Rothstein, The Hippocratic Bargain and Health Information Technology, 38 J.L. Med. & Ethics 7 (2010). Do the costs of the HIPAA privacy regime seem commensurate with the benefits privacy generates for individuals? Are broader social goals served by the Privacy Rule? Are the notice and authorization provisions of HIPAA effective mechanisms for protecting privacy and autonomy or do they merely result in a meaningless flurry of additional paperwork? For a critique, see Fred H. Cate, Protecting Privacy in Health Research: The Limits of Individual Choice, 98 Cal. L. Rev. 1766 (2010).

The Privacy Rule is focused on "covered entities" and "business associates." Some non-health care providers have attempted to establish Web-based medical records databases, arguing that HIPAA rules do not apply to the arrangements. Perhaps to address consumer concerns about privacy, Microsoft named its product "Microsoft Vault." Should these databases be covered by the Privacy Rule? Eric S. Pasternack, HIPAA in the Age of Electronic Health Records, 41 Rutgers L.J. 817 (2010) (suggesting amendment of HIPAA to address electronic medical records companies).

4. *Big Data and Patient Privacy.* To what extent can individuals' personal medical data be used to improve medical care for all patients in keeping with ethical privacy standards? To what extent *should* it be used? HIPAA and the HITECH Act were designed to increase the use of EHRs as a method of reducing costs and improving efficiency and quality of health care, explicitly providing incentive payments to hospitals that effectively utilized EHRs to streamline their care delivery processes. See David Blumenthal & Marilyn Tavenner, The "Meaningful Use" Regulation for Electronic Health Records, 363 New Eng. J. Med. 501 (2010). The power of the data collected through EHRs exceeds the ability to provide more effective care for each specific patient. With the use of predictive analytics, hospitals with access to thousands of patients' medical records will be able to ascertain the probable risk, at any given moment, of harm for any potential patient. This capability would allow hospitals to allocate their resources more equitably and precisely when making rapid, life-or-death decisions.

The privacy concerns that could accompany this broader use of individuals' data, however, are large, and the current HIPAA Privacy Rule may not be well equipped to protect against them. HIPAA's regulations are geared toward protecting data from use and theft by entities outside of the health sphere and include specific provisions designed to protect the security of electronic health records from such threats. 45 C.F.R. §§164.302-.318. Fears of improper use are legitimate given the frequency of breaches, whether intentional, see Doe v. Walgreens, 2010 WL 4823212 (Tenn. Ct. App.) (Walgreens employee wrongfully accessed Walgreens database and shared co-worker's HIV status with others), or merely negligent, see Milt Freudenheim, Breaches Lead to Push to Protect Medical Data, N.Y. Times, May 30, 2011.

In contrast, reliance on big data and predictive analytics will increase the like-lihood that patients' data will be purposefully disseminated within the medical com-munity, against which HIPAA would not guard. There are measures hospitals can take to "launder" the data, that is strip it of most identifying information, but laun-dering the data too carefully may come at the price of reducing its usefulness. How comfortable are we risking the privacy of individuals' personal medical information in exchange for better care across the board? For a discussion of HIPAA's shortcom-ings with respect to intra-hospital data privacy, see Nicolas P. Terry, Big Data Proxies and Health Privacy Exceptionalism, 24 Health Matrix 65 (2014). See also I. Glenn Cohen, et. al., The Legal and Ethical Concerns that Arise from Using Complex Predictive Analytics in Health Care, 33 Health Affairs 1139 (2014) (suggesting addi-tional safeguards, such as establishing a third party to verify when data is sufficiently unlikely to risk re-identification and notifying patients prior to treatment that their data may be used but not necessarily requiring explicit consent).

5. *Genetic Information.* Advances in genetics may create additional privacy con-cerns. Scientists are increasingly able to link human genes with the risk of develop-ing various human maladies. Individuals have a definite interest in maintaining the confidentiality of their genetic predisposition for a variety of ills. At the same time, other affected family members, insurers, and others have an interest in gaining access to this information. Lawrence O. Gostin & James G. Hodge, Jr., Genetic Pri-vacy and the Law: An End to Genetics Exceptionalism, 40 Jurimetrics J. 21 (1999); Mark A. Hall, Legal Rules and Industry Norms: The Impact of Laws Restricting Health Insurers' Use of Genetic Information, 40 Jurimetrics J. 93 (1999). Indeed, researchers have shown that it is possible to re-identify some anonymized genetic samples through using publicly available databases. Melissa Gymrek et al., Identi-fying Personal Genomes by Surname Inference, 339 Science 321, 321 (2013). The federal Genetic Information Nondiscrimination Act of 2008 (GINA), Pub. L. 110-233, 122 Stat. 881, established special rules protecting the confidentiality of genetic information and restricting the use of this information by insurers and employers. See Jessica L. Roberts, Preempting Discrimination: Lessons from the Genetic Infor-mation Nondiscrimination Act, 63 Vand. L. Rev. 439 (2010). In the first case of its kind, two employees were awarded $2.2 million when their employer asked them to undergo a cheek swab and DNA test, in violation of GINA, to determine if they were the employees who had habitually defecated in the warehouse (earning the memorable moniker of "the case of the devious defecator"). Lowe v. Atlas Logistics Grp. Retail Servs. (Atlanta), LLC, 102 F. Supp. 3d 1360 (N.D. Ga. 2015); Daniel Weissner, Georgia Workers Win $2.2 million in "Devious Defecator" Case, Reuters, June 23, 2015. The HIPAA Privacy Rule includes certain types of genetic informa-tion, including information about family members, in the definition of health infor-mation subject to the Rule's protections. 45 C.F.R. §160.103.

6. *The (Limited) Right of Individuals to Control Medical Records.* HIPAA establishes a large reservoir of PHI presumptively under the control of an individual but also establishes significant escape valves through which the flow of PHI is controlled by others. The Rule permitting use of PHI for treatment purposes is a major example: Under this provision no separate patient consent is required. The presumption of confidentiality is reduced in some circumstances where common practices and likely preferences of patients would create a default rule of disclosure. 45 C.F.R. §§164.502(a)(1)(v); 164.510. As noted above, this provision eases disclosure of PHI

in hospital directories; it also facilitates disclosure to family members and friends involved in the patient's care and to disaster relief organizations. The Rule also establishes that disclosures can be made without any authorization or opportunity to agree or object in any one of a dozen important categories of circumstances. As noted above, this provision establishes that PHI can be disclosed where required by law. Other permitted disclosures include: disclosures for public health activities (a broad category including specific examples such as disease surveillance, notification of exposure to contagious diseases, or FDA-related reports of adverse events); disclosures about victims of abuse, neglect, or domestic violence; disclosures for judicial and administrative proceedings; and disclosures for research or law enforcement purposes, among others. See 45 C.F.R. §164.512. See also U.S. v. Wilk, 572 F.3d 1229 (11th Cir. 2009) (law enforcement and judicial proceedings exception).

Given HIPAA's protective purposes, the court in *Miguel* took a narrow approach to interpreting the scope of HIPAA's exceptions. Does the court's analysis seem persuasive? What will be the impact of the court's ruling on New York's ability to carry out the purposes of Kendra's Law? The court suggests that patients could be asked to pre-authorize release of their medical records. Would this approach cure the harm to an individual's right to control disclosure, given that the records were going to be used to mandate treatment over the patient's current objections? The Privacy Rule allows covered entities to rely on an authorization unless it is known to have been revoked; revocations must be written. 45 C.F.R. §164.508.

7. *Patients' Rights and Medical Records.* Medical records have traditionally been deemed the property of the health care provider who creates them, though patients and others may have access to the information within them. EHRs and the collection and transmission of electronic databases of information have created new challenges and opportunities, including questions about who owns the information contained in a record, as distinct from the physical medium in which the information is stored. See, e.g., Mark A. Hall, Property, Privacy, and the Pursuit of Interconnected Electronic Medical Records, 95 Iowa L. Rev. 631 (2010) (arguing that patients should be given right to monetize access and control rights over medical records); Marc A. Rodwin, Patient Data: Property, Privacy & the Public Interest, 36 Am. J.L. & Med. 586 (2010); Frank Pasquale, Grand Bargains for Big Data: The Emerging Law of Health Information, 72 Md. L. Rev. 682 (2013). Cf. Sorrell v. IMS Health, 564 U.S. 552 (2011) (discussing economic value of data on physicians' prescription practices; striking down on First Amendment grounds a state ban on sale of information). The HITECH Act gives patients the right to restrict sale of their PHI. 42 U.S.C. §17935(d); 45 C.F.R. §164.508(a)(4) (authorization required).

The Privacy Rule establishes that patients must be given access to most types of their own PHI, with some exceptions, including psychotherapy notes. 45 C.F.R. §164.524. The Rule establishes timelines and procedures for access, including whether or not the denial of access will be considered to be reviewable and the procedures for review. For example, a correctional facility's denial of access on safety grounds would be unreviewable. Also unreviewable would be a denial of an individual's access to "protected health information created or obtained . . . in the course of research that includes treatment" during the research, "provided that the individual . . . agreed to the denial of access" during the consent process for the research. Id. Among other things, this rule protects the integrity of double-blind clinical trials, see section D. Reviewable grounds for denial of access include concerns that "access . . . is reasonably likely to endanger the life or physical safety of the individual or another person." Id. Reviews generally are conducted by licensed health professionals who were not part of the original access decision.

The Privacy Rule also gives individuals a right to amend PHI held within a particular record set. 45 C.F.R. §164.526. Covered entities can deny a request to amend where, for example, the entity believes the PHI "[i]s accurate and complete." The individual retains the right to submit a written statement disagreeing with the denial; the individual's statement must thereafter be transmitted with the disputed PHI along with any rebuttal from the entity. Where the entity accepts the amendment, the Rule creates a process for communicating the correction to persons or entities identified by the individual.

The Privacy Rule gives patients information about different types of disclosures of their PHI. The concept of disclosing disclosures is called "accounting." 45 C.F.R. §164.528. There are numerous exclusions from the accounting duty. One major exclusion involves disclosures made for treatment, payment, and health care operations. Id. Section 13405(c) of the HITECH Act expanded accounting to include treatment-related disclosures through an EHR. Covered entities argued that the expanded accounting provisions might be unduly onerous, but the more stringent revisions to the Privacy Rule were successfully finalized in January 2013. See 78 Fed. Reg. 5599–5600 (Jan. 25, 2013). The HITECH Act strengthened protections for patients by requiring notification of data breaches. 42 U.S.C. §17932. "Breach" means the "acquisition, access, use or disclosure of" PHI not otherwise permitted under the Privacy Rule "which compromises the security or privacy of" the PHI. 45 C.F.R. §164.402. Certain inadvertent disclosures within the health care environment are excluded. Id. Outside of these exclusions, covered entities or business associates must disclose breaches unless they can "demonstrate [] that there is a low probability that the protected health information has been compromised based on a risk assessment." Id. The risk assessment must consider: "[t]he nature and extent of the . . . [PHI] involved including the types of identifiers and the likelihood of re-identification"; "[t]he unauthorized person who used the . . . [PHI] or to whom the disclosure was made"; "[w]hether the . . . [PHI] was actually acquired or viewed"; and "[t]he extent to which the risk to the . . . [PHI] has been mitigated." Id. Covered entities must notify the individuals and the Secretary of HHS about breaches; "prominent media outlets" must be notified about breaches "involving more than 500 residents." 45 C.F.R. §§164.404-.408; see also §164.410 (notification by business associates).

Notwithstanding the legal protections for patient access to their own records, many patients find securing such access difficult. Elizabeth Rosenthal recounted such an episode in the New York Times: "Many readers were shocked by my recent article about Peter Drier, who received a surprise bill of $117,000 from an out-of-network assistant surgeon who helped out during his back operation. But almost as surprising was how difficult it was during my reporting for Mr. Drier to extract his own records from the hospital." Elizabeth Rosenthal, Medical Records: Top Secret, N.Y. Times Nov. 8, 2014, SR5. As Rosenthal wrote, "Hospitals are computerized, and patients have a right to their own records, so I assumed getting the chart would be easy. I was wrong. The six-week ordeal included requests that needed to be made via regular mail, numerous phone calls, consent forms and an estimate for copying fees that totaled $100. This was topped off by an actual visit to the hospital by Mr. Drier, who sat in an office until he had paper documents in hand."

8. *The Standards for Business Associates.* Covered entities are permitted to disclose PHI to "business associates" after "obtain[ing] satisfactory assurance that the business associate will appropriately safeguard the information." 45 C.F.R. §164.502(e) (1). Business associates perform a range of functions from claims management to quality assurance. 45 C.F.R. §160.103 ("business associate"). Critics argued that permitting disclosure of PHI to business associates created a significant risk, as those entities were not directly subject to regulation under HIPAA. The HITECH Act tightened the rules governing business associates by, among other things, directly imposing both security and privacy standards and civil and criminal penalties for violations. 42 U.S.C. §17934; 45 C.F.R. §164.502(a)(3), (4). Disclosures by business associates remain a significant issue. See Kevin Sack, Medical Data of Thousands Posted Online, N.Y. Times, Sept. 9, 2011.

9. *The Intersection of HIPAA with Other Laws Governing Disclosure.* HIPAA interacts with a wide range of federal and state legislation, such as rules governing financial records, public records laws, and state discovery rules. See, e.g., Holman v. Rasak, 785 N.W.2d 98 (Mich. 2010) (HIPAA does not preempt state discovery rules permitting ex parte discovery from plaintiff's treating physician where "reasonable efforts have been made . . . to secure a protective order that meets" HIPAA requirements); State ex rel. Proctor v. Messina, 320 S.W.3d 145 (Mo. 2010) (en banc) (trial court lacked authority to issue order authorizing ex parte communications under HIPAA); Abbott v. Texas Department of Mental Health and Mental Retardation, 212 S.W.3d 648 (Tex. App. 2006) (HIPAA does not preempt state Public Information Act); State ex rel. Cincinnati Enquirer v. Daniels, 844 N.E.2d 1181 (Ohio 2006) (lead-risk-assessment reports did not count as PHI, and even if they did, the public records law requiring disclosure of lead-risk-assessment reports was permissible under the "required by law" exception to the HIPAA privacy rule); see also Thomas v. 1156729 Inc., 979 F.Supp. 2d 780, 783 (2013) (while HIPAA preempted the state's law regarding ex parte discovery from plaintiff's physician, HIPAA itself "neither prohibits nor permits" ex parte interviews, and therefore granting ex parte discovery subject to a qualified protective order was not inconsistent with HIPAA). That said, even within a jurisdiction, the preemption determination often turns on particularities of the case. Cuyahoga County Board of Health v. Lipson O'Shea Legal Group, 50 N.E.3d 499 (Ohio 2016) distinguishing *Daniels* and holding that the requested "documentation or information of all homes . . . in Cuyahoga County where a minor child was found to have elevated blood levels in excess of 10 [mg/dl]" could qualify as PHI, unlike the information requested in *Daniels*, because the address information could be used to identify specific individuals based on their physical status or condition); see also Brown v. Mortensen, 253 P.3d 522 (Cal. 2011) (analyzing interaction between HIPAA, the federal Fair Credit Act, and state law in claim involving alleged unlawful disclosure of medical records by debt collector). At least one author has proposed that the HIPAA Privacy Rule prohibits "pharmacies from selling de-identified prescription information to data miners for use by drug manufacturers to market their brand-name drugs." Beverly Cohen, Regulating Data Mining Post-Sorrell: Using HIPAA to Restrict Marketing Uses of Patients' Private Medical Information, 47 Wake Forest L. Rev. 1141 (2012).

10. *The Enforcement Record.* The Privacy Rule is enforced by DHHS's Office of Civil Rights (OCR). The incentives created by the HITECH Act appear to have spurred enforcement, with thousands of complaints investigated and resolved each year. In its first use of the civil monetary damages provisions of the HITECH Act, the OCR imposed a $4.3 million civil penalty against Cignet Health in Maryland based on Cignet's refusal to provide 41 patients with access to their medical records and Cignet's failure to cooperate with the OCR investigation. The OCR secured a $1 million settlement from the Massachusetts General Hospital, one of the nation's most prestigious institutions, based on the breach of privacy arising from an employee leaving records of 192 infectious-disease clinic patients on a subway train. And more recently, the OCR made clear that it would also be bringing enforcement actions against both covered business associates and their parent companies. In 2016, HHS imposed fines of $400,000 and $650,000, respectively, against Care New England (for actions taken by its business associate) and the Catholic Health Care Services (CHCS) of the Archdiocese of Pennsylvania (itself a business associate of Catholic Clinical Consultants). The settlement with CHCS marked the OCR's first direct settlement with a business associate. In both cases, OCR implemented a corrective action plan in addition to the fine, involving HHS monitoring of the covered associate for an indefinite period. For more on these enforcement actions, see www.hhs .gov/hipaa/newsroom/.

Notes: Beyond HIPAA — Constitutional, Common Law, and Statutory Duties to Maintain Confidentiality

1. *Overview.* Long before HIPAA, state courts and legislatures grappled with whether and how information arising from the treatment relationship would be protected from disclosure. The Privacy Rule does not displace other laws that are more protective of privacy. Moreover, the absence of a private cause of action in HIPAA means that patients injured by disclosures must look primarily to other sources of law to secure compensation. It is therefore important to (1) understand the scope and implications of the federal Privacy Rule; (2) determine whether other federal and state privacy protections are available; and (3) carefully consider the scope of the privacy protections, the persons or entities subject to duties, the limits of the duties, and the available remedies. There are three major sources of duties to maintain the confidentiality of medical information outside the Privacy Rule: federal and state constitutions, statutes, and the common law.

2. *A Constitutional Right of Confidentiality.* The issue of patient confidentiality is of special importance to state and federal health care providers or agencies. Several courts have found that individuals have a constitutionally protected interest in maintaining the privacy of their medical information. See, e.g., Alfred v. Corrections Corp. of America, 437 Fed. Appx. 281 (5th Cir. 2011) (overturning dismissal of prisoner's claim of potential constitutional violation arising from disclosure of his HIV status to another prisoner); Doe v. City of New York, 15 F.3d 264 (2d Cir. 1994) (individuals have a constitutional right of privacy in their medical information; court employs a balancing test to determine whether the government entity's interest in disclosure is "substantial" enough to outweigh the individual's privacy interest). This "informational privacy" interest has its roots in the Supreme Court's

decision in Whalen v. Roe, 429 U.S. 589 (1977). In that case, the Court upheld a state program that created a centralized data bank with the names of all persons in the state who had been prescribed certain controlled substances. In dicta, however, the Court noted that the state might have some constitutional obligation to maintain the confidentiality of the information it collected.

3. *The Doctrinal Basis for a Common-Law Duty to Maintain Confidentiality.* Most states provide a private cause of action against licensed health care providers who impermissibly disclose confidential information obtained in the course of the treatment relationship to third parties. See Annot., 48 A.L.R.4th 668 (1986). Generally, a physician-patient relationship must be formed before the duty to maintain confidences arises. See Howes v. United States, 887 F.2d 729 (6th Cir. 1989) (psychologist and psychiatrist not liable for disclosing information about husband's drug and alcohol use that had been provided by nonpatient wife). Depending on the jurisdiction, the claim may be phrased as a breach of contract, as an act of malpractice, as a breach of fiduciary duty, as an act of fraud/misrepresentation, or as a breach of a specific civil statute permitting the award of damages. See Biddle v. Warren General Hospital, 715 N.E.2d 518 (Ohio 1999) (finding breach of confidentiality to be an independent tort); Givens v. Mullikin ex rel. Estate of McElwaney, 75 S.W.3d 383 (Tenn. 2002) (implied covenant of confidentiality found in contract for treatment.) The duty to maintain confidentiality generally includes the obligation to have in place policies and procedures designed to reduce the risk of accidental or intentional disclosures. Compare Behringer v. The Medical Center at Princeton, 592 A.2d 1251 (N.J. Super. Ct. Law Div. 1991) (hospital liable for failing to have in place policies to protect the confidentiality of the HIV status of a patient-surgeon), with Rosen v. Montgomery Surgical Center, 825 So. 2d 735 (Ala. 2001) (court rejects invasion of privacy claim based on actions of non-physician employee of hospital) and Doe v. Guthrie Clinic Ltd., 5 N.E.3d 578 (N.Y. 2014) (clinic liability for disclosure limited to reasonably foreseeable acts within scope of employment).

In addition, licensed health care providers who breach the confidentiality of their patients run the risk of professional disciplinary action. See, e.g., Salerian v. Maryland State Board of Physicians, 932 A.2d 1225 (Md. App. 2007) (finding unprofessional conduct where forensic psychiatrist engaged by defense in espionage case disclosed information to subject's wife and media). State privacy rules may also be applied outside the treatment relationship. See Washburn v. Rite Aid Corp., 695 A.2d 495 (R.I. 1997).

The doctrinal basis of the common-law claim can be important to prospective plaintiffs. If the claim arises in contract, plaintiffs will have the benefit of the (generally longer) contract statute of limitations. Plaintiffs alleging breaches of contract will also avoid some of the procedural barriers to malpractice suits established as part of tort reform efforts in many states. See, e.g., Pierce v. Caday, 422 S.E.2d 371 (Va. 1992) (breach of confidentiality claim is subject to notice requirements imposed by malpractice reform statutes). See also Chapter 4.H. A few courts have considered whether breach of confidentiality claims should be subject to the ordinary negligence statute of limitations or the special statute of limitations imposed for malpractice claims. See, e.g., Tighe v. Ginsberg, 540 N.Y.S.2d 99 (App. Div. 1989) (disclosure of medical records is a breach of fiduciary duty subject to the longer negligence statute of limitations). Finally, plaintiffs in contract suits need prove only that the physician failed to honor the degree of confidentiality that was promised. They need not find and present expert medical testimony on the question of whether the health care provider defendant violated the applicable standard of care. Cf. Berger v. Sonneland, 26 P.3d 257 (Wash. 2001) (expert medical testimony required in malpractice claim). Plaintiffs have begun to use the HIPAA Privacy Rule as the source of the standard of care in common-law claims for damages. Compare Byrne v. Avery Center for Obstetrics & Gynecology, PC, 314 Conn. 433 (2014) (HIPAA standards may inform the standard of care) with Sheldon v. Kettering Health Network, 40 N.E.3d 661 (Ohio Ct. App. 2015) (violation of HIPAA standards does not constitute negligence per se). See also Sharona Hoffman & Andy Podgurski, E-Health Hazards: Provider Liability and Electronic Health Record Systems, 24 Berkeley Tech. L.J. 1523, 1558-1560 (2009).

4. *Statutory Protection.* HIPAA is not the only federal statute protecting the confidentiality of information. The federal Privacy Act of 1974 governs the use of information by federal agencies. See, e.g., FAA v. Cooper, 132 S. Ct. 1441 (2012) (interagency exchange of information relating to an individual's HIV status may have violated Act but sovereign immunity applied to bar claims for emotional or mental distress damages). Many states have passed statutes governing the confidentiality of information provided in the health care provider-patient relationship. Some of these state statutes were enacted to build upon the federal Privacy Rule. See Symposium, 2 Yale J. Health Pol'y L. & Ethics 325 (2002). Other state provisions protect certain types of health information. See, e.g., Annot., 12 A.L.R.5th 149 (1993). Do state rules providing additional protection for certain types of health care information, such as information regarding HIV status, represent good public policy?

5. *Confidentiality as a Rule of Evidence.* The confidentiality of patient-physician communications is often also protected under rules of evidence. This evidentiary "privilege" prohibits the discovery of protected information. State rules of evidence almost always provide for a physician-patient privilege. The rule may be invoked by the physician on behalf of the patient or by the patient, but only the patient generally has the power to waive the privilege. See 81 Am. Jur. 2d Witnesses §§444, 452. The privilege may be limited to communications with physicians. In Buchanan v. Mayfield, 925 S.W.2d 135 (Tex. App. 1996), for example, the court held that the statutory privilege accorded to "confidential communications between a physician and a patient" did not apply to the communications between a dentist and a patient.

The Federal Rules of Evidence do not include a physician-patient privilege, see Charles Alan Wright & Kenneth W. Graham, Jr., 25 Fed. Prac. & Proc. Evid. §5521 (RR 504) (discussing the rejection of a physician-patient privilege under the Federal Rules of Evidence); Ralph Ruebner & Leslie Ann Reis, Hippocrates to HIPAA: A Foundation for a Federal Physician-Patient Privilege, 77 Temp. L. Rev. 505 (2004). The Supreme Court recognized a "psychotherapist-patient" privilege under Rule 501 of the Federal Rules of Evidence in Jaffee v. Redmond, 116 S. Ct. 1923 (1996). Justice Stevens, writing for the majority, found that the privilege was "rooted in the imperative need for confidence and trust" and that it served important public and private interests. The majority applied the privilege to shield communications between a police officer and her social worker therapist, who provided counseling after the police officer shot an allegedly innocent person. Justice Scalia's dissent focused on the injustice created by the application of the privilege, including the loss of evidence of possible wrongdoing. There is no dangerous-patient exception to the federal psychotherapist-patient testimonial privilege even though the psychotherapist may have the statutory discretion to disclose confidential information about the patient to prevent harm to a third party or to the patient. U.S. v. Chase, 340 F.3d 978 (9th Cir. 2003).

Is the privilege necessary? Will people seek care from physicians or therapists without its protection? Empirical evidence suggests that perhaps they will. See Daniel W. Shuman, The Origins of the Physician-Patient Privilege and Professional Secret, 39 Sw. L.J. 661, 664-665 (1985) (noting the empirical evidence does not fully support utilitarian proponents of a privilege).

6. *Waiver and Other Exceptions.* The duty to maintain confidentiality is not ordinarily absolute under either common law or statute. Where the duty is derived from medical ethics and practice, for example, it will be limited by policies that permit disclosure for the protection of third parties. Statutes protecting the confidentiality of patient information often contain a general rule of confidentiality and then list situations under which that confidentiality can be breached. The "exceptions" to the duty to maintain confidentiality can be quite broad. Generally, patient information *may* be revealed when the patient consents, or when disclosure is necessary to protect the health and safety of either the patient or third parties. In some circumstances, health care providers may even have a *duty* to breach confidentiality imposed by common law or statute. This issue is discussed in more detail at pages 182-193.

Whether or not a patient has waived his or her right to confidentiality is a significant issue in litigation. See Annot., 21 A.L.R.3d 912 (1968); compare Reda v. Advocate Health Care, 765 N.E.2d 1002 (Ill. 2002) (plaintiff in neurological injury action had not placed mental condition at issue and had not waived privilege with respect to his mental health records) with Deprizio v. Memorial Hospital Association, 12 N.E.3d 782, 790 (Ill. App. Ct. 2014) (plaintiff waived his privilege to confidentiality when he brought an action for pain and suffering and presented evidence referring to his mental health status, including direct references to documents and mental health services). Should asserting one's fitness to be a parent in a child custody dispute constitute a waiver of the psychiatrist-patient privilege? See Laznovsky v. Laznovsky, 745 A.2d 1054 (Md. 2000) (no); Culbertson v. Culbertson, 455 S.W.3d 107, 131-135 (Ct. App. Tenn. 2014) (surveying jurisdictions). See also Annot., 50 A.L.R.4th 714 (1986).

Should a patient be able to gain access to the identity of other patients? Rogers v. New York University Hospitals Cntr., 795 N.Y.S.2d 438 (N.Y. Sup. 2005) (identity of fellow patient can be released without violating HIPAA privacy); Baptist Memorial Hospital-Union County v. Johnson, 754 So. 2d 1165 (Miss. 2000) (hospital must disclose identity of patient who mistakenly breast-fed another patient's baby); Falco v. Institute of Living, 757 A.2d 571 (Conn. 2000) (psychiatrist-patient privilege prevented disclosure of identity of patient who attacked plaintiff in psychiatric hospital). See also Annot., 66 A.L.R.5th 591 (1999).

7. *Adherence to Confidentiality.* Despite the legal rules, studies regularly demonstrate that patient confidentiality is often breached. See, e.g., Elizabeth A. Kitsis, Shining a Light on Shadowing, 305 JAMA 1029 (2011) (shadowing of physicians by university students and patient privacy); Rebecca Shore et al., Report of the AMA Council on Ethical and Judicial Affairs: Professionalism in the Use of Social Media, 22 J. Clin. Ethics 165 (2011) (noting breaches of patient confidentiality); John C. Moskop, From Hippocrates to HIPAA: Privacy and Confidentiality in Emergency Medicine, 45 Ann. Emerg. Med. 60 (2005); P. A. Ubel et al., Elevator Talk: Observational

Study of Inappropriate Comments in a Public Space, 99 Am. J. Med. 190 (1995).
What explains the gulf between legal standards and medical practice in this area?

2. The Duty to Breach Confidentiality

The duty to maintain confidentiality exists in an uneasy equilibrium with a
potentially conflicting duty to breach confidentiality in some circumstances. Recall
that the federal Privacy Rule permits some disclosures without patient authorization
or opportunity to agree or object. Covered entities:

1. "[M]ay use or disclose protected health information to the extent that such use
   of disclosure is required by law";
2. "[M]ay disclose . . . [PHI] for . . . public health activities and purposes . . . to"
   public health authorities for, e.g., disease surveillance activities, prevention of
   child abuse or neglect, or drug safety monitoring;
3. May disclose PHI to "[a] person who may have been exposed to a communicable disease or may otherwise be at risk of contracting or spreading a disease or
   condition, if the covered entity or public health authority is authorized by law to
   notify such person as necessary in the conduct of a public health intervention or
   investigation"; and
4. [M]ay, consistent with applicable law and standards of ethical conduct, use
   or disclose protected health information, if the covered entity, in good faith,
   believes that the use or disclosure: [] [i]s necessary to prevent or lessen a serious
   and imminent threat to the health or safety of a person or the public; and [] [is]
   to a person or persons reasonably able to prevent or lessen the threat, including
   the target of the threat. . . .

45 C.F.R. §164.512 (a), (b), (c), (j).

Health care providers sometimes have not only a common-law or statutory
authority to breach confidentiality; they also have the *duty* to do so. Failure to meet
this obligation can lead to criminal or civil liability. As you read the following materials, consider the perspective of health care providers. Are the rules governing confidentiality and disclosure in hopeless conflict, subjecting health care providers to
"Catch-22" liability? Consider also the perspective of patients. Are the limits of confidentiality clear for patients? Is the protection afforded patient-provider communication sufficient to encourage necessary medical treatment? Finally, consider the
costs to society created by duties to maintain confidentiality and duties to disclose.
When should the interests of third parties be sufficient to outweigh the interests of
patients in the confidentiality of medical information?

Florida provides a typical example of laws regarding the mandatory reporting
of abuse, neglect, or exploitation of vulnerable adults:

(1) Mandatory reporting.—
    (a) Any person, including, but not limited to, any:
        1. Physician, osteopathic physician, medical examiner, chiropractic physician,
    nurse, paramedic, emergency medical technician, or hospital personnel engaged
    in the admission, examination, care, or treatment of vulnerable adults;
        2. Health professional or mental health professional other than one listed in
    subparagraph 1;

3. Practitioner who relies solely on spiritual means for healing;

4. Nursing home staff; assisted living facility staff; adult day care center staff; adult family-care home staff; social worker; or other professional adult care, residential, or institutional staff; . . . who knows, or has reasonable cause to suspect, that a vulnerable adult has been or is being abused, neglected, or exploited shall immediately report such knowledge or suspicion to the central abuse hotline.

Fla. Stat. Ann. §415.1034. Section 415.1034(b) describes specific types of information about the alleged victim, perpetrator, and types of injuries. Persons who knowingly and willfully fail to make reports or who prevent others from doing so are subject to misdemeanor criminal liability. Id. §415.111. Persons who report matters in good faith are immune from statutory liability.

Notes: Statutory Disclosure Obligations

1. *Structure of Statutory Obligations.* Each state imposes disclosure obligations on health care professionals by statute. The statute typically will establish (1) who has the duty to disclose information; (2) the events or information that must be disclosed; (3) to whom the information must be disclosed; and (4) the immunities or liabilities associated with the disclosure obligation. State disclosure obligations generally apply to a wide range of licensed health professions, such as physicians, nurses, nursing home staff members, social workers, and others. The HIPAA Privacy Rules permit providers to make these disclosures. 45 C.F.R. §164.512.

2. *Types of Disclosure Duties.* Most disclosure obligations are associated with the risk of harm to others through criminal activity or the transmission of disease. The Florida statute focuses on the danger of elder abuse, a matter of particular concern in retirement communities. The disclosure duty stems from concerns that members of this group may not be able to communicate their abuse to others. Like other states, Florida imposes a similar disclosure obligation for instances of suspected child abuse. Fla. Stat. Ann. §39.201.

States also require physicians and others to report gunshot or knife wounds to police authorities. See, e.g., N.Y. Penal Law §265.25. See generally Mark A. Hall, Hospital and Physician Disclosure of Information Concerning a Patient's Crime, 63 U. Det. L. Rev. 145 (1985). The disclosure will alert appropriate authorities to the probability that a crime has occurred, but it is not especially helpful in preventing imminent harm. Citizens do not have a general obligation to disclose possible criminal activity; what justifies the existence of a disclosure obligation here? Arguably, the health care provider who gives medical treatment to a gunshot victim is more than a passive bystander, insofar as he or she may help perpetrators to elude law enforcement officers. In addition, the ordinary rules favoring confidentiality may not apply; individuals who have been shot or knifed may be highly motivated to seek health care whether or not their treatment will be confidential.

What about wounds not serious enough to fall within the scope of a reporting statute but which might nonetheless reveal evidence of criminal activity? Suppose that a district attorney serves grand jury subpoenas duces tecum on nearly two dozen hospitals, seeking "[a]ny and all records pertaining to any male Caucasian patient between the ages of 30 to 45 years, . . . [treated during a two-day period] for a laceration, puncture wound or slash, or other injury caused by or possibly caused by a cutting instrument and/or sharp object, said injury being plainly observable to a lay person without expert or professional knowledge. . . ." The subpoenas expressly exclude from discovery information obtained by licensed health care professionals while attending the patient and necessary to provide care for the patient. Should the hospitals comply? See In re Grand Jury Investigation in New York County, 779 N.E.2d 173 (N.Y. 2002) (upholding appellate decision quashing the subpoenas); In re Grand Jury Subpoena for Medical Records of Payne, 839 A.2d 837 (N.H. 2004) (statute requiring physicians to report bodily injuries arising from criminal acts insufficient to provide unilateral authority for government subpoena of medical records). Finally, states also require health care providers to report information about individuals who have been diagnosed with certain contagious or transmissible diseases.

3. *Disclose to Whom?* States require disclosures to different types of state authorities. Some disclosures are made directly to law enforcement personnel. See, e.g., N.Y. Penal Law §265.25 (gunshot wounds disclosed to police). States have also established special "hotlines" for certain types of disclosures, such as those regarding child or elder abuse. See, e.g., Fla. Stat. Ann. §39.201. Contagious or transmissible disease reports are most often directed to state public health authorities. See, e.g., Fla. Stat. Ann. §384.25 (sexually transmissible diseases reported to health department). The statutes generally provide that the confidentiality of some types of reported information will be protected from further disclosure. See, e.g., id. These confidentiality protections may be constitutionally required.

4. *Immunities and Liabilities.* Providers who file mandatory reports about diseases or abuse are usually immune from damages for any mistake and resulting harm. See Zamstein v. Marvasti, 692 A.2d 781 (Conn. 1997). But see Runyon v. Smith, 749 A.2d 852 (N.J. 2000). Less clear is the legal exposure for a professional who is in a position to file a report, but who fails to do so. Under some statutes, a failure to comply with statutory reporting requirements can lead to criminal or civil liability. New York's child abuse reporting statute provides one example of a typical statutory scheme:

> 1. Any person, official or institution required by this title to report a case of suspected child abuse or maltreatment who willfully fails to do so shall be guilty of a class A misdemeanor.
> 2. Any person, official or institution required by this title to report a case of suspected child abuse or maltreatment who knowingly and willfully fails to do so shall be civilly liable for the damages proximately caused by such failure.

N.Y. Social Services Law §420.

Should children injured by a provider's failure to report child abuse be permitted to bring suit in jurisdictions where the reporting statute does not include a specific civil remedy? Courts are divided. See Annot., 73 A.L.R.4th 782 (1989). Should a subsequent child abuse victim be permitted to sue the provider on the theory that if the provider had reported the first victim the second victim would not have been at risk? Marcelletti v. Bathani, 500 N.W.2d 124 (Mich. Ct. App. 1993) (no); Yates v. Mansfield Board of Education, 102 Ohio St.3d 205 (2005) (yes). A provider's failure to follow reporting rules can also spark professional disciplinary action. In the Matter of Schroeder, 415 N.W.2d 436 (Minn. Ct. App. 1988). Should a health care provider have a duty to disclose the limits of confidentiality before providing services to her patients? See Marks v. Tenbrunsel, 910 So. 2d 1255 (Alabama 2005) (patient not permitted to pursue claim against psychologist who reported alleged child abuse even though patient claims he was assured of confidentiality); Hayes v. State, 667 N.E.2d 222 (Ind. Ct. App. 1996) (holding that therapist had no duty to warn client that disclosures of child sexual abuse would be reported to state authorities).

5. *Common-Law Disclosure Requirements.* As the next case reveals, disclosure obligations also arise under common law.

■ BRADSHAW v. DANIEL
854 S.W.2d 865 (Tenn. 1993)

ANDERSON, Justice.

We granted this appeal to determine whether a physician has a legal duty to warn a nonpatient of the risk of exposure to the source of his patient's noncontagious disease — Rocky Mountain Spotted Fever. . . .

On July 19, 1986, Elmer Johns went to the emergency room at Methodist Hospital South in Memphis, Tennessee, complaining of headaches, muscle aches, fever, and chills. He was admitted to the hospital under the care and treatment of the defendant, Dr. Chalmers B. Daniel, Jr. Dr. Daniel first saw Johns on July 22, 1986, at which time he ordered the drug Chloramphenicol, which is the drug of choice for a person in the latter stages of Rocky Mountain Spotted Fever. Johns' condition rapidly deteriorated, and he died the next day, July 23, 1986. An autopsy was performed, and the Centers for Disease Control in Atlanta conclusively confirmed, in late September 1986, that the cause of death was Rocky Mountain Spotted Fever. Although Dr. Daniel communicated with Elmer Johns' wife, Genevieve, during Johns' treatment, he never advised her of the risks of exposure to Rocky Mountain Spotted Fever, or that the disease could have been the cause of Johns' death.

A week after her husband's death, on August 1, 1986, Genevieve Johns came to the emergency room of Baptist Memorial Hospital in Memphis, Tennessee, with similar symptoms of chills, fever, mental disorientation, nausea, lung congestion, myalgia, and swelling of the hands. She was admitted to the hospital and treated for Rocky Mountain Spotted Fever, but she died three days later, on August 4, 1986, of that disease. It is undisputed that no patient-physician relationship existed between Genevieve Johns and Dr. Daniel.

The plaintiff, William Jerome Bradshaw, is Genevieve Johns' son. He filed this suit alleging that the defendant's negligence in failing to advise Genevieve Johns that her husband died of Rocky Mountain Spotted Fever, and in failing to warn her of the risk of exposure, proximately caused her death. . . . Dr. Gelfand [an expert witness for the defense] testified that the medical standard of care did not require a physician treating a patient infected with, or suspected of being infected with, Rocky Mountain Spotted Fever to treat the family of the patient in contact with him, or to warn them of the risk of exposure to the disease or the risk of exposure to ticks or tick bites. The plaintiff responded with the affidavit of Dr. Burt Prater. Dr. Prater testified that because of the clustering effect of the disease, the medical standard of care required that a physician treating a patient with symptoms of Rocky

Mountain Spotted Fever advise the family of the patient as to the incubation period, the symptoms of the disease, and the need for immediate medical attention upon manifestation of the symptoms. Dr. Prater further testified that the defendant, Dr. Daniel, negligently failed to diagnose Elmer Johns' fatal disease of Rocky Mountain Spotted Fever and failed to warn his wife, Genevieve Johns, of the incubation period of the disease, the symptoms, and the need to seek medical treatment upon manifestation of the symptoms. He also testified that the disease, if untreated, has a 40 percent mortality rate, but if treated promptly, has a 4 percent mortality rate. Based on the affidavits, the defendant's motion for summary judgment was denied. The case was . . . tried before a jury, which returned a verdict of $50,000 against the defendant. . . .

LEGAL DUTY

The defendant physician argues that he owed his patient's wife no legal duty because first, there was no physician-patient relationship, and second, Rocky Mountain Spotted Fever is not a contagious disease and, therefore, there is no duty to warn of the risk of exposure.

We begin our analysis by examining how we determine when a legal duty may be imposed upon one for the benefit of another. While duty was not part of the early English common law jurisprudence of tort liability, it has since become an essential element in negligence cases. . . . [T]he imposition of a legal duty reflects society's contemporary policies and social requirements concerning the right of individuals and the general public to be protected from another's act or conduct. Indeed, it has been stated that " 'duty' is not sacrosanct in itself, but is only an expression of the sum total of those considerations of policy which lead the law to say that the plaintiff is entitled to protection." W. Keeton, Prosser and Keeton on the Law of Torts §53 at 358. . . .

The defendant contends that the absence of a physician-patient relationship negates the existence of a duty in this case. While it is true that a physician-patient relationship is necessary to the maintenance of a medical malpractice action, it is not necessary for the maintenance of an action based on negligence, and this Court has specifically recognized that a physician may owe a duty to a nonpatient third party for injuries caused by the physician's negligence, if the injuries suffered and the manner in which they occurred were reasonably foreseeable. Wharton Transport Corp. v. Bridges, 606 S.W.2d 521, 526 (Tenn. 1980) (physician owed duty to third party injured by disabled truck driver's negligence, where the physician was negligent both in his physical examination and certification of the truck driver for the employer).

Here, we are asked to determine whether a physician has an affirmative duty to warn a patient's family member about the symptoms and risks of exposure to Rocky Mountain Spotted Fever, a noncontagious disease. Insofar as we are able to determine, there is no reported decision from this or any other jurisdiction involving circumstances exactly similar to those presented in this case.

We begin by observing that all persons have a duty to use reasonable care to refrain from conduct that will foreseeably cause injury to others. In determining the existence of a duty, courts have distinguished between action and inaction. Professor Prosser has commented that "the reason for the distinction may be said to lie in the fact that by 'misfeasance' the defendant has created a new risk of harm to the plaintiff, while by 'nonfeasance' he has at least made his situation no worse, and has merely failed to benefit him by interfering in his affairs." Prosser, §56 at 373.

Because of this reluctance to countenance nonfeasance as a basis of liability, as a general rule, under the common law, one person owed no affirmative duty to warn those endangered by the conduct of another. Prosser, §56 at 374; Tarasoff v. Regents of University of California, 17 Cal. 3d 425 (1976). To mitigate the harshness of this rule, courts have carved out exceptions for cases in which the defendant stands in some special relationship to either the person who is the source of the danger, or to the person who is foreseeably at risk from the danger. Accordingly,

> while an actor is always bound to prevent his acts from creating an unreasonable risk to others, he is under the affirmative duty to act to prevent another from sustaining harm only when certain socially recognized relations exist which constitute the basis for such legal duty.

Harper & Kime, The Duty to Control the Conduct of Another, 43 Yale L.J. 886, 887 (1934).

One of the most widely known cases applying that principle is *Tarasoff*, supra, in which the California Supreme Court held that when a psychotherapist determines or, pursuant to the standards of his profession, should determine that his patient presents a serious danger of violence to another, the therapist has an affirmative duty to use reasonable care to protect the intended victim against such danger, and the duty may require the physician to warn the intended victim of the danger. The special relationship of the patient to his psychotherapist supported imposition of the affirmative duty to act for the benefit of third persons. . . .

Decisions of other jurisdictions have employed the same analysis and held that the relationship of a physician to his patient is sufficient to support the duty to exercise reasonable care to protect third persons against foreseeable risks emanating from a patient's physical illness. Specifically, other courts have recognized that physicians may be liable to persons infected by a patient, if the physician negligently fails to diagnose a contagious disease, or having diagnosed the illness, fails to warn family members or others who are foreseeably at risk of exposure to the disease. . . . [S]ee generally Annot., 3 A.L.R.5th 370 (1992). . . .

Returning to the facts of this case, first, it is undisputed that there was a physician-patient relationship between Dr. Daniel and Elmer Johns. Second, here, as in the contagious disease context, it is also undisputed that Elmer Johns' wife, who was residing with him, was at risk of contracting the disease. This is so even though the disease is not contagious in the narrow sense that it can be transmitted from one person to another. Both Dr. Daniel and Dr. Prater, the plaintiff's expert, testified that family members of patients suffering from Rocky Mountain Spotted Fever are at risk of contracting the disease due to a phenomenon called clustering, which is related to the activity of infected ticks who transmit the disease to humans. Dr. Prater also testified that Dr. Daniel negligently failed to diagnose the disease and negligently failed to warn his patient's wife, Genevieve Johns, of her risk of exposure to the source of disease. Dr. Daniel's expert disputed these conclusions, but Dr. Daniel conceded there is a medical duty to inform the family when there is a diagnosis of the disease. Thus, this case is analogous to the *Tarasoff* line of cases adopting a duty to warn of danger and the contagious disease cases adopting a comparable duty to warn. Here, as in those cases, there was a foreseeable risk of harm to an identifiable third party, and the reasons supporting the recognition of the duty to warn are equally compelling here.

We, therefore, conclude that the existence of the physician-patient relationship is sufficient to impose upon a physician an affirmative duty to warn identifiable third persons in the patient's immediate family against foreseeable risks emanating from a patient's illness. Accordingly, we hold that under the factual circumstances of this case, viewing the evidence in a light most favorable to the plaintiff, the defendant physician had a duty to warn his patient's wife of the risk to her of contracting Rocky Mountain Spotted Fever, when he knew, or in the exercise of reasonable care, should have known, that his patient was suffering from the disease. Our holding here is necessarily limited to the conclusion that the defendant physician owed Genevieve Johns a legal duty. We express no opinion on the other elements which would be required to establish a cause of action for common-law negligence in this case.

Accordingly . . . this cause is remanded to the trial court for proceedings consistent with this opinion. . . .

Notes: Common-Law Duty to Warn

1. *Overview.* Was Dr. Daniel negligent in his treatment of his patient, Elmer Johns? Daniel appropriately identified the cause of Johns' illness and provided treatment. On what basis can he be held liable for injuries to someone who was not his patient? The court notes that the existence of a physician-patient relationship generally is a prerequisite to the maintenance of a malpractice action. It finds, however, that the absence of a relationship is no barrier to an ordinary negligence action. See Chapter 2.B.1, discussing a physician's duty to third parties. However, the court still must confront whether there is a "special relationship," due to the oft-described distinction between "misfeasance" and "nonfeasance" (creating a risk of harm vs. failing to protect others from a risk of harm created by another). As a general rule, nonfeasance does not constitute actionable negligence. The "special relationship" rule is an exception to this principle. See, e.g., Restatement (Second) Torts §§314, 314A; W. Jonathan Cardi, A Pluralistic Analysis of the Therapist/Physician Duty to Warn Third Parties, 44 Wake Forest L. Rev. 877 (2009); Aaron D. Twerski, The Cleaver, the Violin, and the Scalpel: Duty and the Restatement (Third) of Torts, 60 Hastings L.J. 1 (2008). The key in many third-party liability cases therefore is whether there is a "special relationship" that justifies the imposition of liability for nonfeasance. Note that some jurisdictions are hostile toward the expansion of physicians' duties to third parties. See, e.g., Thapar v. Zezulka, 994 S.W.2d 635 (Tex. 1999).

Once the existence of a duty is established, the court must determine its scope. The scope of the duty is determined in large part by the nature of the risk and the physician's ability to reduce the risk reasonably. Note that in duty to warn situations, some risks can be reduced simply by warning the patient. As an example, suppose that a physician treats a patient for epilepsy and fails to tell the patient to refrain from driving. The patient has a seizure and runs into an oncoming car. Although the physician may have a duty to the driver of the other car, the accident and injury could easily have been avoided by warning the patient not to drive. If the patient had been warned, and had refrained from driving, no breach of confidentiality would have been required and there would have been no conflict between the duty to maintain confidentiality and the duty to protect others from harm. The discussion in this section focuses on the more difficult cases where physicians might have to breach patient confidentiality in order to protect third parties. Note that the federal Privacy Rules permit covered entities to disclose personally identifiable health information in some circumstances to prevent or reduce the risk of a "serious and imminent threat to health and safety" 45 C.F.R. §164.512(j), supra page 182.

Just how far does the duty described in *Bradshaw* extend? The Supreme Court of Connecticut addressed the issue in Jarmie v. Troncale, 306 Conn. 578 (Conn. 2012). In that case, a pedestrian was struck by a car, which the defendant's patient was driving. The victim brought a negligence claim against the doctor for failing to warn his patient that a medication the doctor had prescribed might cause drowsiness. The court concluded that the doctor had no duty to the third party and dismissed the case. Should the outcome have been different if the patient had sued, rather than the third-party victim?

2. *Categorizing Cases: A General Theory of Liability or a Laundry List?* The first problem in these common-law liability cases lies in determining the existence of a "special relationship." The *Bradshaw* court notes that the physician-patient relationship has been used to support the imposition of liability in cases involving dangerous psychiatric patients and patients with contagious illnesses. Courts have also noted the importance of the physician-patient relationship in some automobile and child abuse cases. Does this indicate that physicians will always be held liable for injuries caused by or to their patients? Or are courts developing a list of situations in which physicians may be held liable? If so, what principles or factors determine whether the physician owes a duty to the third party? Are disclosure obligations limited to physicians, or do other types of health care professionals face the same threat of liability?

a. *Contagious Diseases.* One well-developed line of cases holds physicians liable for injuries to nonpatients caused by communicable diseases. Physicians have been held liable for failing to diagnose the contagious condition. See, e.g., Jones v. Stanko, 160 N.E. 456 (Ohio 1928) (physician fails to diagnose smallpox and puts neighbors at risk for infection). But see Ellis v. Peter, 627 N.Y.S.2d 707 (App. Div. 1995) (failure to diagnose TB; no duty to warn). Liability has also been imposed for failure to warn others about the risk of transmission. See, e.g., Skillings v. Allen, 173 N.W. 663 (Minn. 1919) (negligent failure to disclose risk of transmission of scarlet fever); Gammill v. United States, 727 F.2d 950, 954 (10th Cir. 1984) (physician may be found liable for failing to warn persons at risk for exposure of the danger). By contrast, see McNulty v. City of New York, 792 N.E.2d 162 (N.Y. 2003) (defendant physicians did not owe friend of person infected with meningitis a duty to warn her of the risk of infection); Santa Rosa Health Care Corp. v. Garcia, 964 S.W.2d 940 (Tex. 1998) (no duty to warn wife of hemophiliac of risk of HIV). See generally Annot., 3 A.L.R.5th 370 (1992). Note that *Bradshaw* is an extension of this principle — Rocky Mountain Spotted Fever is not contagious but it is likely that others in the patient's household may have come into contact with infected ticks.

The duty to protect third parties from harm in contagious disease cases has become highly controversial because of the risk of HIV transmission. Do physicians have an obligation to warn third parties when their patients continue to engage in activities that present the risk of HIV transmission? The answer is complicated somewhat by the existence of special statutes protecting the confidentiality of

HIV-related information, which may restrict the ability to disclose information even when others may be at risk, and by variations in the risk of transmission related to use of condoms and anti-retroviral therapies. See generally Guion L. Johnstone, A Social Worker's Dilemma When a Client Has a Sexually Transmitted Disease, 49 U. Louisville L. Rev. 111 (2010) (reviewing physician obligations); Bernard Friedland, HIV Confidentiality and the Right to Warn — The Health Care Provider's Dilemma, 80 Mass. L. Rev. 3 (1995).

b. *Mental Illness.* Another set of cases concern a mental health professional's duty to protect third parties from his or her patient. The leading case is Tarasoff v. Regents of University of California, 551 P.2d 334 (Cal. 1976), discussed briefly in *Bradshaw.* In *Tarasoff,* a therapist knew that a patient had made threats of violence toward a young woman. The therapist unsuccessfully attempted to commit the patient for treatment. The patient murdered the young woman, whose parents then sued the patient's mental health care providers. The California Supreme Court, relying in part on Restatement (Second) of Torts §315, supra, held that psychotherapists could be held liable for failing to exercise reasonable care to protect a third party where the therapists know or should know that their patient presents a serious danger of violence to another. The court held that therapists might have an obligation to warn those at risk and specifically rejected the defendants' contention that such a warning would impermissibly breach client confidentiality. *Tarasoff* was much discussed by commentators through the late 1970s and 1980s.

Tarasoff is an important opinion, almost always cited by courts and legislative bodies whether it is followed or rejected. See, e.g., Munstermann v. Alegent Health-Immanuel Medical Center, 716 N.W.2d 73 (Neb. 2006) (establishing scope of psychiatrist's liability to third parties); Powell v. Catholic Medical Center, 749 A.2d 301 (N.H. 2000) (discussing implications of state codification of *Tarasoff*-type rule); Estates of Morgan v. Fairfield Family Counseling Center, 673 N.E.2d 1311 (Ohio 1997) (psychiatrist-outpatient relationship is a "special relationship" justifying imposition of duty to protect third parties).

Many jurisdictions have adopted only a narrow reading of *Tarasoff* or have rejected it completely. See, e.g., Dawe v. Dr. Reuven Bar-Levav & Associates, 780 N.W.2d 272 (Mich. 2010) (statute codifying narrow mental health professional's duties to warn did not completely abrogate common-law duty of care to other patients). Indeed, California itself has partially limited it by statute. Ann. Cal. Civ. Code §43.92. In Nasser v. Parker, 455 S.E.2d 502 (Va. 1995), for example, the court considered whether the defendant physician and hospital had a duty to warn a victim about the impending release of a former boyfriend who had threatened to kill her. The court noted the special relationship rule found in §315, but held that no special relationship existed without an additional showing of an ability to control the patient's conduct:

> Accordingly, we disagree with the holding of *Tarasoff* that a doctor-patient relationship or a hospital-patient relationship alone is sufficient, as a matter of law, to establish a "special relation" under Restatement §315(a). Within the context of the Restatement, there is nothing special about the ordinary doctor-patient relationship or hospital-patient relationship. We think there must be added to those ordinary relationships the factor, required by [Restatement] §319, of taking charge

of the patient, meaning that the doctor or hospital must be vested with a higher degree of control over the patient than exists in the ordinary doctor-patient or hospital-patient relationship before a duty arises concerning the patient's conduct.

Id. at 506. See also Boulanger v. Pol, 900 P.2d 823 (Kan. 1995) (no special relationship between psychiatrist and voluntary mental patient); Thapar v. Zezulka, 994 S.W.2d 635 (Tex. 1999) (no duty to warn). But see Volk v. DeMeerleer, 187 Wash. 2d 241 (2016) (arguably expanding *Tarasoff*-type liability by holding that psychiatrist may be liable to outpatient's foreseeable victims).

c. *Driving Impairments.* Most driving impairment cases involve the physician's obligation to warn the patient about the risks of driving. See, e.g., Weigold v. Patel, 840 A.2d 19 (Conn. App. 2004) (no liability where patient aware of tendency to fall asleep while driving). See generally Annot., 43 A.L.R.4th 153 (1986). Where a state statute requires physicians to report certain driving impairments, physicians can be held liable for injuries to third parties. See, e.g., Harden by Harden v. Allstate Insurance Co., 883 F. Supp. 963 (D. Del. 1995). But see Praesel v. Johnson, 967 S.W.2d 391 (Tex. 1998) (no negligence per se or common-law duty).

d. *Genetic Risks?* How should the duty to warn apply to genetic disorders? Does a physician who diagnoses a hereditary disorder in a person have obligations to disclose that disorder to the patient's children or siblings (often called the "proband")? Compare Pate v. Threlkel, 661 So.2d 278 (Fla. 1995) (physician owed a duty to children of patient diagnosed with a hereditary disease, but that duty was satisfied by warning the patient and did not require warning children directly) with Safer v. Estate of Pack, 677 A.2d 1188 (N.J. Super. 1996) (declining to follow *Pate* because the court could not say that "in all circumstances, the duty to warn will be satisfied by informing the patient. It may be necessary, at some stage, to resolve a conflict between the physician's broader duty to warn and his fidelity to an expressed preference of the patient that nothing be said to family members about the details of the disease.") See also Molloy v. Meier, 679 N.W.2d 711 (Minn. 2004) ("physician's duty regarding genetic testing and diagnosis extends beyond the patient to biological parents who foreseeably may be harmed by a breach of that duty"). Should the law turn on what most patients would want in terms of information? See K. Wolff et al., Confidentiality Versus Duty to Inform—An Empirical Study on Attitudes Toward the Handling of Genetic Information, 143 Am. J. Med. Genet. A. 142 (2007) (most respondents wished to be informed about a hereditary disease in their family; study included consideration of conditions under which breach of confidentiality would be deemed acceptable). Suppose that a sperm bank or egg brokerage later determines that one of its donors has a hereditary disease. Should it have an obligation to track down all the donor-conceived children of that donor? What if doing so would require informing the child that their maternity or paternity is different from what he or she believes?

e. *Incidental Findings in Research.* These materials focus on duties to disclose within a clinical relationship. There is also a well-established literature on somewhat analogous duties in the research context, what are often called "incidental findings." For a good discussion, see Symposium, The Law of Incidental Findings in Human Subjects Research: Establishing Researchers' Duties, 36 J.L. Med. & Ethics 361 (2008). See also, section D. Human Experimentation and Research, below.

3. *A Risk of Harm.* The risk of harm is clear in some cases, particularly those involving serious contagious diseases. The issue is more problematic in the case of psychiatric patients. See, e.g., Douglas Mossman, The Imperfection of Protection Through Detection and Intervention, 30 J. Leg. Med. 109 (2009). Can mental health professionals accurately predict which patients will present a risk of harm to others? The *Tarasoff* court used a professional standard of care to measure the scope of the physicians' obligation to third parties: If the defendant knew or should have known of the risk, using professional judgment, then liability may follow. Tarasoff v. Regents of University of California, 551 P.2d 334 (Cal. 1976). See also Estates of Morgan v. Fairfield Family Counseling Center, 673 N.E.2d 1311, 1325 (Ohio 1997) (psychotherapists need not have perfect predictive power), superseded by statute, Ohio Rev. Code Ann. §2305.51 (West 2014) (expressly limiting mental health professionals' liability for failure to warn to circumstances where the patient has made explicit threats of harm to a clearly identifiable victim and the physician did not take one of four enumerated steps).

4. *Foreseeable and Identifiable Third Parties.* Many contagious disease and psychiatric dangerousness cases suggest that a health care provider's duty to disclose is established by a specific risk to foreseeable and identifiable third parties. See, e.g., *Bradshaw* and *Tarasoff,* supra. This requirement serves at least two purposes: It bolsters the sense that the risk of harm is imminent, and it suggests that a disclosure requirement is reasonable. Where a health care provider knows the identity of the person at risk of harm, it seems reasonable to require that that person be warned about the risk. A few courts have also been willing to impose a duty to breach confidentiality even where the risk is more generalized, however. In Schuster v. Altenberg, 424 N.W.2d 159 (Wis. 1988), the court held that a duty to breach confidentiality existed even in cases where there was no "readily identifiable target" of the patient's violent tendencies. Id. at 172-174. In such cases, the therapist has the duty to inform police so that emergency commitment proceedings can be initiated.

In cases where the claim is based on the physician's failure to disclose information to the *patient* rather than to the injured third parties, courts have not limited liability to situations in which the third party is known or identifiable. See, e.g., Reisner v. Regents of the University of California, 37 Cal. Rptr. 2d 518 (Cal. Ct. App. 1995) (physicians owed a duty to HIV-infected boyfriend to disclose to patient or her parents her HIV status; failure to disclose occurred long before sexual relationship between young people began).

5. *Disclose to Whom?* As noted above, in most cases a physician's duty to third parties is discharged by disclosing the risk to his or her patient. See, e.g., Emerich v. Philadelphia Center for Human Development, Inc., 720 A.2d 1032 (Pa. 1999) (duty satisfied by statement to victim that she should not go to patient's apartment); Pate v. Threlkel, 661 So. 2d 278 (Fla. 1995) ("in any circumstances in which the physician has a duty to warn . . . that duty will be satisfied by warning the patient."). Where the patient presents a risk of harm to an identifiable third party, many jurisdictions also will impose a duty to disclose the risk to that person. See, e.g., *Tarasoff,* supra. Sometimes the provider's disclosure obligation can be met through an institutional disclosure mechanism. In Casarez v. NME Hospital, 883 S.W.2d 360 (Tex. App. 1994), for example, a nurse who allegedly contracted HIV from a patient sued the patient's physician for failing to warn him of the patient's condition. The court held that the

physician complied with his obligations by notifying the hospital's infection control and quality assurance committees of his patient's condition.

In the absence of a statute, should a court require a physician, who knows that a patient presents a risk of harm through driving, to disclose this information to state authorities? What if the patient is informed of the risk and states that she will continue to drive despite the danger?

6. *Zone of Reasonable Judgment.* Given the conflicting nature of the duties to disclose and to protect confidentiality, and the ambiguities associated with each duty, do physicians have enough guidance to allow them to avoid liability? Even if the duties were precisely defined, it would be tricky at best to walk the narrow line between them. But where the extent of each duty is uncertain, it may be impossible to avoid liability. Disclosing may give rise to damages or ethical sanctions for breach of confidentiality, whereas keeping quiet may result in damages for injuries caused to others. What's a doctor to do? Should the law provide for a neutral zone between these two duties, in which disclosure is discretionary, but not mandatory? In other words, doctors would have a qualified privilege to disclose if they do so in the good faith belief that disclosure is necessary to prevent harm, but could not be sued for failing to disclose unless _____. The issue then becomes: How would you fill in the blank? See Mark A. Hall, Hospital and Physician Disclosure of Information Concerning a Patient's Crime, 63 U. Det. L. Rev. 145 (1985) (advocating a qualified privilege with respect to the duty to report serious crimes committed by patients).

7. *Further Reading.* On the *Tarasoff* case and its progeny, see Mark Rothstein, Tarasoff Duties after Newton, 42 J.L., Med. & Ethics 104 (2014); Symposium, *Tarasoff* at Thirty, 75 U. Cin. L. Rev. 497-661 (2006); W. Jonathon Cardi, A Pluralistic Analysis of the Therapist/Physician Duty to Warn Third Parties, 44 Wake Forest L. Rev. 877 (2009); Annot., 83 A.L.R.3d 1201 (1978). On disclosure obligations as to genetic risks, see Mary L. Kovalesky, To Disclose or Not to Disclose: Determining the Scope and Exercise of a Physician's Duty to Warn Third Parties of Genetically Transmissible Conditions, 76 U. Cin. L. Rev. 1019 (2007-2008); Gillian Nycum et al., Intra-Familial Obligations to Communicate Genetic Risk Information: What Foundations? What Forms?, 3 McGill J.L. & Health 21 (2009) (providing international comparisons); Kenneth Offit et al., The "Duty to Warn" a Patient's Family Members About Hereditary Disease Risks, 292 JAMA 1469 (2004).

Discussion Problems

Consider how you would analyze the following problems. What law(s) or regulations would apply in your state? Will the health care provider have a duty to maintain confidentiality, the authority to breach confidentiality, or a duty to disclose the information?

- A 30-year-old woman meets with a physician who had also treated her mother. The woman asks the physician for specific information about her mother's medical history. The woman argues that she needs the information to determine whether she is at a significantly higher risk for (a) cancer, (b) high blood pressure, or (c) glaucoma. Should it matter whether the woman's mother is deceased? On this last point, see 45 C.F.R. §164.502(f) ("A covered entity must comply with the [privacy] requirements . . . with respect to the [PHI] of a deceased individual for a period of 50 years following the death of the individual."); and Jessica Berg, Grave Secrets: Legal and Ethical Analysis of Postmortem Confidentiality, 34 Conn. L. Rev. 81 (2001).

- A drug treatment center's admission form includes the following notice:

  > We understand that persons who have problems with drugs and alcohol may fear that treatment information will be disclosed to others, including family members or employers. Rest assured that your medical treatment information will be protected from disclosure as provided by law.

  A patient undergoes voluntary HIV testing and receives a positive test result. May or must the treatment center disclose the patient's HIV status to other patients? What if it appears that the HIV-infected patient has begun a sexual relationship with another patient? What if the patient is taking anti-retroviral therapies, which reduce the risk of transmission, and claims that she or he is using safer sexual practices?

- Law enforcement officials are concerned about another possible anthrax bioterrorism event. Local authorities approach pharmacies in a particular town, seeking information about recent prescriptions for antibiotics. May the pharmacies release the information to law enforcement officials? Suppose that a physician in the town recently received a call from a patient, inquiring about a prescription for an antibiotic thought to be effective against anthrax. May or must the physician disclose this information to anyone?

C. INFORMED CONSENT

1. Goals, Aspirations, Policies

In Chapter 1.A.2 and in the introduction to this chapter we observed that the physician-patient relationship is characterized by a huge imbalance of power, owing to the vulnerability of illness and treatment and physicians' vastly superior knowledge and skills. This power imbalance may be further accentuated by economic and cultural factors. What should the medical and legal response be to these inequalities in the physician-patient relationship? Historically, or perhaps apocryphally, a patient's reverence for her physician was a source of comfort and an important underpinning to the psychology of a cure. A wide range of factors — perhaps among them the anti-establishment views of the 1960s, the consumer movement of the 1970s, the patient advocacy movements of the 1980s and 1990s, the ready availability of health-related information on the Internet beginning in the 2000s, the startling advances and lingering failures of medical progress, and the expansion of specialties such as "bioethics" and "health law" — have combined to challenge the authority and supremacy of the physician. The most prominent legal tool used by those seeking to reform the physician-patient relationship is the doctrine of informed consent. It is believed that requiring physicians to provide more information to their patients will help to redress the power imbalance problems created by the inequality of knowledge. As you read the materials on informed consent, consider how effective the law has been, or conceivably could be, in accomplishing this reformist mission. Consider also what model the reformists envision for the ideal patient-physician interaction, and whether all (or many) patients actually subscribe to that model.

■PATIENT-CENTERED MEDICINE: A PROFESSIONAL EVOLUTION
Christine Laine & Frank Davidoff*
275 JAMA 152, 152-153 (1996)

In the past, physicians commonly withheld diagnostic information from patients with patients' tacit consent. Hippocrates advocated "concealing most things from the patient while you are attending to him . . . revealing nothing of the patient's future or present condition." . . . The attitude[] of Hippocrates . . . would undoubtedly get [him] into trouble today. Patients increasingly expect to know not only their diagnoses, but also details of pathophysiology, treatment options, and prognosis. . . . Patients expect and often demand information that used to be only within physicians' reach, and physicians increasingly expect to share such information with patients.

The transformation in attitudes surrounding disclosure of diagnoses is particularly striking when one considers cancer. . . . A 1961 study . . . revealed that . . . 90 percent of physicians surveyed preferred not to tell cancer patients their diagnoses. . . . [B]y 1979 . . . 97 percent of physicians surveyed preferred to disclose a diagnosis of cancer. . . .

Beyond "honesty is the best policy," the argument for informing patients is that information enables patients to participate in medical decisions. In more physician-centered days, physicians would decide what was best for their patients, and patient participation was limited to compliance with physicians' orders. As medicine becomes more patient centered, participation begins with the patient helping to decide what the physician will order, and the emphasis shifts from compliance to participation.

■RETHINKING INFORMED CONSENT
Peter H. Schuck**
103 Yale L.J. 899, 900-905 (1994)

The doctrine requiring physicians to obtain a patient's informed consent before undertaking treatment is relatively young, having first appeared in a

* Dr. Laine is Editor in Chief, and Dr. Davidoff is an Editor Emeritus, at the Annals of Internal Medicine, published by the American College of Physicians. Dr. Laine is also affiliated with the Division of Internal Medicine at Jefferson Medical College, Thomas Jefferson University.
** Reprinted by permission of The Yale Law Journal Company and Fred B. Rothman & Company. The author is the Simeon E. Baldwin Professor Emeritus of Law at Yale Law School.

recognizable, relatively robust form only in 1957.[1] Yet the values that underlie the doctrine have an ancient pedigree. The consent norm had occupied a prominent and honored place in our legal thought for many centuries before the courts began to develop a jurisprudence of informed consent in health care.[2] Also well established was the cognate notion that consent must be informed or knowledgeable in some meaningful sense if we are to accord it legal or moral significance. . . .

The doctrine of informed consent in health care shared in the more general expansion of American tort liability that proceeded well into the 1980s and that now appears to have stabilized. Everyone, it seems, favors the principle of informed consent; it is "only" the specific details and applications of the doctrine that arouse serious debate. In order to map and enlarge this debate, it is useful to distinguish three different versions of informed consent doctrine. The first is the letter and spirit of the doctrine as developed primarily by courts—the law "in books." The second is the doctrine as imagined, feared, and often caricatured by some physicians—the law "in the mind." The third version, a consequence both of the gap between the first two and of other situational constraints, is the doctrine as actually practiced by clinicians—the law "in action." (Of course, there are almost as many laws-in-action as there are distinct physician-patient relationships.)

Most commentators on informed consent deploy one or more of these versions of the law. Generally (and crudely) speaking, these commentators fall into two camps: idealists and realists. Informed consent idealists—primarily some judges and medical ethicists—advocate a relatively expansive conception of the physician's obligation to disclose and elicit information about risks and alternatives.[18] More specifically, the idealists tend to define informed consent law's pivotal concepts—materiality of risk, disclosure, alternatives, and causation—broadly and subjectively from the perspective of the individual patient rather than that of the professional, while defining the law's exceptions to the duty narrowly. Perhaps most important, idealists emphasize the qualitative dimension of physician-patient interactions concerning treatment decisions. They insist that these interactions be dialogic rather than authoritative, tailored to the individual patient's emotional needs and cognitive capacities rather than formulaic, aimed at maximizing patient autonomy and comprehension rather than mere information flow, and sensitive to the distortions that can be created by power differentials between physician and patient.

The idealists employ a distinctive rhetorical strategy. Capitalizing on the universal support for the principles and goals of informed consent, they point to the often striking difference between the law in books and the law in action—a difference that I call the "informed consent gap." The existence of this gap, they argue,

1. See Jay Katz, The Silent World of Doctor and Patient 48-84 (1984); see also Ruth R. Faden & Tom L. Beauchamp, A History and Theory of Informed Consent 235-273 (1986).

2. See, e.g., Ford v. Ford, 10 N.E. 474, 475 (Mass. 1887) [assault defined in part by absence of consent].

18. See, e.g., Canterbury v. Spence, 464 F.2d 772, 787 (D.C. Cir. 1972) (principle of informed consent requires that physician disclose information that reasonable patient would wish to know in making treatment decisions); Truman v. Thomas, 611 P.2d 902, 906-907 (Cal. 1980) (patient must be apprised of risks of not undergoing treatment, even if she has refused treatment); see also Katz, supra note 1, at 48-84.

shows that the law in action falls far short of the law in books. Since the law that they think should be in the books is often even more demanding, the true gap is wider still. The problem, then, is not so much the law in books, which tends to demand too little of physicians; rather, it is the laws in action and in the mind. For the idealist, therefore, the goal of reform must be to close the informed consent gap by conforming the law in action, at the very least, to the law now in books.

The realists—primarily practicing physicians—harbor a different vision of informed consent.[20] Although they emphatically do not contest the principle and goals of informed consent, they do question whether most patients really desire the kind of dialogue that the idealists propose. They also question whether, whatever patients desire, the gains in patient autonomy and improved outcomes produced by the dialogue are worth the additional time, money, and needless patient anxiety and confusion that informed consent may entail. Like the idealists, many realists employ a characteristic rhetoric. Rather than master the doctrinal details of the informed consent law in books, they point instead to the law in their minds, which they can easily caricature in order to demonstrate the law's folly. Although some realists do not concede that the law in action actually deviates from the law in their minds, many others readily admit that a gap does in fact exist. To them, however, this gap simply demonstrates how impractical the idealists' vision is and why it cannot be implemented in the demanding world of contemporary clinical practice.

In a real sense, then, informed consent idealists and realists argue past one another, producing a debate that is oblique and inconclusive rather than pointed and fruitful. For several related reasons, it is time to revisit this debate. These reasons include the intense public concern about rising health care costs, the bureaucratization of the physician-patient relationship, and the organization of health care delivery into units with some degree of market power over providers. Is the informed consent gap to be deplored or tolerated? Should physicians' legal obligations to disclose be further expanded, retained in their present form, or reduced? . . .

Notes: The Theory and Practice of Informed Consent

1. *Using Legal Rules to Foster Autonomy.* Peter Schuck suggests that informed consent idealists seek to promote individual autonomy while informed consent realists argue that the goals of complete individual autonomy cannot be met, at least not without great cost. As you read the following materials, identify the interests protected by the informed consent doctrine. A number of commentators have concluded that the doctrine fails to protect individual interests or to promote individual autonomy. See, e.g., Jay Katz, Informed Consent—Must It Remain a Fairy Tale?, 10 J. Contemp. Health L. & Pol'y 69 (1993).

20. Perhaps the most articulate of the realists is Dr. Thomas P. Duffy. See Thomas P. Duffy, Agamemnon's Fate and the Medical Profession, 9 W. New Eng. L. Rev. 21 (1987) (reviewing and criticizing Jay Katz's approach). Dr. Sherwin Nuland advances a more moderate realist position in his . . . book. See Sherwin B. Nuland, How We Die: Reflections on Life's Final Chapter 258-261, 265-267 (1994) (distinguishing inter alia, between family physicians, who can and should engage in meaningful informed consent dialogue with patients, and specialists, who cannot realistically be expected to do so).

Should we blame the law for this shortcoming, or is it inherently incapable of regulating the subtle and minute interactions between doctors and patients? Dr. Jay Katz, one of the law's most visionary and respected advocates of heightened informed consent, believed that "the radically different climate of physician-patient decisionmaking . . . cannot be implemented by judicial, legislative, or administrative orders." Jay Katz, The Silent World of Doctor and Patient 228 (1984). Similarly, a prestigious blue-ribbon ethics commission recognized that

> further evolution of legal standards toward a firmer protection of individual self-determination in medical decisions must be tempered by a recognition of the law's limits as an instrument of social control. . . . [T]he Commission is concerned that efforts to draw the law further into regulating the subtler aspects of relations between patients and health care professionals may prove ineffective, burdensome and ultimately counterproductive.

President's Commission for the Study of Ethical Problems in Medicine and Biomedical and Behavioral Research, Making Health Care Decisions: A Report on the Ethical and Legal Implications of Informed Consent in the Patient-Practitioner Relationship 30, 204, 252 (1982).

2. *Informed Consent in Practice.* Also consider the problems raised by the implementation of the doctrine. The process of health care decisionmaking described in narratives by physicians often suggests the irrelevance of the legal framework. See, e.g., Atul Gawande, Complications: A Surgeon's Notes on an Imperfect Science (2002), which is excerpted at page 295. Has the process of providing informed consent through signed consent forms become as ritualized and meaningless as the exchange of a peppercorn in land transactions? Empirical studies often cast doubt on the efficacy of the practice of informed consent. In one pathbreaking article, Alan Meisel and Loren H. Roth reviewed the empirical data on informed consent. Alan Meisel & Loren H. Roth, Toward an Informed Discussion of Informed Consent: A Review of the Empirical Studies, 25 Ariz. L. Rev. 265 (1983). They found that few patients understood or remembered what they had been told about their medical condition and treatment options. Other research confirms these findings. In one typical study, patients facing either anterior cervical fusion or lumbar laminectomy were given a training session on the procedures by a neurosurgeon and a clinical nurse specialist with a master's degree in neurosurgery. D. A. Herz et al., Informed Consent: Is It a Myth?, 30 Neurosurgery 453 (1992). Patients were given a "simple" written test immediately after the training session; the mean patient score was only 43.5 percent. Six weeks later, the mean test score dropped to 38.4 percent. The authors concluded that health care providers "cannot necessarily expect accurate patient or family recall or comprehension. Fulfillment of the doctrine of informed consent by neurosurgeons may very well be mythical."

There are a number of explanations for the gap between disclosure and comprehension/retention. Patients are often sick or emotionally vulnerable at the time of the disclosure; information may be presented in a highly technical and incomprehensible fashion; patients may not have the intelligence or educational background necessary to understand medical information; and patients may not feel able to ask important follow-up questions. See, e.g., Yael Schenker et al., Interventions to Improve Patient Comprehension in Informed Consent for Medical and Surgical

Procedures: A Systematic Review, 31 Med. Decis. Making 151 (2011). Despite these problems, patients often report that they are satisfied with the informed consent process. See, e.g., F. W. Verheggen et al., Patients' Perceptions on Informed Consent and the Quality of Information Disclosure in Clinical Trials, 29 Patient Educ. Couns. 137 (1996).

Finally, the capacity of patients to understand and to make decisions may be greater than their capacity to participate in carrying out those decisions. A. D. Naik and colleagues note that the "clinical application of the concept of patient autonomy has centered on the ability to deliberate and make treatment decisions (decisional autonomy) to the virtual exclusion of the capacity to execute the treatment plan (executive autonomy)." A. D. Naik et al., Patient Autonomy for the Management of Chronic Conditions: A Two-Component Re-Conceptualization, 9(2) Am. J. Bioethics 23-30 (2009). For responses, see Symposium, 9(2) Am. J. Bioethics 31-35 (2009).

3. *Information That Is Harmful.* Information is not always welcome. Some types of information may increase anxiety and decrease enjoyment of life without appreciably adding to decisionmaking ability. See generally, Symposium, The Right Not to Know, 42 J.L., Med. & Ethics 6-63 (2014). Imagine a genetic condition associated with the early onset of severe dementia and death for which there is no effective preventive treatment. How many people would want to know how and when they are going to die? The empirical evidence is mixed:

> What studies have been done are not at all clear on the psychological effects of predictive genetic testing. Some commentators have suggested that genetic testing can cause depression and suicide. Studies have demonstrated at least some negative impact on family functioning from predictive testing for Huntington's Disease—a test that can confirm with near-certainty whether one will develop this disabling disease. The data are inconclusive, but likely suffer from substantial selection bias. It may well be that living with the knowledge that one will develop an incurable disease turns out to be better than living with uncertainty. At least it may only be different, rather than "worse." When asked what it was like finally to know that she had Huntington's, one young woman replied that " '[i]t's hard to think the other way anymore of not knowing,' . . . 'It's become a part of my life.' "

Christian Turner, The Burden of Knowledge, 43 Ga. L. Rev. 297, 315 (2009).

Assuming that individuals will have different values and preferences in this area, how do you ask whether someone wants to know without tipping them off to the truth? One solution to this dilemma is to have a more elaborate informed consent process before giving the test, in which patients are told that the information obtained might be upsetting or might affect their personal relationships, etc. Then patients could choose not to be tested at all. See Mark E. Robson et al., American Society of Clinical Oncology Policy Statement Update: Genetic and Genomic Testing for Cancer Susceptibility, 28 J. Clin. Oncol. 893 (2010); Consensus Statement, Genetic Testing for Susceptibility to Adult-Onset Cancer: The Process and Content of Informed Consent, 277 JAMA 1467 (1997). This expansive approach to pretest counseling obviously would put a crimp in the approach that many clinicians take toward routine testing, in which screening tests are done with hardly any notice at all, much less with elaborate informed consent.

Advances in genetics raise an additional dilemma. If one patient wants the information and consents to testing, does this invade the privacy of family members who may not want to know the information or even to have the information created? These family members might suffer psychological effects or, absent special legal protections, adverse financial effects from insurance or employment. Professor Roger Dworkin has argued that genetic medicine requires us to adapt our individual autonomy model of informed consent so that it becomes more family centered. Roger B. Dworkin, Medical Law and Ethics in the Post-Autonomy Age, 68 Ind. L.J. 727 (1993). How would one obtain consent from an extended family? Is agreement by every competent adult required, or only a critical mass, or only a single-family matriarch or patriarch?

4. *Do Patients Want Decisional Autonomy?* Several commentators have argued that patients want to be informed but do not actually want to make their own health care decisions. Carl Schneider, a law professor at the University of Michigan, after reviewing empirical studies of patient interest in medical decisionmaking, concluded:

> Taken as a whole, these studies surveyed a considerable variety of populations—from the perfectly well to the dangerously sick. They asked patients about their own conditions and about hypothetical illnesses. They framed their respondent's choices in a variety of ways. And their virtually universal conclusion was that, while patients commonly wish to be informed about their medical circumstances, at least a quite substantial number of them did not want to make their own medical decisions, or perhaps even to participate in those decisions in any very significant way. . . .
>
> One might suppose that if patients were ever to assert their decisional authority it would be after hearing the alarming recitation of risks that characterizes the process of informed consent. Yet a number of studies of that process "strongly suggest that refusals attributable to disclosures are rarely, if ever, seen." Similarly, a study of why patients refuse treatment found an average of 4.6 refusals per 100 patient days. The reasons for refusal were complex, and generally there was more than one "cause" per patient. But two kinds of reasons stood out: first, a failure to tell the patient about the purpose of what was proposed; second, psychological factors, prominently including "characterological factors" (for example, using a refusal to accept treatment as a way of expressing a wish to be cared for) and "other psychoses." While the first of these causes reconfirms the wish for information we have so frequently encountered, neither of them is inconsistent with a reluctance to take control of medical decisions. And the dog that did not bark in the night is the absence of any significant number of patients who heard a doctor's recommendation and reached a different conclusion on the merits.

Carl E. Schneider, Bioethics with a Human Face, 69 Ind. L.J. 1075, 1097, 1099 (1994). Professor Schneider also noted significant evidence that "the more severe a patient's illness, the less likely the patient is to want to make medical decisions." Id. at 1101. See also, Marc D. Ginsberg, Beyond *Canterbury*: Can Medicine and Law Agree about Informed Consent? And Does It Matter? 45 J.L., Med & Ethics 106 (2017). Some have argued that informed consent represents an obsession with Western values and norms that seem less relevant to those from other cultures. See sources cited in note 7 below.

5. *Informed Consent vs. Traditional Malpractice.* Despite academic interest, informed consent theories play a role in a relatively small percentage of claims against physicians, at least as measured by opinions published in computerized databases such as Westlaw. As you read these materials, consider the role that informed

consent theories appear to play in traditional malpractice litigation. Of what relevance is it that informed consent claims are rarely brought alone but are most often seen in cases where plaintiffs also are asserting traditional negligence claims?

6. *The Spectrum of Informed Consent Standards.* Both courts and legislatures have participated in the redefinition of the roles in the physician-patient relationship. They have responded to the inequality of knowledge between providers and patients in at least four distinct ways. Some jurisdictions, about half in fact, use some version of a "material risk" or "reasonable patient" standard, which requires disclosure of risks that a reasonable patient would consider to be material in making a medical treatment decision. An almost equal number use the "professional malpractice" standard, under which physicians are required to disclose to patients that information which would have been disclosed by the reasonable, minimally competent physician. (See Chapter 4 for a detailed discussion of the theory of malpractice claims.) A small number of jurisdictions take an even more protective approach, requiring disclosure of information that a particular patient (as contrasted with a "rational" patient) would have wanted to make his or her decision. Finally, courts seeking tools to regulate the nature of the physician-patient relationship have recently turned to fiduciary law as a source of additional disclosure obligations for physicians.

7. *Additional Commentaries.* The literature on informed consent is voluminous. Some particularly useful commentaries (in addition to those cited in Schuck's article) include Janet L. Dolgin, The Legal Development of Informed Consent Doctrine: Past and Present, 19 Cambridge Q. Healthcare Ethics 97 (2010); Christine Grady, Enduring and Emerging Challenges of Informed Consent, 372 New Eng. J. Med. 855 (2015); Marjorie Maguire Schultz, From Informed Consent to Patient Choice: A New Protected Interest, 95 Yale L.J. 219 (1985). The major treatise is Fay A. Rozovsky, Consent to Treatment: A Practical Guide (2015). There are several important books on the subject, including Carl E. Schneider, The Practice of Autonomy: Patients, Doctors, and Medical Decisions (1998); Ruth R. Faden & Tom L. Beauchamp, A History and Theory of Informed Consent (1986); Jessica W. Berg et al., Informed Consent: Legal Theory and Practice (2001). For general discussions of informed consent, see Annot., 88 A.L.R.3d 1008 (1978).

For a classic **attack on the fundamental theory of informed consent liability**, see Richard Epstein, Medical Malpractice: The Case for Contract, 1976 Am. B. Found. Res. J. 87 (1976). For a critique of informed consent law's application to **racial, religious, and ethnic minority patients**, see Dayna Bowen Matthew, Race, Religion, and Informed Consent—Lessons from Social Science, 36 J.L. Med. & Ethics 150 (2008). For **critiques of prevailing views of patient autonomy** and the physician-patient fiduciary relationship see: Omri Ben-Shahar & Carl E. Schneider, The Failure of Mandated Disclosure, 159 U. Pa. L. Rev. 647 (2011); Roger B. Dworkin, Getting What We Should from Doctors: Rethinking Patient Autonomy and the Doctor-Patient Relationship, 13 Health Matrix 235 (2003); Joan H. Krause, Can Health Law Truly Become Patient-Centered?, 45 Wake Forest L. Rev. 1489 (2010); Symposium, Under Attack: Reconceptualizing Informed Consent, 45 J.L., Med. & Ethics 6-111 (2017); Symposium, Contemporary Challenges in Informed Consent, 44 J.L., Med. Ethics 371-461 (2016).

For more on **informed consent in practice** (note 2), see Lisa I. Iezzoni, Survey Shows That at Least Some Physicians Are Not Always Open or Honest with Patients, 31 Health Aff. 383 (2012) (more than 10 percent of surveyed physicians reported telling "patients something untrue in the previous year"); C.J. Manta, J. Ortiz, B.W. Moulton, and S.S. Sonnad, From the Patient Perspective, Consent Forms Fall Short of Providing Information to Guide Decision Making, _ J Patient Safety _ (Aug. 3, 2016); A. Sherlock & S. Brownie, Patients' Recollection and Understanding of Informed Consent: A Literature Review, 84 ANZ J Surg 207 (2014); J. Bester, C. Cole & E. Kodish, The Limits of Informed Consent for an Overwhelmed Patient: Clinicians' Role in Protecting Patients and Preventing Overwhelm, 18 AMA J. Ethics 869 (2016); Barbara A. Noah, The (Ir)Rationality of (Un)Informed Consent, 34 Quinn. L Rev. 691 (2016); and Ada C. Stefanescu Schmidt, Ami Bhatt & Cass Sunstein, Boundedly Rational Patients? Health and Patient Mistakes in a Behavioral Framework, 1 J. Beh. Econ. for Pol'y 13-17, 19-25 (2017) (Pts 1 & 2).

Exploring various issues **relating to genetics and medical testing** (note 3), see Bartha Maria Knoppers, From the Right to Know to the Right Not to Know, 42 J.L., Med. & Ethics 6 (2014); Gina Kolata, How Do You Live Knowing You Might Have an Alzheimer's Gene?, N.Y. Times, June 7, 2012; Stewart Justman, Uninformed Consent: Mass Screening for Prostate Cancer, 26 Bioethics 143 (2012) (noting that widespread PSA screening creates risk of overdiagnosis and overtreatment for sons of men tested, without demonstrable improvements in health care outcomes).

For **cultural and comparative perspectives** (note 4), see Leslie J. Blackhall et al., Ethnicity and Attitudes Toward Patient Autonomy, 274 JAMA 820 (1995); Joseph A. Carrese & Lorna A. Rhodes, Western Bioethics on the Navajo Reservation: Benefit or Harm?, 274 JAMA 826 (1995); Lawrence O. Gostin, Informed Consent, Cultural Sensitivity, and Respect for Persons, 274 JAMA 844 (1995); George J. Annas & Frances H. Miller, The Empire of Death: How Culture and Economics Affect Informed Consent in the U.S., U.K. and Japan, 20 Am. J.L. & Med. 357 (1994); Kristina Orfali & Elisa J. Gordon, Autonomy Gone Awry: A Cross-Cultural Study of Parents' Experiences in Neonatal Intensive Care Units, 25 Theoretical Med. & Bioethics 329 (2004).

Commentators have been particularly concerned with the role of informed consent in **medical research**. See, e.g., George J. Annas, Questing for Grails: Duplicity, Betrayal and Self-Deception in Postmodern Medical Research, 12 J. Contemp. Health L. & Pol'y 297 (1996); Ruth R. Faden & Tom L. Beauchamp, A History and Theory of Informed Consent 151-232 (1986). The issue is explored in greater depth in section D of this text.

Note: Informed Consent and the First Amendment

The First Amendment to the U.S. Constitution protects "freedom of speech." Yet states directly or indirectly regulate physician speech through the informed consent doctrine as well as through legislative requirements covering disclosures relating to a broad range of conditions or potential therapies. See, e.g., N.J.S. 26:5C-16 (requiring that primary care physicians provide pregnant women with specified information including the recommendation that they undergo testing for HIV). Like state regulation of the medical profession more generally, these disclosure requirements typically are deemed to further the state's compelling interest in the protection of public health. For particularly thoughtful, recent analyses of the relationship between the First Amendment and informed consent, see David

Orentlicher, Abortion and Compelled Physician Speech, 43 J.L., Med. & Ethics 9 (2015); and Nadia N. Sawicki, Toward a Healthy First Amendment, 50 Wash. U. J.L. & Pol'y 11 (2016).

When do governmental efforts to regulate the content of physician-patient communication violate the First Amendment? The "Docs v. Glocks" litigation provides a good example of the complexity of this issue. In 2011, after learning about six anecdotal examples of patients concerned about actions or comments from health care providers related to firearm ownership, Florida enacted the Firearm Owners' Privacy Act (FOPA). F.S. §790.338. The Act prohibited physicians from (a) routinely inquiring about or keeping records of patient firearm ownership; (b) discriminating against patients exercising their "constitutional right to own or possess firearms or ammunition"; or (c) "unnecessarily harassing [] patient[s] about firearm ownership during an examination." Id. Violations of the Act were to be addressed through professional disciplinary action. Wollschlaeger v. Governor, Florida, 848 F.3d 1293, 1303 (11th Cir. 2017) (en banc). Firearm ownership is associated with substantial health risks and various medical organizations recommend that physicians inquire about gun ownership and counsel patients regarding gun safety measures. Id. at 1316. A group of physicians and medical organizations challenged the legislation under the First and Fourteenth Amendments.

The complex procedural history of the case, which includes a divided Court of Appeals panel issuing three different opinions employing three different standards of review, demonstrates significant uncertainty about the intersection of state power over professional regulation with First Amendment protections for physician speech. The Court of Appeals sitting en banc rejected the state's argument that "the First Amendment is not implicated because any effect on speech is merely incidental to the regulation of professional conduct," holding that "we do not think it is appropriate to subject content-based restrictions on speech by those engaged in a certain profession to mere rational basis review." 848 F.3d at 1308, 1311. However, the court determined that it did not need to resolve whether state regulation of professional speech should be tested using heightened scrutiny or strict scrutiny as FOPA's record-keeping, inquiry, and anti-harassment provisions failed the more generous heightened scrutiny review. Id. at 1311. Under the heightened scrutiny standard, states must show that specific speaker- and content-based restrictions directly advance a substantial government interest and that the measures are drawn to achieve that interest and that there is a "fit" between the means and ends chosen by the legislation. Id. at 1311-1312 (citing Sorrell v. IMS Health, Inc, 564 U.S. 552 (2011) (quotations omitted)).

The court found that the record-keeping, inquiry, and anti-harassment provisions did not directly advance the state's asserted substantial interests in protecting citizens' Second Amendment rights, individual privacy or access to health care or its substantial interests in regulating the medical profession. (Of these, the state's interest in regulating the medical profession to protect public health would likely be relevant to the typical informed consent requirement). The court also found that the FOPA measures were not narrowly drawn to achieve these interests. After limiting the FOPA's anti-discrimination provision to apply to "non-expressive conduct," the court upheld the anti-discrimination provision. Id. at 1317. In a second majority opinion, the court also found that the anti-harassment provisions were unconstitutionally vague. Id. at 1319. For more on the case and its implications, see Claudia E. Haupt, Professional Speech and the Content-Neutrality Trap, 127 Yale

L.J. Forum 150 (2017); and Wendy E. Parmet, Jason A. Smith & Matthew Miller, Physicians, Firearms, and Free Speech—Overturning Florida's Firearm-Safety Gag Rule, 376 New Eng. J. Med. 1901 (2017).

For additional examples of the debate about the appropriate scope of state control see King v. Governor of N.J., 767 F.3d 216 (3rd Cir. 2014) (upholding NJ prohibition of use of "sexual orientation change efforts" ("SOCE") therapy to children in an analysis that offers less constitutional protection for professional speech than for public speech or the expression of opinions to patients); Pickup v. Brown, 740 F.3d 1208, 1225-29 (9th Cir. 2013) (upholding California law prohibiting use SOCE therapy to children); and Conant v. Walters, 309 F.3d 629 (9th Cir. 2002) (striking down policy threatening physicians who recommended medicinal use of marijuana with the loss of DEA prescriptive authority).

The power of states to direct physician speech has been particularly tested in the area of abortion. The Supreme Court has upheld the constitutional validity of state laws that impose specific informed consent obligations on physicians performing abortions. Planned Parenthood of Southeastern Pennsylvania v. Casey, 505 U.S. 833, 884 (1992). There have been successive waves of state informed consent regulations involving matters ranging from fetal development and pain to asserted mental health consequences for women who choose to undergo abortion. See Wendy K. Mariner & George J. Annas, Informed Consent and the First Amendment, 372 New Eng. J. Med. 1285 (2015). Courts have typically upheld special abortion-related informed consent requirements against First Amendment challenges so long as the required disclosures are found to be relevant, truthful, and non-misleading.

2. *The Competing Disclosure Standards*

■ CANTERBURY v. SPENCE
464 F.2d 772 (D.C. Cir.), cert. denied, 409 U.S. 1064 (1972)

[Appellant Canterbury, a 19-year-old clerk-typist who had experienced persistent back pain, sought care from Dr. Spence. Dr. Spence conducted a number of tests to determine the cause of the back pain and eventually recommended that Canterbury undergo a laminectomy. According to the court, Canterbury "did not raise any objection to the proposed operation nor did he probe into its exact nature." Dr. Spence spoke with Canterbury's mother by telephone. She asked "if the recommended operation was serious and Dr. Spence replied 'not any more than any other operation.' " It is unclear whether Mrs. Canterbury consented to the operation before it took place; she did sign a consent form afterward. The laminectomy was performed without any apparent difficulties. During the recovery period, however, hospital personnel failed to assist Canterbury during the process of voiding, and Canterbury fell out of his bed while attempting to void. Canterbury developed signs of partial paralysis a few hours after the fall, which were only partially improved by another operation.]

At the time of the trial . . . [he] required crutches to walk, still suffered from urinal incontinence and paralysis of the bowels, and wore a penile clamp. . . . [H]e [had] held a number of jobs, but had constant trouble finding work because he needed to remain seated and close to a bathroom. The damages appellant claims include extensive pain and suffering, medical expenses, and loss of earnings.

Appellant filed suit in the district court on March 7, 1963, four years after the laminectomy and approximately two years after he attained his majority. The complaint stated several causes of action against each defendant. Against Dr. Spence it alleged, among other things, negligence in the performance of the laminectomy and failure to inform him beforehand of the risk involved. Against the hospital the complaint charged negligent postoperative care in permitting appellant to remain unattended after the laminectomy, in failing to provide a nurse or orderly to assist him at the time of his fall, and in failing to maintain a side rail on his bed. . . .

At the close of appellant's case in chief, each defendant moved for a directed verdict and the trial judge granted both motions. . . . The judge did not allude specifically to the alleged breach of duty by Dr. Spence to divulge the possible consequences of the laminectomy.

We reverse. The testimony of appellant and his mother that Dr. Spence did not reveal the risk of paralysis from the laminectomy made out a prima facie case of violation of the physician's duty to disclose which Dr. Spence's explanation did not negate as a matter of law. . . .

Suits charging failure by a physician[6] adequately to disclose the risks and alternatives of proposed treatment are not innovations in American law. They date back a good half-century, and in the last decade they have multiplied rapidly. There is, nonetheless, disagreement among the courts and the commentators on many major questions, and there is no precedent of our own directly in point. For the tools enabling resolution of the issues on this appeal, we are forced to begin at first principles.

The root premise is the concept, fundamental in American jurisprudence, that "[e]very human being of adult years and sound mind has a right to determine what shall be done with his own body. . . ."[12] True consent to what happens to one's self is the informed exercise of a choice, and that entails an opportunity to evaluate knowledgeably the options available and the risks attendant upon each. The average patient has little or no understanding of the medical arts, and ordinarily has only his physician to whom he can look for enlightenment with which to reach an intelligent decision. From these almost axiomatic considerations springs the need, and in turn the requirement, of a reasonable divulgence by physician to patient to make such a decision possible.[15]

6. Since there was neither allegation nor proof that the appellee hospital failed in any duty to disclose, we have no occasion to inquire as to whether or under what circumstances such a duty might arise.

12. Schloendorff v. Society of New York Hospital, 211 N.Y. 125, 105 N.E. 92, 93 (1914). . . .

15. In duty-to-disclose cases, the focus of attention is more properly upon the nature and content of the physician's divulgence than the patient's understanding or consent. Adequate disclosure and informed consent are, of course, two sides of the same coin—the former a sine qua non of the latter. But the vital inquiry on duty to disclose relates to the physician's performance of an obligation, while one of the difficulties with analysis in terms of "informed consent" is its tendency to imply that what is decisive is the degree of the patient's comprehension. As we later emphasize, physician discharges the duty when he makes a reasonable effort to convey sufficient information although the patient, without fault of the physician, may not fully grasp it. . . .

A physician is under a duty to treat his patient skillfully but proficiency in diagnosis and therapy is not the full measure of his responsibility. The cases demonstrate that the physician is under an obligation to communicate specific information to the patient when the exigencies of reasonable care call for it. . . .

A reasonable revelation in these respects is not only a necessity but, as we see it, is as much a matter of the physician's duty. It is a duty to warn of the dangers lurking in the proposed treatment, and that is surely a facet of due care. It is, too, a duty to impart information which the patient has every right to expect. The patient's reliance upon the physician is a trust of the kind which traditionally has exacted obligations beyond those associated with arms length transactions. His dependence upon the physician for information affecting his well-being, in terms of contemplated treatment, is well-nigh abject. As earlier noted, long before the instant litigation arose, courts had recognized that the physician had the responsibility of satisfying the vital informational needs of the patient. More recently, we ourselves have found "in the fiducial qualities of [the physician-patient] relationship the physician's duty to reveal to the patient that which in his best interests it is important that he should know." We now find, as a part of the physician's overall obligation to the patient, a similar duty of reasonable disclosure of the choices with respect to proposed therapy and the dangers inherently and potentially involved.

This disclosure requirement, on analysis, reflects much more of a change in doctrinal emphasis than a substantive addition to malpractice law. It is well established that the physician must seek and secure his patient's consent before commencing an operation or other course of treatment. It is also clear that the consent, to be efficacious, must be free from imposition upon the patient. It is the settled rule that therapy not authorized by the patient may amount to a tort—a common law battery—by the physician. And it is evident that it is normally impossible to obtain a consent worthy of the name unless the physician first elucidates the options and the perils for the patient's edification. Thus the physician has long borne a duty, on pain of liability for unauthorized treatment, to make adequate disclosure to the patient.[36] . . .

Duty to disclose has gained recognition in a large number of American jurisdictions, but more largely on a different rationale. The majority of courts dealing with the problem have made the duty depend on whether it was the custom of physicians practicing in the community to make the particular disclosure to the patient. . . . We agree that the physician's noncompliance with a professional custom to reveal, like any other departure from prevailing medical practice, may give rise to liability to the patient. We do not agree that the patient's cause of action is dependent upon the existence and nonperformance of a relevant professional tradition.

---

36. We discard the thought that the patient should ask for information before the physician is required to disclose. Caveat emptor is not the norm for the consumer of medical services. Duty to disclose is more than a call to speak merely on the patient's request, or merely to answer the patient's questions; it is a duty to volunteer, if necessary, the information the patient needs for intelligent decision. The patient may be ignorant, confused, over-awed by the physician or frightened by the hospital, or even ashamed to inquire. See generally Note, Restructuring Informed Consent: Legal Therapy for the Doctor-Patient Relationship, 79 Yale L.J. 1533, 1545-1551 (1970). . . .

There are, in our view, formidable obstacles to acceptance of the notion that the physician's obligation to disclose is either germinated or limited by medical practice. To begin with, the reality of any discernible custom reflecting a professional consensus on communication of option and risk information to patients is open to serious doubt. We sense the danger that what in fact is no custom at all may be taken as an affirmative custom to maintain silence, and that physician-witnesses to the so-called custom may state merely their personal opinions as to what they or others would do under given conditions. . . . Respect for the patient's right of self-determination on particular therapy demands a standard set by law for physicians rather than one which physicians may or may not impose upon themselves.

More fundamentally, the majority rule overlooks the graduation of reasonable-care demands in Anglo-American jurisprudence and the position of professional custom in the hierarchy. . . .

There is . . . no basis for operation of the special medical standard where the physician's activity does not bring his medical knowledge and skills peculiarly into play. . . .

[T]he physician's duty to disclose is governed by the same legal principles applicable to others in comparable situations, with modifications only to the extent that medical judgment enters the picture. We hold that the standard measuring performance of that duty by physicians, as by others, is conduct which is reasonable under the circumstances.

Once the circumstances give rise to a duty on the physician's part to inform his patient, the next inquiry is the scope of the disclosure the physician is legally obliged to make. The courts have frequently confronted this problem but no uniform standard defining the adequacy of the divulgence emerges from the decisions. . . .

The larger number of courts, as might be expected, have applied tests framed with reference to prevailing fashion within the medical profession. . . .

In our view, the patient's right of self-decision shapes the boundaries of the duty to reveal. That right can be effectively exercised only if the patient possesses enough information to enable an intelligent choice. The scope of the physician's communications to the patient, then, must be measured by the patient's need, and that need is the information material to the decision. Thus the test for determining whether a particular peril must be divulged is its materiality to the patient's decision: All risks potentially affecting the decision must be unmasked. And to safeguard the patient's interest in achieving his own determination on treatment, the law must itself set the standard for adequate disclosure.

Optimally for the patient, exposure of a risk would be mandatory whenever the patient would deem it significant to his decision, either singly or in combination with other risks. Such a requirement, however, would summon the physician to second-guess the patient, whose ideas on materiality could hardly be known to the physician. That would make an undue demand upon medical practitioners, whose conduct, like that of others, is to be measured in terms of reasonableness. Consonantly with orthodox negligence doctrine, the physician's liability for nondisclosure is to be determined on the basis of foresight, not hindsight; no less than any other aspect of negligence, the issue on nondisclosure must be approached from the viewpoint of the reasonableness of the physician's divulgence in terms of what he knows or should know to be the patient's informational needs. . . .

From these considerations we derive the breadth of the disclosure of risks legally to be required. The scope of the standard is not subjective as to either the physician or the patient; it remains objective with due regard for the patient's informational needs and with suitable leeway for the physician's situation. In broad outline, we agree that "[a] risk is thus material when a reasonable person, in what the physician knows or should know to be the patient's position, would be likely to attach significance to the risk or cluster of risks in deciding whether or not to forego the proposed therapy."

The topics importantly demanding a communication of information are the inherent and potential hazards of the proposed treatment, the alternatives to that treatment, if any, and the results likely if the patient remains untreated. The factors contributing significance to the dangerousness of a medical technique are, of course, the incidence of injury and the degree of the harm threatened. A very small chance of death or serious disablement may well be significant; a potential disability which dramatically outweighs the potential benefit of the therapy or the detriments of the existing malady may summon discussion with the patient.

There is no bright line separating the significant from the insignificant; the answer in any case must abide a rule of reason. Some dangers—infection, for example—are inherent in any operation; there is no obligation to communicate those of which persons of average sophistication are aware. Even more clearly, the physician bears no responsibility for discussion of hazards the patient has already discovered, or those having no apparent materiality to patients' decision on therapy. . . .

No more than breach of any other legal duty does nonfulfillment of the physician's obligation to disclose alone establish liability to the patient. An unrevealed risk that should have been made known must materialize, for otherwise the omission, however unpardonable, is legally without consequence. Occurrence of the risk must be harmful to the patient, for negligence unrelated to injury is nonactionable. And, as in malpractice actions generally, there must be a causal relationship between the physician's failure to adequately divulge and damage to the patient.

A causal connection exists when, but only when, disclosure of significant risks incidental to treatment would have resulted in a decision against it. The patient obviously has no complaint if he would have submitted to the therapy notwithstanding awareness that the risk was one of its perils. On the other hand, the very purpose of the disclosure rule is to protect the patient against consequences which, if known, he would have avoided by foregoing the treatment. The more difficult question is whether the factual issue on causality calls for an objective or a subjective determination. . . .

It has been assumed that the issue is to be resolved according to whether the factfinder believes the patient's testimony that he would not have agreed to the treatment if he had known of the danger which later ripened into injury. . . .

In our view, this method of dealing with the issue on causation comes in second-best. It places the physician in jeopardy of the patient's hindsight and bitterness. It places the factfinder in the position of deciding whether a speculative answer to a hypothetical question is to be credited. It calls for a subjective determination solely on testimony of a patient-witness shadowed by the occurrence of the undisclosed risk.

Better it is, we believe, to resolve the causality issue on an objective basis: in terms of what a prudent person in the patient's position would have decided if suitably informed of all perils bearing significance. If adequate disclosure could reasonably be expected to have caused that person to decline the treatment because of the revelation of the kind of risk or danger that resulted in harm, causation is shown, but otherwise not. The patient's testimony is relevant on that score of course but it would not threaten to dominate the findings. . . .

In the context of trial of a suit claiming inadequate disclosure of risk information by a physician, the patient has the burden of going forward with evidence tending to establish prima facie the essential elements of the cause of action, and ultimately the burden of proof—the risk of nonpersuasion—on those elements. . . . The burden of going forward with evidence pertaining to a privilege not to disclose, however, rests properly upon the physician. . . .

We now delineate our view on the need for expert testimony in nondisclosure cases. . . .

The guiding consideration our decisions distill, however, is that medical facts are for medical experts and other facts are for any witnesses—expert or not—having sufficient knowledge and capacity to testify to them. It is evident that many of the issues typically involved in nondisclosure cases do not reside peculiarly within the medical domain. Lay witness testimony can competently establish a physician's failure to disclose particular risk information, the patient's lack of knowledge of the risk, and the adverse consequences following the treatment. Experts are unnecessary to a showing of the materiality of a risk to a patient's decision on treatment, or to the reasonably, expectable effect of risk disclosure on the decision. These conspicuous examples of permissible uses of nonexpert testimony illustrate the relative freedom of broad areas of the legal problem of risk nondisclosure from the demands for expert testimony that shackle plaintiffs' other types of medical malpractice litigation. . . .

This brings us to the remaining question . . . whether appellant's evidence was of such caliber as to require a submission to the jury. [T]he evidence was clearly sufficient to raise an issue as to whether Dr. Spence's obligation to disclose information on risks was reasonably met or was excused by the surrounding circumstances. Appellant testified that Dr. Spence revealed to him nothing suggesting a hazard associated with the laminectomy. His mother testified that, in response to her specific inquiry, Dr. Spence informed her that the laminectomy was no more serious than any other operation. When, at trial, it developed from Dr. Spence's testimony that paralysis can be expected in 1 percent of laminectomies, it became the jury's responsibility to decide whether that peril was of sufficient magnitude to bring the disclosure duty into play. There was no emergency to frustrate an opportunity to disclose, and Dr. Spence's expressed opinion that disclosure would have been unwise did not foreclose a contrary conclusion by the jury. There was no evidence that appellant's emotional makeup was such that concealment of the risk of paralysis was medically sound. Even if disclosure to appellant himself might have bred ill consequences, no reason appears for the omission to communicate the information to his mother, particularly in view of his minority. The jury, not Dr. Spence, was the final arbiter of whether nondisclosure was reasonable under the circumstances. . . .

Reversed and remanded for new trial.

■ CULBERTSON v. MERNITZ
602 N.E.2d 98 (Ind. 1992)

KRAHULIK, Justice.

Roland B. Mernitz, M.D., (Appellee-Defendant) seeks transfer from the Court of Appeals' reversal of a summary judgment entered in his favor. Culbertson v.

Mernitz (1992), Ind. App., 591 N.E.2d 1040. The issue squarely presented in this petition is whether expert medical testimony is required to establish the standard of care of health care providers on the issue of informed consent. . . .

The facts of the case are as follows. Dr. Mernitz first saw Patty Jo Culbertson on March 28, 1988. Her chief complaint was that of uncontrollable leakage of urine and discharge from the vagina. After performing a physical examination, Dr. Mernitz . . . recommend[ed] . . . that she . . . undergo a surgical procedure known as a[n] MMK [Marshall Marchetti Krantz] procedure in order to suspend the bladder and either a hysterectomy or cryosurgery to freeze the infected tip of the cervix. Dr. Mernitz contends that he advised her of the general risks of any surgery, viz. infection, bleeding, and death, and that, with respect to the bladder suspension, he explained to her the risk that the procedure could fail and the possibility that she would be unable to void. . . . Both parties . . . agree that Dr. Mernitz did not advise her of a risk that the cervix could become adhered to the wall of the vagina.

Following this office visit, Mrs. Culbertson decided to proceed with the bladder suspension and cryosurgery. She was admitted to the hospital and underwent these procedures. Post-surgically, Mrs. Culbertson's cervix adhered to the wall of her vagina. Dr. Mernitz prescribed medication for this condition, but Mrs. Culbertson became dissatisfied with his care and saw another surgeon who eventually performed a total abdominal hysterectomy, bilateral salpingo-oophorectomy which involves the removal of both ovaries, and another bladder suspension.

Following this surgery, Mr. and Mrs. Culbertson filed a proposed complaint against Dr. Mernitz with the Indiana Department of Insurance in four counts. . . . Count II alleged that Dr. Mernitz failed to inform Mrs. Culbertson of the alternatives to surgery and the inherent risks and complications of surgery. . . .

A medical review panel was convened and, after submission of evidence to it, issued its written opinion. . . . With respect to the informed consent issue alleged in Count II, the panel ruled:

> The Panel determines that [Dr. Mernitz] did not advise [Mrs. Culbertson] of the complication of cervical adhesion to the vagina; the Panel further determines that such non-disclosure does not constitute a failure to comply with the appropriate standard of care, as such complication is not considered a risk of such surgery requiring disclosure to the patient.

The Culbertsons filed their civil action in a complaint that mirrored the allegations of the proposed complaint. After answering this complaint, Dr. Mernitz moved for summary judgment relying on the expert opinion issued by the medical review panel. The Culbertsons did not file an affidavit or other evidence in opposition to the motion for summary judgment, but argued to the trial court that the "prudent patient" standard should be utilized in evaluating informed consent claims. The trial court entered summary judgment [for the defendants]. . . . [W]e must determine the role, if any, played by expert medical opinion in resolving claims of medical malpractice premised upon a failure to obtain an informed consent.

The courts, historically, have established the standard of care required of physicians when treating patients. The law requires that a physician treating a patient possess and exercise that degree of skill and care ordinarily possessed and exercised by a physician treating such maladies.

. . . In order for a lay jury to know whether a physician complied with the legally prescribed standard of care, expert testimony has generally been held to be required. This requirement was premised on the logical belief that a non-physician could not know what a reasonably prudent physician would or would not have done under the circumstances of any given case. Therefore, an expert familiar with the practice of medicine needed to establish what a reasonably prudent physician would or would not have done in treating a patient in order to set before the jury a depiction of the reasonably prudent physician against which to judge the actions of the defendant physician. An exception was created in cases of res ipsa loquitur on the premise that in such cases a lay jury did not need guidance from a physician familiar with medical practice as to what was required of a reasonably prudent physician because the deficiency of practice "spoke for itself." Kranda v. Houser-Norborg Med. Corp., 419 N.E.2d 1024, 1042 (Ind. App. 1981). This was the settled law of most American jurisdictions, including Indiana, prior to the early 1970s when two cases on the opposite coasts carved out an additional exception to the requirement of expert medical testimony in the area of "informed consent." [The court summarized Cobbs v. Grant, 8 Cal. 3d 229 (1972), and Canterbury v. Spence, 464 F.2d 772 (D.C. Cir.), cert. denied, 409 U.S. 1064 (1972).]

INFORMED CONSENT IN INDIANA JURISPRUDENCE

[The court reviewed Indiana case law and concluded that Indiana followed the medical malpractice standard in informed consent cases. Under this standard, physicians are required to disclose that which the reasonably careful, skillful, and prudent physician would disclose under the same or similar circumstances. In general, medical expert testimony will be required to determine whether a physician has violated her duty, "unless the situation is clearly within the realm of laymen's comprehension."]

Resolution of the issue of the necessity of expert medical testimony in informed consent cases depends on whether the issue is viewed through the eyes of the physician or the patient. When viewed through the eyes of the physician, it is easy to see that a physician should not be required to guess or speculate as to what a hypothetical "reasonably prudent patient" would "need to know" in order to make a determination. A physician should only be required to do that which he is trained to do, namely, conduct himself as a reasonably prudent physician in taking a history, performing a physical examination, ordering appropriate tests, reaching a diagnosis, prescribing a course of treatment, and in discussing with the patient the medical facts of the proposed procedure, including the risks inherent in either accepting or rejecting the proposed course of treatment. From a physician's viewpoint, he should not be called upon to be a "mind reader" with the ability to peer into the brain of a prudent patient to determine what such patient "needs to know," but should simply be called upon to discuss medical facts and recommendations with the patient as a reasonably prudent physician would.

On the other hand, from the patient's viewpoint, the physician should be required to give the patient sufficient information to enable the patient to reasonably exercise the patient's right of self-decision in a knowledgeable manner. Viewed from this vantage point, the patient does not want the medical profession to determine in a paternalistic manner what the patient should or should not be told concerning the course of treatment. Thus, such a patient would view the reasonably prudent physician standard as destroying the patient's right of self-decision and, impliedly, placing such decision under the exclusive domain of the medical profession. While this viewpoint may or may not have been justified in 1972 when *Canterbury* and *Cobbs* were decided, a review of medical ethics standards of care in 1992 should assuage this fear.

The 1992 Code of Medical Ethics, as prepared by the Council on Ethical and Judicial Affairs of the American Medical Association, sets forth the medical profession's standard on informed consent. It reads as follows:

> The patient's right of self-decision can be effectively exercised only if the patient possesses enough information to enable an intelligent choice. The patient should make his own determination on treatment. The physician's obligation is to present the medical facts accurately to the patient or to the individual responsible for his care and to make recommendations for management in accordance with good medical practice. The physician has an ethical obligation to help the patient make choices from among the therapeutic alternatives consistent with good medical practice. Informed consent is a basic social policy for which exceptions are permitted (1) where the patient is unconscious or otherwise incapable of consenting and harm from failure to treat is imminent; or (2) when risk-disclosure poses such a serious psychological threat of detriment to the patient as to be medically contraindicated. Social policy does not accept the paternalistic view that the physician may remain silent because divulgence might prompt the patient to forego needed therapy. Rational, informed patients should not be expected to act uniformly, even under similar circumstances, in agreeing to or refusing treatment.

We recognize this statement as a reasonable statement on the issue of informed consent. There is no need to change Indiana law on this issue. We therefore hold that, except in those cases where deviation from the standard of care is a matter commonly known by lay persons, expert medical testimony is necessary to establish whether a physician has or has not complied with the standard of a reasonably prudent physician.

In the present case we cannot say that the risk of the adherence of the cervix to the vaginal wall is a matter commonly known to lay persons. Therefore, the Culbertsons needed to provide expert medical testimony to refute the unanimous opinion issued by the medical review panel in order to present a material issue of fact as to what a reasonably prudent physician would have discussed concerning this proposed surgery. Without the presentation of such expert medical opinion, the trial court could only conclude that there was no genuine issue of material fact and that summary judgment should be entered for Dr. Mernitz.

[Justice Dickson's dissenting opinion is omitted.]

Notes: Competing Disclosure Standards

1. *The Objective Patient-Centered Standard vs. the Professional Standard.* Why did the *Canterbury* court reject the professional standard of disclosure? One criticism of the malpractice standard is that it measures the scope of required disclosures by customary practice rather than by the patient's need to know. The *Culbertson* court considered and rejected this argument, noting that the 1992 Code of Medical Ethics promulgated by the American Medical Association recognized a physician's

duty to provide information to patients. See also, AMA Code of Medical Ethics 1.1.3 Patient Rights & 2.1 Informed Consent & Shared Decision Making (2016). Does *Canterbury*'s material risk standard provide any significant additional protections given current norms of medical practice? An empirical study suggests that informed consent claims are more likely to succeed in jurisdictions that have adopted the "patient-centered" standard of disclosure. David M. Studdert et al., Geographic Variation in Informed Consent Law: Two Standards for Disclosure of Treatment Risks, 4 J. Empirical Legal Stud. 103 (2007).

2. *The Implications of* Canterbury's *Patient-Centered or Material Risk Standard.* How are providers to know whether a risk should be deemed material? Is there any way for a physician to make this determination before providing care for the patient or before litigating the issue? See American College of Surgeons, Surgical Risk Calculator, at https://riskcalculator.facs.org/RiskCalculator/. What factors does the court suggest are relevant to the determination of materiality? How would you advise a physician who is considering whether to inform patients about the following risks associated with a particular type of cosmetic surgery: (1) a .01 percent risk of death from anesthesia; (2) a 1 percent risk of severe bleeding that would require a blood transfusion (which carries additional risks, ranging from fever to heart failure to transmission of bloodborne pathogens); (3) a 3 percent risk of postoperative infection (which would require treatment by antibiotics, which carry a small risk of adverse reactions); (4) a 5 percent risk of nerve damage that could lead to localized paralysis and/or loss of sensation; and (5) a 10 percent risk that the cosmetic flaw will not be significantly improved.

Some legislatures have provided "safe harbors" for physicians. In Texas, for example, a Medical Disclosure Panel determines what disclosures should be made for certain types of procedures. Physicians disclosing risks pursuant to the Panel's guidelines enjoy a rebuttable presumption that their informed consent obligations have been met. Failure to follow the guidelines creates a rebuttable presumption of negligence. Tex. Civ. Prac. & Rem. Code §74.106. See also Louisiana Medical Disclosure Panel, LSA-R.S. 40:1157.2.

3. *Assessing the Disclosure Landscape.* The patient-centered, material risk standard has been adopted in roughly half of the states and the District of Columbia. The professional disclosure standard has been adopted in the bulk of the remaining states. Two states use a "hybrid" approach. Robin Fretwell Wilson, The Promise of Informed Consent, in the Oxford Handbook of U.S. Health Law 218 (I. Glenn Cohen, Allison K. Hoffman & William M. Sage eds. 2017). In some states, the disclosure standard has been adopted by the courts; in others, it has been imposed by the legislature. In jurisdictions following the professional or reasonable physician disclosure standard, medical practice determines whether a particular type of information will be disclosed to patients. The standard protects physicians from liability so long as they disclose that which would be disclosed by the reasonably prudent physician under like or similar circumstances. In *Culbertson*, the court suggests that the professional malpractice standard will protect individual autonomy because it incorporates the view that individuals must be given enough information to make intelligent decisions. Was Mrs. Culbertson given enough information in this case?

4. *The Subjective Patient-Centered Disclosure Standard.* Note that the material risk standard requires the disclosure of information that a reasonable person would consider material in making a determination about treatment. In most circumstances, physicians are not required to provide information about risks that might

be considered significant by an individual patient. The *Canterbury* court recognizes this potential defect but finds that the imposition of a subjective disclosure standard would pose an "undue burden" on a physician—unless the physician knows of the patient's idiosyncratic views. See, e.g., Stowell v. Huddleston, 643 F.3d 631 (8th Cir. 2011) (applying state informed consent standard requiring disclosure of risks of particular significance to patient); Lugenbuhl v. Dowling, 676 So. 2d 602 (La. Ct. App. 1996) (subjective considerations potentially relevant even in objective standard jurisdiction). The overwhelming majority of those jurisdictions that use the "material risk" standard have followed the *Canterbury* approach by measuring the scope of disclosure by the objective patient. But cf. Macy v. Blatchford, 8 P.3d 204 (Or. 2000) (evidence of sexual relationship between physician and patient relevant to determine whether physician had met his statutory duty to "explain" proposed treatment because of the possible impact of the relationship on the patient's ability to understand).

5. *Expert Testimony Under the Material Risk and Professional Disclosure Standards.* In jurisdictions following the professional disclosure standard, testimony by medical experts obviously will be required to determine whether the defendant met the standard of care. University of Maryland Medical System Corp. v. Waldt, 983 A.2d 112 (Md. 2009) (proposed expert not qualified to testify regarding informed consent claim); Foster v. Oral Surgery Ass'n, 940 A.2d 1102 (Maine 2008) (medical ethicist not qualified as expert). Will a plaintiff in a "material risk" jurisdiction be able to avoid this requirement? Testimony by medical experts will still be required to provide the fact finder with information about the nature and degree of risk associated with particular treatments. See Dunn v. Yager, 58 So. 3d 1171 (Miss. 2011); but see Shortell v. Cavanagh, 15 A.3d 1042 (Conn. 2011) (expert testimony not always required). Experts may also be needed to help the fact finder determine whether the harm suffered by the plaintiff was caused by the procedure or by the plaintiff's underlying injury. See, e.g., Suhadolnik v. Pressman, 254 P.3d 11 (Idaho 2011) (expert testimony and local standard of care); Griffin v. Moseley, 234 P.3d 869 (Mont. 2010) (physician qualified to testify about neurosurgeon's duty to disclose alternative treatments). In some cases, the plaintiff's evidentiary burden can be met through the "expert testimony" provided by the defendant physician. Garcia v. Robinson, 375 P.3d 167 (Hawai'i 2016). See generally Annot., 52 A.L.R.3d 1084 (1973).

6. *Whose Duty? Disclosure as a "Professional" Rather Than "Institutional" Obligation.* Courts typically focus on the physician-patient relationship in establishing and defining disclosure obligations. See, e.g., Shinal v. Toms, 162 A.3d 429 (Pa. 2017) ("physician may not delegate to others his or her obligation to provide sufficient information in order to obtain a patient's informed consent"). Another important consequence of the doctrinal origins of the informed consent claim is that its application has been restricted to a limited range of health care professionals. See, e.g., Blotner v. Doreika, 678 S.E.2d 80 (Ga. 2009) (no common-law informed consent duty applicable to chiropractors); Foster v. Traul, 120 P.3d 278 (Idaho 2005) (physician has duty to obtain informed consent; hospital merely assists in documentation). Should health care institutions have a duty to disclose some types of risks? Should there be an institutional duty to ensure that patients have given their informed consent to care? If so, what should be the doctrinal source of this obligation? The role of hospitals is further discussed infra at page 221 note 4.

7. *Informed Consent and Battery.* Why couldn't claims of this type be resolved using principles from battery cases? Plaintiffs pleading informed consent violations as battery actions have two key advantages: They do not have to prove a deviation

from the standard of care and they have greater access to punitive damages awards. There are drawbacks, of course; a battery theory is difficult to apply where the medical treatment is noninvasive, and a defendant's insurance policy may exclude coverage for intentional torts.

In the typical informed consent claim, the patient has given technical consent to being "touched" by the defendant but argues that consent would not have been given if appropriate disclosures had been made. Courts generally reject battery claims because the patient has "consented" to the touching. In most jurisdictions, battery claims are reserved for those situations in which (1) the patient has not consented to any treatment at all, (2) the health care provider performs a completely different procedure than that for which consent was given, (3) the health care provider performs a procedure on the wrong area of the body, or (4) a different, unconsented-to provider performs the procedure. See, e.g., Coulter v. Thomas, 33 S.W.3d 522 (Ky. 2000) (physician's failure to remove blood pressure cuff as requested by patient addressed in battery claim, not under state informed consent statute); Humboldt Gen. Hosp. v. Sixth Jud. Dist. Ct., 376 P.3d 167 (Nev. 2016) (physician inserted non-FDA approved IUD; battery applicable where consent absent, informed consent governs this dispute over scope); but see Linog v. Yampolosky, 656 S.E.2d 355 (S.C. 2008) (no cause of action for medical battery); and Allison v. Brown, 801 S.E.2d 761 (Va. 2017) (surgeon allegedly improperly operated on both breasts rather than one; plaintiff failed to plead claim for battery and failed to establish proximate cause for informed consent; case remanded for retrial on whether it was negligent to operate without consent); Mayr v. Osborne, 795 S.E.2d 731 (Va. 2017) (claim that physician operated on the "wrong area" by fusing incorrect level of patient's spine properly addressed through informed consent and negligence rather than battery). See generally Annot., 39 A.L.R.4th 1034 (1985). For a discussion from a medical perspective, see David C. Ring et al., Case 34-2010: A 65-Year-Old Woman with an Incorrect Operation on the Left Hand, 363 New Eng. J. Med. 1950 (2010).

8. *Fraud, Misrepresentation and Violation of Consumer Protection Legislation.* Health care providers who misrepresent the risks associated with treatments could be held liable for fraud, misrepresentation, or violation of consumer protection statutes. See, e.g., Annot., 42 A.L.R.4th 543 (1985); Jones v. Clinch, 73 A.3d 80 (D.C. Ct. App. 2013) (noting differential treatment of patient claims under consumer protection legislation in Maryland and D.C.). However, courts are reluctant to permit use of these theories, particularly where they may be asserted in an effort to avoid procedural or substantive requirements applicable to medical negligence claims. See Chapter 4.H. See Sanchez v. Martin, 378 S.W.3d 581 (Tex. App. Dallas 2017).

Notes: The Other Elements of a Nondisclosure Claim

1. *Elements of a Cause of Action.* Plaintiffs in informed consent claims generally will be required to prove (1) that the medical procedure carried a specific risk that was not disclosed, (2) that the physician violated the applicable standard of disclosure, (3) that the undisclosed risk materialized, and (4) that the failure to disclose the information caused the patient's injury.

2. *The Materialization of the Undisclosed Risk.* The plaintiff must show that the undisclosed risk actually materialized into harm. As a result, many failures to disclose information are never litigated. Does this make sense? Can you draw a parallel

to the concept of proximate cause in traditional negligence actions? If the purpose of the informed consent doctrine is to protect individual autonomy and to encourage the transfer of information, doesn't a violation of the disclosure obligation cause a cognizable injury even without a physical harm? See Parris v. Limes, 277 P.3d 1259 (Okla. 2012) (patient who underwent post-surgical treatments alleges physician erred in failing to disclose that surgically removed prostate was cancer free; court finds that the emergence of an undisclosed risk is not required where the patient would not have undergone treatment if he or she had been properly "informed of all the material facts").

Several commentators have argued that individual autonomy would be better protected through the adoption of a "dignitary tort" doctrine, in which the failure to disclose information would be actionable even in the absence of any physical injury. See, e.g., Alan Meisel, A "Dignitary Tort" as a Bridge Between the Idea of Informed Consent and the Law of Informed Consent, 16 L. Med. & Health Care 210, 211-214 (1988); Aaron D. Twerski & Neil B. Cohen, Informed Decision-Making and the Law of Torts: The Myth of Justiciable Causation, 1988 U. Ill. L. Rev. 607, 655; Alan J. Weisbard, Informed Consent: The Law's Uneasy Compromise with Ethical Theory, 65 Neb. L. Rev. 749, 763-764 (1986).

How should damages be measured? "The damages analysis . . . involves a comparison between the condition a plaintiff would have been in had he or she been properly informed and not consented to the risk, with the plaintiff's impaired condition as a result of the risk's occurrence." Howard v. University of Medicine & Dentistry of N.J., 800 A.2d 73 (N.J. 2002). The damages calculations can be more difficult when the patient's initial condition is serious and there are no other alternative treatments.

3. *Objective Causation.* The causation issues associated with informed consent actions are somewhat complex. Most jurisdictions—including those applying the material risk standard—will require proof of objective causation. That is, a plaintiff will be required to show that a reasonable patient would not have undergone the treatment had the material risks been disclosed. Cf. White v. Beeks, 469 S.W.3d 517 (Tenn. 2015) (expert testimony about risks relevant whether or not the risks materialized). Does the informed consent doctrine coupled with an objective causation requirement adequately protect the patient's right to the information necessary to participate in medical decisionmaking? Consider the range of circumstances in which the defendant will be found liable for failing to disclose information. The defendant will be held liable only where he or she suggests that a patient undergo a procedure that, had the true risks been disclosed, a reasonable patient would have refused to undergo. Why wouldn't this simply constitute ordinary malpractice? Should plaintiffs be required to show that they would not have undergone the procedure or is it enough to show that a reasonable patient might have sought another opinion or considered a different provider? Compare Spencer v. Goodill, 17 A.3d 552 (Del. 2011) (jury entitled to consider all options that reasonable person might have considered, including seeking second opinion, a different doctor, or a better equipped hospital, even though same operation might ultimately have been pursued) with Orphan v. Pilnik, 940 N.E.2d 555 (N.Y. 2010) (evidence insufficient where "plaintiff . . . alleged only that, if fully informed, she would have sought second opinion").

How much of the "plaintiff's position" is the jury to consider within the limits of objective causation? See Bernard v. Char, 903 P.2d 667, 675-676 (Haw. 1995) (jury permitted to consider whether a reasonable person who was in great pain and who had no health insurance would have opted for tooth extraction or a more expensive root canal procedure); Ashe v. Radiation Oncology Associates, 9 S.W.3d 119, 123-124 (Tenn. 1999) (fact finder applying objective causation rules may take into account characteristics of plaintiff, including "idiosyncrasies, fears, age, medical condition, and religious beliefs"). At what point does the objective causation standard dissolve into a subjective standard?

4. *The Critique of Objective Causation.* Critics of the objective causation standard argue that it undercuts the goal of protecting individual autonomy. The standard is only a rough approximation or a surrogate device for the protection of individual autonomy because it works only so long as the individual is "reasonable." The Oklahoma Supreme Court has agreed:

> The *Canterbury* view certainly severely limits the protection granted an injured patient. To the extent the plaintiff, given an adequate disclosure, would have declined the proposed treatment, and a reasonable person in similar circumstances would have consented, a patient's right of self-determination is irrevocably lost. This basic right to know and decide is the reason for the full-disclosure rule. Accordingly, we decline to jeopardize this right by the imposition of the "reasonable man" standard. . . .
>
> If a plaintiff testifies he would have continued with the proposed treatment had he been adequately informed, the trial is over under either the subjective or objective approach. If he testifies he would not, then the causation problem must be resolved by examining the credibility of plaintiff's testimony. The jury must be instructed that it must find the plaintiff would have refused the treatment if he is to prevail.
>
> Although it might be said this approach places a physician at the mercy of a patient's hindsight, a careful practitioner can always protect himself by insuring that he has adequately informed each patient he treats. If he does not breach this duty, a causation problem will not arise.

Scott v. Bradford, 606 P.2d 554, 559 (Okla. 1979); see also Parris v. Lime, 277 P.3d 1259 (Okla. 2012). Oklahoma's "subjective causation" approach has not gained many adherents. But see Zalazar v. Vercimak, 633 N.E.2d 1223, 1227 (Ill. App. Ct. 1993) (severely limiting the use of objective causation and expert opinion in informed consent cases arising from cosmetic surgery); and Allison v. Brown, 293 Va. 617 (2017) (noting issue remains open in state). For academic commentaries on the causation problem, see Aaron D. Twerski & Neil B. Cohen, Informed Decision-Making and the Law of Torts: The Myth of Justiciable Causation, 1988 U. Ill. L. Rev. 607; Evelyn M. Tenenbaum, Revitalizing Informed Consent and Protecting Patient Autonomy: An Appeal to Abandon Objective Causation, 64 Okla. L. Rev. 697 (2012).

3. Limiting Liability for Failure to Disclose

■ RIZZO v. SCHILLER
445 S.E.2d 153 (Va. 1994)

HASSELL, Justice.

In this appeal, we consider whether the plaintiffs presented sufficient evidence to establish a prima facie case of medical malpractice against a physician who allegedly failed to obtain the mother's informed consent to use obstetrical forceps to deliver her baby.

Michael Sean Rizzo, Jr., by Pamela Rizzo, his mother and next friend, Pamela Rizzo, individually, and Michael Sean Rizzo, Sr., filed this action against Maurice Schiller, M.D. The plaintiffs alleged that Dr. Schiller, an obstetrician and gynecologist, breached the standard of care owed to them when he assisted Ms. Rizzo with the delivery of Michael. Specifically, the plaintiffs alleged that Dr. Schiller was negligent in the use of obstetrical forceps during the delivery and that he failed to obtain Ms. Rizzo's informed consent to use the forceps.

The case was tried before a jury. The trial court granted Dr. Schiller's motion to strike the plaintiffs' informed consent claim. The case proceeded to the jury on the theory that Dr. Schiller was negligent in the use of the obstetrical forceps. The jury returned a verdict in favor of Dr. Schiller, and we awarded the plaintiffs an appeal on issues related to their informed consent claim.

Pamela Rizzo was admitted to Fairfax Hospital on November 7, 1989, about 9:00 A.M. She was in active labor, and Dr. Schiller was notified of her admission. Upon admission to the hospital, Ms. Rizzo signed the following form:

Authorization for Medical and Surgical Procedures

Patient History No. /P/9456
I hereby authorize Dr. Schiller, and/or other members of the Medical Staff of The Fairfax Hospital of his choice, to perform diagnostic or therapeutic medical and surgical procedures on and to administer anesthetics to Pamela Rizzo. I further authorize The Fairfax Hospital to dispose of any removed tissue or amputated parts.

11/07/89	[Signed] *Pamela S. Rizzo*
(Date)	(Signature)

[Signed] *Vera Thomas*	
(Witness)	(Relationship)

About 12 hours later, Ms. Rizzo's fetal membranes were artificially ruptured at 8:50 P.M., and about 10:00 P.M., she was "pushing with contractions." At 10:15 P.M., Dr. Schiller ordered that Ms. Rizzo be taken to the delivery room. While in the delivery room, Ms. Rizzo made a few, but unsuccessful, attempts to "push" the baby through the birth canal with her abdominal muscles. When Ms. Rizzo's attempts to "push" were unsuccessful, Dr. Schiller told her that he was going to use forceps to deliver the baby. Ms. Rizzo testified that "before I could even get my composure together, ask what they were for, why, [the forceps] were inside me. And my son's head was out, just the head."

[Michael Rizzo developed a subdural hematoma after his birth. Experts testified that the forceps injured his head, causing the hematoma and Michael's subsequently diagnosed cerebral palsy.]

Dr. Arner qualified as an expert witness on the subjects of obstetrics and gynecology and gave the following testimony. Even though Ms. Rizzo had been given certain medication, she was capable of making medical decisions. Ms. Rizzo would have been able to deliver Michael spontaneously, without the use of forceps, had

Dr. Schiller simply waited. If forceps are used in "non-emergent situations," the patient should be informed about the use of the forceps and should be given the opportunity to participate in the decision regarding whether the forceps will be used. Dr. Arner opined that Dr. Schiller breached the standard of care owed to Ms. Rizzo because he failed to allow her to participate in the decision to use forceps.

The plaintiffs contend that the trial court erred by striking their evidence because they established a prima facie case that Dr. Schiller failed to obtain Ms. Rizzo's informed consent for the use of obstetrical forceps during Michael's delivery. Dr. Schiller, however, argues that the plaintiffs' evidence fails to establish a prima facie case and that the plaintiffs failed to present evidence of proximate causation. Furthermore, Dr. Schiller asserts that Ms. Rizzo was allowed to participate in the decision to use forceps because she signed the authorization form. We disagree with Dr. Schiller.

In Hunter v. Burroughs, 96 S.E. 360, 366-367 (1918), we held that "it is the duty of a physician in the exercise of ordinary care to warn a patient of the danger of possible bad consequences of using a remedy," but that the physician's failure to warn "is not per se an act of negligence." Rather, the physician owes a duty to make a reasonable disclosure to the patient of all significant facts under the circumstances. This duty is limited to those disclosures that a reasonable medical practitioner would provide under the same or similar circumstances. Bly v. Rhoads, 222 S.E.2d 783, 785-787 (1976). In most cases, expert testimony is necessary to establish those instances where the duty to disclose arises and what disclosures a reasonable medical practitioner would have made under the same or similar circumstances. Id.

We are of opinion that the plaintiffs presented sufficient evidence to establish a prima facie case that Dr. Schiller failed to obtain Ms. Rizzo's informed consent to use the obstetrical forceps. As we have already mentioned, Dr. Arner testified that the appropriate standard of care required that Dr. Schiller inform Ms. Rizzo about the use of the forceps and that she be given an opportunity to participate in the decision whether to use forceps. Ms. Rizzo testified that Dr. Schiller did not disclose any information to her about the use of the forceps and that he used the forceps without her consent.

It is true that Ms. Rizzo signed a document that purportedly is a consent form. However, this form did not inform her of any specific procedures that Dr. Schiller intended to perform; nor did it inform her of foreseeable risks associated with any procedures or risks in failing to perform any procedures. As Dr. Arner observed, the form is so general in nature that "you could also justify amputating her foot." We hold that the duty imposed upon a physician to obtain a patient's informed consent requires more than simply securing the patient's signature on a generalized consent form, similar to the form present here. The law requires informed consent, not mere consent, and the failure to obtain informed consent is tantamount to no consent.

We are also of opinion that the plaintiffs presented sufficient evidence of proximate causation as an element of their prima facie case. Here, the plaintiffs presented evidence from which the jury might have inferred that had Ms. Rizzo been informed of the possible consequences associated with the use of obstetrical forceps, she would have continued to assist in the birth process by "pushing" and that Michael would have been born spontaneously. The plaintiffs also presented evidence from which the jury could have found that but for the use of the forceps, Michael would not have suffered the brain injury.

Accordingly, we will remand this case for a trial of the plaintiffs' claims of lack of informed consent.

Notes: Limiting Liability for Failure to Disclose

1. *Informed Consent and Competence.* The patient's capacity is an important factor in informed consent cases. Physicians must secure consent from someone who has the legal capacity to give it.

Where the patient is incapable of giving consent him- or herself, substitute decisionmaking methods have been adopted by courts and legislatures. Did Pamela Rizzo have the capacity to make intelligent health care decisions? Her medical expert testified affirmatively.

2. *The Limits of the Duty to Inform.* Courts and commentators have discussed five general limitations to the duty to disclose:

- *Common Knowledge.* There is no duty to disclose risks "of which persons of average sophistication are aware."
- *Patient Knowledge.* The patient cannot recover for the physician's failure to disclose a risk already known by the patient.
- *Emergencies.* There is no duty to disclose information in an emergency situation where the patient is not competent, immediate treatment is required to prevent more serious harm, and no substitute decisionmaker is available. See Stewart-Graves v. Vaughn, 170 P.3d 1151 (Wash. 2007) (physician's continued resuscitation of newborn child fell within emergency exception to informed consent).
- *Therapeutic Privilege.* There is no duty to disclose information where the disclosure process would "foreclose rational decision" or "pose psychological damage" to the patient. The *Canterbury* court was particularly concerned about the need to circumscribe this exception lest it swallow the general rule. The AMA Code of Ethics (2016) limits withholding information from patients. See §2.1.3 ("Except in emergency situation in which a patient is incapable of making an informed decision, withholding information without the patient's knowledge of consent is ethically unacceptable. When information has been withheld in such circumstances, physicians[] should convey that information once the emergency situation has been resolved" in accordance with certain guidelines). For academic commentary on the therapeutic exception, see, e.g., Kathleen M. Boozang, The Therapeutic Placebo: The Case for Patient Deception, 54 Fla. L. Rev. 687 (2002). There are few reported applications of the rule. See, e.g., Barrai v. Betwee, 50 P.3d 946 (Haw. 2002) (psychiatrist fails to establish therapeutic privilege exception); and Marsingill v. O'Malley, 58 P.3d 495 (Alaska 2002) (plaintiffs essentially claim that physician should have applied the therapeutic privilege by withholding information about the likelihood that emergency room treatment would be painful or uncomfortable; patient allegedly suffered injuries from her decision to delay seeking emergency medical assistance after hearing about the nature of the likely treatment).
- *Waiver.* Although there are few court decisions on the issue, the disclosure doctrine's grounding in autonomy suggests that patients should be able to

refuse information offered by the physician. See Spar v. Cha, 907 N.E.2d 974, 983 (Ind. 2009); and Mark A. Hall, A Theory of Economic Informed Consent, 31 Ga. L. Rev. 511 (1997).

These limitations on the duty to disclose may be announced by courts or, in professional disclosure standard jurisdictions, may be established by the testimony of medical experts. The defendant generally has the burden of proving that an exception to the duty to inform is present. For a general discussion of exceptions to the duty to disclose, see Alan Meisel, The "Exceptions" to the Informed Consent Doctrine: Striking a Balance Between Competing Values in Medical Decisionmaking, 1979 Wis. L. Rev. 413.

3. *The "Consent" Process, or the Use of Forms.* Critics of the informed consent process argue that the ideal of a meaningful exchange of information between patient and physician has been replaced with the ritual of the informed consent form. How does the *Rizzo* court analyze the validity of the informed consent document signed by the plaintiff? Why shouldn't a physician be entitled to rely upon informed consent forms as a shield to liability? How was the document defective? Who should draft informed consent documents—health care providers or attorneys? Would a physician relying on the validity of an informed consent form have a malpractice claim against the drafter? Should a physician's failure to obtain a signed consent form give rise to liability? Holley v. Huang, 284 P.3d 81 (Colo. App. 2011) ("because documentation is not required, a failure to document does not constitute a failure to meet the standard of care").

Physician defendants hope that a signed consent form will foreclose any informed consent claim. It is true that a properly completed form can establish at least a presumption that a patient has consented to treatment. Sometimes the presumption is established by statute. See, e.g., Ohio Rev. Code Ann. §2317.54. A form indicating only that a patient has received information and consents is probably not sufficient to benefit from the presumption. See, e.g., Havens v. Hoffman, 902 P.2d 219, 223 (Wyo. 1995) (overturning physician's summary judgment; hospital form is an acknowledgment of the receipt of information but does not indicate the nature of the information disclosed).

4. *Informed Consent Forms in Hospitals.* Hospital employees, such as nurses, often procure patients' signatures on informed consent forms prior to surgery. Does this mean that hospitals have a duty to obtain the informed consent of patients? Courts routinely find that the answer is "no." The duty to obtain informed consent is the physician's; the hospital's involvement in the process normally is considered to be merely facilitative. Annot., 88 A.L.R.3d 1008 (1978). For a cogent critique, see Robert Gatter, The Mysterious Survival of the Policy Against Informed Consent Liability for Hospitals, 81 Notre Dame L. Rev. 1203 (2006). The physician's duty may not be delegable, even to his or her employees. See, e.g., Shinal v. Toms, 162 A.2d 429 (Pa. 2017) ("[A] physician may not delegate to others his or her obligation to provide sufficient information in order to obtain a patient's informed consent. Informed consent requires direct communication between physician and patient, and contemplates a back-and-forth, face-to-face exchange, which might include questions that the patient feels the physician must answer personally before the patient feels informed and becomes willing to consent. The duty to obtain the patient's informed consent belongs solely to the physician.")

5. *Comparative Negligence and Assumption of Risk.* Should patients have an obligation to truthfully disclose information to their physicians? Should the obligation arise only in response to a physician's inquiries, or should patients have a duty to affirmatively disclose matters that a reasonable patient would think might be relevant to his or her medical treatment? In Brown v. Dibbell, 595 N.W.2d 358 (Wis. 1999), the court held that

> for patients to exercise ordinary care, they must tell the truth and give complete
> and accurate information about personal, family, and medical histories to a doctor
> to the extent possible in response to the doctor's requests for information when
> the requested information is material to a doctor's duty as prescribed by . . . [the
> informed consent statute] and that a patient's breach of that duty might, under
> certain circumstances, constitute contributory negligence.

Id. at 368-369. The court did not consider whether patients had a duty to disclose information sua sponte. See also, Piatek v. Beale, 999 N.E.2d 68, 70 (Ind. App. 2013) ("a patient may be contributorily negligent if she gives her doctor false or incomplete information when she is capable of providing an accurate history").

Should a defendant physician be able to argue for contributory or comparative negligence where the plaintiff signs a blank consent form, or signs a consent form without reading it? What if a patient fails to ask for clarifications where the consent documents contain inconsistencies or gaps? See Oghia v. Hollan, 363 S.W.3d 30 (Ky. Ct. App. 2012) (comparative negligence applies to informed consent only in extraordinary circumstances not present in case).

An informed consent form is essentially a written documentation of the patient's assumption of the disclosed risks, assumed in order to achieve a procedure's potential benefits. See Karp v. Cooley, 493 F.2d 408 (5th Cir. 1974) (directed verdict for the defendant affirmed; patient undergoing first attempted implantation of a mechanical heart had been given extensive information and counseling about the experimental nature of the treatment and its risks). Patients ordinarily are not permitted, however, to assume the risk that a procedure will be negligently recommended or performed; they assume only the risks that are non-negligently produced. In the typical case, then, a signed informed consent form signifies that the patient was informed of the required risks and agreed to accept those risks; a form is powerful evidence of a physician's compliance with the duty to disclose but is irrelevant to an ordinary malpractice action brought against a physician for delivering substandard care. See Spar v. Cha, 907 N.E.2d 974 (Ind. 2009) ("a waiver of informed consent does not assume risks associated with negligent performance of the underlying procedure or treatment").

As is often true in legal matters, things are not quite this simple, however. As noted at page 461, informed consent and ordinary malpractice overlap and interact in several important respects. Where there are alternative standards of care or courses of treatment, obtaining informed consent may be important to the physician's malpractice defense that the physician complied with a "respectable minority" point of view. For instance, informed consent can justify departing from customary practice in order to participate in medical research or to try out an untested procedure. Similarly, informed consent might be used to bolster an affirmative defense that the patient assumed the risk or was contributorily negligent. See, e.g., Smith v. Hull, 659 N.E.2d 185 (Ind. Ct. App. 1995) (in a case involving injuries from treatment for baldness, a contributory negligence finding "was supported by evidence that patient sought out physician and hair injection procedure, received extensive literature and discussed risks with physician, and signed consent forms prior to undergoing procedures, . . . leav[ing] us with little doubt that Smith's desire to sport a full head of hair motivated him to pursue remedies that he knowingly undertook at his own peril"); Schneider v. Revici, which is excerpted and discussed at page 447. In traditional malpractice cases not involving informed consent claims, should courts exclude evidence of the consent process to avoid confusion about whether the patient had accepted the risks of his or her injuries? See Brady v. Urbas, 111 A.3d 1155 (Pa. 2015) (yes).

6. *Injury and Causation.* Note that Ms. Rizzo's claim would have failed if the undisclosed risk had not materialized, that is, if the use of forceps had not resulted in her son's injuries. How did Dr. Schiller's failure to disclose the risks associated with using forceps cause Michael Rizzo's injuries? The court holds that the plaintiffs presented sufficient evidence of proximate causation for a jury to decide in their favor. A jury could have decided that Ms. Rizzo, had she been appropriately informed, might have rejected the use of forceps and continued to "push" and that Michael's brain injuries would not have occurred. Assume that you represent the defendant. What types of counter-evidence might you want to present on this issue?

7. *Alternative Treatments.* Under the professional malpractice standard, a physician must disclose treatment alternatives if the reasonable, competent physician would have done so. The existence of alternative treatments would also be considered "material" under the patient-centered standard of disclosure. See, e.g., Allen v. Harrison, 374 P.3d 812 (Okla. 2016) (physician has duty to provide information about all medically reasonable alternatives, including those not being recommended to the patient); Annot., 38 A.L.R.4th 900 (1985). But see Cline v. Kresa-Reahl, 728 S.E.2d 87 (W. Va. 2012) (traditional medical malpractice rather than informed consent applies where physician does not disclose information about non-recommended treatment). What should be the physician's disclosure obligation where a treatment alternative is not readily available, perhaps because of cost considerations or geographic location? See, e.g., Mark Hall, A Theory of Economic Informed Consent, 31 Ga. L. Rev. 511 (1997). Should physicians have an obligation to inform patients about promising but as yet untested potential therapies? See J. Lowenthal, S. C. Hull & S. D. Pearson, The Ethics of Early Evidence—Preparing for a Possible Breakthrough in Alzheimer's Disease, 367 New Eng. J. Med. 488 (2012). Should the physician be required to disclose the option of "doing nothing"? See, e.g., Wecker v. Amend, 918 P.2d 658 (Kan. Ct. App. 1996) (yes).

8. *Precision Medicine.* Recent advances in what is sometimes called "personalized" or "precision" medicine may create additional challenges. Much of the discussion in this section has been premised on the concept of average benefits and risks, such as the likelihood that a particular form of treatment will be successful or that a patient will have an adverse outcome in surgery. An individual patient may not be—and in fact probably is not—"average." A patient's personal risk and benefit profile may differ from the average profile in significant ways. Precision medicine involves first developing and then offering "treatments targeted to the needs of individual patients on the basis of genetic, biomarker, phenotypic, or psychosocial characteristics that distinguish a given patient from other patients with similar clinical presentations." J. Larry Jameson & Dan L. Longo, Precision Medicine—Personalized, Problematic, and Promising, 372 New Eng. J. Med. 2229 (2015). See also, Francis

S. Collins & Harold Varmus, A New Initiative on Precision Medicine, 372 New Eng. J. Med. 793 (2015) (describing plans for significant investment of federal funds). The "development" part of the initiative involves investments in research on the implications of personal factors or characteristics. The "offering" component will require individual physicians to understand when and how to apply a more personalized approach to assessing risks and benefits for patients. As Jameson and Longo note, "[t]he extent to which . . . [advances in precision medicine] are constructive or disruptive depends on our ability to harness vast amounts of new knowledge and treatment options within the framework of everyday clinical practice." Id. at 2233. See also, id. at 2232 (noting the difficulties faced by physicians who must "adapt to this daunting explosion of information and the associated clinical guidelines," suggesting use of informatics and referral pathways for patients from primary care providers to those with expertise in the data and guidelines relevant to the patient's condition); and A. D. Sniderman, R. B. D'Agostino & M. J. Pencina, The Role of Physicians in the Era of Predictive Analytics, 314 JAMA 25 (2015) (discussing importance of understanding individualized risk and implications for clinical practice). What role should the informed consent doctrine play in this process? Will the risk of liability help to "push" physicians to move toward more individualized approaches to the assessment of benefits and risks? How will courts apply the professional standard and material risk standard when patients contend that their physician should have provided a more personalized assessment of treatment alternatives, risks, and benefits? See Gary E. Marchant, Kathryn Scheckel & Doug Campos-Outcalt, Contrasting Medical and Legal Standards of Evidence: A Precision Medicine Case Study, 44 J.L. Med. & Ethics 194 (2016).

9. *Informed Consent and the Therapeutic Placebo.* Physicians and medical researchers have long believed in the "placebo effect," under which some patients appear to improve after the administration of spurious "treatment." Recent research explores the forms and limits of placebo effects. See Damien G. Finniss et al., Placebo Effects: Biological, Clinical, and Ethical Advances, 375 Lancet 686 (2010); Ted J. Kaptchuk & Franklin G. Miller, Placebo Effects in Medicine, 373 New Eng. J. Med. 8 (2015). As noted above, the *Canterbury* court established but sought to limit the therapeutic privilege. Does the informed consent doctrine implicitly prohibit the use of placebos? Can you design a method of using placebos that would allow physicians (and patients) to gain the benefits of the placebo effect without violating the disclosure doctrine?

10. *Misdiagnoses and Diagnostic Tests vs. Treatments.* How should courts view informed consent claims brought in cases involving a health care practitioner's failure to diagnose a patient's condition, which then leads to a failure to provide information about appropriate treatments, alternatives, risks, and benefits? Compare Gomez v. Sauerwein, 331 P.3d 19 (Wash. 2014) (where "provider rules out a particular diagnosis . . . there is no duty to inform the patient on treatment options pertaining to the ruled out diagnosis") with Marsingill v. O'Malley, 58 P.3d 495 (Alaska 2002) (plaintiff may claim both that physician failed to appreciate the seriousness of her condition and that he failed to properly inform her of the risks associated with her condition); and Downs v. Trias, 49 A.3d 180 (Conn. 2012) ("A physician who fails to apprise a patient of a certain fact may . . . be held liable for failing to know the fact in the first place (medical negligence) and for failing to convey the fact to the patient . . . (lack of informed consent)" (emphasis omitted).

Should the duty to disclose alternatives depend on whether a treatment or a diagnostic test is at issue? See Jandre v. Wisconsin Injured Patients and Families

Compensation Fund, 813 N.W.2d 627 (2012). The patient in *Jandre* was brought to the emergency room after he had trouble swallowing his coffee and began drooling; he also experienced slurred speech, facial drooping on the left side, dizziness, and leg weakness. The emergency room physician considered many possible causes, including Bell's Palsy and some form of stroke. She performed a number of diagnostic tests, including using a stethoscope on Jandre's carotid arteries to listen for a blocked artery, but did not order the more reliable carotid ultrasound diagnostic test. She also did not inform Jandre about the availability of the test. The physician incorrectly, but non-negligently, found that Jandre had Bell's palsy. About 11 days after leaving the ER, Jandre suffered a full-blown stroke that caused physical and cognitive injuries. In a fractured decision, the Wisconsin Supreme Court found that the ER physician had a duty to disclose the availability of the carotid ultrasound under the reasonable patient standard. Id. A concurring justice agreed with the result but expressed strong concerns about the policy implications of the decision. Id. at 666. A vigorous dissent warned that the decision would result in strict liability for physicians.

Should physicians be shielded from liability for failure to discuss diagnostic tests for alternative conditions that they have non-negligently eliminated from consideration? Physicians frequently engage in a differential diagnosis analysis, moving from a range of possible conditions of greater or lesser probability to a final diagnosis by analyzing the patient's symptoms, family history, and the results of various diagnostic tests. What are the implications of this decision for physicians engaged in this process? Is the type of fully informed consent the majority imagines a practical possibility in already-overburdened hospital emergency rooms? Will health care costs increase as patients are informed about and demand more diagnostic tests?

11. *Law in Books, Law in Action, and the "New" Model of Shared Decisionmaking.* Does the informed consent duty established under malpractice principles provide adequate protection for patient autonomy? Does it protect physicians from unwarranted intrusions into professional autonomy?

There have been flurries of reformist proposals over the past 15 years exploiting the many weaknesses of the current legal approach to informed consent and advocating some form of "shared medical decisionmaking." New models of "shared decisionmaking" in health care promote a dialogue with physicians providing information about risks and probabilities while patients contribute information about values and preferences with the goal of jointly developing a treatment plan. Although the model has many variations, this description is typical:

> Shared medical decision-making is a process in which the physician shares with the patient all relevant risk and benefit information on all treatment alternatives and the patient shares with the physician all relevant personal information that might make one treatment or side effect more or less tolerable than others. Then, both parties use this information to come to a mutual medical decision.

Jamie Staples King & Benjamin W. Moulton, Rethinking Informed Consent: The Case for Shared Medical Decision-Making, 32 Am. J.L. & Med. 429, 431 (2006) (citations omitted). For a critique, see Carl E. Schneider, Void for Vagueness, Hastings Center Rep. 10 (Jan.-Feb. 2007). Is shared decisionmaking simply a variation on the reasonable patient standard? See Erica S. Spatz, Harlan M. Krumholtz & Benjamin W. Moulton, The New Era of Informed Consent: Getting to a Reasonable-Patient Standard Through Shared Decision Making, 315 JAMA 2063 (2016). Could implementation of shared decisionmaking expand physician liability for failure to disclose low risks that could become relevant in light of a patient's shared values and preferences?

The shared decisionmaking process is often assisted by the use of computer-based or audiovisual "decision aids." This approach may be particularly appropriate for elective procedures or areas in which there are multiple treatment options with varying risks and benefits. Courts typically find, however, that physicians are not required to use any particular means of communicating risk information. Holley v. Huang, 284 P.3d 81 (Colo. App. 2011) ("A doctor may employ any means of communication—such as conversation, writings, video and audio recordings, or some combination of these—that will yield a properly informed consent."). See also Jessica Berg, The E-Health Revolution and the Necessary Evolution of Informed Consent, 11 Ind. Health L. Rev. 589 (2014); Nadia N. Sawicki, Informed Consent Beyond the Physician-Patient Encounter: Tort Implications of Extra-Clinical Decision Support Tools, 21 Ann. Health L. 1 (2012).

Shared decisionmaking has advanced somewhat in recent years through several state and federal initiatives. See Erica S. Spatz, Harlan M. Krumholz & Benjamin W. Moulton, Prime Time for Shared Decision Making, 317 JAMA 1309 (2017). Is shared decisionmaking a recalibration of the role of physicians and patients that addresses the critique of traditional informed consent's focus on information transfer and patient autonomy? For a clinician's contrary view, see Lisa Rosenbaum, The Paternalism Preference—Choosing Unshared Decision Making, 373 New Eng. J. Med. 589 (2015).

12. *Further Reading.* On patients' **competency to consent** (note 1), see S. Boettger et al., Assessment of Decisional Capacity: Prevalence of Medical Illness and Psychiatric Comorbidities, 13 Palliat Support Care 1275 (2015); Laura B. Dunn et al., Assessing Decisional Capacity for Clinical Research or Treatment: A Review of Instruments, 163 Am. J. Psychiatry 1323 (2006); Marsha Garrison, The Empire of Illness: Competence and Coercion in Health-Care Decision Making, 49 Wm. & Mary L. Rev. 781 (2007); Bruce J. Winick, Competency to Consent to Treatment: The Distinction Between Assent and Objection, 28 Hous. L. Rev. 15 (1991); Annot., 25 A.L.R.3d 1439 (1969). Consent issues are particularly acute in the treatment of minors. See generally Note, Mature Minors, Medical Choice, and the Constitutional Right to Martyrdom, 102 Va. L. Rev. 1355 (2016); Jennifer L. Rosato, Let's Get Real: Quilting a Principled Approach to Adolescent Empowerment in Health Care Decision-Making, 51 DePaul L. Rev. 769 (2002).

Regarding **physicians' use of placebos** (note 9), see Kathleen M. Boozang, The Therapeutic Placebo: The Case for Patient Deception, 54 U. Fla. L. Rev. 687 (2002); S. C. Hull et al., Patients' Attitudes about the Use of Placebo Treatments: Telephone Survey, 347 BMJ f3757 (2013) (50–84% of respondents found placebo use acceptable in a range of fact situations; 21.9% found placebo use by physicians unacceptable in all circumstances); Adam J. Kolber, A Limited Defense of Clinical Placebo Deception, 26 Yale L & Pol'y Rev. 75 (2007); Anup Malani, Regulation with Placebo Effects, 58 Duke L.J. 411 (2008); Franklin Miller & Luana Colloca, The Legitimacy of Placebo Treatments in Clinical Practice: Evidence and Ethics, 9 Am. J. Bioethics 39 (2009).

On **shared decisionmaking** (note 11), see Dominick L. Frosch et al., Authoritarian Physicians and Patients' Fear of Being Labeled "Difficult" Among Key

Obstacles to Shared Decision Making, 31 Health Aff. 1030 (2012); Jaime S. King et al., The Potential of Shared Decision Making to Reduce Health Disparities, 39 J.L. Med. & Ethics 30 (2011); Dayna Bowen Matthew, Implementing American Health Care Reform: The Fiduciary Imperative, 59 Buff. L. Rev. 715, 798-800 (2011); Symposium, 70 Med. Care Res. & Rev. 35 (2013).

Discussion Problem: Informed Refusals?

Dr. Claude R. Thomas was Mrs. Rena Truman's personal physician from 1963 to 1969. In 1969, another physician discovered that Mrs. Truman had advanced cervical cancer. Mrs. Truman died in 1970, at the age of 30. Rena Truman's children sued Dr. Thomas for failing to perform a Pap test on Mrs. Truman between 1964 and 1969. Trial testimony indicated that (1) if the Pap smear had been performed during this time period, Mrs. Truman's condition would have been discovered at an earlier stage and she probably would have lived; (2) medical practice required physicians to inform women of the purpose of a Pap test; and (3) Dr. Thomas repeatedly advised Mrs. Truman to undergo the test but did not specifically explain the possible consequences of her refusal. Consider this case under the professional and material risk standards of disclosure. What arguments can you make on behalf of Mrs. Truman's children? What arguments or defenses might you raise on behalf of Dr. Thomas? See Truman v. Thomas, 611 P.2d 902 (Cal. 1980). See also Providence Health Center v. Dowell, 262 S.W.3d 324, 334-335 (Tex. 2008) (O'Neill, dissenting).

4. Fiduciary Obligations, Conflicts of Interest, and Novel Disclosure Obligations

Depending on the jurisdiction, the informed consent doctrine has grown out of the rich soil of cases involving battery, malpractice, and fiduciary law. The doctrine has the potential for continued expansive growth, particularly in those jurisdictions emphasizing a physician's fiduciary obligations over the professional standard of care. In these states, the scope of informed consent is not limited by the current standard of professional conduct. As you read the following cases, consider whether the courts have gone too far or not far enough in regulating the scope of physician disclosure. Does the imposition of liability in these cases seem "just"? Do the courts' decisions seem consistent with the informed consent doctrine they purport to apply? What is the likely impact of these decisions on the nature of physician-patient communications? Are patients more likely to receive important information? What will physicians do to minimize liability?

■AUTONOMY AND PRIVACY: PROTECTING PATIENTS FROM THEIR PHYSICIANS
Mary Anne Bobinski
55 U. Pitt. L. Rev. 291, 347-356 (1994)

. . . Jurisdictions with more generous disclosure requirements typically rely, at least in part, on fiduciary principles as a basis for the disclosure obligation. Fiduciary law thus presents a possible avenue for future growth of a more vibrant disclosure duty. Tort law and the law governing fiduciary relationships are similar in that they impose extra-contractual duties on individuals. The two regulatory schemes, however, differ in conception of those duties. Tort law most often imposes general duties irrespective of the status of the parties. The law of fiduciaries, in contrast, is based on the special character of the relationship between two parties. Courts struggling to define the scope of tort-based disclosure duties have often noted the fiducial characteristics of the doctor-patient relationship as a justification for disclosure. This linkage between ordinary tort and fiduciary principles creates the opportunity for both growth and confusion. Ordinary tort duties may be expanded or amplified because of the perceived relevance of fiduciary principles. To date, few courts have explicitly considered the implications of wholesale acceptance of the doctor-patient relationship as one subject to fiduciary law. There has been little judicial analysis of the appropriateness of applying fiduciary-based disclosure obligations to the physician-patient relationship, and virtually no judicial analysis of the special problems presented by provider-associated risk.

The first question is whether the relationship between physicians and patients is a fiduciary one. Fiduciary relationships are generally described as those in which some aspect of the relationship between the parties [such as an imbalance of power or knowledge] justifies the imposition of special obligations on one of them. Several treatises on fiduciary law name the physician-patient relationship as a fiduciary one and the courts have tended to concur. [See pages 163-164.]

Next, the fiduciary duties that physicians owe to patients must be determined. Generally, a fiduciary must act for the benefit of another, but the specific duties imposed on a fiduciary will vary with the scope of the relationship between the parties. The fiduciary owes a duty of loyalty, "good faith, trust, special confidence and candor" to the other party. Obviously, it is not a breach of the fiduciary relationship for the fiduciary to receive compensation for her services. However, the fiduciary can breach her duty by engaging in self-dealing, by receiving bribes or kickbacks, or by misappropriating that knowledge or property which belongs to the entrustor. The role of disclosure in fiduciary law is somewhat complicated. The fiduciary's failure to disclose information to the entrustor can constitute an independent breach of fiduciary duty when the information was gathered in the course of the fiduciary's duties. Disclosure may also help determine whether an apparent breach of fiduciary duties has been "cured" by the consent of the entrustor. The validity of the entrustor's consent will be the important question because the fiduciary's influence over the entrustor may make any consent presumptively invalid. Disclosure in these cases is of evidentiary significance; it may bolster the fiduciary's claim that the entrustor's consent to the transaction was valid. As a substantive matter, disclosure may not be sufficient where the fiduciary's influence over the entrustor makes any — even informed — consent illusory. . . .

This analysis of fiduciary principles assumes that a breach will provide some effective remedy for patients. A fiduciary is liable to the entrustor for a breach of fiduciary duties. A breach of a fiduciary obligation can be remedied by voiding a transaction, by payment by the fiduciary to the trusting party of any impermissible benefits or profits, or by payment by the fiduciary to compensate the other party for actual damages, which may include compensation for personal injury. Courts are divided on whether the entrustor is required to show some specific injury flowed from the fiduciary's breach of her duties.

The significant number of courts that have applied fiduciary principles to the physician-patient relationship can be deceiving. Most courts have failed to consider the broader policy implications of classifying the physician-patient relationship as a fiduciary one; most have also failed to analyze the range of physicians' required fiduciary duties. Some courts have responded to these problems by hedging, noting that the relationship has fiducial "qualities" or "characteristics" or finding that it is a "confidential" relationship. . . .

The . . . [most important] judicial consideration of common law economic disclosure obligations occurred in Moore v. Regents of the University of California. . . .

■ MOORE v. THE REGENTS OF THE UNIVERSITY OF CALIFORNIA
793 P.2d 479 (Cal. 1990), cert. denied, 499 U.S. 936 (1991)

PANELLI, Justice.

We granted review in this case to determine whether plaintiff has stated a cause of action against his physician and other defendants for using his cells in potentially lucrative medical research without his permission. Plaintiff alleges that his physician failed to disclose preexisting research and economic interests in the cells before obtaining consent to the medical procedures by which they were extracted. . . . We hold that the complaint states a cause of action for breach of the physician's disclosure obligations, but not for conversion.

FACTS

. . . The plaintiff is John Moore (Moore), who underwent treatment for hairy-cell leukemia at the Medical Center of the University of California at Los Angeles (UCLA Medical Center). The five defendants are: (1) Dr. David W. Golde (Golde), a physician who attended Moore at UCLA Medical Center; (2) the Regents of the University of California (Regents), who own and operate the university; (3) Shirley G. Quan, a researcher employed by the Regents; (4) Genetics Institute, Inc. (Genetics Institute); and (5) Sandoz Pharmaceuticals Corporation and related entities (collectively Sandoz).

Moore first visited UCLA Medical Center on October 5, 1976, shortly after he learned that he had hairy-cell leukemia. After hospitalizing Moore and "withdrawing extensive amounts of blood, bone marrow aspirate, and other bodily substances," Golde confirmed that diagnosis. At this time all defendants, including Golde, were aware that "certain blood products and blood components were of great value in a number of commercial and scientific efforts" and that access to a patient whose blood contained these substances would provide "competitive, commercial, and scientific advantages."

On October 8, 1976, Golde recommended that Moore's spleen be removed. Golde informed Moore "that he had reason to fear for his life, and that the proposed splenectomy operation . . . was necessary to slow down the progress of his disease." Based upon Golde's representations, Moore signed a written consent form authorizing the splenectomy.

Before the operation, Golde and Quan "formed the intent and made arrangements to obtain portions of [Moore's] spleen following its removal" and to take them to a separate research unit. Golde gave written instructions to this effect on October 18 and 19, 1976. These research activities "were not intended to have . . . any relation to [Moore's] medical . . . care." However, neither Golde nor Quan informed Moore of their plans to conduct this research or requested his permission. Surgeons at UCLA Medical Center, whom the complaint does not name as defendants, removed Moore's spleen on October 20, 1976.

Moore returned to the UCLA Medical Center several times between November 1976 and September 1983. He did so at Golde's direction and based upon representations "that such visits were necessary and required for his health and well-being, and based upon the trust inherent in and by virtue of the physician-patient relationship. . . ." On each of these visits Golde withdrew additional samples of "blood, blood serum, skin, bone marrow aspirate, and sperm." On each occasion Moore travelled to the UCLA Medical Center from his home in Seattle because he had been told that the procedures were to be performed only there and only under Golde's direction.

"In fact, [however,] throughout the period of time that [Moore] was under [Golde's] care and treatment, . . . the defendants were actively involved in a number of activities which they concealed from [Moore]. . . ." Specifically, defendants were conducting research on Moore's cells and planned to "benefit financially and competitively . . . [by exploiting the cells] and [their] exclusive access to [the cells] by virtue of [Golde's] on-going physician-patient relationship. . . ."

Sometime before August 1979, Golde established a cell line from Moore's T-lymphocytes.[2] On January 30, 1981, the Regents applied for a patent on the cell line, listing Golde and Quan as inventors. "[B]y virtue of an established policy . . . , [the] Regents, Golde, and Quan would share in any royalties or profits . . . arising out of [the] patent." The patent issued on March 20, 1984, naming Golde and Quan as the inventors of the cell line and the Regents as the assignee of the patent. The Regent's patent also covers various methods for using the cell line to produce lymphokines. Moore admits in his complaint that "the true clinical potential of each of the lymphokines . . . [is] difficult to predict, [but] . . . competing commercial firms in these relevant fields have published reports in biotechnology industry periodicals predicting a potential market of approximately $3.01 billion by the year 1990 for a whole range of [such lymphokines]. . . ." [Golde and his associates received several hundred thousand dollars over the next three years plus shares of stock, under agreements with Genetics Institute to develop the cell line products.]

Based upon these allegations, Moore attempted to state 13 causes of action.[4] . . . [T]he superior court sustained a general demurrer to the entire complaint. . . .

---

2. A T-lymphocyte is a type of white blood cell. T-lymphocytes produce lymphokines, or proteins that regulate the immune system. Some lymphokines have potential therapeutic value. If the genetic material responsible for producing a particular lymphokine can be identified, it can sometimes be used to manufacture large quantities of the lymphokine through the techniques of recombinant DNA. . . . Moore's T-lymphocytes were interesting to the defendants because they overproduced certain lymphokines, thus making the corresponding genetic material easier to identify. . . .

4. (1) "Conversion"; (2) "lack of informed consent"; (3) "breach of fiduciary duty"; (4) "fraud and deceit"; (5) "unjust enrichment"; (6) "quasi-contract"; (7) "bad faith breach of

DISCUSSION

A. BREACH OF FIDUCIARY DUTY AND LACK OF INFORMED CONSENT

Moore repeatedly alleges that Golde failed to disclose the extent of his research and economic interests in Moore's cells[6] before obtaining consent to the medical procedures by which the cells were extracted. These allegations, in our view, state a cause of action against Golde for invading a legally protected interest of his patient. This cause of action can properly be characterized either as the breach of a fiduciary duty to disclose facts material to the patient's consent or, alternatively, as the performance of medical procedures without first having obtained the patient's informed consent.

Our analysis begins with three well-established principles. First, "a person of adult years and in sound mind has the right, in the exercise of control over his own body, to determine whether or not to submit to lawful medical treatment." Cobbs v. Grant, 8 Cal. 3d 229, 242 (1972). Second, "the patient's consent to treatment, to be effective, must be an informed consent." Cobbs, 8 Cal. 3d at 242. Third, in soliciting the patient's consent, a physician has a fiduciary duty to disclose all information material to the patient's decision.

These principles lead to the following conclusions: (1) A physician must disclose personal interests unrelated to the patient's health, whether research or economic, that may affect the physician's professional judgment; and (2) a physician's failure to disclose such interests may give rise to a cause of action for performing medical procedures without informed consent or breach of fiduciary duty. . . .

Indeed, the law already recognizes that a reasonable patient would want to know whether a physician has an economic interest that might affect the physician's professional judgment. As the Court of Appeal has said, "[c]ertainly a sick patient deserves to be free of any reasonable suspicion that his doctor's judgment is influenced by a profit motive." Magan Medical Clinic v. Cal. State Bd. of Medical Examiners, 249 Cal. App. 2d 124, 132 (1967). The desire to protect patients from possible conflicts of interest has also motivated legislative enactments. Among these is Business and Professions Code §654.2. Under that section, a physician may not charge a patient on behalf of, or refer a patient to, any organization in which the physician has a "significant beneficial interest, unless [the physician] first discloses in writing to the patient, that there is such an interest and advises the patient that the patient may choose any organization for the purposes of obtaining the services ordered or requested by [the physician]." Similarly, under Health and Safety Code §24173, a physician who plans to conduct a medical experiment on a patient must, among other things, inform the patient of "[t]he name of the sponsor or funding source, if any, . . . and the organization, if any, under whose general aegis the experiment is being conducted."

---

the implied covenant of good faith and fair dealing"; (8) "intentional infliction of emotional distress"; (9) "negligent misrepresentation"; (10) "intentional interference with prospective advantageous economic relationships"; (11) "slander of title"; (12) "accounting"; and (13) "declaratory relief."

6. In this opinion we use the inclusive term cells to describe all of the cells taken from Moore's body, including blood cells, bone marrow, spleen, etc.

It is important to note that no law prohibits a physician from conducting research in the same area in which he practices. Progress in medicine often depends upon physicians, such as those practicing at the university hospital where Moore received treatment, who conduct research while caring for their patients.

Yet a physician who treats a patient in whom he also has a research interest has potentially conflicting loyalties. This is because medical treatment decisions are made on the basis of proportionality—weighing the benefits to the patient against the risks to the patient. As another court has said, "the determination as to whether the burdens of treatment are worth enduring for any individual patient depends upon the facts unique in each case," and "the patient's interests and desires are the key ingredients of the decision-making process." A physician who adds his own research interests to this balance may be tempted to order a scientifically useful procedure or test that offers marginal, or no, benefits to the patient.[8] The possibility that an interest extraneous to the patient's health has affected the physician's judgment is something that a reasonable patient would want to know in deciding whether to consent to a proposed course of treatment. It is material to the patient's decision and, thus, a prerequisite to informed consent. . . .

We acknowledge that there is a competing consideration. To require disclosure of research and economic interests may corrupt the patient's own judgment by distracting him from the requirements of his health.[9] But California law does not grant physicians unlimited discretion to decide what to disclose. . . .

Accordingly, we hold that a physician who is seeking a patient's consent for a medical procedure must, in order to satisfy his fiduciary duty[10] and to obtain the patient's informed consent, disclose personal interests unrelated to the patient's health, whether research or economic, that may affect his medical judgment.

1. Dr. Golde

We turn now to the allegations of Moore's third amended complaint to determine whether he has stated such a cause of action. . . . Moore alleges that Golde actively concealed his economic interest in Moore's cells during this time period.

---

8. This is, in fact, precisely what Moore has alleged with respect to the postoperative withdrawals of blood and other substances.

9. . . . [A] physician who orders a procedure partly to further a research interest unrelated to the patient's health should not be able to avoid disclosure with the argument that the patient might object to participation in research. In some cases, however, a physician's research interest might play such an insignificant role in the decision to recommend a medically indicated procedure that disclosure should not be required because the interest is not material. By analogy, we have not required disclosure of "remote" risks that "are not central to the decision to administer or reject [a] procedure." Truman v. Thomas, 27 Cal. 3d 285, 293 (1980).

10. In some respects the term fiduciary is too broad. In this context the term fiduciary signifies only that a physician must disclose all facts material to the patient's decision. A physician is not the patient's financial adviser. As we have already discussed, the reason why a physician must disclose possible conflicts is not because he has a duty to protect his patient's financial interests, but because certain personal interests may affect professional judgment.

[D]uring each of these visits . . . , and even when [Moore] inquired as to whether there was any possible or potential commercial or financial value or significance of his Blood and Bodily Substances, or whether the defendants had discovered anything . . . which was or might be . . . related to any scientific activity resulting in commercial or financial benefits . . . , the defendants repeatedly and affirmatively represented to [Moore] that there was no commercial or financial value to his Blood and Bodily Substances . . . and in fact actively discouraged such inquiries.

. . . In these allegations, Moore plainly asserts that Golde concealed an economic interest in the postoperative procedures. Therefore, applying the principles already discussed, the allegations state a cause of action for breach of fiduciary duty or lack of informed consent.

We thus disagree with the superior court's ruling that Moore had not stated a cause of action . . . [because he] failed to allege that the operation lacked a therapeutic purpose or that the procedure was totally unrelated to therapeutic purposes. In our view, neither allegation is essential. Even if the splenectomy had a therapeutic purpose, it does not follow that Golde had no duty to disclose his additional research and economic interests. As we have already discussed, the existence of a motivation for a medical procedure unrelated to the patient's health is a potential conflict of interest and a fact material to the patient's decision.

2. The Remaining Defendants

The Regents, Quan, Genetics Institute, and Sandoz are not physicians. In contrast to Golde, none of these defendants stood in a fiduciary relationship with Moore or had the duty to obtain Moore's informed consent to medical procedures. If any of these defendants is to be liable for breach of fiduciary duty or performing medical procedures without informed consent, it can only be on account of Golde's acts and on the basis of a recognized theory of secondary liability, such as respondeat superior. The procedural posture of this case, however, makes it unnecessary for us to address the sufficiency of Moore's secondary-liability allegations. . . .

B. CONVERSION

[In this portion of the opinion, the court rejected Moore's attempt to characterize the invasion of his rights as a conversion. The court reasoned that such an unprecedented extension of property law concepts is not warranted because strict liability would be too threatening to legitimate and socially useful scientific research.] For these reasons, we hold that the allegations of Moore's third amended complaint state a cause of action for breach of fiduciary duty or lack of informed consent, but not conversion.

Mosk, Justice, dissenting.
. . . I disagree with the majority's . . . conclusion that in the present context a nondisclosure cause of action is an adequate — in fact, a superior — substitute for a conversion cause of action. In my view the nondisclosure cause of action falls short on at least three grounds. First, . . . the majority's theory apparently is that the threat of [a damages action based on nondisclosure] . . . will have a prophylactic effect: It

will give physician-researchers incentive to disclose any conflicts of interest before treatment, and will thereby protect their patients' right to make an informed decision about what may be done with their body parts.

The remedy is largely illusory. . . . There are two barriers to recovery. First, the patient must show that if he or she had been informed of all pertinent information, he or she would have declined to consent to the procedure in question. . . . The second barrier to recovery is still higher, and is erected on the first: It is not even enough for the plaintiff to prove that he personally would have refused consent to the proposed treatment if he had been fully informed; he must also prove that in the same circumstances no reasonably prudent person would have given such consent. . . . Few if any judges or juries are likely to believe that disclosure of . . . a possibility of research or development would dissuade a reasonably prudent person from consenting to the treatment. For example, in the case at bar no trier of fact is likely to believe that if defendants had disclosed their plans for using Moore's cells, no reasonably prudent person in Moore's position—i.e., a leukemia patient suffering from a grossly enlarged spleen—would have consented to the routine operation that saved or at least prolonged his life. Here . . . a motion for nonsuit for failure to prove proximate cause will end the matter. In this context, accordingly, the threat of suit on a nondisclosure cause of action is largely a paper tiger.

The second reason why the nondisclosure cause of action is inadequate for the task that the majority assign to it is that it fails to solve half the problem before us: It gives the patient only the right to refuse consent, i.e., the right to prohibit the commercialization of his tissue; it does not give him the right to grant consent to that commercialization on the condition that he share in its proceeds. . . . Third, the nondisclosure cause of action fails to reach a major class of potential defendants: all those who are outside the strict physician-patient relationship with the plaintiff. . . .

In sum, the nondisclosure cause of action (1) is unlikely to be successful in most cases, (2) fails to protect patients' rights to share in the proceeds of the commercial exploitation of their tissue, and (3) may allow the true exploiters to escape liability. It is thus not an adequate substitute, in my view, for the conversion cause of action. . . .

BROUSSARD, Justice, concurring and dissenting.

. . . I disagree with the suggestion in [Justice Mosk's] dissenting opinion that defendants will be able to avoid all liability under the breach-of-fiduciary-duty theory simply by showing that plaintiff would have proceeded with the surgical removal of his diseased spleen even if defendants had disclosed their research and commercial interest in his cells. . . . [I]n this context [of a breach of fiduciary duty]—unlike in the traditional "informed consent" context of *Cobbs*—a plaintiff should not be required to establish that he would not have proceeded with the medical treatment in question if his physician had made full disclosure, but only that the doctor's wrongful failure to disclose information proximately caused the plaintiff some type of compensable damage. . . . [I]n appropriate circumstances, punitive as well as compensatory damages would clearly be recoverable in such an action. Accordingly, [Justice Mosk] underestimates the potential efficacy of the breach-of-fiduciary-duty cause of action in dismissing the action as a "paper tiger."

■HOWARD v. UNIVERSITY OF MEDICINE & DENTISTRY OF NEW JERSEY
800 A.2d 73 (N.J. 2002)

LaVecchia, J.

In this appeal we consider what causes of action will lie when a plaintiff contends that a physician misrepresented his credentials and experience at the time he obtained the plaintiff's consent to surgery. . . .

[The plaintiff suffered serious and progressive back injuries in an automobile accident but decided to forgo recommended surgery. The plaintiff was referred to Dr. Heary, a professor at the defendant University, after the plaintiff sustained additional back injuries in a second car accident.] Dr. Heary had two pre-operative consultations with plaintiff. In the first consultation, Dr. Heary determined that plaintiff needed surgery to correct a cervical myelopathy secondary to cervical stenosis and a significantly large C3 C4 disc herniation. Because of the serious nature of the surgery, Dr. Heary recommended that plaintiff's wife attend a second consultation. The doctor wanted to explain again the risks, benefits, and alternatives to surgery, and to answer any questions concerning the procedure.

Plaintiff returned with his wife for a second consultation, but what transpired is disputed. An "Office Note" written by Dr. Heary detailing the contents of the consultation states that "[a]ll alternatives have been discussed and patient elects at this time to undergo the surgical procedure, which has been scheduled for March 5, 1997." Dr. Heary asserts that he informed plaintiff and his wife that the surgery entailed significant risks, including the possibility of paralysis. Plaintiffs dispute that they were informed of such risks. Further, they contend that during the consultation plaintiff's wife asked Dr. Heary whether he was Board Certified and that he said he was. Plaintiffs also claim that Dr. Heary told them that he had performed approximately sixty corpectomies in each of the eleven years he had been performing such surgical procedures. According to Mrs. Howard, she was opposed to the surgery and it was only after Dr. Heary's specific claims of skill and experience that she and her husband decided to go ahead with the procedure.

Dr. Heary denies that he represented that he was Board Certified in Neurosurgery.[1] He also denies that he ever claimed to have performed sixty corpectomies per year for the eleven years he had practiced neurosurgery.

Dr. Heary performed the surgical procedure on March 5, 1997, but it was unsuccessful. A malpractice action was filed alleging that Mr. Howard was rendered quadriplegic as a result of Dr. Heary's negligence. [The plaintiffs sought leave to add a fraud claim to their complaint. The trial court rejected the motion, the appellate division reversed, and the matter was appealed to the state supreme court.]

Presently, a patient has several avenues of relief against a doctor: (1) deviation from the standard of care (medical malpractice); (2) lack of informed consent; and (3) battery. . . . Plaintiffs' motion to amend the complaint to add a fraud claim

1. Although he was Board Eligible at the time of Mr. Howard's surgery, Dr. Heary did not become Board Certified in Neurosurgery until November 1999. . . .

raises the question whether a patient's consent to surgery obtained through alleged misrepresentations about the physician's professional experience and credentials is properly addressed in a claim of lack of informed consent, or battery, or whether it should constitute a separate and distinct claim based on fraud.

We focus first on the distinction between lack of informed consent and battery as they are recognized in New Jersey. The doctrine of informed consent was tied initially to the tort of battery, but its evolution has firmly established it as a negligence concept. . . . By the mid-twentieth century, as courts began to use a negligence theory to analyze consent causes of action, the case law evolved from the notion of consent to *informed* consent, balancing the patient's need for sufficient information with the doctor's perception of the appropriate amount of information to impart for an informed decision. . . . The doctrine of informed consent continued to be refined. See Natanson v. Kline, 350 P.2d 1093, 1106, modified on other grounds, 354 P.2d 670 (1960) (holding that doctor's required disclosure was "limited to those disclosures which a reasonable medical practitioner would make under the same or similar circumstances," known as the "professional standard"). Eventually, the "prudent patient," or "materiality of risk" standard was introduced. Canterbury v. Spence, 464 F.2d 772, 786-88 (D.C. Cir. 1972), cert. denied, 409 U.S. 1064 (1972). That patient-centered view of informed consent stresses the patient's right to self-determination, and the fiduciary relationship between a doctor and his or her patients. . . . [New Jersey originally followed the professional standard of disclosure but later adopted the patient-centered material risk standard discussed in *Canterbury*.]

Our common law also authorizes a medical battery cause of action where a doctor performs a surgery without consent, rendering the surgery an unauthorized touching. . . . In circumstances where the surgery that was performed was authorized with arguably inadequate information, however, an action for negligence is more appropriate. . . . Thus, although a claim for battery will lie where there has been "ghost surgery"* or where no consent has been given for the procedure undertaken, if consent has been given for the procedure only a claim based on lack of informed consent will lie. A claim based on lack of informed consent properly will focus then on the adequacy of the disclosure, its impact on the reasonable patient's assessment of the risks, alternatives, and consequences of the surgery, and the damages caused by the occurrence of the undisclosed risk. . . .

Few jurisdictions have confronted the question of what cause of action should lie when a doctor allegedly misrepresents his credentials or experience. Research has revealed only one jurisdiction that has allowed a claim based on lack of informed consent under similar circumstances. See Johnson v. Kokemoor, 545 N.W.2d 495 (Wis. 1996) (analyzing doctor's affirmative misrepresentation as claim for lack of informed consent and finding that reasonable person would have considered information regarding doctor's relative lack of experience in performing surgery to have been material in making intelligent and informed decision). Although some suggest that a claim based in fraud may be appropriate if a doctor actively misrepresents his or her background or credentials, we are aware of no court that has so held. . . .

---

* ["Ghost surgery" occurs if the patient consents to a surgical procedure to be performed by Physician A but the surgery actually is performed by Physician B.—EDS.]

The thoughtful decision of the Appellate Division notwithstanding, we are not convinced that our common law should be extended to allow a novel fraud or deceit-based cause of action in this doctor-patient context that regularly would admit of the possibility of punitive damages, and that would circumvent the requirements for proof of both causation and damages imposed in a traditional informed consent setting. We are especially reluctant to do so when plaintiff's damages from this alleged "fraud" arise exclusively from the doctor-patient relationship involving plaintiff's corpectomy procedure. . . . Accordingly, we hold that a fraud or deceit-based claim is unavailable to address the wrong alleged by plaintiff. We next consider whether a claim based on lack of informed consent is the more appropriate analytical basis for the amendment to the complaint permitted by the Appellate Division. . . .

Our case law never has held that a doctor has a duty to detail his background and experience as part of the required informed consent disclosure; nor are we called on to decide that question here. . . . Courts generally have held that claims of lack of informed consent based on a failure to disclose professional-background information are without merit. . . . Although personal credentials and experience may not be a required part of an informed consent disclosure under the current standard of care required of doctors, the question raised in this appeal is whether significant misrepresentations concerning a physician's qualifications can affect the validity of consent obtained. The answer obviously is that they can.

In certain circumstances, a serious misrepresentation concerning the quality or extent of a physician's professional experience, viewed from the perspective of the reasonably prudent patient assessing the risks attendant to a medical procedure, can be material to the grant of intelligent and informed consent to the procedure. See 1 Dan B. Dobbs, *The Law of Torts*, §251 at 660-61 (2001) (citing *Kokemoor, supra*, and discussing that some authority has begun to suggest that patient is entitled to information concerning doctor's experience in performing specific surgery). In *Kokemoor, supra*, the Supreme Court of Wisconsin reviewed a case in which the plaintiff alleged that her surgeon did not obtain her informed consent to perform a surgical procedure because he had misrepresented his experience in response to a direct question during a pre-operative consultation. 545 N.W.2d at 505. At trial, evidence was introduced suggesting that the type of surgery performed—basilar bifurcation aneurysm—was "among the most difficult in all of neurosurgery." Ibid. The court found that evidence of the defendant's lack of experience was relevant to an informed consent claim because "[a] reasonable person in the plaintiff's position would have considered such information material in making an intelligent and informed decision about the surgery." Ibid.

The allegation here is that defendant's misrepresentations concerning his credentials and experience were instrumental in overcoming plaintiff's reluctance to proceed with the surgery. The theory of the claim is not that the misrepresentation induced plaintiff to proceed with unnecessary surgery. . . . Rather, plaintiff essentially contends that he was misled about material information that he required in order to grant an intelligent and informed consent to the performance of the procedure because he did not receive accurate responses to questions concerning defendant's experience in performing corpectomies and whether he was "Board Certified." Plaintiff allegedly was warned of the risk of paralysis from the corpectomy procedure; however, he asserts that if he had known the truth about defendant's qualifications and experience, it would have affected his assessment of the risks of the procedure. Stated differently, defendant's misrepresentations induced plaintiff to consent to a surgical procedure, and its risk of paralysis, that he would not have undergone had he known the truth about defendant's qualifications. Stripped to its essentials, plaintiff's claim is founded on lack of informed consent.

As noted earlier, a patient-specific standard of what is material to a full disclosure does not apply in a claim based on lack of informed consent. Thus, plaintiff's subjective preference for a Board Certified physician, or one who had performed more corpectomies than defendant had performed, is not the actionable standard. Nonetheless, assuming the misrepresentations are proved, if an objectively reasonable person could find that physician experience was material in determining the medical risk of the corpectomy procedure to which plaintiff consented, and if a reasonably prudent person in plaintiff's position informed of the defendant's misrepresentations about his experience would not have consented, then a claim based on lack of informed consent may be maintained.

Modern advances in medicine coupled with the increased sophistication of medical consumers require an evolving notion of the reasonably prudent patient when assessing a claim based on lack of informed consent. . . . That said, most informed consent issues are unlikely to implicate a setting in which a physician's experience or credentials have been demonstrated to be a material element affecting the risk of undertaking a specific procedure. The standard requires proof on which an objectively reasonable person would base a finding that physician experience could have a causal connection to a substantial risk of the procedure. . . .

The alleged misrepresentations in this case about "physician experience" (credentials and surgical experience) provide a useful context for demonstrating the difficulty inherent in meeting the materiality standard required in order for physician experience to have a role in an informed consent case. We recognize that a misrepresentation about a physician's experience is not a perfect fit with the familiar construct of a claim based on lack of informed consent. The difficulty arises because physician experience is not information that directly relates to the procedure itself or one of the other areas of required medical disclosure concerning the procedure, its substantial risks, and alternatives that must be disclosed to avoid a claim based on lack of informed consent. But the possibility of materiality is present. If defendant's true level of experience had the capacity to enhance substantially the risk of paralysis from undergoing a corpectomy, a jury could find that a reasonably prudent patient would not have consented to that procedure had the misrepresentation been revealed. That presumes that plaintiff can prove that the actual level of experience possessed by defendant had a direct and demonstrable relationship to the harm of paralysis, a substantial risk of the procedure that was disclosed to plaintiff. Put differently, plaintiff must prove that the additional undisclosed risk posed by defendant's true level of qualifications and experience increased plaintiff's risk of paralysis from the corpectomy procedure.

The standard for causation that we envision in such an action will impose a significant gatekeeper function on the trial court to prevent insubstantial claims concerning alleged misrepresentations about a physician's experience from proceeding to a jury. We contemplate that misrepresented or exaggerated physician experience would have to significantly increase a risk of a procedure in order for it to affect the judgment of a reasonably prudent patient in an informed consent case. As this case demonstrates, the proximate cause analysis will involve a two-step inquiry.

The first inquiry should be, assuming a misrepresentation about experience, whether the more limited experience or credentials possessed by defendant could have substantially increased plaintiff's risk of paralysis from undergoing the corpectomy procedure. We envision that expert testimony would be required for such a showing. The second inquiry would be whether that substantially increased risk would cause a reasonably prudent person not to consent to undergo the procedure. If the true extent of defendant's experience could not affect materially the risk of paralysis from a corpectomy procedure, then the alleged misrepresentation could not cause a reasonably prudent patient in plaintiff's position to decline consent to the procedure. The court's gatekeeper function in respect of the first question will require a determination that a genuine issue of material fact exists requiring resolution by the factfinder in order to proceed to the second question involving an assessment by the reasonably prudent patient. Further, the trial court must conclude that there is a genuine issue of material fact concerning both questions in order to allow the claim to proceed to trial.

Finally, to satisfy the damages element in a claim based on lack of informed consent, a plaintiff typically has to show a causal connection between the inadequately disclosed risk of the procedure and the injury sustained. . . . If that risk materialized and harmed plaintiff, damages for those injuries are awarded. . . . Here, if successful in his claim based on lack of informed consent, plaintiff may receive damages for injuries caused by an inadequately disclosed risk of the corpectomy procedure. However, as noted, to be successful plaintiff must prove that defendant's allegedly misrepresented qualifications and experience can satisfy the stringent test for proximate causation that is required for physician experience to be material to the substantial risk of the procedure that occurred (paralysis) and injured plaintiff. If he can, then plaintiff may be compensated for that injury caused by the corpectomy irrespective of whether defendant deviated from the standard of care in performing the surgical procedure.

In conclusion, plaintiff's medical malpractice action will address any negligence in defendant's performance of the corpectomy procedure. We hold that in addition plaintiff may attempt to prove that defendant's alleged misrepresentation about his credentials and experience presents a claim based on lack of informed consent to the surgical procedure, consistent with the requirements and limitations that we have imposed on such a claim. . . .

Notes: Fiduciary Principles and the Disclosure of Provider-Associated Risks

1. *Do Fiduciary Principles Add Anything?* Why couldn't the *Moore* court analyze the facts solely using traditional informed consent analysis? Read the opinion to determine (1) the theory underlying the imposition of fiduciary obligations; (2) the scope of the fiduciary duty; (3) the actions that might constitute a breach of the duty; (4) the injury requirements, if any; and (5) the remedies for a breach of fiduciary duty. Do fiduciary duties expand or merely parallel the duties already created under the material risk standard in informed consent cases? What should

Golde have done to avoid liability? Why doesn't the court impose disclosure duties on the other defendants?

2. *Causation Problems in* Moore. Who has the better of the causation and damages arguments between Justice Mosk and Justice Broussard? On remand, Moore's claim was settled before going to trial, so the court never had to resolve these issues. The *Howard* court directly confronts the knotty causation questions created by provider-associated risk disclosure claims. Will Mr. Howard be able to recover on his informed consent claim without expert proof that the surgeon violated the standard of care in the conduct of the surgery? Why or why not? See Starozytnyk v. Reich, 871 A.2d 733 (N.J. Super. 2005) (affirming dismissal of plaintiff's informed consent and fiduciary duty claims due to absence of proximate cause). Would the fiduciary character of the physician-patient relationship be better protected through the adoption of a new statutory claim that would focus on dignitary harm rather than the types of damages ordinarily recognized in malpractice or fiduciary claims? For a proposal see Caroline Forell & Anna Sortun, The Tort of Betrayal of Trust, 42 U. Mich. J.L. Reform 557 (2008-2009).

3. *Disclosure vs. Prohibition.* Provider-associated risks are distinguishable from risks associated with medical treatment because informed patients may be able to avoid a specific risk entirely through, e.g., seeking a second opinion, in the case of conflicts created by financial interests, or by seeking care elsewhere, in the case of other risks. Moreover, physicians might be the most knowledgeable source of information about some types of provider-associated risks and patients might have difficulty accessing this information unless physicians have an affirmative duty to disclose. However, individual patient decisions to avoid some types of risks might have a cumulative negative impact. As one example, physicians will not be able to train and to acquire experience with procedures if patients demand care only from experienced providers. Requiring disclosure of provider-associated risks and benefits can also infringe on the privacy interests of health providers.

The fiduciary conception of the physician-patient relationship suggests that physicians must set aside self-interest to serve their patients' interests. In other fiduciary contexts, some types of conflicts of interest can be addressed through disclosure and knowing acceptance by the vulnerable party. Other types of conflicts are simply prohibited. See infra, at page 241. Should provider-associated risks presumptively be dealt with through one mechanism or the other? What information would you want to have to answer this question? One of many possible areas of research might be to understand better the impact of disclosures on patients. Compare, Roy Spece et al., An Empirical Method for Materiality: Would Conflict of Interest Disclosures Change Patient Decisions?, 40 Amer. J.L. & Medicine 253 (2014) (experiment finds that disclosure of physician financial interests "significantly and substantially increased the probability that the mock patient would reject the conflicted physician's recommendations") with C. P. DiPaola et al., Surgeon-Industry Conflict of Interest: Survey of North Americans' Opinions Regarding Consulting with Industry, 14 Spine J. 584 (2014) (80% of survey respondents "felt it was ethical and either beneficial or of no influence to the quality of health care if surgeons were consultants for surgical device companies"); and Christine Grady et al., The Limits of Disclosure: What Research Subjects Want to Know About Investigator Financial Interests, 34 J.L. Med. & Ethics 592 (2006) (majority of respondents wanted to know about investigators' interest but "only a minority thought such financial information would influence their decisions about research participation in any way"). For recent commentaries on the role of fiduciary principles in medicine, see Maxwell J. Mehlman, Why Physicians are Fiduciaries for Their Patients, 12 Ind. Health L. Rev. 1 (2015). For a thoughtful examination of the problem of provider-associated risk, see Nadia N. Sawicki, Modernizing Informed Consent: Expanding the Boundaries of Materiality, 2016 U. Ill. L. Rev. 821.

Notes: Financial Conflicts of Interest

1. *Financial Conflicts of Interest.* Different types of financial and nonfinancial conflicts of interest permeate medical relationships, as they do most human affairs. (For example, the authors of this book receive modest royalties when their own students purchase it.) How assiduous should physicians be in avoiding or disclosing them? The AMA Code of Ethics provides that "The primary objective of the medical profession is to render service to humanity; reward of financial gain is a subordinate consideration. Under no circumstances may physicians place their own financial interests above the welfare of their patients." AMA Code of Ethics 11.2.2 (2016). This general standard is supplemented by specific statements relating to different types of potential conflicts. The Code provides, for example, that "physicians should . . . [d]isclose any financial and other factors that could affect the patient's care." Id. at 11.2.4. What types of financial arrangements can create a real or perceived conflict of interest? Financial conflicts have been addressed through a number of research studies, working groups, and symposia.

2. *Conflicts Arising from Financial Arrangements Favoring Additional Care.* The issue of conflicts of interest in medical research identified in *Moore* has continued to attract scrutiny and is discussed further infra at page 282. But aside from research studies, what does *Moore* mean for ordinary medical treatment settings? Does it establish a common-law duty for physicians to disclose to patients financial conflicts of interest that could reasonably affect routine treatment recommendations? No one supposes that doctors must disclose the distorting effects of fee-for-service reimbursement, which might result in harms from unnecessary treatment. Cf. Ambach v. French, 216 P.3d 405 (Wash. 2009) (rejecting Consumer Protection Act claim by patient against physician based in part on extra expense of shoulder surgery compared with alternative treatment). Should courts be more receptive to claims based on financial incentives created by additional commercial arrangements? Compare Wright v. Jeckle, 144 P.3d 301 (Wash. 2006) (rejecting claim that physician's direct sale of anti-obesity drug constituted a violation of fiduciary duty under state anti-kickback legislation merely because physician profited from sales) with Bigler-Engler v. Breg, Inc, 7 Cal. App. 5th 276 (2017) (breach of fiduciary duty claim arising from physician recommendation of device to be rented or purchased from his medical group; physician did not disclose his financial interest in the transaction, note that the device was available from other sources, or disclose known risks to the patient).

As *Moore* briefly indicates, statutory law sometimes requires disclosure of certain kinds of financial conflicts of interest. A prime example is when physicians receive payments from third parties related to treatment decisions or have investment or ownership interests in the facilities to which they refer their patients. State and federal laws prohibit or regulate these investment interests in many circumstances. Which approach strikes you as more appropriate: disclosure or prohibition/regulation?

Consider as well the many tactics that drug and medical device companies have used to encourage physicians to prescribe their products. Kickbacks and direct financial incentives are illegal; other types of arrangements have elicited increasing attention. The Affordable Care Act includes "sunshine" provisions that require drug, device, and medical supply companies to report their payments to physicians. 42 U.S.C.A. §1320a-7h. See the CMS Open Payments Web site, www.cms.gove/open-payments. The federal provisions preempt most state statutes or regulations requiring manufacturers to disclose payments but do not preempt disclosure obligations placed on physicians. Can pharmaceutical companies spur sales by redirecting funds toward marketing their wares directly to consumers, who will then pressure their physicians to prescribe the latest cures? See Thomas L. Hafemeister & Richard M. Gulbrandsen, The Fiduciary Obligation of Physicians to "Just Say No" if an "Informed" Patient Demands Services That Are Not Medically Indicated, 39 Seton Hall L. Rev. 335 (2009).

3. *Discussing the Costs of Care.* Curiously, there is virtually no legal or ethical guidance on whether physicians should tell patients how much treatment options cost. In the distant past, this may have been because physicians followed an ethic of treat first and bill later, letting patients pay what they were able. In the more recent past, this may be because insurance usually pays for the majority of costs. In the future, however, these cost-insulating features may soon recede, under the influence of "consumer-driven" health insurance plans that expose patients to much greater cost-sharing obligations. This will likely generate disputes by patients who feel they were not adequately informed about the costs of the treatments to which they agreed. Under the informed consent and fiduciary principles you have learned, should physicians have to volunteer information about costs, or only wait for patients to ask first? Does the answer differ for the costs of the physicians' own services vs. costs charged by other providers, goods, or services the physician may recommend (such as lab tests, drugs, or specialist referrals)?

4. *Conflicts Arising from Incentives to Deny Care.* Should there be a duty to disclose incentives related to managed care? Could you argue that incentives to reduce health care expenses in managed care are "common knowledge"? If there is a financial disclosure obligation on the part of physicians participating in managed care arrangements, how great should the financial incentive be before it is considered "material"? Should the plaintiff be required to prove that the incentive was sufficient to affect physician decisionmaking in individual cases? Or can we presume that managed care companies would not use financial incentives unless they worked, by affecting physician decisions at least to some extent? Managed care physicians might argue that incentives are designed only to reduce unnecessary medical care and are not large enough to induce physicians to refrain from making necessary medical referrals. Even if incentives potentially affect necessary care, isn't the threat of a malpractice claim enough to ensure that physicians will still make appropriate referrals, or a sufficient remedy when they fail to do so? Should any duty to disclose managed care incentives be satisfied by a global disclosure when the patient first enrolls (and perhaps once a year thereafter), or must the incentives be repeated each time the patient seeks treatment? For an argument that disclosure at enrollment satisfies the

fiduciary obligation, or perhaps acts as a waiver of subsequent disclosures, see Mark A. Hall, A Theory of Economic Informed Consent, 31 Ga. L. Rev. 511 (1997).

5. *Fiduciary Duties and Managed Care in the Courts. Moore* appeared to open the door to using informed consent and/or fiduciary theories to protect patients from the risks created by a provider's financial arrangements with third parties, such as managed care organizations. Subsequent courts have tried to push the door shut, at least on some types of claims. In Neade v. Portes, 739 N.E.2d 496 (Ill. 2000), for example, the Illinois Supreme Court rejected the use of fiduciary theories in a case involving managed care incentives. Mr. Neade was only 37 but had a number of significant risk factors for heart disease. Mr. Neade began to experience radiating chest pain and shortness of breath. Mr. Neade's primary physician, Dr. Portes, authorized Mr. Neade's hospitalization. While hospitalized, Mr. Neade underwent a battery of tests that appeared to rule out heart disease. Thereafter, Dr. Portes failed to refer Mr. Neade for more specific tests for heart disease, despite recurring symptoms. Mr. Neade had a heart attack and died. Mr. Neade's estate brought claims for breach of fiduciary duty and medical negligence against Dr. Portes and others. Dr. Portes participated in a risk-sharing agreement with the patient's HMO that arguably gave the physician an incentive to deny referrals to his patients.

Relying in part on some of the language found in the United States Supreme Court's opinion in Pegram v. Herdrich, 530 U.S. 211 (2000) (exploring fiduciary duty under federal ERISA statute), the Illinois Supreme Court rejected the breach of fiduciary duty claim. The Illinois Supreme Court held that a cause of action for breach of fiduciary duty based on a physician's failure to reveal a financial interest in a medical incentive fund essentially duplicated the underlying medical negligence claim:

> [I]t is operative facts together with the injury that we look to in order to determine whether a cause of action is duplicative. In the case at bar, the operative fact in both [the malpractice and fiduciary duty] counts is Dr. Portes' failure to order an angiogram for Mr. Neade. Plaintiff alleges in both counts that Mr. Neade's failure to receive an angiogram is the ultimate reason for his subsequent death. Plaintiff also alleges the same injury in both her medical negligence claim and her breach of fiduciary duty claim, namely, Mr. Neade's death and its effect on plaintiff and her family. We determine that plaintiff's breach of fiduciary duty claim is a representment of her medical negligence claim.
>
> An examination of the elements of a medical negligence claim and breach of fiduciary duty claim illustrates the way in which a breach of fiduciary duty claim would "boil down to a malpractice claim." *Herdrich*, 530 U.S. at —, 120 S. Ct. at 2157. To sustain an action for medical negligence, plaintiff must show: (1) the standard of care in the medical community by which the physician's treatment was measured; (2) that the physician deviated from the standard of care; and (3) that a resulting injury was proximately caused by the deviation from the standard of care. . . . Thus, the standard of care is the relevant inquiry by which we judge a physician's actions in a medical negligence case. . . .
>
> In contrast to an action for medical negligence, in order to state a claim for breach of fiduciary duty, it must be alleged that a fiduciary duty exists, that the fiduciary duty was breached, and that such breach proximately caused the injury of which the plaintiff complains. . . .
>
> In order to sustain a breach of fiduciary duty claim against Dr. Portes, plaintiff would have to allege, inter alia, that: (1) had she known of the Medical Incentive

Fund she would have sought an opinion from another physician; (2) that the other physician would have ordered an angiogram for Mr. Neade; (3) that the angiogram would have detected Mr. Neade's heart condition; and (4) that treatment could have prevented his eventual myocardial infarction and subsequent death. In order to prove the second element, plaintiff would have been required to present expert testimony that the expert, after examining Mr. Neade and considering his history, would have ordered an angiogram. This requirement relates to the standard of care consideration—the first prong in a traditional medical negligence claim—under which a physician is held to "the reasonable skill which a physician in good standing in the community would use." That is precisely what plaintiff must prove to support her breach of fiduciary duty claim. As the Supreme Court stated in *Herdrich*, the breach of fiduciary duty claim "would boil down to a malpractice claim, and the fiduciary standard would be nothing but the malpractice standard traditionally applied in actions against physicians." *Herdrich*, 530 U.S. at —, 120 S. Ct. at 2157. Thus, we need not recognize a new cause of action for breach of fiduciary duty when a traditional medical negligence claim sufficiently addresses the same alleged misconduct. The breach of fiduciary duty claim in the case at bar would be duplicative of the medical negligence claim.

Our decision to refrain from permitting the creation of this new cause of action finds additional support in statutory law. The Illinois legislature has placed the burden of disclosing HMO incentive schemes on HMOs themselves. . . .

Moreover, the outcome that would result if we were to allow the creation of a new cause of action for breach of fiduciary duty against a physician in these circumstances may be impractical. For example, physicians often provide services for numerous patients, many of whom may be covered by different HMOs. In order to effectively disclose HMO incentives, physicians would have to remain cognizant at all times of every patient's particular HMO and that HMO's policies and procedures. See, e.g., Mark Hall, A Theory of Economic Informed Consent, 31 Ga. L. Rev. 511, 525-26 (1997). . . . If we were to recognize a breach of fiduciary duty claim in the context of the case at bar, we fear the effects of such a holding may be unworkable.

Neade v. Portes, 739 N.E.2d. at 502-506. The court also held that evidence of the physician's financial incentives could be relevant on issues relating to interest and bias, in the event that physician testified in the medical negligence trial. Id. at 506.

Chief Justice Harrison dissented:

A complaint against a lawyer for professional malpractice may be couched in either contract or tort. . . . The same rule should apply here. Although this case involves medical rather than legal malpractice, that distinction is insignificant. . . . The right to assert claims for breach of fiduciary duty and negligence in the same professional malpractice action is not unfettered. When the same operative facts support a negligence count and a count for breach of fiduciary duty based on the same injury to the client, the counts are identical and the fiduciary duty count should be dismissed as duplicative. . . . In this case, however, the negligence and breach of fiduciary duty counts asserted by plaintiff are not identical. . . . As the appellate court correctly recognized,

> [i]t is conceivable that a trier of fact could find both that Dr. Portes was within the standard of care and therefore not negligent in relying on the thallium stress test and the EKG in deciding that an angiogram was not necessary and also that Dr. Portes did breach his fiduciary duty in not disclosing his financial

> incentive arrangement and, as a proximate result thereof, Neade did not
> obtain a second opinion, suffered a massive coronary infarction, and died.

Id. at 506.

6. *Institutional Disclosure Obligations Under Fiduciary Law.* Under common-law principles, as *Moore* holds, institutions are generally free from the disclosure duties imposed on physicians. A federal statute, the Employee Retirement Income Security Act of 1974 (ERISA), regulates health plans provided as a benefit of employment. This statute has a number of important implications for the organization and delivery of health care in the United States that are considered in more detail in Chapter 4.G.2. For present purposes, it is enough to note that the Supreme Court's decision in *Pegram* left the door open to efforts to use ERISA's fiduciary principles as a tool for imposing disclosure obligations on managed care employee benefit plans.

7. *Further Reading.* On **financial conflicts of interest generally**, see Maxwell J. Mehlman, Can Law Save Medicine?, 36 J. Legal Med. 121 (2015); Lisa Rosenbaum, Three Part Conflict of Interest Series, 372 New Eng. J. Med. 1860-1864, 1959-1963, 2064-2068 (2015); Special Issue, Conflicts of Interest, 317 JAMA 1705-1797 (2017); Symposium, Conflicts of Interest in the Practice of Medicine, 40 J.L. Med. & Ethics 436-522 (2012). For a popular account by a former long-time reporter for the New York Times, see Elisabeth Rosenthal, An American Sickness: How Healthcare Became Big Business and How You Can Take It Back (2017).

For more about **drug company marketing to physicians** (note 2), see Christopher Robertson, Susannah Rose & Aaron S. Kesselheim, Effect of Financial Relationships on the Behaviors of Health Care Professionals: A Review of the Evidence, 40 J.L. Med. & Ethics 452 (2012); Thomas L. Hafemeister & Sarah P. Bryan, Beware Those Bearing Gifts: Physicians' Fiduciary Duty to Avoid Pharmaceutical Marketing, 57 U. Kan. L. Rev. 491 (2009).

On the ACA's **"sunshine" provisions** (note 2), see Shantanu Agrawal & Douglas Brown, The Physician Payments Sunshine Act—Two Years of the Open Payments Program, 374 New Eng. J. Med. 906 (2016); Charles Ornstein, Public Disclosure of Payments to Physicians from Industry, 317 JAMA 1749 (2017).

Considering whether physicians should discuss **the costs of treatment** (note 3), see Barak D. Richman, Mark A. Hall & Kevin A. Schulman, Overbilling and Informed Financial Consent—A Contractual Solution, 367 New Eng. J. Med. 396 (2012) (noting possible relevance of fiduciary principles); and Nadia N. Sawicki, Modernizing Informed Consent: Expanding the Boundaries of Materiality, 2016 U. Ill. L. Rev. 821, 849-850; Mark A. Hall & Carl E. Schneider, Professional Obligations When Patients Pay Out of Pocket, 58 J. Fam. Prac. E1 (2009).

Regarding **incentives to withhold care** (note 4), see Isaac D. Buck, Furthering the Fiduciary Metaphor: The Duty of Providers to the Payers of Medicare, 104 Cal. L. Rev. 1043 (2016) (arguing that the fiduciary concept should be expanded to include a physician duty of loyalty to Medicare as a payer); Jessica Mantel, A Defense of Physicians' Gatekeeping Role: Balancing Patients' Needs with Society's Interests, 42 Pepp. L. Rev. 633 (2015) (arguing that physicians as gatekeepers have dual duties to patients and society); and Maxwell J. Mehlman, Why Physicians are Fiduciaries for Their Patients, 12 Ind. Health L. Rev. 1 (2015) (critiquing

Neade and contending that physicians' fiduciary duties should be recognized and strengthened).

Notes: Nonfinancial Provider-Associated Risks

1. *Nonfinancial Provider-Associated Risks.* Should physicians have a duty to disclose risks to patients that arise from the identity and characteristics of the provider rather than the type of procedure? In some ways, this topic is the natural corollary of advances in precision medicine, supra at page 223. The development of "big data" means that it is now possible to track experience levels, success rates, and other aspects of physician performance. See, e.g., Nikhil R. Sahni et al., Surgeon Specialization and Operative Mortality in the United States: Retrospective Analysis, 354 BMJ i3571 (2016) ("for six of the eight procedures examined . . . ., we found surgeon specialization to be an important predictor of mortality"). *Howard* is part of a small new line of cases considering whether physicians have any duty to disclose provider risks, as distinguished from procedural risks.

2. *Experience and Success Rates.* Consumers of health care services can now access a wide range of data about the quality of care and health care outcomes produced by health care institutions. As discussed at page 320, health care organizations and purchasers are developing and collecting information about health care outcomes for individual practitioners. Should health care providers have a duty to disclose their own "scorecards" to patients? How does the *Howard* court distinguish between informed consent and misrepresentation claims in this area? Courts generally have considered cases involving misrepresentation of experience under informed consent rather than misrepresentation law. See, e.g., Roderer v. Dash, 233 P.3d 1101 (Alaska 2010); Ray v. Kapiolani Medical Specialists, 259 P.3d 569 (Haw. 2011); Kelly v. Vinzant, 197 P.3d 803 (Kan. 2008); Willis v. Bender, 596 F.3d 1244 (10th Cir. 2010). At least one court has rejected an intentional misrepresentation claim in which the plaintiff did not present expert testimony establishing that his injuries were caused by inexperience. Wooding v. U.S., 2010 WL 781303 (3d Cir. 2010).

For other cases involving physician experience, see Duffy v. Flagg, 905 A.2d 15 (Conn. 2006) (informed consent does not require physician to give detailed account of her past experience with a procedure when answers would not have been relevant to key informed consent issues); DeGennaro v. Tandon, 873 A.2d 191 (Conn. App. 2005) (reasonable patient would consider lack of experience in using equipment, and lack of assistance, to be material information about provider-specific risk); Goldberg v. Boone, 912 A.2d 698 (Md. 2006) (jury should determine whether physician experience is material); Wlosinski v. Cohn, 713 N.W.2d 16 (Mich. App. 2005) ("raw success rates" need not be disclosed; interesting concurring and dissenting opinions); Duttry v. Patterson, 771 A.2d 1255 (Pa. 2001) (physician's personal characteristics and experience irrelevant in informed consent claim; misrepresentation claim possible); Johnson v. Kokemoor, 545 N.W.2d 495 (Wis. 1996) (applying informed consent principles to a case involving a physician's relative lack of experience).

3. *Ghost Surgery and Concurrent Surgery.* The *Howard* court, at page 236, notes that a cause of action for battery may be appropriate to address the issue of "ghost

surgery," where a patient consents to surgery with one surgeon but another actually performs the procedure. The battery claim can often be defeated by demonstrating that the patient signed consent forms that establish that a procedure may be performed by the surgeon or by others. Assuming that a patient has agreed to the possibility that others might be involved in the surgery, would the informed consent doctrine nonetheless require that the original surgeon provide additional information about the likelihood that others will be involved in the surgery, their experience level, and the degree of supervision that will be provided by the original surgeon? See Hurley v. Kirk, 398 P.3d 7 (2017) (physician has "duty to inform the patient 'who' will be performing significant portions of the procedure or surgical tasks"). These questions were brought into focus by the Boston Globe's "Spotlight" team, which released an investigative report on the use of concurrent surgeries at the well-regarded Massachusetts General Hospital. Jenn Abelson et al., Clash in the Name of Care, Boston Globe (2015) (describing controversies arising from scheduling concurrent surgeries, during which a surgeon may move back and forth between two surgical procedures, without disclosure to patients).

4. *Conscience Rights and Disclosure Duties.* Physicians may have personal beliefs and values that affect their views about the delivery of some forms of health care. The "conscience rights" of health care providers are often protected through legislation that allows physicians and others to refrain from participating in care and, in some circumstances, from providing information about types of care, that conflicts with their beliefs. But see Ronit Y. Stahl & Ezekiel J. Emanuel, Physicians, Not Conscripts — Conscientious Objection in Health Care, 376 New Eng. J. Med. 1380 (2017) (arguing that recognition of conscience rights should be limited). Do physicians have an obligation to disclose their beliefs and the possible impact of those beliefs on their treatment recommendations? Would such a requirement be too great an intrusion into the privacy interests of physicians? Could a physician's discussion of moral or religious principles create a different form of harm for patients concerned about the disapproval of their physicians?

5. *Abuse of Drugs or Alcohol.* Would the reasonable patient consider a physician's cocaine addiction to be a material fact in deciding whether or not to undergo surgery? Would the professional standard of care require such a disclosure? Compare Rice v. Brakel, 310 P.3d 16 (Ariz. Ct. App. 2013) (surgeon's failure to disclose prescription drug dependency not actionable under informed consent; plaintiff failed to prove that he would have declined treatment or that defendant's acts caused his injury); and Albany Urology Clinic, P.C. v. Cleveland, 528 S.E.2d 777 (Ga. 2000) (no duty to disclose drug use under common law or state informed consent statute), with Hidding v. Williams, 578 So. 2d 1192 (La. Ct. App. 1991) (physician has duty to reveal his alcoholism; concurring opinion raises interesting causation problem).

6. *Infection with HIV.* In the early years of the HIV epidemic, there was a vigorous debate about whether a physician had or should have a duty to disclose his or her HIV status. See, e.g., Mary Anne Bobinski, Autonomy and Privacy: Protecting Patients from Their Physicians, 55 U. Pitt. L. Rev. 291 (1994). The application of the informed consent doctrine to the problem of HIV disclosure in health care was complicated by the fact that many patients were more fearful about the very low risk of HIV transmission from health care worker to patient than they were about other, larger risks. In addition, persons with HIV infection are protected from discrimination under a variety of statutes, including the Americans with Disabilities

Act, unless they pose a "significant risk" to the health or safety of others. 42 U.S.C. §§12111-12113. From the perspective of the infected physician, disclosure ought not be required unless there is a significant risk of transmission. From the perspective of the patient, even a "less than significant" risk could be avoided by selecting an (apparently) uninfected health care provider. One court resolved the conflict in favor of the patient's right to know:

> [Dr. Behringer, a surgeon] argues: (1) the risk of transmission of HIV from surgeon to patient is too remote to require informed consent, and (2) the law of informed consent does not require disclosure of the condition of the surgeon. . . . [Dr. Behringer] argues that the use of the informed consent form is tantamount to a de facto termination of surgical privileges. [Dr. Behringer] further urges that patient reaction is likely to be based more on public hysteria than on a studied assessment of the actual risk involved.
>
> The answer to these arguments is two-fold. First, it is the duty of the surgeon utilizing the informed consent procedure to explain to the patient the real risk involved. If the patient's fear is without basis, it is likewise the duty of the surgeon to allay that fear. . . .
>
> [Dr. Behringer] further argues that there is no requirement under the doctrine of informed consent that a surgeon's physical condition be revealed as a risk of the surgery itself. The informed consent cases are not so narrow as to support that argument. In [a prior New Jersey Supreme Court case] . . . the court spoke of not only an evaluation of the nature of the treatment, but of "any attendant substantial risks." . . .
>
> [Dr. Behringer] urges that these issues should be dealt with on a case-by-case basis, wherein the hospital or medical staff monitors an HIV-positive surgeon and makes a determination as to the surgeon's ability to perform a particular invasive procedure. . . . The position [Dr. Behringer] seeks to implement is replete with the "anachronistic paternalism" rejected in both Canterbury v. Spence, supra, and by the [New Jersey] Supreme Court. . . .
>
> The obligation of a surgeon performing invasive procedures, such as [Dr. Behringer], to reveal his AIDS condition, is one which requires a weighing of [Dr. Behringer's] rights against the patient's rights. New Jersey's strong policy supporting patient rights, weighed against [Dr. Behringer's] individual right to perform an invasive procedure as a part of the practice of his profession, requires the conclusion that the patient's rights must prevail. At a minimum, the physician must withdraw from performing any invasive procedure which would pose a risk to the patient. Where the ultimate harm is death, even the presence of a low risk of transmission justifies the adoption of a policy which precludes invasive procedures when there is "any" risk of transmission. In the present case, the debate raged as to whether there was "any" risk of transmission, and the informed-consent procedure was left in place. If there is to be an ultimate arbiter of whether the patient is to be treated invasively by an AIDS-positive surgeon, the arbiter will be the fully-informed patient. The ultimate risk to the patient is so absolute—so devastating—that it is untenable to argue against informed consent combined with a restriction on procedures which present "any risk" to the patient.

Estate of Behringer v. Medical Center at Princeton, 592 A.2d 1251, 1279-1283 (N.J. Super. Ct. Div. 1991). The federal Centers for Disease Control issued recommendations in 1991 that advised HIV-infected health care workers seeking to engage in "exposure-prone" procedures to (a) secure advice from an expert review panel; and (b) inform patients of their HIV status. Lawrence O. Gostin, Rights and Duties of

HIV-Infected Health Care Professionals, 10 Health Care Anal. 67 (2002) (recommending revision of national policy). The CDC has since "retired" its guidance on HIV HCWs, and current anti-retroviral therapies can reduce a patient's viral load and ability to transmit HIV to others. How would courts resolve a case involving the disclosure duties of an HIV-infected surgeon today?

7. *Further Reading.* For commentaries on **disclosing experience and success rates** (note 2), see Aaron D. Twerski, The Second Revolution in Informed Consent: Comparing Physicians to Each Other, 94 Nw. U. L. Rev. 1 (1999); Aaron D. Twerski & Neil B. Cohen, Comparing Medical Providers: A First Look at the New Era of Medical Statistics, 58 Brook. L. Rev. 5 (1992); Nadia N. Sawicki, Modernizing Informed Consent: Expanding the Boundaries of Materiality, 2016 U. Ill. L. Rev. 821; Robert Weinstein et al., Infection-Control Report Cards—Ensuring Patient Safety, 353 New Eng. J. Med. 225 (2005); J. Wilks et al., Surgeon with Worst Performance Figures Might Be the Best Option, 323 Brit. Med. J. 1071 (2001).

On **ghost and concurrent surgery** (note 3), see American College of Surgeons, Statements on Principles, www.facs.org/about-acs/statements (2016) (discussing intraoperative responsibility of primary surgeon); and Michelle M. Mello & Edward H. Livingston, Managing the Risks of Concurrent Surgeries, 315 JAMA 1563 (2016).

For a detailed consideration of the issues relating to **disclosing physicians' personal beliefs** (note 4), see Nadia Sawicki, Mandating Disclosure of Conscience-Based Limitations on Medical Practice, 42 Amer. J.L. & Med. 85 (2016).

Problem: *Moore* Liability?

What types of disclosures would be required in the following situations, under either a physician-centered or patient-centered approach? Would the result differ under fiduciary theories?

1. A physician recommending a surgical procedure necessary to save the patient's life will earn about $15,000 from the surgery and follow-up care. What if the surgery is for cosmetic purposes?
2. A physician recommends that a patient see a specialist for her condition. The physician is married to the specialist.
3. A physician providing care for an HMO patient with back pain suggests that the patient take a conservative approach to treatment, delaying expensive diagnostic tests and surgery for as long as possible. The physician's financial arrangements with the HMO include provisions that decrease the physician's income if the physician spends more than an allocated amount on diagnostic tests or hospitalization.
4. A physician describes herself as a social drinker. She only drinks during the evenings and on weekends. On average, she consumes about 21 mixed drinks per week.
5. A surgeon fails to maintain medical malpractice liability coverage despite the fact that coverage is mandatory in the jurisdiction. See Jarrell v. Kaul, 123 A.3d 1022 (N.J. 2015).
6. A physician fails to inform a patient suffering from pancreatic cancer of the patient's low statistical life expectancy. The patient does not make the proper financial arrangements, causing substantial real estate and tax losses. See Arato v. Avedon, 858 P.2d 598 (Cal. 1993).

7. A physician discovers a medical error in a patient's care. Should it matter whether the physician caused the error or whether it occurred under someone else's care? See Chapter 4.A.

D. HUMAN EXPERIMENTATION AND RESEARCH

The *Moore* litigation arose because of the alleged conflicts of interest created by the research interests of the defendants. Media sources and pharmaceutical company advertisements regularly highlight the results of medical research, touting the next great cures for long-feared diseases (as well as informing us about cures for diseases that we never knew existed). Medical research is conducted in a range of public and private settings, funded by public and private sources, and regulated either by different federal regulatory entities or by much more diffuse common-law rules. Funding for medical research totaled $116.5 billion in the United States in 2012. Medical device, biotechnology, and pharmaceutical firms contributed $67.9 billion, or about 58% of the total. The National Institutes of Health contributed $30.9 billion, or 27%. Foundations and charities, state and local government, and non-NIH federal funders contributed $17.6 billion, or 15%. Hamilton Moses et al., The Anatomy of Medical Research: US and International Comparisons, 313 JAMA 174 (2015). The United States is the global leader in spending on medical research, but its share of the world's public and private spending total decreased from 57% in 2004 to 44% in 2012. Id. See also, Justin Chakma et al., Asia's Ascent—Global Trends in Biomedical R & D Expenditures, 370 New Eng. J. Med. 3 (2014).

Medical research involving human experimentation typically takes place in clinical trials, defined as "research stud[ies] in which human volunteers are assigned to interventions (for example, a medical product, behavior, or procedure) based on a protocol (or plan) and then evaluated for effects on biomedical or health outcomes." NIH, ClinicalTrials.gov Background. Data on clinical research has become much more available due to changes in legal requirements, conditions imposed by funders, and new ethical standards that either require or encourage the registration of clinical research trials and in some cases also require the posting of results. The ClinicalTrials.gov database listed 254,668 studies being carried out in 201 countries as of September 2017, with 105,033 studies located in the United States. Millions of people in the United States take part in medical research every year. See "Tom Abate, Experiments on Humans: Business of Clinical Trials Soars, but Risk Unknown, S.F. Chron., Aug. 4, 2002, at A1 (citing "an estimated 20 million Americans tak[ing] part in more than 41,000 clinical trials and uncounted more federally funded experiments").

There are two central concerns in the research context. The first is that experimental treatment is often not done for the patient's immediate benefit. Some patients may approach medical research thinking they will receive better care because it is "state of the art," but this is usually a false impression. Instead, the treatment that is being studied may be riskier; almost certainly its risks are less well known than standard treatment. Also, in randomized controlled trials (RCTs), patients are often "randomized" "blindly" between an "experimental arm" and a "control arm." This means that, by luck of the draw, a significant percentage will receive ordinary treatment or even, in some cases, a placebo; participants generally will not know which type of care they will receive. See generally, Laura E. Bothwell et al., Assessing the Gold Standard—Lessons from the History of RCTs, 374 New Eng. J. Med. 2175 (2016). Moreover, the innovation in treatment may have nothing at all to offer their condition, but may be intended solely to provide an improvement for other patients. The relevant distinction is between "therapeutic" and "nontherapeutic research." Only in the former is there something that a patient might benefit from immediately, but even then, patients are often asked to undergo risks that are greater than the potential rewards in order to further the aims of science.

Fully informed patients may be more than willing to accept these arrangements out of a sense of altruism and a desire to be a part of progress. But there is a second difficulty: How well informed are they, and how freely do they make their decision? Some patients may feel pressured in subtle ways without the knowledge of their physicians. Imagine a physician who eagerly pitches her pet research project, and a patient who fears (irrationally or not?) that disappointing his doctor will jeopardize his treatment. For other patients, coercion could be more overt. The reluctance of well-informed patients to participate in risky experiments might lead researchers either to conceal the experiment or to use patients from vulnerable or socially disadvantaged groups. Cf. Lee Black et al., Physician Recruitment of Patients to Non-Therapeutic Oncology Trials: Ethics Revisited, 4 Frontiers in Pharmacol. 1 (2013).

These concerns are not merely speculative. The history of medical research reveals both astounding advances and disquieting practices. Scientists have sought to expand our knowledge of human biology, illness, and treatment, often at the expense of the least fortunate in society: slaves, the poor, criminals, and other institutionalized persons. Several twentieth-century examples have left a legacy of fear and mistrust. Nazi scientists conducted a vigorous program of medical research on prisoners and internees during World War II. Their appalling lack of respect for human life and humane principles resulted in the Nuremberg Code. The Code's central tenet is a requirement that human research subjects give consent to participation in any research project. See Jonathan D. Moreno, Ulf Schmidt & Steve Joffe, The Nuremberg Code 70 Years Later, 318 JAMA 795 (2017).

Violations of human rights by researchers are not limited, however, to some distant time and far-off place. Two examples of research abuses in the United States have had a profound impact. In the Tuskegee Study, which ran from the 1950s until the early 1970s, researchers studied the effects of untreated syphilis in a group of African-American men. The researchers purported to treat the men for their ailments but never disclosed to their subjects that they continued to suffer from a highly treatable, yet debilitating illness. The researchers' apparently cavalier disregard for their subjects has resulted in a legacy of distrust among minority and poor communities.

In the mid-1990s, the federal government revealed that hundreds of persons had been involuntarily, and in some cases unknowingly, subjected to research in which they were exposed to radiation and harmful substances. President Clinton was forced to announce the adoption of newly strengthened protections for human subjects participating in classified research projects. Strengthened Protections for Human Subjects of Classified Research, 62 Fed. Reg. 26,367 (1997). See generally U.S. Advisory Comm. on Human Radiation Experiments, Final Report of the Advisory Committee on Human Radiation Experiments (Ruth Faden ed., 1996).

More recently, public attention has been drawn to the case of Henrietta Lacks, an African-American woman who died of cancer in 1951. Cell samples extracted from Ms. Lacks for research without her knowledge or consent were used to create the HeLa cell line, which became widely used in biomedical research, including commercial activities. Ms. Lack's family finally became aware of the cell line in the 1970s. Rebecca Skloot, The Immortal Life of Henrietta Lacks (2011). Additional controversy arose in 2013, when researchers published information about the genome of HeLa cells, which raised privacy concerns for Ms. Lacks' living relatives. Kathy L. Hudson & Francis S. Collins, Family Matters, 500 Nature 141 (2013).

A special set of rules governs the disclosure and consent process in medical research. For more than a quarter of a century, medical research has been governed by federal regulations that required an elaborate consent process in order for research to receive federal funding. U.S. Dep't Health & Human Servs. (DHHS), Protection of Human Subjects, 45 C.F.R. Part 46, subparts A through E. Subpart A, originally adopted in 1991, is known as the "Common Rule" because more than a dozen federal agencies and departments agreed to incorporate its provisions into their own regulations or otherwise had agreed to be bound by the same rules. 45 C.F.R. §46.101-.124. Parts B through D of the DHHS regulations provide special protections for specific groups: pregnant women, neonates, and fetuses (subpart B, 45 C.F.R. §46.201-.207), prisoners (subpart C, §46.301-.306), and children (subpart D, §46.401-.409); not all agencies and departments have adopted these provisions. Part E governs the registration of the institutional review boards (IRBs) that are responsible for certain aspects of protecting human research subjects, including particularly the adequacy of the informed consent process. Importantly, the FDA has maintained separate provisions governing the informed consent process. U.S. Food & Drug Admin., 21 C.F.R. §§50.1-.56 (protection of human subjects); 54.1-.6 (financial disclosure by clinical investigators); and 56.101-.124 (IRBs).

Under this long-standing framework, entities that accept federally funded research projects have assured that they would protect human subjects in research projects. 45 C.F.R. §46.103(b). In part due to additional requirements imposed by some federal agencies, entities typically have applied these protections to non-federally-funded research involving human subjects as well. Private foundations usually have similar requirements for funded research projects. The end result has been that the federal regulations effectively have governed most planned medical research in the United States. These federal rules, while influential, do not preempt state laws providing greater protection of human subjects. The federal government announced a process for revising the Common Rule in 2011, and the final regulations were released in early 2017, with most provisions effective as of January of 2018.

■WHY INFORMED CONSENT? HUMAN EXPERIMENTATION AND THE ETHICS OF AUTONOMY
Richard W. Garnett*
36 Cath. Law. 455 (1996)

. . . Why does consent have such moral power? Accept for now that our deference to consent is—perhaps mistakenly—rooted in a commitment to human

---

* Law professor at Notre Dame Law School.

dignity, expressed through respect for autonomy. Is consent's justifying role necessarily required by this commitment to human dignity? Why have we come to think that it is? Does our dignity as persons follow from, or does it instead create and condition, our autonomy? Do we respect consent because one feature of our dignity is that we always know what is best for us? Clearly we do not. . . .

III. REGULATING HUMAN EXPERIMENTATION THROUGH CONSENT

A. THE NUREMBERG CODE AND "INFORMED CONSENT"

The Nuremberg Code and the memory of the Nazi doctors' trial animate and permeate modern thinking about regulation of human experimentation. The Code was our most morally rigorous attempt to limit human experimentation. Its most memorable command was that, in medical research, "[t]he voluntary consent of the human subject is absolutely essential."[70] But while the Code has come to stand for "informed consent," it required more. It focused as much on the experiment itself, on the welfare of the subject, and on the conduct of the researcher as it did on the need for the subject's consent. Sadly, this broad focus has received relatively short shrift, and the consent principle has eclipsed the others.

The Code stands tall in memory but its influence has never lived up to its aims. Seen by many as a product of and reaction to Nazi terror, the Code is often dismissed as a context-bound relic, no longer useful for today's researchers. Pragmatists argue that the Code is simply too demanding, that its standards are too high for necessary research to meet, and that its absolutism cannot compete with the utilitarian and impersonal ethics of modern medicine. . . .

B. REGULATING EXPERIMENTATION AFTER NUREMBERG: THE STANDARD MODEL OF INFORMED CONSENT

. . . Today, human experimentation is regulated by a crazy-quilt of hortatory codes and maxims, scattered federal laws and regulations, and most importantly, by Institutional Review Boards,[85] which provide peer review of proposed experiments. "Informed consent" is still the touchstone, but modern regulations and procedures tolerate and expect deviations from this ideal. Thus, when addressing human experimentation—and they rarely do—courts occasionally mention the [Nuremberg] Code, but generally apply and enforce the more flexible informed consent requirements of later regulations.

The legal doctrine of informed consent as it has developed is quite different from the dignity-based commitment to self-determination animating the Nuremberg Code. The most important feature of today's regulatory regime is that it focuses

---

70. The Nazi Doctors and the Nuremberg Code: Human Rights in Human Experimentation 2 (George J. Annas & Michael A. Grodin eds., 1992).

85. For a complete review of the structure and function of Institutional Review Boards, see, e.g., 45 C.F.R. §§46.107-111 (1994); 21 C.F.R. §§56.101-114 (1994). "IRB approval means the determination of the IRB that the research has been reviewed and may be conducted at an institution within the constraints set forth by the IRB and by other institutional and federal requirements." 45 C.F.R. §46.102(h).

on the subject's state of mind more than on the experiment itself. What is referred to here as the "Standard Model" of informed consent is this subjectively oriented informed consent in the context of peer review. In practice, research peers have proven insufficiently critical when evaluating proposed experiments. In addition, the informed consent "requirement" is viewed as a chore and a ritual, an impersonal incantation, a hurried signing of papers. We know this is true, yet we cherish the myth of informed consent, skating over its lack of real content or impact. But because the Standard Model is a subterfuge aimed more at easing our consciences than at protecting research subjects, it fails both as a necessary condition for proposed experiments and as a justification for them.

IV. THE STANDARD MODEL IN ACTION: INFORMED CONSENT IN HARD CASES

. . . The Standard Model regulates experiments by requiring the subjects' informed consent. Comparatively little attention is given to the nature of the experiment itself—apart from its riskiness—or to the researcher's goals and intentions. Under the Standard Model, concern may be triggered by some characteristic of the subject (age, health, mental capabilities) or by the experiment's location (prison, hospital, university). These characteristics and locations, however, relate less to whether the researcher's plan is itself ethical, than whether the subject's consent was really given, or was truly informed. When experiments are prohibited, it is due to the quality, or lack thereof, of the consent given, not the propriety of the experiment itself. In these situations, whatever it is that gives the subject's consent its justificatory power—the mysterious indicia of autonomy worth respecting—is deemed lacking. To illustrate this dynamic at work, I review below the operation of the Standard Model in three paradigmatically hard cases.

A. PRISONERS

Prisoners have long been conveniently immobile, docile, and hence ideal subjects for research and experimentation. . . . Accordingly, experimentation on prisoners is carefully scrutinized under the Standard Model. The Department of Health and Human Services warns that "prisoners may be under constraints because of their incarceration which could affect their ability to make a truly voluntary and uncoerced decision whether or not to participate as subjects in research." . . .

B. THE TERMINALLY ILL

. . . As with prisoners, experimentation with terminally or grieviously ill patients distorts the Standard Model. Like children or the mentally handicapped, dying persons are often thought of as incapable of making informed decisions; and like prisoners, they are viewed as not "really" free, but instead, captive to the course of their disease and therefore under duress. Even when these patients are lucid, we fear their assessment of an experiment's benefits and risks may be skewed; we worry they might submit to quackery in a hopeless and desperate attempt to beat the inevitable. We also worry that the dying may, having abandoned all hope, submit to immoral experiments out of misplaced or entirely genuine altruism. Finally, we fear that we may be tempted to exploit these subjects' despair, incapacity, or altruism, and to railroad through experiments which might not otherwise pass ethical muster. . . .

C. CHILDREN

The use of children poses even thornier problems for research. We need to experiment on children; their problems and illnesses are often sui generis and can only be solved through experiments on them. However, the Standard Model assumes children cannot give adequate consent, and so it gives in to necessity, though the Nuremberg Code insisted that the subject's consent was essential. Because children cannot, by definition, give consent, we settle for less. In addition, because children are a necessary and unique research class, we are forced to face the steely utilitarian calculus that hides beneath the Standard Model's veneer of respect for persons.

The Standard Model requires someone's consent, and parents are the most obvious candidates. However, even parents might not be able to isolate and protect an individual child's safety and dignity, especially when another child is thrown into the equation. The same considerations that call into question whether a prisoner's consent was voluntary or informed might undermine a desperate parent's consent as well. . . .

■GRIMES v. KENNEDY KRIEGER INSTITUTE, INC.
782 A.2d 807 (Md. 2001)

Opinion by CATHELL, J.

PROLOGUE

We initially note that these are cases of first impression for this Court. For that matter, precious few courts in the United States have addressed the issues presented in the cases at bar. . . .

In these present cases, a prestigious research institute, associated with Johns Hopkins University, based on this record, created a nontherapeutic research program whereby it required certain classes of homes to have only partial lead paint abatement modifications performed, and in at least some instances, including at least one of the cases at bar, arranged for the landlords to receive public funding by way of grants or loans to aid in the modifications. The research institute then encouraged, and in at least one of the cases at bar, required, the landlords to rent the premises to families with young children. In the event young children already resided in one of the study houses, it was contemplated that a child would remain in the premises, and the child was encouraged to remain, in order for his or her blood to be periodically analyzed. In other words, the continuing presence of the children that were the subjects of the study was required in order for the study to be complete. Apparently, the children and their parents involved in the[se] cases . . . were from a lower economic strata and were, at least in one case, minorities.

The purpose of the research was to determine how effective varying degrees of lead paint abatement procedures were. Success was to be determined by periodically, over a two-year period of time, measuring the extent to which lead dust remained in, or returned to, the premises after the varying levels of abatement modifications, and, as most important to our decision, by measuring the extent to which the theretofore healthy children's blood became contaminated with lead, and comparing that contamination with levels of lead dust in the houses over the same periods of time. [Some evidence suggests that families with young children were given priority in renting abated apartments.] . . .

The same researchers had completed a prior study on abatement and partial abatement methods that indicated that lead dust remained and/or returned to abated houses over a period of time. . . . [The researchers also acknowledged that exposure to lead was "particularly hazardous for children."] . . . After publishing this report, the researchers began the present research project in which children were encouraged to reside in households where the possibility of lead dust was known to the researcher to be likely, so that the lead dust content of their blood could be compared with the level of lead dust in the houses at periodic intervals over a two-year period.

Apparently, it was anticipated that the children, who were the human subjects in the program, would, or at least might, accumulate lead in their blood from the dust, thus helping the researchers to determine the extent to which the various partial abatement methods worked. There was no complete and clear explanation in the consent agreements signed by the parents of the children that the research to be conducted was designed, at least in significant part, to measure the success of the abatement procedures by measuring the extent to which the children's blood was being contaminated. It can be argued that the researchers intended that the children be the canaries in the mines but never clearly told the parents. . . .

The researchers and their Institutional Review Board apparently saw nothing wrong with the research protocols that anticipated the possible accumulation of lead in the blood of otherwise healthy children as a result of the experiment, or they believed that the consents of the parents of the children made the research appropriate. Institutional Review Boards (IRB) are oversight entities [that are within the organizational structure of the institution conducting the research]. In research experiments, an IRB can be required in some instances by either federal or state regulation, or sometimes by the conditions attached to governmental grants that are used to fund research projects. Generally, their primary functions are to assess the protocols of the project to determine whether the project itself is appropriate, whether the consent procedures are adequate, whether the methods to be employed meet proper standards, whether reporting requirements are sufficient, and the assessment of various other aspects of a research project. One of the most important objectives of such review is the review of the potential safety and the health hazard impact of a research project on the human subjects of the experiment, especially on vulnerable subjects such as children. Their function is not to help researchers seek funding for research projects.

In the instant case, as is suggested by some commentators as being endemic to the research community as a whole, infra, the IRB involved here, the Johns Hopkins University Joint Committee on Clinical Investigation, in part, abdicated that responsibility, instead suggesting to the researchers a way to miscast the characteristics of the study in order to avoid the responsibility inherent in nontherapeutic research involving children. . . .

While the suggestion of the IRB would not make this experiment any less nontherapeutic or, thus, less regulated, . . . [its action] shows two things: (1) that the IRB had a partial misperception of the difference between therapeutic and nontherapeutic research and the IRB's role in the process and (2) that the IRB was willing to aid researchers in getting around federal regulations designed to protect children used as subjects in nontherapeutic research. An IRB's primary role is to assure the safety of human research subjects—not help researchers avoid safety or health-related requirements. The IRB, in this case, misconceived, at least partially, its own role.

The provisions or conditions imposed by the federal funding entities, pursuant to federal regulations, are conditions attached to funding. As far as we are aware, or have been informed, there are no federal or state (Maryland) statutes that mandate that all research be subject to certain conditions. Certain international "codes" or "declarations" exist (one of which is supposedly binding but has never been so held) that, at least in theory, establish standards. We shall describe them, infra. Accordingly, we write on a clean slate in this case. We are guided, as we determine what is appropriate, by those international "codes" or "declarations," as well as by studies conducted by various governmental entities, by the treatises and other writings on the ethics of using children as research subjects, and by the duties, if any, arising out of the use of children as subjects of research.

Otherwise healthy children, in our view, should not be enticed into living in, or remaining in, potentially lead-tainted housing and intentionally subjected to a research program, which contemplates the probability, or even the possibility, of lead poisoning or even the accumulation of lower levels of lead in blood, in order for the extent of the contamination of the children's blood to be used by scientific researchers to assess the success of lead paint or lead dust abatement measures. Moreover, in our view, parents, whether improperly enticed by trinkets, food stamps, money or other items, have no more right to intentionally and unnecessarily place children in potentially hazardous nontherapeutic research surroundings, than do researchers. In such cases, parental consent, no matter how informed, is insufficient.

While the validity of the consent agreement and its nature as a contract, the existence or nonexistence of a special relationship, and whether the researchers performed their functions under that agreement pursuant to any special relationships are important issues in these cases that we will address, the very inappropriateness of the research itself cannot be overlooked. It is apparent that the protocols of research are even more important than the method of obtaining parental consent and the extent to which the parents were, or were not, informed. If the research methods, the protocols, are inappropriate then, especially when the IRB is willing to help researchers avoid compliance with applicable safety requirements for using children in nontherapeutic research, the consent of the parents, or of any consent surrogates, in our view, cannot make the research appropriate or the actions of the researchers and the Institutional Review Board proper.

The research relationship proffered to the parents of the children the researchers wanted to use as measuring tools, should never have been presented in a nontherapeutic context in the first instance. Nothing about the research was designed for treatment of the subject children. They were presumed to be healthy at the commencement of the project. As to them, the research was clearly nontherapeutic in nature. The experiment was simply a "for the greater good" project.[6] The specific

---

6. The ultimate goal was to find the cost of the minimal level of effective lead paint or lead dust abatement costs so as to help landlords assess, hopefully positively, the commercial feasibility of attempting to abate lead dust in marginally profitable, lower-rent urban housing, in order to help preserve such housing in the Baltimore housing market. . . . The tenants

children's health was put at risk, in order to develop low-cost abatement measures that would help all children, the landlords, and the general public as well. . . .

The research project at issue here, and its apparent protocols, differs in large degree from, but presents similar problems as those in the Tuskegee Syphilis Study conducted from 1932 until 1972 . . . the intentional exposure of soldiers to radiation in the 1940s and 50s . . . the tests involving the exposure of Navajo miners to radiation . . . and the secret administration of LSD to soldiers by the CIA and the Army in the 1950s and 60s. . . . [In] the Tuskegee Syphilis Study . . . patients infected with syphilis were not subsequently informed of the availability of penicillin for treatment of the illness, in order for the scientists and researchers to be able to continue research on the effects of the illness. . . . [P]erhaps [the] most notorious . . . [nontherapeutic research project was] the deliberate use of infection . . . in order to study the degree of infection and the rapidity of the course of the disease in the . . . typhus experiments at Buchenwald concentration camp during World War II. These programs were somewhat alike in the vulnerability of the subjects; uneducated African American men, debilitated patients in a charity hospital, prisoners of war, inmates of concentration camps and others falling within the custody and control of the agencies conducting or approving the experiments. In the present case, children, especially young children, living in lower economic circumstances, albeit not as vulnerable as the other examples, are nonetheless, vulnerable as well.

It is clear to this Court that the scientific and medical communities cannot be permitted to assume sole authority to determine ultimately what is right and appropriate in respect to research projects involving young children free of the limitations and consequences of the application of Maryland law. The Institutional Review Boards, IRBs, are, primarily, in-house organs. In our view, they are not designed, generally, to be sufficiently objective in the sense that they are as sufficiently concerned with the ethicality of the experiments they review as they are with the success of the experiments. . . . Here, the IRB, whose primary function was to insure safety and compliance with applicable regulations, encouraged the researchers to misrepresent the purpose of the research in order to bring the study under the label of "therapeutic" and thus under a lower safety standard of regulation. The IRB's purpose was ethically wrong, and its understanding of the experiment's benefit incorrect.

The conflicts are inherent. This would be especially so when science and private industry collaborate in search of material gains. Moreover, the special relationship

---

involved, presumably, would be from a lower-rent urban class. . . . The children of middle class or rich parents apparently were not involved.

Indeed, the literature on the law and ethics of human experimentation is replete with warnings that all subjects, but especially vulnerable subjects, are at risk of abuse by inclusion [as research subjects]. Those vulnerable subjects included prisoners, who are subject to coercion, . . . children and the elderly . . . and racial minorities, ethnic minorities, and women . . . whom history shows to be the most frequent victims of abuses in human experimentations.

R. Alta Charo, Protecting Us to Death: Women, Pregnancy and Clinical Research Trials, 38 St. Louis U. L.J. 135, 135 (Fall, 1993). . . .

between research entities and human subjects used in the research will almost always impose duties.

In respect to examining that special relationship, we are obliged to further examine its nature and its ethical constraints. In that regard, when contested cases arise, the assessment of the legal effect of research on human subjects must always be subject to judicial evaluation. One method of making such evaluations is the initiation of appropriate actions bringing such matters to the attention of the courts, as has been done in the cases at bar. It may well be that in the end, the trial courts will determine that no damages have been incurred in the instant cases and thus the actions will fail for that reason. In that regard, we note that there are substantial factual differences in the . . . [separate cases under review]. But the actions, themselves, are not defective on the ground that no legal duty can, according to the trial courts, possibly exist. For the reasons discussed at length in the main body of the opinion, a legal duty normally exists between researcher and subject and in all probability exists in the cases at bar. Moreover, as we shall discuss, the consents of the parents in these cases under Maryland law constituted contracts creating duties. Additionally, under Maryland law, to the extent parental consent can ever be effective in research projects of this nature, the parents may not have been sufficiently informed and, therefore, the consents ineffective and, based on the information contained in the sparse records before this court, the research project . . . may have invaded the legal rights of the children subjected to it. . . .

II. FACTS & PROCEDURAL BACKGROUND . . .

The research study [giving rise to these cases] was sponsored jointly by the EPA and the Maryland Department of Housing and Community Development (DHCD). It was thus a joint federal and state project. The Baltimore City Health Department and Maryland Department of the Environment also collaborated in the study. It appears that, because the study was funded and sponsored in part by a federal entity, certain federal conditions were attached to the funding grants and approvals. There are certain uniform standards required in respect to federally funded or approved projects. We, however, are unaware of, and have not been directed to, any federal or state statute or regulation that imposes limits on this Court's powers to conduct its review of the issues presented. None of the parties have questioned this Court's jurisdiction in these cases. Moreover, 45 Code Federal Regulations (C.F.R.) 46.116(e) specifically provides: "The informed consent requirements in this policy are not intended to preempt any applicable federal, state, or local laws which require additional information to be disclosed in order for informed consent to be legally effective." Those various federal or state conditions, recommendations, etc., may well be relevant at a trial on the merits as to whether any breach of a contractual or other duty occurred, or whether negligence did, in fact, occur; but have no limiting effect on the issue of whether, at law, legal duties, via contract or "special relationships" are created in Maryland in experimental nontherapeutic research involving Maryland children. . . .

In summary, KKI conducted a study of five test groups of twenty-five houses each. The first three groups consisted of houses known to have lead present. The amount of repair and maintenance conducted increased from Group 1 to Group 2 to Group 3. The fourth group consisted of houses, which had at one time lead present but had since allegedly received a complete abatement of lead dust. The fifth group consisted of modern houses, which had never had the presence of lead dust. The twenty-five homes in each of the first three testing levels were then to be compared to the two control groups: the twenty-five homes in Group 4 that had previously been abated and the 25 modern homes in Group 5. The research study was specifically designed to do less than full lead dust abatement in some of the categories of houses in order to study the potential effectiveness, if any, of lesser levels of repair and maintenance.

If the children were to leave the houses upon the first manifestation of lead dust, it would be difficult, if not impossible, to test, over time, the rate of the level of lead accumulation in the blood of the children attributable to the manifestation. In other words, if the children were removed from the houses before the lead dust levels in their blood became elevated, the tests would probably fail, or at least the data that would establish the success of the test—or of the abatement results, would be of questionable use. Thus, it would benefit the accuracy of the test, and thus KKI, the compensated researcher, if children remained in the houses over the period of the study even after the presence of lead dust in the houses became evident. . . .

[The consent form for the study provided:]

PURPOSE OF STUDY

As you may know, lead poisoning in children is a problem in Baltimore City and other communities across the country. Lead in paint, house dust and outside soil are major sources of lead exposure for children. Children can also be exposed to lead in drinking water and other sources. We understand that your house is going to have special repairs done in order to reduce exposure to lead in paint and dust. On a random basis, homes will receive one of two levels of repair. We are interested in finding out how well the two levels of repair work. The repairs are not intended, or expected, to completely remove exposure to lead.

We are now doing a study to learn about how well different practices work for reducing exposure to lead in paint and dust. We are asking you and over one hundred other families to allow us to test for lead in and around your homes up to 8 to 9 times over the next two years provided that your house qualifies for the full two years of study. Final eligibility will be determined after the initial testing of your home. We are also doing free blood lead testing of children aged 6 months to 7 years, up to 8 to 9 times over the next two years. We would also like you to respond to a short questionnaire every 6 months. This study is intended to monitor the effects of the repairs and is not intended to replace the regular medical care your family obtains. . . .

BENEFITS

To compensate you for your time answering questions and allowing us to sketch your home we will mail you a check in the amount of $5.00. In the future we would mail you a check in the amount of $15 each time the full questionnaire is completed. The dust, soil, water, and blood samples would be tested for lead at the Kennedy Krieger Institute at no charge to you. We would provide you with specific blood-lead results. We would contact you to discuss a summary of house test results and steps that you could take to reduce any risks of exposure. . . .

On appeal, appellant[s] seek[] review of the Circuit Court's decision granting KKI summary judgment. . . . [They] contend[] that KKI owed a duty of care . . .

based on the nature of its relationship with [the children and parents participating in the study] . . . arising out of: (1) a contract between the parties; (2) a voluntary assumption by KKI; (3) a "special relationship" between the parties; and (4) a Federal regulation. . . . [The appellants argued that KKI was negligent in, for example, failing to notify a parent about elevated lead levels in a rental property for nine months, by which time her child had elevated blood levels of lead.]

III. DISCUSSION

A. STANDARD OF REVIEW

We resolve these disputes in the context of the trial court's granting of the appellee's motions for summary judgment in the two distinct cases. The threshold issues before this Court are whether, in the two cases presented, appellee, KKI, was entitled to summary judgment as a matter of law on the basis that no contract existed and that there is inherently no duty owed to a research subject by a researcher. Perhaps even more important is the ancillary issue of whether a parent in Maryland, under the law of this State, can legally consent to placing a child in a nontherapeutic research study that carries with it any risk of harm to the health of the child. We shall resolve all of these primary issues. . . .

B. GENERAL DISCUSSION

Initially, we note that we know of no law, nor have we been directed to any applicable in Maryland courts, that provides that the parties to a scientific study, because it is a scientific, health-related study, cannot be held to have entered into special relationships with the subjects of the study that can create duties, including duties, the breach of which may give rise to negligence claims. We also are not aware of any general legal precept that immunizes nongovernmental "institutional volunteers" or scientific researchers from the responsibility for the breaches of duties arising in "special relationships." Moreover, we, at the very least, hold that, under the particular circumstances testified to by the parties, there are genuine disputes of material fact concerning whether a special relationship existed between KKI and . . . [the appellants]. Concerning this issue, the granting of the summary judgment motions was clearly inappropriate. When a "special relationship" can exist as a matter of law, the issue of whether, given certain facts, a special relationship does exist, when there is a dispute of material fact in that respect, is a decision for the finder of fact, not the trial judge. We shall hold initially that the very nature of nontherapeutic scientific research on human subjects can, and normally will, create special relationships out of which duties arise. Since World War II the specialness or nature of such relationships has been frequently of concern in and outside of the research community.

As a result of the atrocities performed in the name of science during the Holocaust, and other happenings in the World War II era, what is now known as the Nuremberg Code evolved. Of special interest to this Court, the Nuremberg Code, at least in significant part, was the result of legal thought and legal principles, as opposed to medical or scientific principles, and thus should be the preferred standard for assessing the legality of scientific research on human subjects. Under it, duties to research subjects arise. . . . [The court cited a work by distinguished Boston University Professor George Annas detailing the history of the Nuremberg Code and explaining the lack of U.S. case law regarding the regulation of research under the Nuremberg Code or any other source of regulation.] . . .

In arguing that a fuller disclosure should be made when consent is sought for nontherapeutic research, as opposed to therapeutic research, [ethicist Karine] Morin notes:

> Furthermore, as long as courts continue to interpret the doctrine of informed consent in experimentation as it applies in the context of treatment, the uniqueness of the protection needed for human research subjects will be overlooked. Failing to recognize that subjects who volunteer for the sake of the advancement of science are differently situated from patients who stand to benefit from treatment results in an analysis that misconceives the purpose of disclosure. Beyond informing the patient as to means available to treat him or her, a subject must become a voluntary and willing participant in an endeavor that may yield no direct benefit to him or her, or worse, that may cause harm.

Karine Morin, The Standard of Disclosure in Human Subject Experimentation, 19 J. Legal Med. 157, 220 (1998). . . .

[T]here is no[t] [a] complete record of the specific compensation of the researchers involved. Although the project was funded by the EPA, at the request of KKI the EPA has declined to furnish such information to the attorney for one of the parties, who requested it under the federal Freedom of Information Act. Whether the research's character as a co-sponsored state project opens the records under the Maryland Public Information Act has apparently not been considered. Neither is there in the record any development of what pressures, if any, were exerted in respect to the researchers obtaining the consents of the parents and conducting the experiment. Nor, for the same reason, is there a sufficient indication as to the extent to which the Institute has joined with commercial interests, if it has, for the purposes of profit, that might potentially impact upon the researcher's motivations and potential conflicts of interest—motivations that generally are assumed, in the cases of prestigious entities such as Johns Hopkins University, to be for the public good rather . . . [than] a search for profit.

We do note that the institution involved, the respondent here . . . is a highly respected entity, considered to be a leader in the development of treatments, and treatment itself, for children infected with lead poisoning. With reasonable assurance, we can note that its reputation alone might normally suggest that there was no realization or understanding on the Institute's part that the protocols of the experiment were questionable, except for the letter from the IRB requesting that the researchers mischaracterize the study.

We shall further address both the factual and legal bases for the findings of the trial courts, holding, ultimately, that the respective courts erred in both respects.

C. NEGLIGENCE

It is important for us to remember that appellants allege that KKI was negligent. Specifically, they allege that KKI, as a medical researcher, owed a duty of care to them, as subjects in the research study, based on the nature of the agreements between them and also based on the nature of the relationship between the parties. They contend specifically that KKI was negligent because KKI breached its duty to: (1) design a study that did not involve placing children at unnecessary risk; (2) inform participants in the study of results in a timely manner; and (3) to completely and accurately inform participants in the research study of all the hazards and risks involved in the study. . . .

Because this is a review of the granting of the two summary judgments based solely on the grounds that there was no legal duty to protect the children, we are primarily concerned with . . . whether KKI was under a duty to protect appellants from injury.[33] . . .

The relationship that existed between KKI and both sets of appellants in the case at bar was that of medical researcher and research study subject. Though not expressly recognized in the Maryland Code or in our prior cases as a type of relationship which creates a duty of care, evidence in the record suggests that such a relationship involving a duty or duties would ordinarily exist, and certainly could exist, based on the facts and circumstances of each of these individual cases. . . .

IV. THE SPECIAL RELATIONSHIPS

A. THE CONSENT AGREEMENT CONTRACT

Both sets of appellants signed a similar Consent Form prepared by KKI in which KKI expressly promised to: (1) financially compensate (however minimally) appellants for their participation in the study; . . . (2) collect lead dust samples from appellants' homes, analyze the samples, discuss the results with appellants, and discuss steps that could be taken, which could reduce exposure to lead; and (3) collect blood samples from children in the household and provide appellants with the results of the blood tests. In return, appellants agreed to participate in the study, by: (1) allowing KKI into appellants' homes to collect dust samples; (2) periodically filling out questionnaires; and (3) allowing the children's blood to be drawn, tested, and utilized in the study. If consent agreements contain such provisions, and the trial court did not find otherwise, and we hold from our own examination of the record that such provisions were so contained, mutual assent, offer, acceptance, and consideration existed, all of which created contractual relationships imposing duties by reason of the consent agreement . . . (as well, as we discuss elsewhere, by the very nature of such relationships).

By having appellants sign this Consent Form, both KKI and appellants expressly made representations, which, in our view, created a bilateral contract between the parties. At the very least, it suggests that appellants were agreeing with KKI to participate in the research study with the expectation that they would be compensated, albeit, more or less, minimally, be informed of all the information necessary for the subject to freely choose whether to participate, and continue to participate, and receive promptly any information that might bear on their willingness to continue to participate in the study. This includes full, detailed, prompt, and continuing warnings as to all the potential risks and hazards inherent in the research or that arise during the research. KKI, in return, was getting the children to move into the

---

33. We note that there was little suggestion of actual permanent injury to the children involved with these two cases. Our opinion is not directed to the matter of whether damages can be proven in the present cases.

houses and/or to remain there over time, and was given the right to test the children's blood for lead. As consideration to KKI, it got access to the houses and to the blood of the children that had been encouraged to live in a "risk" environment. In other words, KKI received a measuring tool—the children's blood. Considerations existed, mainly money, food coupons, trinkets, bilateral promises, blood to be tested in order to measure success. "Informed consent" of the type used here, which imposes obligation and confers consideration on both researcher and subject (in these cases, the parents of the subjects) may differ from the more one-sided "informed consent" normally used in actual medical practice. Researcher/subject consent in nontherapeutic research can, and in this case did, create a contract.[35]

B. THE SUFFICIENCY OF THE CONSENT FORM

The consent form did not directly inform the parents of the fact that it was contemplated that some of the children might ingest lead dust particles, and that one of the reasons the blood of the children was to be tested was to evaluate how effective the various abatement measures were.

A reasonable parent would expect to be clearly informed that it was at least contemplated that her child would ingest lead dust particles, and that the degree to which lead dust contaminated the child's blood would be used as one of the ways in which the success of the experiment would be measured. The fact that if such information was furnished, it might be difficult to obtain human subjects for the research, does not affect the need to supply the information, or alter the ethics of failing to provide such information. A human subject is entitled to all material information. The respective parent should also have been clearly informed that in order for the measurements to be most helpful, the child needed to stay in the house until the conclusion of the study. Whether assessed by a subjective or an objective standard, the children, or their surrogates, should have been additionally informed that the researchers anticipated that, as a result of the experiment, it was possible that there might be some accumulation of lead in the blood of the children. The "informed" consent was not valid because full material information was not furnished to the subjects or their parents.

C. SPECIAL RELATIONSHIP

In Case Number 128, Ms. Hughes signed a Consent Form in which KKI agreed to provide her with "specific blood-lead results" and discuss with her "a summary of house test results and steps that [she] could take to reduce any risks of exposure." She contends that this agreement between the parties gave rise to a duty owed by KKI to provide her with that information in a timely manner. She signed the Consent Form on March 10, 1993. The project began almost simultaneously. KKI collected dust samples in the Monroe Street property on March 9, 1993, August 23, 1993, March 9, 1994, September 19, 1994, April 18, 1995, and November 13, 1995. The March 9, 1993 dust testing revealed what the researchers referred to as "hot spots," where the level of lead was "higher than might be found in a completely

---

35. We make no determination as to whether informed consent in a therapeutic medical context can generate contractual obligations.

renovated house." . . . [T]his information was not furnished to Ms. Hughes until December 16, 1993, more than nine months after the samples had been collected and not until after Ericka Grimes's blood was found to contain elevated levels of lead. She contends that not only did KKI have a duty to report such information in a timely manner but that it breached this duty by delaying to such a time that her daughter was allowed to contract lead poisoning. Looking at the relevant facts of Case Number 128, they are susceptible to inferences supporting the position of appellant, Ericka Grimes, and, moreover, that, if true, would create a "special relationship" out of which duties would be created. Therefore, for this reason alone, the grant of summary judgment was improper. . . .

[T]he trial courts appear to have held that special relationships out of which duties arise cannot be created by the relationship between researchers and the subjects of the research. While in some rare cases that may be correct, it is not correct when researchers recruit people, especially children whose consent is furnished indirectly, to participate in nontherapeutic procedures that are potentially hazardous, dangerous, or deleterious to their health. As opposed to compilation of already extant statistics for purposes of studying human health matters, the creation of study conditions or protocols or participation in the recruitment of otherwise healthy subjects to interact with already existing, or potentially existing, hazardous conditions, or both, for the purpose of creating statistics from which scientific hypotheses can be supported, would normally warrant or create such special relationships as a matter of law.

It is of little moment that an entity is an institutional volunteer in a community. If otherwise, the legitimacy of the claim to noble purpose would always depend upon the particular institution and the particular community it is serving in a given case. As we have indicated, history is replete with claims of noble purpose for institutions and institutional volunteers in a wide variety of communities.

Institutional volunteers may intend to do good or, as history has proven, even to do evil and may do evil or good depending on the institution and the community they serve. Whether an institutional volunteer[36] in a particular community should be granted exceptions from the application of law is a matter that should be scrutinized closely by an appropriate public policy maker. Generally, but not always, the legislative branch is appropriately the best first forum to consider exceptions to the tort laws of this State—even then it should consider all ramifications of the policy—especially considering the general vulnerability of subjects of such studies—in this case, small children. In the absence of the exercise of legislative policymaking, we hold that special relationships, out of which duties arise, the breach of which can constitute negligence, can result from the relationships between researcher and research subjects.

36. Moreover, it is not clear that KKI was a mere volunteer in any event. It received funding for developing and conducting the research. Whether it recognized a profit is unknown from the record. The "for profit" nature of some research may well increase the duties of researchers to insure the safety of research subjects, and may well increase researchers' or an institution's susceptibility for damages in respect to any injuries incurred by research subjects.

D. THE FEDERAL REGULATIONS

A duty may be prescribed by a statute, or a special relationship creating duties may arise from the requirement for compliance with statutory provisions. Although there is no duty of which we are aware prescribed by the Maryland Code in respect to scientific research . . . , federal regulations have been enacted that impose standards of care that attach to federally funded or sponsored research projects that use human subjects. See 45 C.F.R. Part 46 (2000). 45 C.F.R. Part 46, Subpart A, is entitled "Basic HHS Policy for Protection of Human Research Subjects" and Subpart D of the regulation is entitled "Additional Protections for Children Involved as Subjects in Research." . . . [T]his study was funded, and co-sponsored, by the EPA and presumably was therefore subject to these federal conditions. These conditions, if appropriate administrative action has been taken, require fully informed consent in any research using human subjects conducted, supported, or otherwise subject to any level of control or funding by any federal department or agency. . . .

These federal regulations, especially the requirement for adherence to sound ethical principles, strike right at the heart of KKI's defense of the granting of the Motions for Summary Judgment. Fully informed consent is lacking in these cases. The research did not comply with the regulations. There clearly was more than a minimal risk involved. Under the regulations, children should not have been used for the purpose of measuring how much lead they would accumulate in their blood while living in partially abated houses to which they were recruited initially or encouraged to remain, because of the study. . . .

Clearly, KKI, as a research institution, is required to obtain a human participant's fully informed consent, using sound ethical principles. It is clear from the wording of the applicable federal regulations that this requirement of informed consent continues during the duration of the research study and applies to new or changing risks. In this case, a special relationship out of which duties might arise might be created by reason of the federally imposed regulations. The question becomes whether this duty of informed consent created by federal regulation, as a matter of state law, translates into a duty of care arising out of the unique relationship that is researcher-subject, as opposed to doctor-patient. We answer that question in the affirmative. In this State, it may, depending on the facts, create such a duty.

Additionally, the Nuremberg Code, intended to be applied internationally, and never expressly rejected in this country, inherently and implicitly, speaks strongly to the existence of special relationships imposing ethical duties on researchers who conduct nontherapeutic experiments on human subjects. The Nuremberg Code specifically requires researchers to make known to human subjects of research "all inconveniences and hazards reasonably to be expected; and the effects upon his health or person which may possibly come from his participation in the experiment." The breach of obligations imposed on researchers by the Nuremberg Code, might well support actions sounding in negligence in cases such as those at issue here. We reiterate as well that, given the facts and circumstances of both of these cases, there were, at the very least, genuine disputes of material facts concerning the relationship and duties of the parties, and compliance with the regulations.

V. THE ETHICAL APPROPRIATENESS OF THE RESEARCH

The World Medical Association in its Declaration of Helsinki . . . included a code of ethics for investigative researchers and was an attempt by the medical community to establish its own set of rules for conducting research on human subjects. . . .[39]

The determination of whether a duty exists under Maryland law is the ultimate function of various policy considerations as adopted by either the Legislature, or, if it has not spoken, as it has not in respect to this situation, by Maryland courts. In our view, otherwise healthy children should not be the subjects of nontherapeutic experimentation or research that has the potential to be harmful to the child. It is, first and foremost, the responsibility of the researcher and the research entity to see to the harmlessness of such nontherapeutic research. Consent of parents can never relieve the researcher of this duty. We do not feel that it serves proper public policy concerns to permit children to be placed in situations of potential harm, during nontherapeutic procedures, even if parents, or other surrogates, consent. Under these types of circumstances, even where consent is given, albeit inappropriately, policy considerations suggest that there remains a special relationship between researchers and participants to the research study, which imposes a duty of care. This is entirely consistent with the principles found in the Nuremberg Code.

Researchers cannot ever be permitted to completely immunize themselves by reliance on consents, especially when the information furnished to the subject, or the party consenting, is incomplete in a material respect. A researcher's duty is not created by, or extinguished by, the consent of a research subject or by IRB approval. The duty to a vulnerable research subject is independent of consent, although the obtaining of consent is one of the duties a researcher must perform. All of this is especially so when the subjects of research are children. Such legal duties, and legal protections, might additionally be warranted because of the likely conflict of interest between the goal of the research experimenter and the health of the human subject, especially, but not exclusively, when such research is commercialized. There is always a potential substantial conflict of interest on the part of researchers as between them and the human subjects used in their research. If participants in the study withdraw from the research study prior to its completion, then the results of the study could be rendered meaningless. There is thus an inherent reason for not conveying information to subjects as it arises, that might cause the subjects to leave the research project. That conflict dictates a stronger reason for full and continuous disclosure. . . .

A special relationship giving rise to duties, the breach of which might constitute negligence, might also arise because, generally, the investigators are in a better position to anticipate, discover, and understand the potential risks to the health of their subjects. . . .

This duty requires the protection of the research subjects from unreasonable harm and requires the researcher to completely and promptly inform the subjects of potential hazards existing from time to time because of the profound trust that participants place in investigators, institutions, and the research enterprise as a whole to protect them from harm. . . .

39. . . . Declaration of Helsinki, World Medical Assembly (WMA) 18th Assembly (June 1964), amended by 29th WMA Tokyo, Japan (October 1975), 35th WMA Venice, Italy (October 1983) and the 41st WMA Hong Kong (September 1989). [Eds. Note: For the current WMA Declaration of Helsinki, see 310 JAMA 2191 (2013).]

While we acknowledge that foreseeability does not necessarily create a duty, we recognize that potential harm to the children participants of this study was both foreseeable and potentially extreme. A "special relationship" also exists in circumstances where such experiments are conducted.

VI. Parental Consent for Children to Be Subjects of Potentially Hazardous Nontherapeutic Research

The issue of whether a parent can consent to the participation of her or his child in a nontherapeutic health-related study that is known to be potentially hazardous to the health of the child raises serious questions with profound moral and ethical implications. What right does a parent have to knowingly expose a child not in need of therapy to health risks or otherwise knowingly place a child in danger, even if it can be argued it is for the greater good? The issue in these specific contested cases does not relate primarily to the authority of the parent, but to the procedures of KKI and similar entities that may be involved in such health-related studies. The issue of the parents' right to consent on behalf of the children has not been fully presented in either of these cases, but should be of concern not only to lawyers and judges, but to moralists, ethicists, and others. The consenting parents in the contested cases at bar were not the subjects of the experiment; the children were. Additionally, this practice presents the potential problems of children initiating actions in their own names upon reaching majority, if indeed, they have been damaged as a result of being used as guinea pigs in nontherapeutic scientific research. Children, it should be noted, are not in our society the equivalent of rats, hamsters, monkeys, and the like. Because of the overriding importance of this matter and this Court's interest in the welfare of children—we shall address the issue.

Most of the relatively few cases in the area of the ethics of protocols of various research projects involving children have merely assumed that a parent can give informed consent for the participation of their children in nontherapeutic research. . . .

It is not in the best interest of a specific child, in a nontherapeutic research project, to be placed in a research environment, which might possibly be, or which proves to be, hazardous to the health of the child . . . in order to test methods that may ultimately benefit all children. . . .

One simply does not expose otherwise healthy children, incapable of personal assent (consent), to a nontherapeutic research environment that is known at the inception of the research, might cause the children to ingest lead dust. It is especially troublesome, when a measurement of the success of the research experiment is, in significant respect, to be determined by the extent to which the blood of the children absorbs, and is contaminated by, a substance that the researcher knows can, in sufficient amounts, whether solely from the research environment or cumulative from all sources, cause serious and long term adverse health effects. Such a practice is not legally acceptable. . . .

In the[se] case[s], no impartial judicial review or oversight was sought by the researchers or by the parents. . . . Science cannot be permitted to be the sole judge of the appropriateness of such research methods on human subjects, especially in respect to children. We hold that in these contested cases, the research study protocols [presented to the court] . . . were not appropriate. . . .

VII. CONCLUSION

We hold that in Maryland a parent, appropriate relative, or other applicable surrogate, cannot consent to the participation of a child or other person under legal disability in nontherapeutic research or studies in which there is any risk of injury or damage to the health of the subject.

We hold that informed consent agreements in nontherapeutic research projects, under certain circumstances can constitute contracts; and that, under certain circumstances, such research agreements can, as a matter of law, constitute "special relationships" giving rise to duties, out of the breach of which negligence actions may arise. We also hold that, normally, such special relationships are created between researchers and the human subjects used by the researchers. Additionally, we hold that governmental regulations can create duties on the part of researchers towards human subjects out of which "special relationships" can arise. Likewise, such duties and relationships are consistent with the provisions of the Nuremberg Code.

The determination as to whether a "special relationship" actually exists is to be done on a case by case basis. . . . The determination as to whether a special relationship exists, if properly pled, lies with the trier of fact. We hold that there was ample evidence in the cases at bar to support a fact finder's determination of the existence of duties arising out of contract, or out of a special relationship, or out of regulations and codes, or out of all of them, in each of the cases.

We hold that on the present record, the Circuit Courts erred in their assessment of the law and of the facts as pled in granting KKI's motions for summary judgment in both cases before this Court. Accordingly, we vacate the rulings of the Circuit Court for Baltimore City and remand these cases to that court for further proceedings consistent with this opinion. . . .

RAKER, J., concurring in result only:

These appeals present the narrow question of whether the Circuit Courts erred in granting summary judgments to appellee, the Kennedy Krieger Institute, a research entity, on the ground that, as a matter of law, it owed no duty to warn appellants, Ericka Grimes and Myron Higgins, et al., human subjects participating in its research study. I concur in the judgment of the Court only and join in the Court's judgment that the Circuit Courts erred in granting summary judgments to appellee. These cases should be remanded for further proceedings.

I concur in the Court's judgment because I find that appellants have alleged sufficient facts to establish that there existed a special relationship between the parties in these cases, which created a duty of care that, if breached, gives rise to an action in negligence. . . . I would hold that a special relationship giving rise to a duty of care, the breach of which would be the basis for an action in negligence, existed in these cases and would remand the cases at bar to the Circuit Courts for further proceedings. I agree with the majority that this duty includes the protection of research subjects from unreasonable harm and requires the researcher to inform research subjects completely and promptly of potential hazards resulting from participation in the study. . . . As a result of the existence of this tort duty, I find it unnecessary to reach the thorny question, not even raised by any of the parties, of whether the informed consent agreements in these cases constitute legally binding contracts. . . .

As I have indicated, this case presents a narrow question of whether a duty in tort exists between the plaintiffs and the defendants. . . . Nonetheless, the majority appears to have decided the issue of whether such duty of care was, in fact, breached as a matter of law, without a hearing or a trial on the merits.

I cannot join in the majority's sweeping factual determinations. . . .

ON MOTION FOR RECONSIDERATION

PER CURIAM.

The Court has considered the motion for reconsideration and the submissions by the various amici curiae. The motion is denied, with this explanation.

Some of the issues raised in this case, in the briefs and at oral argument, were important ones of first impression in this State, and the Court therefore attempted to address those issues in a full and exhaustive manner. The case reached us in the context of summary judgments entered by the Circuit Court, which entailed rulings that the evidence presented by the plaintiffs, for purposes of the motions, even when taken in a light most favorable to them, was insufficient as a matter of law to establish the prospect of liability. We disagreed with that determination. Although we discussed the various issues and arguments in considerable detail, the only conclusion that we reached as a matter of law was that, on the record currently before us, summary judgment was improperly granted—that sufficient evidence was presented in both cases which, if taken in a light most favorable to the plaintiffs and believed by a jury, would suffice to justify verdicts in favor of the plaintiffs. Thus, the cases were remanded for further proceedings in the Circuit Court. Every issue bearing on liability or damages remains open for further factual development, and any relevant evidence not otherwise precluded under our rules of evidence is admissible.

Much of the argument in support of and in opposition to the motion for reconsideration centered on the question of what limitations should govern a parent's authority to provide informed consent for the participation of his or her minor child in a medical study. In the Opinion, we said at one point that a parent "cannot consent to the participation of a child . . . in nontherapeutic research or studies in which there is any risk of injury or damage to the health of the subject." As we think is clear from Section VI of the Opinion, by "any risk," we meant any articulable risk beyond the minimal kind of risk that is inherent in any endeavor. The context of the statement was a non-therapeutic study that promises no medical benefit to the child whatever, so that any balance between risk and benefit is necessarily negative. As we indicated, the determination of whether the study in question offered some benefit, and therefore could be regarded as therapeutic in nature, or involved more than that minimal risk is open for further factual development on remand.

RAKER, Judge, dissenting.

I respectfully dissent from the order denying the motions for reconsideration. I adhere to the views previously expressed in my concurring opinion filed herein. . . . The majority's discussion of the ability of a parent or guardian to consent to the participation of a minor child in a nontherapeutic research study and the discussion regarding the ethics of the research conducted in these cases involve serious public policy considerations. The statements are a declaration of public policy that, in the posture of this case, are best left to the General Assembly. . . .

■ FEDERAL POLICY FOR THE PROTECTION OF HUMAN SUBJECTS
82 Fed. Reg. 7149 (Jan. 19, 2017)

PURPOSE OF THE REGULATORY ACTION

Individuals who are the subjects of research may be asked to contribute their time and assume risk to advance the research enterprise, which benefits society at large. U.S. federal regulations governing the protection of human subjects in research have been in existence for more than three decades. The Department of Health, Education, and Welfare first published regulations for the protection of human subjects in 1974, and the Department of Health and Human Services (HHS) revised them in the early 1980s. During the 1980s, HHS began a process that eventually led to the adoption of a revised version of the regulations by 15 U.S. federal departments and agencies in 1991. The purpose of this effort was to promote uniformity, understanding, and compliance with human subject protections as well as to create a uniform body of regulations across federal departments and agencies (subpart A of 45 Code of Federal Regulations [CFR] part 46), often referred to as the "Common Rule" or "Protection of Human Subjects Regulations." Those regulations were last amended in 2005, and have remained unchanged until the issuance of this final rule.

Since the Common Rule was promulgated, the volume and landscape of research involving human subjects have changed considerably. Research with human subjects has grown in scale and become more diverse. Examples of developments include: an expansion in the number and types of clinical trials, as well as observational studies and cohort studies; a diversification of the types of social and behavioral research being used in human subjects research; increased use of sophisticated analytic techniques to study human biospecimens; and the growing use of electronic health data and other digital records to enable very large datasets to be rapidly analyzed and combined in novel ways. Yet these developments have not been accompanied by major change in the human subjects research oversight system, which has remained largely unaltered over the past two decades.

On July 26, 2011, the Office of the Secretary of HHS, in coordination with the Executive Office of the President's Office of Science and Technology Policy (OSTP), published an advance notice of proposed rulemaking (ANPRM) to request comment on how current regulations for protecting those who participate in research might be modernized and revised to be more effective.

On September 8, 2015, HHS and 15 other federal departments and agencies published a Notice of Proposed Rulemaking (NPRM) proposing revisions to the regulations for protection of human subjects in research.[2] Like the ANPRM, the NPRM sought comment on how to better protect research subjects while facilitating valuable research and reducing burden, delay, and ambiguity for investigators. Public comments on both the ANPRM and the NPRM have informed the final rule that is now being promulgated.

---

2. HHS. Federal Policy for the Protection of Human Subjects. 80 FR 53931 (Sept. 8, 2015). Retrieved from https://www.federalregister.gov/documents/2015/09/08/2015-21756/federal-policy-for-the-protection-of-human-subjects.

The final rule is designed to more thoroughly address the broader types of research conducted or otherwise supported by all of the Common Rule departments and agencies such as behavioral and social science research. It also benefits from continuing efforts to harmonize human subjects policies across federal departments and agencies.

SUMMARY OF THE MAJOR CHANGES IN THE FINAL RULE

The final rule differs in important ways from the NPRM [proposed rule]. Most significantly, several proposals are not being adopted:

- The final rule does not adopt the proposal to require that research involving nonidentified biospecimens be subject to the Common Rule, and that consent would need to be obtained in order to conduct such research. . . .
- The final rule does not expand the policy to cover clinical trials that are not federally funded. . . .
- The final rule does not include the proposed standardized privacy safeguards for identifiable private information and identifiable biospecimens. Aspects of proposals that relied on those safeguards have been modified or are not being adopted.
- The final rule does not adopt the most restrictive proposed criteria for obtaining a waiver of the consent requirements relating to research with identifiable biospecimens.

The final rule makes the following significant changes to the Common Rule:

- Establishes new requirements regarding the information that must be given to prospective research subjects as part of the informed consent process.
- Allows the use of broad consent (i.e., seeking prospective consent to unspecified future research) from a subject for storage, maintenance, and secondary research use of identifiable private information and identifiable biospecimens. Broad consent will be an optional alternative that an investigator may choose instead of, for example, conducting the research on nonidentified information and nonidentified biospecimens, having an institutional review board (IRB) waive the requirement for informed consent, or obtaining consent for a specific study.
- Establishes new exempt categories of research based on their risk profile. Under some of the new categories, exempt research would be required to undergo limited IRB review to ensure that there are adequate privacy safeguards for identifiable private information and identifiable biospecimens.
- Creates a requirement for U.S.-based institutions engaged in cooperative research to use a single IRB for that portion of the research that takes place within the United States, with certain exceptions. This requirement becomes effective 3 years after publication of the final rule.
- Removes the requirement to conduct continuing review of ongoing research for studies that undergo expedited review and for studies that have completed study interventions and are merely analyzing study data or involve only observational follow up in conjunction with standard clinical care.

Other minor changes have been to improve the rule and for purposes of clarity and accuracy. . . .

The Rationale for Modernizing the Common Rule . . .

The Changing Nature of Research

This final rule recognizes that in the past two decades a paradigm shift has occurred in how research is conducted. Evolving technologies—including imaging, mobile technologies, and the growth in computing power—have changed the scale and nature of information collected in many disciplines. Computer scientists, engineers, and social scientists are developing techniques to integrate different types of data so they can be combined, mined, analyzed, and shared. The advent of sophisticated computer software programs, the Internet, and mobile technology has created new areas of research activity, particularly within the social and behavioral sciences. In biomedical science, the Human Genome Project laid the foundation for precision medicine and promoted an environment of data sharing and innovation in analytics and technology, and drew attention to the need for policies that support a changing research landscape. New technologies, including genomic sequencing, have quickly led to exponential growth in the data to which investigators have access. The sheer volume of data that can be generated in research, the ease with which it can be shared, and the ways in which it can be used to identify individuals were simply not possible, or even imaginable, when the Common Rule was first adopted.

Research settings are also shifting. Although much biomedical research continues to be conducted in academic medical centers, more research is being conducted in clinical care settings, thus combining research and medical data. Biospecimen repositories and large databases have made it easier to do research on existing (stored) biospecimens and data. Clinical research networks connected through electronic health records have developed methods for extracting clinical data for research purposes and are working toward integration of research data into electronic health records in a meaningful way. The scientific community recognizes the value of data sharing and open-source resources and understands that pooling intellectual resources and capitalizing on efficient uses of data and technology represent the best ways to advance knowledge.

At the same time, the level of public engagement in the research enterprise has changed. More people want to play an active role in research, particularly related to health.

As technology evolves, so does the nature of the risks and benefits of participating in certain types of research. Many studies do not involve interaction with research subjects, but instead involve secondary analysis of data or biospecimens. Risks related to these types of research studies are largely informational, not physical; that is, harms could result primarily from the inappropriate disclosure of information and not from the research interventions themselves. Nonetheless, those harms can be significant.

Because of these shifts in science, technology, and public engagement and expectations, a wide range of stakeholders have raised concerns about the limitations of the existing regulatory framework, arguing for a re-evaluation of how the fundamental principles of the 1979 Belmont Report that underlie the Common Rule—respect for persons, beneficence, and justice—are applied in practice to the myriad new contexts in which U.S. research is conducted in the 21st century. The changes that are being implemented in the final rule continue to be shaped by those principles. . . .

Finally, it is important to note that, to the extent appropriate, the intent is to eventually amend the other subparts of the HHS human subjects protection regulations in 45 CFR part 46 (subparts B, C, D, and E), and consider the need for updates to FDA regulations and other relevant federal departmental or agency regulations with overlapping scope.

Notes: Human Subjects Research

1. *Federal Regulation.* As described above, most of the field of clinical investigation is now very closely regulated by the DHHS's Office for Human Research Protections, 45 C.F.R. §§46.101 et seq, and the federal Food and Drug Administration (FDA), 21 C.F.R. §§50.1-.56; 54.1-.6; and 56.101-.124. The federal regulatory structure differs from informed consent law in that the penalty for violation is disqualification from federal funding rather than a claim for damages. The regulatory focus, however, mirrors the informed consent themes already introduced in our discussion of fiduciary liability. The federal regulations are designed to safeguard individual autonomy from overreaching by researchers. The mechanism used to provide protection is a combination of mandatory disclosure and individual assent. The researcher is charged with a special obligation to care for his or her research subject and to protect the subject from harm. The federal regulations require prior approval of the informed consent process that typically includes written disclosures and consents. These documents are reviewed by interdisciplinary ethical review committees (called "institutional review boards" or "IRBs") located in hospitals, in other medical research centers, and in universities where research is conducted using human subjects. The Common Rule explicitly preserves from preemption foreign, state, tribal, or local laws providing additional protections. 45 C.F.R. §46.101(f), (g). The relevant federal agency may also permit federal agencies to apply equivalent or more protective internationally recognized protections for human research subjects in research conducted in foreign countries. Id. at §46.101(h).

The Common Rule has played an extremely important role in establishing norms for human subjects research and specific standards for consent. The revision process began with a detailed advance notice of proposed rulemaking in 2011, which was followed by a notice of the proposed rulemaking that offered specific proposed revisions in 2015. These announcements generated significant attention. The proposed rule generated more than 2,100 public comments along with two major reports. See National Research Council of the National Academies, Proposed Revisions to the Common Rule for the Protection of Human Subjects in the Behavioral and Social Sciences (2014); National Academies of Sciences, Engineering, and Medicine, Optimizing the Nation's Investment in Academic Research: A New Regulatory Framework for the 21st Century (2016). The Final Rule differs from the original proposed rule in a number of ways, and further changes are anticipated in related DHHS rules and in the FDA rules governing human subjects research. See, 21st Century Cures Act, P.L. No. 114-255 (2016) (sec. 3023, DHHS and FDA harmonization). The notes in this section will focus on the Common Rule, using the provisions effective as of January 2018, unless otherwise noted.

2. *Basic Definitions: What Is Research?* The federal regulations establish a broad definition of *research* as "a systematic investigation, including research development, testing, and evaluation, designed to develop or contribute to generalizable knowledge." 45 C.F.R. §46.102(l). A "[h]uman subject" is "a living individual about whom an investigator (whether professional or student) conducting research: (i) Obtains information or biospecimens through intervention or interaction with the individual, and uses, studies, or analyzes the information or biospecimens; or (ii) Obtains, uses, studies, analyzes, or generates identifiable private information or identifiable biospecimens." Id. §46.102(e). Is the line between medical treatment and medical research always clear? See Lars Noah, Informed Consent and the Elusive Dichotomy Between Standard and Experimental Therapy, 28 Am. J.L. & Med. 361 (2002).

Although the revised Common Rule maintains the previous broad definition of *research*, the Rule now includes additional provisions carving out activities "deemed not to be research," such as: (1) certain scholarly and journalistic activities (including legal research); (2) specifically defined public health surveillance activities; (3) collection and analysis of information, biospecimens, or records by criminal justice authorities for specific purposes; and (4) authorized operational activities supporting certain "intelligence, homeland security, defense or other national security missions." 45 C.F.R. §46.102(l). The new Common Rule also broadens the category of "exempt research," which generally involves research considered to present low risks to participants, that will ordinarily be exempt from most Part A (Common Rule) requirements. 45 C.F.R. §46.104. One particularly important category of exemptions involves a new process for securing broad consent for secondary use of personally identifiable information or biospecimens, which will be considered further below.

3. *General Requirements for Funded Research.* The federal regulations establish several criteria for approval of most forms of research:

(a) In order to approve research covered by this policy the IRB shall determine that all of the following requirements are satisfied:
(1) Risks to subjects are minimized: (i) By using procedures that are consistent with sound research design and that do not unnecessarily expose subjects to risk, and (ii) Whenever appropriate, by using procedures already being performed on the subjects for diagnostic or treatment purposes.
(2) Risks to subjects are reasonable in relation to anticipated benefits, if any, to subjects, and the importance of the knowledge that may reasonably be expected to result. In evaluating risks and benefits, the IRB should consider only those risks and benefits that may result from the research (as distinguished from risks and benefits of therapies subjects would receive even if not participating in the research). The IRB should not consider possible long-range effects of applying knowledge gained in the research (e.g., the possible effects of the research on public policy) as among those research risks that fall within the purview of its responsibility.
(3) Selection of subjects is equitable. In making this assessment the IRB should take into account the purposes of the research and the setting in which the research will be conducted. The IRB should be particularly cognizant of the special problems of research that involves a category of subjects who are vulnerable to coercion or undue influence, such as children, prisoners, individuals with impaired decision-making capacity, or economically or educationally disadvantaged persons.

(4) Informed consent will be sought from each prospective subject or the subject's legally authorized representative, in accordance with, and to the extent required by, §46.116.

(5) Informed consent will be appropriately documented or appropriately waived in accordance with §46.117.

(6) When appropriate, the research plan makes adequate provision for monitoring the data collected to ensure the safety of subjects.

(7) When appropriate, there are adequate provisions to protect the privacy of subjects and to maintain the confidentiality of data. (i) The Secretary of HHS will, after consultation with the Office of Management and Budget's privacy office and other Federal departments and agencies that have adopted this policy, issue guidance to assist IRBs in assessing what provisions are adequate to protect the privacy of subjects and to maintain the confidentiality of data. . . .

(b) When some or all of the subjects are likely to be vulnerable to coercion or undue influence, such as children, prisoners, individuals with impaired decision-making capacity, or economically or educationally disadvantaged persons, additional safeguards have been included in the study to protect the rights and welfare of these subjects.

45 C.F.R. §46.111 (specific provisions governing research involving "storage or maintenance of identifiable private information or identifiable biospecimens for potential secondary research use" omitted).

Therapeutic research provides the possibility of benefit to the research subject; some risk to the subject might therefore be tolerated so long as it is outweighed by the anticipated benefit and other criteria are met. Nontherapeutic research does not offer a benefit to the subject; the research therefore cannot proceed unless the risks are minimal. The *Grimes* court characterized the lead abatement research as involving more than minimal risk and suggested that parents might not be permitted to consent to nontherapeutic research involving children that poses more than a minimal risk. What is a minimal risk? Federal regulations in place since 1991 provide that "minimal risk means that the probability and magnitude of harm or discomfort anticipated in the research are not greater in and of themselves than those ordinarily encountered in daily life or during the performance of routine physical or psychological examinations or tests." 45 C.F.R. §46.102(j). Is this the definition used by the *Grimes* court? Why didn't the *Grimes* court consider the risk to be minimal, given that children who live in older housing frequently are exposed to the risk of lead paint?

The Rule authorizes "expedited" review (by the IRB chair or one more designated members) for "certain kinds of research involving no more than minimal risk, and for minor changes in approved research." 45 C.F.R. §46.110 (noting that the Secretary of DHHS has published a "list of categories of research that may be reviewed by the IRB through an expedited review procedure" and that "the Secretary will evaluate the list at least every 8 years").

4. *Institutional Review Boards (IRBs).* Under federal law, the membership of an IRB is supposed to be diverse and professionally knowledgeable about research proposals and research ethics. 45 C.F.R. §46.107. IRBs that regularly consider research proposals involving vulnerable subjects should consider including "one or more individuals who are knowledgeable about and experienced in working with these

subjects." Id. The IRB must include at least one member who is unaffiliated with the institution. IRB members may not participate in the review of a research project in which they have a conflict of interest. Id.

The *Grimes* court was skeptical about the independence of IRBs. Commentators have raised many questions about the ability of potentially overworked and conflicted IRBs to safeguard research subjects. The federal government implemented expanded oversight of IRBs in 2009. 45 C.F.R. §46.501-.505. Some of the provisions found in the new Common Rule were designed to allow IRBs to focus attention on higher risk studies. Other mechanisms designed to protect the safety of research subjects include reporting requirements for adverse events and the use of data and safety monitoring committees.

5. *Informed Consent in Research.* The federal regulations focus on the informed consent process as the major tool for protecting human subjects. The informed consent rules are much more detailed in some areas than common-law rules but do not preempt those laws. 45 C.F.R. §46.116. Note that federal law prohibits research sponsors from requiring waivers of liability for negligence. Id. Examine the informed consent form excerpted in the *Grimes* decision: In what way(s) was it deficient?

The Common Rule includes "general," "basic," and "additional" consent requirements. "General" informed consent provisions require (with various exceptions) that (1) human subjects or their legal representatives must provide consent; (2) investigators should ensure that subjects have "sufficient opportunity to discuss and consider" participation and should "minimize the possibility of coercion or undue influence"; (3) information should be provided in "understandable language"; and (4) the information should include what "a reasonable person would want to have in order to make an informed decision . . . and an opportunity to discuss that information." 45 C.F.R. §46.116(a). New provisions also require that, for most forms of consent, the process "begin with a concise and focused presentation of the key information that is most likely to assist a prospective subject . . . in understanding the reasons why one might or might not want to participate in the research. This part of the informed consent must be presented in a way that facilitates comprehension." Id. at §46.116(a)(5). The consent as a whole must provide sufficient detail within an organizational structure that "facilitates the prospective subject's . . . understanding." Id.

The Common Rule establishes "basic elements" of informed consent that should be provided for research not covered by an exception. The basic elements include the purposes of the research, a description of reasonably foreseeable risks and benefits, a disclosure of appropriate alternative procedures or treatments, notice of confidentiality protections, an explanation regarding the availability of compensation for any injuries, contact information for the project, and notice that participation is voluntary. Id. at §46.116(b). In addition, for research involving private information or biospecimens, the consent must include one of two options: "(i) A statement that identifiers might be removed from the identifiable private information or identifiable biospecimens and that, after such removal, the information or biospecimens could be used for future research studies or distributed to another investigator for future research studies without additional informed consent from the subject or the legally authorized representative, if this might be a possibility; or (ii) A statement that the subject's information or biospecimens collected as part of the research, even if identifiers are removed, will not be used or distributed for future research studies." Id. at at §46.116(b)(9).

The Common Rule also includes "additional elements of consent" that are to be provided for research not carried out under one of the Rule's exceptions. Id. at §46.116(c). For example, where appropriate, the consent should include language indicating that the research may involve unforeseeable risks. The new Rule makes some significant additions to this list of potentially required disclosures in areas that had previously created controversy and concern. For example, the consent must provide "[a] statement that the subject's biospecimens (even if identifiers are removed) may be used for commercial profit and whether the subject will or will not share in this commercial profit." Id. at §46.116(c)(7). Where relevant, the new Rule also requires statements about the circumstances, if any, in which "clinically relevant research results, including individual research results, will be disclosed to subjects." Id. at §46.116(c)(8). Potential subjects must also be told whether research involving biospecimens "will or might include whole genome sequencing." Id. at §46.116(c)(9).

Finally, the Common Rule now requires "one IRB-approved informed consent form used to enroll subjects" be posted on a publicly accessible Web site for clinical trials that are "conducted or supported by a Federal department or agency." 45 C.F.R. §46.116(h). This provision will dramatically improve transparency regarding the informed consent process and could result in the development and recognition of model provisions that could reduce the costs of compliance for researchers.

6. *Exceptions to the Regular Informed Consent Principles.* There are a number of important exceptions to the Common Rule's general, basic, and additional informed consent provisions, three of which will be briefly summarized here:

a. *The "Broad Consent" Option.* The new Common Rule offers researchers the option of seeking broad consent for the storage, maintenance, and secondary research use of identifiable private information or identifiable biospecimens (collected for either research studies other than the proposed research or nonresearch purposes). Research carried out using the broad consent provisions that meets certain other requirements, including adequate protection to protect the privacy of subjects and the confidentiality of the data, see §46.111(a)(7), may be found to be exempt under 45 C.F.R. 46.104(d)(8). The broad consent process includes a small subset of the general, basic, and additional consent rules described in Note 5 (e.g., notices regarding the possibility of commercialization or the use of whole genome sequencing) along with seven separate requirements targeting key issues in the use of biospecimens. 45 C.F.R. §46.116(d).

b. *The General Waiver or Alteration of Consent Rule.* The Common Rule permits IRBs to waive or alter consent requirements in certain circumstances. 45 C.F.R. §46.116(f). Before waiving or altering the requirements, the IRB must determine and document that: "(i) The research involves no more than minimal risk to the subjects; (ii) The research could not practicably be carried out without the requested waiver or alteration; (iii) If the research involves using identifiable private information or identifiable biospecimens, the research could not practicably be carried out without using such information or biospecimens in an identifiable format; (iv) The waiver or alteration will not adversely affect the rights and welfare of the subjects; and (v) Whenever appropriate, the subjects or legally authorized representatives will be provided with additional pertinent information after participation." Id. at

§46.116(f)(3). An IRB cannot waive consent for storage, maintenance, or secondary research with identifiable private information or biospecimens where individuals have already declined to provide broad consent. Id. §46.116(f)(1). An IRB approving alteration of some of the consent requirements must still adhere to the general consent requirements (45 C.F.R. §46.116(a)), and, where broad consent is at issue (45 C.F.R. §46.116(d)), may not alter any of the specific broad consent requirements established in the Rule.

　　c. *The Screening or Recruiting Rule.* The Common Rule also authorizes IRBs to permit researchers to "obtain information or biospecimens for the purpose of screening, recruiting, or determining the eligibility of prospective subjects without informed consent" if (1) the researchers "obtain information through oral or written communication with the prospective subject or . . . representative"; or (2) the researchers will obtain the information "by accessing records or stored biospecimens." 45 C.F.R. §46.116(g). Consent must be carried out and documented in accordance with 45 C.F.R. §46.117.

　　7. *Research Involving Biospecimens.* Assume that you are a researcher hoping to use biospecimens in research. Would you be likely to use the Common Rule's much discussed, new broad consent provisions? Or, would you prefer to secure waiver of the consent requirements or de-identification of the biospecimens? See Holly Fernandez Lynch & Michelle Meyer, Hastings Center Rep. 3 (May-June 2017) (arguing that use of broad consent provisions will be limited in light of other mechanisms available within the Rule).

　　The new Common Rule provisions regarding biospecimens defer for the time being a major area of debate involving the "identifiability" of biospecimens, that is, whether most biospecimens are inherently identifiable as they contain genetic material that is uniquely associated with a particular individual. The early drafts of the revised rules would have treated non-identified biospecimens the same as identified biospecimens, considering both to be research involving human subjects. That proposal proved very controversial, as the following explains:

> [T]he use of existing (left over from clinical care or earlier research) human biospecimens (and associated data) traditionally has been deemed not to be human subjects research under the Common Rule if the identity of the subject may not readily be ascertained by the investigator, and to be exempt from most forms of regulatory oversight if the specimens or data are themselves identifiable but information is recorded by the investigator in a non-identifiable manner. This is because the framers of the Common Rule felt confident that these mechanisms of segregating specimens and data from identifiers were adequate to protect any interests of the individuals from which they were derived. Any risk, such as the remote risk of re-identification, was small in comparison to the promise of scientific and medical advances that depended upon the specimens.
>
> 　　Today, this is a matter of considerable controversy. On one hand, technological advances, such as whole-genome sequencing and increasing access to big data, have made it possible for a scientist with access to both sophisticated equipment and a reference key to take an otherwise unidentified human biospecimen and re-identify it using the unique data gleaned from a person's DNA. Although such equipment is expensive and not widely available, and there is no universal reference key of everyone's DNA, the potential for unauthorized re-identification has caused some to argue that there is a pervasive and unavoidable risk of "informational harm" to specimen sources that requires a tightening of the rules. Those

who want more restrictions are concerned about protecting individual liberties and most importantly privacy, and want to maximize the principle of autonomy.

On the other hand are those who advocate for fewer restrictions on and greater sharing of biospecimens and data to maximize their utility in solving important problems. This camp is a mix of scientists, ethicists, and disease-oriented patient advocates, each of whom views the risks of unauthorized re-identification as relatively small and better addressed through penalties for violations rather than tighter restrictions that could impede important scientific progress. People who want fewer restrictions on use of biospecimens typically believe that a more communitarian approach to research will increase beneficence and justice.

Despite the lack of consensus around these issues, millions of human biospecimens are collected and stored each year. Most are obtained during routine clinical encounters with patients for diagnostic and treatment purposes, while a minority are collected with explicit research intent following informed consent by a donor. Regardless of the circumstances, it is not possible to know with certainty at the time of collection all the possible future uses for which a specimen could be of value. Thus, the only way to guarantee full informed consent would be to re-approach donors each time a new use is imagined (which notably is not even possible once a specimen has been de-identified). Science is evolving more quickly than our regulatory procedures can accommodate. A permissive stance would be to allow unforeseen future uses without obtaining new, specific consent unless there is an obvious risk of harm, on the premise that such uses might contribute to important medical discoveries. A conservative approach would be to discard biospecimens immediately following the original use for which they were collected to avoid even the appearance of violating donor's expectations. The current regulatory approach—maintained following revisions finalized in 2017 . . . —requires consent from the specimen source only for the active collection of specimens and data for research use, and for the secondary use of only identified specimens and data. In light of technological advancement and changing patient attitudes, however, the challenge is how best to balance the importance of protecting individual interests against the value of promoting the good of the larger human community.

The federal agencies that oversee human subjects research made an attempt to address this challenge by proposing a major revision to the research rules in 2015 via a Notice of Proposed Rule Making (NPRM) to amend the Common Rule. . . . The NPRM proposed an approach on one side of the spectrum of possibilities and generated substantial dialogue regarding the best path forward. . . .

In particular, the NPRM proposed to expand the definition of the term "human subject" to include a living individual about whom the investigator "obtains, uses, studies, or analyzes biospecimens" even when those biospecimens have been stripped of all the traditional pieces of identifying information. The presumption underlying this proposal was that all genetic material can potentially serve as a unique personal identifier—if not now, then in the relatively near future. The proposal also was based on the notion that individuals have greater autonomy interests in controlling their biospecimens than previously had been acknowledged. The consequence of this regulatory redefinition would be that secondary research with de-identified biospecimens would no longer be permissible without some form of consent, a dramatic change from the status quo. Under the NPRM's proposal, that consent could be "broad," applying to future unspecified use, rather than specific for each study, but the conditions for waiver of consent for biospecimen research would have been dramatically tightened, such that waiver would become "rare."

Suzanne M. Rivera, Barbara E. Bierer, Holly Fernandez Lynch & I. Glenn Cohen, Introduction, in Specimen Science 5-8 (Holly Fernandez Lynch et al. eds. 2017).

Based on numerous comments, the final revised Common Rule reverted to regarding non-identified biospecimens as not constituting "human subjects," meaning that no consent or even IRB review is required, but the issue of what constitutes identifiability remains unresolved. The final Rule requires regulatory agencies, alongside relevant experts, to reexamine the Rule's definition of "identifiable private information" and "identifiable biospecimen" within one year and thereafter at least every four years. Research involving "whole genome sequencing" is likely to be caught up in this review process.

8. *The Role of Randomized Clinical Trials (RCTs) and Placebos.* The randomized clinical trial is a core feature of biomedical research. In an RCT, research subjects are randomly assigned to receive the treatment under study or to receive another form of treatment or, in some cases, no treatment or a placebo. The Common Rule recognizes the use of placebos. 45 C.F.R. §46.102(b) (definition of "clinical trial" includes possible placebo use). From an ethical standpoint, an RCT is justified when there is "clinical equipoise," that is, when the differential benefits of the various forms of treatment or non-treatment are not known or are roughly the same. The legitimacy of equipoise has been challenged, in part because of concerns that it is difficult to know when equipoise truly exists. See, e.g., Franklin G. Miller & Stephen Joffe, Equipoise and the Dilemma of Randomized Clinical Trials, 364 New Eng. J. Med. 476 (2011).

Concerns about RCTs are particularly acute in medical research involving placebos, where some level of patient deception about treatment is inherent in the research design. Does the problem of deception run both ways? Should researchers be able to bring claims against research participants who deceive researchers in order to become eligible to participate in trials? Cf. Rebecca Dresser, Subversive Subjects: Rule Breaking and Deception in Clinical Trials, 41 J.L. Med. & Ethics 829 (2013); David B. Resnik & David J. McCann, Deception by Research Participants, 373 New Eng. J. Med. 1192 (2015).

9. *The Aftermath of* Grimes. The *Grimes* decision was understandably controversial. Imagine how medical researchers might feel about a decision that appears to compare a research study sponsored by the federal government and conducted by a leading research institution with Nazi war crimes. The *Grimes* decision sparked a number of commentaries, including Lainie Friedman Ross, In Defense of the Hopkins Lead Abatement Studies, 30 J.L. Med. & Ethics 50 (2002). See also L. Song Richardson, When Human Experimentation Is Criminal, 99 J. Crim. L. & Criminology 89 (2009) (arguing that medical researchers who "conduct experiments on individuals without their knowledge" or who "deliberately fail to disclose to individuals the known and obvious risks of participation in an experiment" should face criminal punishment).

What did the court actually hold in *Grimes?* The lengthy opinion (more than 70 pages, heavily edited here) explores the broad terrain of human subjects research and appears to hold that (1) parents/surrogates cannot consent to the participation of their children/incompetents in nontherapeutic research where there is any risk of injury or damage to the health of the subject; (2) informed consent agreements in nontherapeutic research trials may create "special relationships," and violation of the agreements may be addressed in breach of contract and negligence; and (3) other sources of the "special relationship" include the researcher-subject relationship itself and governmental research regulations. How much does the court majority take back in the per curiam opinion rejecting reconsideration? The court suggests that the parties are free to present evidence on any of these issues. What evidence would you present for either side? The Maryland courts have subsequently considered a number of claims arising from lead-related research carried out in Baltimore in the 1990s. See, e.g., Smith v. Kennedy Krieger Institute, 2017 WL 1076481 (Md. Ct. App. 2017) (affirming a jury verdict in favor of Kennedy Krieger Institute on claims); and Ward v. White v. Kennedy Krieger Institute, Inc 110 A.3d 724 (Md. Ct. App. 2015) (fraudulent and negligent misrepresentation claims must fail as a matter of law as "lead safe" houses were not presented as "lead free"; institution accurately described lead in homes and did not engage in unfair or deceptive trade practices).

10. *Litigating Claims of Research-Related Harms.* There have been a relatively small number of lawsuits involving experimental medicine using either negligence or informed consent theories, despite the huge volume of activity involving research subjects. A few courts have considered whether clinical trial sponsors owe a fiduciary duty to participants. See, e.g., Suthers v. Amgen Inc., 441 F. Supp. 2d 478 (S.D.N.Y. 2006) (plaintiffs' complaint dismissed in case challenging drug company's decision to terminate clinical trial and deny access to experimental drug; no fiduciary duty owed); and Abney v. Amgen Inc., 443 F.3d 540 (6th Cir. 2006) (no fiduciary duty as the clinical trial sponsors were not acting primarily for the benefit of the participants).

11. *Incidental Findings.* Should researchers have any obligation to inform patients about "incidental findings," such as health issues discovered unexpectedly during the course of research, e.g., tumors discovered during scans for other purposes, or genetic anomalies discovered during testing for something else? Among the "additional elements" for informed consent established in the new Common Rule is a requirement that researchers provide information about whether, and under what conditions, clinically relevant research results will be disclosed to the subjects. 45 C.F.R. §§46.116(c)(8). How should this process be handled in research that might involve biobanks and other forms of archived data sets that may have been collected long ago? Should there be a duty to inform patients that is enforceable under state law? Should different rules apply to international research? Should there be an obligation to inform research subjects if later research reveals that a particular genetic finding is associated with heightened risks to health? Cf. Reed E. Pyeritz, The Coming Explosion in Genetic Testing—Is There a Duty to Recontact?, 365 New Eng. J. Med. 1367 (2011).

12. *Conflicts of Interest.* The *Grimes* court repeatedly expressed concerns about the conflicts of interest between human subjects and researchers. Researchers may have a financial interest in the subject matter of their research that puts their research subjects at risk or affects the reliability of research results. See *Moore,* supra and note 3 at page 240. News stories regularly reveal shocking conflicts of interest that can jeopardize patient safety and the integrity of research results. A number of influential organizations and scholars have focused on methods of identifying and limiting conflicts of interest between researchers and research subjects. See, e.g., Bernard Lo & Marilyn J. Field eds., Conflict of Interest in Medical Research, Education, and Practice (Institute of Medicine, 2009).

Federal regulations require covered institutions to put in place a conflicts of interest policy that includes a requirement that researchers report, and make publicly accessible, significant financial interests (generally $5,000 or more) "that could directly and significantly affect the design, conduct, or reporting of PHS [Public Health Service]-funded research." 42 C.F.R. §50.601-50.607. The Affordable Care

Act includes provisions requiring manufacturers of drugs, biologics, and medical devices to report payments to physicians. 42 U.S.C.A. §1320a-7h; 42 C.F.R. §403.904.

13. *The Economic Interests of Clinical Research Subjects.* As noted above, the Common Rule's consent provisions require that subjects be notified about the possibility that identified or de-identified biospecimens will be used for commercial profit and whether the subject will share in that profit. 45 C.F.R. §46.116(c)(7). Should clinical research subjects share in the economic value of discoveries? The ownership issue, famously raised in Moore v. Regents of the University of California, 793 P.2d 479 (Cal. 1990), supra, at page 229, resurfaced in Washington University v. Catalona, 490 F.3d 667 (8th Cir. 2007). The case arose when a researcher at Washington University accepted a position elsewhere and sought donor consent to take biological specimens that had been donated for research with him to his new position. Universities were keenly interested in the case due to fears that research biobanks would be severely restricted if donor-patients could control the use of their donated tissues. The district court found for the university and the court of appeals agreed, holding that "individuals who make an informed decision to contribute their biological materials voluntarily to a particular research institution for the purpose of medical research" do not "retain an ownership interest allowing the individuals to direct or authorize the transfer of such materials to a third party." 490 F.3d at 673.

The economic interests of research subjects have also been debated in the domain of intellectual property law. See, e.g., Greenberg v. Miami Children's Hospital Research Institute, Inc., 264 F. Supp. 2d 1064 (S.D. Fla. 2003) (dismissing all but unjust enrichment claims brought by families whose samples had been used to develop a genetic test for Canavan's Disease). See also Eliot Marshall, Genetic Testing: Families Sue Hospital, Scientist for Control of Canavan Gene, 290 Science 1062 (2000); Charlotte H. Harrison, Neither *Moore* nor the Market: Alternative Models for Compensating Contributors of Human Tissue, 28 Am. J.L. & Med. 77 (2002).

14. *Research on Vulnerable Populations.* As Professor Richard Garnett notes, much of the controversy in human research has surrounded projects involving groups viewed as particularly vulnerable to coercion or abuse. Historically, the Common Rule addressed the need to ensure equity in the selection of research subjects while being mindful of the risks of research involving "children, prisoners, pregnant women, mentally disabled persons, or economically or educationally disadvantaged persons." 45 C.F.R. §46.111(3) (pre-revision). The revised Rule continues this basic approach while shifting the focus of attention to "subjects who are vulnerable to coercion or undue influence, such as children, prisoners, individuals with impaired decision-making capacity, or economically or educationally disadvantaged persons." Id. (as of January 2018). Where research involves members of vulnerable groups, the study should include additional safeguards to protect the rights and welfare of these subjects. Id. In Parts B–D of the DHHS human subjects have not yet been amended to reflect this new focus, though revisions are anticipated. See 45 C.F.R. §46.201-.207(subpart B pregnant women, neonates, and fetuses), prisoners (subpart C, §46.301-.306), and children (subpart D, §46.401-.409).

Somewhat counterintuitively, the focus on vulnerability is also reflected in concerns about exclusion. Commentators have criticized the failure of medical researchers to include children, women, and members of minority groups in research protocols. Exclusion can be harmful when, for example, conditions particularly affecting disadvantaged or vulnerable groups simply aren't studied or where the exclusion of certain categories of research subjects results in failures to identify possible differences in treatment effectiveness across the population. There are a number of federal initiatives to encourage the inclusion of children, women, minorities, and others in research trials.

a. *Children and Pregnant Women.* The use of children in research presents special problems because the only "consent" available is parental consent, and because the risks of research many may not be fully known or understood. Federal regulations provide special protections for children serving as research subjects. See 45 C.F.R. §§46.401-.409 (DHHS regulations); 21 C.F.R. §§50.50-.56 (FDA regulations). Although pregnant women are no longer automatically considered to be "vulnerable" subjects under the Common Rule, Part B currently still retains specific protections for pregnant women, fetuses, and neonates. 45 C.F.R. §§46.201-.207.

There are conflicting objectives of scientific research involving children: (1) ensuring that children benefit from the progress in medical care made possible by such research and (2) minimizing the risks to children from their participation in scientific research. Many drugs have been tested only in adults, leaving physicians to choose between denying children access to potentially useful medications and guessing about the correct dosage for pediatric use. Congress has become very involved in the issue. The FDA Web site includes a collection of material on pediatric issues, www.fda.gov/cder/pediatric/. Most of the commentaries on research involving children assume the existence of an underlying disease or condition that the research seeks to address. Should research on human enhancement, such as through the use of drugs to improve memory or intelligence, be governed by similar rules? See Maxwell J. Mehlman & Jessica W. Berg, Human Subjects Protections in Biomedical Enhancement Research: Assessing Risk and Benefit and Obtaining Informed Consent, 36 J.L. Med. & Ethics 546 (2008).

b. *Patients with Life-Threatening Illnesses.* Research is an important issue for persons with terminal conditions. Where the current, tested treatments are ineffective, people are often tempted to view "research" as providing the best treatment. They may be particularly vulnerable to coercion and the implicit promises and hopes offered by researchers. On the other hand, of course, research in these areas is extremely important for current and future patients. See, e.g., Michael Malinowski, Throwing Dirt on Doctor Frankenstein's Grave: Access to Experimental Treatments at the End of Life, 65 Hastings L.J. 615 (2014); Jerry Menikoff, The Vulnerability of the Very Sick, 37 J.L. Med. & Ethics 51 (2009).

c. *Individuals with Impaired Decisionmaking Capacity.* Similar concerns exist about whether surrogates can give consent for research on patients with impaired decisionmaking capacity, with the additional concern about who is an appropriate surrogate.

d. *Prisoners.* Should prisoners be permitted to participate in research, even when they "consent"? DHHS regulations provide special protections for prisoners. See 45 C.F.R. §§46.301-.306; and https://humansubjects.nih.gov/prisoners. The special rules require, for example, that a majority of the IRB members have no other association with the prison and that one member be a prisoner or prisoner representative. Another provision requires assurance that parole boards will not take the prisoner's participation into account; prisoners must also be informed of this policy.

15. *Emergency Research.* FDA regulations permit research experimentation on patients who have not consented, personally or through surrogates, in certain circumstances. Under the Rule, an independent physician and an IRB must agree that the clinical trial concerns a life-threatening condition and that there is no proven,

available treatment; that obtaining consent is not feasible; that the research cannot be carried out in another manner; and that the risks and benefits of the experimental procedure are reasonable under the circumstances. 21 C.F.R. §50.24. The emergency research regulations are somewhat controversial because they explicitly abandon the Nuremberg Code's requirement of informed consent. See Nuremberg Code, available at http://ohsr.od.nih.gov/guidelines/nuremberg.html. Some commentators also maintain that these regulations allow research that has no therapeutic benefit for the immediate patient since they include patients who are near death with no hope of recovery.

16. *Research in Other Countries.* As noted above, many trials are conducted in whole or part in countries outside the United States. Cf. ClinicalTrials.gov (listing nearly 150,000 studies located in 200 countries outside of the United States as of September 2017). Proponents of this research argue that it is increasingly difficult to manage drug trials and to recruit a statistically meaningful number of study subjects in the United States and other high income countries. Yet, as noted in the beginning of this section, the history of medical research suggests a need to guard against the risks of exploitation and abuse. Foreign jurisdictions thus have a strong interest in local regulation. For efforts to address alleged abuses through U.S. courts, see Abdullahi v. Pfizer, 562 F.3d 163 (2d Cir. 2009) (permitting claims under Alien Tort Statute, which alleged violation of customary international law norms regarding consent to medical experimentation); and Estate of Alvarez v. Johns Hopkins Univ., 205 F. Supp.3d 681 (D. Md. 2016) (affirming dismissal of claims arising from nonconsensual medical experimentation in Guatemala).

What rules should apply to human subjects research conducted outside the United States by companies affiliated with U.S. companies, or where the study results will be used to seek approval to market a drug in the United States? These concerns gained additional public attention in 2011 with the release of a report by the Presidential Commission for the Study of Bioethical Issues, Research Across Borders, which considered the protections offered to participants in research supported by the federal government and carried out in countries around the world.

The Common Rule applies to federally funded research wherever it is carried out; any applicable foreign laws or regulations "that provide additional protections to human subjects of research" are not preempted. 45 C.F.R. §46.101(f). See also, 21 C.F.R. §50.1(the FDA's protection of human subjects extends to "all clinical investigations regulated by the [FDA under provisions of the Federal Food, Drug, and Cosmetic Act], as well as clinical investigations that support applications for research or marketing permits for products regulated by the [FDA]"). International standards are also important. The CIOMS and Declaration of Helsinki standards offer somewhat different approaches to key issues such as openness to the inclusion of vulnerable subjects in research and the types of community benefits that should be integrated into research projects carried out in moderate- or low-resources countries. Johannes J.M. van Delden & Rieke van de Graaf, Revised CIOMS International Ethical Guidelines for Health-Related Research Involving Humans, 317 JAMA 135 (2017); Joseph Millum, David Wendler & Ezekiel J. Emanuel, The 50th Anniversary of the Declaration of Helsinki: Progress but Many Remaining Challenges, 310 JAMA 2143 (2013).

17. *Resources and Commentaries.* The DHHS's Office for Human Research Protections maintains a Web site with links **to key federal regulations and documents**; www.hhs.gov/ohrp/. Important books on human subjects research in addition to

those noted above include Baruch A. Brody, The Ethics of Biomedical Research: An International Perspective (1998); Claire Foster, The Ethics of Medical Research on Humans (2001); Jerry Menikoff & Edward P. Richards, What the Doctor Didn't Say: The Hidden Truth About Medical Research (2006).

For influential **criticisms of human subjects research**, see the articles cited in *Grimes* and George J. Annas, Questing for Grails: Duplicity, Betrayal and Self-Deception in Research, 12 J. Contemp. Health L. & Pol'y 297 (1996); Carl Elliot, Whatever Happened to Human Experimentation?, Hastings Center Rep. 8 (Jan.-Feb. 2016); Christine Grady et al., Informed Consent, 376 New Eng. J. Med. 856-867 (2017) (reviewing challenges and opportunities for novel, e-technology-based informed consent); Jay Katz, Human Experimentation and Human Rights, 38 St. Louis U. L.J. 7 (1993).

For resources or commentaries on **the revised Common Rule**, see (in addition to the sources cited above) James G. Hodge & Lawrence O. Gostin, Revamping the US Federal Common Rule: Modernizing Human Participant Research Regulations, 317 JAMA 1521 (2017); I. Glenn Cohen & Holly Fernandez Lynch, Human Subjects Research Regulation: Perspectives on the Future (MIT Press 2014); Barbara E. Bierer Mark Barnes & Holly Fernandez Lynch, Revised "Common Rule" Shapes Protections for Research Participants, 36 Health Affairs 784 (2017); and Jerry Menikoff, Julie Kaneshiro & Ivor Pritchard, The Common Rule, Updated, 367 New Eng. J. Med. 613 (2017).

On **safety monitoring** (note 4), see Rachel Berhman Sherman et al., New FDA Regulation to Improve Safety Reporting in Clinical Trials, 365 New Eng. J. Med. 3 (2011); and Charles J. Kowalski & Jan L. Hewett, Data and Safety Monitoring Boards: Some Enduring Questions, 37 J.L. Med. & Ethics 496 (2009).

On the **use of placebos in research** (note 8), compare Clifford J. Rosen & Sundeep Khosia, Placebo-Controlled Trials in Osteoporosis—Proceeding with Caution, 363 New Eng. J. Med. 1365 (2010), with C. Michael Stein & Wayne A. Ray, The Ethics of Placebo in Studies with Fracture End Points in Osteoporosis, 363 New Eng. J. Med. 1367 (2010). See also S.L. Niemansburg et al., Reconsidering the Ethics of Sham Interventions in an Era of Emerging Technologies, 157 Surgery 801 (2015); Elana A. Bertam, How Current Informed Consent Protocols Flunk the Sham Surgery Test: A New Frontier in Medicine and Ethics, 14 Quinnipiac Health L.J. 131 (2010).

On **claims for research-related harms** (note 10), see Valerie Gutmann Koch, A Private Right of Action for Informed Consent in Research, 45 Seton Hall L. Rev. 173 (2015); Paul B. Miller & Charles Weijer, Fiduciary Obligation in Clinical Research, 34 J.L. Med. & Ethics 424 (2006); E. Haavi Morreim, The Clinical Investigator as Fiduciary: Discarding a Misguided Idea, 33 J.L. Med. & Ethics 586 (2005); E. Haavi Morreim, Litigation in Clinical Research: Malpractice Doctrines Versus Research Realities, 32 J.L. Med. & Ethics 474 (2004).

Regarding how to handle **incidental findings** (note 11), see President's Commission for the Study of Bioethical Issues, Anticipate and Communicate: Ethical Management of Incidental and Secondary Findings in the Clinical, Research, and Direct-to-Consumer Contexts (2013); Lisa Eckstein, Jeremy R. Garrett & Benjamin E. Berkman, A Framework for Analyzing the Ethics of Disclosing Genetic Research Findings, 42 J.L. Med & Ethics 190 (2014); Elizabeth Pike, Karen Rothenberg & Benjamin E. Berkman, Finding Fault? Exploring Legal Duties to Return Incidental Findings in Genomic Research, 102 Geo. L.J. 795 (2014).

On researchers' **conflicts of interest** (note 12), see Barry Meier & Duff Wilson, Spine Experts Repudiate Medtronic Studies, N.Y. Times, June 29, 2011; Special Issue, The Evolving Safety Profile of rhBMP-2 Use in the Spine, 11 Spine J. A1-A14, 463-539 (2011); Robin Fretwell Wilson, The Death of Jesse Gelsinger: New Evidence of the Influence of Money and Prestige in Human Research, 36 Am. J.L. & Med. 295-325 (2010); Symposium, Dangerous Liaisons? Industry Relations with Health Professionals, 37 J.L. Med. & Ethics 398-460 (2009); Stacey A. Tovino, Conflicts of Interest in Medicine, Research, and Law: A Comparison, 117 Penn. St. L. Rev. 1291 (2013); Bernard Lo & Marilyn J. Field eds., Conflict of Interest in Medical Research, Education, and Practice (Institute of Medicine, 2009); Robert Steinbrook, Controlling Conflict of Interest—Proposals from the Institute of Medicine, 360 New Eng. J. Med. 2160 (2009); Kevin P. Weinfurt, Disclosure of Financial Relationships to Participants in Clinical Research, 361 New Eng. J. Med. 916 (2009).

Regarding **research on vulnerable populations** (note 14), see Joseph Millum, David Wendler & Ezekiel J. Emanuel, The 50th Anniversary of the Declaration of Helsinki: Progress but Many Remaining Challenges, 310 JAMA 2143 (2013) (noting revised Declaration's greater openness to research involving vulnerable populations but critiquing limitations); Michelle Goodwin, Vulnerable Subjects: Why Does Informed Consent Matter?, 44 J.L. Med. & Ethics 371 (2016); and Symposium, Vulnerability in Biomedical Research, 37 J.L. Med. & Ethics 6-82 (2009). With regard to **children**, see Kristien Hens et al., Children and Biobanks: A Review of the Ethical and Legal Discussion, 130 Hum. Genet. 403 (2011); Valarie Blake et al., Harmonization of Ethics Policies in Pediatric Research, 39 J.L. Med. & Ethics 70 (2011); Ruqaiijah Yearby, Missing the "Target": Preventing the Unjust Inclusion of Vulnerable Children for Medical Research Studies, 42 Amer. J.L. & Med. 797 (2016). Regarding **people with impairments,** see Benedict Carey, An N.Y.U. Study Gone Wrong, and a Top Researcher Dismissed, New York Times, June 27, 2016 (discussing study at psychiatric research center); Carl H. Coleman, Research with Decisionally Incapacitated Human Subjects: An Argument for a Systemic Approach to Risk-Benefit Assessment, 83 Ind. L.J. 743 (2008); P. C. Candia & A. C. Barba, Mental Capacity and Consent to Treatment in Psychiatric Patients: The State of the Research, 24 Curr Opin Psychiatry 442 (2011).

On **making research more inclusive** (note 14), see NIH Human Subjects Policies and Guidance; P. Kanakamedala & S. Haga, Characterization of Clinical Study Populations by Race and Ethnicity in Biomedical Literature, 22 Ethn. Dis. 96 (2012) (though increasingly common, "reporting of race/ethnicity of study populations is relatively low, ambiguous, and inconsistent"); Marianne J. Legato, Paula A. Johnson & JoAnne E. Manson, Consideration of Sex Differences in Medicine to Improve Health Care and Patient Outcomes, 316 JAMA 1865 (2016); and Special Issue, Research Ethics and Minority Populations 103 Am. J. Pub. Health 2118-2199, 2207-2251 (2013). With regard to **women**, see Sara F. Goldkind et al., Enrolling Pregnant Women in Research—Lessons from the H1N1 Influenza Epidemic, 362 New Eng. J. Med. 2241 (2010); Anna C. Mastroianni at al., Research with Pregnant Women, Hastings Center Rep 38 (May-June 2017).

On **research in emergency settings** (note 15), see Gail H. Javitt, Old Legacies and New Paradigms: Confusing "Research" and "Treatment" and Its Consequences in Responding to Emergent Health Threats, 8 J. Health Care L. & Pol'y 38 (2005); Richard S. Saver, Critical Care Research and Informed Consent, 75 N.C. L. Rev. 205

(1996); Symposium, In Case of Emergency: No Need for Consent, 27(1) Hastings Center Rep. 7-12 (1997). See also Ian Roberts et al., Effect of Consent Rituals on Mortality in Emergency Care Research, 377 Lancet 1071 (2011) (arguing that UK rules can be unethical if "consent rituals delay the start of a trial treatment such that the treatment effect could be reduced or obscured").

Discussing research **internationally, including in developing countries** (note 16), see M.K. Mallath & T. Chawla, Investigators' Viewpoint of Clinical Trials in India: Past, Present and Future, 8 Perspect. Clin. Res. 31 (2017); Gerard Porter, Regulating Clinical Trials in India: The Economics of Ethics, __ Dev. World Bioeth. __ (2017); Dennis M. Coyne, International Pharmaceutical Mistrials: Existing Law for the Protection of Human Subjects and a Proposal for Reform, 29 B. U. Int'l L.J. 427 (2011); Darby Hull, Reining in the Commercialized Foreign Clinical Trial, 36 J. Leg. Med. 367 (2015); World Medical Association Declaration of Helsinki: Ethical Principles for Medical Research Involving Human Subjects, 310 JAMA 2191 (2013); and Paul Ndebele, The Declaration of Helsinki, 50 Years Later, 310 JAMA 2145 (2013).

Problem: The SUPPORT Trial

New concerns have arisen about the appropriateness of informed consent procedures for research at least arguably falling with the standard of care. Consider the following facts:

The University of Alabama at Birmingham was the lead study site for a national clinical research trial known as the Surfactant, Positive Pressure, and Oxygenation Randomized Trial ("SUPPORT"). Designed by Dr. Carlo and approved by the IBR Defendants, the SUPPORT study was created to analyze the effects of differing oxygen saturation levels on premature infants. At the time of the study, it was nationally accepted (and neither party contests) that the recognized standard of care was to keep the oxygen saturation levels of low-birth-weight infants at between 85% and 95%. This standard notwithstanding, it was also known that a prolonged period of high oxygen saturation can result in oxygen toxicity which leads to an increased risk of "retinopathy of prematurity".[1] On the other hand, a prolonged period of low oxygen saturation can result in neuro-developmental impairment and death. Given the difficulties of calibrating the optimal oxygen range, the SUPPORT study sought to determine whether, within the accepted standard of care, there was a more precise range of oxygen saturation that would better reduce the risk of exposing an infant to either too much or too little oxygen.

The SUPPORT study randomly divided eligible and enrolled premature infants into two groups. One group was to be kept at an oxygen saturation level between 85-89%, which is the low end of the standard-of-care range, while the other would be kept at an oxygen saturation level between 90-95%, which is the high end of that range. Further, to ensure double-blind data collection, the study would

---

1. Retinopathy of prematurity is a disease that occurs in premature babies. It causes abnormal blood vessels to grow in the retina, and can lead to the retina detaching from the back of the eye, resulting in blindness.

employ specialized oximeters . . . that would "mask" to an onlooker the true oxygen saturation levels of the infants. The oximeters would, however, signal an alarm whenever an infant's oxygen level strayed below 85% or above 95%.

Publishing the results of the study in the New England Journal of Medicine, the study authors concluded that infants in the high-oxygen group were more likely to be diagnosed with retinopathy while infants in the low-oxygen group were more likely to die. There was no statistically significant difference in the incidence of neuro-developmental impairments between the high and low groups.

To enroll in the study, Plaintiffs' guardians had to execute informed consent documents that were drafted and approved by Defendants. After the study's completion, however, the Department of Health and Human Services authored a letter questioning whether these informed consent documents had properly disclosed all of the risks associated with enrollment in the SUPPORT study.

Plaintiffs filed the operative Fifth Amended Complaint in the United States District Court for the Northern District of Alabama asserting claims against Defendants for negligence, negligence per se, breach of fiduciary duty, products liability, and lack of informed consent. Plaintiffs allege that they suffered serious injuries as a result of their participation in the study. Specifically, Plaintiffs Lewis and Malone were assigned to the low-oxygen group, with prolonged periods of low oxygen saturation being associated with neuro-developmental impairment and death. Fortunately, neither infant died, but they did develop neurological issues. Plaintiff Collins was assigned to the high-oxygen group, with prolonged high-oxygen saturation being associated with retinopathy, which can lead to blindness. Plaintiff Collins did develop retinopathy, but fortunately he did not suffer permanent vision loss. Following discovery, Defendants moved for summary judgment asserting that, based on the undisputed material facts, Plaintiffs had failed to demonstrate that participation in the SUPPORT study had caused the injuries alleged in the Complaint. The district court agreed that Plaintiffs had failed to prove that their injuries were caused by participation in the SUPPORT study, as opposed to being a consequence of their premature births.

Looney v. Moore, 861 F.3d 1303, 1306-07 (11th Cir. 2017). The Court of Appeals certified a question to the Alabama Supreme Court regarding whether state law required proof of injury in an informed consent case.

Are you troubled by any aspects of the research trial? The consent forms for the research did not alert parents to the known risks of higher or lower levels of oxygen and instead identified "possible skin breakdown at the oximeter site as the only increased risk of participation in the study." Looney v. Moore, 2015 WL 4773747, *3 (N.D. Ala.). Should parents have been informed about the association of higher or lower levels of oxygen with particular types of risks? Should parents have been informed that their children would not receive individualized treatment in the same way that they would have outside the trial and that the caregivers would not know the infants' oxygen saturation level so long as it was within the broad band of the study? See John D. Lantos, Vindication for SUPPORT, 373 New Eng. J. Med. 1393 (2015); Chana A. Sacks & Celestine E. Warren, Foreseeable Risks? Informed Consent for Studies within the Standard of Care, 372 New Eng. J. Med. 306 (2015); Sabrina Tavernise, Premature Babies Study Raises Debate Over Risks and Ethical Consent, New York Times, Sept. 7, 2015; Robin Fretwell Wilson & Robert John Morse, Realizing Informed Consent in Times of Controversy 44 J.L. Med. Ethics 402 (2016).

Problem: Compensation for Research-Related Injuries

Who should bear the risks of research-related injuries: research subjects, researchers, or society more broadly? Would it make sense to require that clinical trials provide some form of insurance coverage or compensation given the risks borne by participants and the benefits accrued by society? What are the barriers or risks of addressing the compensation issue? The Common Rule prohibits waivers of negligence. 45 C.F.R. §46.116(a)(6). Where risks are more than minimal, participants should ordinarily be provided with "an explanation as to whether any compensation and an explanation as to whether any medical treatments are available if injury occurs and, if so, what they consist of, or where further information may be obtained." 45 C.F.R. §46.116(b)(6). The Helsinki Declaration goes further, providing that "[a]ppropriate compensation and treatment for subjects who are harmed as a result of participating in research must be ensured." Helsinki Declaration, 310 JAMA 2191 (2013) (§15). See also, Elizabeth R. Pike, Recovering from Research: A No-Fault Proposal to Compensate Injured Research Participants, 38 Am. J.L. & Med. 7 (2012).

Problem: Medical Research, Biobanks, and the Privacy Rule

This chapter began with an exploration of the special character of medical information and the complex web of privacy regulations designed to give individuals the right to control use of their protected health information. Privacy concerns pervade medical research. How will medical researchers be able to identify potentially appropriate medical research subjects without having access to medical records? How confidential are the records of medical research projects? These issues are growing increasingly complex, in part due to large-scale research involving medical records, biological samples, and genetic testing. The availability of large sets of patient data and biological samples creates the opportunity to carry out new research strategies that hold great promise for identifying causes and cures for human conditions.

Does the Privacy Rule, discussed supra at section B.1, create inordinate barriers to research, particularly research involving large collections of patient data or biobanking? A study by the Institute of Medicine found that the answer was "yes"; the resulting report made a series of recommendations to address the problem. Institute of Medicine, Beyond the HIPAA Privacy Rule: Enhancing Privacy, Improving Health Through Research (2009). The report recommended that HIPAA's Privacy Rule not be applied to research; that PHI related to direct, interventional research with human subjects be regulated under the Common Rule for research; and that "information-based" research (including biobanks) be regulated under a new scheme that would emphasize administrative safeguards rather than requiring patient consent. As one commentator on the report has noted:

> Autonomy and informed consent are vital ethical and legal principles undergirding . . . experimentation on human subjects. But these principles are implicated less strongly, if at all, by data-based health research—research that is becoming more common and more important as more patient data is captured and stored electronically. . . . [T]here is no ethical principle that requires choice as the basis for research involving patient data, especially if identifying information is masked

and the use of the data is subject to strong, substantive security and privacy requirements. Regulatory insistence on choice is quite literally allowing people to die and
suffer unnecessarily without even providing the benefit of aiding privacy.

Fred Cate, Protecting Privacy in Health Research: The Limits of Individual Choice,
98 Cal. L. Rev. 1765, 1802 (2010). For a pointed critique of the IOM Report, see
Mark A. Rothstein, Improve Privacy in Research by Eliminating Informed Consent? IOM Report Misses the Mark, 37 J.L. Med. & Ethics 507 (2009) (The IOM
Report "underestimates the risk to individuals, . . . fail[s] to justify abandonment
of informed consent . . . overvalues researchers' interests . . . [and] overlook[s] the
betrayal of [patient] trust"). Would you support the IOM Report's approach? Do
you think that the Privacy Rule's authorization process is realistic and viable for
large-scale medical records research projects? Do you think that medical records
research conducted without specific patient authorization would injure patient
autonomy and the trust necessary to the treatment relationship? What types of evidence would you need to answer these questions? Professors Cate and Rothstein
cite to a range of evidence to support their positions, from the meaninglessness of
many patient consumer choices, as evidenced by the ubiquitous clicking of "I agree"
to software licensing notices (noted by Professor Cates) to surveys demonstrating
that most people want to decide whether their PHI is used for research (noted by
Professor Rothstein).

The DHHS has modified the Privacy Rule provisions relating to research,
though not to the extent advocated by the IOM Report. As of 2013, the Privacy Rule
provides three avenues for the use of PHI for research:

1. *De-identification.* The PHI can be "de-identified" by removing more than
   18 types of information, ranging from name to any biometric identifiers.
   De-identified information is not considered to be PHI subject to the protections of the Rule. 45 C.F.R. §164.502(d).
2. *Authorization.* Individuals can provide specific authorization for the use of
   their PHI in research. 45 C.F.R. §164.508. The authorization for research
   now is slightly less demanding than the usual authorization provisions under
   the Privacy Rule. For example, the authorization can be combined with the
   informed consent form for the research study. The provider may require
   completion of the authorization before providing research-related treatment.
   The authorization need not have a specific expiration date, but instead can
   state " 'end of the research study,' 'none,' or similar language . . . if the authorization is for . . . research, including the creation and maintenance of a
   research database or research repository." Id. at §164.508(c)(1)(v). The 2013
   revisions to the federal Privacy Rule moved closer to the Common Rule by,
   for example, 45 C.F.R. §164.508(b)(3) (permitting use of compound authorization for the use of protected health information for research studies with
   a consent to participate in the research or authorization to create a research
   database). See also Mark A. Rothstein, HIPAA Privacy Rule 2.0, 41 J.L. Med. &
   Ethics 525 (2013).
3. *Substituted Consent by IRB or Privacy Board.* The Privacy Rule permits use of
   PHI for research where either an IRB or Privacy Board (as defined in the
   regulations) approves a waiver of the authorization requirement; where

the review is necessary to prepare a research protocol and no PHI will leave the entity; or where the research involves decedent's PHI. 45 C.F.R. §164.512(i). An IRB or Privacy Board may waive authorization where (1) "the use or disclosure . . . involves no more than minimal risk to the privacy of individuals"; (2) "The research could not practicably be conducted without the waiver or alteration"; (3) "The research could not practicably be conducted without access to and use of the protected health information; and (4) certain other procedural requirements have been met." Id.

The Common Rule revision process originally contemplated a number of privacy-related changes. As noted above, at page 272, the "final rule does not include the proposed standardized privacy safeguards for identifiable private information and identifiable biospecimens." Instead, the Rule simply provides that the IRB should ensure [w]hen appropriate, [that] there are adequate provisions to protect the privacy of subjects and to maintain the confidentiality of data." 45 C.F.R. 46.111(a)(7). After consultation, the Secretary of DHHS will issue "guidance to assist IRBs in assessing what provisions are adequate to protect the privacy of subjects and to maintain the confidentiality of data."

Do the current Rules achieve the correct balance between individual control of PHI and the promotion of research, which may improve health care for all? What changes, if any, would you suggest? What types of guidance would be of assistance to IRBs? For international aspects of these issues, see Symposium, Parts I & II: Harmonizing Privacy Law to Enable International Biobank Research, 43 J.L. Med. & Ethics 673-826 (2015) & 44 J.L. of Med. & Ethics 7-172 (2016).

Problem: DNA Research and Indigenous Communities

The Havasupai people, who live in the Grand Canyon, have been embroiled in a conflict with Arizona State University over the use of the tribe's DNA samples. University researchers took DNA samples from the Havasupai with the hope of finding genetic clues to the tribe's high rate of diabetes. The Havasupai believed that the blood samples were collected solely for diabetes research. However, tribe members discovered that their blood samples were used to study many other issues, including mental illnesses and the tribe's historical migration pattern, which threatened to create conflicts with the tribe's traditional beliefs about its origin.

What types of legal claims might be available to the Havasupai? Who would have standing to bring the claims? How would damages be measured? See Amy Harmon, Indian Tribe Wins Fight to Limit Research of Its DNA, N.Y. Times, April 21, 2010; Michelle M. Mello & Leslie Wolf, The Havasupai Indian Tribe Case—Lessons for Research Involving Stored Biologic Samples, 363 New Eng. J. Med. 204 (2010). See also Debra Harry, Indigenous Peoples and Gene Disputes, 84 Chi.-Kent L. Rev. 147 (2009); Bette Jacobs et al., Bridging the Divide Between Genomic Science and Indigenous Peoples, 38 J.L. Med. & Ethics 684 (2010).

4

Medical Malpractice

This chapter addresses those theories of physician and institutional liability that relate directly to the quality of care rendered, in short, classic medical malpractice actions. Other related types of liability arising from somewhat different theories of tort or contract are covered in Chapters 2 and 3; for instance, liability for refusing to accept patients, for releasing confidential medical information, or for failing to obtain informed consent.

This medical malpractice chapter begins with a general overview of what we mean by medical mistakes or bad quality, and what other mechanisms besides tort liability exist for preventing or correcting bad quality. This is intended to prompt you to think about the proper aims of malpractice liability and how the tort system should function in the medical arena. We return to these themes at the end of the chapter with an examination of medical malpractice reform.

The core of the chapter develops the various components of the malpractice cause of action against physicians. It begins with the basic standard of care and how it is proved and then develops alternative theories of liability. Next, causation and affirmative defenses are surveyed, followed by a discussion of damages and settlement. The chapter then explores how these theories of liability apply to hospitals, and finally how hospital liability theories apply to managed care entities such as HMOs. Throughout, we try to achieve a useful mix of (1) explaining the basic elements of legal doctrine and its complexities, (2) outlining the pragmatics of litigating these types of cases, and (3) considering the implications for public policy.

Bibliography

There are several useful texts and treatises on medical malpractice, both from a practicing lawyer perspective and from a public policy perspective. The leading multi-volume treatise is D. Louisell & H. Williams, Medical Malpractice. A good source on trial techniques and medical issues is the multi-volume treatise, Lee S. Goldsmith, Medical Malpractice: Guide to Medical Issues. Another useful resource is D. Danner et al., Medical Malpractice: Checklists and Discovery. For a briefer text addressed to law students, see M. Boumil & Hattis, Medical Liability in a Nutshell Series (3d ed. 2011). A good practical overview is Thomas M. O'Toole et al., The Anatomy of a Medical Malpractice Verdict, 70 Mont. L. Rev. 57 (2009). For a broad theoretical overview, see Alex Stein, Toward a Theory of Medical Malpractice, 97 Iowa L. Rev. 1201 (2012).

For **historical and social accounts** of the development and impact of medical malpractice law, see Kenneth Allen DeVille, Medical Malpractice in Nineteenth-Century America (1990); Iain Hay, Money, Medicine, and Malpractice in American Society (1992); James C. Mohr, American Medical Malpractice Litigation in Historical Perspective, 283 JAMA 1731 (2000); Theodore Silver, One Hundred Years of Harmful Error: The Historical Jurisprudence of Medical Malpractice, 1992 Wis. L. Rev. 1193; Catherine T. Struve, Doctors, the Adversary System, and Procedural Reform in Medical Liability Litigation, 72 Fordham L. Rev. 944 (2004); Robert Field, The Malpractice Crisis Turns 175: What Lessons Does History Hold for Reform, 4 Drexel L. Rev. 7 (2011); Maxwell Mehlman, Professional Power and the Standard of Care in Medicine, 44 Ariz. St. L.J. 1165 (2012); G. Annas, Doctors, Patients and Lawyers: Two Centuries of Health Law, 367 New Eng. J. Med. 445 (2012).

Descriptions and analyses of malpractice **liability systems abroad** can be found in B. A. Koch ed., Medical Liability in Europe (2011); Symposium, 4 Drexel L. Rev. 1-296 (2011); Symposium, 86 Chi.-Kent. L. Rev. 1021-1301 (2011); 87 Chi.-Kent. L. Rev. 1-198 (2012).

A. MEDICAL MISTAKES AND QUALITY

1. The Nature and Extent of Medical Error

We begin with this inquiry: Why do medical mistakes occur, and what kinds of legal responses are appropriate? You should first read or review Chapter 1.A.3, which discusses the nature of medical decisionmaking in general. Then, consider the following accounts of why medical errors and injuries are so widespread.

■HEALTH AND MEDICAL CARE REFORM IN THE UNITED STATES: ETHICAL QUESTIONS AND CONCERNS
Thomas W. Merrill, David G. Miller, Joseph A. Raho & Ginger Gruters
President's Council on Bioethics, Staff Background Paper, 2008

[Read Part III of this excerpt, on pages 38-40.]

■MAKING MEDICAL ERRORS INTO "MEDICAL TREASURES"
David Blumenthal*
272 JAMA 1867 (1994)

Throughout most of this century, the public has granted physicians extraordinary autonomy and power in return for an implied promise that, among other things, physicians would guarantee the quality of care patients receive. Implicit in this social contract was the belief on both sides that physicians have the capability to practice error-free or nearly error-free medicine themselves and to ensure that the rest of the system functions just as well. This belief has served the interests of both parties to this contract. Physicians have enjoyed the resulting status, freedom, and material rewards. Patients have enjoyed the reassuring fantasy that when they are ill, they can expect their physicians to make the health care system perform flawlessly.

Comfortable as this arrangement has been, it is proving dysfunctional. Physicians are encouraged to hold themselves to unattainable standards, to deny evidence of error, and thus to overlook opportunities for improving themselves and the health care system as a whole. When inevitable errors occur, patients feel betrayed and enraged. These feelings fuel the malpractice crisis that is itself a major deterrent to the openness required for quality improvement.

The paradox of modern quality improvement is that only by admitting and forgiving error can its rate be minimized. For error reduction to occur, physicians must become more comfortable with their fallibility, and patients must become more accepting of their own vulnerability.

■COMPLICATIONS: A SURGEON'S NOTES ON AN IMPERFECT SCIENCE
Atul Gawande**
2002

WHEN DOCTORS MAKE MISTAKES

To much of the public—and certainly to lawyers and the media—medical error is fundamentally a problem of bad doctors. The way that things go wrong in medicine is normally unseen and, consequently, often misunderstood. Mistakes do happen. We tend to think of them as aberrant. They are, however, anything but.

At 2 A.M. on a crisp Friday in winter a few years ago, I was in sterile gloves and gown, pulling a teenage knifing victim's abdomen open, when . . . the emergency medical technicians wheeled in a woman who appeared to be in her thirties and to weigh more than two hundred pounds. She lay motionless on a hard orange plastic spinal board—eyes closed, skin pale, blood running out of her nose. . . .

---

*M.D., formally at Massachusetts General Hospital and Harvard Medical School.

**Excerpted with permission, Henry Holt and Company. The author is a physician on the faculty of Harvard's Schools of Medicine and of Public Health. This true story uses fictionalized names.

"What's the story?" I asked.

An EMT rattled off the details: "Unidentified white female unrestrained driver in high-speed rollover. Ejected from the car. Found unresponsive to pain. Pulse a hundred, BP a hundred over sixty, breathing at thirty on her own . . ." This woman's breaths were shallow and rapid. An oximeter, by means of a sensor placed on her finger, measured the oxygen saturation of her blood. The "02 sat" is normally more than 95 percent [but hers was low]. . . .

"She's not oxygenating well," I announced in the flattened-out, wake-me-up-when-something-interesting-happens tone. . . . I got hold of a bag mask, pressed its clear facepiece over her nose and mouth, and squeezed the bellows, a kind of balloon with a one-way valve, shooting a liter of air into her with each compression. After a minute or so, her oxygen came up to a comfortable 98 percent. She obviously needed our help with breathing. "Let's tube her," I said. That meant putting a tube down through her vocal cords and into her trachea, which would insure a clear airway and allow for mechanical ventilation.

Johns, the [supervising physician], wanted to do the intubation. . . . He sucked out about a cup of blood and clot. Then he picked up the endotracheal tube—a clear rubber pipe about the diameter of an index finger and three times as long—and tried to guide it between her [vocal] cords. After a minute, her sat started to fall.

"You're down to seventy percent," a nurse announced.

Johns kept struggling with the tube, trying to push it in, but it banged vainly against the cords. The patient's lips began to turn blue. . . . When you're having trouble getting the tube in, the next step is to get specialized expertise. "Let's call anesthesia," I said. . . . Somewhere in my mind, I must have been aware of the possibility that her airway was shutting down because of vocal cord swelling or blood. If it was, and we were unable to get a tube in, then the only chance she'd have to survive would be an emergency tracheotomy: cutting a hole in her neck and inserting a breathing tube into her trachea. Another attempt to intubate her might even trigger a spasm of the cords and a sudden closure of the airway—which is exactly what did happen.

If I had actually thought this far along, I would have recognized how ill-prepared I was to do an emergency "trache." As the one surgeon in the room, it's true, I had the most experience doing tracheotomies, but that wasn't saying much. . . . I should have immediately called [a more experienced surgeon] for backup. . . . [Then we could have] done a tracheotomy while things were still relatively stable and I had time to proceed slowly. But for whatever reasons—hubris, inattention, wishful thinking, hesitation, or the uncertainty of the moment—I let the opportunity pass.

Johns hunched over the patient, trying intently to insert the tube through her vocal cords. When her sat once again dropped into the 60s, he stopped and put the mask back on. We stared at the monitor. The numbers weren't coming up. Her lips were still blue. Johns squeezed the bellows harder to blow more oxygen in.

"I'm getting resistance," he said.

The realization crept over me: this was a disaster. "Damn it, we've lost her airway," I said. "Trache kit! Light! . . ." I pulled on a gown and a new pair of gloves while trying to think through the steps. . . . [But] I was beset by uncertainty—where should I cut? Should I make a horizontal or vertical incision? . . .

There was no time to wait. Four minutes without oxygen would lead to permanent brain damage, if not death. Finally, I took the scalpel and cut. I hit a vein . . . [Because of the blood], I couldn't see anything . . . I called for suction but the suction wasn't working . . . [W]orking blindly, because of the blood and the poor light—I cut down through the overlying fat and tissue until I felt the blade scrape against the almost bony cartilage . . . I searched with the tip of the knife, walking it along until I felt it reach a gap. I hoped it was the [right spot], and pressed down firmly. I felt the tissue suddenly give, and I cut an inch-long opening. . . [But] was this deep enough? Was I even in the right place?

"I think I'm in," I said, to reassure myself as much as anyone else. "I hope so," [the anesthesiologist] said. "She doesn't have much longer."

I took the tracheostomy tube and tried to fit it in, but something seemed to be blocking it. I twisted it and turned it, and finally jammed it in. Just then [Dr. Ball, the supervising surgeon] arrived. He rushed up to the bed and leaned over for a look. "Did you get it?" he asked. I said that I thought so. The bag mask was plugged onto the open end of the trache tube. But when the bellows were compressed the air just gurgled out of the wound. Ball quickly put on gloves and a gown. . . . "I'm not going to get her an airway in time," he said. . . . Essentially, he was admitting my failure. Trying an oral intubation again was pointless—just something to do instead of watching her die. I was stricken, and concentrated on doing chest compressions, not looking at anyone. It was over, I thought.

And then, amazingly, . . . "I'm in." He had managed to slip a pediatric-size endotracheal tube through the vocal cords. In thirty seconds, with oxygen being manually ventilated through the tube, her heart was back, racing at a hundred and twenty beats a minute. Her [oxygen level] registered at 60 and then climbed. Another thirty seconds and it was at 97 percent. All the people in the room exhaled, as if they, too, had been denied their breath. . . .

We eventually identified the woman, whom I'll call Louise Williams; she was thirty-four years old and lived alone in a nearby suburb. Her alcohol level on arrival had been three times the legal limit, and had probably contributed to her unconsciousness. . . . When Ball came out and talked to family members, he told them of the dire condition she was in when she arrived, the difficulties "we" had had getting access to her airway, the disturbingly long period of time that she had gone without oxygen and thus his uncertainty about how much brain function she still possessed. They listened without protest; there was nothing for them to do but wait. . . .

I felt a sense of shame like a burning ulcer. This was not guilt: guilt is what you feel when you have done something wrong. What I felt was shame: I was what was wrong. And yet I also knew that a surgeon can take such feelings too far. It is one thing to be aware of one's limitations. It is another to be plagued by self-doubt. . . . Even worse than losing self-confidence, though, is reacting defensively. There are surgeons who will see faults everywhere except in themselves. They have no questions and no fears about their abilities. As a result, they learn nothing from their mistakes and know nothing of their limitations. . . .

Consider some other surgical mishaps. In one, a general surgeon left a large metal instrument in a patient's abdomen, where it tore through the bowel and the wall of the bladder. In another, a cancer surgeon biopsied the wrong part of a woman's breast and thereby delayed her diagnosis of cancer for months. A cardiac surgeon skipped a small but key step during a heart valve operation, thereby killing the patient. A general surgeon saw a man racked with abdominal pain in the emergency room and, without taking a CT scan, assumed that the man had a kidney stone; eighteen hours later, a scan showed a rupturing abdominal aortic aneurysm, and the patient died not long afterward.

How could anyone who makes a mistake of that magnitude be allowed to practice medicine? We call such doctors "incompetent," "unethical," and "negligent." We want to see them punished. And so we've wound up with the public system we have for dealing with error: malpractice lawsuits, media scandal, suspensions, firings.

There is, however, a central truth in medicine that complicates this tidy vision of misdeeds and misdoers: all doctors make terrible mistakes. Consider the cases I've just described. I gathered them simply by asking respected surgeons I know—surgeons at top medical schools—to tell me about mistakes they had made just in the past year. Every one of them had a story to tell.

In 1991, the *New England Journal of Medicine* published a series of landmark papers from a project known as the Harvard Medical Practice Study—a review of more than thirty thousand hospital admissions in New York State. The study found that nearly 4 percent of hospital patients suffered complications from treatment which either prolonged their hospital stay or resulted in disability or death, and that two-thirds of such complications were due to errors in care. One in four, or 1 percent of admissions, involved actual negligence. . . . [S]ubsequent investigations around the country have confirmed the ubiquity of error. In one . . . study, mistakes in administering drugs—giving the wrong drug or the wrong dose, say—occur, on average, about once every hospital admission, mostly without ill effects, but 1 percent of the time with serious consequences.

If error were due to a subset of dangerous doctors, you might expect malpractice cases to be concentrated among a small group, but in fact they follow a uniform, bell-shaped distribution. Most surgeons are sued at least once in the course of their careers. Studies of specific types of error, too, have found that repeat offenders are not the problem. The fact is that virtually everyone who cares for hospital patients will make serious mistakes, and even commit acts of negligence, every year. For this reason, doctors are seldom outraged when the press reports yet another medical horror story. They usually have a different reaction: That could be me. The important question isn't how to keep bad physicians from harming patients; it's how to keep good physicians from harming patients.

Medical malpractice suits are a remarkably ineffective remedy. Troyen Brennan, [formerly] a Harvard professor of law and public health, points out that research has consistently failed to find evidence that litigation reduces medical error rates. In part, this may be because the weapon is so imprecise. Brennan led several studies following up on the patients in the Harvard Medical Practice Study. He found that fewer than 2 percent of the patients who had received substandard care ever filed suit. Conversely, only a small minority among the patients who did sue had in fact been the victims of negligent care. And a patient's likelihood of winning a suit depended primarily on how poor his or her outcome was, regardless of whether that outcome was caused by disease or unavoidable risks of care.

The deeper problem with medical malpractice suits is that by demonizing errors they prevent doctors from acknowledging and discussing them publicly. The tort system makes adversaries of patient and physician, and pushes each to offer a heavily slanted version of events. When things go wrong, it's almost impossible for a physician to talk to a patient honestly about mistakes. Hospital lawyers warn doctors that, although they must, of course, tell patients about injuries that occur, they are never to intimate that they were at fault, lest the "confession" wind up in court as damning evidence in a black-and-white morality tale. At most, a doctor might say, "I'm sorry that things didn't go as well as we had hoped."

There is one place, however, where doctors can talk candidly about their mistakes, if not with patients, then at least with one another. It is called the Morbidity and Mortality Conference—or, more simply, M & M—and it takes place, usually once a week, at nearly every academic hospital in the country. This institution survives because laws protecting its proceedings from legal discovery have stayed on the books in most states, despite frequent challenges. . . .

In its way, the M & M is an impressively sophisticated and human institution. Unlike the courts or the media, it recognizes that human error is generally not something that can be deterred by punishment. The M & M sees avoiding error as largely a matter of will—of staying sufficiently informed and alert to anticipate the myriad ways that things can go wrong and then trying to head off each potential problem before it happens. It isn't damnable that an error occurs, but there is some shame to it. In fact, the M & M's ethos can seem paradoxical. On the one hand, it reinforces the very American idea that error is intolerable. On the other hand, the very existence of the M & M, its place on the weekly schedule, amounts to an acknowledgment that mistakes are an inevitable part of medicine.

But why do they happen so often? Lucian Leape, medicine's leading expert on error, points out that many other industries—whether the task is manufacturing semiconductors or serving customers at the Ritz-Carlton—simply wouldn't countenance error rates like those in hospitals. The aviation industry has reduced the frequency of operational errors to one in a hundred thousand flights, and most of those errors have no harmful consequences. The buzz-word at General Electric these days is "Six Sigma," meaning that its goal is to make product defects so rare that in statistical terms they are more than six standard deviations away from being a matter of chance—almost a one-in-a-million occurrence.

Of course, patients are far more complicated and idiosyncratic than airplanes, and medicine isn't a matter of delivering a fixed product or even a catalogue of products; it may well be more complex than just about any other field of human endeavor. Yet everything we've learned in the past two decades—from cognitive psychology, from "human factors" engineering, from studies of disasters like Three Mile Island and Bhopal—has yielded the same insights: not only do all human beings err, but they err frequently and in predictable, patterned ways. And systems that do not adjust for these realities can end up exacerbating rather than eliminating error. . . .

Medicine teems with examples. Take writing out a prescription, a rote procedure that relies on memory and attention, which we know are unreliable. Inevitably, a physician will sometimes specify the wrong dose or the wrong drug. Even when the prescription is written correctly, there's a risk that it will be misread. (Computerized ordering systems can almost eliminate errors of this kind, but only a small minority of hospitals have adopted them.) . . . You can also make the case that onerous workloads, chaotic environments, and inadequate team communication all represent [flaws] in the system. . . . When things go wrong, it is usually because a series of failures conspires to produce disaster. . . . The doctor is often only the final actor in a chain of events that set him or her up to fail. Error experts, therefore, believe that it's the process, not the individuals in it, that requires closer examination and correction. In a sense, they want to industrialize medicine. . . .

But the story doesn't have to end here, as the cognitive psychologists and industrial error experts have demonstrated. . . . It would be deadly for us, the individual actors, to give up our belief in human perfectibility. The statistics may say that someday I will sever someone's main bile duct [while removing a gallbladder], but each time I [do the] operation I believe that with enough will and effort I can beat the odds. This isn't just professional vanity. It's a necessary part of good medicine, even in superbly "optimized" systems. . . .

This may explain why many doctors take exception to talk of "systems problems," "continuous quality improvement," and "process re-engineering." It is the dry language of structures, not people. I'm no exception: something in me, too, demands an acknowledgment of my autonomy, which is also to say my ultimate culpability. Go back to that Friday night in the ER, to the moment when I stood, knife in hand, over Louise Williams, her lips blue, her throat a swollen, bloody, and suddenly closed passage. A systems engineer might have proposed some useful changes. Perhaps a backup suction device should always be at hand, and better light more easily available. Perhaps the institution could have trained me better for such crises, could have required me to have operated on a few more goats. . . .

Yet although the odds were against me, it wasn't as if I had no chance of succeeding. Good doctoring is all about making the most of the hand you're dealt, and I failed to do so. The indisputable fact was that I hadn't called for help when I could have, and when I plunged the knife into her neck and made my horizontal slash my best was not good enough. It was just luck, hers and mine, that [another doctor] somehow got a breathing tube into her in time.

There are all sorts of reasons that it would be wrong to take my license away or to take me to court. These reasons do not absolve me. Whatever the limits of the M & M, its fierce ethic of personal responsibility for errors is a formidable virtue. No matter what measures are taken, doctors will sometimes falter, and it isn't reasonable to ask that we achieve perfection. What is reasonable is to ask that we never cease to aim for it.

Notes: Medical Mistakes

1. *The Extent of Medical Error.* Are you surprised or shocked by the nearly 100,000 annual deaths caused by medical mistakes that is estimated by the Institute of Medicine? This estimate is based primarily on the influential Harvard study, mentioned by Dr. Gawande. Realize, though, that most people who die as the result of medical treatment do not die in the prime of life; many are old or feeble patients whose prospects for long-term survival are dim at best. For full details and analysis, see Paul Weiler et al., A Measure of Malpractice (1993). Similar studies were conducted in California in 1974, and in Utah and Colorado in the late 1990s, producing remarkably similar findings. The Institute of Medicine's report, To Err Is Human: Building a Safer Health System (2000), called widespread attention to these findings, and its recommendations spurred renewed efforts to improve medical care systems to prevent many common mistakes.

Professor Mark Grady reasons that medical mistakes are common because medical science has progressed so rapidly and is capable of much more than it once was. "New technology can enlarge people's opportunities to forget to use precaution and thereby be negligent." Why Are People Negligent? Technology, Nondurable Precautions, and the Medical Malpractice Explosion, 82 Nw. U. L. Rev. 293, 295 (1988). Renowned philosophers Samuel Gorovitz and Alasdair MacIntyre also argue that a high error rate is inevitable in medicine because of the human condition and the limits of technology. Toward a Theory of Medical Fallibility, 5(6) Hastings Center Rep. 13 (Dec. 1975). Lucien Leape (whom Gawande mentions) illustrates from one study of an intensive care unit, which documented "an average of 178 activities per day [for each patient]. The 1.7 errors per day thus indicate that hospital personnel were functioning at a 99 percent level of proficiency. However, a 1 percent failure rate is substantially higher than is tolerated in industry, particularly in hazardous fields such as aviation and nuclear power. As W. E. Deming points out, even 99.9 percent may not be good enough: 'If we had to live with 99.9 percent, we would have: 2 unsafe plane landings per day at O'Hare, 16,000 pieces of lost mail every hour, 32,000 bank checks deducted from the wrong bank account every hour.' " Error in Medicine, 272 JAMA 1851 (1994).

Are these views consistent with commonly held attitudes and expectations about modern medicine as conveyed by mass media? Could there be some therapeutic or social benefit to the blind faith that people sometimes place in their doctors? See Chapter 1.A.2. Viewed in this light, is it good to counter mass delusion by debunking the myth of infallibility?

2. *Conceptual Distinctions.* Roughly a third of malpractice claims are for diagnostic errors (especially failure to diagnose cancer), a third are for surgical errors (improper technique, slip of knife, foreign objects left inside); and a third are for improper medical treatment (e.g., drug reaction, anesthesia error, birth injury). Regardless of the type of medical treatment involved, consider, as you read the cases in the remainder of this chapter, how you would classify the various mistakes that led to injury. One useful analysis distinguishes between skill-based errors ("slips") and those based on decisionmaking (mental "mistakes"). Lucian L. Leape, Error in Medicine, 272 JAMA 1851 (1994). Realize that judgment mistakes might be due to misperception of the problem, choice of the wrong rule of action, or misapplication of the rule. Which kinds of error does Dr. Gawande's account illustrate? As you read the cases in this chapter, consider also whether the errors are the responsibility of any one actor, or do they result from flaws in the overall *system* for coordinating and delivering care? For more on the latter distinction, see Institute of Medicine, supra; Michelle Mello & David Studdert, Deconstructing Negligence: The Role of Individual and System Factors in Causing Medical Injuries, 96 Georgetown L.J. 599 (2008); and a series of articles exploring the nature of medical error, running in the Annals of Internal Medicine (2002-2003).

Renowned medical sociologist Elliot Friedson introduces another distinction in Doctoring Together (1975):

"Normal," excusable mistakes are those that every physician could conceive of making because of lack of information, the uncertainty of medical knowledge, the limitation of available techniques, and the uniqueness of the case. Many physicians would not even call these "mistakes"; in the interviews, some called them "so-called mistakes." Such normal mistakes are less mistakes than they are unavoidable events; they are not so much committed by the doctor as they are suffered or risked. They do not reflect on the physician's competence so much as on his luck. Thus, one should not judge or criticize a colleague's apparent mistakes because "there but for the grace of God go I."

In contrast to normal mistakes are deviant mistakes. Essentially, deviant mistakes seemed to be those that are thought to be due to a practitioner's negligence, ignorance, or ineptitude, reflecting upon his lack of basic or reasonable competence, ethicality, conscientiousness, and judgment. They consist in failures to follow the widely agreed-on rules of good practice. These are the mistakes that are frequently called "blatant" or "gross," "serious" being an adjective more often used to delineate the consequence of a mistake rather than its analytic character.

Timothy Stolzfus Jost, in the article on page 318, introduces two additional relevant distinctions:

A patient may receive a medical procedure that is technically appropriate but . . . [still] suffer a variety of affronts to dignity from health care professionals [such as failure to explain what is happening]. . . . A doctor may be unnecessarily rude or abrupt with a patient, or show contempt for the value of a patient's time. . . . These violations of social values and norms . . . seldom result in litigation or regulatory action, but frequently result in patient dissatisfaction. . . .

Finally, medical errors must be distinguished from medical failures. Some medical failures are not errors in the sense that anyone is culpable for their occurrence. They are simply due to unforeseeable reactions of a particular patient to treatment, unavoidable failure of equipment, the current limits of medical knowledge, or the ultimately intractable complexity of the human body. Even though such failures should in most instances not result in either tort or regulatory sanctions, an effective quality assurance system can discover them, and identify their causes, and perhaps assure they do not happen again.

3. *The Patient's Perspective.* Popular opinion sometimes thinks that malpractice plaintiffs are just trying to capitalize on their misfortune in order to hit the jackpot by suing a rich or well-insured doctor, or that plaintiffs are seduced into this attitude by personal injury lawyers looking for a big contingency fee. Certainly, there is some element of truth in this account, but to a large extent many patients also feel genuinely angry and wronged by how they were treated. In one law office (the one that represented the plaintiff in the first case below), 56 percent of inquiries about malpractice over a ten-year period were prompted by the doctor's referring unpaid bills to a collection agency, and 60 percent of potential clients were told by a nurse that malpractice had occurred. J. Reagan McLaurin et al., Pitfalls for the Practitioner: A Claimant's View of Medical Malpractice, Carolina Health Serv. Res. 97 (Summer 1994). A review of deposition transcripts found that, in 70 percent of the cases, the patients complained of one or more of the following behaviors by the doctor: devaluing patients' views, deserting the patient, and delivering information poorly. See Wendy Levinson, Physician-Patient Communication: A Key to Malpractice Prevention, 272 JAMA 1619 (1994). See also Debra Roter, The Patient-Physician Relationship and Its Implications for Malpractice Litigation, 9 J. Health Care L. & Pol'y 304 (2006).

4. *Physicians' Attitudes Toward Making Mistakes.* A classic study of how medical professionals respond to error is Charles Bosk, Forgive and Remember: Managing Medical Failure (2d ed. 2003). Reflecting on Dr. Gawande's narrative, how would you, or most people, feel if you learned that a perfectly human slip or mental error caused a patient to die or endure great suffering? Would you (or others) be defensive, self-loathing, in denial of your responsibility, deeply regretful and apologetic, "philosophical"? Which of these (or other) attitudes is most constructive? Which help doctors to carry on in the face of inevitability? Which attitudes are likely to lead to constructive change?

5. *Telling Patients and Apologizing.* Dr. Gawande comments that, due to the threat of liability, "it's almost impossible for a physician to talk to a patient honestly about mistakes." See also Sagit Mor & Orna Rabinovich-Einy, Relational Malpractice, 42 Seton Hall L. Rev. 601 (2012). But, should physicians be required, as an aspect of their fiduciary duty to patients, to inform patients when a bad outcome is due to a medical mistake? This question is receiving considerable ethical and public policy attention. The private accreditation body in charge of hospitals (the JCAHO, Joint Commission on the Accreditation of Healthcare Organizations) has instituted a "sentinel events" reporting policy that requires hospitals to make physicians inform patients or their families when unexpected death or serious injury is caused by medical care rather than by the natural course of disease. See Symposium, 35 J. Health L. 179 (2002). A few states require the same. William Sage et al., Bridging the Relational-Regulatory Gap: A Pragmatic Information Policy for Patient Safety and Medical Malpractice, 59 Vand. L. Rev. 1263 (2006).

When doctors reveal medical errors to patients, should they also apologize, either from a genuine feeling of remorse, or as a strategic way to head off medical malpractice litigation?

> Doctors' apologies for medical mistakes may not be a cure-all for litigation, but explaining unforeseen outcomes and making early settlement offers have proven effective, say lawyers who have participated in the process in the last decade. The concept is called "full disclosure/early offer," and it's spreading. The U.S. Department of Veterans Affairs' Veterans Health Administration—as well as a number of hospital systems and insurers across the nation—are among the entities that have adopted variations of the policy. . . . Plaintiffs' and defense attorneys agree that the program—often referred to as Sorry Works! from The Sorry Works! Coalition, . . .—is a sound strategy miscast in the public perception as a touchy-feely ritual. . . . [H]ealth care providers willing to admit when they have made an error and quickly get on top of it cut down on the anger that leads to litigation. . . .
>
> Michael A. Stidham, whose Jackson, Ky., practice includes representing Department of Veterans Affairs (V.A.) patients, has settled three cases with the Veterans Affairs Medical Center in Lexington, Ky.—two on the same morning—and lost a bench trial in a medical malpractice case that involved a suicide. Stidham said that he likes the system and thinks that its wider application could help to reduce docket backlogs. In contrast, a case against a local hospital can take three to four years to get to trial. "The only thing I really find lacking in it at this point is that I don't believe they tell the prospective plaintiffs that they have the right to discuss their offers with an attorney. A lot of men and women don't understand why they're receiving these offers," he said. Stidham noted that "I didn't always get everything I wanted, but I didn't leave with a bad taste in my mouth, and left with a satisfied client, which is the most important thing."

Ginny M. Hamm, the special assistant U.S. attorney assigned to the V.A. medical center in Lexington who worked with the former hospital chief of staff, Dr. Steve S. Kraman, to introduce a centerwide disclosure program in 1987, said that a full and lengthy explanation always precedes an offer. Since Hamm did her first disclosure case in 1989, the "golden rule" has been to tell veterans or their families that they should seek counsel when the hospital meets with them to disclose what went wrong, she said. Kraman, as chief of staff, would speak to the veteran and his family on behalf of the entire medical center, offering an apology and explaining the error, then "hand off to me for the settlement," she said. Hamm added that if the V.A. determined that no mistake was made, it would hold a "closure" meeting explaining its finding to the veteran. Kraman, who now serves on the board of The Sorry Works! Coalition, said that he was aware of only two cases in which angry patients sued for damages. "The vast majority of people respond in kind. If treated honestly, they don't even want money. They want to see that some good comes out of a bad situation," Kraman said.

Peter Geier, Emerging Med-Mal Strategy: "I'm Sorry," National L.J., July 24, 2006.

6. *Physicians' Attitudes Toward Being Sued.* In contrast with their private regret over poor medical outcomes, most doctors view a malpractice suit as an unjustified affront to their professional integrity and reputation, as revealed in the article that follows. Another doctor graphically depicts his feeling of violation after a string of suits in quick succession: "From being a virgin for 20 years, all of a sudden I was gang raped." N. Hupert et al., Processing the Tort Deterrent Signal: A Qualitative Study, 43 Soc. Sci. & Med. 1 (1996). See also Peter Kowey, A Piece of My Mind, 306 JAMA 18 (2011). Does this type of response cause you concern about whether malpractice law is having its intended social effect? How constructive are physicians' responses to this deterrent signal likely to be? Consider how constructive are the suggestions made by the physician in the following article. Also, see page 370 for a discussion of the meaning and extent of the "defensive medicine" caused by the threat of liability.

7. *Bibliography.* For critique of the Institute of Medicine's findings (note 1), see Rodney A. Hayward & Timothy P. Hofer, Estimating Hospital Deaths Due to Medical Errors: Preventability Is in the Eye of the Reviewer, 286 JAMA 415 (2001); Clement J. McDonald et al., Deaths Due to Medical Errors Are Exaggerated in Institute of Medicine Report, 284 JAMA 93 (2000). Additional discussions of the **extent and cause of medical error**, and of **measuring and improving quality**, can be found at Tom Baker, The Medical Malpractice Myth (2005); Michelle M. Mello & Troyen A. Brennan, Deterrence of Medical Errors: Theory and Evidence for Malpractice Reform, 80 Tex. L. Rev. 1595 (2002); Michael Saks, Medical Malpractice: Facing Real Problems and Finding Real Solutions, 35 Wm. & Mary L. Rev. 693 (1994); Peter Jacobson, Medical Liability and the Culture of Technology, *in* Medical Malpractice and the U.S. Health Care System (W. Sage & R. Kersh eds., 2006); Christopher Landrigan et al., Temporal Trends in Rates of Patient Harm Resulting from Medical Care, 363 New Eng. J. Med. 2124 (2011); Rosemary Gibson & Janardan Prasad Singh, Wall of Silence: The Untold Story of Medical Mistakes That Kill and Injure Millions of Americans (2003); Robert M. Wachter & Kaveh G. Shojania, Internal Bleeding: The Truth Behind America's Terrifying Epidemic of Medical Mistakes (2004); Marianne Paget, A Complex Sorrow: Reflections on Cancer and an Abbreviated Life (1993); Symposium, 29(9) Health Aff. (Sept. 2010); Symposium, 22(2) Health Aff. (March

2003); Symposium, 46 Perspect. Biol. Med. 1 (Winter 2003); Symposium, Patient Injury, Medical Errors, Liability and Reform, 29 J.L. Med. & Ethics 248 (2001). For additional discussion, pro and con, of **disclosing and apologizing for medical error**, and whether doing so increases litigation risk (note 5), see K. M. Mazor et al., Communicating with Patients About Medical Errors: A Review of the Literature, 164 Arch. Intern. Med. 1690 (2003); Aaron Lazare, The Healing Forces of Apology in Medical Practice and Beyond, 57 DePaul L. Rev. 251 (2008); Thomas Gallagher et al., Disclosing Harmful Medical Errors to Patients, 356 New Engl. J. Med. 2713 (2007); Symposium, 166 Arch. Intern. Med. 1585 (2006); Symposium, 33(1) Health Aff. 11-52 (Jan. 2014); see Jonathan Todres, Toward Healing and Restoration for All: Reframing Medical Malpractice Reform, 39 Conn. L. Rev. 667 (2006); Richard Bourne, Medical Malpractice: Should Courts Force Doctors to Confess Their Own Negligence to Their Patients?, 61 Ark. L. Rev. 621 (2009); Steven Raper, No Role for Apology: Remedial Work and the Problem of Medical Injury, 11 Yale J. Health Pol'y L. & Ethics 267 (2011); Erin Ann O'Hara, Apology and Thick Trust: What Spouse Abusers and Negligent Doctors Might Have in Common, 79 Chi.-Kent L. Rev. 1055 (2004); Lee Taft, Apology and Medical Mistake: Opportunity or Foil?, 14 Ann. Health L. 55 (2005).

2. Critiquing and Measuring the Malpractice System

■SUITS FOR ALLEGED MALPRACTICE
George W. Gay, M.D.
165 Bos. Med. & Surg. J. 353 (1911)*

Suits at law against reputable physicians for alleged malpractice have attracted unusual attention in late years by reason of their increasing frequency and by the absence of a reasonable foundation of truth and justice in the charges usually brought against the defendant. Litigation, like legislation, was never so rampant as it is today. The multitude of lawyers, the bewildering mass of statutes, and the ever-increasing volume of both only tend to aggravate a condition which would seem already to be too complicated for the public welfare . . . What a large and growing number of litigants want is not a resort to justice, but a resort to chance; not the establishment of truth and the enforcement of whatever rights based on the truth have been infringed upon, but a verdict or a decision obtained from ignorance, prejudice, or favor . . .

[Courts have become so congested] in many states that the President of the United States, the American Bar Association, and many of the acute legal minds of the country are trying to devise some method of correcting this unfortunate state of affairs. . . Thus far, there seems to be no relief from this deplorable state of affairs, nor are the prospects for such relief encouraging . . .

---

*The author was a prominent surgeon in Boston. Thanks to Rob Field for pointing out this gem of an article, a full copy of which can be found on the Web site for this casebook, www.health-law.org. It is fascinating reading.

However faithful and efficient may be the physician . . . [he] is in no way protected from a suit by the fact that the mode of treatment pursued in any case was the one accepted and approved by the leading authorities, or that, from the nature of the disease or injuries, no known method of treatment could have improved the results obtained. These facts do not protect a physician from an unjust, vexatious, and expensive suit . . . Having rendered faithful, skillful service through a long and perhaps critical illness, and having obtained the best result possible under the circumstances, nothing can be more disheartening, more aggravating, and more demoralizing to one's faith in human nature than a suit for malpractice. . . .

To assert that physicians never make mistakes under any circumstances is to claim a degree of perfection which no profession nor vocation possesses. From the nature of our calling and of the conditions with which we have to deal, an occasional error is inevitable. The wonder is that the mistakes are so few. . . . Nature's processes are often obscure, and the danger signals may not be in evidence until too late to avert disaster . . . As the Supreme Court of a neighboring state has well said, "the medical practitioner is necessarily surrounded by doubt and uncertainties and unavoidably exposed to errors and mistakes, which may well furnish a satisfactory explanation of unfavorable results." . . . .

The members of the medical profession stand ready to make reasonable amends for errors and to adjust proper claims. They strongly object, however, to being mulcted and fleeced by sharpers and unreasonable people, as is attempted in a vast majority of the malpractice suits of the present day . . .

Malpractice suits are brought from various motives, as for example, to extort money from the defendant, to escape the payment of his bill, to avenge the disappointment at the termination of the case, to deliberately injure the reputation of the defendant out of spite, and to attract the notice and sympathy of friends and neighbors. The sanctimonious excuse of desiring to protect others from the incompetency of the defendant is occasionally offered as a reason for bringing suit. It is doubtful if a patient of his own motion often brings an action for damages in these cases . . .

A very important factor in many of these cases is the perniciously active attorney, who is constantly on the watch for opportunities to instigate and foment claims of all sorts with little regard to right and justice . . . It would be difficult to devise a scheme, or a mode of procedure, more conducive to the instigation and presentation of bogus claims, than is the so-called contingent suit of the present day. It is a game of chance, a gamble, having stakes that are especially alluring, when the defendants are timid, or rich, or both . . .

Not infrequently, a malpractice suit is brought against the consultant either separately or in conjunction with the attending physician. This is especially noticeable when the former has attachable property, or the reputation of wealth." . . . Holding the consultant equally responsible with the regular attendant for the treatment, especially if the patient be seen but once by the former . . . may be good law, but in many instances, it is neither justice nor common sense . . . It may subject physicians of the highest skill, who have rendered faithful and intelligent service, to the necessity of defending themselves in blackmailing suits against charges having no foundation in fact, or for conditions over which they never had any control and for which they are in no way responsible. It encourages false claims and fake suits . . .

Of course, there is another side to this matter, and no one will deny the fact that malpractice suits are justified under certain conditions [example omitted] . . . This paper makes no plea in defense of such work, but confines itself to those cases in which there is little or no just cause for complaint as to the treatment . . .

The writer much regrets that he is unable to suggest any escape from this unjust and aggravating state of affairs. So long as there are ungrateful patients and pernicious lawyers and doctors, physicians, however accomplished and renowned, must run the risk of being hauled into court upon the most unjust charges and put to the trouble and expense of defending themselves, their reputation, their character, and their bank account, if they be so fortunate as to have one, against the blackmailers and "ambulance chasers" that infest every community . . .

Care, forethought, and discretion would seem to be our only safeguards . . . In the first place, it is essential that the physician . . . should undertake only such cases as he can properly manage with or without available assistance. A reasonably-correct diagnosis is the basis of satisfactory clinical work and no pains should be spared to obtain it. Prompt and repeated consultations should be requested in difficult and obscure cases for the double purpose of avoiding error and dividing responsibility. In these days of highly-developed specialism, it is incumbent upon the family practitioner to avail himself of the services of experts upon all proper occasions, not only for the benefit of the patient, but for his own as well . . .

Let the public understand that reputable physicians . . . will stand by each other in their defense of the right as against the wrong, regardless of time, trouble, and expense; that we mean to do our best for the welfare of our patients, and having done that, we naturally resent being called upon to defend such action at law. Let the people fully comprehend the above facts and conditions, and these unjust and uncalled for suits for alleged malpractice should disappear from the calendars of our courts.

■THE MEDICAL MALPRACTICE MYTH
Tom Baker*

Medical malpractice premiums are skyrocketing. "Closed" signs are sprouting on health clinic doors. Doctors are leaving the field of medicine, and those who remain are practicing in fear and silence. Pregnant women cannot find obstetricians. Billions of dollars are wasted on defensive medicine. And angry doctors are marching on state capitols across the country. All this is because medical malpractice litigation is exploding. Egged on by greedy lawyers, plaintiffs sue at the drop of a hat. Juries award eye-popping sums to undeserving claimants, leaving doctors, hospitals, and their insurance companies no choice but to pay huge ransoms. . . .

This is the medical malpractice myth. . . . None of this bears even a passing resemblance to reality. In fact, the research is so clearly to the contrary that the most interesting question is why the research has not changed people's minds. . . .

Built on a foundation of urban legend mixed with the occasional true story, supported by selective references to academic studies, and repeated so often that even the mythmakers forget the exaggeration, half truth, and outright misinformation employed in the service of their greater good, the medical malpractice myth has filled doctors, patients, legislators, and voters with the kind of fear that short circuits critical thinking.

This fear has inspired legislative action on a nationwide scale three times in my lifetime: [the mid-1970s, the mid-1980s, and the early 2000s]. . . . This time around we have a lot more information. First, we know from [various] studies that the real problem is too much medical malpractice, not too much litigation. . . . The real costs of medical malpractice are the lost lives, extra medical expenses, time out of work, and pain and suffering of tens of thousands of people every year, the vast majority of whom do not sue. . . . "[U]ndeserving" people sometimes bring medical malpractice claims because they do not know that the claims lack merit and because they cannot find out what happened to them (or their loved ones) without making a claim. Most undeserving claims disappear before a trial; most trials end in a verdict for the doctor; doctors almost never pay claims out of their own pockets; and hospitals and insurance companies refuse to pay claims unless there is a good evidence of malpractice. If a hospital or insurance company does settle a questionable claim to avoid a huge risk, there is a very large discount. This means that big payments to undeserving claimants are the very rare exception, not the rule. . . .

This is a book with a mission. My goal is reframing the public discussion about medical malpractice lawsuits . . . [so that] the people who know a lot about medicine and the people who know a lot about law can start to talk *to* each other, rather than *at* each other, about the role that law can play in improving the quality of health care.

Notes: Facts and Figures

1. *The History and "Epidemiology" of Malpractice Suits.* Are you surprised by the fact that Dr. Gay wrote his article a century ago? His perspective is still shared by a large portion of the medical profession today. To appreciate the concern that doctors have about being sued in the modern legal climate, consider that, prior to 1960, only one in seven doctors had ever been sued in their entire career. Today, claims are filed against about one in seven doctors *each year*. This explains why malpractice law is often the focal point for discussion of tort reform in state and federal legislatures, and why tort reform is one of the AMA's highest legislative priorities, sometimes appearing to rank above other social concerns such as universal access to health care.

Although most doctors complain about the threat of malpractice suits, they are not all equally affected. Malpractice claims are not spread uniformly. Some specialties (surgery, anesthesiology, obstetrics, and emergency medicine) produce claims much more frequently than others and some doctors within the same specialty are sued more often than others.

2. *Plaintiffs' Lawyers.* As Prof. Baker summarizes, and as his book thoroughly documents, a flurry of empirical research over the past decade or more allows us to address the contentious debate over malpractice litigation with something more than anecdotal opinion. For instance, the claim Dr. Gay made a century ago that

too many frivolous suits are filed is belied today by the fact that most experienced malpractice lawyers are very selective in the cases they agree to take, due to the costs of litigation and the uncertainty of prevailing. In one study of six firms, 502 potential plaintiffs called over a ten-day period. Of these, 85 (17 percent) were selected for expert review of the medical records. Sixty-two percent of these were rejected, usually for insufficient damages, and only one-quarter for lack of negligence. For callers who were rejected without medical review, the overwhelming reason (73 percent) was insufficient damages. L. Huycke & M. Huycke, Characteristics of Potential Plaintiffs in Malpractice Litigation, 120 Ann. Intern. Med. 792 (1994). Naturally, less established malpractice attorneys may decide not to be this selective.

3. *Jury Bias.* It appears that physicians' concerns about juries being biased in favor of injured patients are exaggerated. For the most part, research findings are much more supportive of juries than is popular opinion. When malpractice complaints go to trial, plaintiffs win only 20 to 30 percent of the time. This compares with an overall success rate of about 50 percent for plaintiffs in general civil litigation. Interviews with jurors in malpractice cases also confirm that, generally speaking, they enter the case sympathetic to doctors and suspicious of plaintiffs' motives to "make a fast buck." Neil Vidmar, Medical Malpractice and the American Jury (1995).

Although doctors win most of the time, how accurate these verdicts are is another question. Accuracy, of course, is in the eye of the beholder, since there is no agreement on what the proper "gold standard" should be for evaluating jury verdicts. The best that researchers can do is to ask expert neutral physicians whether the medical records reveal any substandard care causing injury. When they do so, researchers find a statistically significant, but far from perfect, correlation between the expert reviewer's opinion and the jury's verdict in the same case. For instance, one study compared how cases were resolved by juries with how the physician-run insurer had evaluated the case before trial for purposes of settlement negotiations. It found that plaintiffs won 42 percent of the cases that the insurer's consultants considered "indefensible," but plaintiffs won only 21 percent of those considered "defensible." This study also found that wins and losses were not influenced by the severity of injury, indicating that juries were not swayed purely by sympathy for the plaintiff. The amount of damages did vary with the strength of the liability case, even after controlling for the severity of the injury. Therefore, the expected value of a malpractice claim (i.e., the expected award times the chances of winning) was 25 times larger for claims that reviewers judged to be meritorious than for ones they judged to be without merit. This gives contingent fee lawyers a strong incentive to weed out weaker or "frivolous" claims. Mark I. Taragin et al., The Influence of Standard of Care and Severity of Injury on the Resolution of Medical Malpractice Claims, 117 Ann. Intern. Med. 780 (1992). Other studies show that, when plaintiffs win, damages are appropriately correlated with the patients' age and severity of injury.

Finding a statistical association between jury results and expert opinion means only that jury verdicts as a whole are not entirely random or unpredictable. Results in individual cases are still highly erratic. Also, as the numbers from the study by Taragin and colleagues reflect, depending on how one conceives of the correct "gold standard," juries produce a large number of both false positives (incorrect findings of negligence) and false negatives (incorrect findings of no liability), perhaps more of the latter than the former. The materials in section D outline alternatives for liability determination other than the jury trial that rely more on expert opinion. Even if these alternatives were to produce greater accuracy, what other values would they sacrifice?

Another measure of the accuracy and rationality of the malpractice system is lawyers' behavior in settling cases. As discussed in section F, many more cases settle than go to trial. Lawyers take their clues for when and how much to settle by observing how juries behave. If juries don't reach accurate results or if their behavior is unpredictable, then settlement decisions are not likely to be accurate. As summarized in Philip G. Peters, Jr., What We Know About Malpractice Settlements, 92 Iowa L. Rev. 1783 (2007), "weak claims are much less likely to result in a settlement payment than strong claims. Only 10% to 20% of the weak cases result in a payment, and it is typically only a token amount, such as forgiveness of any unpaid doctor bills. Strong cases settle at a much higher rate (85% to 90%) and for a much larger average payment. Borderline cases fall in the middle." See also David M. Studdert et al., Claims, Errors, and Compensation Payments in Medical Malpractice Litigation, 354 New Eng. J. Med. 2024 (2006) (malpractice claims involving verifiable errors are much more likely to result in a payment to the patient, and such payments are substantially higher than in claims without medical errors that are settled).

4. *Further Reading*. On medical **malpractice attorneys and their case selection** (note 2), see Kenneth DeVille, Act First and Look Up the Law Afterward? Medical Malpractice and the Ethics of Defensive Medicine, 19 Theoretical Med. & Bioethics 569 (1998) (an excellent overview, both for doctors and lawyers, of the factors that influence patients' decisions to consult a lawyer, lawyers' decisions to bring a case, the chances of success, and the likely recovery); L. Laska, Medical Malpractice Cases Not to File, 20 Mem. St. U. L. Rev. 27 (1989); Catherine T. Harris et al., Who Are Those Guys? An Empirical Examination of Medical Malpractice Plaintiffs' Attorneys, 58 SMU L. Rev. 225 (2005); Stephen Daniels & Joanne Martin, Plaintiff's Lawyers, Specialization, and Medical Malpractice, 59 Vand. L. Rev. 1051 (2006).

For additional views and research on **jury bias and accuracy** (note 3), see Philip G. Peters, The Role of the Jury in Modern Malpractice Law, 87 Iowa L. Rev. 911 (2002) (thorough review of the evidence, concluding that juries, on balance, reach defensible results and are not biased against physicians; if anything, juries are biased in doctors' favor); Philip G. Peters, Doctors and Juries, 105 Mich. L. Rev. 1453 (2007) (multiple studies are "startlingly consistent," that "the probability of a plaintiff's verdict grows as the evidence of negligence improves"); Thomas M. O'Toole et al., The Anatomy of a Medical Malpractice Verdict, 70 Mont. L. Rev. 57 (2009); William M. Sage & Rogan Kersh, Medical Malpractice and the U.S. Health Care System (2006); Frank Sloan & Lindsey M. Chepke, Ill-Suited? Medical Malpractice at a Crossroads (2008); David A. Hyman & Charles Silver, Medical Malpractice Litigation and Tort Reform: It's the Incentives, Stupid, 59 Vand. L. Rev. 1085 (2006); Symposium, 4 J. Empirical Legal Stud. 1 (2007). Compare Jeffrey O'Connell & Christopher Pohl, How Reliable Is Medical Malpractice Law? A Review of "Medical Malpractice and the American Jury," 12 J.L. & Health 359 (1998) (insightful review of both Neil Vidmar's research of jury verdicts and the Harvard study findings, concluding that malpractice law is not well designed to

Relationship Between Injuries & Claims

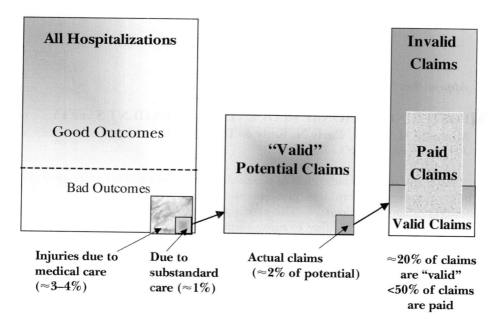

Note: Diagram scale is only approximate.

produce accurate and fair results, and advocating instead a no-fault compensation system), with David A. Hyman, Medical Malpractice and the Tort System: What Do We Know and What (If Anything) Should We Do About It?, 80 Tex. L. Rev. 1639 (2002) (criticizing malpractice system but also expressing skepticism about no-fault compensation).

5. *Piecing It All Together.* Based on the data and concepts discussed in these notes, Randall Bovbjerg has created the accompanying diagram above, adapted from an earlier version by Don Harper Mills (who ran the California study). The diagram is conceptual, not to scale, but it provides some rough scope for the issues addressed throughout this chapter.

In any medical encounter, there is a considerable chance of a disappointing outcome. However, most of these poor results are the unavoidable consequence of the disease itself and the inherent limits of medical science. Of all hospital admissions, only about 4 percent involve an injury caused by medical treatment. Of these, only about one-fourth (1 percent of the total) are the result of substandard care. Only about 2 percent of negligent injuries result in claims being filed with insurers. In part, this is because the great majority of these injuries are temporary or minor. Importantly, however, most claims are for injuries not caused by negligence. Fewer than half of all claims result in payment, usually through settlement.

6. *Looking Ahead.* The next reading considers the full range of possible legal responses that are available for medical mistakes and other deficiencies in the

quality of health care delivery. As you read it, consider which responses are appropriate for which types of mistakes, and how malpractice suits compare with other types of legal oversight.

3. Approaches to Improving Quality of Care

■ FOSTERING RATIONAL REGULATION OF PATIENT SAFETY
Michelle M. Mello, Carly N. Kelly & Troyen A. Brennan
30 J. Health Pol. Pol'y & L. 375 (2005)

After decades of inattention to the problem of medical injuries, patient safety is now occupying a prominent place on the health policy agenda and garnering renewed regulatory interest. . . . This article reviews the evolution of the regulatory environment for patient safety, examines some of the tensions and challenges that currently dene patient safety oversight, and suggests strategies for more rational and responsive regulation. . . .

Historically, the relationship between government and the health care industry has been characterized by an unparalleled faith in the ability of medical professionals to regulate themselves. Recently, however, three developments have invigorated policy makers' interest in health care quality oversight. First, the Institute of Medicine's (IOM's) reports on patient safety (Kohn, Corrigan, and Donaldson 2000) and quality of care (Institute of Medicine 2001) have focused public attention on the current deficiencies in health care and, by implication, the deciencies of existing regulatory efforts. These wake-up calls have created signicant political momentum for new forms of regulation. Second, the steady erosion of professionalism in medicine has suggested to legislators and the public that physicians are no longer equipped to self-regulate. Third, the escalating intrusion of the market into health care has raised public suspicion about corner cutting by prot-driven entities. . . .

In this article, we seek to assess the new regulation of patient safety. We dene regulation broadly to include any organized and deliberate leveraging of power or authority to effect changes in the behavior of health care providers. . . . *Patient safety* specically refers to prevention of iatrogenic injury—that is, injuries caused by medical management as opposed to the patient's underlying disease process. Quality assurance aims more broadly at improving health outcomes by improving care processes, with an emphasis on basing medical decisions on the best available evidence and ensuring that patients receive needed services. . . . Safety focuses on inadvertent harm to patients, whereas effectiveness focuses on the production of afrmative benet. Yet the two are frequently conflated. . . .

[S]everal major studies conducted over the past thirty years have gradually built an empirical case that iatrogenic injuries are a serious public health problem warranting intervention. The 2000 IOM report on medical errors catapulted this research into the public eye and energized public and private regulators to undertake such interventions. . . . [I]n the mid-1980s, a group of [Harvard] investigators . . . undertook a review of thirty thousand medical records and sixty-seven thousand malpractice claims (Weiler et al. 1993). The results, which were . . . replicated in Utah and Colorado in the late 1990s by some of the same investigators, . . .

were strikingly similar: 3 percent of hospitalizations resulted in an adverse event and about 1 percent involved an adverse event attributable to negligence (Thomas et al. 2000). . . . The IOM's report on medical errors, which extrapolated injury prevalence gures from the Harvard studies, generated publicity at a level virtually unparalleled in health services research. In particular, the IOM's estimate that for- ty-four thousand to ninety-eight thousand deaths per year were attributable to med- ical errors shocked the public. . . .

The science of error prevention in other industries turns out to produce few ready-made solutions to medical injuries. . . . [U]nlike nuclear plant failures or air crashes, medical injuries are diffuse and often difcult to disentangle from bad outcomes unrelated to medical management. . . . Thus, we must begin by acknowl- edging that there is presently very little evidence of measures that can give rise to patient safety regulation. This nearly ensures that the regulation will be a compli- cated story, as the enthusiasm of regulators exceeds the range of tools available to them. With this background in mind, we now turn to that story as it has unfolded to date.

THE PLURALISTIC REGULATORY ENVIRONMENT

The current regulatory environment for patient safety is highly pluralistic in nature. Traditional, top-down forms of regulation such as statutes and agency oversight are supplemented with private and quasi-private, bottom-up approaches including tort law and the market. Individually, each of these regulatory mecha- nisms has well-recognized strengths and weaknesses, but often overlooked are the interactive effects. . . .

Government regulation of health care quality has traditionally been limited, dominated by a philosophy that medical professionals can and should regulate themselves. Historically, quality assurance in hospitals was largely left to the medical staff, whose primary mechanism for ensuring quality was the careful selection and oversight of the clinicians who were given staff privileges. . . . Hospitals' medical leadership reviews the credentials of physician applicants, admits only those who are believed to meet high standards, and periodically reviews the care provided by individual doctors to determine whether to continue their staff privileges.

Hospitals have also self-regulated through accreditation by the Joint Com- mission on Accreditation of Healthcare Organizations (JCAHO). . . . Although the JCAHO has influential lay commissioners, it remains dominated by hospital and physician representatives. . . . States formally retain responsibility for hospi- tal licensure decisions, but most states have incorporated JCAHO accreditation standards into their licensure standards, and the large majority accepts JCAHO accreditation as the basis for a license. Similarly, the federal government has made JCAHO accreditation a sufficient condition for certification for Medicare participation. . . .

The JCAHO inspects hospitals every two to three years to ensure that they are in compliance with a series of structural and process-oriented quality measures. . . . It is not clear that the[se] standards address the problems that are most important for patient safety. . . . The standards may have been favored because most of them are relatively easy to articulate and measure. . . . Some have expressed doubts that its accreditation inspections have meaningful effects on hospital quality. . . .

To some extent, research and policy organizations are beginning to step in to address the information deficiency and assist policy makers in crafting substantive patient safety legislation. For example, the National Quality Forum (NQF), a public-private partnership in Washington, DC, has begun to develop a list of adverse events that should not occur and should be reported to governmental—as well as a list of safety-enhancing interventions. However, many of the proposed interventions are from the effectiveness domain, and quite a few of those from the safety domain are admittedly best shots rather than evidence based. . . .

BOTTOM-UP REGULATION

Tort Law. Tort law, or personal injury law, is intended to serve two regulatory functions. First, it provides a social insurance function; that is, it is a mechanism to compensate injured persons for the costs of injuries caused by the inadequate precaution taking of others. Second, it serves a deterrent function: in requiring that a defendant pay money to persons injured by the defendant's conduct, tort liability creates an economic incentive for safer behavior.

Tort law is a bottom-up regulatory approach because it relies upon individual patients to initiate malpractice claims. Although it bears little resemblance to statutory and administrative regulation in terms of its source or scope of application, in our view it can reasonably be considered a form of regulation. . . . Beginning in the 1940s, leading judges began to modify existing tort doctrine by eliminating principles that made it difficult for patients to sue doctors (Weiler 1991). Making lawsuits more attractive to potential plaintiffs was part of a general strategy to strengthen the deterrent signal tort law sent to health care providers. By 1960, these changes in malpractice law had led to a significant increase in claims frequency. These changes have had the intended effect of making providers more conscious of the threat of malpractice litigation, but whether this awareness has translated into improved patient safety is hotly disputed.

Tort law has certain advantages over other forms of health care regulation. Unlike agency oversight, litigation is not vulnerable (except at the margins) to capture by the regulated parties, fluctuations in political and bureaucratic agendas, or underfunded regulatory mandates. Unlike industry self-regulation, it is not constrained by the inherent conflict of interest involved in policing one's own profession.

However, several factors have made the relationship between tort law and patient safety a troubled and increasingly uncomfortable one. First, courts face significant structural constraints in serving as regulators. Judges lack specic expertise about health care quality and must rely on litigants to supply the facts of disputes and suggest remedies. In contrast, agency regulators typically have extensive experience in health care. Courts cannot engage in problem detection and initiate cases on their own; they must wait for an aggrieved litigant to present himself or herself—after the harm has already been done. Furthermore, they are limited in the remedies at their disposal: whereas agencies can promulgate new rules that will apply to all providers under their jurisdiction, and conduct inspections and impose sanctions for violating the rules, court decisions in tort cases bind only the particular defendant at bar (though landmark rulings may influence the behavior of other providers). All of these design features of the judiciary make tort law a relatively inefcacious mechanism in general. Several additional problems make it especially problematic for regulating patient safety.

One concern is that there is scant evidence that physicians process the deterrent signal sent by malpractice litigation in a constructive way (Danzon 1985; Mello and Brennan 2002). Physicians have long maintained that most malpractice suits are unwarranted, that patterns of suing are haphazard, and that as a result malpractice litigation does not create a rational and systematic deterrent signal. Contributing to the perception of haphazardness are findings from the California, New York, and Utah/Colorado studies showing that most patients who are injured due to negligence never bring claims, whereas a large proportion of malpractice claims do not actually involve a negligent injury. . . .

As a result, rather than viewing lawsuits as an indication that their clinical practices require modification, physicians tend to view suits as unrelated to the quality of care rendered. This is largely a modern view. Prior to the dissemination of the [Harvard study's] New York results, physician groups were more inclined to consider patient safety improvement a good risk-management strategy. Certainly there is no better example of this than . . . anesthesiologists responding to the mid-1980s tort crisis with a massive effort to understand and reduce anesthesia injuries. In contrast, providers in today's malpractice crisis seek merely to limit their liability. . . .

Finally, the deterrent signal is weakened by the fact that nearly all health care providers carry professional liability insurance and are therefore insulated from at least the economic consequences of malpractice (Danzon 1985). Experience rating—adjusting premiums to reflect an insured's claims experience—can get around this problem, but is not considered feasible for individual physicians (Mello and Brennan 2002). Owing to these and other problems, tort law as a form of regulation has not had much of an impact on patient safety. Although few systematic studies of the deterrent value of the tort law have been conducted, the existing analyses provide only very limited evidence that providers who experience malpractice claims have fewer adverse events and instances of negligence in the future. . . .

[T]he critical twist on the tort crisis today is that it has begun to create a siege mentality among physicians. This in turn has led to increased defensiveness regarding any initiative designed to bring more awareness to medical injuries, in particular patient safety initiatives that aim to encourage physician self-reporting of adverse events (Liang 2000). There is a dynamic tension between the general belief that greater transparency about adverse events is a good thing and the need to keep information about reported adverse events confidential in order to encourage reporting.

. . . We expect the conflict between patient safety regulation and malpractice to persist, because both are impelled by the increasingly widely accepted notion that patients are endangered by errors in medical care. The tort system presumes that punishment through economic sanctions is the best approach to deterrence, especially because the tort system is essentially uncapturable by the regulated industry. Members of the patient safety movement within the health care industry, however, rely on motivated professional commitment and a sanction-free environment to cultivate greater safety. As the public's awareness of errors deepens, plaintiffs' attorneys will grow more empowered and aggressive, which will in turn increase the pressure of the tort crisis and the defensiveness of the medical profession.

Market and Business Approaches. Regulation is usually contrasted with the market as an approach to social change, so it is perhaps odd to describe market approaches in an article on regulation. But if regulation is conceived of broadly as a rational structure of incentives set in place to accomplish a particular purpose, then regulation can proceed through market forces. . . . It has become de rigueur to refer to this regulatory strategy as building a "business case for quality."

The theory of value-based purchasing is that purchasers—employers, the government, health care organizations, and, to a lesser extent, individual patients—can gather, analyze, and use quality, safety, and cost information on health care providers for the purpose of selectively contracting with providers based on their performance. Individual patients in a consumer-driven health care marketplace can vote with their feet by choosing health plans or hospitals based on quality and safety report cards. Employers and the government can mandate or encourage providers to pursue specific objectives through the use of contractual provisions, direct financial incentives, and ongoing quality monitoring.

How well does this theory translate into practice? With regard to shopping behavior by individual patients, the findings are rather discouraging. Considerable energy has been spent generating quality report cards on health care organizations and making this information available to consumers, . . . [but] few consumers actually use quality information in selecting providers. For the most part, patients continue to pick their providers based on personal recommendations or convenience. . . .

[V]alue-based purchasing is presently being pursued vigorously by only a handful of large employers and employer coalitions. Other employers have been reluctant to venture down this path due to a number of obstacles including inadequate manpower and expertise, the difficulty of collecting quality and outcomes data, questions about the credibility of existing quality measures, and financial constraints that drive employers to shop for providers and health plans primarily based on cost rather than quality. Additionally, employers in small markets or markets dominated by small businesses generally do not have sufficient leverage with hospitals to successfully push for improved patient safety.

Some employers have attempted to increase their collective bargaining power by forming coalitions to pursue patient safety initiatives. One coalition that has garnered considerable attention is the Leapfrog Group, a consortium of more than one hundred large employers . . . representing more than 31 million employees. [The] Leapfrog Group has announced the intention of steering these employees toward health care institutions that have instituted specic safety measures. Rather than rating [or picking] individual hospitals, the group has chosen to give consumers information about comparative institutional performance on three processes or practices believed to be associated with high-safety care: [computerized entry of physicians' orders, referral of patients for high-risk procedures to hospitals that perform a high volume of these procedures, and round-the-clock coverage of intensive care units by ICU physician specialists]. . . .

It appears that Leapfrog chose clear standards, for which compliance can be readily monitored to be able to rely largely on self-reporting. But the evidence that the standards themselves are the most effective approaches to improving safety has been questioned. . . . [Also, the] investments required to implement Leapfrog's recommendations are substantial, and the business case requires strong evidence that Leapfrog certification will raise market demand for a hospital's services enough to recoup these expenditures. . . . To create strong financial incentives for hospitals, initiatives such as Leapfrog need to significantly expand their purchaser and patient base and select safety standards that are possible for most or all hospitals to meet with a reasonable investment.

. . . Business-case advocates discouraged by this situation might articulate a business case along a second angle: rather than emphasizing the potential for increased market share as a result of safety improvement, as Leapfrog does, they might emphasize the costs of medical injuries and the potential for hospitals to avoid those costs by reducing injuries. . . . However, an often-missed nuance is that medical injury costs generally do not redound in a significant way to hospitals. Most of these costs—which include additional acute care costs, the cost of long-term care and maintenance of the disabled, lost income, and lost household production—fall on patients and their families, their health insurers, their employers, and state disability and income-support programs. Although the costs of poor safety are largely externalized to other parties, the costs of implementing safety improvement fall squarely on hospitals. For this reason . . . hospitals have little to gain financially from putting improvements in place. . . .

Presently, the tort system focuses liability heavily on individuals; the circumstances in which health care organizations are held liable are relatively limited. This approach makes sense if we believe that individual negligence is responsible for most preventable medical injuries. But if research reveals that errors often tend to be attributable not to individual carelessness or incompetence but to breakdowns in larger systems of care (which hospitals are in a much better position than individuals to x), then the wisdom of regulating patient safety through our current tort system may be cast into doubt. Such a finding would suggest, at a minimum, the need to refashion tort doctrine to incorporate greater enterprise liability. . . .

THE IMPLICATIONS OF REGULATORY PLURALISM

We have described a regulatory landscape in patient safety consisting of two streams of regulation—one from the top down and one from the bottom up—each of which is populated by multiple regulators. State and federal legislatures, state and federal administrative agencies, industry accrediting, professional and peer review organizations, courts and litigants, and purchaser organizations are all active regulators of patient safety today. Pluralistic regulation is a choice, not an inevitability. In other industries in which safety is a concern, we have limited the number of regulators. Dedicated national-level agencies have exclusive jurisdiction over nuclear power and aviation, for example; and the tort liability system has been largely eliminated as a regulator of workplace safety, replaced by the workers' compensation system and agency oversight. Who should regulate patient safety?

There is reason to hope that greater coordination and consensus on effective safety measures will emerge naturally over time, because many of the same experts advise the various regulators and because so much of this regulatory activity is quite new. There are already signs of moves in this direction: the JCAHO, [National Quality Forum, Agency for Healthcare Research and Quality] and Leapfrog are now collaborating on various measures and standards. However, all are adding new requirements, and there is still the sense on the part of the entities that they have a responsibility to serve the public by issuing mandates, even if that means that they cannot always wait for evidence to develop. . . .

All of the regulators on the scene today have a valuable contribution to make to safety improvement. However, as we have articulated, their collective impact has been somewhat enervated by lack of coordination and evidence-based standard setting. An optimal model of regulatory pluralism would address these concerns by better leveraging the distinctive institutional strengths of the various regulators. This capacity-leveraging model, as it might be called, recognizes that evidence-based patient safety regulation proceeds through a number of distinct steps, each of which calls for particular kinds of expertise and institutional capabilities. . . .

It is worth noting that despite its historical preeminence as a patient safety regulator, the tort liability system['s] . . . ability to set new standards for patient safety is circumscribed by the continued reliance of most states' courts on medical custom to set the standard of care. . . . The courts' ability to enforce compliance with standards is [also] limited by the fact that they can only address cases of noncompliance that come before them, and only a tiny fraction of patients injured by negligence le lawsuits. Thus, it is a mistake to rely on the tort system as a frontline regulator of patient safety. At best, it is a regulator of last resort, seeking to make whole those who have suffered injuries that other forms of regulation have tried and failed to prevent. . . .

REFERENCES

Danzon, P. 1985. *Medical Malpractice: Theory, Evidence, and Public Policy*. Cambridge, MA: Harvard University Press.
Institute of Medicine. 2001. *Crossing the Quality Chasm: A New Health System for the Twenty-First Century*. Washington, DC: National Academies Press. 2002. *Fostering Rapid Advances in Health Care: Learning from System Demonstrations*. Washington, DC: Institute of Medicine.
Kohn, L. T., J. M. Corrigan, and M. S. Donaldson, eds. 2000. *To Err Is Human: Building a Safer Health System*. Washington, DC: National Academies Press.
Liang, B. A. 2000. Risks of Reporting Sentinel Events. *Health Affairs* 19(5): 112-120.
Mello, M. M., and T. A. Brennan. 2002. Deterrence of Medical Errors: Theory and Evidence for Malpractice Reform. *University of Texas Law Review* 80: 1595-1637.
Studdert, D. M., M. M. Mello, and T. A. Brennan. 2004. Medical Malpractice. *New England Journal of Medicine* 350: 283-292.
Thomas, E. J., D. M. Studdert, H. R. Burstin, E. J. Orav, T. Zeena, E. J. Williams, K. M. Howard, P. C. Weiler, and T. A. Brennan. 2000. Incidence and Types of Adverse Events and Negligent Care in Utah and Colorado. *Medical Care* 38: 261-271.
Weiler, P. C. 1991. *Medical Malpractice on Trial*. Cambridge, MA: Harvard University Press.
Weiler, P. C., H. H. Hiatt, J. P. Newhouse, W. G. Johnson, T. A. Brennan, and L. L. Leape. 1993. *A Measure of Malpractice: Medical Injury, Malpractice Litigation, and Patient Compensation*. Cambridge, MA: Harvard University Press.

■ THE NECESSARY AND PROPER ROLE OF REGULATION TO ASSURE THE QUALITY OF HEALTH CARE*
Timothy Stolzfus Jost
25 Hous. L. Rev. 525 (1988)

A consideration of strategies for quality assurance should begin with an examination of the meaning of quality and error. Donabedian, the leading theorist of

*This excerpt is a combination of three articles, the second one entitled Regulatory Approaches to Problems in the Quality of Medical Care: Diagnosis and Prescription (Copyright © 1989 by the Regents of the University of California), and the third one entitled Oversight of the Quality of Medical Care: Regulation, Management, or the Market? They are reprinted with permission. Headings, footnote numbering, and to some extent the structure of the argument have been altered from the original.

health care quality, . . . categorizes [quality] evaluation mechanisms in his famous typology as concerned with structure, process, or outcome.[2] A structural evaluation (e.g., a licensure examination) focuses on underlying capacity to deliver quality care: How much does the doctor know; how well is the hospital equipped? . . . [S]tructural aspects of care are the easiest to define and to evaluate; thus, many strategies rely, at least in part, on structural evaluation.

Process evaluation studies the process through which care is delivered. It considers, for example, whether a drug was properly prescribed in the appropriate dosage given the patient's symptoms. Process is more difficult to evaluate than structure. Process evaluation is usually based on professional consensus as to appropriate procedures for a given problem. It forms the basis for many peer review programs. It has been criticized as overemphasizing the technical nature of care and contributing to health care cost inflation through this emphasis. Moreover, process norms are model treatments for model cases. It is difficult to adapt them to address the wide variations found in patients and their conditions.

Finally, outcome analysis considers the results of care: Did the patient get better; did the condition improve? Comparing hospital mortality and morbidity statistics for treatment of a particular condition is a form of outcome analysis. Outcome analysis is the most difficult form of quality evaluation because the duration, timing, or extent of outcomes of optimal care are often hard to specify. Data on the outcomes of care delivered by professionals or institutions cannot be compared usefully unless adjustments are made for variations in case mix and severity of conditions. It is often difficult to relate a specific outcome to a particular medical intervention, and outcomes are often clear only when it is too late to affect practice. Yet outcome analysis looks at the ends of medical care rather than the means, and is thus ultimately most telling. The medical malpractice system has always begun its inquiry with a bad outcome, though it ultimately relies on process analysis. . . .

Notes: Quality Measurement and Control

1. *Overview.* The purpose of this section is to put in broader context the role that malpractice law plays in the deterrence and punishment of medical error and in the improvement of medical quality. To sharpen your focus, review the types of bad medical outcomes identified earlier, the dimensions of quality surveyed by Jost, and the various social and legal responses available, noting which responses are addressed to which types and dimensions of poor quality. Based on the resulting patterns and gaps, how would you articulate the strongest case for the role of tort law? What types of medical mistakes should it be most concerned with? Which types should it ignore?

2. *Medical Licensure.* Professor Mello and colleagues fail to mention another source of medical quality regulation — physician licensure. Each state has a disciplinary process to consider complaints against physicians from either patients or

2. Donabedian, Criteria and Standards for Quality Assessment and Monitoring, 12 Quality Rev. Bull. 99 (1986); Donabedian, Commentary on Some Studies on the Quality of Care, Health Care Fin. Ref., 1987 Supp., at 75, 76-77; 1 A. Donabedian, Explorations in Quality Assessment and Monitoring: The Definition of Quality and Approaches to Its Assessment 4-6 (1980).

other physicians. Much like state bars for attorney discipline, these boards of medical examiners are composed of other physicians and therefore are subject to the limits of self-regulation noted above. As summarized by Prof. Sawicki in the article excerpted at page 124, "medical boards rarely take disciplinary action on the basis of incompetent medical practice or poor quality of care." Instead, many of their actions are based on financial misdeeds, substance abuse, or inappropriate relationships with patients. Character, Competence, and the Principles of Medical Discipline, 13 J. Health Care L. & Pol'y 285 (2010).

3. *Donabedian's Categories.* To sharpen your understanding of the structure/process/outcome categories developed by Donabedian, consider which category best describes the way that each of the following measures ensures the quality of motor vehicle driving: (1) requiring drivers to pass a written exam; (2) requiring an on-road test; (3) vehicle inspection laws that check brake lights, windshield wipers, etc.; (4) enforcing speed limits; (5) increasing insurance premiums when drivers are involved in accidents.

4. *The Information Explosion.* Other influential standards-setting organizations, in addition to those that Professor Mello and colleagues mention, include the National Committee for Quality Assurance (NCQA), which focuses on performance measures for HMOs and other health plans using what is known as the Health Plan and Employer Data and Information Set (HEDIS). HEDIS entails measures such as consumer satisfaction, rates of childhood immunization and cancer screening, and management of asthma and diabetes. Medicare does something similar using its Consumer Assessment of Health Plans and Systems (CAHPS) survey.

The federal government has also taken strides to rank hospitals according to how well their patients do. The Center for Medicare and Medicaid Services (CMS), which oversees Medicare and Medicaid, rewards hospitals that report a variety of quality measures focused on process steps in caring for heart attacks, pneumonia, and surgery patients. CMS also reports hospital mortality statistics, adjusted for various risk factors (so that hospitals are not rated poorly simply for treating sicker patients). In addition to simply reporting this information, CMS is implementing payment policies that reward better-performing hospitals or penalize worse ones. See the casebook Web site for further details, www.health-law.org.

So far, these "report card" efforts have not extended (much) to physicians. Medicare is beginning to move in this direction, but a variety of concerns will likely slow progress. Physician organizations have objected to (1) the burden of providing all the relevant information, and (2) how valid the information is. On validity, consider the situation of a physician who complains that his poor surgical outcomes scorecard is due to the fact that his colleagues refer him the most difficult cases, in recognition of his being the very best in the community at what he does. A related concern is that, if outcome measures (like death) are not appropriately adjusted for patient risk factors, then physicians will avoid patients who are likely to hurt their scorecards. See Timothy Hofer et al., The Unreliability of Individual Physician "Report Cards" for Assessing the Costs and Quality of Care of a Chronic Disease, 281 JAMA 2098 (1999) (finding that report cards "were unable to detect reliably true practice differences" and that their use "may foster an environment in which physicians can most easily avoid being penalized by avoiding . . . [more difficult patients who have not responded well to treatment]").

5. *Total Quality Management.* Central to any comprehensive discussion of health care quality is the concept of "continuous quality improvement" (CQI), also known as "total quality management" (TQM). This is a managerial concept imported from manufacturing industries that owes its popularity to management gurus whose ideas were first implemented by Japanese companies and are considered an important reason why they so quickly surpassed American quality standards in consumer electronics and automobile manufacturing. In health care, CQI signals a paradigm shift away from identifying isolated mistakes and deterring malefactors, to improving the quality of all outcomes through systems improvements. CQI assumes that professionals generally are diligent and well motivated and so only need better information and support in order to do a better job. Its philosophy is captured in the title of the first reading in this chapter, Making Medical Errors into "Medical Treasures," since it views mistakes as opportunities to learn, not occasions for blame and punishment. CQI attempts to target the entire range of medical outcomes, not simply to eliminate the "bad apples," and it sees errors as resulting more from system flaws than from individual misfeasance. Institute of Medicine, Crossing the Quality Chasm: A New Health System for the Twenty-first Century (2001).

Troyen Brennan, co-author with Professor Mello, supra, teamed up with Donald Berwick, a proponent of quality improvement who now heads CMS, to write New Rules: Regulation, Markets, and the Quality of American Health Care (1996). They argue that the entire legal regime is antithetical to the philosophy of quality improvement. Can you imagine how that might be the case? For a contrary argument, see David A. Hyman & Charles Silver, The Poor State of Health Care Quality in the U.S.: Is Malpractice Liability Part of the Problem or Part of the Solution?, 90 Corn. L. Rev. 893 (2005).

6. *Bibliography.* On **modernizing quality regulation in the information age** (note 4), see Kristin Madison, Regulating Health Care Quality in an Information Age, 40 U.C. Davis L. Rev. (2007); Kristin Madison, Donabedian's Legacy: The Future of Health Care Quality Law and Policy, 10 Ind. Health L. Rev. 325 (2013); William M. Sage, Regulating Through Information: Disclosure Laws and American Health Care, 99 Colum. L. Rev. 1701 (1999); Symposium, 31 J. Leg. Med. 9 (2010); Symposium, 24(1) Health Aff. (Jan. 2005); Symposium, 23 Health Aff. (Oct. 2004) (special supp.).

For studies that examine the **impact of comparative outcomes measures on actual consumer and provider behavior**, see Mark Chassin, Achieving and Sustaining Improved Quality, 21(4) Health Aff. 40 (July 2002) (finding some impact); Ashish K. Jha & Arnold M. Epstein, The Predictive Accuracy of the New York State Coronary Artery Bypass Surgery Report-Card System, 25(3) Health Aff. 844 (June 2006) (finding no impact); David Dranove et al., Is More Information Better? The Effects of "Report Cards" on Health Care Providers, 111 J. Pol. Econ. 555 (2003) (finding negative impact by prompting physicians and hospitals to avoid sicker or more severe cases); Symposium, 35 Health Aff. 563 (2016).

On **quality measurement and improvement generally**, see Stephen R. Latham, System Responsibility: Three Readings of the IOM Report on Medical Error, 27 Am. J.L. & Med. 145 (2001); 335 New Eng. J. Med., issues 12-15 (1996); Symposium, 16(3) Health Aff. (May 1997); Symposium, 12 Widener L. Rev. 1 (2005); Katharine Tassell, Harmonizing the Affordable Care Act with the Three Main National Systems for Healthcare Quality Improvement, 78 Brook L. Rev. 883 (2013).

B. PHYSICIAN LIABILITY

1. *The Custom-Based Standard of Care*

■ **McCOURT v. ABERNATHY**
457 S.E.2d 603 (S.C. 1995)

SHAW, Acting Associate Justice.

[The following facts are quoted from Wendy McCourt's medical record: "This patient is a 23-year-old white female who was admitted to the hospital with shortness of breath and chest wall pain. The patient states about five days prior to admission, she was working with some horses doing castrations. While trying to hold a horse, the horse suddenly bolted and hyperextended her left shoulder. . . . The patient also relates that about two days prior to the horse incident, she pricked her finger with a pin. She continued working around manure and other agents in the barns with the horses. She had developed a slight redness around the pin prick over the fat pad of the left second finger."]

[Doctors Abernathy and Clyde are board certified family practitioners who practice together in Anderson, South Carolina.] . . . There is evidence Wendy was seen by Dr. Abernathy in his office at the time [of the horse incident] and was treated for a pulled muscle. [Three or four days later,] on Sunday, March 13, her condition worsened and Wendy went to the Anderson Memorial Hospital emergency room. She was experiencing greater pain and had difficulty breathing. Dr. Clyde examined Wendy at that time and treated her for a pulled chest muscle. There is evidence Dr. Clyde treated the puncture wound to Wendy's finger at that time.[2] She was given prescriptions for Motrin and Co-Tylenol. She returned to her home.

The following day, March 14, Wendy's condition became significantly worse and she again sought treatment at the emergency room. She was examined by an emergency room physician who ran some blood tests. This physician indicated an immediate need to admit Wendy to the hospital. He telephoned Dr. Abernathy and was given permission to admit Wendy. At 6:30 that evening, Dr. Abernathy examined Wendy and observed the injured finger, for which he prescribed Keflex, an oral antibiotic.

At 9:00 the following morning, both Dr. Abernathy and Dr. Clyde saw Wendy while making rounds at the hospital. By that time, Wendy's condition had worsened yet more and the doctors consulted Dr. Kovaz, an internist. Although appellants requested a consult from Dr. Kovaz, they did not express any urgency in his seeing her. After examining Wendy, Dr. Kovaz immediately moved her to the intensive care unit with a diagnosis of sepsis, a bacterial infection. Although treatment with intravenous antibiotics was begun at that time, her condition continued to deteriorate. Over the next four days, her skin began to slough off, her eyes filled with blood,

---

2. Steven McCourt testified Dr. Clyde pointed out the puncture wound on Wendy's finger which Dr. Clyde proceeded to clean and dress. He stated the finger was red and swollen to almost twice the normal size, and was having some sort of discharge. He further testified the wound was very noticeable and Wendy indicated it was a result of a pin prick that occurred a couple of days earlier.

her feet turned black, she bled from her nose, mouth and pores, and she became bloated beyond recognition. On March 19, 1988, Wendy McCourt died from beta strep septicemia with multiple organ system failure secondary to the sepsis.*

Respondent presented expert testimony from Dr. Neal Craine and Dr. Kenneth DeHart. Dr. Craine stated Wendy's illness was caused by "an unfortunate circumstance where transient bacteria in the bloodstream landed in an area already traumatized by the injury with the horse." He testified, assuming, as the "Death Summary" indicates, Dr. Abernathy saw Wendy on the ninth, she had a puncture wound to the finger and it was known she was working around horses, he should have put her on preventive antibiotics on that day. He stated it would also have been below the standard of care for Dr. Clyde to have observed an infected finger on the thirteenth and not treat her with antibiotics nor order laboratory tests. He stated he felt Wendy had a 100 percent chance of survival on the thirteenth had she been started on antibiotics at that time. Based on the test results received on the afternoon of the fourteenth, he stated that a doctor should know the patient was seriously ill and should have suspected sepsis. He concluded Wendy's life could have been saved if antibiotics had been started on the ninth, which would have prevented or treated an early infection of the finger. He also stated, more likely than not, Wendy could have been saved on the thirteenth by treatment with antibiotics as well as on the fourteenth with aggressive antibiotic therapy. He stated it was also below the standard of care to wait until the fifteenth to call in a specialist.

Dr. DeHart likewise testified [that] . . . failure to treat [the infected finger] prophylactically fell below the standard of care. . . . As to Dr. Abernathy's treatment on the fourteenth, he testified it was "profoundly below the standard of care," not because he missed the diagnosis, but because he failed to order aggressive observation and failed to request consultation intervention.

This matter was tried by a jury and on January 7, 1993 the jury returned the following verdicts for appellant: [$700,000 in actual damages and $1,000,000 in punitive damages against Dr. Abernathy, and $350,000 in actual damages and $500,000 in punitive damages against Dr. Clyde.] TOTAL VERDICTS: $2,550,000. . . .

Appellants first contend the trial judge erred in failing to charge several jury instructions relating to mistake in diagnosis or error in judgment in a medical malpractice cause of action.[4] . . . [T]he appellants assert all of the charges stand for

---

*[In the popular press, beta strep is known as the "flesh-eating" bacteria, as described by Dr. Gawande at page 31. Septicemia is an extremely serious condition in which an infection invades the bloodstream and spreads throughout the body, much like a localized cancer can metastasize. — EDS.]

4. Oral request #1: When a physician exercises ordinary care and skill in keeping within recognized and proven methods, he is not liable for the result of a bona fide mistake of judgment. There is no responsibility unless it is negligent, as I have defined that to you, so as to be inconsistent with that degree of skill which is the duty of every physician practicing in his specialty to possess and use. . . . Request #13: Ladies and Gentlemen, when a physician exercises ordinary care and skill in keeping within recognized and proven methods, he is not liable for the result of a mere mistake of judgment or for a bad result which does not occur because of any negligence on his part. There is no responsibility for error of judgment or for a bad result unless it is so negligent as to be inconsistent with that degree of skill which it is the duty of every practitioner practicing in his specialty to possess.

the proposition that a physician is not liable for a mistake in diagnosis or error in judgment if he acts within the appropriate standard of care. . . . We disagree. . . . [T]he requested charges may have a tendency to confuse the jury. Some of the charges imply to the jury that an error in judgment is actionable only if made in bad faith. Such an instruction would impose an unrealistic burden on the plaintiff to prove the doctor's judgment was rendered with less than good faith.

. . . [T]he trial judge gave the following relevant charges:

> . . . The mere fact that the plaintiff's expert may use a different approach is not considered a deviation from the recognized standard of medical care. Nor is the standard violated because the expert disagrees with a defendant as to what is the best or better approach in treating a patient. Medicine is an inexact science, and generally qualified physicians may differ as to what constitutes a preferable course of treatment. Such differences due to preference . . . do not amount to malpractice.
>
> I further charge you that the degree of skill and care that a physician must use in diagnosing a condition is that which would be exercised by competent practitioners in the defendant doctor's field of medicine. In South Carolina the question of whether a physician, in making a diagnosis deviated from the applicable standard of care either by not employing a particular procedure or by not ordering a particular test is to be determined by what an ordinary careful and prudent physician would have done under the same or similar circumstances. . . .
>
> Negligence may not be inferred from a bad result. Our law says that a physician is not an insurer of health, and a physician is not required to guarantee results. He undertakes only to meet the standard of skill possessed generally by others practicing in his field under similar circumstances.

Even if we were to assume the appellants' requested charges were the current and correct law of the state, we find the instructions [given] as a whole clearly intimate that a mere mistake in diagnosis or error in judgment alone is insufficient to support a finding of malpractice. Accordingly, we find no error.

Appellants next contend the trial judge erred in denying their motions for new trial . . . on the basis of the excessiveness of the punitive damages awards. They contend the damages are excessive and, because there was no evidence of conduct rising to the level of recklessness, the verdict was the result of passion and prejudice. We disagree.

In order for a plaintiff to recover punitive damages, there must be evidence the defendant's conduct was willful, wanton, or in reckless disregard of the plaintiff's rights. A conscious failure to exercise due care constitutes willfulness. . . .

We find the record before us contains evidence that both Dr. Abernathy and Dr. Clyde consciously failed to exercise due care in treating Wendy. This evidence includes, but is not limited to: (1) failure to properly diagnose and treat Wendy within the standard of care on three separate occasions; (2) failure to order timely diagnostic tests in light of continual complaints and no improvement of Wendy's condition; (3) failure to appreciate the seriousness of Wendy's deteriorating condition in the face of highly abnormal blood work; (4) failure to aggressively monitor Wendy's deteriorating condition; and (5) failure to promptly seek the immediate aid of a specialist once the seriousness of Wendy's condition became apparent. While the evidence indicates a more severe degree of culpability on the part of Dr. Abernathy than Dr. Clyde, the record contains sufficient evidence of conduct on the part of both doctors to support the awards of punitive damages. The jury's determination of damages is entitled to substantial deference. We find no abuse of the trial judge's discretion in this respect. . . . Affirmed.

■LOCKE v. PACHTMAN
521 N.W.2d 786 (Mich. 1994)

M ALLETT, Justice.

In this medical malpractice action, the trial judge granted defendants' motion for a directed verdict at the close of the plaintiff's proofs. The court of appeals affirmed, finding that plaintiff had failed to make a prima facie showing of the standard of care related to defendants' allegedly negligent conduct. We affirm.

I

On August 5, 1981, plaintiff Shirley Locke underwent a vaginal hysterectomy with entocele and rectocele repair at the University of Michigan Hospital.* The procedure was performed by defendant, Dr. Judith Pachtman, then a fourth-year resident in gynecology. Codefendant, Dr. James Roberts, was the attending physician and was present for most of the surgery.**

Dr. Pachtman testified that she performed the first two procedures, the hysterectomy and entocele repair, without complication, although the entocele repair took longer than expected. Following the entocele repair, Dr. Roberts left the room to attend another operation that had been previously scheduled.

Dr. Pachtman then began the rectocele repair. Upon Dr. Pachtman's initial insertion into the levator ani muscle, the needle she was using broke. One-half to two-thirds of the needle, a length of about 1.5 cm, broke off and lodged somewhere within that muscle. Dr. Pachtman searched unsuccessfully for the broken portion of the needle for 15 to 20 minutes. At that time, Dr. Roberts returned and joined Dr. Pachtman in searching for the needle fragment.

Drs. Pachtman and Roberts utilized a silver probe to X-ray the affected area, in an attempt to locate the broken portion of the needle. After ascertaining the approximate location of the fragment, they decided to close the old incision and to continue their search through a new incision. After unsuccessfully searching for the needle for another 45 minutes to one hour, they abandoned the search and closed the second incision. Both doctors indicated that they felt it was in the plaintiff's best

---

*As explained at trial, an entocele is an out-pouching or hernia of the peritoneal cavity where the bowel protrudes into the area between the vagina and the rectum. A rectocele is a hernial protrusion of the rectum through the posterior vaginal wall.

**At trial, Dr. Roberts explained that he was the senior medical officer involved in the procedure. However, he also stated that, as attending physician, his role was to act as assistant and consultant to Dr. Pachtman, who actually performed the surgery. Dr. Pachtman essentially agreed with Dr. Roberts' characterization of his role in the procedure, but asserted nevertheless that, as attending physician, Dr. Roberts had "ultimate responsibility" for the surgery.

interest to terminate the surgery at that point, even though they had failed to locate the needle fragment.

Plaintiff testified that after the surgery Dr. Pachtman informed her of the needle breakage and stated that the needle was entrenched in the muscle and therefore could remain there without causing her any problems. However, after experiencing considerable pain and discomfort, plaintiff consulted with another physician, Dr. Frances Couch. Dr. Couch advised removing the needle fragment, and, subsequently, she performed the surgical procedure, successfully locating and removing the broken portion of the needle.

Plaintiff filed suit against Drs. Pachtman and Roberts, alleging negligence on various grounds, including the use of a needle that they knew or should have known was too small and failing to locate and remove the needle fragment. Plaintiff claimed that she suffers from severe pain, disfigurement, and limitation of body movement and functions, as well as experiencing mental and emotional distress. Plaintiff's husband, Danny Locke, filed a derivative claim.

In testimony presented at trial, plaintiff's expert witness, Dr. Couch, was unable to identify any negligent conduct on the part of either Dr. Pachtman or Dr. Roberts. Dr. Couch also stated that she could not give an opinion regarding the adequacy of the needle size, because she had never viewed the needle intact. She explained that she could not identify the size of the needle without viewing the needle in its entirety.

When questioned generally regarding the cause of needle breakage and its relation to the standard of care, Dr. Couch made two separate statements. At one point Dr. Couch stated that the standard of care did not relate to needle breakage at all, but rather to how one dealt with it, suggesting that needle breakage was simply one of the risks of surgery. Later, without relating this point to a standard of care, she noted that a surgeon's "incorrect technique" often causes a needle to break. When asked to describe what she meant by incorrect technique, Dr. Couch described instances in which a surgeon fails to manipulate the needle correctly, such as by inserting it at the wrong angle or applying too much force. Dr. Couch also testified that she had previously had a needle break while performing surgery.

In addition to Dr. Couch's expert testimony, plaintiff introduced evidence regarding a number of statements allegedly made by Dr. Pachtman following the surgery. Plaintiff's brother, Reverend Gary Heniser, testified that, while he was at the hospital visiting his sister, Dr. Pachtman told him, " 'I knew the needle was too small when I used it.' " Coplaintiff Danny Locke testified that Dr. Pachtman had also spoken to him about the surgery: "[S]he told me that it was her fault, that she used the wrong needle, and she was sorry." Finally, Shirley Locke testified that Dr. Pachtman had told her: "I knew that needle was too small when the new scrub nurse handed it to me. It wasn't her fault because she was new, but I chose to use it anyway and it's my fault and I am really sorry. . . ."

Both Dr. Pachtman and Dr. Roberts testified at trial. Neither acknowledged any negligent behavior in the choice of needle, the needle breakage, or their subsequent search for the needle fragment.

At the close of plaintiff's proofs, the trial court granted defendants' motion for directed verdict on the ground that plaintiff had failed to make a prima facie showing regarding the standard of care. Plaintiff's motion for a new trial was denied, and, in a divided opinion, the court of appeals affirmed. . . .

II

Proof of a medical malpractice claim requires the demonstration of the following four factors: (1) the applicable standard of care, (2) breach of that standard of care by the defendant, (3) injury, and (4) proximate causation between the alleged breach and the injury.[6] To survive a motion for directed verdict, the plaintiff must make a prima facie showing regarding each of the above elements.

Plaintiff argues that the lower courts erred in finding that she had failed to demonstrate the standard of care applicable to defendants' conduct. Plaintiff contends that expert testimony was sufficient to establish this point, and, further, that the standard of care and breach of that standard were inferable under the doctrine of res ipsa loquitur and because the alleged negligence was within the common understanding of the jury.

We agree with the lower courts' determination that no prima facie showing was made, and therefore we affirm the directed verdict entered for the defendants.

A

. . . Plaintiff argues first that the standard of care attributable to Dr. Pachtman was established by way of expert testimony. This court has long recognized the importance of expert testimony in establishing a medical malpractice claim, and the need to educate the jury and the court regarding matters not within their common purview. As we have previously explained:

> In a case involving professional service the ordinary layman is not equipped by common knowledge and experience to judge of the skill and competence of that service and determine whether it squares with the standard of such professional practice in the community. For that, the aid of expert testimony from those learned in the profession involved is required.

While we have recognized exceptions to this requirement, the benefit of expert testimony, particularly in demonstrating the applicable standard of care, cannot be overstated.

In this case, plaintiff contends that the standard of care applicable to Dr. Pachtman was established by Dr. Couch's expert testimony. For this point, plaintiff relies on Dr. Couch's statement that needle breakage often occurs because of the surgeon's "incorrect technique." Plaintiff asserts that this testimony, coupled with

---

6. [Michigan statutes state:]

In an action alleging malpractice the plaintiff shall have the burden of proving that in light of the state of the art existing at the time of the alleged malpractice: (a) The defendant, if a general practitioner, failed to provide the plaintiff the recognized standard of acceptable professional practice in the community in which the defendant practices or in a similar community, and that as a proximate result of the defendant failing to provide that standard, the plaintiff suffered an injury. (b) The defendant, if a specialist, failed to provide the recognized standard of care within that specialty as reasonably applied in light of the facilities available in the community or other facilities reasonably available under the circumstances, and as a proximate result of the defendant failing to provide that standard, the plaintiff suffered an injury.

Dr. Pachtman's admissions regarding use of a needle she knew to be too small, were sufficient to establish the standard of care and breach of that standard.

Dr. Couch's testimony with regard to the standard of care associated with needle breakage was rather confused. At one point she suggested that needle breakage was merely one of the risks of surgery, and that needle breakage did not ordinarily signal a violation of the standard of care. . . . Dr. Couch later testified that needle breakage may be attributable to a surgeon's "incorrect technique":

Q. From your experience and your training can the manner in which a surgeon utilizes a needle cause it to break?
A. I would say most of the time that's the case. It's a matter of incorrect technique.
Q. Could you discuss that?
A. Well, a needle is curved. If you forget the needle is curved and you push against the curve instead of with the curve the needle will break. If you try to put a needle through an instrument it doesn't go through steel. If it's not positioned correctly in a tissue and you're trying to draw it through against a clamp it will break. . . . Generally, that's most of the reason why they break. You are putting force against where it wasn't made to be put against.

As the lower courts found, it is indeed questionable whether Dr. Couch's latter testimony on this point was sufficient to establish a standard of care with regard to "incorrect technique." Dr. Couch, while presenting one way in which needles break, never went so far as to relate that discussion to a standard of care. In effect, she never explained what a reasonably prudent surgeon would do, in keeping with the standards of professional practice, that might not have been done by Dr. Pachtman. Accordingly, the jury would have had no standard against which to measure Dr. Pachtman's conduct. This factor, coupled with the conflicting nature of Dr. Couch's testimony, leads us to believe that the standard of care was not sufficiently established. . . .

B

Plaintiff next argues that the statements allegedly made by Dr. Pachtman were themselves sufficient to establish the standard of care and breach of that standard. Plaintiff contends that her case is governed by this court's decision in Orozco v. Henry Ford Hosp., 408 Mich. 248, 290 N.W.2d 363 (1980). . . . Plaintiff's reliance upon *Orozco* is misplaced. In *Orozco*, the plaintiff testified that during his hernial surgery he heard one of the surgeons say, "Oops, I cut in the wrong place." Following the surgery, one of his testicles atrophied. At trial, an expert witness testified that this injury was likely due to an impairment of the blood supply to the testicles during the surgery.

At the close of Orozco's proofs, the trial court granted the defendants' motion for a directed verdict, and the court of appeals affirmed, finding that the plaintiff had failed to make a prima facie showing of the applicable standard of care.[9] This court reversed the court of appeals by per curiam opinion. The court found that

9. In reaching this conclusion, the court of appeals relied on Lince v. Monson. In Lince, this court held that expert testimony was required in order for the jury to determine whether the defendants violated the standard of care when they mistakenly sutured the plaintiff's ureter in responding to excessive bleeding. 363 Mich. at 142, 108 N.W.2d 845.

expert testimony was not necessary because jury members would be able to determine, from their own common knowledge, whether the defendants' actions violated the applicable standard of care. As the court explained:

> Here Orozco offered the fact of the injury, a medical explanation of how that injury likely occurred, and an admission by the surgeon that he cut in the wrong place. Paraphrasing *Lince*, "[t]he question is whether the action of defendants conformed to standards of good practice in the community. Common knowledge and the experience of ordinary laymen do . . . equip them to give the answer in a case such as this" when an expert testifies that the likely cause of injury was an impairment of the blood supply to the testicles in the course of the operation and the plaintiff testifies that the surgeon said, "Oops, I cut in the wrong place."

. . . This decision was in line with previous case law holding that expert testimony is not normally required where the defendant mistakenly treated or did injury to a portion of the body that was free of disease and not designated for treatment. Sullivan v. Russell, 417 Mich. 398, 408, 338 N.W.2d 181 (1983) (no expert testimony was necessary where a dentist mistakenly ground three of the plaintiff's teeth not intended for treatment); Higdon v. Carlebach, 348 Mich. 363, 374, 83 N.W.2d 296 (1957) (expert testimony was not required where a dentist, using a rotating disk to separate two of the plaintiff's teeth, mistakenly cut into her tongue).

Turning to the present case, we hold that the lower courts correctly concluded that Dr. Pachtman's statements were insufficient to make a prima facie showing. While the statements may have indicated Dr. Pachtman's belief that she made a mistake or acted in error, a jury could not reasonably infer from those statements alone that Dr. Pachtman's actions did not conform to the standard of professional practice for the community as a whole.

Unlike the situation presented in *Orozco*, the standard of care associated with needle choice and needle breakage is not accessible to the jury absent expert guidance. Plaintiff has provided no guidance with regard to what options were available to Dr. Pachtman and which of them she should have chosen. In short, there was no testimony regarding what a reasonably prudent surgeon would have done in Dr. Pachtman's situation. We agree with the court of appeals determination that the jury should not be left to speculate in this regard. It is precisely to avoid such speculation that expert testimony is ordinarily required. . . .

E

Plaintiff asserts liability against Dr. Roberts on grounds . . . [of] negligent supervision. However, . . . plaintiff's negligent supervision claim is also not supported by the record. There was uncontroverted testimony, including testimony from plaintiff's own expert, to the fact that it was not unusual for an attending physician at University of Michigan Hospital to leave a resident alone during portions of a procedure. There was no testimony suggesting that such action was violative of a standard of care, nor do we find that point inferable by the jury. Therefore this claim is also without merit. . . .

Cavanagh, C.J., and Riley, Brickley, Boyle, and Robert P. Griffin, JJ., concur.

Levin, Justice (dissenting). . . .

The question presented is whether Pachtman's statements—in effect admitting error but not in lawyer jargon such as "standard medical practice in this community"—are prima facie evidence of the standard of care and breach. . . .

The majority concludes that Pachtman's statements may have expressed her belief that she violated her personal standard of care, and her personal standard of care may have been higher than the prevailing standard of care among physicians in the community. . . . It is no more probable, however, that the statements concerned her personal standard of care than that they concerned the generally applicable standard of care. The statements refer neither to a personal nor a general standard of care. The statements can reasonably be read either way, and a jury should decide the meaning of Pachtman's statements.[10] . . . This is not a case in which a physician merely expressed general dissatisfaction with her overall performance or merely expressed regret.

Cases from other jurisdictions indicate that statements like Pachtman's—that confess error with reasonable specificity—are prima facie evidence of the standard of care and breach.

In Greenwood v. Harris, 362 P.2d 85, 87-88 (Okla. 1961), the plaintiff alleged that the physician erroneously diagnosed her pregnancy as a tumor, and then performed unnecessary surgery that left the plaintiff with an unsightly and painful scar. The plaintiff's only evidence concerning the standard of care was the physician's statements to the plaintiff and her husband that he "should have made more tests," and that he "wasn't satisfied with the lab report [and] should have had the tests run again, . . . should have made some other tests." The Oklahoma Supreme Court held that those statements alone were prima facie evidence of the standard of care and breach. The court said: We can interpret these statements in no other way than as an admission that a faulty diagnosis had been made due to the failure of the defendant to use and apply the customary and usual degree of skill exercised by physicians in the community. . . .

In Sheffield v. Runner, 163 Cal. App. 2d 48, 328 P.2d 828 (1958), a physician's statement that he should have put the patient in a hospital was held to be prima facie evidence of the standard of care and breach. In Wickoff v. James, 159 Cal. App. 2d 664, 324 P.2d 661 (1958), a physician's statement that he "sure messed up" was held to be prima facie evidence of the standard of care and breach. In Robertson v. LaCroix, 534 P.2d 17, 19 (Okla. App., 1975), a physician's statement that he "just made a mistake and got over too far" during surgery was held to be prima facie evidence of the standard of care and breach. . . .

Other state supreme courts have found that the standard of care was not established by statements that fail to explain with relative precision what the physician should have done. . . . In Maxwell v. Women's Clinic, 102 Idaho 53, 54, 625 P.2d 407 (1981), the plaintiff claimed that the defendant physician negligently performed a

10. In Wooten v. Curry, 50 Tenn. App. 549, 552, 554, 362 S.W.2d 820 (1961), as distinguished from the instant case, the physician, under the law of Tennessee, was subject to liability for malpractice if his conduct fell below his personal standard of care. . . . [See also Burton v. Brooklyn Doctor's Hospital, 452 N.Y.S.2d 875 (1982) (modifying treatment to conduct a medical experiment violates duty to exercise physicians' best judgment, even though treatment rendered was within existing standard of care).]

tubal ligation. The plaintiff's only evidence regarding the standard of care was the physician's statement that he "obviously messed up." The Idaho Supreme Court held that summary judgment against the plaintiff was properly granted because the plaintiff did not present sufficient evidence of breach of the standard of care. In Cobbs v. Grant, 104 Cal. Rptr. 505, the physician's statement that he "blamed himself for [the plaintiff] being back in there [the hospital]" was held not to be prima facie evidence of the standard of care and breach. In both *Maxwell* and [*Cobbs*], the physicians' statements did not explain relatively precisely—as did Pachtman's—how they had erred.

I conclude, consistent with precedent from other jurisdictions, that Pachtman's statement satisfied Locke's burden of presenting prima facie evidence of the standard of care and breach.

■ THE ROLE OF THE JURY IN MODERN MALPRACTICE LAW
Philip G. Peters, Jr.
87 Iowa L. Rev. 909 (2002)

A. TRADITIONAL DEFERENCE TO MEDICAL CUSTOMS

For more than a century, courts have given physicians the power to set their own standard of care. This delegation of standard-setting authority to private parties dramatically distinguished malpractice actions from other negligence litigation. . . . In most negligence actions, the defendant's compliance with industry customs is simply one factor for the jury to consider. . . . Since the late nineteenth century, courts have treated physicians quite differently. Medical customs are not merely admissible; they define the physician's legal standard of care.[2] In the words of Dean Prosser, the custom-based standard of care "gives the medical profession . . . the privilege, which is usually emphatically denied to other groups, of setting their own legal standards of conduct, merely by adopting their own practices."

By deferring conclusively to medical customs, the courts materially changed the function that the jury would perform in malpractice actions. In an ordinary negligence action, the jury must consider all of the evidence adduced and then determine whether the defendant has behaved reasonably under the circumstances. To do so, the jury must make important judgments about the value of life and personal safety and about the proper level of safety precautions. In a malpractice action, by contrast, the jury does not make these value judgments. Instead, they have been

---

2. See, e.g., James A. Henderson, Jr. & John A. Siliciano, Universal Health Care and the Continued Reliance on Custom in Determining Medical Malpractice, 79 Cornell L. Rev. 1382, 1384 (1994) (stating custom is rule in medical malpractice); Alan H. McCoid, The Care Required of Medical Practitioners, 12 Vand. L. Rev. 549, 560, 605-606 (1959) (same); Clarence Morris, Custom and Negligence, 42 Colum. L. Rev. 1147, 1158 (1942) (stating custom normally should define standard of care); Theodore Silver, One Hundred Years of Harmful Error: The Historical Jurisprudence of Medical Malpractice, 1992 Wis. L. Rev. 1193, 1212 (stating custom determines standard of care).

delegated to the medical profession. The jury's job is merely to determine whether the defendant has complied with the norms set by the industry.

B. The Recent Retreat from a Custom-Based Standard

Gradually, quietly and relentlessly, state courts are abandoning the custom-based standard of care.* Thus far, a dozen states have expressly refused to equate reasonable care with customary practices. . . . These states now use a "reasonable physician" test. Another nine states, although not explicitly addressing the role of custom, have also endorsed the "reasonable physician" test. In these states, . . . the jury decides whether the physician behaved reasonably, not whether she complied with custom. Although experts still battle in the courtroom, they argue about what physicians *should* do, not what physicians *ordinarily* do.

In addition to the states that have moved to a reasonability standard, several other states have case law that is too ambiguous or inconsistent to classify confidently. As a consequence, the fraction of states that unambiguously endorse the custom-based standard of care has fallen from a clear majority to a shrinking plurality.

Finally, courts in states that purportedly endorse the custom-based standard often allow plaintiffs more latitude than the law on the books would imply. Plaintiffs in these states commonly reach a jury even when their experts have stated only that the defendant's conduct is not "acceptable" or "appropriate" or fails to meet the "standard of care." The experts in these cases have not been required to testify that the defendant deviated from customary practice. . . .

Whatever the explanation, it is clear today that courts defer less to physicians than they once did and are less willing to erect special rules for health care providers. For example, physicians are no longer exempt from the antitrust laws. In many states, physicians no longer enjoy the protection from corporate competition once provided by the corporate practice prohibitions. In tort law, physicians have lost the protection of the strict locality rule and are also required to obtain informed consent. In addition, courts appear to be retreating from some of the special "no duty" rules that once typified medical malpractice law, such as the rule that pharmacists have no duty to warn patients about incompatible prescriptions and the rule that "on call" doctors have no duty to emergency patients until they establish a physician-patient relationship. Abandonment of the custom-based standard of care is consistent with this trend away from special rules for health care providers. The weakening of support for the custom-based standard of care is also consistent with the gradual movement of twentieth century tort law away from special duties tailored for specific social contexts and toward a general obligation of reasonable care. . . .

D. Implications

Whether de jure or de facto, the shift away from the customary standard and to a reasonable physician standard takes the task of standard-setting away from the

---

*This migration away from the custom-based standard of care is described at much greater length in Philip G. Peters, Jr., The Quiet Demise of Deference to Custom: Malpractice Law at the Millennium, 57 Wash. & Lee L. Rev. 163, 166-168 (2000).

profession and assigns it to the jury. The centrality of this doctrinal shift cannot be overstated. The delegation of standard-setting authority to the professions is unique in tort law. It is the foundation upon which the field of medical malpractice law has been built. Under the custom-based standard of care, . . . the jury determines what the customary practice *is*. It does not decide what the custom *ought* to be. The law assigns the normative judgment to the medical profession. . . . Under the jury-applied reasonable physician standard, by contrast, the *jury* determines what a reasonable physician would have done under similar circumstances, not the profession. Medical customs, to the extent that they exist, are admissible, but they are not binding on the jury. . . . The crucial unanswered question is whether jurors can handle that task responsibly. . . .

E. CONFIDENCE IN MEDICAL CUSTOMS

Scholars and courts have articulated two quite distinct rationales for trusting clinical practices. The first is faith in the professionalism of physicians. The second is faith in the power of the market to make medical practices efficient. In the real world, however, medical practices live up to neither ideal. Historically, both courts and scholars have trusted physicians to put the welfare of patients above all other interests. . . .

Regrettably, much of this confidence in physician norms is misplaced. Recent research demonstrates that physicians, like the rest of us, are driven not only by science and fidelity to patient interests, but also by habit, self-interest and other competing considerations. . . . As a result, medical customs have a veneer of scientific validity that is too often undeserved. . . . Medicine has also undergone a recent structural transformation. . . . Insurers are using a variety of strategies to make physicians more cost-conscious. . . .

Under these circumstances, it seems reasonable to revisit the assumption that medical customs are uniquely reliable. The unwavering faith that the law once placed in physicians was probably naive from the outset and predictably has weakened in a more realistic and cynical age. . . .

[Moreover, the] argument in favor of a custom-based standard of care turns on [a] fundamental assumption . . . that medical customs will be readily ascertainable. . . . In reality, however, medical practices rarely provide [a] stable, ascertainable benchmark. . . . In the past few decades, medical researchers have learned that clinical practices vary dramatically and inexplicably. A number of studies, starting with the classic work of John Wennberg,* have demonstrated that physician practices vary widely, even within narrow geographic limits. . . . [A] Medicare study found that procedure rates varied by more than three hundred percent for more than one-half of the procedures studied.

In addition to the geographic variation that permeates clinical medicine, the highly-differentiated nature of medical problems is also a barrier to the formation of medical customs. Patients vary in ways that resist standardization. This variation in patients is matched by a similar variety in possible therapeutic responses, each with its own mix of benefits, risks and costs. At the same time, physicians vary in their

---

*See, e.g., John Wennberg, Dealing with Medical Malpractice Variations: A Proposal for Action, Health Aff. 6, 7 (1984).

preferences and in their knowledge of the medical literature. Finally, the movement of many employers away from fee-for-service health plans and toward managed care plans has produced significant differences among health plans in their resources and their cost-containment philosophies. Under these circumstances, there will rarely be a "custom" that provides a clear rule of decision. . . .

There is an additional erroneous assumption underlying the idea that a custom-based standard will provide a more ascertainable and predictable standard. In truth, few trial experts can be expected to have an accurate sense of what most physicians are doing. As David Eddy notes, "[I]t is a major research task to figure out what practitioners in a community are doing."* As a consequence, experts who are asked questions about the standard of care are unlikely to have a reliable understanding of customary norms across the nation or even in similar communities. Instead, their testimony is more likely to be a barometer of their own practices. . . .

H. SUMMARY OF POTENTIAL ADVANTAGES OF JURY STANDARD-SETTING

Abandonment of the custom-based standard of care in favor of a reasonable physician standard offers several potential advantages. Most importantly, the reasonable physician standard assigns the task of legal standard-setting to representatives of the community, rather than to the regulated industry. Jury decision-making is more likely to incorporate community values. Moreover, the flexibility of the reasonable physician standard provides more protection for innovators and less shelter for those adhering to antiquated customs. Furthermore, the reasonable physician standard is a more honest way to accomplish these goals than bending the custom-based standard to cure its shortcomings. The reasonable physician standard of care also gives the health care industry an incentive to engage the community in a dialogue about health care resources. At the same time, it allows the courts to supervise the influence of the managed care industry on clinical practices.

Notes: The Custom-Based Standard of Care

1. *Overview.* These readings introduce a number of complexities and nuances in the basic malpractice standard of care: the error-in-judgment rule, the standard of care for residents and specialists, the availability of punitive damages, the liability of consulting and attending physicians, admissions of error, and sensitivity to resource constraints. These detailed issues are taken up later in this chapter. The main focus of these notes is this more general inquiry: How does malpractice law define which bad results are compensated and which are not? On this point, in what respects are *McCourt* and *Locke* in agreement? In what respects do they disagree? If each of their respective facts and procedural histories were presented to the other court, would you expect a similar result?

2. *Verbal Formulations.* Courts constantly tinker with the precise verbal formulation of the basic standard of care that should be instructed to the jury and uttered by the expert witnesses. This creates havoc for the imprecise lawyer or judge. Illustrative is McCarty v. Mladineo, 636 So. 2d 377 (Miss. 1994), where the court reversed

---

*David M. Eddy, The Use of Evidence and Cost Effectiveness by the Courts: How Can It Help Improve Health Care?, 26 J. Health Pol. Pol'y & L. 387, 396 (2001).

a verdict in favor of the defendant physician, holding that it was error to instruct that the standard is that of a "minimally competent physician." Instead, the court ruled that the jury should be instructed in terms of the "reasonably prudent, minimally competent" physician.

An error in the opposite direction occurred in the trial in Smith v. Menet, 530 N.E.2d 277 (Ill. App. Ct. 1988). There, the plaintiff's lawyer had his favorable verdict reversed because, in questioning his expert witness, he asked whether the defendant's conduct "fell within the standard of *good* medical care." Because the only negative testimony was in response to this defective question, the court ruled there was insufficient evidence to sustain the verdict, explaining, "when good is interpreted to mean better than average, it contradicts the applicable standard," even though in prior cases the same court had used phrases such as "the reasonable skill which a physician in good standing would use."

Deposition testimony Dr. Abernathy gave in the *McCourt* case indicates that he was on academic probation for a time while a student at the University of South Carolina Medical School. Are "below average" doctors automatically liable for their mistakes, or are we to suppose that, as in Garrison Keillor's Lake Wobegon, most doctors are at or above average? The focus on "average" skill and judgment should not mislead one into thinking that any sort of numerical dividing line or litmus test exists. See Hood v. Phillips, 554 S.W.2d 160, 165 (Tex. 1977) (rejecting an instruction to the jury that creates the impression that "the standard for malpractice is to be determined by a poll of the medical profession").

Similarly, it has been observed that the custom-based standard is not strictly determined by actual practice. Instead, it is one that inquires whether existing practices are "accepted" within the profession. Professor Joseph King explains that the distinction between accepted and actual practice is the focus of much of this linguistic debate. Joseph King, In Search of a Standard of Care for the Medical Profession: The "Accepted Practice" Formula, 28 Vand. L. Rev. 1213 (1975). By way of analogy, consider whether, if the automobile driving standard of care were determined by custom, should someone who speeds up through a yellow light be found negligent? Many, or even a majority, of drivers in some communities may actually do this, but we all know they are not supposed to.

3. *Supervising Physicians.* As *Locke* indicates, supervising physicians are liable under a standard of care for reasonable supervision. Other cases explore the extent of liability when a physician is consulted on an informal basis. Consider, for instance, a doctor discussing a difficult case with her colleagues in the physician's lounge, or in a passing conversation in the hallway. These cases frequently turn on whether any doctor-patient relationship was ever established, for, as explained in Chapter 2.B.1, no professional duty of care attaches unless such a relationship was formed.

4. *Saying You're Sorry.* Dr. Pachtman is lucky that her expression of regret at making a mistake was not used against her in court. Other jurisdictions are more willing to do so. David M. Studdert et al., Disclosure of Medical Injury to Patients: An Improbable Risk Management Strategy, 26(1) Health Aff. 215 (Jan. 2007). Accordingly, there is a movement to enact "apology shield" statutes that protect physicians who disclose errors to patients and/or express regret for bad outcomes. However, most of these statutes cover only statements of sympathy but not admissions of responsibility. Anna Mastroianni et al., The Flaws in State "Apology" and "Disclosure" Laws Dilute Their Intended Impact, 29(9) Health Aff. 1611 (2010). Ronan v. Sanford Health, 809 N.W.2d 834 (S.D. 2012) applied one such statute

to exclude a hospital employee's statements to a bereaved wife that "I'm sorry we failed you, we let you down. [The doctor] got the whole thing off on the wrong track and it snowballed. . . . [That's what happens] when people don't do their jobs." Without this evidence, the jury issued a defense verdict.

5. *Is Medical Consensus Real or Imagined?* What do you think about Prof. Peters's argument that the law often imagines a professional consensus that in fact does not exist? Here are the similar views of a practicing physician:

> To be quite candid, I have no idea what the standard of care really is, and my point is that neither does anyone else. . . . The implementation of the term in the judicial setting . . . disregards in large part the intangible and interpersonal patient variables that so often affect the medical outcome. . . . In fact, there is no standard of care. The medical body of knowledge contains both fact and opinion. Each case must be assessed on its individual merits, including intangible factors and only from a prospective viewpoint.

Robert P. Nirschl, Delving into the Myth of "Standard of Care," Am. Med. News, Dec. 16, 1988, at 24. If law really is this disconnected from reality, what difficulties and dangers does this create? Consider the issue from both the plaintiff's and the defendant's perspectives.

Suppose the "snowflake" attitude in the previous quote (every patient is unique) is correct. Does this mean that the custom-based standard is entirely a figment of the judicial imagination? Even if custom is not nearly so unitary and precise as we might sometimes imagine, does this negate the fact that, for any set of clinical facts, however unique, there are decisions or actions that virtually no doctor would find acceptable? In other words, do these sentiments do anything more than establish that, in many cases, the actual standard of care is very broad and allows for major differences of opinion?

Assuming the latter is correct, how do we make sure that expert witnesses are honestly testifying to a breach of (or compliance with) the standard of care and not merely expressing a strong personal preference or opinion? See Travers v. District of Columbia, 672 A.2d 566 (D.C. 1996) (holding that the expert testimony established only personal preference or opinion, not prevailing custom). More than this, even experts' personal opinions may overstate what they themselves do in actual practice. Several studies have shown that most doctors are actually less thorough, prompt, or accurate than experts have claimed they are in particular lawsuits. William Meadow & Cass Sunstein, Statistics, Not Experts, 51 Duke L.J. 629 (2001). These authors conclude, therefore, that proof of custom should be even more rigorous, using statistical or survey evidence rather than expert opinion. See also Tim Cramm et al., Ascertaining Customary Care in Malpractice Cases: Asking Those Who Know, 37 Wake Forest L. Rev. 699 (2002). However, others agree with Prof. Peters that the persistent failure of actual practice to measure up to accepted medical standards reinforces the case for a reasonable physician standard for liability. Richard Lempert, Following the Man on the Clapham Omnibus: Social Science Evidence in Malpractice Litigation, 37 Wake Forest L. Rev. 903 (2002).

Keep these problems in mind as we consider the locality rule, respectable minority rule, and evidentiary rules introduced in later readings.

6. *Punitive Damages.* Do you think Drs. Abernathy and Clyde in the *McCourt* case deserved to be hit with punitive damages? In many states, public policy forbids

liability insurance from covering punitives because this would dilute the intended impact on the defendant, so punitives have to be paid from the doctors' own personal assets. Would this change your opinion?

Regardless of your opinion about the *McCourt* case, it contains (according to allegations in the plaintiffs' brief) several inflammatory elements that are frequently seen in cases that receive punitives: failure to treat aggressively a seriously ill patient; failure to admit promptly and candidly to the seriousness of the mistake; and suggestions that the medical records might have been altered after the fact. Compare this with the account from Dr. Gawande at page 30, whose patient appears to have had a very similar kind of infection.

Punitive damages are still rare in medical malpractice cases, owing to the complexity of medical judgment, the good motives of virtually all doctors, and the high regard in which most juries hold doctors in general. However, there is a noted trend toward more punitive damage awards against doctors—in large cities, they are now awarded in over 10 percent of malpractice cases that reach a verdict. In recent years, a number of states have enacted limits on the amount of punitives relative to compensatory damages (for instance, no more than three times compensatory damages).

In a rare decision, one court reduced from $5 million to $2 million a punitive award against a nursing home for the death of a patient, finding that there was no evidence of recklessness, and that the amount was ten times the compensatory damage and several times the defendant's net worth. Stogsdill v. Healthmark Partners, 377 F.3d 827 (8th Cir. 2004).

7. *Further Reading.* On the **standard of care** generally, see Page Keeton, Medical Negligence: The Standard of Care, 10 Tex. Tech. L. Rev. 351 (1979); 18 A.L.R.4th 603 (1982); Leonard J. Nelson, Helling v. Carey Revisited: Physician Liability in Age of Managed Care, 25 Seattle U. L. Rev. 775 (2002); Ben A. Rich, Medical Custom and Medical Ethics: Rethinking the Standard of Care, 14 Cambridge Q. Healthcare Ethics 27 (2005); and the sources cited in n.2 of the Peters article.

On the **empirical basis for the standard of care** (note 5), see Symposium, 37 Wake Forest L. Rev. 663 (2002) (thorough discussion of the problem, with multiple critiques and proposals for reform); Bryan A. Liang, Medical Malpractice: Do Physicians Have Knowledge of Legal Standards and Assess Cases as Juries Do?, 3 U. Chi. L. Sch. Roundtable 59, 90 (1996); Caroline Young, Medico-Legal Research Using Evidence-Based Medicine, 102 Law Libr. J. 449 (2010); Lars Noah, Medicine's Epistemology: Mapping the Haphazard Diffusion of Knowledge in the Biomedical Community, 44 Ariz. L. Rev. 373 (2002).

On **punitive damages** in medical malpractice cases (note 6) see Frank M. McClellan, Medical Malpractice: Law, Tactics, and Ethics ch. 8 (1994); M. Rustad & T. Koenig, Reconceptualizing Punitive Damages in Medical Malpractice: Targeting Amoral Corporations, Not "Moral Monsters," 47 Rutgers L. Rev. 975 (1995); Robert Shaw, Punitive Damages in Medical Malpractice: An Economic Evaluation, 81 N.C. L. Rev. 2371 (2003).

2. *Variations in the Standard of Care*

The black-letter law is simple to utter, but more difficult to implement. Physicians are judged by the standard of care that is established by prevailing practice and professional consensus. But seldom can one find a monolithic, clearly defined "right way" of doing things that almost all doctors agree to. Medical practice is highly variable and judgmental. This leads us to consider which variations in practice or opinion can legitimately be used to adjust the standard of care in a given case, and which cannot. The following materials explore variations that are structured around (1) schools of thought and training, (2) practice location and specialization, and (3) source of payment.

■ JONES v. CHIDESTER
610 A.2d 964 (Pa. 1992)

Papadakos, Justice.

We granted review in this case in order to reexamine our test for the defense of the so-called two schools doctrine in a medical malpractice case arising in the context of a jury instruction. The necessity of our reexamination arises from the vacillation of the Superior Court and our court in applying the appropriate standard.

A medical practitioner has an absolute defense to a claim of negligence when it is determined that the prescribed treatment or procedure has been approved by one group of medical experts even though an alternate school of thought recommends another approach, or it is agreed among experts that alternative treatments and practices are acceptable. The doctrine is applicable only where there is more than one method of accepted treatment or procedure. In specific terms, however, we are called upon in this case to decide once again whether a school of thought qualifies as such when it is advocated by a "considerable number" of medical experts or when it commands acceptance by "respect[ed], reputable and reasonable" practitioners. The former test calls for a quantitative analysis, while the latter is premised on qualitative grounds.

The facts indicate that in November, 1979, Appellant, Billy Jones, underwent orthopedic surgery on his leg performed by Dr. John H. Chidester. In order to create a bloodless field for the surgery, the surgeon employed a tourniquet which was elevated and released at various intervals. Because of subsequent problems with the leg, the patient was referred to a neurosurgeon who determined that Jones had suffered nerve injury to the leg. Additional examinations by other doctors confirmed that the nerve injury had resulted in a condition known as "drop foot."

At trial in June, 1988, Jones complained, inter alia, that his nerve injury was the result of Dr. Chidester's use of the tourniquet. Both sides presented testimony by medical experts supporting their positions. Unsurprisingly, Dr. Chidester's experts told the court and jury that his technique was acceptable medically in this particular case, and the plaintiffs' experts insisted that it constituted unacceptable practice. At the close of the evidence, the court gave the following instruction to the jury:

> . . . Ladies and gentlemen, I instruct you upon this additional principle of law known as the two schools of thought doctrine. This principle provides that it is improper for a jury to be required to decide which of two schools of thought as to proper procedure should have been followed in this case, when both schools have their respective and respected advocates and followers in the medical profession. . . . Thus, under the two schools of thought doctrine, a physician in the position of Dr. Chidester will not be held liable to a plaintiff merely for exercising his judgment in applying the course of treatment supported by a reputable and respected body

of medical experts, even if another body of medical experts' opinion would favor a different course of treatment. . . .

The jury returned a verdict in favor of Dr. Chidester. . . . On appeal, Jones argues that under Pennsylvania law, the test for the doctrine is "considerable number" rather than "reputable and respected" as the court had charged the jury.

We note at the outset of our analysis that there appears to be confusion and contradiction in the use of these standards—a confusion apparent even between the trial court's charge to the jury ("reputable and respected") and its subsequent opinion denying the post-trial motion ("considerable number"). . . . The initial modern case in this jurisdiction on the subject of the two schools of thought doctrine was Remley v. Plummer, 79 Pa. Superior Ct. 117 (1922). Relevant portions of that opinion are as follows:

> The question actually passed upon by the jury was not whether the defendants, in their handling of the case, had been guilty of negligence in not following a well-recognized and established mode of treatment, but rather, which of two methods, both having their respective advocates and followers of respectable authority, was the safer and better from a surgical standpoint. . . . Where competent medical authority is divided, a physician will not be held responsible if in the exercise of his judgment he followed the course of treatment advocated by a considerable number of his professional brethren in good standing in his community. . . .
>
> Thus practitioners of a reputable school of medicine are not to be harassed by litigation and mulcted in damages because the course of treatment prescribed by that school differs from that adopted by another school: (citations omitted) . . . As we said in Patten v. Wiggin, "The jury are not to judge by determining which school, in their judgment, is the best." "If the treatment is in accordance with a recognized system of surgery, it is not for the court or jury to undertake to determine whether that system is best, nor to decide questions of surgical science on which surgeons differ among themselves:" . . . The testimony clearly showed a difference of medical opinion expressed by physicians and surgeons of unquestioned standing and reputation, and the defendants were not negligent for having adopted the view held by the majority of their brethren who testified.

. . . Other jurisdictions also appear to waffle between the two standards. . . . In Borja v. Phoenix General Hospital, Inc., 727 P.2d 355 (Az. 1986), the court [held] that the doctrine requires only support by a "respectable minority." California has defined its standard as one where "a physician chooses one of alternative accepted methods of treatment, with which other physicians agree." Meier v. Ross General Hospital, 445 P.2d 519 (Cal. 1968). Florida has adopted the "respectable minority" test in Schwab v. Tolley, 345 So. 2d 747 (Fla. App. 1977), while Arkansas accepts the doctrine when any alternative "recognized method" is employed by the physician. Rickett v. Hayes, 511 S.W.2d 187 (Ark. 1974). . . .

It is incumbent upon us to settle this confusion. The "two schools of thought doctrine" provides a complete defense to malpractice. It is therefore insufficient to show that there exists a "small minority" of physicians who agree with the defendant's questioned practice. Thus, the Superior Court's "reputable and respected by reasonable medical experts" test is improper. Rather, there must be a considerable number of physicians, recognized and respected in their field, sufficient to create another "school of thought." . . . A school of thought should be adopted not only by "reputable and respected physicians" in order to insure quality but also by a "considerable number" of medical practitioners for the purpose of meeting general acceptance even if it does not rise to the level of a majority. . . .

In recognizing this doctrine, we do not attempt to place a numerical certainty on what constitutes a "considerable number." The burden of proving that there are two schools of thought falls to the defendant. The burden, however, should not prove burdensome. The proper use of expert witnesses should supply the answers. Once the expert states the factual reasons to support his claim that there is a considerable number of professionals who agree with the treatment employed by the defendant, there is sufficient evidence to warrant an instruction to the jury on the two "schools of thought." It then becomes a question for the jury to determine whether they believe that there are two legitimate schools of thought such that the defendant should be insulated from liability.

Reversed and remanded for a new trial consistent with this opinion.

McDERMOTT, Justice, concurring.

. . . [W]hether it [is] best to chill or heat, use medicines, intervene with scalpel or await nature, or approach from back, front, top or bottom to reach the site of ill, are questions over which doctors disagree. One group of doctors of skill and competence may withhold the scalpel, another group of equal competence may believe in quick response. When each group has its advocates, and each has its arguable reasons, a doctor of either cannot be faulted if he properly administers the one to his knowledge and experience seems the better, so long as that group is comprised of a sufficient number of reputable and respected members.

Thus, an isolated expert cannot argue it was his own belief that a procedure was inappropriate, because then this belief would be elevated, against experience and knowledge, to a separate level, though a considerable portion of the world of medicine be against it.

I join in the opinion of the majority.

ZAPPALA, Justice, concurring.

While I join in the opinion, I vehemently disagree with the majority that the existence of two schools of medical thought may ever be a question of fact to be submitted to a jury. . . . It is the responsibility of the trial judge to determine in the first instance whether there are two schools of medical thought so that competent medical authority as to a course of treatment is divided. It is a question of law for the trial judge. It is not a question of fact. In all other respects, I agree with the majority's analysis of the two schools of medical thought doctrine.

■ CHAPEL v. ALLISON
785 P.2d 204 (Mont. 1990)

SHEEHY, Justice.

. . . Lawrence A. Chapel was injured when he was kicked by a horse on February 18, 1983. He was taken to the emergency room at Livingston Memorial Hospital where he was treated by Dr. James G. Allison [for a severe leg fracture]. . . . He applied a long leg cast extending from Chapel's mid-thigh down to and including

his foot. . . . The cast was removed May 2, 1983. Chapel's leg exhibited a varus defor-
mity (bow-leggedness) which required surgery, a procedure called an "osteotomy,"
to straighten the bowed leg. . . .

Chapel had been a patient of Dr. Allison's for nearly 20 years, the doctor treating ailments from common illnesses up to and including sprains, fractures, and an
initial treatment for a ruptured disc. Chapel's injury was of the kind which would fall
within the area of practice of an orthopedic surgeon. It would also fall within the area
of practice of a properly qualified general practitioner. . . . Dr. Allison claimed during
the litigation that he possessed the requisite degree of knowledge for treating Chapel
because of his 24 years of practice in which he had treated 1,000 fractures, 50 of which
involved the tibia and 15 of which involved the tibial plateau, and one instance of the
same injury, but without the wound overlying the fracture site.

The expert testimony produced by the plaintiff Chapel came from an orthopedic surgeon from Denman, Massachusetts, Dr. Stephen Sand, board-certified in
the specialty of orthopedic surgery. His testimony was as follows:

Q.   Based upon what you have learned by reviewing all of the documents that we men-
     tioned, have you been able to form a reasonable judgment on what the standards
     of care are in the Livingston-Bozeman area in Montana for the care and treatment
     of an injury such as was sustained by Mr. Chapel by a general practitioner? . . .
A.   My opinion, based on the review of the information that you have stated, and
     my contact with a general practitioner in the area, is that a general practitioner
     would not, under ordinary circumstances, handle this type of case or injury.

. . . At the close of Chapel's case in chief, . . . the court granted Dr. Allison's
motion for a directed verdict. . . . The district court said that proof of the competency of Dr. Sand to testify in the matter was "very shaky"; that the plaintiff did not
call Dr. Kurtz, a Bozeman doctor, upon whom Dr. Sand had relied for information
as to the area of practice for a general practitioner; that Dr. Allison had testified
that in his opinion Chapel was bow-legged before the accident and despite the leg
injury and disc surgery the same year, that Chapel was able to go elk hunting in the
mountains for a two-week period; that the other doctors whose testimony appeared
in the case have all in effect said that there was no fault. . . .

During pretrial procedures before the district court, the plaintiff made a
motion in limine that the "same locality rule" (infra) was not applicable in this case.
The court denied the motion, saying:

> The court specifically determines that the rule applicable in this case is that
> Dr. Allison will be held to the standard of care in February 1983 of a licensed gen-
> eral practitioner, who is not board certified, in the same or similar communities
> within Montana. Provided, however, experts from elsewhere and in other specialties
> will be considered competent to testify if they are medically qualified and if they are
> in fact familiar with the standards for a general practitioner in Livingston or similar
> communities in Montana at the time in question. . . .

Formerly, the standard of care required of a physician or surgeon in treating
a patient was to exercise as reasonable care and skill which "is usually exercised by
physicians or surgeons of good standing of the same system or school of practice in

the community in which he resides, having due regard to the condition of medical or surgical science at that time." The "same locality rule" restricted the geographical area from which the degree of care exercised by a physician or surgeon could be determined to the community in which the doctor resided.

In Tallbull v. Whitney, 564 P.2d 162 (Mont. 1977), this court examined the "same locality rule" and determined that the foundation for it no longer existed. The reasons given were that the accessibility of medical literature, the frequency and availability of national, regional and state medical meetings, advances of communication of medical knowledge, transportation advances, and the opportunity for rural community doctors to gain medical knowledge in the same manner as doctors in more populous regions in the state, all made the "same locality rule" outdated. In *Tallbull*, this court expanded the rule saying:

> For the foregoing reasons, we hold that Montana's "locality rule" imposes on a physician undertaking the care of a patient the legal duty of possessing and exercising that reasonable and ordinary degree of learning, skill and care possessed and exercised by physicians of good standing of the same school of practice in the same or similar locality in Montana. A similar locality in Montana within the meaning of this rule is a locality of similar geographical location, size and character in a medical context.

The *Tallbull* rule was modified insofar as it applied to an orthopedic surgeon in Aasheim v. Humberger, 695 P.2d 824 (Mont. 1985). There, this court recognized that the defendant was a nationally board-certified orthopedic surgeon and had received comparable training and passed the same national board certification tests as all other board-certified orthopedic specialists in the nation. On that basis, this Court held that when a defendant in a medical negligence action was a board-certified specialist, his skill and learning would be measured by "the skill and learning possessed by other doctors in good standing, practicing in the same specialty and who hold the same national board certification." Thenceforth, board certified specialists in Montana would be subject to a national standard of care.

In Glover v. Ballhagen, 756 P.2d 1166 (Mont. 1988), . . . the doctor was a board-certified family practitioner. In *Glover*, we concluded that: ". . . the standard of care to which a board certified family practitioner will be held is that skill and learning possessed by other doctors in good standing, practicing with the same national board certification." . . .

Not answered in the foregoing cases, and raised as an issue in this case, is whether a non-board-certified general practitioner, practicing in a Montana community, who treats a patient for an injury of a kind which would fall within an area of practice of an orthopedic surgeon should be held to the degree of care, knowledge and skill of the specialist. . . . Because of the broad implications to the medical community and to injured patients lurking in whatever decision we made on this issue, we ordered rebriefing and oral argument on the issue and invited briefs from amici curiae. Here are the arguments marshalled by each side:

Counsel for Chapel maintains that in an age of increasing specialization, a doctor in general practice is under a legal duty, in diagnosing or treating a patient, to seek consultation with or refer a patient to a specialist when the doctor knows or should know in the exercise of reasonable care that the services of a specialist are indicated. Chapel further argues that if there is another mode of treatment that is likely to be more successful for which the physician does not have the facilities or the training to administer, but which is available from specialists, it is the doctor's duty to so advise the patient, and failure to apprise the patient of these facts would constitute a breach of that duty. . . .

Dr. Allison contends that restricting the degree of care to the same or similar communities in Montana is proper because he confronts illnesses and injuries in serving his community whereas practitioners in a larger city devote much of their practice to initial diagnoses with referral to a specialist for anything beyond routine care. Dr. Allison also contends that it would be impracticable to require a general practitioner to be held to the standard of care of whatever area of expertise in which his treatment might fall, including an orthopedic surgeon, a dermatologist, a neurologist, an obstetrician, an internist, and so on.

An amicus brief filed by the Montana Trial Lawyers Association . . . contend[s] that there is a trend away from the locality rule in most states which apply a national standard of care, typically defined as "a physician is under a duty to use that degree of care and skill which is expected of a reasonable competent practitioner in the same class to which it belongs, acting in the same or similar circumstances." Trial Lawyers contend that the phrase "the same or similar circumstances" allows the trier of fact to take into account and to weigh local conditions when the standard is applied, so as to reflect the same "general facilities, services, and options" which were available to the treating doctor. . . .

An amicus brief was received from the Montana Hospital Association. Essentially, this brief points out the rather dire prospects faced by rural hospitals in Montana. It states that all of Montana's 64 hospitals were only marginally profitable for the past five years but that rural hospitals experienced increasing financial losses. The losses are occurring primarily because of reduced utilization of rural hospitals. Some of the reductions are due to public policies and issues undertaken at both the federal and state levels with cutbacks in federal and state Medicare and Medicaid programs. The importance of a rural doctor to a rural hospital is emphasized in the brief and the hospitals contend that the similar locality rule is needed in rural areas to keep physicians there providing essential health services and utilizing local rural hospital services. . . .

The brief of the Montana Medical Association recognizes the implications of the problem and seems to be seeking a middle ground for its resolution. Thus, with regard to general practitioners, its brief recommends that we continue to adopt the "same or similar locality" standard, without geographical limitations for general practitioners but allow the "national" specialist standard to be applied to any physician who holds himself or herself out as a specialist. . . . The brief suggests that the elimination of the Montana boundary restriction on the locality rule is warranted. . . . It points out that if the "same or similar locality" rule for general practitioners is any locality similar in the United States, sound policy reasons support such a change, including . . . the increased availability of expert witnesses, the lack of which would be some justification for alterations in the law. The brief contends for a balance to be struck between the right of a negligently injured patient to receive compensation through the availability of expert testimony and the right of a doctor to due process and a fair hearing, by insuring that those experts who do testify possess solid practical experience in the type of practice at issue.

On balance, the position asserted by the Montana Medical Association as to the standard of care applicable in cases of this type, with slight modification, appears suitable for adoption by us. . . . [W]e abandon the "locality" rule which is limited to Montana communities. . . . The geographical restriction of the state boundary is too narrow in view of the necessity of expert testimony; yet, as the Association contends, the national standard should not exclude local considerations which face rural general practitioners. Accordingly, we hold that a non-board-certified general practitioner is held to the standard of care of a "reasonably competent general practitioner acting in the same or similar community in the United States in the same or similar circumstances." See Shilkret v. Annapolis Emergency Hospital Association, 349 A.2d 245 (Md. 1975). "Similar circumstances" permits consideration by the trier of fact of legitimate local factors affecting the ordinary standard of care including the knowledge and experience of the general practitioner, commensurate with the skill of other competent physicians of similar training and experience, with respect to the type of illness or injury he confronts and the resources, facilities and options available to him at the time. . . . This opinion applies only to general practitioners, and does not affect board-certified specialists or board-certified general or family practitioners. . . .

Reversed and remanded for further proceedings in accordance with this opinion.

Notes: Variations in the Standard of Care — Location, Schools of Thought, Experiments, and Specialization

1. *The Respectable Minority Rule.* Reaching a different result from that in *Jones* on the quantitative vs. qualitative standard is Hood v. Phillips, 554 S.W.2d 160 (Tex. 1977). Even more demanding than Jones, see Yates v. Univ. of W. Virginia Bd. of Trustees, 549 S.E.2d 681 (W. Va. 2001) (doctrine does not apply unless the alternative method "enjoys such substantial support within the medical community that it is, in fact, widely and generally recognized").

Intertwined with the "respectable minority" or "two schools of thought" doctrine is the "error in judgment" concept discussed in the *McCourt* case (page 322), since it conveys the same notion of absence of negligence when doctors make an educated choice among two or more reasonable paths. Many courts shy away from the "error in judgment" language, however, because it seems to convey to the jury that doctors are liable only if they act in bad faith, but other courts find the instruction permissible. Reviewing jurisdictions, in a divided opinion, see Passarello v. Grumbine, 87 A.3d 285 (Pa. 2014). Some scholars have argued that doctors should be given discretion similar to business managers to make mistakes as long as they act in good faith. E.g., Jeffrey O'Connell & Andrew S. Boutros, Treating Medical Malpractice Claims Under a Variant of the Business Judgment Rule, 77 Notre Dame L. Rev. 373 (2002); Charles Caldwell & Evan Seamone, Excusable Neglect in Malpractice Suits Against Radiologists, 16 Ann. Health L. 43 (2007).

2. *Medical Experiments.* Does the "considerable number" formulation allow sufficient room for medical experimentation? Requiring that a sizeable number of doctors follow a practice means that the first few to innovate do so at their own risk. Is strict liability an appropriate standard for medical experimentation? Early decisions generally held "yes," but most modern courts say "no," holding that doctors

are bound by a standard of reasonable experimentation. Brook v. St. John's Hickey Memorial Hospital, 380 N.E.2d 72 (Ind. 1978) (no liability for hitting a nerve while injecting needle in the leg instead of the arm; "therapeutic innovation has long been recognized as permissible; . . . even where there is an established mode of treatment, the physician may be permitted to innovate somewhat if he can establish that, in his best judgment, this was for the benefit of his patient"); Hood v. Phillips, 554 S.W.2d 160 (Tex. 1977) ("physicians should be allowed to experiment in order that medical science can provide greater benefits for humankind"; jury should have been allowed to decide based on expert testimony that controversial surgery was unreasonable and discredited). In order for this justification to hold, however, the innovation must be done for therapeutic reasons, not purely for research curiosity. This usually means the deviation from standard therapy is fairly minor or existing treatment is wholly inadequate. As a German authority explains:

> [T]hree different types of procedure must be distinguished: (i) *Therapeutic treatment,* whereby the patient is treated with [one of the] normal and approved (or orthodox) procedures; (ii) *Therapeutic experiments,* whereby the patient is treated with new methods and techniques for primarily (though not exclusively) therapeutic purposes. This is also known as therapeutic research or "innovative therapy"; (iii) *Research experiments,* whereby persons, either patients or test subjects, are treated with new methods and drugs for purely scientific purposes.

Dieter Giesen, Civil Liability of Physicians for New Methods of Treatment and Experimentation: A Comparative Examination, 3 Med. L. Rev. 22 (1995). See also Nancy King, Experimental Treatment: Oxymoron or Aspiration?, 25(4) Hastings Center Rep. 6 (July 1995).

Liability for experimental deviations from customary practice is more often avoided by resorting to informed consent law. Because modern experiments are usually accompanied by careful disclosure of the risks and procedures, in most instances the patient has been informed of the therapy's experimental status and has consented to the increased risks. In order for this consent to be effective, is it sufficient to disclose simply (1) the risks of the experimental therapy (which, by definition, are not well known), (2) the fact that this is an experiment, or also (3) the comparative risks and benefits of the alternative, standard procedure? In practice, only (1) and (2) are usually done. Nevertheless, the consent is usually sufficient to avoid liability, unless of course the procedure itself was improperly performed. See Slater v. Optical Radiation Corp., 961 F.2d 1330 (7th Cir. 1992) (experiment okay if patient is informed of risks); Karp v. Cooley, 493 F.2d 408 (5th Cir. 1974) (first patient to receive an artificial heart expressly consented to all aspects of operation); Fiorentino v. Wenger, 280 N.Y.S.2d 373 (N.Y. 1967) (doctor liable where he failed to disclose he was the only one in the country who performed a discredited operation).

Even if doctors and hospitals are not legally obligated to compensate fully informed patients who are injured in medical experiments, should they do so voluntarily, as a matter of public policy, considering the sacrifice the patient has made for the benefit of science? Many hospitals and drug companies agree to pick up at least the costs of treatment for injuries in experiments they conduct or fund.

3. Excessive Innovation. A contrasting concern is that the custom standard unduly speeds up adoption of expensive and unproven innovations. Prof. Gibson argues that the custom standard creates a "feedback effect" in which some doctors first start to use unproven precautions, such as electronic fetal heart monitoring, in order to, rightly or wrongly, reduce the likelihood of suit, then others start to do the same, which creates the basis for an emerging new custom, which then forces all doctors to follow suit. "Instead of discouraging wasteful practices, then, the law feeds them back into doctrine, . . . ratcheting up the standard of care. Overcautious physicians consequently have to do even more to steer clear of liability, and the cycle begins anew." James Gibson, Doctrinal Feedback and (Un)reasonable Care, 94 Va. L. Rev. 1641 (2008). See also Michelle Lewis et al., The Locality Rule and the Physician's Dilemma: Local Medical Practices vs. the National Standard of Care, 297 JAMA 2633 (2007) (claiming that a locality standard might be more demanding than a national standard, when local physicians' practices are excessive). Does that seem plausible? If so, is there any way to modulate or restate the custom standard to avoid that effect?

4. *Unorthodox Medicine.* Less frequently litigated is whether the "schools of thought" doctrine protects doctors who practice completely unorthodox or unscientific medicine, such as homeopathy, naturopathy, or even faith healing. If the practitioner is not a licensed M.D., then presumably only the standards of that group apply. If a physician incorporates alternative theories, or uses them exclusively, then a tougher issue is presented. In the leading, and virtually the only, case — one involving a cancer patient who died after her doctor treated her with nutritional therapy — the court held that "we see no reason why a patient should not be allowed to make an informed decision to go outside currently approved medical methods in search of an unconventional treatment." Schneider v. Revici, 817 F.2d 987 (2d Cir. 1987). In that case, the doctor had carefully documented a consent form that advised the patient to seek conventional treatment as well, and the jury rejected the claim that the doctor had fraudulently misrepresented the prospects of success for the treatment. In a licensing case not involving malpractice, however, the court held that a doctor who uses homeopathic medicines prepared from "moss, the night shade plant, and various other . . . substances" can be disciplined for engaging in unprofessional conduct, even though his patients were fully informed and there was no evidence that he posed a risk of harm to anyone. In re Guess, 393 S.E.2d 833 (N.C. 1990). See also Brown v. Shyne, 151 N.E. 197 (N.Y. 1926) (chiropractor who practices medicine will be held to the standard of a physician). See generally Michael H. Cohen, Complementary and Alternative Medicine: Legal Boundaries and Regulatory Perspectives (1998); J. Brad Kallmyer, A Chimera in Every Sense: Standard of Care for Physicians Practicing Complementary and Alternative Medicine, 2 Ind. Health L. Rev. 225 (2005).

5. *Legal Effect of Schools-of-Thought Rules.* In conventional cases, more important than how exactly the "two schools" or "error in judgment" rules are phrased is their legal effect. Do you agree with the majority or with Justice Zappala's concurrence in *Jones*? Also, do you agree that the defendant should bear the burden of proof; in other words, is this doctrine an affirmative defense, or must the plaintiff negate the existence of alternative schools as part of his prima facie case? If the defendant bears the burden and the doctrine merely results in instructing the jury, how does one avoid the concern expressed in Justice McDermott's concurrence in *Jones* that an "isolated expert" should not be allowed to elevate his mere personal belief to a binding standard of care?

A minority of courts give the doctrine greater force by using it to direct a verdict where the conflicting expert testimony merely shows a "difference of opinion" and not that the defendant was beyond the bounds of any respectable practice. See, e.g., Chumbler v. McClure, 505 F.2d 489 (6th Cir. 1974) (directed verdict for defendant is proper despite conflict in testimony and the fact that Dr. McClure was the only doctor in town who followed the disputed practice; "the test for . . . community standards is not to be determined solely by a plebiscite").

Even if this harder stance is taken, however, it is still relatively simple for the plaintiff's expert to create a jury issue on the question of "respectability." Consider which of the following is sufficient to get the case in front of the jury:

1. "I would never do it that way."
2. "No one I know of does it that way."
3. "In my opinion, no respectable doctor should do it that way; some may do so, but that's not considered good medical practice."

How difficult do you suppose it is for an expert who starts at the first position to move to the third?

6. *Locality Rules.* A classic statement of the reasons for the old "strict" locality rule can be found in Small v. Howard, 128 Mass. 131, 136 (1880) ("It is a matter of common knowledge that a physician in a small country village . . . [is] but seldom called upon as a surgeon to perform difficult operations. He would have but few opportunities of observation and practice in that line such as public hospitals or large cities would afford."). Have these conditions really changed that much? Another reason the strict locality rule has been overturned is that the "conspiracy of silence" among medical professionals made it extremely difficult for a plaintiff to find a qualified expert witness, even in cases of egregious negligence. The seminal decision on liberalizing the locality rule is Pederson v. Dumouchel, 431 P.2d 973 (Wash. 1967) ("The fact that several careless practitioners might settle in the same place cannot affect the standard of [care]. . . . Negligence cannot be excused on the ground that others in the same locality practice the same kind of negligence. No degree of antiquity can give sanction to usage bad in itself.").

Chapel indicates that the differences among the modern locality rules may be more in appearance than in substance. A national standard tends to be "lowered" (or, more properly, varied) by its inclusion of a "similar circumstances" qualifier, while a local standard tends to be "raised" (or universalized) when applied to board-certified specialists. The meaning and significance of board certification is explained further below. Of the following three factors, which do you think is *most* relevant in defining "similarity" of location or circumstances: (1) population density; (2) medical facilities (consider similar towns with and without a teaching hospital); or (3) socioeconomics, such as portion of population without insurance or on Medicaid? See generally Annots., 18 A.L.R.4th 603 (1982); 99 A.L.R.3d 1133 (1980).

It may be possible to raise even the strict locality standard to a national level with testimony in the particular case that local doctors follow the national practice. Idaho is one of the few states to retain the strict locality standard, where it is codified by statute. Plaintiff's efforts to circumvent it by attempting to qualify national experts have resulted in about a dozen state supreme court decisions clarifying when national standards apply. Symposium, 44 Idaho L. Rev. 291 (2008). At first, it appeared the court had adopted the Montana rule that board certification automatically invokes a national standard, but it later retreated to holding that this depends on the testimony in each case. See Grimes v. Green, 746 P.2d 978 (Idaho 1987). See also Henning v. Thomas, 366 S.E.2d 109 (Va. 1988) (expert from another part of the country allowed to testify to a statewide standard of care for orthopedic surgeons by asserting that uniform national standards apply in all states).

As these cases indicate, the primary significance of the locality dimension of the standard of care is not the influence these words have when instructed to the jury, but instead is on who is qualified to testify on both sides of the case. Issues of witness qualification are discussed below. It suffices for now to observe that, in most jurisdictions today, experts need not actually practice in the specialty or locational category that defines the standard of care, they need only demonstrate some acquaintance with the relevant standard of care. This liberalization in expert qualification may be just as or more important in practical effect than how the standard of care is defined in theory.

7. *The Specialization Dimension of the Standard of Care.* In addition to geography and schools of practice, the custom-based standard is adjusted according to the physician's specialization. Thus, a surgeon or obstetrician is held to a higher standard than is a general practitioner who performs the same procedure. Specialty practice is usually designated by "board certification," meaning that the physician has passed special training and testing requirements set by one of the two dozen American Boards of Medical Specialties. Observe how the *Chapel* court deals with the question of board certified family practitioners. Do you agree, considering that family practice is one of the classic forms of general practice?

What about subspecialties? Rather than just general surgery, suppose a physician is regarded as a specialist in cardiac surgery, or pediatric cardiac surgery, or in a particular heart valve replacement for children. How does one square the notion that the standard is elevated for specialists with the rule that the standard should not be elevated simply because the defendant is more highly skilled or experienced than average? In resolving this dilemma, it may help to observe that one basis for elevating the standard of care to begin with—to that of a reasonably prudent physician as opposed to a reasonably prudent person—is that doctors hold themselves out as specially trained professionals. If this is key to the initial elevation, then how doctors hold themselves out as specialists and subspecialists may determine how many further gradations are possible. See, e.g., Aves v. Shah, 997 F.2d 762 (10th Cir. 1993) (general practitioner held to an obstetrics standard because she considered herself a specialist, and so did her patient).

Plaintiffs sometimes attempt to elevate a generalist standard by arguing that a doctor should be held to a specialist standard if she extends her practice to procedures or conditions that are not within the competence of an ordinary generalist, thereby becoming a de facto specialist. Although this does not usually succeed in just these terms, plaintiffs sometimes are able to conflate the generalist and specialist standards to some extent by arguing, as in *Chapel*, that, although a generalist might have rendered treatment as well as could be expected, he failed to recognize his own limitations and call in a specialist when one was needed.

Locke v. Pachtman, in the prior set of cases, raises the additional complication of what standard applies to a doctor-in-training. Licensure of M.D.s occurs only after they complete four years of medical school and pass a series of standardized exams.

They then go through a period of apprenticeship, partially or wholly in a hospital setting, in which they are known as "residents" (the older term is "interns"). Those who seek board certification go through much longer residencies. Even though residents have just received their M.D.s and practice only under supervision, most courts, as in *Locke*, hold them to at least a normal standard of care for general practitioners, reasoning that, if they aren't ready to practice as full-fledged doctors, they should not be represented as such to patients. Many courts go further and hold them to an elevated standard, somewhere between generalists and specialists, since they are usually in specialty training at highly sophisticated teaching and research hospitals. See Justin Ward, Medical Residents: Should They Be Held to a Different Standard of Care?, 22 J. Leg. Med. 283 (2001). See, e.g., Jistarri v. Nappi, 549 A.2d 210 (Pa. Super. Ct. 1988) (orthopedic resident held to an intermediate standard of care). Prof. King argues that, following informed consent principles, residents who disclose their status as trainees should be held to a trainee standard, whereas those who don't should be held to a fully practicing specialist standard. Joseph H. King, The Standard of Care for Residents and Other Medical School Graduates in Training, 55 Am. U. L. Rev. 683-751 (2006). See also Phelps v. Physicians Insurance Co. of Wisconsin, Inc., 698 N.W.2d 643 (Wis. 2005) (holding first-year obstetrics resident to standard of care of other such residents).

8. *Further Reading.* For additional discussion of **medical experimentation** (note 2), see Chapter 3.C.4; President's Commission, Compensating for Research Injuries (1982); Comment, 78 Wash. L. Rev. 229 (2003); Anna Mastroianni, Liability, Regulation and Policy in Surgical Innovation, 16 Health Matrix 351 (2006); Michael D. Greenberg, Medical Malpractice and New Devices: Defining an Elusive Standard of Care, 19 Health Matrix 423 (2009); Anna Laakmann, When Should Physicians Be Liable for Innovation?, 36 Cardozo L. Rev. 913 (2015). For historical discussion of the **locality rule** (note 6), see T. Silver, One Hundred Years of Harmful Error: The Historical Jurisprudence of Medical Malpractice, 1992 Wis. L. Rev. 1193 (arguing that locality originally was just a relevant factor but mistakenly was converted into an absolute rule); Marc Ginsberg, The Locality Rule Lives!, 61 Drake L. Rev. 321 (2013).

Problem: What Is the Standard of Care?

Imagine a law school grading regime in which your final grade could be docked from one to five points each time you failed to answer correctly a question posed to you in class, but only if you had failed to meet the prevailing "standard of care" in preparation for the class. (In other words, you are penalized only if you are at "fault" for not knowing, with fault defined as not preparing.) Write a statement of what you view as the prevailing standard of care in your school for class preparation. What is the highest standard to which you might be held? Are there "accepted" alternative or "minority" standards? Does the standard vary according to 1L vs. 2L vs. 3L, or for first vs. second semester 1Ls, or according to full-time vs. night students? Should the prevailing standard differ in top-ten national schools as opposed to non-ABA-accredited schools?

In an evidentiary hearing, who should be allowed to testify about such a standard: only current students at the same school; students at another school; anyone who has graduated from law school within ten years; faculty; administrators?

Would such a regime cause you to prepare excessively, that is, more than you needed to in order to do well on the exam?

■ MURRAY v. UNMC PHYSICIANS
   806 N.W.2d 118 (Neb. 2011)

GERRARD, J.

This case involves a failure to provide medical treatment. The treatment at issue is a very expensive drug that must be administered indefinitely. But it also may cause serious and even deadly symptoms if its administration is interrupted. In this case, the patient's treating physicians, wary of those health risks, decided not to administer the drug until the patient's insurer approved it or another source of payment could be found. But, regrettably, the patient died before either happened. The question presented in this appeal is whether under such circumstances, an expert medical witness is permitted to opine that under the customary standard of care, a physician should consider the health risks to a patient who may be unable to pay for continued treatment. We conclude that such testimony is admissible and, therefore, reverse the district court's order granting a new trial. . . .

Pulmonary arterial hypertension is a chronic medical condition in which the blood vessels in the lungs constrict, and the resulting pressure on the heart leads to heart failure. Flolan is a vasodilator that relaxes blood vessels and prevents blood clotting. It is administered by a pump, connected to a port and catheter usually inserted above the collarbone. Flolan is very expensive and short-acting, so patients on Flolan treatment need a constant supply of the drug, because if its administration stops, pulmonary blood pressure rebounds and can be life threatening. And because Flolan is a chronic treatment, patients who begin Flolan need to remain on it, essentially, for the rest of their lives—it must be administered 24 hours a day and costs approximately $100,000 a year. The parties do not seem to disagree that generally, Flolan therapy is the appropriate course of treatment for chronic pulmonary arterial hypertension. . . .

The course of treatment relevant to this case began in late June 2006, as [Mary Murray's] treating physician, Austin Thompson, M.D., was preparing to treat Mary's pulmonary arterial hypertension with Flolan. . . . [After evaluating Mary's condition, Dr. Thompson approved her for Flolan.] She was discharged [to wait for insurance approval] and was supposed to begin Flolan after port placement the following week. But on July 10, she reported to the emergency room with a rapid heartbeat and shortness of breath. She began to seize, then her heartbeat stopped, and medical efforts failed to resuscitate her.

At trial, the parties disputed both the cause of Mary's death and whether [the University of Nebraska Medical Center (UNMC)] had breached the standard of care. Robert [Murray, Mary's husband,] presented expert medical testimony that . . . UNMC's treatment of Mary fell below the relevant standard of care after June 29, because the medical center should have paid for and provided Flolan by July 4 or 5—in other words, that the standard of care for a patient as sick as Mary was to start Flolan and obtain insurance approval afterward. UNMC's witnesses, on the other hand, testified that . . . their practice was to wait for insurance approval before beginning Flolan, because most patients are not able to pay for the drug without insurance and it can be more dangerous if treatment is started and then stopped. . . . [Dr.] Thompson testified to "horror stories" about patients who had been forced to discontinue treatment, and he said it would be "irresponsible" not to have lifelong financial support for the drug, because it could be "devastating" if discontinued. . . .

The jury returned a general verdict for UNMC. But Robert filed a motion for new trial that the district court granted. The court explained:

> . . . that, as a matter of law, a medical standard of care cannot be tied to or controlled by an insurance company or the need for payment. The "bean counters" in an insurance office are not physicians. Medicine cannot reach the point where an insurance company determines the medical standard of care for the treatment of a patient. Nor, can we live in a society where the medical care required is not controlled by the physicians treating the patient. The position advanced by [UNMC's] expert tells us that the standard of care is different for those with money than for those without. This is neither moral nor just. It is wrong. . . .

ANALYSIS

It is important, from the outset, to carefully note what issues this appeal does *not* present. This appeal arises against a backdrop of increasing concern about the costs of health care, among health care providers, insurers, government officials, and consumers. That concern has prompted a great deal of discussion, among commentators and in the public arena, about what should be done to control health care costs or to allocate potentially limited resources. As we will explain below, the question presented in this appeal is narrow and does not require us to address the more sweeping issues that are the subject of greater public policy debate. But some discussion of the broader picture will help us clarify what this case is about—or, more precisely, what it is not about.

In Nebraska, [the legislature has adopted the standard similar to the locality rule]. That standard is consistent with the general common-law rule and is a so-called unitary, or wealth-blind, standard of care. In other words, the standard of care is found in the customary practices prevailing among reasonable and prudent physicians and must not be compromised simply because the patient cannot afford to pay.[8] That standard of care, however, developed in a world of fee-for-service medicine and persisted while health insurance still primarily provided first-dollar unlimited coverage.[9] . . .

But "[b]ecause tort law expects physicians to provide the same standard of care regardless of patients' ability to pay, and because this standard sometimes encompasses costly technologies no longer readily available for the poorest citizens," physicians are "caught in a bind between legal expectations and economic realities."[11] Courts have been accused of being "oblivious to the costs of care, essen-

---

8. See E. Haavi Morreim, Cost Containment and the Standard of Medical Care, 75 Cal. L. Rev. 1719 (1987); John A. Siliciano, Wealth, Equity, and the Unitary Medical Malpractice Standard, 77 Va. L. Rev. 439 (1991).

9. See E. Haavi Morreim, Stratified Scarcity: Redefining the Standard of Care, 17 L. Med. & Health Care 356 (1989).

11. E. Haavi Morreim, Medicine Meets Resource Limits: Restructuring the Legal Standard of Care, 59 U. Pitt. L. Rev. 1, 4-5 (1997).

tially requiring physicians to commandeer resources that may belong to other parties, regardless of whether those other parties owe the patient these resources." *Id.*

It has been suggested that at a fundamental level, a unitary, wealth-blind standard of care cannot be reconciled with the growth of technology and the stratification of available health care. Custom is increasingly difficult to identify in today's medical marketplace, as resource distinctions produce fragmentation and disintegration.[13] It has also been suggested that maintaining a unitary standard of care disadvantages those who may not be able to pay for health care. Physicians remain free, for the most part, to decline to treat those who cannot pay, and "an outright refusal to treat an indigent patient, in contrast to a decision to treat in a manner inconsistent with the unitary malpractice standard, rarely creates the threat of liability." Siliciano, supra note 8, at 457. So, it has been argued that rather than assume the burden of paying for a patient's treatment, or the potential liability of providing some but not all possible care, the unitary standard makes it more likely that "providers will now sidestep the entire problem simply by refusing to accept some, or all, of such patients for treatment." *Id.*

On the other hand, it has been argued that permitting physicians to make medical decisions based on resource scarcity would compromise the fiduciary relationship between patient and physician, creating a conflict of interest because the patient's well-being would no longer be the physician's focus.[16] The question is how the value judgments inherent in the development of the standard of care might evolve in response to a societal interest in controlling health care costs. It has been explained that . . .

> [p]hysicians do not do everything conceivably possible in caring for a patient—they draw what they consider to be reasonable boundary lines. For example, physicians do not order every diagnostic test available for a patient that requests a physical examination, even though doing so might reveal interesting information. Instead, they order tests which are indicated given the age and physical characteristics of the patient. Hirshfeld, *supra* note 16, at 1835.

A physician's initial value judgment, in other words, is constrained by reason but does not include a societal interest in conserving costs or resources, and certainly does not include weighing the physician's own economic interests.

In short, the traditional ethical norms of the medical profession and the legal demands of the customary standard of care impose significant restrictions on a physician's ability to consider the costs of treatment, despite significant and increasing pressure to contain those costs. Whether the legal standard of care should change to alleviate that conflict, and how it might change, has been the subject of considerable discussion. It has been suggested that the customary standard of care could

---

13. See James A. Henderson, Jr. & John A. Siliciano, Universal Health Care and the Continued Reliance on Custom in Determining Medical Malpractice, 79 Cornell L. Rev. 1382 (1994).

16. See Maxwell J. Mehlman, The Patient-Physician Relationship in an Era of Scarce Resources: Is There a Duty to Treat?, 25 Conn. L. Rev. 349 (1993); Edward B. Hirshfeld, Should Ethical and Legal Standards for Physicians Be Changed to Accommodate New Models for Rationing Health Care?, 140 U. Pa. L. Rev. 1809 (1992).

evolve to permit the denial of marginally beneficial treatment—in other words, when high costs would not be justified by minor expected benefits.[20] Others have suggested that the standard of care should evolve to consider two separate components: (1) a skill component, addressing the skill with which diagnoses are made and treatment is rendered, that would not vary by a patient's financial circumstances and (2) a resource component, addressing deliberate decisions about how much treatment to give a patient, that would vary so as to not demand more of physicians than is reasonable.[21] . . . And many have suggested that custom should no longer be the benchmark for the standard of care; instead, practice standards or guidelines could be promulgated that would settle issues of resource allocation.[24]

All of the concerns discussed above are serious, and they present difficult questions that courts will be required to confront in the future. But we do not confront them here, because under the unique facts of this case, they are not presented. Contrary to the district court's belief, this is not a case in which insurance company "bean counters" overrode the medical judgment of a patient's physicians or in which those physicians allowed their medical judgment to be subordinated to a patient's ability to pay for treatment.[26] Nor is this a case in which the parties disputed the cost-effectiveness of the treatment at issue. Rather, UNMC's evidence was that its decision to wait to begin Flolan treatment was not economic—it was a medical decision, based on the health consequences to the patient if the treatment is interrupted. . . .

UNMC's witnesses testified that UNMC's treatment of Mary was consistent with the statutory standard of care—in other words, that health care providers in the same community or in similar communities and engaged in the same or similar lines of work would ordinarily defer Flolan treatment until payment for a continuous supply had been secured. We cannot depart from the customary standard of care on policy grounds, even if it is subject to criticism, because the standard of care is defined by statute and public policy is declared by the Legislature. . . .

Finally, and more fundamentally, the district court's concerns about health care policy, while understandable, are misplaced in a situation in which the patient's ability to continue to pay for treatment is still a *medical* consideration. . . . This case does not involve a conflict of interest between the physician and patient—there was no evidence, for instance, of a financial incentive for UNMC's physicians to control costs. As explained by UNMC's witnesses, the decision to defer Flolan treatment was not based on its financial effect on UNMC, or subordinating Mary's well-being to the interests of other patients, or even considering Mary's own financial interest. Instead, when making its initial value judgment regarding Mary's treatment,

20. See Mark A. Hall, Rationing Health Care at the Bedside, 69 N.Y.U. L. Rev. 693 (1994).

21. See Mark A. Hall, Paying for What You Get and Getting What You Pay For: Legal Responses to Consumer-Driven Health Care, 69 Law & Contemp. Probs. 159 (Autumn 2006).

24. See Daniel W. Shuman, The Standard of Care in Medical Malpractice Claims, Clinical Practice Guidelines, and Managed Care: Towards a Therapeutic Harmony?, 34 Cal. W. L. Rev. 99 (1997); Peter H. Schuck, Malpractice Liability and the Rationing of Care, 59 Tex. L. Rev. 1421 (1981).

26. Compare Wickline v. State, 192 Cal. App. 3d 1630 (1986) [which is excerpted at page 507 infra].

UNMC's physicians were not weighing the risk to Mary's health against the risk to her pocketbook, or UNMC's budget, or even a general social interest in controlling health care costs. UNMC's physicians were weighing the *risk to Mary's health* of delaying treatment against the *risk to Mary's health* of potentially interrupted treatment. . . .

As explained by [Mary's doctors], the reason for waiting to begin Flolan until after insurance approval had been obtained was out of concern for the health of the patient. That was not meaningfully different from any number of other circumstances in which a health care provider might have to base a treatment decision upon the individual circumstances of a patient. For instance, a physician with concerns about a particular patient's ability to follow instructions, or report for appropriate followup care, might treat the patient's condition differently in the first instance. And a health care provider who is told that a patient cannot afford a particular treatment may recommend a less expensive but still effective treatment, reasoning that a treatment that is actually used is better than one that is not. These are difficult decisions, and there may be room to disagree, but it is hard to say they are unreasonable as a matter of law, or that an expert cannot testify that such considerations are consistent with the customary standard of care. . . .

UNMC's evidence and opinion testimony reflect difficult medical decisions— but still *medical* decisions. Therefore, the scope of our holding is limited. We need not and do not decide whether the standard of care can or should incorporate considerations such as cost control or allocation of limited resources. Although the decision (or lack thereof) of a third-party payor contributed to the circumstances of this case, UNMC's decisions were still (according to its evidence) premised entirely upon the medical well-being of its patient. In a perfect world, difficult medical decisions like the one at issue in this case would be unnecessary. But we do not live in a perfect world, and we cannot say as a matter of law that UNMC's decisions in this case violated the standard of care.

Notes: The Impact of Economic Constraints

1. *Damned If You Do.* It may seem surprising that more courts have not previously considered more squarely a question as fundamental as whether the costs of treatment can affect the legal standard of care. The one case that comes closest to being on point is Wickline v. State, 239 Cal. Rptr. 810 (Cal. Ct. App. 1986), cited in *Murray* and reprinted at page 507. It found that no malpractice occurred when a Medicaid patient lost her leg as the result of being released from the hospital in four days rather than the eight days her doctors requested. The treating physicians blamed the state Medicaid program because it refused to pay for any more than four days. The court's rejection of liability says very little about the legal standard of care, however, since the patient chose not to sue her doctors, only Medicaid. She relied on her doctors as her expert witnesses against the state, and they naturally were not willing to testify that they gave her substandard medicine. Therefore, the key issue was not litigated. This case does illustrate, however, that there is often a wide range in acceptable standards of practice from the minimum to the optimal—here, from four to eight days—so that there may be plenty of room to accommodate economically constrained practice patterns within existing standards of care, especially under the "respectable minority rule."

The absence of case law on point is also due to the fact that defense counsel are highly reluctant to raise resource constraints as an excuse for omitting potentially beneficial treatment, for fear that plaintiffs might turn this defense against them by inflaming the jury to impose punitive damages, as discussed at page 516. Indeed, in a series of lawsuits, plaintiffs' lawyers have argued that an HMO physician's decision to withhold treatment, such as a Pap smear or biopsy to detect cancer, was inappropriately influenced by how the doctor was paid. The common law is still undeveloped because most of these cases have been settled or dismissed for procedural reasons prior to trial. In the few reported decisions, one court ruled that it was proper to exclude evidence that profit motivation might have caused an HMO physician to fail to hospitalize a patient with labor complications, observing that such evidence "was only marginally relevant [to malpractice] and potentially very prejudicial." Madsen v. Park Nicollet Medical Center, 419 N.W.2d 511, 515 (Minn. Ct. App. 1988), rev'd on other grounds, 431 N.W.2d 855 (Minn. 1988). However, Neade v. Portes, 739 N.E.2d 496 (Ill. 2000), ruled that evidence of economic motivation is admissible in a medical malpractice case. Is it possible to reconcile these conflicting decisions by observing that, where negligent treatment exists, a financial inducement can be found to be a contributing factor, but, standing alone, it does not constitute an independent tort? Would the second point hold true, however, if the financial inducement is not known to the patient? The discussion at page 241 addresses whether an informed consent cause of action exists for failure to disclose payment methods that create a conflict of interest.

2. *Ducking the Hard Questions.* Are you convinced by the *Murray* court's assertion that the doctor's decision was purely medical? Why would treatment necessarily need to stop just because insurance might not pay? If the patient refuses treatment because of the costs, then of course doctors must comply. Mark Hall & Carl Schneider, When Patients Say No (To Save Money): An Essay on the Tectonics of Health Law, 41 Conn. L. Rev. 743 (2009). But what if the Murrays would have wanted to continue the treatment and try to find ways to raise the funds? What would the law of "patient abandonment," discussed in Chapter 2.B.3, say about stopping treatment against the patient's wishes simply because they cannot pay?

In any event, the *Murray* court suggests that the custom rule provides leeway to consider costs, when doctors in fact think that it is medically relevant to consider costs. Does the similar locality version of the custom rule provide more leeway for this defense—by allowing lawyers to argue that physicians who practice under unconstrained, fee-for-service insurance are not from sufficiently similar situations to give relevant testimony in more cost-constrained settings? How would you evaluate such an argument based on the cases above? In Moss v. Miller, 625 N.E.2d 1044 (Ill. App. Ct. 1993), the court reversed a defense verdict against a prisoner who alleged negligent failure to refer him to a specialist. The fatal flaw in the trial was simply the inclusion of an ordinary similar locality standard in the jury instructions. The court was concerned that the jury would be misled, in light of counsel's arguments that prisons are a distinct locality. The court held:

> [T]hose practicing the medical arts in the penitentiary are held to the same standard of care as [other doctors]. To hold otherwise would be to abandon reason and common sense. . . . [W]e recognize constraints necessarily exist in correctional institutions which may well have a negative effect on the ability to delivery medical

services. . . . However, those types of constraints, while interfering with proper medical care, do not lessen the standards required of the medical arts practitioner.

Are these questions easier if patients are thought to have a choice over the matter? Consider, for instance, whether subscribers to an HMO plan should be allowed to contractually specify a lower but acceptable standard of care than that which prevails elsewhere in their community, so that their health insurance will be more affordable. That topic is discussed further at page 459.

3. *Bibliography.* In 1975, Randall Bovbjerg first analyzed these issues in relation to HMOs: The Medical Malpractice Standard of Care: HMOs and Customary Practice, 1975 Duke L.J. 1375. In 1981, the Texas Law Review published a lengthy debate among James Blumstein, Rand Rosenblatt, and Peter Schuck about precisely this set of issues. Symposium, 59 Tex. L. Rev. 1345 (1981). Haavi Morreim collects and expands her several articles (cited in *Murray*) into the book, Holding Health Care Accountable (2001). Considering how the issues take shape in the era of increased patient cost-sharing, see Isaac Buck, The Cost of High Prices: Embedding an Ethic of Expense into the Standard of Care, 58 B.C. L. Rev. 101 (2017) (developing the concept of "financial toxicity" as justification for physicians to consider costs to patients).

Problem: Economic Malpractice

You are legal counsel to Metropolis Inner City Hospital (MICH), a public facility that is bound by statute to treat all patients regardless of their ability to pay. Naturally, the hospital is chronically strapped for funds. Controversy is fast developing within the medical staff over the use of high osmolar contrast media (HOCM) vs. low osmolar contrast media (LOCM) in diagnostic imaging procedures, such as angiography. This is an invasive procedure to visualize the blockage in blood vessels by injecting a substance that shows up under X-ray (the "contrast media"). The substance's "osmolarity" affects its safety, with lower being better. Toxic effects are usually temporary (pain, nausea, altered kidney or nervous functions), but some are permanent, and some deaths have been documented. Although HOCMs are approved as safe and effective by the FDA, they have osmolarities of up to seven times that of blood plasma and consequently produce undesirable effects in some patients. Concerns over the toxicity of HOCMs led to the development of LOCMs, the first of which became commercially available ten years ago. Although all adverse reactions can be reduced by using LOCMs instead of HOCMs, HOCMs are usually well tolerated and affected patients respond quickly to treatment. Fortunately, fatal adverse reactions appear to be very infrequent. However, on a purely medical basis, with no cost considerations taken into account, there is no scientific reason to use anything other than LOCMs owing to the significant reduction in the prevalence of all degrees of adverse reactions.

The higher incidence of adverse reactions to HOCMs can be reduced by identifying patients at highest risk, such as those with asthma, allergies, renal or cardiac impairment, diabetes, etc. The American College of Radiology issued a set of guidelines for use of HOCMs vs. LOCMs based on various risk factors. However, risk stratification schemes cannot identify all persons who will react adversely to HOCMs. There is still a statistical benefit that can be realized by giving LOCM to patients who are placed in a low-risk category.

Both HOCMs and LOCMs produce images of similar quality. LOCMs, however, are about 10 to 20 times higher cost per dose than HOCMs ($20 vs. $200–$400). Although the higher cost may not be viewed as outrageous per procedure, if all procedures at MICH were to use LOCMs, costs would total over $500,000 a year.

Five years ago, about 9 percent nationally of radiological exams requiring contrast media were done with LOCMs. By this year, this number had climbed to 70 percent. Previously, MICH has used LOCMs only for high-risk patients. Physicians at MICH have expressed liability concerns about the continued use of HOCMs for any patients. Despite adherence to risk stratification procedures, the very availability of LOCMs concerns them. LOCM manufacturers have helped to fuel these concerns by telling the radiologists that the use of any contrast agent other than LOCMs could constitute malpractice.

How would you advise the hospital on the physicians' demands to eliminate all use of HOCMs? See Jacobson & Rosenquist, The Introduction of Low-Osmolar Contrast Agents in Radiology, 260 JAMA 1586 (1988).

3. Res Ipsa and Negligence Per Se

■LOCKE v. PACHTMAN
521 N.W.2d 786 (Mich. 1994)

[The facts are stated in the main excerpt at page 325. Briefly, a long, flexible needle broke off while Dr. Pachtman was performing surgery. After searching, she could not find it, and so a second operation was required to remove it. The court held there was insufficient expert testimony from the plaintiff for the case to go to the jury.]

Plaintiff next argues that even if expert testimony was insufficient, her case against Dr. Pachtman should have proceeded to the jury on the theory of res ipsa loquitur. Specifically, plaintiff contends, under this doctrine, a prima facie case was made, with regard to both the needle breakage and the fact that defendant terminated the surgery without having recovered the needle. The lower courts rejected these arguments, as do we. . . .

The following four factors a[re] necessary to a res ipsa loquitur claim:

(1)   the event must be of a kind which ordinarily does not occur in the absence of someone's negligence;
(2)   it must be caused by an agency or instrumentality within the exclusive control of the defendant;
(3)   it must not have been due to any voluntary action or contribution on the part of the plaintiff . . .
(4)   [e]vidence of the true explanation of the event must be more readily accessible to the defendant than to the plaintiff.

In the medical malpractice context, the crucial element, and that most difficult to establish, will often be the first factor, i.e., that the event is of a kind that does not ordinarily occur in the absence of negligence. A bad result will not itself be sufficient to satisfy that condition. . . . This does not mean that a bad result cannot be presented by plaintiffs as part of their evidence of negligence, but, rather, that, standing alone, it is not adequate to create an issue for the jury. Something more is required, be it the common knowledge that the injury does not ordinarily occur without negligence or expert testimony to that effect. . . . Neither standard was met here. . . . Even plaintiff's own expert acknowledged at one point that needle breakage is one of the risks of surgery, suggesting that faulty equipment might be a cause of breakage. . . .

Plaintiff relies on this court's holding in LeFaive v. Asselin, 262 Mich. 443, 247 N.W. 911 (1933). In *LeFaive*, the court held that a jury could determine, without the aid of expert testimony, that the defendant's action in inadvertently leaving a needle within the plaintiff's incision violated the applicable standard of care. Plaintiff's analogy to *LeFaive* is inapposite. In *LeFaive*, the act of leaving the needle within the incision was one of carelessness, from which negligence may easily be discerned. However, a far different situation is presented where a needle breaks off, and the surgeon, despite attempts to locate the fragment is unable to. One could not reasonably conclude, on the basis of common knowledge, that such an event does not ordinarily occur in the absence of negligence. . . .

Notes: Res Ipsa Loquitur and Negligence Per Se

1. *Other Examples. Locke* is an example of one of several typical, recurring situations in which courts will sometimes allow the case to go to the jury without expert testimony on deviation from customary practice. Other typical scenarios involve: leaving other foreign objects behind after surgery, such as clamps and sponges; injury to a part of the body that was not involved in the operation; and removal of the wrong organ or appendage. These cases are argued and decided under several doctrinal categories that overlap with res ipsa loquitur: "negligence per se"; the "common knowledge rule"; and "obvious negligence." As noted in Flowers v. Torrance Memorial Hospital Medical Center, 35 Cal. Rptr. 2d 685 (Cal. 1994), the gist of all these doctrines is captured in Bob Dylan's *Subterranean Homesick Blues* (Columbia Records 1965): "[Y]ou don't need a weatherman to know which way the wind blows." In the words of a Tennessee court, however, the medical negligence must be "as plain as a fly floating in a bowl of buttermilk." German v. Nichopoulos, 577 S.W.2d 197 (Tenn. Ct. App. 1978).

These various doctrinal categories are not all identical, however, and they are often applied somewhat differently in medical malpractice cases than they are in conventional tort cases. The "common knowledge" rule allows the jury to make simple factual findings from its own experience and knowledge base. It allows some facts to be found even though there are gaps in the supporting evidence, but it usually does not allow a finding of negligence without any expert testimony at all. Res ipsa loquitur is a stronger rule because it does allow this result, in proper circumstances. Negligence per se is stronger still; it can result in the judge directing a verdict of negligence as a matter of law. Note that this use of negligence per se differs from the standard application, which finds negligence as a matter of law only when a statute is violated; here, no statutory violation is required. Negligence per se in malpractice cases tends to be restricted, however, to certain extreme factual situations, such as incorrect sponge counts or amputating the wrong leg, in which negligence is so obvious as to be beyond dispute. Compare Guilbeau v. St. Paul Fire and Marine Insurance Co., 325 So. 2d 395 (La. Ct. App. 1976) ("the general rule . . .

is that a surgeon's failure to remove a sponge or pad before closing an incision may be regarded as negligence per se" justifying a directed verdict for plaintiff), with Nazar v. Branham, 291 S.W.3d 599 (Ky. 2009) (res ipsa, and not negligence per se, applies to foreign object cases due to the complexity who precisely is responsible within surgical teams for counting and retrieving surgical objects). For a case-by-case comparison among these rules, see Annot., 49 A.L.R.4th 63 (1986); Joseph H. King, The Common Knowledge Exception to the Expert Testimony Requirement for Establishing the Standard of Care in Medical Malpractice, 59 Ala. L. Rev. 51 (2007).

Notice how these three doctrines, without meaning to do so, tend to shift the focus from what physicians ordinarily do in similar cases, to what the jury thinks was reasonable in the particular case. Therefore, these doctrines do not simply overcome a gap in the evidence; they tend to alter the substantive standard of liability.

2. *Doctrinal Variations.* Res ipsa loquitur potentially applies to any type of medical mistake, as long as the elements of the rule are met. Because some of these elements are matters that are not usually in the common knowledge of jurors, however, plaintiffs frequently need expert testimony to establish them, as illustrated in *Locke.* Res ipsa loquitur in such cases allows the jury to fill in by inference the gaps that remain in expert testimony rather than displacing expert testimony entirely.

For a contrasting view that takes a more expansive approach than *Locke* to the availability of res ipsa loquitur and the "common knowledge rule," see Jones v. Harrisburg Polyclinic Hospital, 437 A.2d 1134 (Pa. 1981) (res ipsa applies whenever there is a "fund of common knowledge" from which to draw lay inferences), and an excellent student note on the case, 21 Duq. L. Rev. 547 (1983). Compare generally De Leon Lopez v. Corporacion Insular de Seguros, 931 F.2d 116 (1st Cir. 1991) (expert not needed where hospital switched babies born at same time), and Seavers v. Methodist Medical Center, 9 S.W.3d 86 (Tenn. 1999) (where patient suffered nerve damage in arm while being restrained in a hospital bed, res ipsa applies even when the issue is not within "the fund of common knowledge" but requires expert testimony to establish its elements), and Toppino v. Herhahn, 673 P.2d 1297 (N.M. 1983) (it is common knowledge that reconstructive breast surgery should result in breast of same size and shape as the other one), with Miller v. Jacoby, 33 P.3d 68 (Wash. 2001) (res ipsa applies to failure to fully remove a surgical drain but not to negligence in inserting the drain), and Sisson v. Elkins, 801 P.2d 722 (Okla. 1990) (res ipsa does not apply to surgeon who cut the wrong blood vessel, despite testimony he was negligent), and Bearfield v. Hauch, 595 A.2d 1320 (Pa. Super. Ct. 1991) (severing nerve during gallbladder surgery does not raise inference of negligence absent expert testimony to that effect, because usual results from this surgery are not within "fund of common knowledge").

Is the first element of res ipsa satisfied by the mere fact that, statistically speaking, a harmful effect rarely occurs if the procedure is performed properly? See Clark v. Gibbons, 426 P.2d 525 (Cal. 1967) (the rarity of the problem alone is not enough, but coupled with actual evidence of possible negligent acts this does suffice to support a jury verdict; operation had to be terminated prematurely because anesthesia wore off too early).

The factor requiring exclusive control is often not applied literally in medical malpractice actions, under the reasoning that it is unduly demanding considering that the team approach to treatment often means that no single defendant is exclusively responsible and the plaintiff is often not in a position to observe who performs which tasks. The classic case is Ybarra v. Spangard, 208 P.2d 445 (Cal. Ct. App. 1949), which allowed res ipsa to be instructed where a patient suffered a shoulder injury while under anesthesia for an appendectomy. The court observed that it should be the defendants' burden to come forward with evidence about who among those present in the operating room was and was not responsible for the injury. For a review of the application of these rules in cases of multiple medical defendants, see Annot., 67 A.L.R.4th 544 (1989).

3. *Legal Effect.* Locke v. Pachtman focuses on the conditions required for applying the res ipsa doctrine. Also at issue in these cases are the legal effects of the doctrine when it does apply. In *Locke*, the doctrine would have resulted in presenting the case to the jury. Other courts go further and use the doctrine to instruct the jury to find liability against at least one of the defendants, although this is much more controversial. See, e.g., Anderson v. Somberg, 338 A.2d 1 (N.J. 1975) (adopting this approach in a case similar to *Locke*, over a heated dissent accusing the majority of forcing the jury to act without "any semblance of rationality, . . . as the whimsy of the moment dictates, . . . no more a rational process than were trial by ordeal or trial by combat"). But see Salgo v. Leland Stanford Jr. University Board of Trustees, 317 P.2d 170 (Cal. Ct. App. 1957) (improper to direct verdict for plaintiff where factual dispute existed over whether needle injection hit the spinal cord and where experts disagreed over whether such a mistake would constitute negligence). An intermediate approach, followed by a substantial minority of states, is to create some type of rebuttable presumption or shift in the burden of proof when the elements of res ipsa are met.

4. *"Never Events."* Medicare now has a policy of not paying for certain "never events"—those that should never happen, such as administering the wrong drug or dosage or operating on the wrong body part. Should this federal payment rule determine state courts' applications of negligence per se or res ipsa loquitur? Somewhat surprisingly, the federal list also includes patients injured by falling, certain infections resulting from treatment, and pulmonary embolisms (blood clots to the lung) caused by certain surgeries.

5. *Legal Trend.* In earlier years, many legal commentators urged that res ipsa loquitur and similar liberalizing rules were necessary to aid plaintiffs with legitimate claims who were confronted with "the conspiracy of silence" on the part of physicians refusing to appear as expert witnesses. See, e.g., *Salgo*, supra. In more recent times, now that it is much easier to find qualified experts, the attitudes of commentators in both legal and medical journals have all but completely reversed. These rules are now often described as unfair to defendant physicians. Many of the statutory reforms adopted in the mid-1970s and mid-1980s include modifications of the res ipsa loquitur doctrine in medical malpractice litigation. See references and discussion in section H. A particularly outspoken expression of the modern view is found in Priest v. Lindig, 583 P.2d 173, 175 n.7 (Alaska 1976), where the court asserted that the legislative history of the Alaska statute abolishing res ipsa loquitur in medical malpractice cases was intended to counteract "the *intolerable* rule of law resulting in astronomically high malpractice insurance rates" (emphasis added). For commentary on these rules, see K. Albin, Res Ipsa Loquitur and Expert Opinion Evidence in Medical Malpractice Cases, 82 Va. L. Rev. 325 (1996).

4. *Ordinary Negligence*

It is one thing to argue that medical custom is common knowledge or its violation can be presumed from the outrageousness of the doctor's behavior. It is another thing altogether to argue that liability should be imposed *regardless* of medical custom or *contrary* to known medical custom. That is the result in the following decision, which is the most infamous of all medical malpractice cases.

■ HELLING v. CAREY
519 P.2d 981 (Wash. 1974)

HUNTER, Associate Justice.

This case arises from a malpractice action instituted by the plaintiff (petitioner), Barbara Helling.

The plaintiff suffers from primary open angle glaucoma. Primary open angle glaucoma is essentially a condition of the eye in which there is an interference in the ease with which the nourishing fluids can flow out of the eye. Such a condition results in pressure gradually rising above the normal level to such an extent that damage is produced to the optic nerve and its fibers with resultant loss in vision. The first loss usually occurs in the periphery of the field of vision. The disease usually has few symptoms and, in the absence of a pressure test, is often undetected until the damage has become extensive and irreversible.

The defendants (respondents), Dr. Thomas F. Carey and Dr. Robert C. Laughlin, are partners who practice the medical specialty of ophthalmology. Ophthalmology involves the diagnosis and treatment of defects and diseases of the eye.

The plaintiff first consulted the defendants for myopia, nearsightedness, in 1959. At that time she was fitted with contact lenses. She next consulted the defendants in September, 1963, concerning irritation caused by the contact lenses. Additional consultations occurred in October, 1963; February, 1967; September, 1967; October, 1967; May, 1968; July, 1968; August, 1968; September, 1968; and October, 1968. Until the October 1968 consultation, the defendants considered the plaintiff's visual problems to be related solely to complications associated with her contact lenses. On that occasion, the defendant, Dr. Carey, tested the plaintiff's eye pressure and field of vision for the first time. This test indicated that the plaintiff had glaucoma. The plaintiff, who was then 32 years of age, had essentially lost her peripheral vision and her central vision was reduced to approximately 5 degrees vertical by 10 degrees horizontal.

Thereafter, in August of 1969, after consulting other physicians, the plaintiff filed a complaint against the defendants alleging, among other things, that she sustained severe and permanent damage to her eyes as a proximate result of the defendants' negligence. During trial, the testimony of the medical experts for both the plaintiff and the defendants established that the standards of the profession for that specialty in the same or similar circumstances do not require routine pressure tests for glaucoma upon patients under 40 years of age. The reason the pressure test for glaucoma is not given as a regular practice to patients under the age of 40 is that the disease rarely occurs in this age group. Testimony indicated, however, that the standards of the profession do require pressure tests if the patient's complaints and symptoms reveal to the physician that glaucoma should be suspected.

The trial court entered judgment for the defendants following a defense verdict. . . .

We find this to be a unique case. The testimony of the medical experts is undisputed concerning the standards of the profession for the specialty of ophthalmology. It is not a question in this case of the defendants having any greater special ability, knowledge and information than other ophthalmologists which would require the defendants to comply with a higher duty of care than that "degree of care and skill which is expected of the average practitioner in the class to which he belongs, acting in the same or similar circumstances." Pederson v. Dumouchel, 72 Wash. 2d 73, 79, 431 P.2d 973 (1967). The issue is whether the defendants' compliance with the standard of the profession of ophthalmology, which does not require the giving of a routine pressure test to persons under 40 years of age, should insulate them from liability under the facts in this case where the plaintiff has lost a substantial amount of her vision due to the failure of the defendants to timely give the pressure test to the plaintiff.

The defendants argue that the standard of the profession, which does not require the giving of a routine pressure test to persons under the age of 40, is adequate to insulate the defendants from liability for negligence because the risk of glaucoma is so rare in this age group. The testimony of the defendant, Dr. Carey, however, is revealing as follows:

Q. Now, when was it, actually, the first time any complaint was made to you by her of any field or visual field problem?
A. Really, the first time that she really complained of a visual field problem was the August 30th date. [1968.]
Q. And how soon before the diagnosis was that?
A. That was 30 days. We made it on October 1st.
Q. And in your opinion, how long, as you nor have I the whole history and analysis and the diagnosis, how long had she had this glaucoma?
A. I would think she probably had it ten years or longer.
Q. Now, Doctor, there's been some reference to the matter of taking pressure checks of persons over 40. What is the incidence of glaucoma, the statistics, with persons under 40?
A. In the instance of glaucoma under the age of 40, is less than 100 to one percent. The younger you get, the less the incidence. It is thought to be in the neighborhood of one in 25,000 people or less.
Q. How about the incidence of glaucoma in people over 40?
A. Incidence of glaucoma over 40 gets into the 2 to 3 percent category, and hence, that's where there is this great big difference and that's why the standards around the world has been to check pressures from 40 on.

The incidence of glaucoma in one out of 25,000 persons under the age of 40 may appear quite minimal. However, that one person, the plaintiff in this instance, is entitled to the same protection, as afforded persons over 40, essential for timely detection of the evidence of glaucoma where it can be arrested to avoid the grave and devastating result of this disease. The test is a simple pressure test, relatively inexpensive. There is no judgment factor involved, and there is no doubt that by giving the test the evidence of glaucoma can be detected. The giving of the test is harmless if the physical condition of the eye permits. The testimony indicates that although the condition of the plaintiff's eyes might have at times prevented the defendants from administering the pressure test, there is an absence of evidence in the record that the test could not have been timely given.

Justice Holmes stated in Texas & Pac. Ry. v. Behymer, 189 U.S. 468, 470, 23 S. Ct. 622, 623, 47 L. Ed. 905 (1903): "What usually is done may be evidence of what ought to be done, but what ought to be done is fixed by a standard of reasonable prudence, whether it usually is complied with or not." In The T. J. Hooper, 60 F.2d 737, on page 740 (2d Cir. 1932), Justice Hand stated: "(I)n most cases reasonable prudence is in fact common prudence; but strictly it is never its measure; a whole calling may have unduly lagged in the adoption of new and available devices. It never may set its own tests, however persuasive be its usages. *Courts must in the end say what is required; there are precautions so imperative that even their universal disregard will not excuse their omission.*" (Italics ours.)

Under the facts of this case reasonable prudence required the timely giving of the pressure test to this plaintiff. The precaution of giving this test to detect the incidence of glaucoma to patients under 40 years of age is so imperative that irrespective of its disregard by the standards of the opthalmology profession, it is the duty of the courts to say what is required to protect patients under 40 from the damaging results of glaucoma.

We therefore hold, as a matter of law, that the reasonable standard that should have been followed under the undisputed facts of this case was the timely giving of this simple, harmless pressure test to this plaintiff and that, in failing to do so, the defendants were negligent, which proximately resulted in the blindness sustained by the plaintiff for which the defendants are liable.

There are no disputed facts to submit to the jury on the issue of the defendants' liability. Hence, a discussion of the plaintiff's proposed instructions would be inconsequential in view of our disposition of the case.

The judgment of the trial court and the decision of the court of appeals is reversed, and the case is remanded for a new trial on the issue of damages only.

■MEDICAL UNCERTAINTY, DIAGNOSTIC TESTING, AND LEGAL LIABILITY*
Eric E. Fortess & Marshall B. Kapp
13 L. Med. & Health Care 213 (1985)

Health care cost considerations exert increasing influence today over clinical decisionmaking. One way to help contain costs while maintaining the quality of

*Reprinted with the permission of the American Society of Law, Medicine & Ethics.

health care may be to increase among both physicians and patients an acknowledg-ment of, and tolerance for, a reasonable degree of medical uncertainty. By medical uncertainty we mean here those clinical situations in which, based on available data, absolute scientific proof regarding some aspect of a patient's health status cannot be obtained. . . .

For a variety of reasons, physicians are generally reluctant to acknowledge openly the existence and role of uncertainty in medical care. Traditional medi-cal training does not go deeply into the theory, mathematics, and management of uncertainty. Moreover, physicians tend to insist on maintaining professional control and dominance, to believe in the potential therapeutic efficacy of both the patients' and the professionals' unquestioning confidence in a treatment, and to perceive that many patients will not accept a physician who claims not to be omniscient. . . . The main impetus for physicians' overuse of diagnostic and therapeutic modalities is their intellectual desire to know as much as possible about the facts of each case, whether or not any of the additional data generated will materially affect the course of treatment or the ultimate outcome. Other factors are the Western philosophy that action is superior to inaction and the "technological imperative" perspective that whatever technology can do should be done. See V. Fuchs, Who Shall Live? Health, Economics and Social Change (1974). . . .

A physician comfortable with his or her own uncertainty can usually con-vince the patient to accept incomplete or indefinite answers and explanations. This acceptance implies a change in emphasis from a Mechanistic Paradigm to a . . . Probabilistic Paradigm. This conceptual framework recognizes that absolute cer-tainty is neither obtainable, identifiable, nor always desirable. . . . Put simply, past a certain point, the chance of achieving a small gain in certainty is not worth the costs—in any respect—of the effort. . . .

Most physicians appreciate the logic of diagnostic and therapeutic restraint in the face of inescapable medical uncertainty. Yet many argue that such restraint could result in patient-initiated medical malpractice suits predicated on provision of less than maximal care. To protect themselves, they resort to "defensive medicine," one cause of rising health care costs. "Defensive medicine" is an ambiguous, often care-lessly used term for which Hershey has supplied the most useful working definition: "Poor practice (a deviation from what the physician believes is sound practice and which is generally so regarded) induced by a threat of liability." N. Hershey, The Defensive Practice of Medicine: Myth or Reality, Milbank Memorial Fund Quarterly 50(1):69, 72 (January 1972). A 1983 American Medical Association study claims that 40 percent of the AMA's members prescribe additional tests and 27 percent provide additional treatment at least in part because of the perceived threat of litigation. . . .

Most importantly, our public policymakers assume that uncontrolled health care costs are indeed due partially to a medical malpractice system that engenders defensive medicine. This perception has led to the introduction in Congress of bills that would substantially alter the medical malpractice system in an attempt to con-trol one aspect of federal health care costs.

In spite of the furor over defensive medicine, cost-effective medical practice and the prudent management of legal risks can co-exist. An examination of mal-practice jurisprudence supports this thesis and refutes many widespread but incor-rect perceptions. . . . By expressly recognizing that the same clinical problem can be approached in a range of different but equally acceptable ways (based either on the physician's philosophical convictions or on recognition of the limited state of medical knowledge), the legal system in essence respects and condones medical uncertainty and embraces the Probabilistic Paradigm. . . .

Contrary to popular medical belief, the mere existence of a particular diagnostic or treatment technology does *not* automatically create a legal imperative to use that technology indiscriminately. . . . The case most often cited to prove that rampant judicial intervention has wreaked havoc with medical standard-setting and necessitated the defensive practice of medicine is Helling v. Carey. . . . The medical profession reacted to the *Helling* decision with somber predictions that the quality of medical practice would fall and the cost of health care would rise, due to the overuse and misuse of diagnostic testing. It was argued that money, time, and other resources would be diverted from real needs and that patients would be unnecessarily exposed to iatrogenic risks. These predictions have in large measure gone unfulfilled. Whatever surge in defensive medicine and costs can be traced directly to *Helling* is attributable to a misperception, rather than to an accurate appraisal of the current status of the law and its requirements.

Basically, the *Helling* case, for all its attendant publicity, simply represents a legal anomaly. With the exception of *Gates v. Jensen*, 595 P.2d 919 (Wash. 1979), in which the same Washington Supreme Court ignored a legislative attempt to return to the professional standard and instead ratified the *Helling* approach, the *Helling* precedent has not been applied in any reported malpractice lawsuit in any jurisdiction. . . .

[Nevertheless], *Helling*, as almost the sole example of direct legal intervention in setting the stringency of a medical standard, bears closer scrutiny. . . . We propose the following method of analysis, based on the mathematics of diagnostic testing, as a model . . . that may be applied to other tests to demonstrate that cost-effective medicine is also legally defensible. . . .

[Glaucoma] is diagnosed with one or more of three tests: tonometry, to measure intraocular pressure; perimetry, to evaluate the patient's field of vision; and funduscopy of the optic disc to detect "cupping" of the head of the optic nerve. In screening for glaucoma, ophthalmologists customarily use a tonometric test first. Tonometry usually involves light contact of the pressure-measuring instrument, the tonometer, on the anesthetized eye. If a pressure greater than 22 millimeters of mercury is found, the other tests may then be used to confirm or reject a diagnosis of glaucoma. Diagnosis is complicated by the fact that some people can have glaucoma without high intraocular pressure, while others can have high pressure (ocular hypertension) without developing glaucoma. . . . If glaucoma is diagnosed, treatment may include drugs to lower intraocular pressure, laser therapy, or surgery.

The diagnostic tests for glaucoma are thus not perfect, and actual disease states do not correspond totally with test results. Two major types of diagnostic error can occur: false negative test results with diseased patients and false positive test results with disease-free individuals. The ability of a test to correctly identify people with a disease is called its *sensitivity*, and its ability to correctly identify people without disease is its *specificity*. A test with few false negative results is highly sensitive, while one with few false positives is very specific. [Screening tests, like the tonometry pressure test used to detect possible glaucoma, are usually designed to err on the side of false positives, considering that false negatives — missing an actual case — are worse than falsely suspecting a number of healthy cases. In addition, even a low false positive *rate*, that is, very good test specificity, will produce a high *number* of false positives if the underlying incidence of the disease is very low, because lots of people have to be tested in order to ferret out the few true positives.] . . .

How do the probabilities of diagnostic testing relate to the *Helling* case? . . . Let us consider a hypothetical population of 25,000 individuals under age forty, of whom one has glaucoma. . . . Applying the estimates representing the best test performance, sensitivity of 70 percent and specificity of [95] percent, to our hypothetical population produces 1,250 false positive results. . . . If one is a true positive and 1,250 are false positives, then we can calculate that [the probability of truly having glaucoma when there is a positive test result is about 0.0008.] . . . Repeating the test, or performing the other two tests—perimetry and funduscopy, each with its own imperfect sensitivity and specificity—will shrink the pool of [false positives] but may never separate the one diseased person from the others. [Therefore, all may need to be treated. In addition, we must consider, even the one true positive may not be detected because of the rate of false negatives. Finally, when detected, treatment for the one true positive may not be safe and effective.] . . .

We have seen that in our hypothetical population, tonometry will probably produce [1,251] positive test results, of which only one truly identifies a person with glaucoma. Several disturbing issues arise. . . . What does the physician do with these patients, over 99.99 percent of whom don't have glaucoma? Does the physician have a duty to inform every patient of the possibility of glaucoma, causing great anxiety in many? Must the physician carefully monitor the thousands of patients identified as being at "increased risk" for glaucoma? What are the costs to society of mislabeling many people as "at risk" and then following and retesting them, perhaps for years? . . .

In retrospect, the *Helling* plaintiff should have been tested on the basis of her complaints and symptoms, despite her youth. But what would constitute good practice in one specific and unusual medical situation should not in itself be sufficient reason to institute a broad policy to test [all] young people for glaucoma.

■ ONE HUNDRED YEARS OF HARMFUL ERROR: THE HISTORICAL JURISPRUDENCE OF MEDICAL MALPRACTICE*
Theodore Silver
1992 Wis. L. Rev. 1193

A medical malpractice action is identical in all vital respects to any and every suit sounding in negligence. That simple truth, however, has been lost in a maze of judicial mistakes one century in the making. . . . Courts do not frequently offer a rationale for the professional custom rule. A few have suggested that medicine is too complex and the human body too temperamental to allow that a doctor be held to the simple standard of reasonableness. . . . Such explanations might at first seem sensible, but sensible they surely are not. First, medicine is no more complex than scores of other professional undertakings. . . . Organ transplantation is glamorous, but surely it is no more complicated or unpredictable in outcome than

*Reprinted by permission of the Wisconsin Law Review.

taming wild animals, designing a nation-wide marketing plan, or evaluating a new corporate security. All these pursuits are prey to the unknown and unknowable, and all demand expertise of a high order. With regard to medicine, complexity and uncertainty provides no greater reason for fashioning a standard of care after custom than they would in any other professional endeavor. . . .

Negligence is nothing more nor less than a failure to do what a reasonable person would under the prevailing circumstance. From a more refined perspective it is a failure to assess reasonably the costs and benefits associated with a given course of conduct, and thus to decide on its advisability. Justice Learned Hand . . . reduced the matter to quasi-mathematical terms, creating the famed Hand calculus: "Possibly it serves to bring this notion into relief to state in algebraic terms: if the probability be called P; the injury, L; and the burden, B; liability depends upon whether B is less than L multiplied by P: i.e., whether $B < PL$." Conway v. O'Brien, 111 F.2d 611 (2nd Cir. 1940).

The complexity of any technical field, medicine included, may well disable a lay juror who seeks independently to assess the relative risks and benefits attending a given course of conduct. That, however, only means that the juror needs advice from experts (genuine experts) who can identify the risks and benefits at issue. Thus informed, there is no reason that a juror cannot and should not pass on the appropriateness of anyone's conduct, including a physician's.

Without expert assistance, a lay juror cannot determine whether it is negligent to discharge a particular cardiac patient from the hospital without prescribing anti-coagulants. Yet, to make the determination, the juror requires only that an expert explain how the omission affects the matter of risks and benefits. An expert might explain that, according to standard medical wisdom, anticoagulants present a variety of risks and adverse effects, and, to the extent competent information allows, he might provide estimates of such risks in quantitative terms. . . . Armed with this knowledge, the jury would be competent to determine, as it does in any other negligence suit, whether the defendant physician had acted with reasonable care. . . .

Notes: Ordinary Negligence and the "Hand Formula"; Defensive Medicine

1. *Helling* met with an immediate storm of criticism in the legal and medical literature and upset the insurance industry even more, causing many insurers to feel that the deluge of expanded legal liability had reached revolutionary levels of social and political policy. This decision, along with the concurrence printed below, was credited with contributing to the withdrawal in the mid-1970s of many insurers from the medical malpractice market and the resulting "crisis" in medical malpractice, discussed in section H.

Is *Helling* really all that revolutionary? Can it be justified, for instance, using the res ipsa loquitur and negligence per se rules articulated in the previous notes, or is it simply an example, noted above at page 331, of courts rejecting a medical custom standard of liability in favor of a reasonable physician standard? See, e.g., United Blood Services v. Quintana, 827 P.2d 509 (Colo. 1992) (plaintiff is entitled to show that blood bank's methods for screening for AIDS virus, which were standard at the time, were not sufficiently protective because blood banks had failed to quickly adopt new safer methods). There is an obvious difference, however, between allowing a plaintiff to reach the jury without an expert on a contested question of fact and conceding that all medical opinion is opposed to the plaintiff's position. There is also an obvious difference between allowing the case to go to the jury and finding negligence as a matter of law. Did the defendant have a fair chance to present the data described in the Fortess and Kapp article? Do you think this information would have mattered to the *Helling* court? Prof. Peters explains that

> in one respect, the *Helling* decision was and remains genuinely aberrant. No other court has endorsed the Washington Supreme Court's decision to take the issue of medical negligence away from the jury and to rule, without the benefit of expert testimony, that a customary practice is negligent as a matter of law. This aspect of *Helling* was deeply flawed and has justly contributed to its reputation as a rogue case. However, *Helling*'s rejection of customary norms was not aberrant. Not only has *Helling*'s rejection of customary standards survived in Washington with the eventual blessing of the legislature, but many other courts have reached the same conclusion. Although few of these courts have expressly relied on *Helling*, perhaps because of its notoriety, many have agreed with its rejection of customary standards.

Philip G. Peters, The Quiet Demise of Deference to Custom: Malpractice Law at the Millennium, 57 Wash. & Lee L. Rev. 163, 171 (2000).

Immediately following *Helling*, the Washington legislature attempted to explicitly overrule it by a statute, but the state supreme court interpreted the statute as being consistent with its decision in *Helling*, since the statute refers to the skill and care "possessed" by physicians rather than "practiced" by them. Gates v. Jensen, 595 P.2d 919 (Wash. 1979). A subsequent decision clarifies, however, that "absent exceptional circumstances such as were present in *Helling*, expert testimony will be necessary to show whether or not a particular practice is reasonably prudent" and to clarify what skill and knowledge Washington physicians actually possess. Harris v. Groth, 663 P.2d 113 (Wash. 1983). The net effect, then, is to adopt the same "reasonable physician" standard that exists in many other states.

2. *The Technological Imperative.* It is often said that medicine in general, and doctors in particular, operate under a "technological imperative," which compels the use of all available technology, regardless of the economic, and sometimes even the medical, costs. This imperative is reinforced by the threat of liability, because doctors who want to obtain and use a new piece of equipment or new surgical technique that others are using can always point to the liability concerns of being the last one on the block to innovate. For instance, in Washington v. Washington Hospital Center, 579 A.2d 177 (D.C. 1990), a brain-damaged patient won $4.5 million because the hospital failed to acquire a newer, better machine for monitoring oxygen levels during surgery. The monitor was in use in some, perhaps many, other hospitals, but not in all, and the plaintiff's expert equivocated on whether the new monitor was required by the standard of care at the time of the injury. However, there was evidence that the hospital's chief anesthesiologist, prior to the accident, had asked the hospital to purchase the new monitor, citing as support the potential legal threat of not complying with the emerging national standard of care.

When the technology in question is diagnostic, it produces information relevant to additional courses of treatment. This information often leads to a "clinical cascade," in which further testing is required to confirm or reject the initial test, and then to various paths of treatment. Along the way, other potential or actual problems are often uncovered or created, which precipitate additional testing or treatment. Thus, early intervention and additional information in medicine often spawns greater, not lesser, costs. For instance, one study found that women undergoing annual mammograms have a 50 percent chance of receiving a false positive result over the course of ten years, and a 19 percent chance of undergoing an unnecessary biopsy. One HMO spent $33 to evaluate false positive results for every $100 spent on breast cancer screening. J. G. Elmore et al., Ten-Year Risk of False Positive Screening Mammograms and Clinical Breast Examinations, 338 New Eng. J. Med. 1089 (1998). An accompanying editorial argues that these results do not justify refusing to do routine mammograms for women under age 50, but they do support informing younger women of these odds and giving them the opportunity to decline. Are there any practical difficulties in resolving these issues simply by presenting the choice to patients? See H. Gilbert Welch, Informed Choice in Cancer Screening, 285 JAMA 2776 (2001) (criticizing this approach). Reviewing the evidence, the U.S. Preventive Services Task Force initially recommended routine mammograms starting at age 40. Then, in late 2009, in the midst of national debate over federal health care reform, the Task Force recommended against routine mammograms below age 50. A storm of controversy erupted, amid shouts that government was already starting to ration health care, so the government quickly clarified that the recommendation still leaves doctors and patients free to opt for mammogram screening at younger ages and that most insurance would still continue to pay for this, but the controversy still has not been quelled. See Jessica Mantel, Setting National Coverage Standards for Health Plans Under Healthcare Reform, 58 UCLA L. Rev. 221 (2010).

Given the financial and professional impetus for doing all that is possible in medicine, why do you suppose eye doctors in 1974 had restrained themselves from routinely testing all patients for glaucoma? How likely is this collective restraint to be exercised after *Helling*? Is this kind of collective restraint—selective use of new technology—good or bad for society? Who should make these decisions: doctors, patients, courts, or regulators?

A questionnaire administered several years after *Helling* revealed that it had not affected ophthalmology practice as much as had been expected. Doctors reported that they often performed the glaucoma test on patients under 40, but this was true both within and outside Washington State, and both before and after the court's decision. It appears that the testimony given in the case, that routine testing for younger patients was never done, was simply wrong. Jerry Wiley, The Impact of Judicial Decision on Professional Conduct: An Empirical Study, 55 S. Cal. L. Rev. 345 (1982). In 2005, the U.S. Preventive Services Task Force reviewed all available evidence and concluded that there was "insufficient evidence to recommend for or against screening adults for glaucoma." Due to "uncertainty of the magnitude of benefit from early treatment and given the known harms of screening and early treatment," the task force "could not determine the balance between the benefits and harms of screening for glaucoma." What does this suggest about the accuracy and utility of using tort law to evaluate and regulate medical practice?

3. *The Hand Formula.* Consider how the Hand formula might actually come out in the *Helling* case, using the numbers in Fortess and Kapp and additional reasonable assumptions. Start with the value for L, which represents the injury loss.

What do you think reasonable compensation would be for the partial loss of vision Helling suffered (tunnel vision, but still functional eyesight) — $100,000, $250,000, $500,000, or more? What are the possible values for the other factors? Starting with B, the burden of injury prevention, assume 25,000 people are screened at a cost of $10 each. How much should be added to B for the unnecessary treatment and anxiety caused by false positives — $100 per person? $200? $500? Next, what value should be used for P, the probability of loss prevention? Realize that screening all 25,000 does not guarantee detecting the one bad case, and if it is detected, it is not always possible to treat it effectively. Suppose detection and treatment are only 70 percent effective. Suppose they are only 50 percent effective. What would the value of the loss have to be in order to balance out these costs and probabilities? See Schwartz & Komesar, Doctors, Damages and Deterrence, infra.

4. *Defensive Medicine.* Despite all the controversy, some type of pressure testing has in fact become routine in all eye exams. Perhaps the costs are lower than supposed or the sensitivity and specificity have been improved. Or perhaps this is an example of the phenomenon described as "defensive medicine." This phrase is often used by doctors in a highly pejorative way to accuse the legal system of fostering unnecessary or harmful medical practice adopted solely to avoid liability and not for patient welfare. On the other hand, defensive medicine might be characterized as a perfectly appropriate result of the deterrent effect of liability, which encourages safer practices and more vigilance against error. In the middle ground, defensive medicine might be defined as medical practices adopted for liability reasons that are marginally or potentially beneficial but that, on balance, are wasteful. One must try to be clear in this debate about which understanding of the term is meant.

One place to start is to ask why the worst form of defensive medicine would ever occur. Since nonbeneficial medical procedures impose medical risks from side effects and cost more money, why don't these counterpressures force doctors to resist the legal pressures? One answer is that, under fee-for-service reimbursement, the economic costs of extra procedures are borne by insurance and contribute to doctors' revenues. Observe that liability concerns conceivably could also manifest themselves through lengthier counseling with patients (to acquire greater insight into their lifestyle habits and past medical history) or through more library research (to learn more about difficult, borderline cases) — much like we see in law firms that are paid by the hour — but this is not the sort of behavior complained of. Instead, it is said that physicians manifest defensive concerns by increasing the number of tests and procedures — no surprise since they are paid on a fee-for-service basis. Given this, is defensive medicine likely to abate, or at least assume a different form, as payment shifts to a different form? See Daniel Kessler & Mark McClellan, Malpractice Law and Health Care Reform: Optimal Liability Policy in an Era of Managed Care, 84 J. Public Econ. 175 (2002) (finding that managed care restrictions and liability reforms have similar and reinforcing effects in reducing defensive practices, which suggests that both payment incentives and liability pressures contribute to excess medical costs); Michael Frakes, The Surprising Relevance of Medical Malpractice Law, 82 U. Chicago L. Rev. 317 (2015) (arguing that medical costs would be more responsive to legal rules if underlying payment methods were not so inflationary).

Another reason doctors may minimize or ignore the medical risks created by nonbeneficial defensive medicine is that these risks may be less likely to result in large damage verdicts. A single omitted diagnosis concentrates the harms of omission in a single case. A mild side effect spreads the harms of commission over a large number of cases, none of which is likely to result in suit. Also, side effects from unnecessary procedures may be more difficult to prove. Consider, for instance, that while too many X-rays may cause an increased risk of cancer, it is almost impossible to detect the specific origin of any particular case of cancer. Occasionally, however, one does see a successful suit for the harmful effects of unnecessary treatment, especially surgery. E.g., Riser v. American Med. Int'l, 620 So. 2d 372 (La. Ct. App. 1993) (liability for unnecessary arteriogram that caused patient to die from a stroke).

5. *The Extent of Defensive Medicine.* How precisely to define defensive medicine and the extent to which it contributes to the total costs of health care are still matters very much in debate. Based on estimates of tens of billions of dollars, the AMA and other interest groups continue to press for sweeping federal relief from state malpractice laws as one means to lower health care costs, but others sharply criticize the methodology behind the estimates. Also, they note that even tens of billions of dollars is considerably less than 10 percent of the nation's $2.5 trillion health care bill.

6. *Negative Defensive Medicine.* Perhaps the most serious harm of defensive medicine, however, is when it operates in the opposite direction, to discourage doctors from doing certain procedures. This is known as "negative" defensive medicine. Because the malpractice liability threat is especially high for labor and delivery, many general practitioners have stopped delivering babies, some obstetricians refuse to take certain high-risk cases or restrict their practice to gynecology, and others refuse to accept Medicaid patients for whom the reimbursement is too low to compensate for the liability risk. This aggravates the serious shortage of physicians in rural areas and creates barriers to care for other disadvantaged population groups who are more prone to premature births or to being on Medicaid.

A large and prominent medical group in San Diego adopted a policy of transferring patients and all their family members if they filed a malpractice claim. In one case, the court ruled that this could constitute illegal abandonment, interference with the doctor-patient relationship, and breach of fiduciary duties if the transfer hampered access to care or lacked sufficient notice and opportunity to find a new physician. Scripps Clinic v. Superior Court, 108 Cal. App. 4th 917, 134 Cal. Rptr. 2d 101 (Cal. App. 2003). In Williams v. St. Joseph Hospital, 629 F.2d 448 (7th Cir. 1980), the court found that this could constitute an antitrust violation.

7. *Further Reading.* For discussion of **technological imperative** issues (note 2) relating to electronic fetal monitoring during childbirth, see Note, 51 Stan. L. Rev. 807 (1999); James Gibson, Doctrinal Feedback and (Un)reasonable Care, 94 Va. L. Rev. 1641 (2008). See generally, H. Gilbert Welch et al., Overdiagnosed: Making People Sick in the Pursuit of Health (2011); Richard A. Deyo, Cascade Effects of Medical Technology, 23 Ann. Rev. Pub. Health 23 (2002).

For additional discussion of the **empirical issues in *Helling*,** see J. F. Bovin et al., Cost-Effectiveness of Screening for Primary Open Angle Glaucoma, 3 J. Med. Screening 154 (1996); Comment, Rational Health Policy and the Legal Standard of Care: A Call for Judicial Deference to Medical Practice Guidelines, 77 Cal. L. Rev. 1483 (1989); William Schwartz & Neil Komesar, Damages and Deterrence: An Economic View of Medical Malpractice, 298 New Eng. J. Med. 1282 (1978).

For additional discussion of **defensive medicine** and physicians' perceptions of the legal system (note 5), see page 304; Tom Baker, The Medical Malpractice

Myth (2005); Michelle Mello et al., National Costs of the Medical Liability System, 29(9) Health Aff. 1569 (Sept. 2010) (estimating defensive costs of (only) $45 billion); James Reschovsky & Cynthia Saiontz-Martinez, Malpractice Claim Fears and the Costs of Treating Medicare Patients, Health Serv. Res. (2017) (estimating that physicians' liability concerns add $1,000-$2,000 per year to the cost of Medicare patients); William Thomas et al., Low Costs of Defensive Medicine, Small Savings from Tort Reform, 29(9) Health Aff. 1578 (Sept. 2010); Troyen A. Brennan et al., Liability, Patient Safety, and Defensive Medicine, *in* Medical Malpractice and the U.S. Health Care System 93, 109-110 (W. Sage & R. Kersh eds., 2006); David Studdert et al., Defensive Medicine Among High-Risk Specialist Physicians, 293 JAMA 2609 (2005); D. Kessler & M. McClellan, Do Doctors Practice Defensive Medicine?, 8 Q. J. Econ. 353 (1996).

Problem: To Test or Not to Test

Older women are at higher risk of giving birth to children with certain congenital defects such as Down syndrome. Amniocentesis, the test for these defects, itself poses risks of causing a miscarriage. The universal, accepted practice for pregnant women without a family history of defects is to use amniocentesis routinely only for women age 35 or over. The logic is that, under 35, the statistical risk of miscarriage is greater than the chance of detecting serious birth defects. Also, amniocentesis can have false positives, which can result in erroneously aborting a healthy fetus.

How would you evaluate the age-35 rule of thumb under *Helling*? Under the Hand formula? Under informed consent law? Consider this both from the situation of a younger woman who is not tested who delivers a baby with Down syndrome, and an older woman who is tested, resulting in the miscarriage of a healthy fetus.

C. QUALIFICATION AND EXAMINATION OF MEDICAL EXPERTS

Earlier editions of this casebook devoted hundreds of pages to issues of medical proof in civil and criminal litigation generally. Medical and similar scientific expertise is critical in areas as diverse as criminal law, paternity disputes, and competency hearings. Lawyers in these cases draw from countless scientific disciplines and specific techniques such as autopsies, genetics and DNA fingerprinting, polygraphs, and hypnosis-induced memory. See generally D. H. Kaye, Science in Evidence (1997); David Faigman et al., Modern Scientific Evidence (1997); Federal Judicial Center, Reference Manual on Scientific Evidence (1994); Jason Payne-James et al. eds., Encyclopedia of Forensic and Legal Medicine (2006). Earlier in this century, issues like these dominated the field of law and medicine, which was then known as "medical jurisprudence." See James C. Mohr, Doctors and the Law: Medical Jurisprudence in Nineteenth-Century America (1993). Today, it is no longer possible to adequately summarize each of these branches of forensic medicine. Instead, they are addressed in the law school curriculum as specialized aspects of advanced evidence law, or of law and science more generally. For those who are interested, a sampling of these issues can be found on the Web site for this book, www.health-law. org, where we have provided an edited version of the Supreme Court's landmark decision on scientific evidence, Daubert v. Merrell Dow Pharmaceuticals, Inc., 509 U.S. 579 (1993), with notes relevant to medical issues.

Even though medical proof in general is no longer a major part of this course, it is still important to understand the fundamentals of medical proof as one aspect of litigating medical malpractice cases. For this reason, we survey in this section a variety of common evidentiary and discovery issues encountered in malpractice litigation, primarily, how litigants in medical malpractice cases prove or dispute the standard of care.

■ TREES v. ORDONEZ
311 P3d 848 (Or. 2013)

BALMER, C. J.

In this medical malpractice case, . . . Plaintiff presented expert testimony from a biomechanical engineer familiar with use of the medical device installed on plaintiff's cervical spine by defendant, a neurosurgeon. For the reasons set out below, we conclude that plaintiff introduced sufficient evidence from an expert witness who is not a medical doctor to present a jury question on at least one aspect of her negligence claim.

Dr. Ordonez, a neurosurgeon, performed surgery on plaintiff that involved installing a plate made by Synthes on plaintiff's cervical spine . . . Plaintiff brought this negligence action against Dr. Ordonez . . . alleging, among other things, that Dr. Ordonez had failed to properly place and secure the Synthes plate and its screws, resulting in damage to plaintiff's esophagus that led to other injuries. At trial, plaintiff presented expert testimony from Dr. Tencer, a biomechanical engineer who is not a medical doctor, about the design, use, and installation of the Synthes plate; however, no medical doctor testified that defendant had breached the standard of care. At the close of plaintiff's evidence, the court granted defendant's motion for a directed verdict on the standard of care and breach because, although Dr. Tencer's testimony established the "ideal" placement of the Synthes plate, the court determined that defendant's conduct had to be compared to that of other neurosurgeons . . . We conclude that Dr. Tencer's testimony was sufficient for plaintiff to survive a motion for a directed verdict, and we reverse . . .

The Synthes plate that defendant used is a titanium plate designed to provide stability to allow for cervical fusion . . . To install the plate, the surgeon inserts a set of two screws into each of the six holes in the plate . . . For plaintiff's surgery, defendant used the smallest available plate, ...

At trial, plaintiff presented expert testimony from Dr. Tencer, a biomechanical engineer who works as a professor in the Department of Orthopedic Surgery at the medical school at the University of Washington. Dr. Tencer has a Ph.D. in mechanical engineering and is not a medical doctor. He testified, however, that there is overlap between the two disciplines because biomechanical engineering involves "engineering devices for the human body," and "surgeon[s] put[ ] in mechanical devices to hold bones together."

In his current position as a professor, Dr. Tencer lectures medical residents who are learning to become orthopedists on various topics, including "what types of things to watch out for" when using implants, and he guides some of those residents through research projects. He acts as a scientific reviewer for a variety of academic journals, including the journal Spine, and he has lectured to the National Association of Orthopedic Surgeons. In addition, he conducts his own research and has developed an implant system for spinal surgeries. Dr. Tencer testified that in the course of conducting research comparing the Synthes plate to other similar devices, he had watched and participated in the placement of a Synthes plate on a cadaver, but had not participated in such a surgery involving a living person . . . Outside the research and patient care context, Dr. Tencer testified that he also had experience with Synthes devices because he had done biomechanical testing of some of those devices as part of the FDA approval process, and he had helped Synthes come up with ways to improve their products.

Dr. Tencer testified about . . . defendant's placement of the plate on plaintiff's cervical spine, and he identified two related concerns. His first concern was that, unlike a correctly installed plate, the plate had not been bent to follow the curvature of plaintiff's spine. As a result, the plate was not close enough to the cervical spine to allow the screws to be fully seated in the plate. His second concern was that some of the screw heads protruded above the plate.

Dr. Tencer focused on the second concern, testifying that the plate that defendant had selected was the incorrect size. The plate was too short, and, as a result, the screws used to secure the plate were "over angled," and five of the six screws did not sit flush with the plate. Dr. Tencer went on to state that "it's very well defined as a step that the screw head must sit underneath down below the plates so it doesn't present any sharp edges" because "obviously [sharp edges] can lead to damage to the tissue." Specifically, he noted that a protruding screw head could come into contact with the esophagus. Given that risk, Dr. Tencer testified that, because there were screws protruding above the plate used on plaintiff, "it's pretty clear it's a go/no-go situation. In other words, any protrusion above the plate is essentially no-go, because it's clear that it can cause damage of some type, and it's very well described in all the literature that there should be no protrusion.". . .

[T]he issue is whether the testimony of an expert who is not a medical doctor can establish "that degree of care, skill and diligence that is used by ordinarily careful physicians . . . in the same or similar circumstances" and a breach of that standard. . . . [Oregon Rule of Evidence 702] provides that "a witness qualified as an expert by knowledge, skill, experience, training or education" may testify "[i]f scientific, technical or other specialized knowledge will assist the trier of fact to understand the evidence or to determine a fact in issue." . . .

Other jurisdictions have split on the issue: some jurisdictions have required expert testimony from a medical doctor to establish the standard of care, and others have held that experts who are not medical doctors may, in certain cases, provide testimony sufficient to establish the standard of care for a medical doctor. Compare Bell v. Hart, 516 So.2d 562, 570 (Ala.1987) (finding pharmacist and psychologist could not testify to standard of care in negligent prescription case against physician because "the standard of care must be established by medical testimony," meaning "testimony by physicians or properly introduced medical treatises"), with Thompson v. Carter, 518 So.2d 609, 614–15 (Miss.1987) (toxicologist and pharmacologist should have been allowed to testify regarding the standard of care for physician prescribing a drug because an expert on the standard of care must possess medical knowledge, but need not possess a medical degree) . . .

This court's medical malpractice cases . . . focus on whether the expert has the necessary knowledge to support his or her testimony, rather than whether the expert has a particular degree or specialty. See, e.g., Sheppard v. Firth, 334 P.2d 190 (Or. 1959) (finding that trial court erred in allowing orthopedic surgeon, who had no training in treatment using chiropractic adjustments, to testify that chiropractor's treatment was improper). For example, unlike decisions from some other jurisdictions, our cases have allowed experts from schools of medicine different from the defendant's to testify to the standard of care, if they have the necessary knowledge . . .

In Creasey v. Hogan, 637 P.2d 114 (Or. 1981), for example, this court held that two orthopedic surgeons could testify regarding the standard of care for a podiatrist in performing a bunionectomy. The court based its decision on evidence that orthopedic surgeons as well as podiatrists perform bunionectomies, use similar methods of treatment, rely on some of the same texts, and attend the same medical conferences. The court also noted that at least one of the methods that the podiatrist had used in that case was commonly used by both disciplines. Thus, in determining the qualifications of experts in medical malpractice cases, our cases have looked to substance, rather than form, and have focused on the knowledge of the expert, see id., rather than on an expert's particular medical degree or area of specialty . . .

Based on our cases, testimony from a qualified expert, who has knowledge about the standard of care that is helpful to the trier of fact, is admissible, and we see no principled reason why such testimony is necessarily insufficient to establish the standard of care in a medical malpractice case merely because that testimony comes from an expert who is not a medical doctor. . . . [M]any of defendant's concerns about allowing a nonphysician to establish the standard of care can be addressed through cross-examination of the nonphysician experts and through a defendant doctor's own testimony or that of his or her experts. That is, a defendant can challenge the weight that the trier of fact should afford to testimony from an expert who is not a medical doctor, and then the jury—not this court—ultimately must determine what weight to afford that testimony . . .

Based on Dr. Tencer's testimony, a reasonable jury could infer that an "ordinarily careful" surgeon would not leave screws protruding above the plate because that would present a "no-go" situation, particularly when those screws specifically are designed to sit below the surface of the plate due to the risk of damage to the soft tissue . . . [Thus], the evidence that the screw heads in this case were protruding above the plate could allow a jury to find that defendant breached the standard of care . . . .

■ CRUZ-VAZQUEZ v. MENNONITE GENERAL HOSPITAL
613 F.3d 54 (1st Cir. 2010)

Lipez, Circuit Judge.

In this action filed pursuant to Puerto Rico's medical malpractice law, . . . the district court excluded the testimony of the plaintiffs' lone expert witness at trial. [We reverse.] . . .

The plaintiffs brought this [malpractice] action against Mennonite General Hospital, two physicians, and several others, alleging that the defendants' negligence caused the premature birth of their daughter and her death two days later. . . . [T]he plaintiffs proposed to introduce testimony from one expert witness, Dr. Carlos E. Ramírez. . . . In response to an oral motion by the defendants, however, the court . . . ruled that Dr. Ramírez was not a qualified expert and would not be permitted to testify. The court then determined that the plaintiffs lacked evidence to support their claims and granted the defendants' motion for judgment as a matter of law on that basis. . . .

[T]he judge's task in determining whether to admit or exclude expert testimony is "to ensure that the expert's testimony 'both rests on a reliable foundation and is relevant to the task at hand.' " Although a district court has substantial discretion to make admissibility determinations on expert testimony, that discretion is not without bounds. An expert "with appropriate credentials and an appropriate foundation for the opinion at issue must be permitted to present testimony as long as the testimony has a 'tendency to make the existence of any fact that is of consequence to the determination of the action more probable or less probable than it would be without the evidence.' " (quoting Fed. R. Evid. 401). Generally, if an expert has "scientific, technical, [and] other specialized knowledge" that "will assist the trier better to understand a fact in issue," and that knowledge "rests on a reliable foundation," that testimony must be admitted.

Dr. Ramírez received his medical degree in 1981 from the University of Puerto Rico, . . . [and] became board certified in obstetrics and gynecology in 1987 and was re-certified in 1997. . . . Dr. Ramírez served as a [part-time] faculty member in gynecology and obstetrics for twenty-six years [at the University of Puerto Rico, and did both general gynecology and obstetrics]. In 2000, after being diagnosed with cancer, Dr. Ramírez left his private practice. . . . Since that time, he has . . . served as an expert witness in approximately 150 medical malpractice cases in the past ten years . . . primarily for plaintiffs because . . . defendants are reluctant to hire experts who have testified for plaintiffs in medical malpractice actions.

The district court excluded Dr. Ramírez's testimony on the ground that Dr. Ramírez was biased in favor of plaintiffs in medical malpractice cases. . . . The court also highlighted the fact that "Dr. Ramírez has begun collaborating with the distinguished attorney for Plaintiffs in this case . . . to give lectures regarding medical-malpractice and EMTALA." The Court noted that those lectures were "for profit, thereby focusing [Dr. Ramírez's] work further on assisting plaintiffs who seek to sue doctors and hospitals for various alleged violations of the law." This too "indicate[d] to the Court that Dr. Ramírez is not an impartial witness" because "he has a significant stake in the successful outcome of cases brought by alleged victims of medical malpractice."

In a similar vein, the Court described . . . a "trend" in which "supposed experts" do not "utiliz[e] scientific methods to render an opinion" but instead "twist[] scientific methods to produce a result that will support the case of those footing the bill." [T]he district court explained that it evaluated such experts "with a highly critical eye in order to preserve the sanctity of the common law legal system." . . .

The district court cited as the basis for excluding Dr. Ramírez's testimony aspects of his work that are typically established through cross-examination of an expert witness at trial in an effort to discredit his or her testimony. The court's reasoning had nothing to do with the scientific validity of the opinion that Dr. Ramírez proposed to offer or the principles that underlie it. . . . By excluding Dr. Ramírez's testimony due to its own determination that Dr. Ramírez would be a biased witness on the grounds cited, the district court abused its discretion. Assessing the potential bias of an expert witness, as distinguished from his or her specialized training or knowledge or the validity of the scientific underpinning for the expert's opinion, is a task that is "properly left to the jury." . . . Thus, considerations such as an expert witness's pecuniary interest in the outcome of a case, or his status as an expert witness only for one side of an issue, or the extent to which a doctor currently sees patients, go to the probative weight of testimony, not its admissibility. Furthermore, specific credentials, such as an up-to-date board certification, are not required for an expert to be qualified to testify. . . . The judgment is therefore vacated.

Notes: Qualification and Impeachment of Experts

1. *The Practice Dimension.* Observe that the requirements for qualifying an expert to testify on the standard of care are distinct from those for testifying about causation or extent of injuries. The former is our primary focus here. On the latter, see sections E.1 and F.

As the *Trees* court explains, the American courts are split on the issue of the competency of nonphysicians to testify on the standards of patient care required of medical practitioners. For other examples of the more restrictive viewpoint see Boehm v. Mayo Clinic Rochester, 690 N.W.2d 721 (Minn. 2005) (nurse practitioner lacked sufficient training or practical experience to testify about the standard of care for restraining the head movement of a patient after surgery by a thoracic surgeon); Wexler v. Hecht, 928 A.2d 973 (Pa. 2007) (under state statute, podiatrist may not testify about bunion surgery done by orthopedist).

Similar objections can be lodged against physicians as well. See, e.g., Williams v. Wadsworth, 503 N.W.2d 120 (Minn. 1993) (cardiologist who had not performed lymphangiogram in ten years could not testify against endocrinologist); Chase v. Mary Hitchcock Memorial Hospital, 668 A.2d 50 (N.H. 1995) (general practitioner who did not usually handle premature deliveries could not testify against obstetrician). However, most courts do not require physician experts to practice in precisely the same specialty as the defendant.

It is also curious to observe how courts react when physicians are called to testify against nonphysicians. Again, decisions are split. Creekmore v. Maryview Hospital, 662 F.3d 686 (4th Cir. 2011) (physician may testify about nursing standard for monitoring high-risk maternity patient); Sullivan v. Edward Hospital, 806 N.E.2d 645 (Ill. 2004) (physician may not testify about the standard of care for nurses in restraining a patient from falling out of bed); Wilkins v. Conn. Childbirth & Women's Ctr., 104 A.3d 671 (Ct. 2014) (physician may testify against a nurse midwife); Hankla v. Postell, 749 S.E.2d 726 (Ga. 2013) (physician who does not supervise or train nurse midwives may not testify against them).

2. *The Geographic Dimension.* Another dimension of an expert's qualification in addition to specialty and licensure is geographic location of practice. Where the jurisdiction follows a local or statewide standard of care, is it necessary for the expert to actually live and practice in that location? Generally, no; courts allow experts to assert knowledge of local practices through professional contacts in addition to actual practice. In Idaho, this has been elevated to a high art form in about a half dozen state supreme court cases that clarify precisely what extent of local inquiry will suffice for properly educating an out-of-area expert. See Symposium, 44 Idaho

L. Rev. 291 (2008); Suhadolnik v. Pressman, 254 P.3d 11 (Idaho 2011) (expert's bare statement that he is familiar with local practice does not suffice; must show he talked with a local specialist; not sufficient merely to review medical records and depositions in the case); Gubler v. Boe, 815 P.2d 1034 (Idaho 1991) (plaintiff must show that the local doctors his expert consulted were practicing in the same town the year the treatment was rendered). See also Shipley v. Williams, 350 S.W.3d 527 (Tenn. 2011) (lengthy opinion explaining all the ways in which an out-of-state expert can show actual knowledge of local practice). Another technique for qualifying out-of-state experts is for them to assert that national standards apply equally in every location. See, e.g., Henning v. Thomas, 366 S.E.2d 109 (Va. 1988). But see Falcon v. Cheung, 848 P.2d 1050 (Mont. 1993) (university physician may not testify to rural standard of care if he has never practiced in that setting).

3. *Impeaching Hired Guns.* Cruz-Vazquez v. Mennonite General Hospital adopts the prevailing approach of allowing "professional experts" to testify, subject to impeachment. Some courts go further, however, by restricting insinuations of an "opinion for sale." For instance, one court ordered a new trial where plaintiff's counsel unfairly characterized the hospital's expert as a " 'hired gun' who peddles his expertise randomly" and where plaintiff's counsel introduced extensive evidence about all of the defense expert's various sources of income, including fees from patient care and from consulting unrelated to malpractice litigation. The court reasoned that "there must be, and is, a point beyond which inquiry is/will be held to be prejudicial, too intrusive and only serving to divert the case into collateral matters." Mohn v. Hahnemann Medical College, 515 A.2d 920-923 (Pa. Super. Ct. 1986).

For a survey of legal and regulatory actions that can be taken to reprimand or control medical experts, see Gary N. McAbee, Improper Expert Medical Testimony: Existing and Proposed Mechanisms of Oversight, 19 J. Leg. Med. 257 (1998); Fred L. Cohen, The Expert Medical Witness in Legal Perspective, 25 J. Leg. Med. 185 (2004). See also Austin v. American Ass'n of Neurological Surgeons, 253 F.3d 967 (7th Cir. 2001) (expert witness had no right to challenge his suspension from a professional medical association for giving "irresponsible" testimony). For a general analysis and critique, with proposals for reform, see Jody Menon, Adversarial Medical and Scientific Testimony and Lay Jurors, 21 Am. J.L. & Med. 282 (1995).

4. *Statutory Reforms.* A number of states have cracked down on the perceived abuses of hired-gun, out-of-state, and inexperienced experts by enacting statutes that set more demanding qualifications. Common examples include requiring the expert (1) to reside in or near the state; (2) to have been in active practice in recent years (which excludes full-time teachers and researchers as well as "consultants"); (3) to practice in the same or overlapping specialty, or to have performed the same type of procedure, in recent years; and/or (4) to be licensed in the same professional category. Following these criteria, courts are becoming more stringent about expert qualifications. One court, for instance, refused to allow an osteopathic family physician to testify against another osteopathic family physician because their board certifications were from different professional organizations. Dale v. Kolb, 61 So. 3d 251 (Ala. 2010). See also Stowell v. Huddleston, 643 F.3d 631 (Minn. 2011) (refusing to allow an ophthalmologist to testify against a surgeon regarding failure to warn a patient about the risk of blindness from a procedure).

These statutes often contain "escape valves" that give trial courts limited discretionary authority to waive these requirements for just cause. See, e.g., Jackson

v. Qureshi, 671 S.E.2d 163 (Va. 2009) (out-of-state pediatrician may testify against a pediatric emergency physician); Sutphin v. Platt, 720 S.W.2d 455 (Tenn. 1986) (upholding constitutionality of residency rule because escape clause avoided hardship). But, where there is no judicial escape valve, one court has declared statutory restrictions on expert qualifications to be unconstitutional because they invaded the judiciary's "sole . . . province" to determine procedural matters. Broussard v. St. Edward Mercy Health System, Inc., 386 S.W.3d (Ark. 2012).

■ DAUBERT v. MERRELL DOW PHARMACEUTICALS, INC.
509 U.S. 579 (1993)

Justice BLACKMUN delivered the opinion of the Court.

In this case we are called upon to determine the standard for admitting expert scientific testimony in a federal trial.

Petitioners Jason Daubert and Eric Schuller are minor children born with serious birth defects. They and their parents sued respondent in California state court, alleging that the birth defects had been caused by the mothers' ingestion of Bendectin, a prescription anti-nausea drug marketed by respondent. Respondent removed the suits to federal court on diversity grounds.

After extensive discovery, respondent moved for summary judgment, contending that Bendectin does not cause birth defects in humans and that petitioners would be unable to come forward with any admissible evidence that it does. In support of its motion, respondent submitted an affidavit of Steven H. Lamm, physician and epidemiologist, who is a well-credentialed expert on the risks from exposure to various chemical substances. Doctor Lamm stated that he had reviewed all the literature on Bendectin and human birth defects—more than 30 published studies involving over 130,000 patients. No study had found Bendectin to be a human teratogen (i.e., a substance capable of causing malformations in fetuses). On the basis of this review, Doctor Lamm concluded that maternal use of Bendectin during the first trimester of pregnancy has not been shown to be a risk factor for human birth defects.

Petitioners did not (and do not) contest this characterization of the published record regarding Bendectin. Instead, they responded to respondent's motion with the testimony of eight experts of their own, each of whom also possessed impressive credentials. These experts had concluded that Bendectin can cause birth defects. Their conclusions were based upon "in vitro" (test tube) and "in vivo" (live) animal studies that found a link between Bendectin and malformations; pharmacological studies of the chemical structure of Bendectin that purported to show similarities between the structure of the drug and that of other substances known to cause birth defects; and the "reanalysis" of previously published epidemiological (human statistical) studies.

The District Court granted respondent's motion for summary judgment. The court stated that scientific evidence is admissible only if the principle upon which it is based is "sufficiently established to have general acceptance in the field to which it belongs." The court concluded that petitioners' evidence did not meet this standard. Given the vast body of epidemiological data concerning Bendectin, the court held, expert opinion which is not based on epidemiological evidence is not admissible to establish causation. Thus, the animal-cell studies, live-animal studies, and chemical-structure analyses on which petitioners had relied could not raise by themselves a reasonably disputable jury issue regarding causation. Petitioners' epidemiological analyses, based as they were on recalculations of data in previously published studies that had found no causal link between the drug and birth defects, were ruled to be inadmissible because they had not been published or subjected to peer review.

The United States Court of Appeals for the Ninth Circuit affirmed. Citing Frye v. United States, 54 App.D.C. 46, 47, 293 F. 1013, 1014 (1923), the court stated that expert opinion based on a scientific technique is inadmissible unless the technique is "generally accepted" as reliable in the relevant scientific community. . . . The court emphasized that other Courts of Appeals considering the risks of Bendectin had refused to admit reanalyses of epidemiological studies that had been neither published nor subjected to peer review. . . .

In the 70 years since its formulation in the *Frye* case, the "general acceptance" test has been the dominant standard for determining the admissibility of novel scientific evidence at trial. Although under increasing attack of late, the rule continues to be followed by a majority of courts, including the Ninth Circuit.

The *Frye* test has its origin in a short and citation-free 1923 decision concerning the admissibility of evidence derived from a systolic blood pressure deception test, a crude precursor to the polygraph machine. In what has become a famous (perhaps infamous) passage, the then Court of Appeals for the District of Columbia described the device and its operation and declared:

> Just when a scientific principle or discovery crosses the line between the experimental and demonstrable stages is difficult to define. Somewhere in this twilight zone the evidential force of the principle must be recognized, and while courts will go a long way in admitting expert testimony deduced from a well-recognized scientific principle or discovery, the thing from which the deduction is made must be sufficiently established to have gained general acceptance in the particular field in which it belongs. Because the deception test had "not yet gained such standing and scientific recognition among physiological and psychological authorities as would justify the courts in admitting expert testimony deduced from the discovery, development, and experiments thus far made," evidence of its results was ruled inadmissible.

The merits of the *Frye* test have been much debated, and scholarship on its proper scope and application is legion. See, e.g., Green, Expert Witnesses and Sufficiency of Evidence in Toxic Substances Litigation: The Legacy of Agent Orange and Bendectin Litigation, 86 Nw. U. L. Rev. 643 (1992) (hereinafter Green). Petitioners' primary attack, however, is not on the content but on the continuing authority of the rule. They contend that the *Frye* test was superseded by the adoption of the Federal Rules of Evidence. We agree. . . . Rule 702, governing expert testimony, provides:

> If scientific, technical, or other specialized knowledge will assist the trier of fact to understand the evidence or to determine a fact in issue, a witness qualified as an expert by knowledge, skill, experience, training, or education, may testify thereto in the form of an opinion or otherwise.

Nothing in the text of this Rule establishes "general acceptance" as an absolute prerequisite to admissibility. . . . [A] rigid "general acceptance" requirement would be at odds with the "liberal thrust" of the Federal Rules and their "general approach of relaxing the traditional barriers to 'opinion' testimony." Beech Aircraft Corp. v. Rainey, 488 U.S., at 169, 109 S.Ct., at 450 (citing Rules 701 to 705). . . .

That the *Frye* test was displaced by the Rules of Evidence does not mean, however, that the Rules themselves place no limits on the admissibility of purportedly scientific evidence. . . . The adjective "scientific" implies a grounding in the methods and procedures of science. Similarly, the word "knowledge" connotes more than subjective belief or unsupported speculation. . . . Of course, it would be unreasonable to conclude that the subject of scientific testimony must be "known" to a certainty; arguably, there are no certainties in science. But, in order to qualify as "scientific knowledge," an inference or assertion must be derived by the scientific method. . . .

Rule 702 further requires that the evidence or testimony "assist the trier of fact to understand the evidence or to determine a fact in issue." This condition goes primarily to relevance. . . . See United States v. Downing, 753 F.2d 1224, 1242 (CA3 1985) ("An additional consideration under Rule 702—and another aspect of relevancy—is whether expert testimony proffered in the case is sufficiently tied to the facts of the case that it will aid the jury in resolving a factual dispute"). This consideration has been aptly described by Judge Becker as one of "fit." "Fit" is not always obvious, and scientific validity for one purpose is not necessarily scientific validity for other, unrelated purposes. . . .

That these requirements are embodied in Rule 702 is not surprising. Unlike an ordinary witness, see Rule 701, an expert is permitted wide latitude to offer opinions, including those that are not based on first-hand knowledge or observation. Presumably, this relaxation of the usual requirement of first-hand knowledge—a rule which represents "a 'most pervasive manifestation' of the common law insistence upon 'the most reliable sources of information,' " Advisory Committee's Notes on Fed.Rule Evid. 602—is premised on an assumption that the expert's opinion will have a reliable basis in the knowledge and experience of his discipline.

Faced with a proffer of expert scientific testimony, then, the trial judge must determine at the outset whether the expert is proposing to testify to (1) scientific knowledge that (2) will assist the trier of fact to understand or determine a fact in issue. This entails a preliminary assessment of whether the reasoning or methodology underlying the testimony is scientifically valid and of whether that reasoning or methodology properly can be applied to the facts in issue. We are confident that federal judges possess the capacity to undertake this review. Many factors will bear on the inquiry, and we do not presume to set out a definitive checklist or test. But some general observations are appropriate.

Ordinarily, a key question to be answered in determining whether a theory or technique is scientific knowledge that will assist the trier of fact will be whether it can be (and has been) tested. . . . K. Popper, Conjectures and Refutations: The Growth of Scientific Knowledge 37 (5th ed. 1989) ("[T]he criterion of the scientific status of a theory is its falsifiability, or refutability, or testability").

Another pertinent consideration is whether the theory or technique has been subjected to peer review and publication. Publication (which is but one element of peer review) is not a sine qua non of admissibility; it does not necessarily correlate with reliability, and in some instances well-grounded but innovative theories will not have been published. Some propositions, moreover, are too particular, too new, or of too limited interest to be published. But submission to the scrutiny of the scientific community is a component of "good science," in part because it increases the likelihood that substantive flaws in methodology will be detected. The fact of publication (or lack thereof) in a peer-reviewed journal thus will be a relevant, though not dispositive, consideration in assessing the scientific validity of a particular technique or methodology on which an opinion is premised.

Additionally, in the case of a particular scientific technique, the court ordinarily should consider the known or potential rate of error, see, e.g., United States v. Smith, 869 F.2d 348 (7th Cir. 1989) (surveying studies of the error rate of spectrographic voice identification technique), and the existence and maintenance of standards controlling the technique's operation.

Finally, "general acceptance" can yet have a bearing on the inquiry. . . . Widespread acceptance can be an important factor in ruling particular evidence admissible, and a known technique that has been able to attract only minimal support within the community may properly be viewed with skepticism.

The inquiry envisioned by Rule 702 is, we emphasize, a flexible one. Its overarching subject is the scientific validity—and thus the evidentiary relevance and reliability—of the principles that underlie a proposed submission. The focus, of course, must be solely on principles and methodology, not on the conclusions that they generate.

Throughout, a judge assessing a proffer of expert scientific testimony under Rule 702 should also be mindful of other applicable rules. Rule 703 provides that expert opinions based on otherwise inadmissible hearsay are to be admitted only if the facts or data are "of a type reasonably relied upon by experts in the particular field in forming opinions or inferences upon the subject." Rule 706 allows the court at its discretion to procure the assistance of an expert of its own choosing. Finally, Rule 403 permits the exclusion of relevant evidence "if its probative value is substantially outweighed by the danger of unfair prejudice, confusion of the issues, or misleading the jury. . . ." Judge Weinstein has explained: "Expert evidence can be both powerful and quite misleading because of the difficulty in evaluating it. Because of this risk, the judge in weighing possible prejudice against probative force under Rule 403 of the present rules exercises more control over experts than over lay witnesses." Weinstein, 138 F.R.D., at 632.

. . . Vigorous cross-examination, presentation of contrary evidence, and careful instruction on the burden of proof are the traditional and appropriate means of attacking shaky but admissible evidence. See Rock v. Arkansas, 483 U.S. 44, 61, 107 S. Ct. 2704, 2714, 97 L. Ed. 2d 37 (1987). Additionally, in the event the trial court concludes that the scintilla of evidence presented supporting a position is insufficient to allow a reasonable juror to conclude that the position more likely than not is true, the court remains free to direct a judgment, and likewise to grant summary judgment. Cf., e.g., Turpin v. Merrell Dow Pharmaceuticals, Inc., 959 F.2d 1349 (CA6) (holding that scientific evidence that provided foundation for expert testimony [about Bendectin], viewed in the light most favorable to plaintiffs, was not sufficient to allow a jury to find it more probable than not that defendant caused plaintiff's injury). These conventional devices, rather than wholesale exclusion under an uncompromising "general acceptance" test, are the appropriate safeguards where the basis of scientific testimony meets the standards of Rule 702. . . .

Accordingly, the judgment of the Court of Appeals is vacated and the case is remanded for further proceedings consistent with this opinion.

Notes: Forensic Medicine and Epidemiological Evidence

1. *Forensic Science.* Earlier editions of this casebook devoted hundreds of pages to issues of medical proof in civil and criminal litigation generally. Medical and similar scientific expertise is critical in areas as diverse as criminal law, paternity disputes, and competency hearings. Lawyers in these cases draw from countless scientific disciplines and specific techniques such as autopsies, genetics and DNA fingerprinting, polygraphs, and hypnosis-induced memory. See note 7. Earlier in the twentieth century, issues like these dominated the field of law and medicine, which was then known as "medical jurisprudence." See James C. Mohr, Doctors and the Law: Medical Jurisprudence in Nineteenth-Century America (1993). Today, these topics are covered in more depth in specialized courses on advanced evidence law, or on law and science more generally.

2. *Genetic Tests and Beyond.* Regarding forensic use of clinical genetic tests, consider the following scenarios, offered by Diane E. Hoffmann & Karen H. Rothenberg, Judging Genes: Implications of the Second Generation of Genetic Tests in the Courtroom, 66 Md. L. Rev. 858 (2007):

> Case 1. In a non-capital sentencing proceeding of a twenty-eight-year-old man convicted of a violent homicide, the prosecutor requests that you compel the defendant to have a genetic test for a gene mutation that predisposes an individual to exhibit bouts of extreme rage. Between fifty and sixty percent of individuals with this mutation exhibit these behavioral abnormalities before the age at which the defendant committed the crime. With this test result the prosecutor wishes to show that the defendant has a proclivity toward violence ("future dangerousness"). The defendant objects to being compelled to have the test.
>
> Case 2. In the damages phase of a products liability case, the defendant requests that you compel the twenty-one-year-old plaintiff to have a genetic test for Neurofibromatosis type II (NF-2), as his father died of the disease at the age of forty. NF-2 is a rare, inherited disorder characterized by the development of benign tumors on both auditory nerves and by the development of malignant central nervous system tumors. The disease is unrelated to the injury caused by the defendant's product. Virtually everyone who has the mutation develops the disease; however, the severity of symptoms differs from person to person, and the gene is not predictive of such disparities. An expert testifies that the average age of onset of NF-2 is between eighteen and twenty-four and that the average age of death of those with the disease is thirty-six. At present, the plaintiff has no symptoms of the disease.

As these authors note, "soon, judges across the country may face questions similar to the ones posed by these two hypothetical scenarios. Would you compel the test in either case?" See generally D. H. Kaye, The Double Helix and the Law of Evidence (2010).

Neuroimaging (or brain imaging) using techniques such as PET scanning is a rapidly growing new area of forensic medicine. See generally Symposium, 33 Am. J.L. & Med. 163 (2007).

3. *The Relevance of* Daubert. The relevance of *Daubert*, a products liability case against a drug manufacturer, to medical malpractice cases against doctors may not be readily apparent. This case appears in these materials for two main reasons: (1) law and medicine has strong historical roots in the field of forensic science; and (2) epidemiological and statistical evidence of the sort at issue in *Daubert* is increasingly important in medical and other litigation. *Daubert* has generated extensive debate over the range of experts and topics of testimony to which it applies. Rule 702 allows expert testimony on an unlimited range of technical or specialized topics; scientific knowledge is only one subset. For a time, courts and commentators thought *Daubert* might be limited to only scientific theories or techniques. However, in Kumho Tire Co. v. Carmichael, 526 U.S. 137 (1999), the Court clarified that *Daubert* also applies to "technical or other specialized knowledge," and so it sustained a trial court's decision to exclude as unreliable the proffered testimony of an expert on tire failure, in a case claiming that a manufacturing defect caused a tire to blow out. Similarly, it seems clear that *Daubert* factors can be used to evaluate economic testimony going to damages calculations in medical malpractice cases (i.e., the extent and measure of injuries) and medical expertise on causation issues (whether the injuries resulted from the physician's error or would have happened anyway). Consider, for instance, that in the Bendectin controversy, plaintiffs had one physician, Dr. Palmer, who was willing to state unequivocally that the drug caused the plaintiff's defects. He stated:

> It is my opinion . . . that [animal in vivo and in vitro studies, and epidemiological and other human data] shows that Bendectin and specifically its component, doxylamine succinate, has teratogenic properties. . . . I have also examined the medical records pertaining to Brandy Turpin and it is my opinion . . . that Bendectin did cause the limb defects from which she suffers.

Nevertheless, the 9th Circuit in *Daubert* agreed with the 6th Circuit in *Turpin* (which the Supreme Court cites favorably) in concluding that this failed to create a jury issue: "This testimony is [no]thing more than a personal belief or opinion. . . . Dr. Palmer does not testify on the basis of the collective view of his scientific discipline, nor does he take issue with his peers and explain the grounds for his differences. Indeed, no understandable scientific basis is stated. Personal opinion, not science, is testifying here." 959 F.2d 1349.

Just this type of qualitative opinion testimony is exactly what malpractice litigants almost always rely on, however. See Marsh v. Valyou, 977 So. 2d 543 (Fla. 2007) (Daubert does not apply to medical causation testimony that is based simply on medical opinion and conventional clinical reasoning); Marcum v. Adventist System/ West, 193 P.3d 1 (2008) (same). More rigorous quantitative proof is seldom available because the medical mistake at issue is rarely common and widespread enough to be subjected to the large epidemiological studies that the courts favor in suits against pharmaceutical companies. Presumably, more is demanded in the drug cases because better evidence is available. E.g., Samaan v. St. Joseph Hosp., 670 F.3d 21 (1st Cir. 2012) (upholding *Daubert* exclusion of physician testimony on causation, in the failure to administer the correct drug for a stroke patient). Is this a correct application of *Daubert*, or should scientific evidence that is admissible in any case be admitted in every case (assuming it is equally relevant to a fact in issue)? Is weak scientific evidence "prejudicial" just because a jury might use it to reject stronger evidence?

Much more controversial is whether *Daubert* might be used to block expert testimony on the medical standard of care. Although this requires a certain type of scientific or technical expertise, it relates to standards of professional practice and clinical judgment, not the use of a scientific method to arrive at conclusions about facts in the case, and so courts generally decline to apply a *Daubert* analysis to such testimony. See, e.g., Dickenson v. Cardiac & Thoracic Surgery, 388 F.3d 976 (6th Cir. 2004); Adams v. Laboratory Corporation of America, 760 F.3d 1322 (11th Cir. 2014). See generally Jerome P. Kassierer & Joe S. Cecil, Inconsistency in Evidentiary Standards for Medical Testimony, 288 New Eng. J. Med. 1392 (2002).

4. *Junk Science.* *Daubert* was decided after several years of controversy over whether judges were allowing too much "junk science" to prevail in court. The accusation is frequently made that a paid expert can always be found to testify on both sides of any proposition. See, e.g., Peter W. Huber, Galileo's Revenge: Junk Science in the Courtroom (1991). The Bendectin drug is often cited as a leading example of how the unjustified threat of liability can cause a beneficial medical product to be pulled from the market even though virtually the entire scientific community believes it is safe.

One way to conceive of the difference between *Frye* and *Daubert* is that *Frye* deferred to the collective opinion of the scientific community, whereas *Daubert* asks judges themselves to determine what constitutes "good science," employing factors such as those mentioned in the opinion. Are judges up to this task? How does this compare with how the medical standard of care is determined?

Some commentators, harshly critical of the way the adversarial system distorts scientific truth, call for more sweeping reforms. One possibility is greater use of neutral, court-appointed experts or special masters, which is standard practice in Europe and was long ago the norm in the United States. In the United States, this practice is still allowed by the federal rules but is infrequently done. Another potential reform is to create specialized tribunals (often called "science courts") composed of adjudicators who themselves possess scientific expertise.

5. Daubert's *Impact.* Initially, it was thought that *Daubert* made it easier for "junk science" to be introduced than was the case under the *Frye* rule. Increasingly, it appears, however, that *Daubert* may have had just the opposite effect. Bert Black et al., Science and the Law in the Wake of *Daubert*: A New Search for Scientific Knowledge, 72 Tex. L. Rev. 715, 722 (1994). On remand, the 9th Circuit reaffirmed its prior opinion. It reasoned: (1) the plaintiffs' experts had developed their positions specifically in response to litigation and therefore deserved heightened skepticism; (2) no independent scientists agreed with them; and (3) the evidence flunked *Daubert's* "fit" test because it showed at most only an increased risk, not actual causation of birth defects for any of these particular plaintiffs. Daubert v. Merrell Dow Pharmaceuticals, 43 F.3d 1311. Does this violate the Supreme Court's command not to confuse the underlying methods with the scientists' conclusions? In a subsequent decision, the Court affirmed a trial judge's decision to exclude opinion testimony from established scientists based on animal studies and epidemiological evidence that the plaintiff's lung cancer was caused by his exposure to PCBs. The Court held that it was not an abuse of discretion for the judge to conclude that "there [was] simply too great an analytical gap between the data and the opinion proffered." General Electric Co. v. Joiner, 522 U.S. 136 (1997).

Recognize that *Daubert* states only federal law. Prior to *Daubert*, the majority of states adhered to the *Frye* rule, and following *Daubert*, of those that have reconsidered the issue, almost half have reaffirmed *Frye.* Joseph R. Meaney, From *Frye* to *Daubert:* Is a Pattern Unfolding?, 35 Jurimetrics 191 (1995) ("*Frye* supporters can send get well cards, but the funeral has been postponed.").

6. *Epidemiological Evidence.* Focusing on the kind of epidemiological evidence that prevailed in the Bendectin case, consider situations where that evidence favors the plaintiff. How strong a statistical association must be shown before causation is actually proven? If the study is well designed, it will control for "confounding factors" that might offer an innocent explanation for the observed harm. A good study also uses an observation technique that attempts to sample objectively a random or representative selection from the population at large. Even when these criteria for sound methodology are met, a difficulty arises from using probability figures for a large number of cases to decide what happened in the particular case under litigation. A pressing example of this dilemma comes from past litigation over silicone breast implants. A larges study (400,000 respondents and 10,000 patients), conducted at Harvard, showed a 24 percent increased risk of "connective tissue disease," amounting to 1 in 3000 women each year attributable to the implants. The authors interpreted this study as ruling out any "large hazard," but plaintiffs' attorneys hailed it as confirming their previously discredited allegations. Numerous other physicians were willing to testify that they are convinced that implants cause these illnesses because their patients often improved markedly when the implants were removed. N.Y. Times, Feb. 28, 1996, at A14. Is this the type of evidence that should go to the jury? On remand, the 9th Circuit in *Daubert* agreed with a number of other courts that, under a civil standard (preponderance of the evidence), plaintiffs must show an increased risk of at least 200 percent in order to create a jury issue on causation, because only then can it be said with scientific certainty that the hazardous agent "more likely than not" caused the injury compared with all other possible causes. In medical malpractice cases, many of these difficulties over statistical uncertainty are avoided using the "loss of chance" theory discussed in section E. below, which allows partial recovery even when causation is less likely than not. Also, contrast the different levels of proof necessary to justify regulation as opposed to compensation in tort. Even a slight and uncertain elevated risk may be sufficient to ban or regulate a carcinogen, environmental hazard, or medical drug.

7. *Bibliography.* On **forensic science generally**, see David Faigman et al., Modern Scientific Evidence (annual updates); Federal Judicial Center, Reference Manual on Scientific Evidence (3d ed. 2011); Symposium: Forensic Science for the 21st Century, 50 Jurimetrics J. 1 (2009); Symposium, Lessons from the Lab: Implications of the 2009 National Academy of Sciences Report on the Future of Forensic Science, 2010 Utah L. Rev. 221-442; Erin Murphy, The New Forensics, 95 Cal. L. Rev. 721 (2007).

For an introduction to proposals for **science courts** (note 4), see James Martin, The Proposed "Science Court," 75 Mich. L. Rev. 1058 (1977); Samuel Gross, Expert Evidence, 1991 Wis. L. Rev. 1113 (1991); Symposium, Expert Evidence, 16 Law & Human Behav. 253-379 (1992); K. Kreiling, Managing Expert Evidence: An Overview, 36 Jurimetrics J. 121 (1996); Margaret Farrell, Coping with Scientific Evidence: The Use of Special Masters, 43 Emory L.J. 927 (1994).

For general **commentary on *Daubert*** and its progeny, see Ronald Allen & Esfand Nafisi, Daubert and its Discontents, 76 Brook. L. Rev. 131 (2010); Symposium, 36

New Eng. L. Rev. 573 (2002); Symposium, 15 Cardozo L. Rev. 1745 (1994); Lee Loevinger, Science as Evidence, 35 Jurimetrics J. 153 (1995); Note, 116 Harv. L. Rev. 2142 (2003); Note, 113 Harv. L. Rev. 1467 (2000).

■TRIAL TACTICS AND METHODS*
Robert E. Keeton**
1973

Plaintiff Peter Park alleges that Defendant David Dell, an anesthesiologist, negligently injected liquid anaesthesia into tissues of plaintiff's arm rather than into the vein, causing damage to nerves and producing disability. At trial, a professor of neurology, who did not treat plaintiff and does not have personal knowledge of the relevant medical history, is called as an expert witness for the plaintiff. [The following demonstrates how] hypothetical questions [might] be framed as to the cause of plaintiff's disability and as to whether the defendant's conduct failed to measure up to professional standards:

Doctor, as the basis for my next question, please assume the following as facts:

(1) Peter Park, on January 6, 19X3, went to the Dental Clinic of Ames Memorial Hospital for an operation to be conducted by Dr. John Rogers, an oral surgeon, the operation having been scheduled to treat a serious infection of Peter Parks' gums, which had been diagnosed by Dr. Rogers as advanced gingivitis;

(2) Defendant, Dr. David Dell, was the attending anesthesiologist at that operation;

(3) Defendant, Dr. Dell, began to anesthetize Peter Park for the operation by an injection of a liquid anesthesia, called Brevitol, into Peter Park's left arm;

(4) The first injection produced no effect of drowsiness; also, immediately after that injection, Peter Park complained of severe pain in the arm and requested that the proposed operation not be done and that he be released;

(5) Defendant, Dr. David Dell, with the assistance of others, restrained Peter Park forcefully, and, without checking again to be sure the needle was properly seated, so as to cause the injection to go into the vein where it was supposed to go Dr. Dell injected additional liquid anesthesia, called Brevitol, into plaintiff's left arm;

(6) After the second injection of Brevitol failed to produce the intended effect, Dr. Dell and others again restrained Peter Park forcibly, and Dr. Dell administered gas as an anesthetic;

(7) Dr. Rogers, the oral surgeon, then proceeded with the operation;

(8) Peter Park remained at the Dental Clinic after the operation for about four hours, and during that time continued to complain of pain in his left arm and of what he described to attendants as a crawling sensation in the fingers of his left hand and in his left arm; . . .

---

*Adapted from materials developed by the Instructors in Trial Practice at Harvard Law School. Reprinted with permission.

**Formerly Professor at Harvard Law School and subsequently a trial court judge.

(9) The pain gradually went away during the next few days, but Peter Park was, and is, still not able to straighten into the full open position the third and fourth fingers of his left hand;

(10) In February, 19X3, Peter Park came to you, on the recommendation of a friend, and his condition was as you found it to be and as you have described it in your testimony today in this court, including sensory and motor deprivation in the left arm, centering in the region of the third and fourth fingers, and damage to the ulnar and median nerves.

Doctor, given these assumptions and findings, have you an opinion, with reasonable certainty, as to the cause of the condition of Peter Park's arm?

Yes, I do.

What is that opinion?

Brevitol injected into his arm missed the vein and entered the tissues, causing nerve damage.

Doctor, given the same set of assumptions and findings, have you an opinion, with reasonable certainty, as to whether the attending anesthesiologist, Dr. Dell, acted in accordance with the professional standards of medical practice among anesthesiologists in this and similar communities while attending Peter Park on January 6, 19X3?

I do.

What is that opinion?

He did not.

Please explain in what way Dr. Dell did not act in accordance with these professional standards.

He missed the vein with the needle, shot a batch of Brevitol into the tissues of the arm, and failed to check the placement of the needle before injecting a second batch, after the first failed to have its expected effect.

■McCOURT v. ABERNATHY
457 S.E.2d 603 (S.C. 1995)

[The following is part of the examination of one of the plaintiff's experts in the case excerpted at page 322, taken from the trial court record. The expert is a physician practicing emergency medicine in South Carolina.]

Q. Did you have an opportunity to go over the medical records thoroughly?

A. I have.

Q. Did you have an opportunity to read the deposition of Steve McCourt?

A. I have.

Q. Did you have an opportunity to read the deposition of Dr. David Potts?

A. Yes.

Q. Would you tell the jury, please, what your opinions are in regards to the treatment that Mrs. McCourt received on March the 9th, if you have any opinions in that regard?

A. The opinion I form is based on the information that has been given to me; in part the death summary, and in part the comments that have been made today.

But I feel that indeed if an infectious finger was presented on the 9th, if indeed the individual was evaluated on the 9th, I feel that it falls below the standard of care not to have treated that prophylactically.

Q. All right. Tell us what the standard of care, meaning the proper practice, for March the 9th would have been if done correctly.

A. . . . I would view this as a dirty wound . . . or contaminated. There are a number of guidelines promulgated in part by the American College of Surgeons and others that would suggest that individuals who are showing signs of infection, which could be localized tenderness or pain, with a contaminated wound, would benefit from prophylactic antibiotics.

■STANG-STARR v. BYINGTON
532 N.W.2d 26 (Neb. 1995)

CAPORALE, Justice. . . .

Pursuant to verdict, the district court dismissed this action wherein [] Teri Stang-Starr claims she was damaged by the negligent failure of [] Dr. Robert T. Byington to properly diagnose and treat abnormalities in her cervix. [Over a period of eight months, Byington obtained three Pap smears. The first showed moderate cellular abnormalities. The second report incorrectly stated no malignant cells were present. The lab made a mistake and should have said the sample was unsatisfactory and therefore the evaluation was inconclusive. The third Pap smear, followed by a biopsy, found stage IV cervical cancer. The defense disputed whether a correct diagnosis would have made a difference, arguing that it was not possible for moderate abnormalities to progress to full scale cancer so quickly. The jury found in favor of the defendant doctor.] Stang-Starr . . . here asserts that the district court erred by refusing to permit her to question her medical experts regarding medical texts and treatises upon which they relied in their testimony. . . .

During the trial, Stang-Starr called two physicians to testify on her behalf as expert witnesses: Dr. Manford Oliphant and Dr. William Woodard. . . . Based on his knowledge and information obtained from textbooks, medical literature, and personal experience, Oliphant formed an opinion, to a reasonable medical probability, as to the standard of care required of a board-certified obstetrician in May 1986 in Lincoln or similar communities. He then testified that he had read a particular technical bulletin issued by the [American College of Obstetrics] as a predicate to formulating some of the opinions on dysplasia to which he had testified. When Stang-Starr offered that bulletin into evidence, Byington successfully interposed a hearsay objection.

Stang-Starr then made an offer of proof of the bulletin and of material found in more than 12 textbooks concerning gynecology and colposcopy. She proposed that Oliphant would identify the text as authority in the field, identify the text as a basis of opinion, and identify and read specific passages of the material upon which Oliphant relied in testifying. The district court sustained Byington's hearsay objections to the offers.

Woodard then took the stand and testified that in forming his opinion, he had reviewed five or six textbooks, other specifically named textbooks, 15 to 18 journal articles, and the college bulletin identified earlier. In making an offer of proof, Stang-Starr represented that were Woodard allowed to respond to questions about those medical authorities, he would describe the textbooks by title, author, and date of publication, but would not attempt to quote from the actual text. Byington's hearsay objection to the offer was sustained. . . .

On cross-examination, Woodard testified generally as to what the medical literature suggested. When asked on cross-examination whether he had experienced a patient's cancer to progress from normal to invasive within nine months, he replied that the "literature suggests that the original Pap smear was improper or was one of those false negatives, from 15 to 40 percent, and that the cancer doesn't go that rapidly." . . .

On redirect examination, Woodard was asked whether in his opinion there existed in May 1986 diagnostic chaos as to how a gynecologist should have responded to moderate dysplasia in Pap smears. Woodard responded that there was no confusion as to what to do about dysplasia from a gynecologist's standpoint. When asked what the basis for his statement was, Woodard began to reply about the technical bulletin referred to earlier. Byington objected on the basis of hearsay and lack of foundation. Stang-Starr then withdrew the question, and the redirect examination continued with the following questions and answers: . . .

Q. Okay. Let me hand you, Dr. Woodard, a copy—first of all, will you verify what's been marked as . . . the . . . technical bulletin . . . and refer you to page 3 under "Evaluation of Abnormalities." . . .

Q. Do those two paragraphs address the approach to an abnormal Pap smear when the report comes back?

A. Yes, they do.

Q. Would you please give us your interpretation of those two paragraphs from that . . . bulletin? . . .

The objection was sustained. . . .

When offered to prove the truth of matters asserted in them, learned writings, such as treatises, books, and articles regarding specialized areas of knowledge, are clearly hearsay. 2 McCormick on Evidence §321 (John W. Strong 4th ed. 1992). There was no exception for learned treatises at common law, and medical textbooks and professional articles are not admissible to prove the substantive facts stated therein. . . . We have permitted the use of standard medical texts and other authorities for the purpose of impeaching, contradicting, or discrediting a witness through cross-examination. . . . We have not, however, permitted the use of such materials as independent evidence of the opinions and theories advanced by the parties. As explained in Van Skike v. Potter, 73 N.W. 295, 299 (Neb. 1887):

> [E]ven if they are regarded as authoritative, [medical texts] cannot be read to the jury as independent evidence of the opinions and theories therein expressed or advocated. One objection to such testimony is that it is not delivered under oath; a second objection is that the opposite party is thereby deprived of the benefit of a cross-examination; and a third and perhaps a more important reason for rejecting such testimony is that the science of medicine is not an exact science. There

are different schools of medicine, the members of which entertain widely different views, and it frequently happens that medical practitioners belonging to the same school will disagree as to the cause of a particular disease, or as to the nature of an ailment with which a patient is afflicted, even if they do not differ as to the mode of treatment. Besides, medical theories, unlike the truths of exact science, are subject to frequent modification and change, even if they are not altogether abandoned. For these reasons it is very generally held that when, in a judicial proceeding, it becomes necessary to invoke the aid of medical experts it is safer to rely on the testimony of competent witnesses who are produced, sworn, and subjected to a cross-examination, than to permit medical books or pamphlets to be read to the jury.

. . . While it is likely that the practice of medicine is more of a science today than it was almost a century ago when we decided *Van Skike*, the fact remains that the *Van Skike* reasoning continues to be sound. We are thus not persuaded that we should abandon our longstanding rule in this regard.

Nor does the fact that the out-of-court statements contained in the authorities were offered in the guise of forming the bases for the testifying experts' opinions alchemically transmute them from inadmissible hearsay into admissible nonhearsay. When Stang-Starr attempted to elicit testimony from her witness concerning what a particular authority has reported about an issue, she was attempting to use her witness to recite the opinion of each authority cited instead of eliciting her witness' expert opinion derived from the witness' own knowledge and experience. The witness was merely seeking to act as a conduit for inadmissible hearsay. The recitation of a passage by a nontestifying authority, even if such is in conformity with the opinion of the testifying expert, is hearsay.

As observed in United States v. Williams, 431 F.2d 1168, 1172 (5th Cir. 1970):

> If the witness has gone to only one hearsay source and seeks merely to summarize the content of that source, then he is acting as a summary witness, not an expert. . . . When, however, the witness has gone to many sources — although some or all be hearsay in nature — and rather than introducing mere summaries of each source he uses them all, along with his own professional experience, to arrive at his opinion, that opinion is regarded as evidence in its own right and not as an attempt to introduce hearsay in disguise.

. . . Accordingly, the district court did not err in sustaining Byington's objections to the proffered evidence or the offers of proof made in regard to the evidence. . . .

Notes: Examination of Experts; Introduction of Treatises and Guidelines

1. *Hypothetical Questions.* The rigors of evidence rules governing the questioning of expert witnesses have been considerably loosened over the past two generations. The excerpt from Robert Keeton's 1973 book displays the older form in which (1) each factual underpinning for the expert's opinion was explicitly stated hypothetically prior to eliciting the expert's opinion, and (2) each hypothetical foundation point had to be independently proved in evidence. This hypothetical question approach produced a horribly complex chain of thought for the jury to absorb and, for lawyers, meant agonizing decisions about strategy and heightened chances for

error. The lawyer's task was to decide whether to state as part of the hypothetical basis for an expert's opinion facts in dispute or facts based on evidence that might not be admitted. If the jury were to find that one of the subsidiary assumptions was false, or the court were to exclude the source of evidence for that point, then it could easily be argued that the expert's entire testimony was worthless.

The modern approach, embodied in Federal Rules of Evidence 701, 702, 703, and 705, and followed now in most states, is demonstrated in the testimony taken from the *McCourt* case. Both aspects of the older approach stated above are now rejected. Instead, experts' opinions may be based on information that is not in evidence if it is the type of information experts in that field normally rely on in forming opinions. These foundation points do not have to be disclosed before giving an opinion. All of these matters are left to cross-examination by the opposing lawyer. Still, do you think some of the older technique might be valuable in direct examination? Selective restatement of the foundational points, either prior to or following the expert's statement of opinion, could help to reinforce strengths in the case and how well reasoned the opinion is. For additional discussion, see David M. Malone & Paul J. Zwier, Effective Expert Testimony (3d ed. 2014).

2. *Learned Treatises.* Modern practice has also loosened somewhat with respect to the use of learned treatises. The emerging approach, adopted in Federal Rules of Evidence 803(18), is to allow testimony, either in direct or cross-examination, from learned treatises, guidelines, or other similar authoritative sources that the expert acknowledges are reliable. The court may also take judicial notice of their reliability. However, these statements may not be received as exhibits but only read into evidence. Naturally, the states vary in the extent to which they have adopted this liberalization. They also vary considerably in the extent to which, under the older practice, these authorities could be used in cross-examination. Some states require the expert to admit he relied on the authority; others require only that he acknowledge the general authoritativeness of the treatise or other written source. See Annot., 38 A.L.R.2d 77 (1958 & Supp.).

3. *Practice Guidelines.* One type of documentary evidence that has unique status in medical malpractice actions is the "package inserts" for prescription drugs (compiled in the Physicians' Desk Reference (PDR)), which contain FDA-required warnings and instructions for use. As noted at page 425, these written guidelines are directly admissible as independent evidence on the standard of care under the hearsay exception for tabulations, lists, and directories generally relied on by persons in particular occupations. Fed. R. Evid. 803(17). Some courts treat package inserts as especially authoritative by declaring that they are prima facie proof of the standard of care, subject to rebuttal that physicians commonly depart from the instructions in particular situations.

Observe in *Stang-Starr* that it is much more difficult to introduce other officially promulgated statements of medical standards adopted by professional societies such as the AMA and the various certification boards for medical specialties. These "practice guidelines" are also being issued in greater numbers by government research agencies such as the National Institutes of Health (NIH), which convene experts in the field to deliberate on an area of medical practice and issue a consensus statement advising physicians of the best approach to particular clinical situations. Should explicit statements of consensus standards of care from these authoritative national sources be subjected to the same hearsay hurdles as medical treatises and scholarly articles written by only one or a few individuals? Even under the modern treatment of medical authorities illustrated in the McCourt v. Abernathy testimony, courts often rule that practice guidelines can only be referred to and recited by testifying experts, not introduced directly as independent proof. Many commentators, however, argue that if the source is sufficiently authoritative, and the guidelines sufficiently relevant, they should not only be admitted as independent evidence of the standard of care, they should be taken as conclusive, or at least presumptive, proof of the standard of care.

Practice guidelines are usually used offensively by plaintiffs against doctors who deviate from them, but they can also be used defensively by doctors to justify their treatment decisions. Thousands of these detailed practice guidelines currently exist, and their numbers are rapidly proliferating as a consequence of the perceived need to bring greater rationality and standardization to medical practice. Guidelines issued by government agencies and professional societies are used not only to advise physicians of proper practice, but increasingly are being adapted by public and private insurers as a basis for conducting utilization review activities that determine what treatments are paid for by health insurance. These newer guidelines are geared toward determining when treatment is unnecessary, and therefore are more relevant to defending than to prosecuting a malpractice claim. Some states have viewed these guidelines as a possible way to blunt the impact of defensive medicine—the tendency of physicians to perform unnecessary procedures out of a fear of liability. Maine was the first state to declare by statute (which is no longer in effect) that certain officially promulgated guidelines were directly admissible and create an "affirmative defense," but Maine did not allow plaintiffs to use these designated guidelines unless they were put in issue by the defense. Is this differential weight justifiable? Consider the argument in Mark A. Hall, The Defensive Effect of Medical Practice Policies in Malpractice Litigation, 54 Law & Contemp. Probs. 119 (Spring 1991):

> This difference in the [offensive vs. defensive] posture of the [case] is critical because of the possibility that two schools of practice might prevail. With this possibility in mind, it makes eminent sense to hold that it is not conclusive for a plaintiff to establish that the defendant violated *one* established standard. However, the opposite holds for a defendant who complies with at least one established professional guideline: Because it is not necessary for a doctor to show that unanimous professional consensus supports his conduct, a defense is sufficiently established if the doctor shows only that she complied with *at least* one respectable body of opinion.

Observe also that most guidelines purport to state optimal, not minimally acceptable, practice. Does this mean, though, that guidelines should be inadmissible by plaintiffs or only receive lesser weight?

If authoritative medical practice guidelines were to be given special weight in more states, then one must consider which organizations have authoritative stature. Are guidelines issued by a national association or government agency relevant under a similar locality standard in a rural setting? May guidelines adopted by insurers (including HMOs) be considered? In many hospitals and HMOs, efforts are being made to develop treatment protocols that are based on specific scientific evidence from actual patients at the facility rather than being based on broad professional opinion. This movement toward evidence-based, institution-specific guidelines is seen as desirable for three reasons: (1) decentralized efforts will generate many more guidelines, (2) these guidelines are likely to be more useful because they are more clinically specific, and (3) physicians who participate in their development are more likely to comply with them. What objections do you imagine, however, from the plaintiff's lawyer when a physician attempts to defend himself with the institution's own guideline? See Adams v. Laboratory Corporation of America, 760 F.3d 1322 (11th Cir. 2014) (refusing to follow "litigation guideline" from pathology association that required "blinded" review of challenged slides (to determine whether original misreading was negligent), because this "industry group has promulgated a set of guidelines that attempts to define and limit the evidence courts should accept when the group's members are sued.").

4. *Physician Report Cards.* Another emerging source of evidence are the "report cards" discussed in section A.3 that are beginning to emerge on individual doctors. These reports contain statistics on the number of good and bad outcomes for particular types of high-profile treatment such as cardiac bypass surgery. These statistics are not unlike the kind of information hospital peer review committees traditionally compile on infection rates, blood loss, tissue analysis, and other technical aspects of surgery, but those sources of information are cloaked in the peer review privilege discussed at page 400, which keeps them confidential. The newer report cards are discoverable, but are they admissible? One commentator predicts not, based on irrelevance. Courts are cautious about admitting evidence of previous similar wrongdoing because of the potential for undue prejudice and the reluctance to greatly expand the scope of litigation. This type of evidence is generally limited to instances involving the very same mistake. See Paul D. Rheingold, The Admissibility of Evidence in Malpractice Cases: The Performance Records of Practitioners, 58 Brook. L. Rev. 75 (1992).

5. *Empirical Evidence of Medical Custom.* With so many available and emerging sources of empirical evidence regarding medical custom, one must wonder why courts have not been more demanding regarding the foundation for experts who testify about medical custom. Courts traditionally have allowed experts to testify based on their general experience and opinion rather than requiring them to show they have actually studied or researched in a scientific or methodical fashion how physicians usually behave in similar circumstances. Perhaps this is a holdover from a century ago when, under a local standard of care, nothing more could be expected. However, as noted above, at page 369, this often results in testimony that is demonstrably inaccurate. Accordingly, several scholars have advocated either allowing or encouraging experts to conduct surveys of physicians, or to analyze databases reflecting actual physician practices, in order to support their expert opinions. Could this help to overcome difficulties that plaintiffs face in finding qualified experts? Might this be *required* as a basic element of the scientific validity of experts' assertions about professional practice, under Daubert v. Merrell Dow Pharmaceuticals, Inc., 509 U.S. 579 (1993)? See Adams v. Laboratory Corporation of America, 760 F.3d 1322 (11th Cir. 2014) (suggesting not, because *Daubert* allows qualified experts to rely on their "experience and general knowledge in the field"). For a thorough analysis of these proposals and their many problems, see Symposium, Empirical Approaches to Proving the Standard of Care in Medical Malpractice Cases, 37 Wake Forest L. Rev. 663 (2002).

6. *Further Reading.* For various analyses and critiques of existing law regarding **practice guidelines** (note 3), and proposals for change, see generally Michelle Mello & Allen Kachalia, Medical Malpractice: Evidence on Reform Alternatives and Claims Involving Elderly Patients (MedPac, 2016); Maxwell Mehlman, Professional Power and the Standard of Care in Medicine, 44 Ariz. St. L.J. 1165 (2012); K. Van Tassel, Harmonizing the Accountable Care Act with the Three Main National Systems for Healthcare Quality Improvement, 78 Brook. L. Rev. 883 (2013); Ronen Avraham, Clinical Practice Guidelines: The Warped Incentive in the U.S. Healthcare System, 37 Am. J.L. & Med. 7 (2011); Ronen Avraham, Private Regulation, 34 Harv. J.L. & Pub. Pol'y 543 (2011); S. Mangalmurti et al., Medical Malpractice in the Age of Electronic Health Records, 363 New Eng. J. Med. 2060 (2010); Jodi Finder, The Future of Practice Guidelines: Should They Constitute Conclusive Evidence of the Standard of Care?, 10 Health Matrix 67 (2000); R. E. Leahy, Rational Health Policy and the Legal Standard of Care: A Call for Judicial Deference to Medical Practice Guidelines, 77 Cal. L. Rev. 1483 (1989); Michelle Mello, Of Swords and Shields: The Use of Clinical Practice Guidelines in Medical Malpractice Litigation, 149 U. Pa. L. Rev. 645 (2000); Note, 61 Wash. & Lee L. Rev. 479 (2004); Arnold J. Rosoff, The Role of Clinical Practice Guidelines in Health Care Reform, 5 Health Matrix 369 (1995).

On the use of **physician report cards** in litigation (note 4), see Symposium, 58 Brook. L. Rev. 85 (1992); Aaron S. Kesselheim et al., Will Physician-Level Measures of Clinical Performance Be Used in Medical Malpractice Litigation?, 295 JAMA 1831 (2007).

Problem: Practice Guidelines

Jane Austere is a 62-year-old female with a history of severe diabetes and high blood pressure. She lives in a small town in a rural county of a state that follows the national standard of care for specialists. Following surgery on her left knee performed under general anesthesia at the local public hospital, she was suddenly unable to speak normally. This is consistent with brain damage caused by decreased oxygen to the brain, among other possible causes. Jane brings a medical malpractice action against her anesthesiologist.

Several national organizations have issued guidelines for monitoring ventilation (breathing) during surgery. Two years before Jane's operation, the anesthesiology department at the hospital studied all these guidelines and adopted the following as its view of the best compromise among all their various nuances:

> Every patient receiving general anesthesia shall have the adequacy of ventilation evaluated regularly and frequently. Quantitative monitoring of the CO2 content and the volume of expired gas is encouraged, but not required. . . . These guidelines are not intended to displace the physician's discretion to conform treatment to the particular clinical circumstances of the individual patient.

Jane's anesthesiologist admits that he did not perform quantitative measures of CO_2 and volume of exhaled air because he considers visual observation of breathing to be sufficient in all cases. Jane's expert testifies that she could have suffered decreased oxygen because her breathing slowed or paused for a minute or two. In his opinion, quantitative measures are advisable for a patient in Jane's condition. The hospital had recently purchased new equipment that can make these measures continuously and much less obtrusively than was the case before.

The defense lawyer tries to introduce this hospital guideline as evidence of the standard of care. What objections are likely, and what response would you make? If the guidelines were admitted, what instruction should the judge give to the jury, assuming this jurisdiction follows a national standard of care?

■ DUQUETTE v. SUPERIOR COURT
778 P.2d 634 (Ariz. App. 1989)

CONTRERAS, Judge.

In this special action, we consider the issue of whether defense counsel in a medical malpractice action may engage in *ex parte* communications with the plaintiff's treating physicians without having obtained plaintiff's consent. . . .

[One-year-old Eric Lamberty] was diagnosed as having a dermoid tumor in and around his spinal column. The tumor required surgery. . . . Following the surgery, the Lambertys filed a civil action against Dr. Duquette alleging that he committed medical malpractice by failing to: (1) treat Eric properly during his birth hospitalization, and (2) diagnose the tumor in a timely fashion. Scottsdale Memorial Hospital was also a named defendant under an agency theory of liability.

In the summer of 1987, defense attorneys for petitioners conducted *ex parte* interviews of approximately thirteen of plaintiff's treating physicians without the express consent of plaintiff, his parents, or his counsel. . . . [P]laintiffs filed a motion to bar testimony and to disqualify counsel. . . . Petitioners seek special action review of that portion of Judge Moroney's order barring plaintiff's treating physicians from testifying as expert witnesses unless first offered as witnesses by plaintiffs. . . .

[P]etitioners first contend that the *ex parte* communications between plaintiff's treating physicians and defense attorneys were not improper because the physician-patient privilege had been waived. . . . The Arizona statute precludes a physician from being examined about any communications made by the patient concerning his condition or any knowledge of the condition obtained through personal examination of the patient without the consent of the patient. . . . [P]etitioners contend that the real parties in interest waived the privilege when they: 1) placed Eric's medical condition in issue by filing suit, and 2) claimed Eric's medical expenses as damages in their civil complaint. . . .

[T]he Arizona Supreme Court [has] stated that when a plaintiff "places a particular medical condition at issue by means of a claim or affirmative defense, . . . then the privilege will be deemed waived with respect to that particular medical condition." In accordance with [this ruling], we conclude that Eric's parents have waived the physician-patient privilege by placing their son's medical condition at issue through initiation of litigation.

This waiver is not absolute however, and we believe petitioners' reliance on implied waiver in support of the propriety of *ex parte* communications is misplaced. In this regard, we agree with those cases which conclude that even where the physician-patient privilege has been impliedly waived, the holder of the privilege waives only his right to object to discovery of pertinent medical information which is sought through the formal methods of discovery authorized by the applicable Rules of Civil Procedure. . . .

Those courts which have taken the view that a defendant's counsel may interview the plaintiff's treating physicians *ex parte* have identified a number of factors and policies for allowing such informal methods of discovery. These include decreased litigation costs, the potential to eliminate non-essential witnesses, early evaluation and settlement of claims, the ease of scheduling interviews as opposed to depositions, and greater spontaneity and candor in the interview than in the deposition. Annot., 50 A.L.R. 4th 714.

Those courts which have taken an opposite view and have held that the defendant's counsel is limited to the formal methods of discovery listed within the Rules of Civil Procedure have based their decisions on varying propositions. Among the reasons relied upon in refusing to grant permission for informal *ex parte* interviews are the broad privacy interest underlying the physician-patient relationship, the potential tort liability of physicians for breach or invasion of privacy, the potential that defense counsel may seek to improperly influence plaintiff's treating physicians or may discourage the physician from testifying, the duty of loyalty from the physician to the patient, and the view that discovery rules determine the extent of the physician-patient privilege. Id. . . .

We note, . . . that a ban on *ex parte* communications does not preclude defense attorneys from contacting plaintiff's treating physicians. Rather, such a ruling merely limits the methods of contact available to the defense attorney to those methods authorized by our Rules of Civil Procedure. . . .

[W]e believe that the unique nature of the physician-patient relationship justifies a ban on *ex parte* communications. We recognize that such a ban allows the plaintiff to engage in *ex parte* communications with his physician witnesses while it prohibits the defendant from gaining equal access. However, this inequality of access to the physician witnesses does not preclude the defendant from availing himself of the full panoply of discovery devices. . . . [W]e do not believe that such practical concerns as cost efficiency and ease of scheduling are of paramount concern to a proper resolution of the issue. . . . We believe the public has a widespread belief that information given to a physician in confidence will not be disclosed to third parties absent legal compulsion, and we further believe that the public has a right to have this expectation realized. See Petrillo v. Syntex Laboratories, Inc., 499 N.E.2d 952, 959-62 (1986). We agree with the *Petrillo* court when, in limiting physician disclosure to court authorized methods of discovery, it stated:

> Discussion of the patient's confidences under any other circumstances, such as the *ex parte* conference, could be inconsistent with the duties of a fiduciary for the physician would, in effect, engage in conduct which may be contrary to a fiduciary's obligation of good faith and, in addition, may be potentially harmful to the interests of the patient which are unrelated and irrelevant to the mental or physical condition placed at issue in the lawsuit. . . .

A second set of considerations supporting a prohibition on *ex parte* communications involves the pressure brought to bear on the physician. . . . Although the physician is free to reject such a request and thereby force the defense attorney to utilize formal methods of discovery, we believe that this option does not acceptably reduce the pressure on the physician. . . . [A] substantial number of physicians are insured by a single "doctor owned" insurer. Realistically, this factor could have an impact on the physician's decision. In other words, the physician witness might feel compelled to participate in the *ex parte* interview because the insurer defending the medical malpractice defendant may also insure the physician witness.

An additional factor that must be taken into consideration is that a physician who allows himself to be interviewed *ex parte* embarks, perhaps unknowingly, on a course which may involve a breach of professional ethics and potential liability. First, participation in an *ex parte* interview may constitute a breach of the physician's professional code of ethics. . . . Thus, the physician's voluntary participation in the *ex parte* interview may subject him or her to professional discipline as well as potential tort liability. . . .

An additional consideration supporting a ban on *ex parte* interviews involves the practical difficulty in determining the scope of the waiver of the physician-patient privilege. The scope of the waiver is often in dispute, and absent court participation in the discovery process, resolution of that dispute is left to the defense attorney and the physician witness. We believe that this scenario places both the defense attorney and the physician in an untenable position. As the Iowa Supreme Court stated in Roosevelt Hotel Ltd. Partnership v. Sweeney, 394 N.W.2d 353, 357 (1986):

> Placing the burden of determining relevancy on an attorney, who does not know the nature of the confidential disclosure about to be elicited, is risky. Asking the physician, untrained in the law, to assume this burden is a greater gamble and is unfair to the physician. We believe this determination is better made in a setting in which counsel for each party is present and the court is available to settle disputes. . . . Accordingly, we hold that defense counsel in a medical malpractice action may not engage in non-consensual *ex parte* communications with plaintiff's treating physicians.

We now consider the sanction imposed by the trial court. . . . Prior to today's decision, the law on this issue in the State of Arizona was unsettled. . . . Given this situation, we believe that it was an abuse of discretion for the trial court to summarily impose the sanction of preclusion of testimony. . . .

Remanded.

Notes: Discovery and Confidentiality

1. *Medical Records.* Investigation of a potential malpractice claim by a plaintiff's lawyer starts with obtaining and reviewing his client's own medical records. The initial review may be conducted inside the law firm by someone such as a nurse paralegal who has some medical training, but thorough investigation usually entails sending the record out for expert review prior to initiating suit. Hospital medical records are too large, complex, and various to adequately summarize in the context of this book. An illustration of the types of documents and sorts of information one might find in a typical hospital chart can be found on the Web site for this book, www.health-law.org, which contains excerpts from the trial record in McCourt v. Abernathy, page 322. Take a look at these samples. On first inspection, they may

be hard to digest, but see if you can read them in a way that tells a story. The usual components of a medical story are: (1) history and symptoms; (2) exam, testing, and diagnosis; (3) treatment; and (4) outcome. Following that structure, see if you can identify in these records how Wendy first presented her symptoms, what additional symptoms her physicians observed, what tests they performed and why, where the diagnosis went wrong, and what the resulting effect was on her treatment.

2. *Spoliation of Evidence.* Medical malpractice cases frequently contain allegations that medical records have been altered to cover up mistakes. If true, this obviously creates problems for the defense, which is then subject to various damaging presumptions or waivers of defenses, if not penalties for outright fraud and deceit. See generally Comment, Spoliation of Evidence and Medical Malpractice, 14 Pace L. Rev. 235 (1994).

3. *Waiver of Confidentiality.* Although a malpractice plaintiff waives her right to confidentiality in the medical records and treatment relationship at issue in the litigation, that waiver does not extend to any treatment the plaintiff might have ever received, even by the same doctor. Courts tailor the waiver to fit the allegations of the complaint in order to avoid deterring suit by unnecessarily forcing a plaintiff to expose all embarrassing or private aspects of her medical past. See, e.g., R.K. v. Ramirez, 887 S.W.2d 836 (Tex. 1994).

4. *Ex Parte Interviews.* In *Duquette,* the court declined to impose a penalty the first time the prohibition on ex parte interviews was announced in the state. Other courts, however, have barred defendants from using physician witnesses who were improperly contacted. Additional penalties might include a tort action against the interviewed physician for breach of confidence, or a disciplinary action against the lawyer.

The waiver of the physician-patient privilege, and the corresponding prohibition of informal discovery, apply equally to any civil action, such as automobile accidents or products liability, in which the plaintiff's medical condition is placed at issue. As should be obvious, the prohibition against contacting the plaintiff's doctor informally applies only to *non-party* physicians. A defendant doctor can talk all he wants with his own lawyer. Acosta v. Richter, 671 So. 2d 149 (Fla. 1996). The issue is cloudier, however, if the defendant and non-party doctors practice together in the same partnership, or if they both work at the same hospital that is named in the suit. Testin v. Dryer Medical Clinic, 605 N.E.2d 1070 (Ill. App. 1992), applied the ban on ex parte interviews to a plaintiff's subsequent treating physician who was director of the clinic in which the defending physician worked. Ritter v. Rush Presbyterian-St. Luke's Med. Ctr., 532 N.E.2d 327 (Ill. App. 1988), applied the ban to a hospital lawyer's communication with other treating physicians in the same hospital but observed in dictum that this prohibition should not be carried so far as to "effectively prevent [a] hospital from defending itself by barring communication with [a] physician for whose conduct the hospital is allegedly liable." What strategy does this suggest for a plaintiff's lawyer in deciding whether to name a hospital as a defendant? In deciding how many physicians to name as defendants? What may a hospital lawyer safely investigate when the plaintiff's precise allegations and theories of liability are unknown? According to Keith Emmons, an Illinois lawyer, "the best present option would appear to be the early identification of all potentially liable practitioners and entities and the appointment of separate defense counsel for [each one] even before they become named defendants." Each lawyer can interview her own client, and nothing in the ex parte rule appears to prevent the lawyers from talking among themselves, or does it?

There is debate over whether the HIPAA federal privacy rule might affect state law on ex parte communications. See Beverly Cohen, Reconciling the HIPAA Privacy Rule with State Laws Regulating Ex Parte Interviews of Plaintiffs' Treating Physicians, 43 Hous. L. Rev. 1091 (2006). Some courts have ruled, for instance, that HIPAA prevents a defense lawyer from informally interviewing the plaintiff's other treating physicians, even though state law would not prohibit this ex parte communication. Moreland v. Austin, 670 S.E.2d 68 (Ga. 2008); Proctor v. Messina, 320 S.W.3d 145 (Mo. 2010). Going the other direction, one high court has encouraged informal contact between defense counsel and plaintiffs' physicians, in the interests of litigation efficiency. Arons v. Jutkowitz, 850 N.Y.S.2d 345 (NY 2007). See also Holman v. Rasak, 785 N.W.2d 98 (Mich. 2010) (HIPAA is no bar if ex parte communications occur under judicially issued protective orders (which set the allowable conditions and scope for informal discovery); In re Collins, 286 S.W.3d 911 (Tx. 2009) (same). For commentary and analysis, see Comment, 34 Cap. U. L. Rev. 775 (2006); Annot., 50 A.L.R.4th 714 (1986).

5. *Peer Review Confidentiality.* Other sources of confidentiality and evidentiary privilege protect the defendant in a malpractice action. The primary sources are: (1) peer review confidentiality statutes; (2) the attorney-client communication privilege; and (3) the lawyer's work product privilege. We will discuss only the first of these, and only briefly. See the Web site for this book, www.health-law.org, for additional information.

Peer review confidentiality attaches by statute in most states to various standing hospital committees that investigate the competence of individual practitioners and the quality of care rendered within the institution. In order to ensure candor and vigorous participation in these activities, state statutes protect from discovery any records generated by these committees. A few decisions have recognized a common-law privilege protecting self-evaluation or self-improvement efforts even in the absence of such statutes. The peer review confidentiality statutes produce a steady stream of litigation over precisely which committees and records they cover. See generally Annots., 60 A.L.R.4th 1273 (1988); 81 A.L.R.3d 944 (1977).

One major area of dispute concerns "incident reports" and investigations conducted by hospital risk management departments. Compare Krusac v. Covenant Medical Center, 865 N.W.2d 908 (Mich. 2015) (incident reports are privileged), with Valley Health System v. Eighth Judicial District Court, 252 P.3d 676 (Nev. 2011) (some incident reports are discoverable). The hospital might also seek to protect these reports as attorney work product, or to protect the communications they report under the attorney-client privilege. These claims are not always successful, for reasons summarized on the Web site. See, e.g., Collins v. Braden, 384 S.W.3d 154 (Ky. 2012) (hospital lawyers who interviewed nurse witnesses were not acting as lawyers for the nurses, only for the hospital).

Out of concern that state law too narrowly protects the ability of health care institutions to investigate, correct, and report medical safety issues, Congress adopted a discovery privilege and liability protection in 2005. The Patient Safety and Quality Improvement Act protects from discovery any reports of medical errors made by health care providers to certified "patient safety organizations," such as the JCAHO. However, any such records must be maintained only for patient safety evaluation purposes, and not for patient care or billing purposes. The goal is to encourage efforts to improve medical quality in arenas outside the traditional peer review process, for instance, by sharing information among different facilities or with private accreditation organizations.

6. *The Costs of Litigation.* The complexity of medical malpractice cases, and the costs of medical expertise, mean that these are expensive cases to litigate, often costing at least $50,000 in out-of-pocket expenses. Overall, less than half of medical malpractice premiums collected end up in the pockets of injured patients.

7. *Further Reading.* For commentary and analysis of **ex parte contacts** (note 4), see Beverly Cohen, Reconciling the HIPAA Privacy Rule with State Laws Regulating Ex Parte Interviews of Plaintiffs' Treating Physicians, 43 Hous. L. Rev. 1091 (2006); Comment, 34 Cap. U. L. Rev. 775 (2006); Annot., 50 A.L.R.4th 714 (1986).

On **peer review confidentiality and immunity** (note 5), see Gregory Nowakowski et al., Health Care Quality Improvement Act: Peer Review, Procedure, Process, and Privacy, 33 Cooley L. Rev. 1 (2016); Lisa M. Nijm, Pitfalls of Peer Review, 24 J. Leg. Med. 541 (December 2003); Gail Friend et al., Identifying and Protecting the Peer Review and Medical Committee Privilege, 49 Baylor L. Rev. 607 (1997); Comment, 11 Mich. St. U. J. Med. & L. 177 (2007); Note, 17 Health Matrix 319 (2007); Note, 4 Ind. Health L. Rev. 151 (2007).

Attacking the view that **liability exposure deters error reporting or quality improvement** (note 5), see David A. Hyman & Charles M. Silver, The Poor State of Health Care Quality in the U.S.: Is Malpractice Liability Part of the Problem or Part of the Solution?, 90 Cornell L. Rev. 893 (2005); Stephan Landsman, Reflections on Juryphobia and Medical Malpractice Reform, 57 DePaul L. Rev. 221 (2008).

D. ALTERNATIVE THEORIES OF LIABILITY

Observing the difficulties that plaintiffs often have in qualifying expert witnesses and proving a breach of the standard of care, it is understandable that their lawyers are eager to find theories of liability that do not rely on the custom-based standard of care. The following readings survey several such theories.

1. Breach of Contract

■ SULLIVAN v. O'CONNOR
296 N.E.2d 183 (Mass. 1973)

KAPLAN, Justice.

The plaintiff patient secured a jury verdict of $13,500 against the defendant surgeon for breach of contract in respect to an operation upon the plaintiff's nose. . . . The declaration was in two counts. In the first count, the plaintiff alleged that she, as patient, entered into a contract with the defendant, a surgeon, wherein the defendant promised to perform plastic surgery on her nose and thereby to enhance her beauty and improve her appearance; that he performed the surgery but failed to achieve the promised result; rather the result of the surgery was to disfigure and deform her nose, to cause her pain in body and mind, and to subject her to other damage and expense. The second count, based on the same transaction, was in the conventional form for malpractice, charging that the defendant had been guilty of negligence in performing the surgery. . . . The jury returned a verdict for the plaintiff on the contract count, and for the defendant on the negligence count. The judge then instructed the jury on the issue of damages.

As background to the instructions and the parties' exceptions, we mention certain facts as the jury could find them. The plaintiff was a professional entertainer, and this was known to the defendant. The agreement was as alleged in the declaration. More particularly, judging from exhibits, the plaintiff's nose had been straight, but long and prominent; the defendant undertook by two operations to reduce its prominence and somewhat to shorten it, thus making it more pleasing in relation to the plaintiff's other features. Actually, the plaintiff was obliged to undergo three operations, and her appearance was worsened. Her nose now had a concave line to about the midpoint, at which it became bulbous; viewed frontally, the nose from bridge to midpoint was flattened and broadened, and the two sides of the tip had lost symmetry. This configuration evidently could not be improved by further surgery. The plaintiff did not demonstrate, however, that her change of appearance had resulted in loss of employment. Payments by the plaintiff covering the defendant's fee and hospital expenses were stipulated at $622.65. . . .

By his exceptions, the defendant contends that the judge erred in allowing the jury to take into account anything but the plaintiff's out-of-pocket expenses (presumably at the stipulated amount). The defendant excepted to the judge's refusal of his request for a general charge to that effect, and, more specifically, to the judge's refusal of a charge that the plaintiff could not recover for pain and suffering connected with the third operation or for impairment of the plaintiff's appearance and associated mental distress. . . . We conclude that the defendant's exceptions should be overruled.

It has been suggested on occasion that agreements between patients and physicians by which the physician undertakes to effect a cure or to bring about a given result should be declared unenforceable on grounds of public policy. But there are many decisions recognizing and enforcing such contracts, see annotation, 43 A.L.R.3d 1221, and the law of Massachusetts has treated them as valid, although we have had no decision meeting head on the contention that they should be denied legal sanction. These causes of action are, however, considered a little suspect, and thus we find courts straining sometimes to read the pleadings as sounding only in tort for negligence, and not in contract for breach of promise, despite sedulous efforts by the pleaders to pursue the latter theory.

It is not hard to see why the courts should be unenthusiastic or skeptical about the contract theory. Considering the uncertainties of medical science and the variations in the physical and psychological conditions of individual patients, doctors can seldom in good faith promise specific results. Therefore, it is unlikely that physicians of even average integrity will in fact make such promises. Statements of opinion by the physician with some optimistic coloring are a different thing, and may indeed have therapeutic value. But patients may transform such statements into firm promises in their own minds, especially when they have been disappointed in the event, and testify in that sense to sympathetic juries.[2] If actions for breach of promise can be readily maintained, doctors, so it is said, will be frightened into practising "defensive medicine." On the other hand, if these actions were outlawed, leaving only the possibility of suits for malpractice, there is fear that the public might be exposed to the enticements of charlatans, and confidence in the profession might ultimately be shaken. See Miller, The Contractual Liability of Physicians and Surgeons, 1953 Wash. L.Q. 413, 416-423. The law has taken the middle of the road position of allowing actions based on alleged contract, but insisting on clear proof. Instructions to the jury may well stress this requirement and point to tests of truth, such as the complexity or difficulty of an operation as bearing on the probability that a given result was promised. See annotation, 43 A.L.R.3d 1225, 1225-1227.

If an action on the basis of contract is allowed, we have next the question of the measure of damages to be applied where liability is found. Some cases have taken the simple view that the promise by the physician is to be treated like an ordinary commercial promise. . . . Thus in Hawkins v. McGee, 84 N.H. 114, 146 A. 641, the defendant doctor was taken to have promised the plaintiff to convert his damaged hand by means of an operation into a good or perfect hand, but the doctor so operated as to damage the hand still further. The court, following the usual expectancy formula, would have asked the jury to estimate and award to the plaintiff the difference between the value of a good or perfect hand, as promised, and the value of the hand after the operation. . . . Other cases, including a number in New York, without distinctly repudiating the *Hawkins* type of analysis, have indicated that a different and generally more lenient measure of damages is to be applied. . . .

The factors, already mentioned, which have made the cause of action somewhat suspect, also suggest moderation as to the breadth of the recovery that should be permitted. Where, as in the case at bar and in a number of the reported cases, the doctor has been absolved of negligence by the trier, an expectancy measure may be thought harsh. We should recall here that the fee paid by the patient to the doctor for the alleged promise would usually be quite disproportionate to the putative expectancy recovery. To attempt, moreover, to put a value on the condition that would or might have resulted, had the treatment succeeded as promised, may sometimes put an exceptional strain on the imagination of the factfinder. . . .

The question of recovery on a reliance basis for pain and suffering or mental distress requires further attention. We find expressions in the decisions that pain and suffering (or the like) are simply not compensable in actions for breach of contract. The defendant seemingly espouses this proposition in the present case. True, if the buyer under a contract for the purchase of a lot of merchandise, in suing for the seller's breach, should claim damages for mental anguish caused by his disappointment in the transaction, he would not succeed; he would be told, perhaps, that the asserted psychological injury was not fairly foreseeable by the defendant as a probable consequence of the breach of such a business contract. See Restatement: Contracts, §341, and comment *a*. But there is no general rule barring such items of

---

2. Judicial skepticism about whether a promise was in fact made derives also from the possibility that the truth has been tortured to give the plaintiff the advantage of the longer period of limitations sometimes available for actions on contract as distinguished from those in tort or for malpractice.

damage in actions for breach of contract. It is all a question of the subject matter and background of the contract, and when the contract calls for an operation on the person of the plaintiff, psychological as well as physical injury may be expected to figure somewhere in the recovery, depending on the particular circumstances. . . .

In the light of the foregoing discussion, all the defendant's exceptions fail: The plaintiff was not confined to the recovery of her out-of-pocket expenditures; she was entitled to recover also for the worsening of her condition, and for the pain and suffering and mental distress involved in the third operation. . . .

Notes: Liability Based on Contract or Fraud

1. *Strategic Choice of Theories.* The application of a contractual theory of liability in medical malpractice is rare, and, as illustrated in *Sullivan,* the courts usually impose a very high standard for proving a contractual breach. Nevertheless, plaintiffs persist for four reasons: raising the standard of care and avoiding the need to produce expert medical testimony; seeking a longer statute of limitations; avoiding restrictions imposed by medical malpractice reform statutes; and avoiding doctrines of sovereign or charitable immunity. Even where a contract action exists, the second and third strategies do not always work. Courts tend to impose the tort-law requirements when an action sounds in medical malpractice, regardless of the precise legal theory, and many statutory reforms define "medical malpractice actions" to include both tort and contract theories.

2. *Promises, Imagined and Real.* The *Sullivan* case involves an allegation of contractual guarantee of a particular result in plastic surgery. Another common situation involves a woman who conceives a child following a sterilization procedure. See generally Annot., 43 A.L.R.3d 1221 (1972 & Supp.). Courts express hostility to these and other contract theories in a variety of ways. In addition to raising the standard of proof to clear and convincing evidence and lowering damages to a reliance rather than an expectation measure, some courts also require the plaintiff to show separate consideration for the promise of a cure, apart from the doctor's normal fee for performing the procedure, or they require the guarantee to be in writing. See, e.g., Herrera v. Roessing, 533 P.2d 60 (Colo. 1975). Other states have achieved the same policy by statute. But see Burns v. Wannemaker, 343 S.E.2d 27 (S.C. 1986) (no separate consideration required for dentist's breach of express warranty with respect to fitting dentures).

What type of communication is sufficient to meet a clear and convincing proof standard? Compare Ferlito v. Cecola, 419 So. 2d 102 (La. Ct. App. 1982) (dentist's promise to "make your teeth real pretty" does not create a promise of complete satisfaction with respect to repairing crooked and discolored teeth), and Anglin v. Kleeman, 665 A.2d 747 (N.H. 1995) (alleged statements that surgery would make knee stronger and enable patient to resume football were opinions and not promises), with Doerr v. Villate, 220 N.E.2d 767 (1966) (assurance that sterilization will prevent pregnancy sufficient to support contract cause of action). As a practical matter, most surgeons avoid these disputes by including in the signed informed consent form a statement that specifically denies any guarantee of results and asserts only that the surgeon will use his professional skills in the accepted manner. After signing such a document, can the patient claim not to have understood its plain language? Is such a document similar to a release or covenant not to sue, which generally are not enforced? See section E.3 and Chapter 2.B.2.

3. *Advertising.* HMOs and other forms of managed care insurance create an arena in which contractual theories may have much greater prominence. Garden variety contract claims naturally arise when HMO subscribers complain that deliberate decisions to refuse treatment breached the promise of covered services contained in their insurance contract. Where the complaint sounds more in classic malpractice due to poorly performed treatment, mistaken diagnoses, or the like, contract theory might be based on advertising or promotional statements. Explicit image-building efforts with the public at large were once a rarity in medicine, but now there is a glut of ads in newspapers, on billboards, and over the airwaves touting the quality of various medical institutions such as hospitals or HMOs. Even if these and similar assertions cannot be taken as warranting specific results from particular procedures, they can be argued to heighten the ordinary standard of care. Consider, for instance, an HMO that advertises "total health care" or that it has "over 1000 of the best doctors" in the region. See Allan S. Brett, The Case Against Persuasive Advertising by HMOs, 326 New Eng. J. Med. 1353 (1992). As George Anders explains,

> HMOs don't present themselves as the medical equivalent of a tawdry motel chain or a discount clothing store in a rundown part of town, blithely selling an inferior product in the name of having the cheapest possible price. Managed-care companies promise to uphold standards through their cost cutting, simply by targeting wasteful practices.

Health Against Wealth: HMOs and the Breakdown of Medical Trust 59 (1996).

Should the same concerns expressed in *Sullivan* about allowing doctors to give "therapeutic assurances" cause courts to take a protective view of quality assurances issued by medical institutions? Giordano v. Ramirez, 503 So. 2d 947 (Fla. Dist. Ct. App. 1987), held that a health care plan that promised a "high standard of competence, care, and concern for the welfare and needs of subscribers" did not undertake a higher than normal standard of care. However, in Dunn v. Praiss, 656 A.2d 413 (N.J. 1995), the court accepted for purposes of argument that a contractual theory might be maintained based on language in an HMO's description of benefits that "Plan members receive health care from a large number of well-qualified, highly trained physicians." Nevertheless, the court dismissed the claim on technical grounds for failure to raise it in time. See also McClellan v. Health Maintenance Organization of Pennsylvania, 604 A.2d 1053 (Pa. Super. Ct. 1992) (allowing patient to plead HMO breached contract by misrepresenting that physicians were qualified and would make appropriate referrals).

4. *Abandonment and Switching Doctors.* Contractual theories also arise frequently in the form of allegations that physicians "abandoned" a patient by totally neglecting the patient or by failing to give the required attention. Abandonment claims may sound like negligence, but they also can be said to be grounded in the contractual obligation to attend the patient properly and continuously until care for the particular illness is no longer needed. In this respect, the physician has failed to provide the personal professional services demanded under the contract of medical care. See Chapter 2.B.3. Employing a somewhat different theory, Maryland's high court ruled that a breach of contract action can be stated, based on informed consent principles, against a doctor who allows a training physician to perform part of

an operation, where the patient alleges that the more experienced doctor expressly stated he would do the operation. Dingle v. Belin, 749 A.2d 157 (Md. 2000).

5. *Fraud.* Closely related to the contract and guarantee situations represented by *Sullivan* are situations where a physician is accused of fraudulent statements or intentional misrepresentation of the results that can be expected from treatment. Most of these cases involve unethical practices and criminal activities by charlatans who are not licensed physicians or are persons who have had medical licenses revoked in the past for improper practices. There are many alleged "doctors" who offer unorthodox treatment for weight loss, baldness, cancer, or other conditions where afflicted patients are especially susceptible to false hopes for cure. The most well-known action in this field was the prosecution of a chiropractor "faith healer" for murder in the case of a young child with cancer in her eye. The prosecutor obtained a conviction for first-degree murder under a felony-murder theory that characterized the chiropractor's false promises as "grand theft." The California Supreme Court reversed, asserting that grand theft is not the type of felony that usually creates personal danger to human life and so could not support the felony-murder rule. People v. Phillips, 414 P.2d 353 (Cal. 1966). The case did not end at this point, however. The prosecutor persisted and in a second jury trial the chiropractor was convicted of second-degree murder. On appeal, the intermediate appellate court upheld the conviction on grounds that the defendant maliciously caused the child's death by fraudulently discouraging the parents from seeking proper treatment. People v. Phillips, 270 Cal. App. 2d 381, 75 Cal. Rptr. 720 (Cal. Ct. App. 1969). For a review of the background of the case see W. Curran, Law-Medicine Notes—Program in Medicolegal Relations 161-164 (1989).

Some cases do not involve frankly criminal conduct but rather overzealous assurances to patients before or after treatment, or both. In order to sustain liability for fraud, however, the plaintiff would be required to prove that statements of fact, not opinion, were knowingly false. Practitioners can often claim they have an honest belief based on a few documented "miraculous" cures. See, e.g., Schneider v. Revici, excerpted at page 447.

6. *Implied Warranties.* Contractual theories based on express statements should be distinguished from those based on implied warranties. Implied warranties that arise automatically from the sale of consumer products do not generally attach to professional services. Where products are involved in medical care, they are usually considered by the courts as incidental to medical services and therefore as not giving rise to implied warranties or other forms of products liability on the part of doctors or hospitals. Products liability theories may, however, be stated against manufacturers of medical drugs and devices. For additional discussion, see section D.3.

2. Vicarious Liability

■ FRANKLIN v. GUPTA
567 A.2d 524 (Md. App. 1990)

WILNER, Judge.

. . . Appellant, an unfortunate soul with a host of physical and emotional problems, also developed carpal tunnel syndrome—a condition that causes pain in the wrist and muscle weakness in the hand. He consulted Dr. Shanker L. Gupta, a general surgeon, who recommended surgical treatment for that condition.

. . . Dr. Herbert S. T. Lee, an anesthesiologist, and Gary J. Sergott, a certified registered nurse anesthetist, were assigned by the hospital to administer and monitor the anesthesia. Unfortunately, Dr. Lee was also scheduled to administer and monitor anesthesia to another patient in another operating room at the hospital at the same time. Dr. Lee chose to tend to the other patient, and so the actual administration and monitoring of the anesthesia to appellant fell to Nurse Sergott. As we shall see, things did not go as planned. The anesthesia administered by Nurse Sergott was not only not effective, but appellant suffered certain physical and emotional trauma from it, and the surgery was eventually cancelled.

As a result of this experience, appellant filed a claim with the Health Claims Arbitration Office against Dr. Gupta, Dr. Lee, Nurse Sergott, and the hospital. After an evidentiary hearing, the arbitration panel found no liability on the part of any of the defendants and entered an award in their favor. Appellant rejected the award and filed suit in the Circuit Court for Baltimore City.

After a de novo trial, the jury agreed with the arbitration panel that there was no liability on the part of Dr. Gupta, but it concluded that the other defendants were culpable. It returned a verdict in favor of Dr. Gupta but against Dr. Lee, Nurse Sergott, and the hospital in the amount of $375,000. . . . [The trial court granted the three losing defendants' motions for a new trial or, in the alternative, remittitur of all but $50,000, citing the failure of appellant to show convincing evidence that the treatment rendered caused most of his injuries. Plaintiff appealed.]

I. Underlying Facts

We mean no disrespect when we say that appellant was not a picture of health when he presented himself at the hospital on July 16, 1981—the day before his scheduled surgery. He had a history of syncope (temporary blackouts), asthma, emphysema, bronchitis, hyperthyroidism, chronic depression, and a nervous condition. He was also excessively—"morbidly"—obese; five feet, five inches tall, he weighed 295 pounds. He was permanently and totally disabled from employment and subsisted from Social Security disability benefits.

Dr. Lee, as we indicated, was designated by the hospital as the anesthesiologist for appellant's surgery, along with Nurse Sergott. Dr. Lee visited appellant on the afternoon of the 16th for an "anesthesia evaluation." Because of the patient's asthma, obesity, and hyperthyroidism, Dr. Lee recognized that appellant was a "high risk patient for anesthesia"; he therefore decided against a general anesthesia and opted instead for an axillary or brachial block.[1] He did not, however, . . . discuss the case in any way with Nurse Sergott. . . . Nurse Sergott independently decided to use a brachial block; he decided, by himself, which drug to use for that purpose; and he also decided, by himself, what analgesic to use and how it was to be administered. . . .

---

1. An axillary or brachial block is designed to anesthetize the entire arm, but nothing more.

At some point, shortly after administering the third dose of [local anesthesia], Nurse Sergott noticed that the block was "patchy"—i.e., "[t]he media flesh was not completely blocked on his hand." He wanted to give appellant another block, but Dr. Gupta insisted that he put appellant to sleep. Believing that general anesthesia was inappropriate and that, "being a surgeon, [Dr. Gupta] is not aware of anesthesia," Nurse Sergott decided to consult Dr. Lee who, . . . then busy with another patient under anesthesia and unable to leave, agreed that appellant should be given another brachial block and not put to sleep.

. . . While Nurse Sergott was conferring with Dr. Lee, appellant's breathing became shallow. Indeed, according to the medical record, he became cyanotic—i.e., his skin turned blue because of lack of oxygen in the body. He then became bradycardic (slow heartbeat) and had a period of asystole (his heart stopped beating entirely). . . . Appellant was promptly intubated and given Atropine and cardiopulmonary resuscitation, and his heartbeat returned to normal. At that point, Dr. Lee appeared and instructed Dr. Gupta to cancel the surgery.

Appellant remained in the hospital until his discharge on July 21, 1981. He never did have the surgery on his wrist. [He alleged that the delay caused by the nurse anesthesist's indecision and inability to properly anesthetize him aggravated his underlying medical conditions and caused permanent injury. . . .]

IV. JURY INSTRUCTIONS

. . . At the close of the evidence, appellant submitted . . . Proposed Instruction No. 11, captioned "Responsibility and Liability of Surgeon—the Captain of the Ship Doctrine." The relevant part of it is as follows:

> While Mr. Franklin was being prepared to undergo surgery, Dr. Gupta, the surgeon, is ordinarily regarded in law as having the exclusive responsibility and control over the case. . . . [H]e can thus be held responsible for any acts of negligence committed during the operation by any nurse anesthetist or assisting physician who is under his direction, no matter whether or not such assistant is an employee of [the] Hospital. For the purposes of the surgery, nurse Sergott and the other members of the operating room staff are referred to as "borrowed servants" for whose acts the surgeon and the employer ([the] Hospital) must be responsible. . . .

The court declined to give . . . instructions . . . about any vicarious liability on the part of Dr. Gupta for the acts or omissions of Dr. Lee or Nurse Sergott. Instead, it told the jury, in relevant part that . . . "Dr. Gupta is to be judged in his capacity as a surgeon. Dr. Lee is to be judged in his capacity as an anesthesiologist; and Mr. Sergott is to be judged in his capacity as a certified, registered nurse anesthetist. . . ."

[No] expert witness asserted any direct negligence on the part of Dr. Gupta. Nor did . . . any expert witness assert, as a matter of standard medical or hospital practice, that Dr. Gupta, as the surgeon employed to operate on appellant's wrist, had the expertise, the duty, or the right to supervise or control the method of anesthesia, the agents used to achieve the anesthesia, the dosages of those agents, the preoperative examination and evaluation of appellant by Lee and/or Sergott, the extent of communication and collaboration between them, or the precise manner in which Sergott conducted himself in the holding area and in the operating room.[5] There was no evidence that Dr. Gupta actually exercised, or attempted to exercise, any such supervision or control. Proposed Instruction No. 11, then, was not based on any factual predicate but on an assumed principle of law.

The principle underpinning the instruction has become popularly—and sometimes erroneously or misleadingly—called the "captain of the ship" doctrine. As explained in Thomas v. Raleigh General Hosp., 358 S.E.2d 222, 224 (W. Va. 1987): "Under this doctrine, a surgeon is likened to the captain of a ship, in that it is his duty to control everything going on in the operating room. Thus, liability is imposed by virtue of the surgeon's status and without any showing of actual control by the surgeon." As pointed out by Price, The Sinking of the "Captain of the Ship," 10 J. Legal Med. 323 (1989), this "Captain of the Ship" doctrine is but one of several theories of vicarious liability on the part of hospitals and surgeons for acts of negligence committed in the operating room. It is helpful, in examining the doctrine, to consider its context, its purpose, its scope, and how the courts have dealt with it.

A hospital, like any "master" or employer, is liable under agency principles for the negligence of its servants or employees. That would include nurses, physicians, and other medical and nonmedical personnel employed by it. Until fairly recently, however, in Maryland and in many states, this vicarious liability under agency law was of little assistance to plaintiffs injured by malpractice because of the eleemosynary (or governmental) immunity enjoyed by most hospitals. See Annotation, 25 A.L.R.2d 29 (1952).

Whether for that reason or whether because hospitals in earlier days were regarded less as comprehensive health care providers in their own right than as "innkeeper[s], providing a facility for patients to be treated by their privately retained physicians" (Price, supra, 10 J. Legal Med. at 340), courts began to impose liability on the surgeon for what went on in the operating room. The first theory employed was the traditional "borrowed servant" doctrine now expressed in Restatement (Second) of Agency §227.[6] The notion was that the surgeon acted as a special employer who borrowed nurses and other attendants from their general employer—the hospital—and thus became liable for their negligence. See, in general, Annotation, 12 A.L.R.3d 1017 (1967). Liability under that doctrine, of course, requires a showing that the surgeon actually controlled or had a right to control the details of the servant's conduct.

In McConnell v. Williams, 361 Pa. 355, 65 A.2d 243 (1949), the Pennsylvania Court essentially applied that doctrine, but in doing so it likened the surgeon to the captain of a ship. Unfortunately, that simile came to receive more attention than the actual holding in the case. The defendant was an obstetrician employed to attend the plaintiff during her pregnancy. The delivery, by cesarian section, was a difficult one. When the baby was removed from the womb, the defendant handed

---

5. Dr. Gupta . . . conceded only that it was part of his duty to see that the patient is properly anesthetized before beginning to operate.

6. A servant directed or permitted by his master to perform services for another may become the servant of such other in performing the services. He may become the other's servant as to some acts and not as to others.

her to an intern to tie the cord and administer silver nitrate to the eyes. The intern performed the latter task negligently; he put too much solution in the eyes and failed to irrigate, thereby causing severe damage to the child's eyes. The intern was a hospital employee but had been designated by the obstetrician to assist. The action against the obstetrician was based solely on a theory of vicarious liability for the intern's negligence. At the time the case reached the Pennsylvania Supreme Court, the hospital enjoyed charitable immunity and therefore could not be made to answer for the intern's negligence.

Unlike most cases, the obstetrician acknowledged in his testimony that his liability "was to continue until the baby was turned over to the family doctor" and that "he had complete control of the operating room and of every person within it while the operation was in progress." It was in that light that the court, after reciting the general law relating to borrowed servants, including the requirement of control, made the statement that

> it can readily be understood that in the course of an operation in the operating room of a hospital, and until the surgeon leaves that room at the conclusion of the operation . . . he is in the same complete charge of those who are present and assisting him as is the captain of a ship over all on board, and that such supreme control is indeed essential in view of the high degree of protection to which an anaesthetized, unconscious patient is entitled. . . . [I]f operating surgeons were not to be held liable for the negligent performance of the duties of those then working under them, the law would fail in large measure to afford a means of redress for preventable injuries sustained during the course of such operations.

McConnell is sometimes credited with having spawned a new "separate and independent concept of agency" in hospital settings. Price, supra, 10 J. Legal Med. at 331. That may be giving *McConnell* too much credit. . . . [T]he *McConnell* court made clear that the issue of control by the surgeon was one of fact, not of law. In its concluding paragraph, it said that "[i]t is for the jury to determine whether the relationship between defendant and the intern, at the time the child's eyes were injured, was that of master and servant." 65 A.2d at 48.

Some courts that seemingly have made surgeons strictly liable for the negligence of others in the operating room, or that have used the expression "captain of the ship," have in reality done nothing more than apply res ipsa loquitur or a doctrine of negligence per se to the physician. Most of these cases involved the leaving of sponges or other foreign substances in the body, and the court adopted the view that, in such circumstances, negligence on the part of the surgeon can be inferred from the mere happening of the event. The surgeon's negligence, in other words, was direct, not vicarious. References in these cases to the "captain of the ship" are usually in the context of rejecting as a defense to such inferred negligence that the surgeon relied on an erroneous sponge count by the nurse.

In summary, a careful analysis of the cases cited as "captain of the ship" cases generally reveals that the court has applied traditional agency concepts and that, where the surgeon has been held liable, the liability has either been direct (even if inferred) or based on evidence that the negligent actors were, in fact, under his direct supervision and control. As in *McConnell*, the rhetoric often tends to obscure the factual underpinning of the holding.[7]

To the extent that the doctrine is regarded as an expansion of the traditional borrowed servant rule, most courts have either expressly rejected it or have declared it inapplicable when the negligent actor is an anesthesiologist or nurse anesthetist. Two theories have been advanced for the rejection or limitation. The first was well expressed in Thomas v. Raleigh General Hosp., supra, 358 S.E.2d 222, 225:

> We reject the captain of the ship doctrine. The trend toward specialization in medicine has created situations where surgeons do not always have the right to control all personnel within the operating room. . . . An assignment of liability based on a theory of actual control more realistically reflects the actual relationship which exists in a modern operating room.[8]

. . . Compare Baird v. Sickler, 69 Ohio St. 2d 652, 433 N.E.2d 593 (1982) (surgeon could be liable for the negligent conduct of a nurse anesthetist where the evidence showed that the surgeon "exercised and possessed" the right to control the nurse's actions and actually "participated in the administering of the anesthetic.")

The second theory, applied by some courts, is that, with the curtailment or abolition of the hospital's charitable or governmental immunity, by statute or judicial decision, an expanded liability on the part of the surgeon is no longer necessary. . . .

Maryland ventured into these waters only once—76 years ago. In Hunner v. Stevenson, supra, 122 Md. 40, 89 A. 418, . . . [the plaintiff] sued the doctor,

7. The Texas Court in Sparger v. Worley Hospital, Inc., 547 S.W.2d 582, 584 (Tex. 1977), put its judicial finger on the problem:

> way of being canonized and of growing until they can stand and walk independently of the usual general rules. Mr. Justice Frankfurter once wrote concerning such phrase-making in judicial opinions: "The phrase . . . is an excellent illustration of the extent to which uncritical use of words bedevils the law. A phrase begins life as a literary expression; its felicity leads to its lazy repetition; and repetition soon establishes it as a legal formula, undiscriminatingly used to express different and sometimes contradictory ideas." Tiller v. Atlantic Coast Line R. Co., 318 U.S. 54, 68, 63 S. Ct. 444, 452, 87 L. Ed. 610 (1943). The result in the use of captain of the ship is that a surgeon or physician may be held liable, not as others upon the basis of the general rule of borrowed servant, but as captain of the ship.

8. May v. Broun, 261 Or. 28, 492 P.2d 776, 781 (1972), also espoused the first theory, pointing out at 781:

> Changes have also been occurring in the confines of operating rooms. Surgeons are operating more and more in a highly-mechanized environment wholly created by hospitals. Much highly technical equipment, now considered necessary, is furnished by the hospital and operated by personnel which the hospital hires and trains. As a result, in most instances, a surgeon cannot actually have direct supervision or control over such equipment and the persons who operate it even when he is present, if he is going to give the concentration and attention to the surgery which his patient has the right to expect.

not for anything he did or didn't do directly, but on the theory that, as the surgeon, he was responsible for the negligence of other hospital personnel in the postoperative treatment and dressing of the wound. The court said as to that issue: . . . "It would be unreasonable to expect such a one as the record shows the appellant to be—performing operations in five different hospitals in Baltimore, and in one at Frederick, in addition to his other practice—to continue to dress the wounds and have personal charge of the after-treatment in all cases until the patient is discharged from the hospital."

. . . From our analysis of how other courts have dealt with the issue at hand, we reject any "captain of the ship" theory of liability. . . . The correct doctrine to apply is the traditional "borrowed servant" rule. Where the evidence suffices to support a finding that the surgeon in fact had or exercised the right to control the details of another person's work or conduct in the operating room and the other elements of the rule are satisfied, the trier of fact may find that the surgeon was the "special employer" and is therefore liable for the negligence of the borrowed servant.

That was not the case here, however. As we indicated, there was no evidence that Dr. Gupta in any way supervised or controlled, attempted to supervise or control, or had the right or power to supervise or control, the conduct and decisions of Dr. Lee or Nurse Sergott. Proposed Instruction No. 11 was therefore properly rejected. . . .

Notes: Physicians' Vicarious Liability; "Captain of the Ship"

1. *The* Franklin *Case.* Cutting against the grain of *Franklin* and other modern cases, a California court reasoned that the "captain of the ship" doctrine still survives, even without evidence of actual control, in a case involving a sponge left behind due to negligence of the nurse who conducted the sponge count. The court reasoned that, even though it is not the surgeon's responsibility to conduct or check the sponge count, a "helpless patient on the operating table who cannot understand or control what is happening reasonably expects a surgeon to oversee her care and to look out for her interests. We find this special relationship sufficient justification for . . . [a] nondelegable duty to remove all sponges from the patient's body." The court contrasted this situation with anesthesia, which it acknowledged is conducted by "an independent specialist. . . . By contrast, an assisting nurse is obligated to follow the commands of a surgeon. . . ." Baumgardner v. Yusuf, 144 Cal. App. 4th 1381 (2006).

Similarly, under *Franklin*'s borrowed servant rule, acknowledging that Dr. Gupta did not actually determine which anesthesia to use and how to administer it, are you convinced beyond any reasonable dispute that he lacked the *right* and *power* to do so? It was agreed that he could at least halt the operation if he was not satisfied. What about Dr. Lee, the anesthesiologist? Was he any more responsible, in actuality or in theory, for what the nurse did wrong? As it turns out, he and the nurse were found liable, along with the hospital (albeit, for only $50,000). How strong is the "captain of the ship" case against Dr. Lee? See generally Nancy King, The Physician as Captain of the Ship: A Critical Appraisal (1988); Annot., 12 A.L.R.3d 1017 (1967).

2. *The Effect on Hospital Liability.* "Captain of the ship" and borrowed servant are not only theories of liability against doctors, they are also theories of defense

asserted by hospitals. Where a surgeon controls a negligent nurse, hospitals assert that they are not vicariously liable even though they are the nurse's employer because they lent their "servant" to the physician. See Krane v. St. Anthony Hospital System, 738 P.2d 75 (Colo. Ct. App. 1987). However, most courts hold the hospital jointly liable unless the doctor instructs the nurse to do an act that is not within the general scope of duty. Restatement (Second) of Agency §227; Annot., 29 A.L.R.3d 1065 (1970).

The erosion of hospitals' charitable immunity and the rise of complex, technologically dependent team treatment are discussed further in section H.1. Are there any other theories of liability that you think should be affected by these developments? Some in the academic and public policy community contend that hospitals should be *exclusively* liable for all negligent medical care rendered on their premises, without regard to the physician's specialty or relationship with the hospital, thus absolving individual physicians from any liability, even for their own mistakes. See page 518.

3. *Professional Corporations.* Physicians' vicarious liability is not restricted to the borrowed servant rule. It can also arise by virtue of being an employer of or partner with the medical professional who makes a negligent mistake. In the partnership setting, doctors are not individually liable for negligence committed by their colleagues unless they are involved in the treatment. The partnership as an entity however, is, liable, and doctors who are general partners have unlimited individual liability for making good the partnership's debts, so the liability exposure effectively exists in general partnerships. See Annot., 85 A.L.R.2d 889 (1962 & Supp.). This is one reason doctors seek to organize as professional corporations, which combine the tax advantages of a partnership with the liability protections of a corporate form. However, many state professional corporations' statutes protect physicians only from contractual or business obligations, not tort obligations, or have been interpreted in this fashion by restrictive court decisions. Thus, physicians continue to be jointly and severally liable for the professional torts of member physicians. See, e.g., Pediatric Neurosurgery v. Russell, 44 P.3d 1063 (Colo. 2002).

More recently, states have enacted "limited liability corporation" statutes that make it even easier to combine the tax benefits of partnerships with the liability protections of the corporate form. These have proven to be wildly popular. Although they retain the same constraints on the ability to avoid professional liability, some of these statutes adopt the innovation that physicians are vicariously liable only if they supervise the physician at fault.

Moreover, these liability rules affect only the obligation to patients. They can always be altered internally by indemnification agreements among partnering physicians or with their corporate entities.

3. Strict Liability, Products Liability, and Preemption

This chapter focuses on the professional liability of those who deliver health care services: doctors, hospitals, and HMOs. Also important in the medical arena is the institutional liability of those who manufacture and sell medical drugs and equipment. Length constraints do not allow an in-depth treatment of these additional sources of liability, so we provide only a cursory survey of products liability.

For more, see also Lars Noah, This Is Your Products Liability Restatement on Drugs, 74 Brook. L. Rev. 839 (2009).

Also, because products liability is a form of strict liability, we consider here whether conventional negligence liability could be replaced or supplemented by some form of "no-fault" liability. Finally, this intersection of issues also raises the question of federal preemption of state tort law.

Rather than attempt to master all the twists and turns of these various complex doctrines, read this case and the following notes with these more general questions in mind: Why is strict liability justified for medical products but not for medical services? Where products liability exists, how is it shared among the responsible parties (manufacturer, hospital, and physician)? Should doctors and hospitals also be subject to a form of no-fault liability? Should regulatory oversight of medical safety displace the traditional role that juries play in balancing the competing concerns over cost, quality, fairness, and innovation?

■ BRUESEWITZ v. WYETH
562 U.S. 223 (2011)

SCALIA, J.

For the last 66 years, vaccines have been subject to the same federal premarket approval process as prescription drugs, and compensation for vaccine-related injuries has been left largely to the States. Under that regime, . . . vaccines became, one might say, victims of their own success. They had been so effective in preventing infectious diseases that the public became much less alarmed at the threat of those diseases, and much more concerned with the risk of injury from the vaccines themselves.

Much of the concern centered around vaccines against diphtheria, tetanus, and pertussis (DTP), which were blamed for children's disabilities and developmental delays. This led to a massive increase in vaccine-related tort litigation. Whereas between 1978 and 1981 only nine product-liability suits were filed against DTP manufacturers, by the mid-1980's the suits numbered more than 200 each year. This destabilized the DTP vaccine market, causing two of the three domestic manufacturers to withdraw; and the remaining manufacturer, Lederle Laboratories, estimated that its potential tort liability exceeded its annual sales by a factor of 200. . . .

To stabilize the vaccine market and facilitate compensation, Congress enacted the [National Childhood Vaccine Injury Act of 1986 (NCVIA)]. The Act establishes a no-fault compensation program designed to work faster and with greater ease than the civil tort system. A person injured by a vaccine, or his legal guardian, may file a petition for compensation. . . . A special master then makes an informal adjudication of the petition. . . . [After appeal to an administrative court], a claimant has two options: to accept the court's judgment and forgo a traditional tort suit for damages, or to reject the judgment and seek tort relief from the vaccine manufacturer. Fast, informal adjudication is made possible by the Act's Vaccine Injury Table, which lists the vaccines covered under the Act; describes each vaccine's compensable, adverse side effects; and indicates how soon after vaccination those side effects should first manifest themselves. Claimants who show that a listed injury first manifested itself at the appropriate time are prima facie entitled to compensation. No showing of causation is necessary; the [government] bears the burden of disproving causation. A claimant may also recover for unlisted side effects, and for listed side effects that occur at times other than those specified in the Table, but for those the claimant must prove causation. Unlike in tort suits, claimants under the Act are not required to show that the administered vaccine was defectively manufactured, labeled, or designed.

Successful claimants receive compensation for medical, rehabilitation, counseling, special education, and vocational training expenses; diminished earning capacity; pain and suffering; and $250,000 for vaccine-related deaths. Attorney's fees are provided, not only for successful cases, but even for unsuccessful claims that are not frivolous. These awards are paid out of a fund created by an excise tax on each vaccine dose.

The *quid pro quo* for this, designed to stabilize the vaccine market, was the provision of significant tort-liability protections for vaccine manufacturers. The Act requires claimants to seek relief through the compensation program before filing suit for more than $1,000. Manufacturers are generally immunized from liability for failure to warn if they have complied with all regulatory requirements (including but not limited to warning requirements) and have given the warning either to the claimant or the claimant's physician. . . . And most relevant to the present case, the Act expressly eliminates liability for a vaccine's unavoidable, adverse side effects:

> No vaccine manufacturer shall be liable in a civil action for damages arising from a vaccine-related injury or death associated with the administration of a vaccine after October 1, 1988, if the injury or death resulted from side effects that were unavoidable even though the vaccine was properly prepared and was accompanied by proper directions and warnings.

The vaccine at issue here is a DTP vaccine. . . . Hannah Bruesewitz was born on October 20, 1991. Her pediatrician administered doses of the DTP vaccine according to the Center for Disease Control's recommended childhood immunization schedule. Within 24 hours of her April 1992 vaccination, Hannah started to experience seizures. She suffered over 100 seizures during the next month, and her doctors eventually diagnosed her with "residual seizure disorder" and "developmental delay." Hannah, now a teenager, is still diagnosed with both conditions. . . .

A Special Master denied [the parents'] claims on various grounds, . . . [and the Bruesewitzes elected to file suit in state court]. Their complaint alleged (as relevant here) that defective design of [Wyeth's] DTP vaccine caused Hannah's disabilities, and that [Wyeth] was subject to strict liability, and liability for negligent design, under Pennsylvania common law. [The complaint also made claims based upon failure to warn and defective manufacture, but those were no longer at issue. After removal to federal court, the case was dismissed], holding that the Pennsylvania law providing those causes of action was preempted by [the NCVIA]. . . .

[Under the statute], [p]rovided that there was proper manufacture and warning, any remaining side effects, including those resulting from design defects, are deemed to have been unavoidable. State-law design-defect claims are therefore preempted. . . . The language of the provision thus suggests that the *design* of the vaccine is a given, not subject to question in the tort action. What the statute establishes as a complete defense must be unavoidability (given safe manufacture and warning) *with respect to the particular design.* Which plainly implies that the design itself is not open to question.[1]

A further textual indication leads to the same conclusion. Products-liability law establishes a classic and well known triumvirate of grounds for liability: defective manufacture, inadequate directions or warnings, and defective design. If all three were intended to be preserved, it would be strange to mention specifically only two, and leave the third to implication. . . . *Expressio unius, exclusio alterius.* . . .

Petitioners' and the dissent's textual argument also rests upon the proposition that the word "unavoidable" in [the statute] is a term of art that incorporates comment *k* to Restatement (Second) of Torts §402A (1963-1964). The Restatement generally holds a manufacturer strictly liable for harm to person or property caused by "any product in a defective condition unreasonably dangerous to the user." Comment *k* exempts from this strict-liability rule "unavoidably unsafe products." An unavoidably unsafe product is defined by a hodge-podge of criteria and a few examples, such as the Pasteur rabies vaccine and experimental pharmaceuticals. Despite this lack of clarity, petitioners seize upon one phrase in the comment *k* analysis, and assert that by 1986 a majority of courts had made this a *sine qua non* requirement for an "unavoidably unsafe product": a case-specific showing that the product was "quite incapable of being made safer for [its] intended . . . use."[2]

We have no need to consider the finer points of comment *k*. Whatever consistent judicial gloss that comment may have been given in 1986, there is no reason to believe that [the NCVIA] was invoking it. . . . The structure of the NCVIA and of vaccine regulation in general reinforces what the [statutory] text suggests. A vaccine's license spells out [in great detail] the manufacturing method that must be followed and the directions and warnings that must accompany the product. Manufacturers ordinarily must obtain the Food and Drug Administration's (FDA) approval before modifying either. . . . Design defects, in contrast, do not merit a single mention in the NCVIA or the FDA's regulations. Indeed, the FDA has never even spelled out in regulations the criteria it uses to decide whether a vaccine is safe and effective for its intended use. And the decision is surely not an easy one. Drug manufacturers often could trade a little less efficacy for a little more safety, but the safest design is not always the best one. Striking the right balance between safety and efficacy is especially difficult with respect to vaccines, which affect public as well as individual

---

1. The dissent advocates for another possibility: "[A] side effect is 'unavoidable' . . . where there is no feasible alternative design that would eliminate the side effect of the vaccine without compromising its cost and utility." . . . We have no idea how much more expensive an alternative design can be before it "compromis[es]" a vaccine's cost or how much efficacy an alternative design can sacrifice to improve safety. Neither does the dissent. And neither will the judges who must rule on motions to dismiss.

2. Restatement §402A, Comment *k*, p. 353. Petitioners cite, *inter alia, Kearl* v. *Lederle Labs.*, 218 Cal. Rptr. 453, 463-464 (1985); *Belle Bonfils Memorial Blood Bank* v. *Hansen*, 665 P.2d 118, 122 (Colo. 1983). Though it is not pertinent to our analysis, we point out that a large number of courts disagreed with that reading of comment *k*, and took it to say that manufacturers did not face strict liability for side effects of properly manufactured prescription drugs that were accompanied by adequate warnings. See, *e.g., Brown* v. *Superior Court*, 751 P.2d 470 (Cal. 1988); . . .

health. Yet the Act, which in every other respect micromanages manufacturers, is silent on how to evaluate competing designs, . . . leaving the universe of alternative designs to be limited only by an expert's imagination.

Jurors, of course, often decide similar questions with little guidance, and we do not suggest that the absence of guidance alone suggests preemption. But the lack of guidance for design defects combined with the extensive guidance for the two grounds of liability specifically mentioned in the Act strongly suggests that design defects were not mentioned because they are not a basis for liability. . . . And, of course, whenever the FDA concludes that a vaccine is unsafe, it may revoke the license.

These provisions for federal agency improvement of vaccine design, and for federally prescribed compensation, once again suggest that [the statute's] silence regarding design-defect liability was not inadvertent. It instead reflects a sensible choice to leave complex epidemiological judgments about vaccine design to the FDA and the National Vaccine Program rather than juries. . . .

The dissent's legislative history relies on the following syllogism: A 1986 House Committee Report states that [the statute] "sets forth the principle contained in Comment *k* of Section 402A of the Restatement of Torts (Second);" in 1986 comment *k* was "commonly understood" to require a case-specific showing that "no feasible alternative design" existed; Congress therefore must have intended [the statute] to require that showing. The syllogism ignores . . . [that] Comment *k* did not have a "commonly understood meaning" in the mid-1980's. Some courts thought it required a case-specific showing that a product was "unavoidably unsafe"; many others thought it categorically exempted certain types of products from strict liability. . . .

For the foregoing reasons, we hold that the National Childhood Vaccine Injury Act preempts all design-defect claims against vaccine manufacturers brought by plaintiffs who seek compensation for injury or death caused by vaccine side effects.

Justice SOTOMAYOR, Justice GINSBURG joins, dissenting.

Vaccine manufacturers have long been subject to a legal duty, rooted in basic principles of products liability law, to improve the designs of their vaccines in light of advances in science and technology. Until today, that duty was enforceable through a traditional state-law tort action for defective design. . . . [The Court's] decision leaves a regulatory vacuum in which no one ensures that vaccine manufacturers adequately take account of scientific and technological advancements when designing or distributing their products. . . .

Blackletter products liability law generally recognizes three different types of product defects: design defects, manufacturing defects, and labeling defects (e.g., failure to warn). The reference in the "even though" clause to a "properly prepared" vaccine "accompanied by proper directions and warnings" is an obvious reference to two such defects — manufacturing and labeling defects. . . . [I]t follows that the "even though" clause requires a vaccine manufacturer in each civil action to demonstrate that its vaccine is free from manufacturing and labeling defects to fall within the liability exemption of [the NCVIA]. Given that the "even though" clause requires the absence of manufacturing and labeling defects, the "if" clause's reference to "side effects that were unavoidable" must refer to side effects caused by something other than manufacturing and labeling defects. The only remaining kind of product defect recognized under traditional products liability law is a design defect. Thus, "side effects that were unavoidable" must refer to side effects caused by a vaccine's *design* that were "unavoidable." . . . Accordingly, . . . Congress must also have intended a vaccine manufacturer to demonstrate in each civil action that the particular side effects of a vaccine's design were "unavoidable." . . .

The legislative history . . . expressly adopts comment *k* of §402A of the Restatement of Torts (Second) (1963-1964) (hereinafter Restatement), which provides that "unavoidably unsafe" products—i.e., those that "in the present state of human knowledge, are quite incapable of being made safe for their intended and ordinary use"—are not defective.[3] As "[a]n outstanding example" of an "[u]navoidably unsafe" product, comment *k* cites "the vaccine for the Pasteur treatment of rabies, which not uncommonly leads to very serious and damaging consequences when it is injected"; "[s]ince the disease itself invariably leads to a dreadful death, both the marketing and the use of the vaccine are fully justified, notwithstanding the unavoidable high degree of risk which they involve." Comment *k* thus provides that "seller[s]" of "[u]navoidably unsafe" products are "not to be held to strict liability" provided that such products "are properly prepared and marketed, and proper warning is given." As the [legislative history of the NCVIA] explains, Congress intended that the "principle in Comment K regarding 'unavoidably unsafe' products" apply to the vaccines covered in the bill. . . . By the time of the Vaccine Act's enactment in 1986, numerous state and federal courts had interpreted comment *k* to mean that a product is "unavoidably unsafe" when, given proper manufacture and labeling, no feasible alternative design would reduce the safety risks without compromising the product's cost and utility.[4] . . . By explaining what

---

3. Comment *k* provides as follows: "*Unavoidably unsafe products.* There are some products which, in the present state of human knowledge, are quite incapable of being made safe for their intended and ordinary use. These are especially common in the field of drugs. An outstanding example is the vaccine for the Pasteur treatment of rabies, which not uncommonly leads to very serious and damaging consequences when it is injected. Since the disease itself invariably leads to a dreadful death, both the marketing and the use of the vaccine are fully justified, notwithstanding the unavoidable high degree of risk which they involve. Such a product, properly prepared, and accompanied by proper directions and warning, is not defective, nor is it *unreasonably* dangerous. The same is true of many other drugs, vaccines, and the like, many of which for this very reason cannot legally be sold except to physicians, or under the prescription of a physician. It is also true in particular of many new or experimental drugs as to which, because of lack of time and opportunity for sufficient medical experience, there can be no assurance of safety, or perhaps even of purity of ingredients, but such experience as there is justifies the marketing and use of the drug notwithstanding a medically recognizable risk. The seller of such products, again with the qualification that they are properly prepared and marketed, and proper warning is given, where the situation calls for it, is not to be held to strict liability for unfortunate consequences attending their use, merely because he has undertaken to supply the public with an apparently useful and desirable product, attended with a known but apparently reasonable risk."

4. . . . See 1 L. Frumer & M. Friedman, Products Liability §§8.07[1]-[2], pp. 8-277 to 8-278 (2010) (comment *k* applies "only to defects in design," and there "must be no feasible alternative design which on balance accomplishes the subject product's purpose with a lesser risk" (internal quotation marks omitted)). To be sure, a number of courts at the time of the

Congress meant by the term "unavoidable," moreover, the [Congressional] Report also confirms that whether a side effect is "unavoidable" . . . involves a specific inquiry in each case as to whether the vaccine "in the present state of human skill and knowledge cannot be made safe,"—i.e., whether a feasible alternative design existed that would have eliminated the adverse side effects of the vaccine without compromising its cost and utility. . . . Accordingly, I believe [the statute] exempts vaccine manufacturers from tort liability only upon a showing by the manufacturer in each case that the vaccine was properly manufactured and labeled, and that the side effects stemming from the vaccine's design could not have been prevented by a feasible alternative design that would have eliminated the adverse side effects without compromising the vaccine's cost and utility.

[T]he majority's position elides a significant difference between state tort law and the federal regulatory scheme. . . . [N]either the Act nor any other provision of federal law places a legal duty on vaccine manufacturers to improve the design of their vaccines to account for scientific and technological advances. Indeed, the FDA does not condition approval of a vaccine on it being the most optimally designed among reasonably available alternatives, nor does it (or any other federal entity) ensure that licensed vaccines keep pace with technological and scientific advances.[5] Rather, the function of ensuring that vaccines are optimally designed in light of existing science and technology has traditionally been left to the States through the imposition of damages for design defects. Cf. *Wyeth v. Levine*, 555 U.S. 555 (2009) (noting that the FDA has "traditionally regarded state law as a complementary form of drug regulation" as "[s]tate tort suits uncover unknown drug hazards and provide incentives for drug manufacturers to disclose safety risks promptly"). . . .

I respectfully dissent.

Notes: Designing a No-Fault Liability System

1. *Overview.* The type of no-fault compensation programs used for childhood vaccines has also received considerable discussion as a possible basis for an administrative compensation system that could apply to all medical injuries, including those caused by physicians or hospital staff. These no-fault liability proposals resemble the workers' compensation schemes that replaced negligence suits against employers in the first half of the twentieth century. The basic structure is to define a range of

---

Vaccine Act's enactment had interpreted comment *k* to preclude design defect claims categorically for certain kinds of products, see *Hill v. Searle Labs.*, 884 F. 2d 1064, 1068 (CA8 1989) (collecting cases), but as indicated by the sources cited above, the courts that had construed comment *k* to apply on a case-specific basis generally agreed on the basic elements of what constituted an "unavoidably unsafe" product. . . .

5. See, *e.g., Hurley v. Lederle Labs.*, 863 F.2d 1173, 1177 (CA5 1988) ("[T]he FDA is a passive agency: it considers whether to approve vaccine designs only if and when manufacturers come forward with a proposal"); . . . Conk, Is There a Design Defect in the Restatement (Third) of Torts: Products Liability? 109 Yale L.J. 1087, 1128-1129 (1999-2000) ("The FDA does not claim to review products for optimal design. . . . FDA review thus asks less of drug . . . manufacturers than the common law of products liability asks of other kinds of manufacturers").

compensable events, establish a schedule of economic and noneconomic damages, and create an administrative system for filing claims and resolving factual disputes and questions of interpretation. See generally Paul C. Weiler, Medical Malpractice on Trial (1991). Each of these components offers potential advantages over current tort law, but also presents sources of controversy and difficulties in design and implementation, as explored in the following notes.

2. *Defining Compensable Events.* Defining compensable events in terms of negative medical outcomes, without regard to fault or the standard of care, has the advantages of greater simplicity, the reduction of pejorative accusations against well-meaning professionals, and the increased social justice of covering seriously injured patients regardless of the behavior that caused the injury. Proponents of no-fault argue that traditional malpractice liability does a poor job of deterrence because doctors perceive lawsuits as largely random and uncontrollable events, medical malpractice insurance is widespread and not experience-rated, and deterrent signals create unnecessary and costly "defensive medicine." See generally Michelle M. Mello & Troyen A. Brennan, Deterrence of Medical Errors: Theory and Evidence for Malpractice Reform, 80 Tex. L. Rev. 1595 (2002). The hope is that a well-crafted no-fault system could correct some or all of these deficiencies. Sagit Mor & Orna Rabinvich-Einy, Relational Malpractice, 42 Seton Hall L. Rev. 610 (2012).

The difficulty with designing a no-fault compensation system, however, is defining exactly which events trigger compensation. As vaccine injuries illustrate, medical causation is complex and not all failures to achieve perfect results are avoidable. Subjecting these questions to litigation would prove costly, but they are essential to defining the scope of strict liability. Therefore, causation and injury questions continue to complicate no-fault systems even though they are designed to be simple and expedient. Claims to the vaccine compensation program, for instance, have become increasingly litigious and protracted. Betsy Grey, The Plague of Causation in the National Childhood Vaccine Injury Act, 48 Harv. J. on Legis. 343 (2011); Peter H. Meyers, Fixing the Flaws in the Federal Vaccine Injury Compensation Program, 63 Admin. L. Rev. 785 (2011).

Moreover, in the context of physician care, it is difficult to define which bad results are avoidable or unexpected without allowing concepts of fault to creep back in, since a less than perfect outcome is compensable only if "correct" medical procedures would have avoided it. Consider, for instance, how you would determine which of various versions of the following events is subject to no-fault compensation: misdiagnosis; adverse drug reactions; and post-surgical infections. Can you make such a determination without suggesting the doctors did something wrong? Can you do so without alluding to what most other doctors do in the same situation?

One way to circumvent these difficulties is simply to list for each major category of treatment or illness which outcomes are considered abnormal enough to warrant compensation as a medical injury. This is what the vaccine compensation fund does, but doing this for all of medicine would be a huge, complex undertaking. Still, methods have been proposed, as documented in note 6.

3. *Costs and Administrative Efficiency.* The other two components of proposals for no-fault compensation attempt to make damages more predictable and dispute resolution speedier and less costly. These advantages are articulated further

in sections E.4 and H. Of particular note is the fact that, under the conventional tort system, less than 50 percent of malpractice insurance premiums end up in the pockets of injured patients. Aaron Carroll et al., The Impact of Defense Expenses in Medical Malpractice Claims, 40 J.L. Med. & Ethics 135 (2012). The hope is that savings in administrative and legal costs and the somewhat lower awards from a no-fault system will largely offset the increase in the number of claims that are filed, so that the total costs of the system remain the same but it covers more people and operates more fairly. These virtues alone are substantial enough that in the 1980s the AMA proposed a *fault-based* administrative compensation system. There is the potential, however, that as the system becomes less costly and more accessible, the number of claims will skyrocket, since research has shown that the number of patients who now sue is a tiny fraction (1 to 2 percent) of the total number who are injured by medical care. Accordingly, the AMA has stopped promoting its administrative reform proposal. However, the idea has been taken up by others, in the form of resolving malpractice disputes through administrative hearings or specialized "health courts." See note 6.

The other drawback to no-fault schemes is their costs and how they are distributed. Even with administrative efficiencies, full compensation for all medical injuries would be much more expensive in total than the present system because so many injuries now are entirely uncompensated. To keep a no-fault system affordable, proponents usually set tight caps on total recoverable damages. As discussed in section F, this resolution of the funding dilemma in essence shifts compensation from the most severely to the least severely injured victims of medical error.

4. *Childbirth Injuries.* All-encompassing administrative no-fault systems for the full range of medical injuries have been adopted in Sweden, Finland, and New Zealand (the latter as part of a compensation system for all accidental injuries). See K. Oliphant & R. Wright eds., Medical Malpractice and Compensation in Global Perspective (2013); J. Dute et al. eds. No-Fault Compensation in the Health Care Sector (2004).

In the United States, the closest real-world application of these ideas has occurred in Florida and Virginia, with their limited no-fault schemes that cover only designated injuries from child birth—the arena that produces the greatest liability exposure. Both programs cover only severe, permanent brain damage. Other injuries in obstetrics such as death, birth defects, and non-neurological physical injury are left to the regular tort system. Because of this limited scope, few claims have been filed or paid. See note 6. Compensation for these cases is focused primarily on the unreimbursed costs of medical care; compensation for lost earnings and for pain and suffering are severely limited.

5. *Neo-No Fault.* A final variation is no fault by voluntary agreement, also known as "neo-no fault." Jeffrey O'Connell is the architect of this idea, in Neo-No Fault Remedies for Medical Injuries: Coordinated Statutory and Contractual Alternatives, 49 Law & Contemp. Probs. 125 (Spring 1986). The gist is that if doctors or hospitals promptly volunteer to cover the uncompensated economic consequences of a medical injury, then patients would be precluded from suing in tort for noneconomic damages (or, in other versions, they would be taxed various costs if they then sued and failed to recover more than the offer). If you had as a client the doctors in the *Locke* case (page 325), would you advise making this type of voluntary offer of payment?

4 ■ Medical Malpractice

6. *Bibliography.* On the pros and cons of **no-fault** (note 3), see Catherine Struve, Doctors, the Adversary System, and Procedural Reform in Medical Liability Litigation, 72 Fordham L. Rev. 943 (2004); Eleanor D. Kinney, Administrative Law Approaches to Medical Malpractice Reform, 49 St. Louis U. L.J. 45 (2004); Michelle Mello et al., "Health Courts" and Accountability for Patient Safety, 84 Milbank Q. 459 (2006); Maxwell Mehlman & Dale Nance, Medical Injustice: The Case Against Health Courts (2007); Philip G. Peters, Jr., Health Courts? 88 B.U. L. Rev. 227 (2008); Note, 7 Yale J. Health Pol'y L. & Ethics 387 (2007); Symposium, 33 J. Health Pol. Pol'y & L. 725 (2008); Symposium, J. Health Care L. & Policy 217 (2006).

On **childbirth injury compensation** programs (note 4), see Randall R. Bovbjerg & Frank A. Sloan, No Fault for Medical Injury: Theory and Evidence, 67 Univ. Cin. L. Rev. 53 (1998); David M. Studdert et al., The Jury Is Still In: Florida's Birth-Related Neurological Injury Compensation Plan After a Decade, 25 J. Health Pol. Pol'y & L. 499 (June 2000); Gil Siegal et al., Adjudicating Severe Birth Injury Claims in Florida and Virginia, 34 Am. J.L. & Med. 493 (2008). For additional discussion of the federal vaccine compensation program, see Peter H. Meyers, Fixing the Flaws in the Federal Vaccine Injury Compensation Program, 63 Admin. L. Rev. 785 (2011).

On "neo-no fault" (note 5), see Jeffrey O'Connell & Evan Stephenson, Binding Statutory Early Offers by Defendants, Not Plaintiffs, *in* Personal Injury Suits, 54 DePaul L. Rev. 233 (2005); J. Hersch et al., An Empirical Assessment of Early Offer Reform for Medical Malpractice, 36 J. Leg. Stud. 119 (2007).

Notes: Products Liability for Defective Drugs and Medical Devices

1. *Mass Torts.* Defective drugs and devices have given rise to several massive rounds of litigation when it was discovered that a widely used drug or medical device has a previously unknown potential harm. Notable examples include DES (prenatal miscarriage prevention), Vioxx (arthritis treatment), silicone breast implants, Bendectin (a pregnancy antinausea drug), Dalkon Shield (an intrauterine contraceptive device), and the birth control pill. Some manufacturers, such as Dow-Corning in the breast implant cases, have declared bankruptcy when faced with billions of dollars in liability claims. See generally Michael D. Green, Bendectin and Birth Defects: The Challenges of Mass Toxic Substances Litigation (1996); Jonathan Van O'Steen, The FDA Defense: Vioxx and the Argument Against Federal Preemption of State Claims for Injuries Resulting from Defective Drugs, 48 Ariz. L. Rev. 67 (2006); Frank M. McClellan, The Vioxx Litigation: A Critical Look at Trial Tactics, the Tort System, and the Roles of Lawyers in Mass Tort Litigation, 57 DePaul L. Rev. 509 (2008).

2. *Medical Devices.* The only example comment *k* cites of unavoidably unsafe products is medical drugs, but its rationale might also apply to medical devices such as pacemakers and various artificial implants. Is there any basis on which to distinguish these two categories of medical products? Most courts conclude "no," and so refuse to apply strict liability to medical devices as well. See Tansy v. Dacomed Corp., 890 P.2d 881 (Okla. 1994) (penile implant that failed due to overuse); Annot., 70 A.L.R.4th 16 (1989). Should the same be true for medical devices available to consumers in stores, such as thermometers, heating pads, and crutches? Are tampons "medical devices"? What about condoms? Where do each of these lie on the line

drawn by one court between products "used to make work easier or to provide pleasure" vs. those "necessary to alleviate pain and suffering" or prevent illness? Brown v. Superior Court, 751 P.2d 470 (Cal. 1988). See O'Gilvie v. International Playtex Inc., 821 F.2d 1438 (10th Cir. 1987) (applying ordinary strict liability to toxic shock syndrome allegedly caused by tampons); Artiglio v. Superior Court, 27 Cal. Rptr. 2d 589 (Ct. App. 1994) (comment *k* covers breast implants despite their use for cosmetic purposes); Hufft v. Horowitz, 5 Cal. Rptr. 2d 377 (Ct. App. 1992) (distinguishing implanted medical devices that, like drugs, are available only from physicians and go inside the body, from ordinary commercial medical products such as wheelchairs).

3. *Litigating Unavoidability. Bruesewitz* resolves what "unavoidably unsafe" means under the childhood vaccine statute, but controversy still rages in state courts, where common-law products liability still prevails. Notice the reference in *Bruesewitz* to two distinct positions: (1) *per se*: all drugs and devices covered by comment *k* are free from design defect claims; (2) *case-by-case*: each case inquires whether the particular drug or device could have been designed more safely without sacrificing any substantial benefit or cost advantage. For a while, the case-by-case rule appeared to be the majority position, but the newer Restatement (Third) of the Law of Torts: Products Liability (1998) leans more heavily in favor of the per se rule. Still, it is not decisive, so debate continues.

4. *Blood Shield Statutes.* The one instance where manufacturers and distributors of medical supplies have avoided strict liability even for *manufacturing* defects is contaminated blood transfusions. Despite careful screening, a certain portion of donated or purchased blood is contaminated with impurities such as hepatitis or AIDS viruses. For a while, courts wrestled with whether blood banks or hospitals that sell defective blood are selling a product or instead only performing a service. See Brody v. Overlook Hospital, 332 A.2d 596 (N.J. 1975) (blood banks not subject to strict liability; reversing contrary decision by lower court). To resolve the legal uncertainty produced by these inconsistent holdings, virtually all states have enacted "blood shield" statutes declaring that blood products are not subject to strict products liability. These statutes often apply as well to human organs and tissues used for transplants. Annot., 75 A.L.R.5th 229 (2000); Annot., 24 A.L.R.4th 508 (1982); Comment, 2 Ind. Health L. Rev. 295 (2005).

Several courts have ruled that these statutes do not cover companies that manufacture drugs from blood products, such as the "clotting factor" that pharmaceutical companies produce to keep hemophiliacs from bleeding. See In re Rhone-Poulenc Rorer, Inc., 51 F.3d 1293 (7th Cir. 1995). Because this manufacturing process requires combining blood from many different donors in order to distill a single batch of clotting factor, virtually all severe hemophiliacs—some 10,000 in all—were infected with the AIDS virus during the early 1980s before adequate screening tests were available. The manufacturers agreed to settle a class action suit for roughly $100,000 for each person infected. See Conk, infra, 109 Yale L.J. 1087 (2000).

5. *Hospital and Physician Liability.* The comment *k* defense applies only to design and warning defects. When drugs and medical devices suffer from manufacturing defects, strict products liability clearly applies, but only to manufacturers and distributors, not to hospitals or doctors, so long as the product is not altered by the provider. Consider, for instance, the needle that broke during surgery in the

Locke v. Pachtman case (page 325). If the needle had broken due to a manufacturing flaw, as opposed to misuse, the hospital and doctor would not have been responsible, even though they were in the chain of distribution. The reason is that, in this context, the needle is seen as merely a supply that is incidental to the sale of a service, and therefore the doctor, not the patient, is the end user. Magrine v. Krasnico, 97 N.J. 228 (1967) (dentist not responsible for broken needle); Note, The Physician as Consumer, 79 Nw. U. L. Rev. 460 (1984); Annot., 100 A.L.R.3d 1205 (1980). The same reasoning does not apply as strongly when considering other medical supplies such as pacemakers and neck braces that are more clearly sold by hospitals as individual products. Most courts, however, find that hospitals generally are not covered by products liability law for defects in their supplies or equipment that are used directly for patient care. See, e.g., Cafazzo v. Central Medical Health Service, Inc., 668 A.2d 521 (Pa. 1995) (neither doctor nor hospital strictly liable for defective prosthesis implanted in patient's jaw). Naturally, hospitals can be held liable for failing to reasonably inspect and maintain equipment and medical devices.

6. *Learned Intermediaries and Direct-to-Consumer Advertising.* Warnings for prescription drugs generally need to be given only to doctors, not to patients. Under tort law's "learned intermediary" rule, it is up to physicians to determine how these warnings should be incorporated into their treatment decisions and which warnings should be passed along to patients. Reyes v. Wyeth Labs, 498 F.2d 1264 (5th Cir. 1974). The learned intermediary rule does not apply to "over-the-counter" drugs purchased directly by consumers, however, and several courts have held it does not apply to mass immunization vaccines or to prescription drugs that are commonly available just for the asking, without any particular medical problem. The classic instance of the latter is the birth control pill. In these situations, manufacturers can be sued for failures to warn consumers directly. See Davis v. Wyeth Labs, 399 F.2d 121 (9th Cir. 1968) (polio); MacDonald v. Ortho Pharmaceutical Corp., 475 N.E.2d 65 (Mass. 1985) (birth control pills).

Increasingly, drug companies are advertising directly to the public a wide range of pharmaceuticals for common maladies, encouraging people to ask their doctor to prescribe drugs for seasonal allergies, baldness, and heartburn, for instance. This is partly in response to restrictions imposed by managed care insurers. Symposium, 346 New Eng. J. Med. 523 (2002). One influential court has held, with respect to birth control implants, that advertising directly to consumers precludes application of the learned intermediary rule. Perez v. Wyeth Laboratories, 734 A.2d 1245 (N.J. 1999). In a potentially groundbreaking decision, the West Virginia Supreme Court went much further, holding that the learned intermediary doctrine no longer applies generally, due to the pharmaceutical industry's widespread use of direct-to-consumer advertising. State v. Karl, 647 S.E.2d 899 (W. Va. 2007). Criticizing this decision, see Note, 48 Jurimetrics J. 285 (2008).

7. *Package Inserts and "Off-Label" Use.* Where the learned intermediary rule applies, patients can still sue drug manufacturers for inadequate warnings to their physicians, and naturally patients can also sue their physicians who ignore drug risks or fail to warn them personally. These suits against physicians are brought as standard negligent practice or breach of informed consent actions, however. In such actions, the FDA's required warning to physicians, known as the "package insert," becomes one possible source of evidence against the physician. The instructions on

package inserts do not strictly bind physicians; FDA law allows them to use approved drugs in any fashion they want, even if the particular use is not approved (so-called off-label use). This is particularly common, for instance, in cancer treatment and, to a lesser extent, AIDS treatment. Nevertheless, as discussed above at page 392, most courts have held that plaintiffs may introduce package inserts directly into evidence on the standard of care as an exception to the hearsay rule, and a few have held that package inserts create a rebuttable, prima facie case for liability when the defendant doctor deviates from the instructions, shifting the burden of proof to the doctor to show that the departure was accepted practice. See Hyman & Armstrong, P.S.C. v. Gunderson, 279 S.W.3d 93 (Ky. 2008) (package insert admissible but not conclusive of standard of care); Cuc Thi Ngo v. Queen's Med. Ctr., 358 P.3d 26 (Hawaii 2015) (same); Garvey v. O'Donoghue, 530 A.2d 1141 (D.C. App. 1987) (package insert is prima facie evidence of standard of care); Note, 51 Stan. L. Rev. 1343 (1999). If physicians intentionally and nonnegligently use a drug for purposes other than those approved by the FDA, or in a manner that contradicts the manufacturer's warnings, does this absolve the manufacturer from products liability? See K. Stoffelmayr, Products Liability and "Off-Label" Uses of Prescription Drugs, 63 U. Chi. L. Rev. 275 (1996) (finding that the cases split into five different lines, from no liability, to liability if off-label use is widespread, to full liability).

8. *"Detail Men."* The FDA requires pharmaceutical manufacturers to continue monitoring adverse reactions to their products even after approval, and to change or intensify warnings if different or greater risks materialize. As described in Sterling Drug, Inc. v. Yarrow, 408 F.2d 978 (8th Cir. 1969), this information is collected and these after-market warnings are distributed through pharmaceutical "detail men" who permeate hospitals and doctors' offices trying to encourage doctors to use their products. The court upheld a jury verdict finding a manufacturer liable for failing to use this means of communication where, one year prior to the plaintiff's starting treatment with the drug, medical publications began to report an association between the drug and certain serious side effects:

> Appellant usually communicates its product information to physicians prescribing its products: (1) by "detail men," who are specially trained field representatives engaged in selling and promoting the use of its products by personal calls in which oral presentations are made and literature and samples delivered, (2) by listings of drugs in an annually published advertising medium known as Physicians' Desk Reference, (3) by "product cards" which are mailed and distributed by detail men to physicians and are available at medical conventions and hospital exhibits, and (4) by special letters mailed to physicians. . . . Nevertheless, the detail men who made regular personal calls on prescribing physicians and customers were never, in the relevant period, instructed to invite attention of the physicians and customers to the reported dangers. . . . The warnings of side effects . . . were limited to the product cards, the Physicians' Desk Reference and to the "Dear Doctor" letter dated February 1963 . . . [that were sent] to all [248,000] physicians and hospital personnel in the United States. . . .
>
> The direct and circumstantial evidence amply supports a finding that . . . Dr. Olson (and other general practitioners) receive so much literature on drugs that it is impossible to read all of it; that Dr. Olson relied on detail men, medical conventions, medical journals and conversations with other doctors for information

on drugs he was prescribing; that Dr. Olson was inundated with literature and product cards of various manufacturers; that a change in literature and an additional letter were insufficient to present new information to Dr. Olson; that detail men visit physicians at frequent intervals and could give an effective warning which would affirmatively notify the doctor of the dangerous side effects of chloroquine phosphate on the retina. These findings of fact were not clearly erroneous. . . .

This does not mean that every physician in the United States must have been given an immediate warning by a personal messenger. But it does mean that the trial court was justified in finding that it was unreasonable to fail to instruct the detail men, at least, to warn the physicians on whom they regularly called of the dangers of which appellant had learned, or in the exercise of reasonable care should have known. . . . [Moreover], the "Dear Doctor" letter could have been reasonably found to be lacking in emphasis, timeliness and attention inviting qualities. A reasoning mind could find that appellant's warning actions were unduly delayed, reluctant and lacking in a sense of urgency.

Drug company "detail men" can also be a source of liability when they minimize the significance of official warnings in their eagerness to sell their product. See, e.g., Incollingo v. Ewing, 282 A.2d 206 (Pa. 1971) (official warning ineffective where detail men emphasized antibiotic's effectiveness and wide acceptance while downplaying known side effects). For additional discussion, see the incredible saga of the 15-year litigation (two trials and three state supreme court decisions) in Feldman v. Lederle Labs, 625 A.2d 1066 (N.J. 1993), concerning the failure to warn that a common antibiotic can cause teeth to turn gray.

9. *Computerized Medicine.* The computerization of medicine creates novel opportunities for design defect and related theories of products liability. Physicians and nurses increasingly are using software programs that prescribe or recommend diagnostic and treatment decisions, for instance, by analyzing lists of symptoms and assigning probabilities to alternative diagnoses. If these computer algorithms are found to contain an error, perhaps the designer, seller, or hospital purchaser can be found liable. Related issues arise from medical information or advice given on Web sites that are proliferating rapidly. For discussion and analysis, see B. H. Lamkin, Medical Expert Systems and Publisher Liability: A Cross-Contextual Analysis, 43 Emory L.J. 731 (1994); Nicolas P. Terry, Cyber-Malpractice: Legal Exposure for Cybermedicine, 25 Am. J.L. Med. 327 (1999); S. Mangalmurti et al., Medical Malpractice in the Age of Electronic Health Records, 363 New Eng. J. Med. 2060 (2010); Nadia Sawicki, Patient Protection and Decision-Aid Quality: Regulatory and Tort Law Approaches, 54 Ariz. L. Rev. 621 (2012).

10. *Federal Preemption.* Displacement of state tort law might also result from FDA regulation. The FDA imposes extensive testing requirements for safety and effectiveness before prescription drugs and potentially dangerous medical devices can be marketed. After approval, the FDA also extensively regulates the labeling instructions and warnings that manufacturers must give doctors. Is there any basis in public policy for holding manufacturers liable for design defects or warning deficiencies that the FDA finds acceptable? Consider the discussion in Chapter 2.C.3 of the FDA approval process, which notes that the FDA relies primarily on information supplied by and tests commissioned by the pharmaceutical manufacturers themselves, rather than the FDA conducting its own investigations.

FDA regulation might absolve manufacturers of liability in one of two ways. First, regulatory compliance might act as a substantive defense to liability under state tort law by demonstrating actual reasonableness or nondefectiveness. Second, federal law might be found to preempt state tort liability. There are different responses to these two arguments. For the substantive defense, state courts usually allow regulatory compliance only as evidence, but not as conclusive proof, of reasonable care. A few states by statute declare that regulatory compliance creates a rebuttable presumption of nonliability or protects manufacturers from punitive damages. See Garcia v. Wyeth-Ayerst Labs., 385 F.3d 961 (6th Cir. 2004); Note, 84 N.C. L. Rev. 737 (2006).

As for federal preemption, courts' positions are complex, differing between drugs and devices and between different types of claimed defects. For drugs, most cases find no federal preemption because the federal statute overrides state law only where "there is a direct and positive conflict." Such a conflict might be found with respect to warnings of risk if the FDA labeling requirements were exclusive, that is, if the FDA were to preclude any additional warnings than those it imposes. See Pliva, Inc. v. Mensing, 131 S. Ct. 1672 (2011) (state law preempted for labeling of *generic* drugs because generic manufacturers must use the same labels as those approved for brand name equivalents). But, for non-generic drugs, the FDA has been unclear about whether its labeling requirements can be varied by manufacturers or whether its labeling rules preempt state tort law. Given this uncertainty, the Court held in Wyeth v. Levine, 555 U.S. 555 (2009), that FDA oversight does not preempt a suit claiming inadequate warning for a drug administered by injection. Nevertheless, manufacturers remain reluctant to depart from the FDA script. Could that be because doing so might itself expose them to suit? How so?

For medical devices, the preemptive effect of federal regulation is equally complex. The Food, Drug and Cosmetics Act appears to expressly preempt state law in §360k(a), which declares that states may not impose any "requirement which is different from or in addition to" those imposed by the FDA. Based on this, a number of circuit courts found products liability actions preempted, but others did not. The Supreme Court ruled 5-4 that no preemption occurs for medical devices that receive only cursory FDA review. Medtronic Inc. v. Lohr, 518 U.S. 470 (1996). The precise reasoning is obscure due to fractured voting, but preemption still does hold for devices that receive more thorough pre-market review by the FDA. E.g., Riegel v. Medtronic, 552 U.S. 312 (2008) (suit preempted regarding balloon catheter that burst during surgery). Also, claims that device manufacturers were not honest with the FDA in obtaining approval are preempted. Buckman Co. v. Plaintiffs' Legal Committee, 531 U.S. 341 (2001).

11. *Further Reading.* On **design defects** (note 3), see George W. Conk, Is There a Design Defect in the Restatement (Third) of Torts: Products Liability?, 109 Yale L.J. 1087 (2000); James A. Henderson & Aaron D. Twerski, Drug Designs Are Different, 111 Yale L.J. 151 (2001); Symposium, 30 Seton Hall L. Rev. 202 (1999).

On **direct-to-consumer advertising** (note 6), see Richard C. Ausness, Will More Aggressive Marketing Practices Lead to Greater Tort Liability for Prescription Drug Manufacturers?, 37 Wake Forest L. Rev. 97 (2002); Jack Karns, Direct Advertising of Prescription Drugs: The Duty to Warn and the Learned Intermediary Rule, 3 DePaul J. Health Care L. 273 (2000); Note, 51 Stan. L. Rev. 1343 (1999).

On federal preemption (note 10), see Symposium, 32 Hamline L. Rev. 657 (2009); Richard Epstein, What Tort Theory Tells Us About Federal Preemption: The Tragic Saga of Wyeth v. Levine, 65 N.Y.U. Ann. Surv. Am. L. 485 (2010); Catherine M. Sharkey, What *Riegel* Portends for FDA Preemption of State Law Products Liability Claims, 103 Nw. U. L. Rev. 437 (2009); Mary J. Davis, The Battle over Implied Preemption: Products Liability and the FDA, 48 B.C. L. Rev. 1089 (2007); William Dreier, Liability for Drug Advertising, Warnings, and Frauds, 58 Rutgers L. Rev. 615 (2006); Richard Ausness, Should the Courts Defer to the FDA's New Interpretation of the Medical Device Amendments?, 80 Tul. L. Rev. 727 (2006); Note, Cardozo L. Rev. 38 (2005); Annot., 98 A.L.R. Fed. 124 (1990).

Review Questions: Products Liability

Under the majority rule, what is the potential liability of the manufacturer (Mfg.) and the physician (Dr.) or hospital in each of the following situations? What attitudes of public policy support liability or nonliability in each situation?

1. Dr. implants a pacemaker. Before doing so, he fails to ascertain that it is operational. It turns out to be a dud.
2. With FDA approval, Mfg. markets a new, powerful chemotherapy drug for kidney cancer. The package insert warns that it is not intended for use in any other cancer. Dr. decides to use the drug for pancreatic cancer, which, using standard treatment, currently has an extremely dim prognosis (10 percent chance of survival). The drug's toxic effects kill the cancer patient. Dr. obtains only generic, routine informed consent ("We'll be treating you with various chemical agents that have a significant risk of toxic side effects, including death"), but does not say anything about using a new drug intended for a different purpose.
3. Korkafine is a widely used and recommended over-the-counter drug for hay-fever-type allergies. Mfg. widely advertises it both to the public under the brand name Snuffle, and also directly to physicians, since many people consult physicians about their allergies. After five years on the market, it was discovered that, when korkafine is taken in conjunction with okra (a southern vegetable), a bizarre chemical reaction occasionally happens that causes mild hair loss. After some deliberation, the FDA allows the drug to remain on the market as long as Mfg. adds the okra warning to others on the package and in any written promotional materials. Three years later, suit is brought against Mfg. by a rapidly balding Southerner who, with his Dr.'s knowledge, decided to use Snuffle every spring and fall during pollen season.

E. CAUSATION AND AFFIRMATIVE DEFENSES

Having surveyed numerous theories that can be used to establish a physician's breach of duty, we now turn to other elements of the basic medical malpractice cause of action: causation, affirmative defenses, and damages.

1. Causation

■ HERSKOVITS v. GROUP HEALTH COOPERATIVE OF PUGET SOUND
664 P.2d 474 (Wash. 1983)

DORE, Justice.

. . . The personal representative of Leslie Herskovits' estate initiated this survivorship action against Group Health Cooperative of Puget Sound (Group Health), alleging failure to make an early diagnosis of her husband's lung cancer. Group Health moved for summary judgment for dismissal on the basis that Herskovits probably would have died from lung cancer even if the diagnosis had been made earlier, which the trial court granted.

The complaint alleged that Herskovits came to Group Health Hospital in 1974 with complaints of pain and coughing. . . . Plaintiff contends that Herskovits was treated thereafter only with cough medicine. . . . In the early spring of 1975, Mr. and Mrs. Herskovits went south in the hope that the warm weather would help. Upon his return to the Seattle area with no improvement in his health, Herskovits visited Dr. Jonathan Ostrow on a private basis for another medical opinion. Within three weeks, Dr. Ostrow's evaluation and direction to Group Health led to the diagnosis of cancer. In July of 1975, Herskovits' lung was removed, but no radiation or chemotherapy treatments were instituted. Herskovits died 20 months later, on March 22, 1977, at the age of 60.

At hearing on the motion for summary judgment, plaintiff was unable to produce expert testimony that the delay in diagnosis "probably" or "more likely than not" caused her husband's death. . . . Dr. Ostrow testified that if the tumor was a "stage 1" tumor in December 1974, Herskovits' chance of a five-year survival would have been 39 percent. In June 1975, his chances of survival were 25 percent assuming the tumor had progressed to "stage 2". Thus, the delay in diagnosis may have reduced the chance of a five-year survival by 14 percent. . . . It is Group Health's contention that plaintiff must prove that Herskovits "probably" would have survived had the defendant not been allegedly negligent; that is, the plaintiff must prove there was at least a 51 percent chance of survival. . . .

This court has held that a person who negligently renders aid and consequently increases the risk of harm to those he is trying to assist is liable for any physical damages he causes. Restatement (Second) of Torts §323. . . . This court heretofore has not faced the issue of whether, under §323(a), proof that the defendant's conduct increased the risk of death by decreasing the chances of survival is sufficient to take the issue of proximate cause to the jury. Some courts in other jurisdictions have allowed the proximate cause issue to go to the jury on this type of proof. These courts emphasized the fact that defendants' conduct deprived the decedents of a "significant" chance to survive or recover, rather than requiring proof that with absolute certainty the defendants' conduct caused the physical injury. The underlying reason is that it is not for the wrongdoer, who put the possibility of recovery beyond realization, to say afterward that the result was inevitable.

Other jurisdictions have rejected this approach, generally holding that unless the plaintiff is able to show that it was more likely than not that the harm was caused by the defendant's negligence, proof of a decreased chance of survival is not enough to take the proximate cause question to the jury. These courts have concluded that the defendant should not be liable where the decedent more than likely would have died anyway. . . .

III

We are persuaded by the reasoning of the Pennsylvania Supreme Court in *Hamil v. Bashline*, 392 A.2d 1280 (Pa. 1978). While *Hamil* involved an original survival chance of greater than 50 percent, we find the rationale used by the *Hamil* court to apply equally to cases such as the present one, where the original survival chance is less than 50 percent. The plaintiff's decedent was suffering from severe chest pains. His wife transported him to the hospital where he was negligently treated in the emergency unit. The wife, because of the lack of help, took her husband to a private physician's office, where he died. In an action brought under the wrongful death and survivorship statutes, the main medical witness testified that if the hospital had employed proper treatment, the decedent would have had a substantial chance of surviving the attack. The medical expert expressed his opinion in terms of a 75 percent chance of survival. . . .

The *Hamil* court distinguished the facts of that case from the general tort case in which a plaintiff alleges that a defendant's act or omission set in motion a force which resulted in harm. In the typical tort case, the "but for" test, requiring proof that damages or death probably would not have occurred "but for" the negligent conduct of the defendant, is appropriate. In *Hamil* and the instant case, however, the defendant's act or omission failed in a duty to protect against harm from another source. Thus, as the *Hamil* court noted, the factfinder is put in the position of having to consider not only what did occur, but also what might have occurred. "Such cases by their very nature elude the degree of certainty one would prefer and upon which the law normally insists before a person may be held liable." . . . The *Hamil* court held that once a plaintiff has demonstrated that the defendant's acts or omissions have increased the risk of harm to another, such evidence furnishes a basis for the jury to make a determination as to whether such increased risk was in turn a substantial factor in bringing about the resultant harm.

. . . The following quotation from *Hicks v. United States*, 368 F.2d 626, 632 (4th Cir. 1966), is frequently cited in cases adopting loss of a chance because it succinctly defines the doctrine:

> Rarely is it possible to demonstrate to an absolute certainty what would have happened in circumstances that the wrongdoer did not allow to come to pass. The law does not in the existing circumstances require the plaintiff to show to a certainty that the patient would have lived had she been hospitalized and operated on promptly. . . .

The recent case of *James v. United States*, 483 F. Supp. 581 (N.D. Cal. 1980), concerned the failure to diagnose and promptly treat a lung tumor. The court concluded that the plaintiff sustained its burden of proof even without statistical evidence, stating:

As a proximate result of defendant's negligence, James was deprived of the opportunity to receive early treatment and the chance of realizing any resulting gain in his life expectancy and physical and mental comfort. *No matter how small that chance may have been*—and its magnitude cannot be ascertained—no one can say that the chance of prolonging one's life or decreasing suffering is valueless.

. . . We hold that medical testimony of a reduction of chance of survival from 39 percent to 25 percent is sufficient evidence to allow the proximate cause issue to go to the jury. . . . To decide otherwise would be a blanket release from liability for doctors and hospitals any time there was less than a 50 percent chance of survival, regardless of how flagrant the negligence. . . . We reverse the trial court and reinstate the cause of action.

PEARSON, Justice (concurring).

. . . In medical malpractice cases such as the one before us, cause in fact must usually be established by expert medical testimony, and must be established beyond the balance of probabilities. In a case such as this, medical testimony must be relied upon to establish the causal relationship between the liability-producing situation and the claimed physical disability resulting therefrom. The evidence will be deemed insufficient to support the jury's verdict, if it can be said that considering the whole of the medical testimony the jury must resort to speculation or conjecture in determining such causal relationship. In many recent decisions of this court we have held that such determination is deemed based on speculation and conjecture if the medical testimony does not go beyond the expression of an opinion that the physical disability "might have" or "possibly did" result from the hypothesized cause. To remove the issue from the realm of speculation, the medical testimony must at least be sufficiently definite to establish that the act complained of "probably" or "more likely than not" caused the subsequent disability.

The issue before the court, quite simply, is whether Dr. Ostrow's testimony satisfies th[is] standard. . . . In order to make this determination, we must first define the "subsequent disability" suffered by Mr. Herskovits. Therein lies the crux of this case. . . .

If the injury is determined to be the death of Mr. Herskovits, then under the established principles of proximate cause plaintiff has failed to make a prima facie case. Dr. Ostrow was unable to state that probably, or more likely than not, Mr. Herskovits' death was caused by defendant's negligence. On the contrary, it is clear from Dr. Ostrow's testimony that Mr. Herskovits would have probably died from cancer even with the exercise of reasonable care by defendant. . . .

If, on the other hand, we view the injury to be the reduction of Mr. Herskovits' chance of survival, our analysis might well be different. Dr. Ostrow testified that the failure to diagnose cancer in December 1974 probably caused a substantial reduction in Mr. Herskovits' chance of survival. The . . . standard of proof is therefore met.

I note here that two other problems are created by the latter analysis. First, we have never before considered whether the loss or reduction of a chance of survival is a compensable injury. And second, this analysis raises the issue of whether an action for reduction of the chance of survival can be brought under the wrongful death statute. Confronted with these problems, . . . I turn to consider how other jurisdictions have dealt with similar cases. . . .

Having concluded this somewhat detailed survey of the cases cited by plaintiff, what conclusions can we draw? First, the critical element in each of the cases is that the defendant's negligence either deprived a decedent of a chance of surviving a potentially fatal condition or reduced that chance. To summarize, in Hicks v. United States the decedent was deprived of a probability of survival; in Jeanes v. Milner the decedent's chance of survival was reduced from 35 percent to 24 percent; in O'Brien v. Stover, the decedent's 30 percent chance of survival was reduced by an indeterminate amount; in McBride v. United States the decedent was deprived of the probability of survival; in Kallenberg v. Beth Israel Hospital the decedent was deprived of a 20 percent to 40 percent chance of survival; in Hamil v. Bashline the decedent was deprived of a 75 percent chance of survival; and in James v. United States the decedent was deprived of an indeterminate chance of survival, no matter how small.

The three cases where the chance of survival was greater than 50 percent (*Hicks, McBride,* and *Hamil*) are unexceptional in that they focus on the death of the decedent as the injury, and they require proximate cause to be shown beyond the balance of probabilities. Such a result is consistent with existing principles in this state, and with cases from other jurisdictions cited by defendant. The remaining four cases allowed recovery despite the plaintiffs' failure to prove a probability of survival. . . . I am convinced that these cases reflect a trend to the most rational, least arbitrary, rule by which to regulate cases of this kind. I am persuaded to this conclusion not so much by the reasoning of these cases themselves, but by the thoughtful discussion of a recent commentator. King, Causation, Valuation, and Chance in Personal Injury Torts Involving Preexisting Conditions and Future Consequences, 90 Yale L.J. 1353 (1981).

King's basic thesis is explained in the following passage, which is particularly pertinent to the case before us:

> . . . A plaintiff ordinarily should be required to prove by the applicable standard of proof that the defendant caused the loss in question. What caused a loss, however, should be a separate question from what the nature and extent of the loss are. This distinction seems to have eluded the courts, with the result that lost chances in many respects are compensated either as certainties or not at all. . . . A more rational approach, however, would allow recovery for the loss of the chance of cure even though the chance was not better than even. The probability of long-term survival would be reflected in the amount of damages awarded for the loss of the chance. . . .

Under the all or nothing approach, typified by Cooper v. Sisters of Charity of Cincinnati, Inc., 27 Ohio St. 2d 242, 272 N.E.2d 97 (1971), a plaintiff who establishes that but for the defendant's negligence the decedent had a 51 percent chance of survival may maintain an action for that death. The defendant will be liable for all damages arising from the death, even though there was a 49 percent chance it would have occurred despite his negligence. On the other hand, a plaintiff who establishes that but for the defendant's negligence the decedent had a 49 percent chance of survival recovers nothing. . . .

These reasons persuade me that the best resolution of the issue before us is to recognize the loss of a less than even chance as an actionable injury. Therefore, I would hold that plaintiff has established a prima facie issue of proximate cause by producing testimony that defendant probably caused a substantial reduction in Mr. Herskovits' chance of survival.

The decedent's personal action for loss of this chance will survive to his personal representatives. The family of the decedent should also be allowed to maintain an action for the lost chance of recovery by the decedent. I would interpret the wrongful death statute to apply to cases of this type. Under this interpretation, a person will "cause" the death of another person whenever he causes a substantial reduction in that person's chance of survival.

Finally, it is necessary to consider the amount of damages recoverable in the event that a loss of a chance of recovery is established. Once again, King's discussion provides a useful illustration of the principles which should be applied:

> To illustrate, consider a patient who suffers a heart attack and dies as a result. Assume that the defendant-physician negligently misdiagnosed the patient's condition, but that the patient would have had only a 40 percent chance of survival even with a timely diagnosis and proper care. Regardless of whether it could be said that the defendant caused the decedent's death, he caused the loss of a chance, and that chance-interest should be completely redressed in its own right. Under the proposed rule, the plaintiff's compensation for the loss of the victim's chance of surviving the heart attack would be 40 percent of the compensable value of the victim's life had he survived (including what his earning capacity would otherwise have been in the years following death). The value placed on the patient's life would reflect such factors as his age, health, and earning potential, including the fact that he had suffered the heart attack and the assumption that he had survived it. The 40 percent computation would be applied to that base figure. . . .

BRACHTENBACH, Justice (dissenting).

. . . Malpractice suits represent a class of controversies where extreme caution should be exercised in relaxing causation requirements. The physician serves a vital function in our society, a function which requires the assumption of a duty to the patient. Yet, his profession affords him only an inexact and often experimental science by which to discharge his duty. Moreover, the tendency to place blame on a physician who fails to find a cure is great. Thus, policy considerations do not, on balance, weigh in favor of abandoning the well-established requirements of proximate cause.[13]

. . . Usually the substantial factor test has been applied only in situations where there are two causes, either of which could have caused the event alone, and it cannot be determined which was the actual cause. For example, A and B both start separate fires which combine to burn C's house. Either fire alone would have caused the same result, but C cannot prove that "but-for" the negligence of either A or B the house would not have burned. Therefore, to prevent both A and B being relieved

---

13. There is also a difference between the standard of proof for proximate cause to show liability and the standard of proof to show the amount of damages after liability is established. Courts are willing to relax proof requirements on the issue of damages, once liability is shown. Therefore, statistical data may be of greater value at the damage stage, especially with regard to future damages that are necessarily subject to some uncertainties and contingencies.

of liability, the "but-for" test is abandoned, and the question becomes whether the conduct of A or B was a substantial factor in causing the fire that injured C. Under this test, either A or B could be held liable for the damage. Except in situations where there are coequal causes, however, defendant's act cannot be a substantial factor when the event would have occurred without it. . . .

Thus, I would not resolve the instant case simply by focusing on the 14 percent differentiation in the chance to survive five years for the different stages of cancer. Instead, I would accept this as an admissible fact, but not as proof of proximate cause. To meet the proximate cause burden, the record would need to reveal other facts about the patient that tended to show that he would have been a member of the 14 percent group whose chance of five years' survival could be increased by early diagnosis. . . .

Other statistics admitted into evidence also tend to show the inconclusiveness of the statistics relied on by the majority. One study showed the two-year survival rate for this type of cancer to be 46.6 percent for stage one and 39.8 percent for stage two. Mr. Herskovits lived for 20 months after surgery, which was 26 months after defendant allegedly should have discovered the cancer. Therefore, regardless of the stage of the cancer at the time Mr. Herskovits was examined by defendant, it cannot be concluded that he survived significantly less than the average survival time. Hence, it is pure speculation to suppose that the doctor's negligence "caused" Mr. Herskovits to die sooner than he would have otherwise. . . .

Cases alleging misdiagnosis of cancer are increasing in number, perhaps because of the increased awareness of the importance of early detection. These cases, however, illustrate no more than an inconsistency among courts in their treatment of the problems of proof. See Annot., Malpractice in Connection with Diagnosis of Cancer, 79 A.L.R.3d 915 (1977). Perhaps as medical science becomes more knowledgeable about this disease and more sophisticated in its detection and treatment of it, the balance may tip in favor of imposing liability on doctors who negligently fail to promptly diagnose the disease. But, until a formula is found that will protect doctors against liability imposed through speculation as well as afford truly aggrieved plaintiffs their just compensation, I cannot favor the wholesale abandonment of the principle of proximate cause. For these reasons, I dissent.

Notes: Causation and Loss of Chance

1. *Life Is Complicated.* Unlike conventional personal injury litigation where the victim first encounters the defendant in a generally healthy condition, malpractice plaintiffs usually start out sick. Moreover, the injury is more often failure to improve rather than a more garden-variety bodily injury. These factors, coupled with the complexities of human biology, result in causation issues demanding as much or more of a lawyer's time and attention as do issues regarding standard of care.

2. *The Traditional Test.* Under the traditional "more likely than not test," plaintiffs sometimes lose on summary judgment or have their verdicts overturned because the expert testimony is expressed in terms of "reasonable possibility" rather than "probability." A few courts have gone further, however, and required expert testimony of a "reasonable medical certainty." See, e.g., Steineke v. Share Health Plan of Nebraska, 518 N.W.2d 904 (Neb. 1994). One court insisted:

The issue is not merely one of semantics. There is a logical reason for the rule [requiring "reasonable medical certainty"]. For a factfinder to award damages for a particular condition to a plaintiff, he must find as a fact that the condition was legally caused by the defendant's conduct. Here, the only evidence offered was that it was "probably caused," and that is not enough. Perhaps in the world of medicine nothing is absolutely certain. Nevertheless, doctors must make decisions in their own profession every day based on their own expert opinions. Physicians must understand that it is the intent of our law that if the plaintiff's medical expert cannot form an opinion with sufficient certainty so as to make a medical judgment, there is nothing on the record with which a jury can make a decision with sufficient certainty so as to make a legal judgment.

McMahon v. Young, 276 A.2d 534 (Pa. 1971). Going in the other direction, one court allowed a physician to testify that a radiologic dye caused an injury despite the long statistical odds against this happening, based on the expert's "differential diagnosis" that concluded that other possible causes were not present, so the dye was the most likely cause. Marcum v. Adventist System/West, 193 P.3d 1 (2008). See generally Jeff Lewin, The Genesis and Evolution of Legal Uncertainty About "Reasonable Medical Certainty," 57 Md. L. Rev. 380 (1998).

3. *The Concurrence.* Oddly, Justice Pearson's concurring opinion is actually the plurality opinion since it garnered four votes, in contrast with the two votes for Justice Dore. The dissent had three. Subsequently, the Washington Supreme Court endorsed the plurality's opinion, and extended the rule to cover cases where a patient is disabled but does not die. Mohr v. Grantham, 262 P.3d 490 (Wash. 2011). What is the difference between Justice Pearson's and Justice Dore's conception of the loss-of-chance theory? Does this conceptual debate make any practical difference in the fact patterns that are actionable, the case's procedural posture, or the measure of damages? The concurrence specifies the measure of damages rather clearly (or does it)? How should damages be measured under the main opinion?

Most courts agree that full damages should not be awarded under a loss-of-chance theory, but rather should be discounted by the portion of chance that was lost. What is the correct portion in *Herskovits*, however: 39 percent, 25 percent, or 14 percent? Some courts might reason that he lost all, not just a portion, of his preexisting 39 percent since he in fact died. Even if this is not correct in theory, in practice it may be difficult to know the precise chance of survival that results *after* the mistake (i.e., in this case, the 25 percent). Absent this evidence, do damages become too speculative to award? Note the comment in note 13 of the dissent. For thoughtful analysis generally, see Lars Noah, An Inventory of Mathematical Blunders in Applying the Loss-of-a-Chance Doctrine, 70 Mo. L. Rev. (2005); Robert Rhee, Loss of Chance, Probabilistic Cause, and Damage Calculations, 1 Suffolk U. L. Rev. 39 (2013).

Why should damages be discounted only if the chance of survival was less than 50 percent? Aren't full damages at 51 percent but half damages at 49 percent just as arbitrary as the causation/no-causation line the plurality complains of? Despite this concern, there has been no movement to reduce full damages under ordinary but-for causation.

4. *Wrongful Death Actions.* Another complication, noted by the concurrence, is whether the loss-of-chance theory applies under wrongful death statutes, in contrast

with the patient's own survival action. Consider, again, whether it matters which theory of loss of chance one adopts, the majority or concurrence. These statutes vary in their precise wording and the precise theory of damages, so predictably courts reach different results. For a contrasting view, see Kramer v. Lewisville Memorial Hospital, 858 S.W.2d 397 (Tex. 1993).

5. *Causation vs. Breach of Duty.* Observe that loss of chance is not, strictly speaking, a theory of liability. It is a theory of causation or injury. Breach of duty must still be positively demonstrated under the normal "more likely than not" standard. Thus, testimony that if a procedure or test had been done the patient's chances would have improved does not suffice to establish that the treatment is required by the standard of care.

6. *Fear of Death or Disease.* Following the argument in the *Herskovits* concurrence, can a loss-of-chance theory be applied even if the loss has not yet occurred? Most courts have not yet taken loss of chance this far. In Fabio v. Bellomo, 504 N.W.2d 758 (Minn. 1993), the court held that a delayed diagnosis of cancer was not actionable where chemotherapy successfully brought the cancer into remission, even though the patient might prove that the delay shortened her life expectancy by increasing the odds that cancer would recur. The obstacle in such actions is that the loss complained of—shortened life—has not yet happened, but query whether there has not been some loss of the "chance interest" described in the *Herskovits* concurrence. Following that logic, the same court that decided *Fabio* subsequently allowed a loss-of-chance theory (over a vigorous dissent) in a case where delay in cancer diagnosis reduced the patient's chance of survival from 60 to 40 percent, but the patient remained in remission at the time of suit. Dickhoff v. Green, 836 N.W.2d 321 (Minn. 2013). But such cases remain rare.

Contrast this mistake-without-injury scenario with cases where there is some actual, present medical injury. Then, plaintiffs may recover for the possibility that the harms may get worse in the future. For instance, Fein v. Permanente Medical Group, excerpted at page 462, allowed recovery for the economic costs from a shortened life expectancy and increased risk of disease caused by the misdiagnosis of a heart attack that left the patient in a weakened condition. These elements of damage do not require any unique theory of liability since actual injury is already established and the only issue is its full extent. Also, where there is present injury, it may be possible to recover as an element of damages the emotional distress over worrying about future death or disease.

It may be possible to avoid showing present injury if the only damages being sought are economic, for the costs of monitoring future health problems caused by increased risk of disease. See, e.g., Sutton v. St. Jude Medical S.C., Inc., 419 F.3d 568 (6th Cir. 2005) (recognizing a right to recover for increased risk of future harm when a possibly defective implanted medical device required medical monitoring). These "medical monitoring" theories have been tested in a number of lawsuits, usually involving toxic exposures rather than medical errors. Victor E. Schwartz et al., Medical Monitoring: Should Tort Law Say Yes?, 34 Wake Forest L. Rev. 1057 (1999); Symposium, 88 Va. L. Rev. 1921 (2002); Comment, 32 Wm. Mitchell L. Rev. 1095 (2006).

Recovery is not as readily available, however, where the *only* injury is *emotional.* In such cases, another body of precedent addresses whether tort actions can be maintained for negligent infliction of a purely emotional injury. Traditionally this was not actionable except in specialized cases such as the mishandling of a corpse. In recent decades, however, courts have liberalized this theory of action, but in a highly complex and contradictory fashion that is impossible to summarize here. See Andrew R. Klein, Fear of Disease and the Puzzle of Futures Cases in Tort, 35 U.C. Davis L. Rev. 965 (2002). In general, courts require that the distress be especially severe and that some special relationship or characteristic exist that limits the range of potential claimants. In the medical context, the doctor-patient relationship and the act of medical treatment can easily satisfy the special relationship requirement. The severe distress element has been found to be satisfied in two notable medical situations: fear of cancer and fear of AIDS. A few cases have ruled that doctors or institutions can be sued when their negligence reasonably causes patients to fear they have a dread disease, even if the evidence fails to establish that negligence worsened their prospects. Hedgepeth v. Whitman Walker Clinic, 22 A.2d 789 (D.C. Cir. 2011) (en banc); Roes v. FHP, Inc., 985 P.2d 661 (Haw. 1999); 50 A.L.R.4th 12 (1986). See S. Lochlann Jain, Fear of Cancer, 44 Loy. L.A. L. Rev. 233 (2010).

Fear of AIDS exposure has produced considerable litigation. The typical scenario involves a patient who discovers after surgery that her doctor carried the AIDS virus (HIV) and the patient then suffers a period of great distress until receiving a series of conclusive negative HIV tests. Courts are divided on whether these claims are actionable (usually stated as informed consent actions), with disputes centering on whether the fear is reasonable in light of the extent of actual exposure during treatment. Another version of AIDS phobia involves a false positive HIV test result such that, for a period of time, the patient falsely thinks he has AIDS. With certain limitations, courts have allowed these versions of negligent infliction of distress actions as well. See Chizmar v. Mackie, 896 P.2d 196 (Alaska 1995) (actionable despite no physical injury); R.J. v. Humana of Florida, 652 So. 2d 360 (Fla. 1995) (actionable if some physical harm can be shown from unnecessary treatment).

7. *Other States.* Most jurisdictions to consider the issue have accepted some form of the loss-of-chance doctrine. For a particularly thorough review of decisions and theories, see Delaney v. Cade, 873 P.2d 175 (Kan. 1994). One loss-of-chance case allowed this theory to go to the jury even though the deceased patient had only a 10 percent chance of survival, at best. Wendland v. Sparks, 574 N.W.2d 327 (Iowa 1998). For an example of a contrary decision, see Williams v. Spring Hill Memorial Hospital, 646 So. 2d 1373 (Ala. 1994). A compromise position is to allow recovery for an increased risk of harm, but only if there is "reasonable medical certainty" that the defendant's negligence caused the increased risk. Holton v. Memorial Hospital, 679 N.E.2d 1202 (Ill. 1997). A full collection of decisions is contained in Annot., 54 A.L.R.4th 10 (1987). For recent commentary, see Todd Aagaard, Note, Identifying and Valuing the Injury in Lost Chance Cases, 96 Mich. L. Rev. 1335 (1998); David A. Fischer, Tort Recovery for Loss of a Chance, 36 Wake Forest L. Rev. 60 (2001); Margaret Berger & Aaron D. Twerski, Uncertainty and Informed Choice, 104 Mich. L. Rev. 258 (2005).

Problem: Loss of a Chance

Group Health, the *Herskovits* defendant, is an HMO. HMOs attempt to reduce costs of medical care by eliminating marginal tests, where the potential "yield" of the tests in accurate findings of disease is low compared to the unit cost of the diagnostic testing. If these cost containment policy decisions render some "missed diagnoses" statistically inevitable, should the health care provider be liable under the "lost chance" doctrine? Consider, for instance, Pap smears, which detect cervical cancer. Suppose the HMO were to calculate that testing every second year rather than every year would save $5 million for its population of 50,000 women patients and, statistically, would increase the number of untreatable cases from ten to eleven per year and decrease the treatable cases from ten to nine per year. That is, assume that, in this population, the HMO can expect 20 cases of cervical cancer a year. With testing every year, ten could be detected in time and successfully treated, but with testing every two years, only nine could be. Can any woman covered by the HMO who then has untreatable cervical cancer sue under a loss-of-chance theory? Assume that, once incurable cervical cancer is found, there is no way after the fact to be sure whether it is one of the cases that could have been successfully detected and treated.

2. Statutes of Limitations

■ RATHJE v. MERCY HOSPITAL
745 N.W.2d 443 (Iowa 2008)

CADY, J.

On March 19, 1999, Kelly and Richard Rathje admitted their sixteen-year-old daughter, Georgia, to an outpatient alcohol abuse treatment center at Mercy Hospital in Cedar Rapids. Part of the treatment plan developed for Georgia called for the [ongoing] administration of a drug called Antabuse [twice a week]. This drug causes the body to produce an alcohol sensitivity that results in a highly unpleasant reaction to the ingestion of beverages containing alcohol. . . . Around a week later [back at home], Georgia began to feel sick and nauseated [even though she was not consuming any alcohol]. She also began to experience cramps and was constipated. . . . [T]he family's physician, Dr. Jerome Janda . . . prescribed medication for Georgia's stomach pain.

[Still], Georgia would not eat or drink. She was suffering from abdominal pain and was vomiting a green substance. She was also fatigued. . . . On April 26, Georgia returned to Dr. Janda's office. She had been bedridden for most of the time since the previous office visit on April 23. She was nauseated, vomiting, and constipated. At this visit, Dr. Janda noticed Georgia's skin color was "mildly yellow or jaundiced and the whites of her eyes were yellowish or icteric." . . . Georgia was admitted to St. Luke's Hospital [the next day, where] Dr. Janda consulted with a surgeon about his concern that Georgia could have gallbladder stones. . . . The gastroenterologist determined the jaundice and elevated liver enzymes experienced by Georgia were secondary to hepatitis. He believed Georgia's condition might be a "drug-induced hepatitis secondary to Antabuse." He recommended Georgia stop taking all prior medications. Georgia['s] . . . condition continued to deteriorate over the passing days. On May 5, she was transferred to the University of Iowa Hospitals and Clinics Pediatric Intensive Care Unit. She later received a liver transplant as a result of end-stage liver disease secondary to Antabuse.

On April 26, 2001, Georgia and her parents filed a petition against numerous health care providers, including Mercy and Dr. Dwight Schroeder, the medical director at the Alcohol Treatment Center at Mercy. The lawsuit claimed Dr. Schroeder and the hospital were negligent in prescribing Antabuse and in their treatment of Georgia for alcohol abuse, and this negligence was the cause of her irreversible liver damage and transplant. . . . The district court granted summary judgment for Mercy Hospital and Dr. Schroeder. It found the facts were undisputed that Georgia's injury had physically manifested itself well prior to April 26, 1999, more than two years before the Rathjes filed suit. Consequently, it concluded the lawsuit filed by the Rathjes was barred by the statute of limitations. . . .

III. STATUTE OF LIMITATIONS FOR MEDICAL MALPRACTICE ACTIONS.

This case requires us once again to visit the medical malpractice statute of limitations and apply it to the facts of a particular case. We have done this on a number of occasions since the special statute was enacted in 1975, . . . [y]et, this law has raised some questions about the fairness of the outcome of a number of these cases. This perception has not gone unnoticed by us, for we have freely acknowledged the statute can "severely restrict[] the rights of unsuspecting patients." Nevertheless, we have declined to change course, recognizing it is the role of the legislature to "address this problem."

It is, of course, the role of the legislature to write [and amend] statutes, . . . [y]et, these general principles of separation of powers and fundamental duties do not totally absolve us from our continued responsibility to interpret applicable statutes in each case and, more importantly, to revisit our past interpretations if we are convinced they have not clearly captured the intent of our legislature. . . .

We begin . . . by returning to the original statute of limitations for personal injury actions enacted by our legislature in the Nineteenth Century, . . . [which] used the "accrual" of the claim as a starting point for the limitation period. In doing so, the legislature determined a two-year period was sufficient for a reasonably diligent person to file a [tort] claim with the judicial system. . . . While the legislature prescribes the period of limitation, courts have generally been called upon to determine when a claim accrues to start the running of the statute of limitations. This task has been formidable, largely due to the manifold sequences in which the elements of a tort action can unfold and become discernible to a plaintiff as a signal to pursue a legal remedy for a wrong.

The first rule to emerge from our early statute-of-limitations cases was that a claim accrued when the injured party had a "right to institute and maintain a suit." This approach meant the statute was triggered when the commission of a tortious act caused a legally recognized injury. It reflected the general rule of law around the country. We also observed early on that the tortious act committed by a defendant was not always immediately followed by the resulting injury. Thus, in response to a number of statute-of-limitations cases in which the injury did not occur until long after the wrongful act, our general rule for the accrual of a claim was more specifically described to commence the running of the statute of limitations for personal injury actions at the time the injury occurred. This approach was logical because the injury would not always occur at the same time as the wrongful act, but no cause of action could accrue until the injury occurred. . . . Of course, there was no change in the rule that the statute of limitations began to run even if the plaintiff had not discovered the injury or its cause. The early case of [Ogg v. Robb, 181 Iowa at 147 (1917)] illustrates this approach.

In *Ogg*, the plaintiff suffered burns on his arms as a result of x-rays taken by the doctor after he broke his wrist. This event occurred in 1901. In 1912, the plaintiff developed cancer in his arm, resulting in amputation. In 1915, he brought a negligence action against the doctor, alleging the x-rays caused the cancer. After finding no evidence of fraudulent concealment of the tort by the physician, the court concluded the cause of action accrued at the time of the burn in 1901, and the action was therefore barred by the statute of limitations. This approach reaffirmed the bright-line rule, but frequently left victims who were unable to discover their injuries within the statute-of-limitations period, through no fault of their own, without any remedy.

[This "injury" rule] was followed well into the Twentieth Century. The individual hardship visited on those plaintiffs who failed to discover the injury before the end of the statute-of-limitations period was largely considered to be the price paid to achieve the greater societal goals of the statute of limitations. *See* W. Page Keeton et. al, *Prosser and Keeton on the Law of Torts* §30, at 165 (5th ed. 1984). . . . Other jurisdictions, however, began to apply [a] "discovery rule" . . . in response to the harshness of the prevailing rule to unsuspecting plaintiffs who were blamelessly ignorant of their legal rights. In the same year we rejected the discovery rule in *Ogg*, Maryland became the first . . . state in the nation to apply the discovery rule to a medical malpractice case. In *Hahn v. Claybrook*, 130 Md. 179 (1917), a plaintiff brought a malpractice action against her doctor, claiming the doctor negligently prescribed argentum oxide for a six-year period between 1904 and 1910. The plaintiff claimed the excessive quantities of the drug caused silver poisoning, a chronic discoloration of the skin. . . . Consequently, the court held the statute of limitations began to run at the time the plaintiff first noticed her skin discoloration in 1908, not when the doctor began prescribing the drug. . . .

[Eventually], Iowa joined the parade of states to apply the discovery rule to the general statute of limitations. . . . We also observed with approval that the discovery rule as defined in other jurisdictions meant the statute of limitations did not begin to run until the date "the wrongful act" was discovered or should have been discovered. Yet, we ultimately held that actions for negligence do not accrue until the plaintiff discovers or should have discovered "the injury to his interest." The distinction between "the wrongful act" and "the injury" as the triggering event went unnoticed.

. . . In *Baines v. Blenderman*, 223 N.W.2d 199 (Iowa 1974), the plaintiff, Baines, awoke from surgery on a herniated disk and was unable to see out of his right eye. The surgery took place on March 30, 1970. A treating physician told Baines the condition was temporary. Baines, however, was eventually examined by another doctor on July 15, 1970. This doctor informed Baines his vision loss could have been caused by the deprivation of blood to his eye during the surgery and his condition was permanent. Baines filed an action against the surgeon more than two years after the surgery but less than two years after he was informed of the probable cause of his condition and that his condition was permanent. . . . Baines claimed he was unaware of his cause of action . . . until he was informed on July 15, 1970, that his injury was permanent and he learned how it likely occurred. The doctor claimed the statute of limitations began to run when Baines awoke from surgery because this was the date he knew of his injury (blindness) and knew it resulted from surgery.

. . . [W]e held a plaintiff must not only discover the injury and its cause, but must also discover the physician was negligent. Yet, we reached this conclusion without acknowledging the rule followed in [some] other jurisdictions that discovery [simply] of the injury and its factual cause triggers the statute of limitations. . . . Conceptually, the national movement responsible for introducing the discovery rule into the statute of limitations merely transformed the commencement of the limitation period from the date the elements of the cause of action *occurred* to the date the elements were [or reasonably should have been] *discovered.* The difficult subissue, however, was how the discovery rule should be applied to the elements of the claim, i.e. whether or not it should be applied to *all* of the elements. Most state courts, as we did in *Baines*, triggered the discovery rule upon knowledge of the cause of action, including at least some knowledge that the conduct of the physician was negligent or wrongful. Other courts interpreted the discovery rule more narrowly to require only knowledge of the injury and its factual cause, without requiring discovery of any negligence or possible wrongdoing. In fact, many courts made the choice between the two theories without recognizing there was even a choice to be made, and others vacillated back and forth with little recognition they were doing so, . . . [or] failed to precisely describe the full meaning of their rule governing the breadth of knowledge required to trigger the statute of limitations, which has made it difficult at times to discern which rule was actually followed. . . . This phenomenon was aptly described by the New Hampshire Supreme Court:

> One might read several discovery cases and conclude that the courts are applying two substantively distinct rules. In most cases the courts frame the rule in terms of the plaintiff's discovery of the causal relationship between his injury and the defendant's conduct. In some cases, . . . a court will state simply that, under the discovery rule, a cause of action accrues when the plaintiff discovers or should have discovered his injury. Still other courts use both statements of the rule within the same case. The reason for these apparent differences is that in most cases in which the court states the rule in terms of the discovery of the injury, the injury is the kind that puts the plaintiff on notice that his rights have been violated. Thus, there is no reason for the court to express the rule in terms of the discovery of the causal connection between the harm and the defendant's conduct. . . .

Raymond v. Eli Lilly & Co., 117 N.H. 164 (1977).

The national trend of using the term "injury" to describe the triggering event under the discovery rule . . . gave rise to the suggestion from time to time that the discovery rule only looked to the injury to commence the running of the period of limitation, without any requirement of knowledge of its cause or the physician's wrongdoing. . . . [But no] court at the time [actually] expressed a principled notion that the cause of action accrued under the discovery rule based on mere knowledge of the injury.

The second circumstance of importance at the time *Baines* was decided was the concomitant drumbeat of tort reform sweeping the country, predicated on claims of a mounting medical malpractice crisis. One common reform centered on the need to tighten the statute of limitations to reduce a physician's exposure to future liability for malpractice lawsuits. In particular, as the popularity of the discovery rule . . . picked up steam in the 1960s, the medical malpractice insurance industry began to increase premiums to protect against the resulting "long tail" of potential liability. In response to this problem, various state and national commissions recommended placing an outside limit on the discovery rule in medical malpractice cases. As a result, statutes of repose, which bar medical malpractice claims after a specific period of time regardless of the date of discovery, were proposed to reduce malpractice premiums by eliminating the insurance companies' inability to predict future claims and losses. . . .

In 1975, one year following *Baines,* the Iowa legislature enacted Iowa Code section 614.1(9)(a) as a specific exception to the general statute of limitations for malpractice actions against a specific group of medical personnel and medical facilities. The statute maintained the two-year limitation period, adopted the discovery rule, and placed a six-year period of repose on the applicability of the discovery rule as proposed by the reform movement. The statute of repose provided an outside limitation for all lawsuits, even though the injury had not been discovered.

Since the enactment of the statute, the dispute in Iowa has not involved the adoption of the discovery rule or the six-year period of repose. Instead, the dispute has mostly centered on the extent to which the legislature intended to restrict the triggering event for the two-year limitation. While the Iowa legislature adopted the discovery rule concept, it defined the rule to begin the two-year statute of limitations when the patient "knew, or through the use of reasonable diligence should have known . . . *the injury or death* for which damages are sought in the action" [emphasis added]. In contrast, the definition of the discovery rule in *Baines* provided for the cause of action to accrue not only upon the discovery of the injury and its cause, but also the discovery of the negligent conduct.

In our first cases to address section 614.1(9) following its enactment, we . . . focused on the triggering event used by the legislature under the statute—injury or death—and found neither the plain language of the statute nor the history of the statute permitted us to inject any modifying language that the injury or death be wrongful. . . . We also formally read inquiry notice into the application of the statute and indicated the duty to investigate begins "once a person is aware that a problem exists." The "injury" claimed to have been suffered in [one case] was posttraumatic stress disorder allegedly caused, in part, by the rude bedside statements of a treating psychiatrist. The plaintiff's "problem" surfaced so as to give rise to a duty to investigate at the time the conduct of the psychiatrist hurt her feelings, even though she did not understand the medical reasons why the conduct adversely affected her. . . . [In another case, we] concluded that the constant pain experienced by [the patient] following [an] operation was sufficient to put her on notice of the injury for which she claimed damages.

We next faced the statute in *Schlote v. Dawson,* 676 N.W.2d 187 (Iowa 2004). In that case, the patient brought a malpractice action against a physician based on a claim that the physician negligently treated a throat condition by unnecessarily removing his voice box. However, the patient did not discover the surgery may have been unnecessary until more than two years later and, consequently, filed the lawsuit more than two years after the voice box was removed. . . . [We] determined the legislature intended the word "injury," to refer to its common dictionary meaning of physical harm, as opposed to its legal meaning involving the violation of a right or protected interest. . . . Consequently, we found the statute of limitations began to run when the plaintiff knew the fact of his injury, even though the plaintiff did not know of the physician's wrongful conduct. . . .

In applying this case law to the undisputed facts of the summary judgment proceedings in this case, it is clear the Rathjes were placed on inquiry notice when Georgia was suffering from physical harm prior to April 26, 1999, more than two years prior to filing the petition. She was experiencing increasing signs of physical harm to her body, which an investigation revealed within two years from the time of the onset of the symptoms was caused by the administration of Antabuse. Under the rule applied in *Schlote*, the Rathjes failed to timely file their petition, even though they had no idea of the cause of the harm prior to the commencement of the statute of limitations. . . .

Understanding the consequences of this state of the law, the Rathjes attempt to sidestep this result by arguing the relevant injury for the purpose of the statute of limitations is not the symptoms Georgia experienced prior to April 26, 1999, but the later damage to her liver. They claim the liver damage is the injury that is the basis for the lawsuit, and this injury was not discovered, or could not have been reasonably discovered, until after April 26, 1999. The approach advocated by the Rathjes gives rise to concerns about allowing plaintiffs to separate injuries [or "split causes of action"] and only leads to additional problems in an already troubled area of the law. . . .

Clearly, the [Iowa] legislature intended to reject discovery of the physician's negligence as a triggering event for the discovery rule, but there was . . . no indication our legislature sought to narrow the triggering event to something other than the two prevailing schools of thought. . . . This dispute over the triggering event was aptly illustrated in *U.S. v. Kubrick*, 444 U.S. 111 (1979). In *Kubrick*, a patient brought a medical malpractice action under the Federal Tort Claims Act to recover for a loss of hearing that allegedly resulted from prior treatment he received for an infection to his leg. The patient knew of his hearing loss more than two years before filing his petition and knew it was most likely caused by the drug used to irrigate the leg infection. However, the patient did not discover the treating physician should have known that using the drug to treat the infection would cause hearing loss until less than two years before filing the petition. . . . [The Court] explained the rationale for only using discovery of the injury and its factual cause to trigger the discovery rule for purposes of the statute of limitations instead of also requiring knowledge of negligent treatment, as follows:

> That [the plaintiff] has been injured in fact may be unknown or unknowable until the injury manifests itself; and the facts about causation may be in the control of the putative defendant, unavailable to the plaintiff or at least very difficult to obtain. The prospect is not so bleak for a plaintiff in possession of the critical facts that he has been hurt and who has inflicted the injury. He is no longer at the mercy of the latter. There are others who can tell him if he has been wronged, and he need only ask. If he does ask and if the defendant has failed to live up to minimum standards of medical proficiency, the odds are that a competent doctor will so inform the plaintiff. . . .

In some instances, the cause of medical malpractice injuries may be evident from facts of the injury alone, but in other cases it may not. Yet, in all cases, a plaintiff must at least know the cause of the injury resulted or may have resulted from medical care in order to be protected from the consequences of the statute of limitations by seeking expert advice from the medical and legal communities. . . . Thus, the discovery of relevant facts about the injury to commence the statute of limitations must include its cause in order to justify the commencement of the limitation period. . . .

We think it is clear our legislature intended the medical malpractice statute of limitations to commence upon actual or imputed knowledge of both the injury and its cause in fact. Moreover, it is equally clear this twin-faceted triggering event must at least be identified by sufficient facts to put a reasonably diligent plaintiff on notice to investigate. This approach rejects the claim made by the Rathjes that "the injury" that will trigger the statute can be separated into different degrees of harm or different categories of harm that separately give rise to different triggering dates. The statute does not work in that manner. We adhere to the rule that a plaintiff does not need to know the full extent of the injury before the statute of limitations begins to run. The statute begins to run only when the injured party's actual or imputed knowledge of the injury and its cause reasonably suggest an investigation is warranted. *See* Annot., 101 A.L.R. Fed. 27 (1991). The symptoms experienced by a patient can be sufficient to alert a reasonable person to the existence of the injury, but those symptoms may not always alert the plaintiff to the cause of the injury. These elements must be considered together to allow the statute of limitations to operate in its intended manner to protect unsuspecting plaintiffs.

The general approach we adopt today is consistent with the framework followed in other jurisdictions. . . . While these jurisdictions reach different conclusions on the question whether discovery of causation involves the relationship between the injury and the factual cause or the relationship between the injury and negligence (or some evidence of wrongdoing), they all recognize causation to be an essential component of the analysis. Although some courts appear to state a rule, from time to time, that the statute of limitations begins to run upon discovery of the injury alone, as we have done in the past, the validity of those holdings are suspect. . . .

In applying the medical malpractice statute of limitations, as we now interpret it, to the undisputed facts in this case, it is clear the Rathjes knew Georgia was suffering from physical harm. However, a reasonable jury could find they did not know the cause of the harm until, at the earliest, April 27, 1999, the date the gastroenterologist made a diagnosis of "drug-induced hepatitis secondary to Antabuse." . . .

Notes: Statutes of Limitations

1. *Discovery Rule.* Why exactly did Georgia's earlier visits to Dr. Janda (the family doctor) not indicate actual notice of a possible injury related to taking Antabuse? There was no suggestion that Georgia was consuming alcohol at home, so perhaps it was because Dr. Janda believed the cause might be an unrelated gallstone problem. But, don't doctors usually consider a variety of possible causes? Perhaps a more definitive diagnosis is required because only then might it be reasonable to consult a lawyer. Is that really what a reform-minded legislature probably intended, in contrast with a rule that a patient simply must have reason to think that something isn't right? Compare Wilson v. El-Daief, 964 A.2d 354 (Pa. 2009) (excruciating pain after

surgery is sufficient notice where patient admitted that she thought "something was wrong"). And, do you agree with the Iowa court's resolution that these questions should be resolved by a jury's factual determinations rather than by the court as a matter of law? The debate surely will continue, even in Iowa.

Notice how the Iowa court's resolution differs from the formulation advanced by the Rathjes. Rather than argue that they failed to discover the cause of an earlier injury, they argued that the actual injury in question did not occur until later, as the effects of the drug became serious enough to destroy Georgia's liver. Therefore, no discovery rule is needed to extend the limitations period. Other courts have been more receptive to creative attempts to "split the cause of action." See, e.g., Cleaveland v. Gannon, 655 S.E.2d 662 (2007) (when undiagnosed cancer started to metastasize, this restarted the clock because spreading cancer constitutes a new "injury"). Also consider situations (like those reviewed by the Iowa court) where the slowly growing nature of an injury means that it accrues over a period of time. See generally Annots., 70 A.L.R.3d 7 (1976); 50 A.L.R.4th 250 (1986); Neal F. Eggeson, Snatching Confusion from the Jaws of Clarity: The Puzzling Evolution of the Discovery Rule, 8 Ind. Health L. Rev. 95 (2011).

2. *Statute of Repose; Fraudulent Concealment.* Notice that the six-year outer limit would bar suit regardless of any failure to discover injury. It runs from the "date on which occurred the act or omission . . . [alleged] to have been the cause of the injury." Although Iowa creates an exception for foreign objects left in the body (which remain subject to an indefinite discovery rule), other states apply their statutes of repose even to those situations. See, e.g., Walters v. Cleveland Regional Medical Center, 307 S.W.3d 292 (Tex. 2010) (ten-year statute of repose is absolute, even in foreign object case). Statutes of repose usually do not apply, however, in situations of "fraudulent concealment." When might that arise in medical malpractice cases? What if, during follow-up treatment, a doctor simply fails to tell the patient the full extent of injury or its true cause?

3. *Constitutional Challenges.* Several state supreme courts have struck down shortened statutes of limitations as unconstitutional, usually on grounds of equal protection, because they target only one type of tort action—medical malpractice. Some of these decisions find an absence of rational basis for this selective restriction, while others justify fundamental-interest heightened scrutiny based on an "open courts" constitutional provision that guarantees the right to sue for personal injury. See, e.g., Kenyon v. Hammer, 688 P.2d 961 (Ariz. 1984) (shorter limitations period for medical malpractice than for other tort cases violates equal protection); Martin v. Richey, 711 N.E.2d 1273 (Ind. 1999) (a two-year period does not give a reasonable opportunity to sue for a patient who claimed that her physician negligently failed to diagnose breast cancer that she did not discover until three years later). Contra Deen v. Egleston, 597 F.3d 1223 (11th Cir. 2010) (applying a two-year limitation to a mentally incompetent patient is constitutional under the rational basis test); Jennings v. Burgess, 917 S.W.2d 790 (Tex. 1996) (statute valid if it does not produce unreasonable result in the particular case). For discussion of the Indiana case, see Symposium, Indiana's Medical Malpractice Reform, 31 Ind. L. Rev. 1043 (1998). See generally section H of this chapter.

4. *Continuing Treatment.* Another tolling doctrine adopted by some state courts is the "continuing course of treatment" rule, which suspends the clock as long as a patient continues to receive treatment from the defendant doctor (or institution).

Courts differ on whether this rule survives the malpractice reform statutes. Compare Forshey v. Jackson, 671 S.E.2d 748 (W. Va. 2008) (continuing treatment rule is still in effect) with Dickey v. Vermette, 960 A.2d 1178 (Me. 2008) (rule implicitly abolished by statute). See Note, 62 Ala. L. Rev. 439 (2011).

Where the rule applies, there are two versions: The conventional one applies even to a single act of negligence. It holds that the statute does not start to run until treatment for the same condition has been completed. The rationale is well stated in Watkins v. Fromm, 488 N.Y.S.2d 768 (App. Div. 1985):

> It would be absurd to require a wronged patient to interrupt corrective efforts by serving a summons on the physician or hospital superintendent. . . . [T]he trust and confidence that marks the physician-patient relationship puts the patient at a disadvantage to question the doctor's techniques and gives the patient the right to rely upon the doctor's professional skill without the necessity of interrupting a continuing course of treatment by instituting suit. The exception not only provides the patient with the opportunity to seek corrective treatment from the doctor, but also gives the physician a reasonable chance to identify and correct errors made at an earlier stage of treatment.

The second version applies only where there is continuing negligence, such as a doctor who repeatedly prescribes the wrong medication. Here, the rationale for the doctrine is more formal: it is to operationalize the statutory definition of the injury event that triggers the statute running. Strictly speaking, then, this second version is not a tolling doctrine; it is a rule about when injury actually occurs. Where the mistake is failure to diagnose, does the negligence continue until the doctor makes the correct diagnosis? Fabio v. Bellomo, 504 N.W.2d 758 (Minn. 1993) (no, for failure to diagnose lump as breast cancer, even though patient saw her doctor 60 times over four years and misdiagnosis was repeated several times); Sander v. Geib, Elseton, Frost P.A., 506 N.W.2d 107 (S.D. 1993) (yes, where incorrect reading of a Pap smear was repeated and subsequent visits were for general gynecological exams); Chambers v. Conaway, 883 S.W.2d 156 (Tex. 1993) (yes, under similar facts, even past the point where misdiagnosis was repeated).

Under the first version of the doctrine, what kind of treatment will toll the statute? Treatment for any condition, or only for the condition in question? Consider the various rationales for the doctrine, and what they would suggest. See Konstantikis v. Kassipidis, 602 N.Y.S.2d 67 (App. Div. 1993) (no continuing treatment occurred for surgery that accidentally caused infertility where subsequent treatment of infertility addressed other problems).

What if the subsequent negligence is not by the same exact doctor, but by someone the doctor practices with? In Watkins v. Fromm, supra, the court held that continued treatment by a medical group tolled the statute against two doctors even though the two doctors left the group more than three years before it concluded its treatment of the patient.

3. Affirmative Defenses

All of the standard affirmative defenses available in other tort actions can be used in medical malpractice cases. The following decision reviews a number of these, as well as other strands of doctrine from earlier in the chapter. Focus your attention on the aspects of the case that concern release from liability, contributory negligence or comparative fault, and assumption of risk.

■ SCHNEIDER v. REVICI
817 F.2d 987 (2d Cir. 1987)

MINER, Circuit Judge.

Emanuel Revici, M.D. and the Institute of Applied Biology, Inc. (the "Institute") appeal from a judgment . . . arising from Dr. Revici's treatment of plaintiff Edith Schneider's breast cancer with unconventional, noninvasive cancer therapy, after she had been advised by numerous doctors to undergo a biopsy and had refused to do so. Edith Schneider and her husband asserted . . . : (1) fraud, premised on Dr. Revici's alleged promise to cure Mrs. Schneider of breast cancer; and (2) medical malpractice. . . . After the district judge refused to charge the jury on the affirmative defense of express assumption of risk, the jury . . . awarded Edith Schneider and her husband $1,000,000.00 and $50,000.00 respectively. Because the jury found that Mrs. Schneider was equally responsible, through her own culpable conduct, for the damages she suffered, the awards were halved to $500,000.00 and $25,000.00, pursuant to New York's comparative negligence statute.

On appeal, Dr. Revici and the Institute challenge the district court's refusal to charge with respect to an alleged covenant not to sue and express assumption of risk as affirmative defenses, either of which would serve as a total bar to recovery. Appellants also contend that numerous evidentiary rulings were erroneous. . . .

I. BACKGROUND

In October 1981, Dr. Cocoziello discovered a lump in appellee Edith Schneider's right breast during her annual gynecological checkup. . . . Mrs. Schneider was examined by Dr. Abessi and Dr. Volke, who both separately advised her to undergo a biopsy and possibly a partial mastectomy, depending upon the analysis of the biopsied tissue. She refused.

In November 1981, Mrs. Schneider consulted with Dr. Emanuel Revici, . . . a physician and researcher who treats cancer patients with "non-toxic," noninvasive methods that have not been adopted by the medical community. Mrs. Schneider had learned of Dr. Revici and his novel cancer therapy from a radio program. After Mrs. Schneider signed a detailed consent form,[1] Dr. Revici diagnosed cancer of

---

1. Mrs. Schneider signed a consent form that reads as follows: Dr. Revici testified that Mrs. Schneider had told him that she had not seen other doctors and had not yet had a mammogram. He testified that because of this, he explained the consent form to her in great detail. . . .

. . . I fully understand that some of the treatment procedures and medications are still investigatory awaiting further research and submission for F.D.A. approval. . . . I am aware that the practice of medicine is not an exact science and I acknowledge that no guaranties have been made to me as to the results of the treatment procedures the right breast and began treatment with selenium [a nonmetallic element used in electronic devices] and dietary restrictions. . . . After 14 months of treatment, the tumor had increased in size, and cancer had spread to her lymph system and left breast. Mrs. Schneider finally underwent a bilateral mastectomy at Memorial Sloan-Kettering Hospital in January 1983, followed by 16 months of conventional chemotherapy. . . .

A. EVIDENTIARY RULINGS

. . . The trial court excluded records of patients successfully treated by Dr. Revici on the grounds that the issue in medical malpractice is not whether a particular treatment is effective but whether that treatment is a deviation from accepted medical practice in the community. The trial court's statement of the law of medical malpractice is correct. However, evidence as to the effectiveness of Dr. Revici's treatment method was relevant to show that he did not make a false representation with intent to defraud. Any error in excluding the patient records was clearly harmless, however, in light of the jury's finding that Dr. Revici was not liable on the claim of common law fraud. Dr. Revici's sole liability was founded on medical malpractice, which is amply supported by the record, and the evidence of the effectiveness of his treatment was not relevant to that issue. . . .

Defendants' expert witness, Gerhard Schrauzer, had testified about the nutritional value of selenium — testimony directed at negating the fraud claim against Dr. Revici. To rebut that testimony, plaintiffs called Victor Herbert, M.D., who authored two books concerning health and nutrition fads. . . . Appellants object to the trial court's failure to strike his testimony in the following exchange:

Q. Could you tell us whether Dr. Emanuel Revici is recognized by the National Council Against Health Fraud and in what manner? [Objection]
A. We recognize him as a quack, we recognize his treatment as snake oil. We consider him, in quotes, one of the cruelest killers in the United States.

. . . The labels applied to Dr. Revici by Dr. Herbert should not have been countenanced by the district judge. Dr. Herbert was entitled to furnish his opinion on the efficacy of Dr. Revici's treatment and on the consequences likely to befall patients who accepted it in lieu of traditional treatment. These views could have been forcefully expressed without the incendiary labels "quack" and "one of the cruelest killers." However, viewing the testimony in the context of the emphatic opinions that were properly expressed, we do not believe the failure to strike the use of inflammatory characterizations warrants reversal. The labels, though improper, added but slight impact to the force of Dr. Herbert's testimony.

We have considered the other evidentiary arguments of appellants and find them to be without merit.

---

and medications. . . . I therefore release Dr. Emanuel Revici from all liabilities to me, including all claims and complaints by me or by other members of my family. I am here because I wish to try the Revici methods and preparations for disease control. . . .

B. COVENANT NOT TO SUE

New York law recognizes the efficacy of a covenant not to sue in the context of medical treatment:

> Specifically, where a patient voluntarily agrees to undergo an experimental and inherently dangerous surgical procedure, the parties may covenant to exempt the physician from liability for those injuries which are found to be the consequences of the non-negligent, proper performance of the procedure. . . . That is to say, that an experimental procedure which, because of its inherent dangers, may ordinarily be in and of itself a departure from customary and accepted practice (and thus possibly actionable as malpractice) even if performed in a non-negligent manner, may be rendered unactionable by a covenant not to sue.

Colton v. New York Hospital, 414 N.Y.S.2d 866, 876 (Sup. Ct. 1979), and cases there cited. However, New York requires that "a covenant not to sue . . . must be strictly construed against the party asserting it. Moreover, its wording must be 'clear and unequivocal.' " The form signed by Mrs. Schneider lacks the precision required by New York law.

In the first place, the form was not labeled a covenant or agreement not to sue but was instead captioned "CONSENT FOR MEDICAL CARE." . . . Second, the one paragraph of the consent form that bears on legal liability is not "clear and unequivocal." . . . To "release . . . from all liabilities" can plausibly be understood only to relinquish claims currently existing, rather than to promise not to sue in the future on claims that may subsequently arise. . . .

The district judge did not err in declining to submit the covenant not to sue issue to the jury.

C. ASSUMPTION OF RISK

. . . In 1975, New York adopted a comparative negligence statute eliminating contributory negligence as a total bar to recovery. Prior to adoption of the statute a plaintiff was required to be free of any negligence contributing in the slightest degree to his injury, in order to recover. The plaintiff's own negligence was viewed as an intervening cause, between the defendant's negligent act and the plaintiff's injury, which prevented any recovery. Dowd v. New York, Ontario & W. Ry. Co., 63 N.E. 541 (N.Y. 1902). See generally Arbegast v. Board of Educ., 480 N.E.2d 365, 368 (N.Y. 1985).

The doctrine of assumption of risk was a defense to an action for the recovery of damages for personal injuries, prior to the adoption of the comparative negligence statute. . . . While assumption of risk, like contributory negligence, barred recovery, it was predicated on a theory of contract rather than on a theory of culpable conduct: the plaintiff's agreement, either express or implied, to absolve the defendant from responsibility. "Express" assumption of risk resulted from an advance agreement that the defendant need not use reasonable care for the plaintiff's benefit. "Implied" assumption of risk, on the other hand, was founded on plaintiff's unreasonable and voluntary consent to the risk of harm from defendant's conduct with full understanding of the possible harm. Restatement (Second) of Torts §§496B, 496E.

In 1975, New York's Civil Practice Law and Rules were amended by the addition of a pure comparative negligence statute. . . . In accord with the plain language of the statute . . . commentators assumed that under the new comparative negligence statute assumption of risk was no longer a total bar to recovery, but simply diminished the amount of damages recoverable. . . . [However,] [i]n 1985, the Court of Appeals of New York . . . held that express assumption of risk would provide a complete defense, while implied assumption of risk was subsumed by [the comparative negligence statute]: "[The statute] requires diminishment of damages in the case of an implied assumption of risk but, except as public policy proscribes an agreement limiting liability, does not foreclose a complete defense that by express consent of the injured party no duty exists and, therefore, no recovery may be had." Arbegast, 480 N.E.2d at 371. . . .

In the case before us, appellees contend that it is against public policy for one expressly to assume the risk of medical malpractice and thereby dissolve the physician's duty to treat a patient according to medical community standards. . . . [W]e see no reason why a patient should not be allowed to make an informed decision to go outside currently approved medical methods in search of an unconventional treatment. While a patient should be encouraged to exercise care for his own safety, we believe that an informed decision to avoid surgery and conventional chemotherapy is within the patient's right "to determine what shall be done with his own body," Schloendorff v. Society of the New York Hospital, 105 N.E. 92 (N.Y. 1914) (Cardozo, J.). . . .

While we do not determine, in the case before us, whether Mrs. Schneider expressly assumed the risk of Dr. Revici's treatment, we hold that there existed sufficient evidence—in the language of the Consent for Medical Care form that she signed, and in testimony relating to specific consent informed by her awareness of the risk of refusing conventional treatment to undergo the Revici method—to allow the jury to consider express assumption of risk as an affirmative defense that would totally bar recovery. It was therefore error for the district court to deny the defendants' request for a jury charge on the issue, and we reverse and remand for that reason.

Notes: Affirmative Defenses

1. Schneider v. Revici introduces a complex thicket of doctrines that overlap to a large extent but that are also conceptually distinct: (1) the standard of care for experimental care or "alternative" practitioners; (2) informed consent (the discussion of which is omitted in this excerpt); (3) release from liability, or waiver of the right to sue; (4) contributory negligence or comparative fault; and (5) assumption of risk. (1) and (2) are explored elsewhere because they go to basic elements in the cause of action. See section B.2 and Chapter 3.C. In addition, the fraud action mentioned in the decision is explored at page 406, and the evidentiary point is addressed in section C.

The focus here is on the affirmative defenses stated in (3), (4), and (5). Observe the extent of both overlap and independence among these. Even though the release was not effective, the court still found the consent form could establish assumption of risk. And even though there was no instruction on assumption of risk, the jury found 50 percent comparative fault. For a contrasting decision from over a century ago, see Nelson v. Harrington, 40 N.W. 228 (Wis. 1888) (patient not contributorily negligent in seeking care from "clairvoyant physician" even though he knew in advance what the treatment was; "the proposition that one holding himself out as a medical practitioner, . . . because he resorts to some peculiar method . . . [is] exonerated from all liability for unskillfulness on his part, no matter how serious the consequences may be, cannot be entertained" and is contrary to public policy).

2. *Waiver of Liability.* Generally speaking, releases of liability or waivers of the right to sue for medical negligence, signed at the time of treatment, are unenforceable as contrary to public policy, even if they are correctly worded. The seminal decision is Tunkl v. Regents, discussed in the next case and excerpted at page 110. See Annot., 6 A.L.R.3d 704 (1966 & Supp.). *Revici* is consistent with this law because it holds only that a release of liability prior to a claim arising is potentially valid only to the extent that it specifies *nonnegligent* performance of nonstandard care. Releases are also commonly obtained and enforced when patients leave the hospital against medical advice ("AMA").

Releases from liability or covenants not to sue for negligent care are also valid if signed *after* the harm occurs and the claim arises. This is how parties settle a dispute. A critical aspect of legal practice is to correctly distinguish between the two forms—release vs. covenant—because of the effect on the liability of joint tortfeasors. Many malpractice actions are brought against more than one defendant—several doctors or a hospital as well as the doctors. Plaintiffs often agree to settle with one or more of the less culpable or less well insured parties while keeping the others on the hook. At common law, a release from liability of one joint tortfeasor had the automatic effect of releasing all the others, even if the release stated to the contrary, because it was seen as extinguishing a single, indivisible cause of action; covenants not to sue do not have this effect, however. This rule has been reversed in most states, but releases are still dangerous in some states. See, e.g., Gilbert v. Sycamore Municipal Hospital, 622 N.E.2d 788 (Ill. 1993) (settlement with doctor extinguishes vicarious liability of hospital even though settling parties expressly reserved the right to sue hospital); Fiakpoey v. Middlesworth, 118 A.D.3d 743 (NY App. Div. 2014) (release of hospital also releases independent physician who is agent of hospital).

3. *Contributory Fault and Mitigation of Damages.* *Revici* addresses comparative fault and contributory negligence only in passing, but this was obviously a large part of the case since it resulted in halving the jury verdict. Presumably, this finding was based on Ms. Schneider's foolishness in believing Dr. Revici's claims and ignoring advice to seek conventional treatment at the same time.[1] What other actions might constitute contributory fault, either during, before, or following treatment? Notice in note 1 that Ms. Schneider misled Dr. Revici about her medical history. See also Fall v. White, 449 N.E.2d 628 (Ind. Ct. App. 1983) (patient contributed to his own

---

1. Subsequent studies have shown, however, that selenium in fact inhibits several types of cancer. In one study, it cut cancer deaths in half. The benefit was so dramatic, the researchers felt compelled to halt the placebo wing of the study. Graham Colditz, Selenium and Cancer Prevention: Promising Results Indicate Further Trials Required, 276 JAMA 1984 (1996). On the other hand, Dr. Revici also treated cancer patients with vinegar, baking soda, soft boiled eggs, and coffee. See Revici v. Comm'r of Educ., 546 N.Y.S.2d 240 (1989) (upholding revocation of Dr. Revici's medical license).

death by heart attack when he failed to reveal to the doctor that he was experiencing chest pains); Annot., 33 A.L.R.4th 790 (1984). Consider also that, where a doctor is given an inaccurate or incomplete medical history, this may also negate any primary finding of negligence on the doctor's part.

In other cases, courts have found contributory fault where the patient blatantly ignored doctors' orders or failed to return for follow-up visits, as instructed. See Dennis v. Jones, 928 A.2d 672 (D.C. 2007) (patient may have contributed to her post-surgical complications by continuing to smoke contrary to doctor's instructions); Shinholster v. Annapolis Hospital, 685 N.W.2d 275 (Mich. 2004) (patient is 20 percent at fault for failure to diagnose mini-strokes leading to massive stroke because she failed to take her prescribed blood pressure medication); Harlow v. Chin, 545 N.E.2d 602 (Mass. 1989) (13 percent fault found where patient failed to contact doctor when pain got much worse. But see Tobia v. Cooper Hospital University Medical Center, 643 A.2d 1 (N.J. 1994) (doctors' duty of care includes protecting patients from harming themselves, in a case where an 85-year-old fell off a stretcher trying to go to the bathroom unattended); Durphy v. Kaiser Foundation Health Plan, 698 A.2d 459 (D.C. 1997) (patient's failure to follow instructions, resulting in foot amputation, does not bar recovery for prior act of negligence by doctor). See generally Michele Goodwin & L. Richardson, Patient Negligence, 72 Law & Contemp. Probs. 223 (Fall 2009); Annot., 84 A.L.R.5th 619 (2000). Patient negligence that occurs *after* the doctor's can also go to mitigation of damages rather than mitigation of fault. See George Washington University v. Waas, 648 A.2d 178 (D.C. 1994) (patient's failure to follow instructions and cooperate with follow-up treatment mitigates damages from failure to diagnose cancer but does not bar recovery).

Can patients be found at fault for their behavior *leading up to* their medical condition? In general, no. Doctors take their patients as they find them. See Mercer v. Vanderbilt University, Inc., 134 S.W.3d 121 (Tenn. 2004) (no contributory fault by patient who suffered brain damage from a negligent medical mistake during treatment for a car accident caused by the patient's own alcohol consumption); Jensen v. Archbishop Bergan Mercy Hospital, 459 N.W.2d 178 (Neb. 1990) (no contributory negligence even though patient's failure to lose weight may have caused the pulmonary embolism that was negligently treated). But see Cobo v. Raba, 495 S.E.2d 362 (N.C. 1998) (a patient who was also a doctor could be found contributorily negligent for engaging in repeated unprotected homosexual intercourse with prostitutes and for delays in seeking treatment once he became HIV-infected). Similarly, in the context of mitigation of damages, patients do not have to submit to risky surgery or medication to correct a negligent injury, even if medically advised. See, e.g., Robins v. Katz, 391 N.W.2d 495 (Mich. Ct. App. 1986) (patient could refuse second foot surgery to correct mistakes made the first time). But see Corlett v. Caserta, 562 N.E.2d 257 (Ill. App. Ct. 1990) (Jehovah's Witness who refused blood transfusion to correct gastric bleeding following colon surgery must "bear a proportionate share of tort liability").

4. *Good Samaritans.* Another affirmative defense of unique importance to medical malpractice is the "Good Samaritan" immunity statutes enacted in all states. These laws are intended to encourage doctors to come to the aid of injured strangers ("Is there a doctor in the house?") by reducing the standard of care to gross negligence or recklessness when they respond to an emergency or render first aid.

Usually, one thinks of these accident scenes occurring on the highway or in public places, but because the wording of these statutes varies, it is sometimes possible to argue they apply in hospital settings or in doctors' offices. See Annot., 68 A.L.R.4th 294 (1989); Paul A. Hattis, Overcoming Barriers to Physician Volunteerism, 2004 U. Ill. L. Rev. 167. The case for this interpretation is stronger if the physician who claims immunity is a true volunteer, that is, not the patient's usual doctor and not assigned to emergency care. In a few states, these statutes cover all types of treatment, not just emergencies, but they apply to ordinary medical care only when physicians treat indigent patients for free. See, e.g., Rodas v. Seidlin, 56 F.3d 610 (7th Cir. 2011) (salaried physicians at low-income clinic not entitled to immunity).

These statutes first arose during the 1960s after a flurry of press reports discussing the legal vulnerability of doctors who aid accident or heart attack victims on the scene. In fact, there were no recorded malpractice suits against doctors in such situations. William J. Curran, The Not-So-Good Samaritan Laws, 270 New Eng. J. Med. 1003 (1964). What about physicians who respond to a public health emergency, such as bioterrorism or a flu pandemic? Some scholars are concerned that existing laws and precedents do not protect sufficiently against liability claims in those potential doomsday scenarios. Sharona Hoffman, Responders' Responsibility: Liability and Immunity in Public Health Emergencies, 96 Geo. L.J. 1913 (2008); Eleanor Kinney et al., Altered Standards of Care for Health Care Providers in the Pandemic Influenza, 6 Ind. Health L. Rev. 1 (2009); Victoria Sutton, Is There a Doctor (and a Lawyer) in the House? Why Our Good Samaritans Laws Are Doing More Harm Than Good for a National Public Health Security Strategy: A Fifty-State Survey, 6 J. Health & Biomed. L. 261 (2010); Comment, 14 J. Health Care L. & Pol'y 209 (2011).

5. *Hospital Immunity.* Other sources of potential immunity have more relevance for hospitals than for physicians and so are discussed later in this chapter. These include charitable immunity for nonprofit facilities, and governmental immunity for state and municipal facilities. In most states, these immunities have disappeared or have been greatly scaled back.

4. Arbitration and Waiver of Liability

The next case concerns arbitration. It is important in its own right, since various forms of alternative dispute resolution are increasingly being used for medical care. But it has broader importance as well. It explains the legal framework in which contractual agreements might be used to alter the core standard of care or to waive malpractice liability entirely. The key question is how far this precedent might extend in those directions.

■ MADDEN v. KAISER FOUNDATION HOSPITAL
552 P.2d 1178 (Cal. 1976)

TOBRINER, Justice.
Defendants appeal from an order denying enforcement of an arbitration provision in a medical services contract entered into between the Board of

Administration of the State Employees Retirement System (hereafter board) and defendant Kaiser Foundation Health Plan. Plaintiff, a state employee who enrolled under the Kaiser plan, contends that she is not bound by the provision for arbitration. The instant appeal presents the issue whether an agent or representative, contracting for medical services on behalf of a group of employees, has implied authority to agree to arbitration of malpractice claims of enrolled employees arising under the contract. . . .

When plaintiff first enrolled under the Kaiser plan in 1965, it did not contain an arbitration provision. On April 1, 1971, however, the Kaiser Foundation Health Plan, anticipating the inclusion of an arbitration provision, mailed to all subscribers a brochure which, in describing the terms and benefits of the plan, stated that claims involving professional liability and personal injury must be submitted to arbitration. Shortly thereafter, on May 28, 1971, the Kaiser Foundation Health Plan and the board amended their contract in several respects and included a provision for binding arbitration of "any claim arising from the violation of a legal duty incident to this Agreement."[2]

On August 1, 1971, plaintiff underwent a hysterectomy at the Kaiser Hospital in Los Angeles. During the surgery, her bladder was perforated; blood transfusions were required; plaintiff thereafter contracted serum hepatitis.

Plaintiff filed a malpractice complaint against Kaiser and the blood banks. Kaiser moved to stay the action and compel arbitration. Opposing this motion, plaintiff filed a declaration stating that because of absence from work by reason of illness she had not received the April 1971 brochure, that she was not aware of the execution of the arbitration agreement in May of 1971, and thus had no knowledge that the Kaiser plan, at the time of her operation, required arbitration of malpractice claims. By order of April 22, 1974, the trial court denied the motion to stay the action and compel arbitration. Kaiser appeals from that order.

2. The board, as agent for the employees, had implied authority to provide for arbitration of malpractice claims.

Government Code §§22774, 22790 and 22793 authorize the board to negotiate contracts for group medical plans for state employees. In negotiating such agreements and amendments the board acts as the agent or representative of the employees. . . .

We shall explain that although the courts in the past regarded arbitration as an unusual and suspect procedure, they now recognize it as an accepted method of settlement of disputes. Since Civil Code §2319 grants an agent the authority to do whatever is "proper and usual" to carry out his agency, the board enjoyed an implied authority to agree to arbitration of malpractice claims of enrolled employees. . . .

In Crofoot v. Blair Holding Corp., 260 P.2d 156, 170 (Cal. App. 1953), Justice Peters summarized the evolution of legal attitudes toward arbitration.

---

2. The arbitration agreement stated that it was retroactive to April 1, 1971, the date of the Kaiser brochure advising subscribers of the arbitration clause. Since plaintiff's claim arose after May 28, 1971, we need not consider whether the agreement can be retroactively effective to require arbitration of claims arising before it was finally approved.

Arbitration has had a long and troubled history. The early common law courts did not favor arbitration, and greatly limited the powers of arbitrators. But in recent times a great change in attitude and policy has taken place. Arbitrations are now usually covered by statutory law, as they are in California. Such statutes evidence a strong public policy in favor of arbitrations, which policy has frequently been approved and enforced by the courts.

Subsequent decisions confirm the self-evident fact that arbitration has become an accepted and favored method of resolving disputes, praised by the courts as an expeditious and economical method of relieving overburdened civil calendars.

The transformation of legislative and judicial attitudes toward arbitration has encouraged a dramatic development in the use of this procedure. A 1952 study estimated that "aside from personal injury cases and cases in which the government is a party, more than 70 percent of the total civil litigation is decided through arbitration rather than by the courts" (Mentschikoff, The Significance of Arbitration—A Preliminary Inquiry (1952) 17 Law & Contemp. Prob. 698). In the following decades arbitration further expanded its role to encompass in certain circumstances disputes requiring evaluation of personal injury claims: California and many other states now require arbitration of uninsured motorist claims, and proposals for no-fault automobile insurance frequently provide for arbitration. . . .

The matter becomes even clearer if we narrow our focus to arbitration of disputes arising under group contracts. In collective bargaining agreements, which, like the present contract, are negotiated by elected representatives on behalf of a group of employees, arbitration has become a customary means of resolving disputes. . . .

Finally, we observe the growing interest in and use of arbitration to cope with the increasing volume of medical malpractice claims. Henderson, Contractual Problems in the Enforcement of Agreements to Arbitrate Medical Malpractice, 58 Va. L. Rev. 947, 956 (1972). . . .

We therefore conclude that an agent or other fiduciary who contracts for medical treatment on behalf of his beneficiary retains the authority to enter into an agreement providing for arbitration of claims for medical malpractice.[11]

3. *The principles that govern contracts of adhesion do not bar enforcement of the arbitration amendment.*

---

11. Amicus suggests that we should fashion a new rule to the effect that no arbitration provision in a group insurance policy will bind the beneficiary absent proof of the beneficiary's actual knowledge of that provision. In the present case, Kaiser provided plaintiff with a brochure describing the Kaiser plan, including the arbitration provision. Apart from plaintiff's own testimony, neither the board nor Kaiser have any way of proving whether or not plaintiff read all or part of that brochure. The orderly administration of the plan would be impossible if it were to depend on such proof. Amicus acknowledges as much; it does not maintain that no provision of the Kaiser plan can be enforced against a beneficiary who enrolls without actual knowledge of that provision; it would, instead provide only that arbitration provisions cannot be enforced without actual knowledge. But Amicus' proposal for a special rule which discriminates against enforcement of arbitration clauses would be viable only if arbitration were an extraordinary procedure, and one especially disadvantageous for the beneficiary—propositions which we have rejected in . . . cases cited in this opinion.

. . . Contending that the Kaiser contract is one of adhesion, plaintiff argues that the courts should refuse to enforce its arbitration clause on the ground that the clause is inconspicuous, unexpected, and disrupts the members' reasonable expectation that a malpractice claim will be adjudicated by trial by jury. We explain our reason for concluding that the principles governing adhesion contracts do not cover the present case. . . .

In the characteristic adhesion contract case, the stronger party drafts the contract, and the weaker has no opportunity, either personally or through an agent, to negotiate concerning its terms. The Kaiser plan, on the other hand, represents the product of negotiation between two parties, Kaiser and the board, possessing parity of bargaining strength. Although plaintiff did not engage in the personal negotiation of the contract's terms, she and other public employees benefitted from representation by a board, composed in part of persons elected by the affected employees, which exerted its bargaining strength to secure medical protection for employees on more favorable terms than any employee could individually obtain.

In many cases of adhesion contracts, the weaker party lacks not only the opportunity to bargain but also any realistic opportunity to look elsewhere for a more favorable contract; he must either adhere to the standardized agreement or forego the needed service. Plaintiff, on the other hand, enjoyed the opportunity to select from among several medical plans negotiated and offered by the board, some of which did not include arbitration provisions, or to contract individually for medical care. . . .

To support her contract of adhesion argument, plaintiff points to Tunkl v. Regents of University of California, 383 P.2d 441 (Cal. 1963); that decision, however, serves instead to illuminate by contrast the nonoppressive character of the contract in the present case. In *Tunkl*, defendant hospital presented to all incoming patients a document entitled "Conditions of Admission," which provided that the patient release the hospital from liability for negligent or wrongful acts. We observed that the "would-be patient is in no position to reject the proffered agreement, to bargain with the hospital, or in lieu of agreement to find another hospital." Thus, the patient had no realistic choice but to assent to a standardized agreement under which he waived his right to recover for negligently inflicted injuries.

As we have explained, plaintiff, in contrast to *Tunkl*, benefitted from the board's assertion of equal power on her behalf, enjoyed the opportunity to choose from among alternative medical plans, and waived no substantive right. We conclude that *Tunkl* is not controlling in the instant setting; the principles of adhesion contracts, as elucidated and applied in *Tunkl* and the other cases we have cited, do not bar enforcement of terms of a negotiated contract which neither limit the liability of the stronger party nor bear oppressively upon the weaker. Accordingly, such principles do not bar enforcement of the arbitration amendment against plaintiff Madden.

4. *Enforcement of the arbitration provision does not violate constitutional or statutory protections of the right to trial by jury.* . . .

Plaintiff further contends that the arbitration provision in the Kaiser contract fails because it does not expressly waive the parties' constitutional right to jury trail. But to predicate the legality of a consensual arbitration agreement upon the parties' express waiver of jury trial would be as artificial as it would be disastrous.

When parties agree to submit their disputes to arbitration they select a forum that is alternative to, and independent of, the judicial—a forum in which, as they well know, disputes are not resolved by juries. Hence there are literally thousands of commercial and labor contracts that provide for arbitration but do not contain express waivers of jury trial. Courts have regularly enforced such agreements; in [one case], for example, we unanimously affirmed an order compelling an employer to submit a contract dispute to arbitration, although the arbitration provision did not expressly waive the employer's right to trial by jury. Relying on this consistent pattern of judicial decision, contracting parties, such as Kaiser and the board in the case at bar, continue to draft arbitration provisions without express mention of any right to jury trial. Before today no one has so much as imagined that such agreements are consequently invalid; to destroy their viability upon an extreme hypothesis that they fail expressly to negative jury trials would be to frustrate the parties' interests and destroy the sanctity of their mutual promises. . . .

We conclude that the trial court erred in denying Kaiser's motion to compel arbitration and in refusing to stay the action against Kaiser. . . .

Mosk, Justice (dissenting).
I dissent. . . .
It must be emphasized that the plaintiff enrolled in the Kaiser plan in 1965, at a time when the master contract between Kaiser and the Board of Administrators of the State Employees Retirement System contained no arbitration clause and apparently none was contemplated. . . . Six years after plaintiff's original enrollment in the plan, without her knowledge or consent, the board purporting to act on her behalf agreed with Kaiser to amend the master contract to provide that plaintiff's claims must be submitted to arbitration. . . . Had the original master contract executed by the board and Kaiser provided for arbitration, plaintiff might have been bound thereby when she signed a written enrollment in the program. But six years after enrollment by plaintiff an amendment providing for abdication of fundamental rights can be effective only if plaintiff consents thereto in writing. This is manifest when the two rights purportedly abandoned by the board on behalf of plaintiff are as fundamental as recourse to the courts of the state and trial by jury. . . .

Notes: Alternative Dispute Resolution; Contractually Set Standards of Care

1. *Pros and Cons of Arbitration.* Professor Thomas Metzloff explains:

Arbitration in and of itself does not radically change how a dispute is litigated apart from the identity of the decisionmaker. Discovery may be somewhat limited and the hearing itself is hopefully shorter. But beyond such tinkering, the use of an arbitration format does not usually alter many of the procedural elements that malpractice defenders find objectionable. . . . Significantly, arbitration does not change the basic tort theory of liability.

Thomas B. Metzloff, The Unrealized Potential of Malpractice Arbitration, 31 Wake Forest L. Rev. 203, 215 (1996). Where arbitration differs is in the formality of the proceedings and the length of the hearing. Based on the experience at Kaiser, when cases are arbitrated they are resolved in about half the time and the hearings often last only one or two days. However, arbitration can also be more expensive because the parties have to split the costs of the arbitrators, in contrast with the judicial system, which is essentially free. Arbitration also tends to produce different results than litigation. Plaintiffs win about 50 percent more often than in jury trials; however, very large recoveries are rare. Conventional wisdom is that arbitration more often produces "compromise verdicts," although Metzloff's experience is to the contrary.

Professor Metzloff explains that, "in the simplistic nature of the tort reform debates, patient advocates are against [arbitration] because doctors are for it; arbitration has become a prisoner of war." Accordingly, arbitration of medical malpractice disputes is rare, except in the HMO context. Even then, it is still the exception. To understand why, consider whether, on balance, arbitration really is pro-plaintiff or pro-defendant? Does it depend on the facts of the case? Consider small claims vs. very large ones; cases where liability is hotly disputed; the parties' feelings about justice and vindication; and the interests of the lawyers on each side. If litigation truly were made speedier, less costly, and more predictable, would you expect an increase or decrease in the number of claims submitted? See generally Marc Ginsberg, The Execution of an Arbitration Provision as a Condition Precedent to Medical Treatment: Legally Enforceable? Medically Ethical?, 42 Mitchell Hamline L. Rev. 273 (2016); Kenneth DeVille, The Jury Is Out: Pre-Dispute Binding Arbitration Agreements for Medical Malpractice Claims, 28 J. Leg. Med. 333 (2007); Kathy L. Cerminara, Contextualizing ADR in Managed Care: A Proposal Aimed at Easing Tensions and Resolving Conflict, 33 Loy. U. Chi. L.J. 547 (2002); Symposium, 74 Law & Contemp. Probs. 1 (Summer 2011); Symposium: Medical Malpractice Dispute Resolution, 28 Cap. U. L. Rev. 249 (2000); Annot., 24 A.L.R.5th 1 (1994).

2. *Mediation.* In contrast with the *Madden* setting, agreements to arbitrate made after a claim arises are not controversial; this is a standard form of alternative dispute resolution. Also of growing significance are voluntary agreements to mediate malpractice disputes. In mediation, the parties go through a structured process designed to sharpen their understanding of the other side's perspective and to search for common ground. The process is entirely nonbinding, but some jurisdictions mandate that parties pursue mediation before litigating. Lydia Nussbaum, Trial and Error: Legislating ADR for Medical Malpractice Reform, 76 Md. L. Rev. 247 (2017). In contrast with voluntary binding arbitration and voluntary nonbinding mediation are mandatory nonbinding screening panels. As discussed in section H, many states require malpractice parties to submit their disputes to panels composed of doctors and lawyers that render advisory opinions on the merits, with the hope of encouraging settlement or early dismissal. This has proven to be a failure. Can you see why?

3. *Varying the* Madden *Facts.* Is it crucial to the holding in *Madden* that the plaintiff had several insurance options available, not all of which required arbitration? What about an employee who is offered only a single HMO insurance policy at work? If an employer chooses a single plan for workers that requires arbitration, is the employer doing this as the workers' agent? See Siopes v. Kaiser Foundation Health Plan, 312 P.3d 869 (Haw. 2013) (no, unless workers are specifically informed of the provision). Many state statutes encouraging malpractice arbitration allow these agreements to be revoked retroactively within one to three months of signing.

Does this provide the element of choice required to avoid adhesion contract characterization? What if revocation is allowed only prospectively, that is, for disputes that have not yet arisen or treatment not yet rendered?

More controversial than the *Madden* setting are agreements to arbitrate signed at the point of treatment, that is, upon admission to the hospital or when arriving at the doctor's office. Typically, the patient is given no obvious choice (although in fact the provider may provide treatment anyway if the patient refuses to sign). In different versions of this context, courts have been more inclined to follow *Tunkl* and find unconscionability. See, e.g., Sosa v. Paulos, 924 P.2d 357 (Utah 1996) (unconscionable where given to patient when she was already in surgical gown, even though she had right to revoke within 14 days). The Supreme Court, however, has ruled that states go too far in declaring point-of-treatment arbitration illegal as a matter of law, since doing so contravenes the Federal Arbitration Act, which declares that arbitration agreements connected with commerce are enforceable. Marmet Health Care Center, Inc. v. Brown, 132 S. Ct. 1201 (2012). Similarly, the Trump administration has proposed that nursing homes participating in Medicare be allowed to require binding arbitration, reserving a ban on arbitration that the government had imposed during the last months of the Obama administration.

These federal rules, however, do not preclude a state court finding that a particular agreement's terms are unconscionable. For instance, King v. Bryant, 795 S.E.2d 340 (N.C. 2017) refused to enforce an arbitration agreement with a surgeon because it was too obscure for the patient to notice or understand, and Gessa v. Manor Care of Florida, Inc., 86 So. 3d 484 (Fla. 2011) invalidated an arbitration agreement by a nursing home patient because it precluded any award of punitive damages. But see Hayes v. Oakridge Home, 908 N.E.2d 408 (Ohio 2009) (over a vigorous dissent, enforcing an arbitration agreement and waiver of punitive damages signed by a 95-year-old nursing home resident).

In one decision, the court struck down an arbitration agreement as applied, ruling that Kaiser fraudulently ran its arbitration process to strategically gain an unfair advantage on the panel and to create needless delay so that the plaintiff would die before the decision, resulting in lower damages. Engalla v. The Permanente Medical Group, 938 P.2d 903 (Cal. 1997). See also Sosa v. Paulos, supra (agreement unconscionable where losing claimant is required to pay all the arbitration costs, but requiring all the arbitrators to be physicians is not per se unconscionable).

4. *Altering Tort Law by Contract.* The *Tunkl* decision discussed in *Madden* is excerpted at page 111. It states the general law that providers cannot enforce waivers of malpractice liability. In contrast with total waivers, however, are agreements to alter the prevailing legal standards. If parties can agree to arbitrate, can they also agree to change the substantive rules that determine liability during arbitration, assuming that other elements of unconscionability are avoided (adequate notice and some element of choice)? Clark Havighurst is the leading advocate of contractually determined standards of care. He proposes the following language to be included in HMO-type health insurance contracts:

> Because the costs of unlimited legal rights (and their enforcement) must ultimately be borne by you and other plan subscribers, you agree that, in any legal action brought by you against a Plan Provider for injury suffered in the course of your treatment, you will be entitled to recover damages only if such injury was caused

by gross negligence on the part of the Provider. Gross negligence is distinguishable from ordinary negligence and is characterized by willful neglect of your personal well-being or reckless disregard for the consequences of some act or omission.

Health Care Choices: Private Contracts as Instruments of Health Reform 296 (1995).

Would the assumption of risk doctrine applied in Schneider v. Revici, page 447, validate these types of agreement? What else might be determined by contract? Consider: the statute of limitations; the allowable elements of recoverable damages; who is entitled to testify as an expert; and anything else from the long list of legal reforms discussed in section H. Even if these are not contrary to public policy, is it plausible to assume that ordinary consumers will focus their attention on this many discrete elements of their insurance policies or hospital admission forms? Even if these are noticed by consumers, can it be said they have meaningful choice if they lack the opportunity to bargain over each component of the package? In theory, the private market could offer a differentially priced checklist of legal options, but in practice this is never done. Why not? See generally Mark A. Hall, Making Medical Spending Decisions ch. 7 (1997).

5. *Consumer-Directed Health Care.* As discussed at page 19, health insurers and employers are turning more to types of coverage that place more responsibility on patients to pay for treatment themselves out of pocket. If a patient refuses treatment his physician recommends due to expense, what defenses might protect the physician if he or she continues to treat the patient with less effective care (assuming that the less expensive treatment does not work or causes harm)? For in-depth discussion, see Mark Hall & Carl Schneider, When Patients Say No (To Save Money): An Essay on the Tectonics of Health Law, 41 Conn. L. Rev. 743 (2009); Haavi Morreim, High-Deductible Health Plans: New Twists on Old Challenges from Tort and Contract, 59 Vand. L. Rev. 1207 (2006); Mark A. Hall, Paying for What You Get and Getting What You Pay For, 69 Law & Contemp. Prob. 159 (Autumn 2006).

6. *Further Reading.* On **different forms of ADR for medical malpractice** generally (notes 1 and 2), see Nussbaum supra; Kathy L. Cerminara, Contextualizing ADR in Managed Care: A Proposal Aimed at Easing Tensions and Resolving Conflict, 33 Loy. U. Chi. L.J. 547 (2002); Symposium, 74 Law & Contemp. Probs. 1 (Summer 2011); Symposium: Medical Malpractice Dispute Resolution, 28 Cap. U. L. Rev. 249 (2000).

On the **enforceability of arbitration** (note 3), Marc Ginsberg, The Execution of an Arbitration Provision as a Condition Precedent to Medical Treatment: Legally Enforceable? Medically Ethical?, 42 Mitchell Hamline L. Rev. 273 (2016); Kenneth DeVille, The Jury Is Out: Pre-Dispute Binding Arbitration Agreements for Medical Malpractice Claims, 28 J. Leg. Med. 333 (2007); Annot., 24 A.L.R.5th 1 (1994).

On **contractual specification** of the standard of care (note 4), see Richard A. Epstein, Medical Malpractice: The Case for Contract, 1976 Am. B. Found. Res. J. 87 (1976). Professor Maxwell Mehlman is a leading opponent of these agreements, arguing that principles of fiduciary contracting prohibit them. M. Mehlman, Fiduciary Contracting: Limitations on Bargaining Between Patients and Health Care Providers, 51 U. Pitt. L. Rev. 365 (1990). See also Chapter 2.B.2; Jennifer Arlen, Contracting over Liability: Medical Malpractice and the Cost of Choice, 158 U. Pa. L. Rev. 957 (2010); Tom Baker & Timothy Lytton, Allowing Patients to Waive the

Right to Sue for Malpractice: A Response to Thaler and Sunstein, 104 Nw. U. L. Rev. 233 (2010); Note, 83 N.Y.U. L. Rev. 850 (2009).

5. *Informed Consent Law*

Informed consent law is covered in Chapter 3. This body of law is usually not thought of as a defense to malpractice liability; rather, it is an alternative theory of liability. Nevertheless, we mention informed consent law here because its principles have important similarities to various defenses, and because the complex relationship between informed consent liability and ordinary malpractice liability cannot be fully understood until this point. See generally Jerry Menikoff, Demanded Medical Care, 30 Ariz. St. L.J. 1091 (1998).

Earlier, we saw that a number of alternative theories of physician liability potentially avoid the need for expert testimony about the standard of care. Informed consent liability is another such alternative theory, and it is the one that is most frequently tried. Typically, plaintiffs' lawyers allege breach of informed consent along with breach of the standard of care. Liability rarely is found to rest exclusively on this allegation, however, separate from ordinary malpractice. This is because informed consent liability is distinct from negligence liability only within a limited range of circumstances. This can be illustrated by distributing physicians' competency in responding to any given condition across a range of treatment options, as follows:

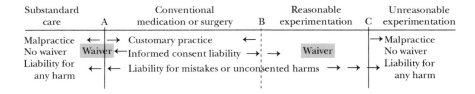

Ordinary malpractice liability exists for harms that result from doing less than or more than what most reasonable physicians would do (to the left of A and the right of C), or for making a mistake while giving conventional treatment (between A and C). Ordinary malpractice liability does not exist for unavoidable side effects that result from conventional treatment done competently. Informed consent liability, in contrast, might apply across this full range of treatment options. Where it overlaps with ordinary malpractice, however, it is mostly redundant. Deviations from customary practice are negligent, regardless of the presence or absence of consent. We have just seen that the prevailing standard of care generally speaking cannot be waived.

For the most part, then, informed consent law has unique effect only where treatment decisions comply with customary practice. The main exceptions to this generalization are for treatments at the two borders between customary and non-standard care. At the right-hand border, B, which leads into experimental treatment, physicians who are purposefully more aggressive than is customary can avoid malpractice liability if they obtain informed consent for experiments that are considered reasonable innovations. At point C, however, experiments become too radical to permit consent.

Informed consent law also operates at the left-hand border with customary care, to help resolve ambiguous cases in what in fact is a large gray zone rather than a bright line. For instance, where there are competing schools of thought or alternative courses of acceptable treatment, informed consent can play a strong defensive role for a physician who follows an unorthodox approach or one subscribed to by only a minority of physicians. An example is found above in Schneider v. Revici. Finally, informed consent can be used defensively by physicians to disclaim any promise of a guaranteed result, thereby foreclosing possible contract liability as discussed in section D.1.

We return now to the middle zone, where informed consent operates separately from ordinary malpractice. Informed consent liability attaches to unavoidable side effects from competent treatment if the harms were not sufficiently disclosed to the patient. The key question is what standard of disclosure applies? This is discussed at length in Chapter 3, as part of the law that defines the structure of the physician-patient relationship. There, we learn that informed consent law has four different doctrinal foundations: battery law; custom-based negligence; patient-centered negligence; and fiduciary law. Only one of these four—custom-based negligence—determines disclosure obligations according to what other doctors commonly disclose to their patients, thereby requiring expert testimony just like regular medical malpractice. The other theories can be established through patient testimony and common knowledge. But the custom-based version of informed consent liability prevails in many, perhaps most, states. Moreover, in all states informed consent liability is difficult to demonstrate because, in order for causation to be established, it must be shown that the patient would have opted to decline treatment that is generally acceptable. Also, the jury must conclude that the alternative treatment would not have caused a worse outcome due to its own risks of failure or side effects.

F. DAMAGES AND SETTLEMENT

■ FEIN v. PERMANENTE MEDICAL GROUP
695 P.2d 665 (Cal. 1985)

Kaus, Justice.

In this medical malpractice action, both parties appeal from a judgment awarding plaintiff about $1 million in damages. Defendant claims that the trial court committed reversible error . . . in failing to order that the bulk of plaintiff's award be paid periodically rather than in a lump sum. Plaintiff . . . maintains that the trial court, in fixing damages, should not have applied two provisions of the Medical Injury Compensation Reform Act of 1975 (MICRA): Civil Code §3333.2, which limits noneconomic damages in medical malpractice cases to $250,000, and Civil Code §3333.1, which modifies the traditional "collateral source" rule in such litigation. Plaintiff's claims are based on a constitutional challenge similar to the challenges to other provisions of MICRA that we recently addressed and rejected in

Roa v. Lodi Medical Group, Inc., 695 P.2d 164 (Cal. 1985) [upholding the following limits on lawyers' contingency fees in medical malpractice cases: 40 percent of the first $50,000, 33 percent of the next $50,000, 25 percent of the next $100,000, and 10 percent of any amounts above $200,000]. We conclude that the judgment should be affirmed in all respects.

I

On Saturday, February 21, 1976, plaintiff Lawrence Fein, a 34-year-old attorney, . . . felt a brief pain in his chest as he was riding his bicycle to work. [The pain returned several times and worsened over the next few days. He saw two doctors and a nurse practitioner with the defendant, which is affiliated with Kaiser-Permanente, but each time the pain was treated as a muscle spasm. It turned out to be a heart attack.] . . .

Following a period of hospitalization and medical treatment without surgery, plaintiff returned to his job on a part-time basis in October 1976, and resumed full-time work in September 1977. By the time of trial, he had been permitted to return to virtually all of his prior recreational activities — e.g., jogging, swimming, bicycling and skiing.

In February 1977, plaintiff filed the present action, alleging that his heart condition should have been diagnosed earlier and that treatment should have been given either to prevent the heart attack or, at least, to lessen its residual effects. The case went to judgment only against Permanente. . . .

At trial, Dr. Harold Swan, . . . testified to the damage caused by the attack. He stated that as a result of the attack a large portion of plaintiff's heart muscle had died, reducing plaintiff's future life expectancy by about one-half, to about 16 or 17 years. Although Dr. Swan acknowledged that some of plaintiff's other coronary arteries also suffer from disease, he felt that if plaintiff had been properly treated his future life expectancy would be decreased by only 10 to 15 percent, rather than half. . . .

The jury awarded $24,733 for wages lost by plaintiff to the time of trial, $63,000 for future medical expenses, and $700,000 for wages lost in the future as a result of the reduction in plaintiff's life expectancy.[1] Finally, the jury awarded $500,000 for "noneconomic damages," to compensate for pain, suffering, inconvenience, physical impairment and other intangible damages sustained by plaintiff from the time of the injury until his death. . . .

The trial court . . . reduced the noneconomic damages to $250,000, reduced the award for past lost wages to $5,430 — deducting $19,303 that plaintiff had already received in disability payments as compensation for such lost wages — and ordered defendant to pay the first $63,000 of any future medical expenses not covered by medical insurance provided by plaintiff's employer, as such expenses were incurred. At the same time, the court declined to order that the award for future lost wages or noneconomic damages be paid periodically pursuant to Code of Civil Procedure §667.7, determining that the statute was not "mandatory" and that

---

1. Plaintiff did not claim that the heart attack would reduce his earning capacity during his lifetime.

"under the unique facts and circumstances of this case" a periodic payment award of such damages would "defeat[ ] rather than promote[ ]" the purpose of §667.7. [The following excerpt focuses on how these various components of damages were calculated. Other portions of the opinion address whether the statutory limits are constitutional.] . . .

V

Defendant . . . argues that the trial court erred in permitting the jury to award damages for the loss of earnings attributable to plaintiff's so-called lost years, i.e., the period of time by which his life expectancy was diminished as a result of defendant's negligence. We believe that this was clearly a proper element of plaintiff's damages. . . . [R]ecovery of such damages is consistent with the general rule permitting an award based on the loss of future earnings a plaintiff is likely to suffer because of inability to work for as long a period of time in the future as he could have done had he not sustained the accident.[10] . . .

Defendant alternatively argues that the jury should have been instructed to deduct from plaintiff's prospective gross earnings of the lost years, the "saved" cost of necessities that plaintiff would not incur during that period. Although there is some authority to support the notion that damages for the lost years should be assessed on the basis of plaintiff's "net" loss, we need not decide that issue in this case because defendant neither requested such an instruction at trial nor presented any evidence of anticipated cost savings that would have supported such an instruction. . . .

After the jury returned its verdict, defendant requested the trial court to enter a judgment—pursuant to §667.7 of the Code of Civil Procedure—providing for the periodic payment of future damages, rather than a lump-sum award. . . . The statute provides that "[i]n any [medical malpractice action], a superior court shall, at the request of either party, enter a judgment ordering that money damages or its equivalent for future damages of the judgment creditor be paid in whole or in part by periodic payments rather than by a lump-sum payment if the award equals or exceeds fifty thousand dollars ($50,000) in future damages."[11] . . .

---

10. The comments in the Restatement 2d Torts §924 state:

d. Loss or impairment of earning capacity for the future. The extent of future harm to the earning capacity of the injured person is measured by the difference, viewed as of the time of trial, between the value of the plaintiff's services as they will be in view of the harm and as they would have been had there been no harm. This difference is the resultant derived from reducing to present value the anticipated losses of earnings during the expected working period that the plaintiff would have had during the remainder of his prospective life, but for the defendant's act. Accordingly, the trier of fact must ascertain, as nearly as can be done in advance, the difference between the earnings that the plaintiff would or could have received during his life expectancy but for the harm and the earnings that he will probably be able to receive during the period of his life expectancy as now determined. . . .

11. Section 667.7 provides in relevant part:

As a condition to authorizing periodic payments of future damages, the court shall require the judgment debtor who is not adequately insured to post security adequate to assure full payment of such damages awarded by the judgment. . . . Such payments

Nonetheless, for several reasons relating to the specific facts of this case, we conclude that the trial court judgment should not be reversed on this ground. To begin with, although the court formally rejected defendant's motion for a periodic payment order, its judgment did provide for the periodic payment of the damages which the jury awarded for plaintiff's future medical expenses, directing the defendant to pay such expenses "as [they] are incurred up to the amount of $63,000."

Second, with respect to the award of noneconomic damages, . . . the jury was not instructed to designate the portion of the noneconomic damage award that was attributable to future damages, and it did not do so. Instead, it returned an undifferentiated special verdict awarding noneconomic damages of $500,000. Because of defendant's failure to raise the periodic payment issue earlier, plaintiff was deprived of the opportunity to seek a special verdict designating the amount of "future noneconomic damage." . . .

Third and finally, there is the question of the $700,000 award for lost future earnings. Although in general lost future earnings are a type of future damage particularly suitable to a periodic payment judgment, this case presents a somewhat unusual situation because the damages awarded are solely attributable to the earnings of plaintiff's lost years. If the trial court had ordered such damages paid periodically over the time period when the loss was expected to be incurred, the damages would have been paid in their entirety after plaintiff's expected death, and thus—if the life expectancy predictions were accurate—plaintiff would not have received any of this element of damages. . . .

Thus, in sum, we conclude that none of the defendant's contentions call for a reversal of the judgment.

VII

We now turn to plaintiff's contentions.

As noted, although the jury by special verdict set plaintiff's noneconomic damages at $500,000, the trial court reduced that amount to $250,000 pursuant to Civil Code §3333.2. Plaintiff challenges this ruling, contending that §3333.2 is unconstitutional on a number of grounds. In many respects, plaintiff's argument tracks

---

shall only be subject to modification in the event of the death of the judgment creditor. . . . However, money damages awarded for loss of future earnings shall not be reduced or payments terminated by reason of the death of the judgment creditor, but shall be paid to persons to whom the judgment creditor owed a duty of support, as provided by law, immediately prior to his death. . . . By authorizing periodic payment judgments, it is the further intent of the legislature that the courts will utilize such judgments to provide compensation sufficient to meet the needs of an injured plaintiff and those persons who are dependent on the plaintiff for whatever period is necessary while eliminating the potential windfall from a lump-sum recovery which was intended to provide for the care of an injured plaintiff over an extended period who then dies shortly after the judgment is paid, leaving the balance of the judgment award to persons and purposes for which it was not intended. It is also the intent of the legislature that all elements of the periodic payment program be specified with certainty in the judgment ordering such payments and that the judgment not be subject to modification at some future time which might alter the specifications of the original judgment.

the constitutional objections to other provisions of MICRA that we have recently rejected in *Roa.* . . .

For similar reasons, plaintiff's constitutional challenge to Civil Code §3333.1 — which modifies this state's common law "collateral source" rule — is also without merit. Under the traditional collateral source rule, a jury, in calculating a plaintiff's damages in a tort action, does not take into consideration benefits — such as medical insurance or disability payments — which the plaintiff has received from sources other than the defendant — i.e., "collateral sources" — to cover losses resulting from the injury. Under §3333.1, subdivision (a), a medical malpractice defendant is permitted to introduce evidence of such collateral source benefits received by or payable to the plaintiff; when a defendant chooses to introduce such evidence, the plaintiff may introduce evidence of the amounts he has paid — in insurance premiums, for example — to secure the benefits. Although §3333.1, subdivision (a) — as ultimately adopted — does not specify how the jury should use such evidence, the legislature apparently assumed that in most cases the jury would set plaintiff's damages at a lower level because of its awareness of plaintiff's "net" collateral source benefits. . . .

In addition, §3333.1, subdivision (b) provides that whenever such collateral source evidence is introduced, the source of those benefits is precluded from obtaining subrogation either from the plaintiff or from the medical malpractice defendant. As far as the malpractice plaintiff is concerned, subdivision (b) assures that he will suffer no "double deduction" from his tort recovery as a result of his receipt of collateral source benefits; because the jury that has learned of his benefits may reduce his tort award by virtue of such benefits, the legislature eliminated any right the collateral source may have had to obtain repayment of those benefits from the plaintiff. . . .

[T]he legislature clearly did not act irrationally in choosing to modify the collateral source rule as one means of lowering the costs of malpractice litigation. In analyzing the collateral source rule more than a decade ago, we acknowledged that most legal commentators had severely criticized the rule for affording a plaintiff a "double recovery" for "losses" he had not in reality sustained, and we noted that many jurisdictions had either restricted or repealed it. . . .

The judgment is affirmed.

■ ROBERTS v. STEVENS CLINIC HOSPITAL
345 S.E.2d 791 (W. Va. 1986)

NEELY, Justice.

In this appeal we decide whether we should sustain a McDowell County Circuit Court $10,000,000 jury award [for compensatory damages] in favor of the parents and two siblings of Michael Joseph Roberts, a 2 1/2-year-old child who died as the result of medical malpractice. [A surgeon punctured his bowel trying to correct a problem that was causing severe diarrhea. He died from the resulting infection.] . . .

Kenneth and Joyce Roberts are a young couple who . . . gave birth to Michael Joseph Roberts. . . . Michael was the darling of the whole family. He was both an intelligent and happy little boy who was particularly close to his mother. The jury had before it substantial evidence that since Michael's death Joyce has been overwhelmed by grief and that the Roberts' family is no longer a happy household. . . . Joyce spent many nights crying and writing poems to Michael, and there was evidence that she continues to suffer from chronic diarrhea and vomiting. . . .

At trial the plaintiff introduced into evidence a professionally prepared, twenty minute, videotape that combined "home movie" video recordings of Michael taken by a neighbor with a series of still, colored, photographs of Michael and the family. The audio background for this video presentation consisted of tape recordings of the child's voice as well as Joyce's voice singing and talking to the child. It is the defendant's contention that this film was a "theatrical" presentation that artistically highlighted certain aspects of Michael's life and Joyce's relationship to Michael in an inaccurate way.

We have reviewed the tape in its entirety and we find nothing inflammatory or prejudicial about it. . . . The purpose of the videotape was to demonstrate that Michael was a healthy, intelligent, enthusiastic, and well-loved child. So, as a preliminary matter, the videotape was relevant. In our review of the tape, we find no artistic highlighting that emphasizes some scenes or photographs more than others, and we find no merit in the defendant's assertion that because the mother's voice went on several seconds after the screen turned black, an unduly sentimental atmosphere was evoked that would have prejudiced the jury.

This court has not previously addressed the admissibility of videotape "Day-in-the-Life" films. . . . We are not unmindful of the potential dangers inherent in such presentations. As one court has explained: Almost always an edited tape necessarily raises issues as to every sequence portrayed of whether the event shown is fairly representative of fact, after the editing process, and whether it is unduly prejudicial because of the manner of presentation. Bolstridge v. Central Maine Power Co., 621 F. Supp. 1202 (D.C. Me. 1985) (plaintiff's "Day-in-the-Life" videotape excluded when open court testimony could demonstrate similar evidence, and admission of videotape would create risk of distracting jury and unfairly prejudicing defendant). . . . But, we shall not reverse a trial court's decision in these matters unless the record shows a clear abuse of discretion. . . .

We now come to the most serious problem in this case, namely the closing argument of plaintiff's counsel. In a nutshell, the reason that we are compelled to reduce the jury's award from $10,000,000 to $3,000,000 is that plaintiff's counsel implied, in his closing argument, that the duty of the jury was to place a value on Michael's life. No objection along those lines, however, was made during the closing argument, and for that reason we are undisposed to reverse the entire trial because, technically, the error was waived.[5] . . .

[Plaintiff's counsel] argued that if a $10,000,000 race horse had been killed through the negligence of a veterinary hospital, the measure of damages would be exactly $10,000,000. At another point in the argument counsel asked what would have happened if someone had approached Michael's parents with an envelope containing ten, $1,000,000 winning lottery tickets and asked the parents if they would trade Michael's life for the tickets. Finally, counsel made reference to the

---

5. . . . In the roughly seven seconds available to counsel to make the strategic decision whether to object, it probably dawned on counsel that an objection and "curative" instruction would serve only to reinforce plaintiff's counsel's point.

American space program where billions of dollars are spent to avoid the loss of a single life. Representative excerpts from counsel's closing argument are as follows:

> . . . Now if Michael were a race horse and the Stevens Clinic Hospital operated a veterinarian hospital and a race horse named Michael died as a result of the negligence of a veterinary doctor, you wouldn't have any trouble in returning a verdict for millions of dollars because you know that that's what race horses are worth. You tell me, you tell the family, are horses entitled to better care than children? And are children less valuable than horses? . . .

Our wrongful death statute specifically sets forth the losses for which damages can be recovered.[8] Obviously, if the measure of damages were the value of a human life then, arguably, no jury verdict could be excessive. The death of a family member, particularly a child, involves inconsolable grief for which no amount of money can compensate. . . . We believe that our conclusion in this regard is grounded in sound public policy, which we now proceed to discuss.[9] . . .

[B]ecause less than 6 percent of all serious lawsuits are tried, the most important thing that courts do is to cast a shadow of legal rules within which litigants can craft their own custom-made settlements. . . . Without the occasional jury award that is at least ten times greater than what the parties would have settled for immediately after the tragedy, there would be no incentive on the part of clients to temper the . . . anti-settlement proclivities of their lawyers by urging quick payment of just claims. . . .

Ideally, in a case such as the one before us where the negligence of the defendants is palpable, some just compensation for Michael's death would have been forthcoming within 30 days. Yet Michael died in July, 1982 and it is now April, 1986 without the Roberts' having received any compensation whatsoever for Michael's loss.

When the defendants moved for leave to file an appeal in this court, the court asked the parties to describe the settlement negotiations that preceded the trial. Such information is generally inadmissible and incompetent to show liability or set the measure of damages. But we believe that settlement discussions have some bearing on the necessarily subjective criteria that appellate courts use to

---

8. W. Va. Code §55-7-6 [1982] provides:

The verdict of the jury shall include, but may not be limited to, damages for the following: (A) Sorrow, mental anguish, and solace which may include society, companionship, comfort, guidance, kindly offices and advice of the decedent; (B) compensation for reasonably expected loss of (i) income of the decedent, and (ii) services, protection, care and assistance provided by the decedent; (C) expenses for the care, treatment and hospitalization of the decedent incident to the injury resulting in death; and (D) reasonable funeral expenses. . . .

9. While the plaintiffs furnished us with a number of cases where jury verdicts of this magnitude have been approved, the plaintiffs in those cases had suffered severe personal injuries that necessitated enormous future medical care costs and also loss of earning capacity. These elements are absent in this case.

determine a proper remittitur, because such a determination affects future settlement negotiations. . . .

About two months before trial plaintiff's counsel made a written offer to both defendants to settle for $5,000,000, which was approximately half of the total available insurance coverage of $10,250,000. No response was received from the defendants until the Friday afternoon before the Monday morning trial date! At that time defendant Magnus offered $100,000 and the offer was rejected. The next day the offer was increased to $125,000, and after one week of trial, when most of the plaintiff's evidence was in, and both defendants had reason to expect a substantial verdict, defendant Magnus increased the offer to $220,000.

In light of the statistically demonstrable fact that settlement rather than litigation is the true cynosure of the whole judicial process, in this case, then, we not only ask ourselves how much money the Roberts family should receive to compensate them for the losses enumerated under the Wrongful Death Statute; we also ask ourselves what jury award in a case of this type will establish the proper climate for out-of-court settlements. . . . Accordingly, . . . the case is remanded to the circuit court with directions to enter a remittitur of $7,000,000 and enter judgment on the verdict for $3,000,000 or, in the alternative, at the option of the plaintiff, to award a new trial.

Reversed and remanded with directions.

Notes: Damages; Wrongful Life Cases

1. *Hedonic Damages.* Damages for loss of enjoyment of life are sometimes referred to as "hedonic damages." One must distinguish carefully among versions of hedonic damages in order to make an accurate statement of the law. The situation in which they are the most readily recoverable is as an element of pain and suffering, where an injury has left the plaintiff alive and aware but disabled. The situation in which they are least recoverable is where the plaintiff is killed or left comatose. The inability to experience the loss of life's pleasures usually means that they cannot be claimed as a form of pain and suffering. But a few courts disagree. For a thorough review of the law with majority and dissenting views, see generally McDougald v. Garber, 536 N.E.2d 372 (N.Y. 1989). See also Annot., 34 A.L.R.4th 293 (1984). *Fein* presents a third situation, where a plaintiff is fully abled in the present, but is likely to die early. Here, it is possible to receive some form of compensation for lost enjoyment of life by characterizing the damages as distress and anguish in the present over realizing that one's life is shortened. The traditional view, however, is that no recovery is allowed for the value of life itself, under the view that it is impossible or unseemly to place a value on life.

Measurable *economic* damages, however, do pertain to a shortened life. Review *Fein* to clarify the difference between economic damages during life and as a result of a shortened life. Which set of economic damages raises the possibility of a "necessities-of-living" offset? Which set relies on diminished earning capacity?

Other exceptions to the general rule that loss of life is not compensated arise by virtue of wrongful death statutes. Review the version of this statute in the *Roberts* case and the components of damages that were recognized and rejected there. You will observe that these statutes do not directly overturn the general rule. How, then, do they justify noneconomic damages in cases of instantaneous death?

2. *Wrongful Life and Wrongful Birth.* "Wrongful life" and "wrongful birth" cases are where these concepts are put to their greatest test in medical malpractice litigation. In contrast to wrongful death actions that ask what is the value of a *lost* life, wrongful life and birth actions ask what are the damages for a life *brought into being* that *should not* have been. There are two typical scenarios. First, if a doctor fails to identify or avoid a birth defect, a claim can result for the expenses and anguish of living life with a severe handicap. Second, if a sterilization procedure fails, an action can result for the expenses of raising a normal, healthy child, as well as for any harms attendant to pregnancy and childbirth.[1] The first scenario presents the greatest conceptual difficulties.

The first difficulty is causation. Usually, the only way to avoid a birth defect once it is detected is by aborting. Of course, there is always the question whether the parents would have made this decision, but there is the more fundamental realization that the only way *this* child could have avoided the severe defect is to not be born at all. Therefore, one must measure damages by comparing the two states of severe disability with nonexistence.

At first, these causation and damages difficulties were insurmountable for the courts. Shortly after abortions became commonplace, however, courts began to allow limited forms of these actions. See William J. Curran, Genetic Counseling and Wrongful Life, 68 Am. J. Public Health 501 (1978). They distinguished between "wrongful life" actions, which are the child's own claims for the suffering and expenses of being alive, and "wrongful birth" actions, which are the parents' claims for having to raise a handicapped child. Most courts allow only the latter—the parents' claim—and even then limit the damages to mostly economic ones, such as the "extraordinary" costs of intensive care and treatment. (Query why not the "ordinary" costs as well?) Emotional distress damages are not recoverable in a number of states because it is thought that the emotional benefits of having a child at all outweigh the emotional harms of the severe handicap. Again, it is usually not factually possible to make a claim for failure to have a healthy child. Nevertheless, a number of other states allow juries to weigh the competing benefits and burdens of having the child at all and award damages for a net emotional loss.

A very few states also allow the handicapped child to maintain his own action, but the damages are similarly constrained to the economic costs of managing life as a disabled adult. The leading case is Turpin v. Sortini, 643 P.2d 954 (Cal. 1982). This is no different, however, than allowing the parents to recover the costs of care for the child's *entire* lifetime rather than for only the years of dependency. A very few courts have rejected both causes of action entirely. See, e.g., Atlanta Obstetrics & Gynecology Group v. Abelson, 398 S.E.2d 557 (Ga. 1990). Also, several state legislatures, motivated by antiabortion sentiments, have restricted or abolished these causes of action. Note, Wrongful Birth Actions: The Case Against Legislative Curtailment, 100 Harv. L. Rev. 2017 (1987) (arguing these statutes are unconstitutional).

In "wrongful conception" cases (i.e., those involving failed sterilizations), courts usually allow only the medical expenses of birth but not the economic costs

---

1. A third scenario, which entails wrongfully maintaining an existing life by refusing to disconnect life support, is presented in Anderson v. St. Francis-St. George Hospital, 671 N.E.2d 225 (Ohio 1996).

of raising a normal, healthy child. Although child-rearing costs clearly result from the failed sterilization, as a matter of social policy most courts are not willing to allow a jury to find that children, on balance, are a burden. Other courts, however, allow recovery of both the economic and the emotional costs of having an unexpected child, subject to the jury's views on the value of offsetting benefits. One court went so far as to allow recovery of child-rearing costs with no offset, under the view that emotional benefits are usually offset only against emotional, not economic, burdens. Marchiniak v. Lundborg, 450 N.W.2d 243 (Wis. 1990).

There are a host of cases, and almost as many law review articles, on this topic. For a sampling of the latter, see note 8. For cases, see Annot., 74 A.L.R.4th 798 (1989).

The potential for wrongful life litigation is greatly increasing with the explosion in genetic tests, not only for congenital defects but also for "normal" diseases later in life such as cancer. Far-reaching genetic mapping projects currently under way are likely to increase exponentially our current ability to detect predisposition to genetic conditions.

3. *The Size of Awards.* Most years, medical malpractice cases regularly produce some of the highest verdicts in the country, in the range of $20 million to $50 million or more. Usually, these involve severely damaged newborns. But, focusing on these extreme cases gives a false impression of what typical damages awards are in medical malpractice cases. Even a more systematic reading of reported decisions can give a false impression since only the rare claim reaches appellate review and review is more likely when the actual or potential damages award is high. Substantial empirical research sheds considerable light on the experience in more typical malpractice claims.

When claims are filed, only about a third result in payment, most by settlement. Fewer than 10 percent of malpractice claims are tried, and only about 20 to 30 percent of these produce plaintiff verdicts. Most jury verdicts are well below $1 million. A study of verdicts from large cities in 2001 found that the median award was $77,000 for temporary injuries, $412,000 for permanent injuries, and $837,000 for death; no plaintiff with a temporary injury received a jury verdict exceeding $1 million. David A. Hyman & Charles Silver, Medical Malpractice Litigation and Tort Reform: It's the Incentives, Stupid, 59 Vand. L. Rev. 1085, 1105 (2006). Considering all of this, injured patients have difficulty finding a lawyer willing to take their case when their potential damages are less than $50,000. Id.

Combining both jury verdicts and claims settled outside of litigation, the average payment in 2015 was about $400,000 nationally, but this does not represent the typical case because the average is skewed by a relatively few number of very high awards. More representative is the median payout, which (in 2015) was $225,000. Settlement amounts have held fairly steady over the past decade, but the number of paid claims has dropped by about 40 percent since 2005. See note 8.

4. *Settlements.* Additional research indicates that, when cases go to trial, the variation in jury awards *in the aggregate* is broadly consistent with the severity of injury, although for a given category of injury, *individual* jury awards are highly erratic, varying by a factor of ten or more. See Symposium, 54 Law & Contemp. Probs. 1 (Winter 1991). This unpredictability makes it difficult to settle cases, even where liability is relatively clear. Also, doctors are often reluctant to settle because of the negative publicity and their desire for personal vindication. Accordingly,

medical malpractice cases are twice as likely to go to trial as are other personal injury suits. Michael Saks, Do We Really Know Anything About the Behavior of the Tort Litigation System—And Why Not?, 140 U. Pa. L. Rev. 1147, 1128 (1992).

Nevertheless, most malpractice awards are obtained through settlement. Settlement amounts are influenced by the reputation and experience of the particular lawyers and expert witnesses representing plaintiffs, with lawyers receiving significantly more if their track record in front of juries shows they are able to land sizeable verdicts. Also, studies show that settlement amounts tend to correlate with the strength of a case, although the degree of injury has more influence than the degree of fault. For sources, see note 8.

On the other hand, settlement tends to suppress the average amount of the award. Settlements rarely are for amounts greater than the limits of physicians' liability insurance, so physicians almost never have to use personal assets to pay claims. In a study from Florida, only about a fifth of paid claimants recovered more than their economic loss, and most recovered less, on account of the discounting that occurs in settlement negotiations. The average pretrial settlement paid about half of economic losses. Even those who won at trial recovered on average only 22 percent more than economic losses. Frank Sloan et al., Suing for Medical Malpractice (1993). Again, this is due in part to settlement. Plaintiffs often settle even after receiving favorable jury verdicts, since a post-trial settlement avoids the cost and delay of an appeal. The vast majority of $1 million-plus verdicts are settled for somewhat less. An insurer is likely to insist on appealing only if it is confident in the merits or if it sees the case as a good opportunity to set a favorable precedent for future cases. Review the facts in McCourt v. Abernathy at page 322. As defense counsel, what would you have settled the case for after trial?

5. *Dropping a Claim.* As just noted, over half of malpractice claims filed are closed (resolved) without payment, some by court dismissal, but many because the insurer refuses to pay and the plaintiff simply drops the claim. See Dwight Golann, Dropped Medical Malpractice Claims, 30(7) Health Aff. 1343 (2011). How can a lawyer ethically drop a case, though, once she learns it is not possible to settle? Generally, there are two options: (1) have an agreement (preferably written) with the client that the case is being taken on for purposes of settlement only; (2) seek the judge's permission to withdraw. The latter is necessary only if suit has been filed. Many judges will be reluctant to grant this permission if diligent investigation before suit would have disclosed the case's weaknesses.

6. *Scheduled Damages.* One notable proposal to make jury awards more predictable is to create a schedule of pain and suffering damages according to a matrix of the following factors: whether the injury is temporary or permanent; life expectancy; and whether the injury is minor, significant, major, or grave. These scheduled damages could then either be mandated, given to the jury as advisory guidelines, or used by the judge to police excessively large or small verdicts. Moreover, the scheduled amounts could be based on a collection of actual prior jury verdicts rather than on legislative or administrative assessments. See note 8.

7. *The Collateral Source Rule.* It may seem difficult on the surface to justify the traditional collateral source rule that allows plaintiffs double recovery of their medical bills or lost income, but in theory this is sensible because most third-party health

and disability insurers have a contractual right of subrogation that allows them to be reimbursed for their payments from the tort award. In practice, however, such subrogation claims are fairly rare, owing to the difficulty in allocating lump sum tort awards or settlements among various damages components. Moreover, many states have statutes that limit or preclude the ability of insurers to enforce these contractual provisions. A more practical justification for not offsetting collateral source recoveries is the need to provide plaintiffs a source for paying their attorneys' fees. This is also a practical justification for unlimited pain and suffering awards. This perhaps best explains why physicians push so strongly for malpractice reform statutes that limit these elements of damage, since they go a long way toward removing lawyers' economic motivation for taking the case in the first place. Note that the *Roa* case decided the same day as *Fein* upheld California's statutory limits on the size of contingency fees.

Recall from section A.1 the research that indicates many injured patients sue because they are worried primarily about the costs of medical treatment or in response to hospitals' or doctors' attempts to collect on their overdue bills. How does this information bear on this debate? Would you advise hospitals and doctors to voluntarily pick up the costs of extended treatment for injured patients without admitting liability?

8. *Bibliography.* For discussion of **wrongful life/birth** cases and related theories (note 2), see Alexander M. Capron, Tort Liability in Genetic Counseling, 79 Colum. L. Rev. 618 (1979); Wendy F. Hensel, The Disabling Impact of Wrongful Life and Wrongful Birth Actions, 40 Harv. C.R.-C.L. L. Rev. 141 (2005); Daniel Whitney & Kenneth Rosenbaum, Recovery of Damages for Wrongful Birth, 32 J. Leg. Med. 167 (2011); Dov Fox, Reproductive Negligence, 117 Colum. L. Rev. 149 (2017).

On the **size of awards** (note 3) and **settlements** (4), see Michelle Mello & Allen Kachalia, Medical Malpractice: Evidence on Reform Alternatives and Claims Involving Elderly Patients (MedPac, 2016); David A. Hyman et al., Settlement at Policy Limits and the Duty to Settle, 8 J. Empirical Legal Stud. 48 (2011); Catherine Harris et al., Placing "Standard of Care" in Context: The Impact of Witness Potential and Attorney Reputation in Medical Malpractice Litigation, 3 J. Empirical Legal Stud. 467 (2006); Catherine Harris et al., Does Being a Repeat Player Make a Difference?, 8 Yale J. Health Pol'y L. & Ethics 253 (2008); Philip Peters, What We Know About Malpractice Settlements, 92 Iowa L. Rev. 1783 (2007); Kathryn Zeiler et al., Physicians' Insurance Limits and Malpractice Payments, 36 J. Leg. Stud. 9 (2007); Neil Vidmar et al., Million Dollar Medical Malpractice Cases in Florida: Post-Verdict and Pre-Suit Settlements, 59 Vand. L. Rev. 1343 (2006); David Hyman et al., Do Defendants Pay What Juries Award?, J. Empirical Legal Stud. 3 (2007).

Regarding **hedonic damages** (note 1), see generally R. Pallin & B. Danninger, Hedonic Damages: Proving Damages for Lost Enjoyment of Living (1990); Eric A. Posner & Cass R. Sunstein, Dollars and Death, 72 U. Chi. L. Rev. 537 (2005). On **scheduled damages** (note 6), see Randall R. Bovbjerg et al., Valuing Life and Limb in Tort: Scheduling "Pain and Suffering," 83 Nw. U. L. Rev. 908 (1989); David M. Studdert et al., Rationalizing Noneconomic Damages, 74 Law & Contemp. Probs. 57 (Summer 2011). On the **collateral source rule** (note 7), see Adam Todd, An Enduring Oddity: The Collateral Source Rule in the Face of Tort Reform, the Affordable

Care Act, and Increased Subrogation, 43 McGeorge L. Rev. 965 (2012); Comment, 60 UCLA L. Rev. 736 (2013).

Exercise: "A Day in the Life"

Interview someone you know who suffers from a physical or mental infirmity, or someone who lives with such a person. Write a script for a demonstrative exhibit (video, charts, still photographs, etc.) that details a day or week in the life of this individual. Explain your strategic decisions regarding what to highlight or dramatize and what to leave out or avoid, in order to maximize the exhibit's emotional impact without having it excluded altogether.

Exercise: Damages Settlement

Conduct a settlement negotiation with one of your classmates in the following hypothetical:*

> Joe Jenks is paralyzed from the waist down as a result of negligently performed surgery on his back. At the time of the surgery he was 30 years of age and employed as a forklift operator for Wheeling Manufacturing Co. He graduated from high school at age 18, spent two years in the army (receiving an honorable discharge), and immediately after discharge went to work for Wheeling. Before the surgery he was in good health, except for chronic back pain that plagued him for six months after he fell while playing basketball. He earned $40,000 as a forklift operator in the year before the accident. In addition, that same year he earned $30,000 moonlighting as a security guard on evenings and weekends. He has never been married and lives alone. He was a below-average student in high school, graduating at the bottom of his class. He was, however, a well-liked and ambitious young man who had a strong aptitude for mechanics. His paralysis is permanent.

Take the lawyer's position on one side or the other in a suit against the orthopedic surgeon. Make up and stick to the client facts you need that aren't given. Assume that investigating and trying the case will cost the plaintiff's lawyer $50,000 in out-of-pocket expenses and will cost the doctor's insurer $150,000 in legal fees and expenses. Assume further that your jurisdiction has no damages cap, but does have statutes that allow period payments and offset of collateral source payments. Engage in negotiations attempting to reach a definite settlement. If successful, then reveal to the other side the actual "bottom line" or "top dollar" you would have been willing to agree to. If you haven't reached a settlement after half an hour, then determine how far apart you are by stating your final best offers.

*This is adapted from Frank M. McClellan, Medical Malpractice: Law, Tactics, and Ethics (1994). Another excellent source for practical trial techniques is Thomas M. O'Toole et al., The Anatomy of a Medical Malpractice Verdict, 70 Mont. L. Rev. 57 (2009).

BLEDAY v. OUM GROUP
645 A.2d 1358 (Pa. Super. Ct. 1994)

HUDOCK, Judge.

. . . Appellants secured malpractice insurance through Insurers for the period of February, 1988, through February, 1989. The policy obtained by Appellants contained the following [provision]:

> The company shall have the right and duty to defend any suit against the insured seeking damages because of such injury even if any of the allegations of the suit are groundless, false or fraudulent. The company may make such investigation and settlement of any claim or suit as it deems expedient.

Within the time period covered by said policy, Tracey Worchesky (Worchesky) instituted an action against Appellants. The nature of her claim was that she had to seek corrective surgery from another podiatrist because she never properly recovered from surgery performed by Dr. Bleday. . . . [O]ver the objection of Appellants, Insurers settled Worchesky's claim for $10,000.[1] Insurers stated that the settlement was a result of a business decision which was made to "avoid the cost of litigation and the uncertainties of a jury trial."

. . . Appellants filed a complaint against Insurers and Adjusters . . . alleg[ing] that Insurers breached their duty of good faith to Appellants by settling Worchesky's claim without their consent. . . . With respect to damages, Appellants assert that they will be subjected to increased insurance premiums, loss of earnings, and harm to reputation since Dr. Bleday's name will be placed on the National Physician Data Bank, a list of doctors who have been involved in malpractice actions. . . . The trial court granted the [defendants' motion to dismiss]. . . . Appellants assert that Insurers, despite the policy language "deems expedient," have the duty to act in good faith in the handling of its claims. . . .

After a thorough review of case law from other jurisdictions, we conclude that, although judicial deference must be given to the decision of an insurance company to settle a claim within the policy limits, a claim for bad faith may, in limited circumstances, be asserted against the insurance company notwithstanding a "deems expedient" provision. A "deems expedient" provision in an insurance contract cannot be interpreted to convey to an insurance company an absolute right to settle a claim within the policy limits if such settlement was contrary to the intent and expectation of the parties. However, after a thorough review of the complaint filed by Appellants, we find that Appellants did not sufficiently plead a cause of action in bad faith against Insurers, and, thus, the trial court properly granted Insurers' preliminary objections.

Several jurisdictions hold that a "deems expedient" provision in an insurance contract conveys to an insurer an absolute right to settle the claims of the

---

1. As one of the grounds for objecting to the settlement, Appellants assert that Worchesky, at no time, submitted an expert report to support her claim of injury. The only expert report was secured by [Insurers], and it stated that Dr. Bleday was not negligent.

insured within the insurance policy limits. . . . In Feliberty v. Damon, 527 N.E.2d 261 (N.Y. 1988), a medical malpractice panel found that the appellant committed malpractice and was liable in the amount of $743,000. Before judgment was entered and without his consent, the appellant's insurer settled the claim for $700,000, an amount within the policy limits. The appellant sought compensatory and punitive damages from the insurer, asserting that his reputation was damaged as a result of the settlement. The New York court, in granting the insurer's motion to dismiss the complaint, held that the insurance company had an absolute right to settle under the language of the policy. . . .

In Shuster v. South Broward Hospital, 591 So.2d 174 (Fla. 1992), . . . the court opined:

> The language of the ["deems expedient"] provision is clear and the insured was put on notice that the agreement granted the insurer the exclusive authority to control settlement and to be guided by its own self-interest when settling the claim for amounts within the policy limits. The obvious intent behind placing the provision in the agreement was to grant the insurer the authority to decide whether to settle or defend the claim based on its own self-interest, and this authority includes settling for the nuisance value of the claim. Therefore, we interpret the provision as granting the insurer the discretion to settle cases for amounts within the policy limits, regardless of whether the claim is frivolous or not. . . .

However, the court further stressed that every contract that is entered into requires the good faith performance of its provisions, and, thus, the "deems expedient" provision is not absolute. . . .

Based on the facts in the case herein, we find that Appellants have not sufficiently pled a cause of action in bad faith. . . . We believe, as the Supreme Court of Florida did in *Shuster*, that something more is required to maintain a cause of action for bad faith when a claim is settled within the policy limits. However, we leave for another day to define what circumstances constitute bad faith; it is enough to say that they are not present in the instant case. . . .

■ REGULATORY SYSTEM IN SHAMBLES; NEGLIGENT DOCTORS STAY ON JOB
Bruce Butterfield & Gerard O'Neill
Boston Globe, Oct. 2, 1994*

A nine-month investigation of malpractice by the Boston Globe Spotlight Team examined more than 1,000 court cases of scores of doctors across the state who have been sued repeatedly over the last ten years—some more than ten times. Yet nearly all continue to practice virtually unregulated and unpenalized. . . . Records of the most-sued doctors reveal a malpractice trail of anguish and suffering across the

*This is the first of a five-part series of articles. The last two paragraphs of this excerpt are from another article in the same series, Brian C. Mooney, Doctors with Dubious Records Start Fresh in Other States, *Boston Globe*, Oct. 5, 1994.

state: children maimed for life; babies dead from botched deliveries; women dying needlessly of breast and cervical cancers; patients left paraplegic, incontinent or crippled. . . . In case after case, the story is the same. Doctors at the center of the malpractice problem are frequently sued, but never admit wrongdoing regardless of the severity of the case.

And there is nobody willing to force them: not fellow doctors, not medical insurers, and not even the courts where settlements are almost always subject to secrecy agreements. . . . Deficient doctors in Massachusetts rarely lose their licenses. They never lose malpractice insurance. When they get in trouble in one hospital, they are often passed to another. The result is a medical monitoring system turned on its head. . . .

Take the case of Dr. Grahshyam P. Massand—currently practicing at Somerville Hospital. Massand has been sued 10 times since 1985, been subject to hospital restrictions on his work, lost privileges at one hospital, and moved to another. . . . If patients should have been able to find out about any problem doctor, it should have been about Massand. His record was well known by medical, regulatory and insurance officials alike. But in many cases, the slow-footed Board of Registration in Medicine doesn't even know who the repeatedly sued doctors are. Insurers know, but shroud nearly everything they do—and everything they fail to do—in confidentiality. The agency that insures two-thirds of all doctors is the quasi-public Massachusetts Professional Insurance Association, established in the mid-1970s and dominated by doctors and hospital executives who sit on its board of directors. Despite its public mission, it is protective and secretive to its core. . . . Its executives say they process the paper and pay the bills, but don't get involved with discipline. "I mean, it's not our job," says Tracy Gehan Leu, spokeswoman for the agency.

The real job of disciplining bad doctors is left to the Board of Registration in Medicine. But the board's efforts on the malpractice front have all but collapsed. Massand is one of only a handful of repeatedly sued doctors who have been formally charged by the board. Still, after a decade marked by disastrous cases, he continues to hang onto his license.

Far more common are doctors like Sherman Stein—untouched by the board despite frequent and severe malpractice complaints. . . . Stein was sued for negligence, and his insurers settled in a secret agreement in 1992. By then, Stein had left a trail of lawsuits and patients claiming they were injured or maimed by him. But he was no longer around—he had moved on to become head of neurosurgery at Cooper Hospital in Camden, N.J., with an ostensibly spotless record. In all, Stein has had 11 malpractice suits filed against him since 1985, and a twelfth filed only months before that—one of the worst records of any doctor in the state. At least six of those suits resulted in secret settlements to avoid trial. . . .

Judges as well as lawyers routinely sidestep a 1986 state law banning confidential settlements, which occur in about one third of all medical malpractice suits. . . . [I]n the overwhelming majority of cases in which plaintiffs are paid, the settlement is masked by a bland order "stipulating dismissal" of the complaint and a patient's promise not to talk about it under a threat of forfeiture. . . . In many cases, the record is a sham: Judgment is recorded for the doctor even though the insurer paid a substantial sum to the plaintiff. . . .

These clamps on the flow of information to the public outrage activists in the small but growing health consumer movement. "This is ultimately a question of the right to know," said U.S. Rep. Ron Wyden (D.-Or.), principal sponsor of the bill that created the national data bank and cosponsor of a pending bill that would open up some of its information to the public. . . . Wyden's bill, opposed by the AMA, would disclose information about physicians and others who have had medical privileges restricted or had two or more payouts in malpractice suits.

Notes: Settlement; National Practitioner Data Bank; Insurance

1. *Bleday* reflects the prevailing law that insurers with "deems expedient" language control the decision to settle. Other courts have ruled, however, that as soon as the defendant's lawyer determines that the insurer and the doctor are at odds on settlement, the lawyer has a conflict of interest and therefore a duty to notify the doctor and give him a chance to obtain other counsel. Even if the doctor cannot block the insurer's decision, he might want to release the insurer from further involvement and bear the costs of defending himself. Breach of this duty to disclose could result in an action for legal malpractice. Rogers v. Robson, Masters, Ryan, Brumund & Belon, 407 N.E.2d 47 (Ill. 1980). The physician-owned malpractice insurers that exist in many states are more sympathetic to allowing physicians to control the decision to go to trial than are independent, "commercial" insurers. In many states, insurance is available with language that requires the doctor's consent to settle, but in other states, insurers prohibit such clauses because they deter settlement. Interestingly, where such clauses exist, they increase the cost of insurance by 1 to 3 percent, which physicians are often willing to pay so they can have more control over whether they will be reported to the National Practitioner Data Bank (NPDB). For an exploration of the psychology of settlement in this context, see Ralph Peeples et al., Settlement Has Many Faces: Physicians, Attorneys and Medical Malpractice, 41 J. Health & Soc. Behav. 333 (2000). See generally Scott Thomas, An Insurer's Right to Settle Versus Its Duty to Defend Nonmeritorious Medical Malpractice Claims, 16 J. Leg. Med. 545 (1995).

When doctors want to settle, they have more legal leverage because insurers can be held liable for exposing doctors to uninsured damages beyond their policy limits. See generally Kent D. Syverud, The Duty to Settle, 76 Va. L. Rev. 1113 (1990); Annot., 18 A.L.R.5th 474 (1995).

2. *Secrecy.* As the *Boston Globe* article reflects, some doctors very much want to settle malpractice suits to avoid attracting attention. Even though the NPDB was implemented in 1989 to require disclosure of all payments in claims against doctors, defense lawyers are often able to avoid these laws by (1) stipulating that payment will come from an institutional defendant such as a hospital or medical clinic rather than the doctor; (2) stipulating that the doctor is not at fault; and (3) presenting an uncontested motion to seal the court records for cause. See Haavi Morreim, Malpractice, Mediation, and Moral Hazard: The Virtues of Dodging the Data Bank, 27 Ohio St. J. on Disp. Resol. 1 (2012). Query whether it is ethically permissible for a plaintiff's lawyer to participate in such a stipulation or motion that neither she nor her client actually believes.

Public outrage following the *Boston Globe*'s investigative reporting led to a 1996 law in Massachusetts requiring the medical licensing board to collect and provide on request information about each complaint against a doctor in which any payment is made to the plaintiff. Well over a dozen other statutes have followed suit, and most require that this information be made available to the public through the Internet. See this casebook's Web site for links, www.health-law.org, and see generally E. Helland, Bargaining in the Shadow of the Website: Disclosure's Impact on Medical Malpractice Litigation, 12 Am. L. & Econ. Rev. 423 (2010); Matthew E. Brown, Redefining the Physician Selection Process and Rewriting Medical Malpractice Settlement Disclosure Webpages, 31 Am. J.L. & Med. 479 (2005). Many commentators view these mandatory reporting requirements as an obstacle to settlement. E.g., William Sage et al., Bridging the Relational-Regulatory Gap: A Pragmatic Information Policy for Patient Safety and Medical Malpractice, 59 Vand. L. Rev. 1263 (2006). But see Helland, supra. At present, the NPDB requires settlements of *any* size to be reported, even those of "nuisance value." Unlike the Massachusetts system, however, the NPDB does not allow public access to this information. Instead, the information is collected only for use by state licensing boards or by medical institutions when they review physicians' competence for licensing or credentialing purposes. Litigants have access only in cases that allege a hospital was negligent in allowing a doctor to use its facilities.

3. *Malpractice Insurance.* One might think that physicians who are repeatedly sued would be put out of business because they could no longer afford their malpractice insurance, much like high-risk automobile drivers. Malpractice insurance, however, is not generally "experience-rated," that is, premiums usually are not set according to each doctor's track record. Instead, premiums are usually adjusted only for the doctor's location and practice specialty. Premiums can vary by as much as fivefold based on location and tenfold based on specialty. See Frank Sloan et al., Insuring Medical Malpractice (1991); William M. Sage, Medical Malpractice Insurance and the Emperor's Clothes, 54 DePaul L. Rev. 463 (2005). For the most part, the lack of a rating system for physicians individually is in keeping with empirical evidence that malpractice claims, on average, are largely unpredictable events. In one study, doctors who were sued in a six-year baseline period had only a 3 percent chance of being sued in a subsequent three-year period. Randall R. Bovbjerg & Kenneth R. Petronis, The Relationship Between Physicians' Malpractice Claims History and Later Claims, 272 JAMA 1421 (1994). Of course, this does not excuse the failure of physician-owned insurers to do something about the few doctors who are sued and lose repeatedly. Additional discussion about the structure of the medical malpractice insurance market is in section H.

G. INSTITUTIONAL LIABILITY

While most doctors are well insured, some are not; and even those who are do not always make the most attractive targets for suit. Moreover, many medical errors do not result from physicians' mistakes. Therefore, plaintiffs are sometimes eager to hold the institutions in which physicians practice responsible for bad medical outcomes. There are two prominent institutions: hospitals and insurers, especially HMOs. These institutional targets of suit entail both unique theories of liability and unique defenses against liability, which the following sections explore.

You will learn shortly that two distinct theories of liability have emerged: vicarious and direct. In the former, the institution is held strictly liable for acts of negligence by member physicians, based on the physician's relationship with the institution. Observe how this branch of liability takes shape according to differ-ences in how types of physicians are connected with hospitals. Direct liability, the second branch, depends on showing some wrongdoing by the institution's manage-ment with respect to physician competence and patient care. Here, the issue is what responsibility is it realistic to assign to lay managers with respect to clinical matters? Overarching this development of legal doctrine is an evolution in judicial and pub-lic attitudes about the role that institutions play in the delivery of health care. This change has occurred both with respect to hospital liability and in the migration of liability from hospitals to HMOs. To set these materials in their historical context, then, we begin with a now outmoded but still seminal decision.

1. Hospital Liability

■ SCHLOENDORFF v. SOCIETY OF NEW YORK HOSPITAL
105 N.E. 92 (N.Y. 1914)

CARDOZO, J.

In the year 1771, by royal charter of George III, the Society of the New York Hospital was organized for the care and healing of the sick. During the century and more which has since passed, it has devoted itself to that high task. It has no capital stock; it does not distribute profits; and its physicians and surgeons, both the visiting and the resident staff, serve it without pay. Those who seek it in search of health are charged nothing if they are needy, either for board or for treatment. The well-to-do are required by its by-laws to pay $7 a week for board, an amount insufficient to cover the per capita cost of maintenance. Whatever income is thus received is added to the income derived from the hospital's foundation, and helps to make it possible for the work to go on. The purpose is not profit, but charity. . . .

To this hospital, the plaintiff came in January, 1908. She was suffering from some disorder of the stomach. She asked the superintendent or one of his assistants what the charge would be, and was told that it would be $7 a week. She became an inmate of the hospital, and after some weeks of treatment, the house physician, Dr. Bartlett, discovered a lump, which proved to be a fibroid tumor. He consulted the visiting physician, Dr. Stimson, who advised an operation. The plaintiff's testi-mony is that the character of the lump could not, so the physicians informed her, be determined without an ether examination. She consented to such an examination, but notified Dr. Bartlett, as she says, that there must be no [surgical removal]. She was taken at night from the medical to the surgical ward and prepared for an oper-ation by a nurse. On the following day ether was administered, and, while she was unconscious, a tumor was removed. Her testimony is that this was done without her consent or knowledge. She is contradicted both by Dr. Stimson and by Dr. Bartlett, as well as by many of the attendant nurses. For the purpose of this appeal, how-ever, since a verdict was directed in favor of the defendant, her narrative, even if improbable, must be taken as true. Following the operation, and, according to the testimony of her witnesses, because of it, gangrene developed in her left arm, some of her fingers had to be amputated, and her sufferings were intense. She now seeks to charge the hospital with liability for the wrong.

Certain principles of law governing the rights and duties of hospitals, when maintained as charitable institutions have, after much discussion, become no longer doubtful. It is the settled rule that such a hospital is not liable for the negligence of its physicians and nurses in the treatment of patients. Hillyer v. St. Bartholomew's Hospital, [1909] 2 K.B. 820. This exemption has been placed upon two grounds. The first is that of implied waiver. It is said that one who accepts the benefit of a charity enters into a relation which exempts one's benefactor from liability for the negligence of his servants in administering the charity. The hospital remains exempt, though the patient makes some payment to help defray the cost of board. Such a payment is regarded as a contribution to the income of the hospital, to be devoted, like its other funds to the maintenance of the charity. The second ground of the exemption is the relation subsisting between a hospital and the physicians who serve it. It is said that this relation is not one of master and servant, but that the physician occupies the position, so to speak, of an independent contractor, following a separate calling, liable, of course, for his own wrongs to the patient whom he undertakes to serve, but involving the hospital in no liability, if due care has been taken in his selection. On one or the other, and often on both of these grounds, a hospital has been held immune from liability to patients for the malpractice of its physicians. The reasons that have led to the adoption of this rule are, of course, inapplicable where the wrong is committed by a servant of the hospital and the sufferer is not a patient. It is therefore also a settled rule that a hospital is liable to strangers—i. e., to persons other than patients—for the torts of its employees committed within the line of their employment.

In the case at hand, the wrong complained of is not merely negligence. It is trespass. Every human being of adult years and sound mind has a right to determine what shall be done with his own body; and a surgeon who performs an operation without his patient's consent commits an assault, for which he is liable in damages. This is true, except in cases of emergency where the patient is unconscious, and where it is necessary to operate before consent can be obtained. The fact that the wrong complained of here is trespass, rather than negligence, distinguishes this case from most of the cases that have preceded it. . . . [The plaintiff] had never waived the right to recover damages for any wrong resulting from this operation, for she had forbidden the operation. In this situation, the true ground for the defendant's exemption from liability is that the relation between a hospital and its physicians is not that of master and servant. The hospital does not undertake to act through them, but merely to procure them to act upon their own responsibility. . . .

The wrong was not that of the hospital; it was that of physicians, who were not the defendant's servants, but were pursuing an independent calling, a profession sanctioned by a solemn oath, and safeguarded by stringent penalties. If, in serving their patient, they violated her commands, the responsibility is not the defendant's; it is theirs. There is no distinction in that respect between the visiting and the resident physicians. Whether the hospital undertakes to procure a physician from afar, or to have one on the spot, its liability remains the same. . . .

It is true, I think, of nurses, as of physicians, that, in treating a patient, they are not acting as the servants of the hospital. The superintendent is a servant of the hospital; the assistant superintendents, the orderlies, and the other members of the administrative staff are servants of the hospital. But nurses are employed to carry out the orders of the physicians, to whose authority they are subject. The hospital undertakes to procure for the patient the services of a nurse. It does not undertake, through the agency of nurses, to render those services itself. The reported cases make no distinction in that respect between the position of a nurse and that of a physician and none is justified in principle. If there are duties performed by nurses foreign to their duties in carrying out the physician's orders, and having relation to the administrative conduct of the hospital, the fact is not established by this record, nor was it in the discharge of such duties that the defendant's nurses were then serving. The acts of preparation immediately preceding the operation are necessary to its successful performance, and are really part of the operation itself. They are not different in that respect from the administration of the ether. Whatever the nurse does in those preliminary stages is done, not as the servant of the hospital, but in the course of the treatment of the patient, as the delegate of the surgeon to whose orders she is subject. The hospital is not chargeable with her knowledge that the operation is improper any more than with the surgeon's.

If, however, it could be assumed that a nurse is a servant of the hospital, . . . [w]as she to infer from the plaintiff's words that a distinguished surgeon intended to mutilate the plaintiff's body in defiance of the plaintiff's orders? Was it her duty, as a result of this talk, to report to the superintendent of the hospital that the ward was about to be utilized for the commission of an assault? I think that no such interpretation of the facts would have suggested itself to any reasonable mind. The preparation for an ether examination is to some extent the same as for an operation. The hour was midnight, and the plaintiff was nervous and excited. . . . There may be cases where a patient ought not to be advised of a contemplated operation until shortly before the appointed hour. To discuss such a subject at midnight might cause needless and even harmful agitation. About such matters a nurse is not qualified to judge. She is drilled to habits of strict obedience. She is accustomed to rely unquestioningly upon the judgment of her superiors. No woman occupying such a position would reasonably infer from the plaintiff's words that it was the purpose of the surgeons to operate whether the plaintiff forbade it or not. I conclude, therefore, that the plaintiff's statements to the nurse on the night before the operation are insufficient to charge the hospital with notice of a contemplated wrong. . . .

The conclusion, therefore, follows that the trial judge did not err in his direction of a verdict. A ruling would, indeed, be an unfortunate one that might constrain charitable institutions, as a measure of self-protection, to limit their activities. A hospital opens its doors without discrimination to all who seek its aid. It gathers in its wards a company of skilled physicians and trained nurses, and places their services at the call of the afflicted, without scrutiny of the character or the worth of those who appeal to it, looking at nothing and caring for nothing beyond the fact of their affliction. In this beneficent work, it does not subject itself to liability for damages, though the ministers of healing whom it has selected have proved unfaithful to their trust.

Notes: Hospital Liability; Charitable and Governmental Immunity

1. Schloendorff. For a fascinating account of the history of this famous case, see Paul Lombardo, Phantom Tumors and Hysterical Women: Revising Our View of the Schloendorff Case, 33 J.L. Med. Ethics 791 (2005). He reveals that the unconsented operation was a hysterectomy.

Is Justice Cardozo's rejection of hospital liability as absolute as it first appears? What about the qualification, "if due care has been taken in [the doctor's] selection"? What if the court were more demanding about the nurse's duty to speak up? Compare these potential theories of liability with those introduced in the modern landmark case of Darling v. Charleston Community Hospital, excerpted at page 491.

2. *Charitable Immunity.* The rule of charitable immunity was subjected to an increasing number of exceptions—distinguishing between paying and nonpaying patients, patients and strangers, and administrative vs. professional acts—until it eventually crumbled in most states. The leading decision is President of Georgetown College v. Hughes, 130 F.2d 810 (D.C. Cir. 1942), which observed that charitable hospitals could simply purchase insurance to protect themselves from economic catastrophe. The gist of this changed attitude is best captured in a colorful dissent by the renowned Pennsylvania Justice Musmanno in Michael v. Hahnemann Medical College and Hospital of Philadelphia, 172 A.2d 769 (Pa. 1961):

> Hospitals then were little better than hovels in which the indigent were gathered for the primitive cures available. The wealthy and the well-to-do were cared for in their homes. The hospital or infirmary was more often than not part of the village parish. Charity in the biblical sense prevailed. And if it happened that some poor mortal was scalded by a sister of mercy, who exhausted from long hours of vigil and toil, accidentally spilled a ladle of hot soup on a hand extended for nourishment, there was no thought of lawsuits against the philanthropists who made the meager refuge possible. But if, following such a mishap, litigation should have been initiated in the courts, it is not difficult to understand why judges would be reluctant to honor such a complaint, convinced on the basis of humanity, that an enterprise utterly devoid of worldly gain should be exempt from liability. A successful lawsuit against such a feeble structure might well have demolished it and have thus paralyzed the only helping hand in the world of unconcern for the rag-clothed sick and the crutchless disabled.
>
> The situation today is quite different. Charitable enterprises are not housed in ramshackle wooden structures. They are not mere storm shelters to succor the traveler and temporarily refuge those stricken in a common disaster. Hospitals today, to a large extent, are mighty edifices, in stone, glass and marble. They maintain large staffs, they use the best equipment that science can devise, they utilize the most modern methods of helping themselves to the noblest purpose of man, that of helping one's stricken brother. But they do all this on a business basis, and properly so. . . . And if the hospital is a business for the purpose of collecting money, it must be a business for the purpose of meeting its obligations. . . .

So be it for hospitals, but what about physician groups? In an unusual but important decision, the Virginia Supreme Court considered whether faculty at the state's premier medical school qualified for charitable immunity. The Court held no, despite the organization's charitable tax exemption, because it operated much more as a normal for-profit business than as a charity. University of Virginia Health Services Foundation v. Morris, Va., 657 S.E.2d 512 (Va. 2008). Despite this shift in attitude, a number of states retain a version of charitable immunity in statutes that limit the amount of damages that can be recovered against nonprofit hospitals or charities generally. See Conners v. Northeast Hospital Corp., 439 Mass. 469 (2003) ($20,000 cap on damages against any charitable corporation protects a hospital in a suit by someone who slipped in its icy parking lot); Annot., 25 A.L.R.4th 517 (1983).

3. *Governmental Immunity.* Public hospitals might also claim governmental immunity under the common-law concept that "the king can do no wrong." See, e.g., Withers v. University of Kentucky, 939 S.W.2d 340 (Ky. 1997) (university hospital is a "state agency" immune from suit). Most states, however, have abrogated governmental immunity to some degree by statute, as has the federal government. This abrogation is often limited, though, to "ministerial" or "proprietary" functions, thus preserving many of the same arcane distinctions that arose under charitable immunity and the *Schloendorff* rule. See, e.g., Moser v. Heistand, 681 A.2d 1322 (Pa. 1996) (immunity exists only for suits based simply on physician error, not for suits based on failures in administration that result in physician error). See generally John Akula, Sovereign Immunity and Health Care: Can Government Be Trusted?, 19(6) Health Aff. 152 (Dec. 2000). Substantial immunity is still common in many states for psychiatric hospitals, and full immunity is still preserved for injuries suffered during the course of active military duty. See Feres v. United States, 340 U.S. 135 (1950). In sharp contrast, Veterans Administration (VA) hospitals are subject by statute to a form of strict liability, without regard to negligence. See Brown v. Gardner, 513 U.S. 113 (1994).

4. *Subsequent Developments in Vicarious Liability.* The refusal to apply ordinary principles of respondeat superior even to employed nurses gave way in later decades to a rule that held the hospital responsible for "administrative" errors, in contrast with errors in medical judgment. What resulted was a string of arcane distinctions and inconsistent decisions concerning such routine medical acts as administering medication, giving injections, and applying casts. For instance, giving a blood transfusion to the wrong patient was considered "administrative," whereas giving the wrong blood to the right patient was labeled an error of medical judgment. See generally Bing v. Thunig, 143 N.E.2d 3 (N.Y. 1957). As will be seen in the next case, these cracks in hospitals' liability armor eventually led to the outright reversal of *Schloendorff* by *Bing.* The modern issue, then, becomes how does standard respondeat superior apply to physicians who are not, strictly speaking, employees.

On the modern status of hospital liability generally, see James Smith, Hospital Liability; Mary Bertolet & Lee Goldsmith, Hospital Liability: Law and Practice; Aspen Hospital Law Manual. Documenting a sharp rise in suits against nursing homes, see David G. Stevenson & David M. Studdert, The Rise of Nursing Home Litigation: Findings from a National Survey of Attorneys, 22(2) Health Aff. 219 (Mar. 2003).

■ DIGGS v. NOVANT HEALTH, INC.
628 S.E.2d 851 (N.C. App. 2006)

GEER, Judge.

In September 1999, plaintiff, who was in her early eighties, was diagnosed [with gall stone disease]. . . . Plaintiff chose to have [a surgeon] perform the gall bladder surgery [who] had hospital privileges at Forsyth Medical Center ("FMC") . . . [which] in turn is owned by Novant Health Inc. Plaintiff's gall bladder surgery required general anesthesia. Piedmont Anesthesia & Pain Consultants, P.A. ("Piedmont") had a contract . . . that granted Piedmont the exclusive right to provide anesthesia services at FMC. Piedmont employees Dr. Joseph McConville and nurse Sheila Crumb were responsible for administering anesthesia to plaintiff through an induction and intubation process. Ms. Crumb performed the intubation, which involved inserting a tube into plaintiff's trachea, under the supervision of Dr. McConville. Ms. Crumb made three attempts before successfully completing the intubation. At some point during the attempts, Ms. Crumb perforated plaintiff's esophagus, a fact that was not discovered until many hours after the gall bladder surgery was over. Plaintiff contends that as a result of that perforation, she has suffered severe and permanent injuries.

On 11 October 2002, plaintiff filed suit against not only the hospital defendants, but also Ms. Crumb, Dr. McConville, and Piedmont, . . . [alleging] that the hospital defendants were vicariously liable for the anesthesiology defendants' negligence, as well as the negligence of the hospital floor nurses who, following plaintiff's surgery, failed to immediately notice the perforation. . . . [The trial court granted summary judgment for the hospital defendants.]

A. Liability Based on Actual Agency

As this Court has held, "[u]nder the doctrine of *respondeat superior,* a hospital is liable for the negligence of a physician or surgeon acting as its agent. There will generally be no vicarious liability on an employer for the negligent acts of an independent contractor." This Court has established that "[t]he vital test in determining whether an agency relationship exists is to be found in the fact that the employer has or has not retained the right of control or superintendence over the contractor or employee as to details." Specifically, the principal must have the right to control *both the means and the details of the process* by which the agent is to accomplish his task in order for an agency relationship to exist.

In arguing that an agency relationship existed, plaintiff relies exclusively on two contracts entered into between Piedmont and FMC: the Anesthesia Agreement and the Anesthesia Services Agreement. The Anesthesia Services Agreement specifically provided, however, that FMC "shall neither have nor exercise any control or direction over the methods by which [Piedmont] or any Physician shall perform it or his work and functions." . . . Further, under the agreements, (1) the physicians associated with Piedmont are not prohibited from practicing outside of the Hospital; (2) Piedmont and the hospital bill patients separately for their respective services; (3) Piedmont is responsible for meeting its own hiring needs; and (4) Piedmont is responsible for managing its own scheduling. . . .

We hold that the provisions in the agreements between Piedmont and FMC are materially indistinguishable from those in . . . *Hoffman v. Moore Reg'l Hosp., Inc.,* 114 N.C. App. 248, 251, 441 S.E.2d 567, 569 (1994) (upholding grant of summary judgment when the physician was a member of a private group, the physician's schedule was determined by the group rather than the hospital, and the patient was billed for the physician's services by the group and not the hospital). . . . Plaintiff has, therefore, failed to present sufficient evidence to establish a *prima facie* case of actual agency.

B. Liability Based on Apparent Agency

It is well-established that even in the absence of an agency relationship, "'[w]here a person, by words or conduct, represents or permits it to be represented that another is his agent, he will be estopped to deny the agency as against third persons, who have dealt, on the faith of such representation, with the person so held out as agent, even if no agency exists in fact.' " This doctrine of apparent agency was first considered by our Supreme Court as a basis for hospital liability for malpractice in *Smith v. Duke Univ.*, 14 S.E.2d 643 (NC 1941): . . . [Citing *Schloendorff*, the court rejected both actual and apparent agency on the part of Duke University, even though it employed the doctor in question as a member of its medical school faculty, because he was employed to teach and treat indigent patients, and this patient was seen as part of his private practice, for which the patient paid the doctor separately.] . . .

Our Supreme Court has since recognized that, in the years following *Smith*, the nature of hospitals has substantially changed. After observing that the *Smith* assumptions regarding hospitals were "no longer appropriate in this era," the Court explained: "First of all, hospitals are now in the business of treatment. As stated in [Bing v. Thunig, 143 N.E.2d 3 (NY 1957), which overturned *Schloendorff*]:

> The conception that the hospital does not undertake to treat the patient, does not undertake to act through its doctors and nurses, but undertakes instead simply to procure them to act upon their own responsibility, no longer reflects the fact. Present day hospitals, as their manner of operation plainly demonstrates, do far more than furnish facilities for treatment. They regularly employ on a salary basis a large staff of physicians, nurses and internes [sic], as well as administrative and manual workers, and they charge patients for medical care and treatment, collecting for such services, if necessary, by legal action. Certainly, the person who avails himself of hospital facilities' expects that the hospital will attempt to cure him, not that its nurses or other employees will act on their own responsibility.

In applying the doctrine of apparent agency, courts throughout the country have struggled with this change in the nature of hospitals from institutions providing only facilities to institutions actually providing medical services, such as emergency room care or, as in this case, anesthesia. In *Sword v. NKC Hosps., Inc.*, 714 N.E.2d 142 (Ind. 1999), the Indiana Supreme Court . . . noted that courts have employed apparent agency to hold hospitals liable for the negligence of independent contractors in both emergency room and anesthesia contexts. The court . . . pointed out that some jurisdictions ask whether the plaintiff reasonably believed that the hospital was providing the pertinent medical care, while other jurisdictions presume reliance. Over all, the court concluded that "[c]entral to both of these factors—that is, the hospital's manifestations and the patient's reliance—is the question of whether the hospital provided notice to the patient that the treating physician was an independent contractor and not an employee of the hospital." . . . According to *Sword*, . . . "a hospital generally will be able to avoid liability by providing meaningful written notice to the patient, acknowledged at the time of admission." The court noted, however, that written notice might not suffice if the patient did not have an adequate opportunity to make an informed choice, such as in the case of a medical emergency.

After conducting a similar survey of the development of the law nationwide, the South Carolina Supreme Court also chose to adopt [an apparent agency] approach. *Simmons v. Tuomey Reg'l Med. Ctr.*, 533 S.E.2d 312, 322 (SC 2000). . . . The court limited application of this test "to those situations in which a patient seeks services at the hospital as an institution, and is treated by a physician who reasonably appears to be a hospital employee." It stressed that its holding did "not extend to situations in which the patient is treated in an emergency room by the patient's own physician after arranging to meet the physician there. Nor does our holding encompass situations in which a patient is admitted to a hospital by a private, independent physician whose only connection to a particular hospital is that he or she has staff privileges to admit patients to the hospital. Such patients could not reasonably believe his or her physician is a hospital employee." Comparable tests have been adopted in numerous other jurisdictions, particularly with respect to the rendering of anesthesia or emergency services. . . .

Defendants point to [our prior decision in] *Hoffman* as establishing a different test. . . . Although the plaintiff in *Hoffman*, who was admitted to a hospital at the request of her private physician for a particular procedure, did not choose the doctor who would perform that procedure, the consent form specifically listed five possible doctors and the patient was looking to one of those doctors to provide her care. The case fell squarely within the traditional *Smith* analysis regarding treating physicians. There was no indication in the opinion that the hospital was holding itself out as providing the services involved as opposed to simply providing facilities for the performance of the procedure by private practitioners. Under those circumstances, this Court required evidence "that Mrs. Hoffman would have sought treatment elsewhere or done anything differently had she known for a fact that [the doctor] was not an employee of the hospital."

When, however, a hospital does hold itself out as providing services, we . . . are . . . persuaded by the weight of authority from other jurisdictions. Under this approach, a plaintiff must prove that (1) the hospital has held itself out as providing medical services, (2) the plaintiff looked to the hospital rather than the individual medical provider to perform those services, and (3) the patient accepted those services in the reasonable belief that the services were being rendered by the hospital or by its employees. A hospital may avoid liability by providing meaningful notice to a patient that care is being provided by an independent contractor. *See, e.g., Cantrell v. Northeast Ga. Med. Ctr.*, 235 Ga. App. 365, 368, 508 S.E.2d 716, 719-20 (1998) (concluding that trial court did not err in granting a directed verdict to hospital when "conspicuous signage was posted and forms signed by the patient or representative revealed the independent contractor status of the doctor").

Plaintiff has submitted sufficient evidence to meet this test. The hospital had a Department of Anesthesiology with a Chief of Anesthesiology and a Medical Director, a fact that a jury could reasonably find indicated to the public that FMC was providing anesthesia services to its patients. Further, defendants chose to provide those services by contracting with Piedmont to provide anesthesia services to the hospital on an exclusive basis. Piedmont doctors served as the hospital's Chief of Anesthesiology and anesthesia Medical Director. As Dr. McConville put it, his group "provide[d] the anesthesia services for the operating room at Forsyth." . . . Plaintiff and other surgical patients had no choice as to who would provide anesthesia services for their operations.

Plaintiff's affidavit states that she was unaware that Dr. McConville and Ms. Crumb were not employees of the hospital. . . . In addition, plaintiff pointed to the form on FMC letterhead that she signed entitled "Consent to Operation and/or Other Procedures." The form specified: "I therefore authorize *my physician*, his or her associates or assistants to perform such surgical procedures as they, in the exercise of their professional judgment, deem necessary and advisable." (Emphasis added.) By contrast, with respect to anesthesia services, the form stated: "I authorize the administration of such anesthetics as may be necessary or advisable *by the anesthetist/anesthesiologist responsible for this service and I request the administration of such anesthetics.*" . . . A jury could decide based on this form that plaintiff was, through this form, requesting anesthesia services from FMC and that—given the distinction made between plaintiff's personal physician and the unnamed anesthesiologist—plaintiff was accepting those services in the reasonable belief that the services would be provided by the hospital and its employees. . . .

Given the current record, we hold that the trial court erred in granting summary judgment with respect to plaintiff's claims based on apparent agency. . . . Plaintiff has also argued (1) that the hospital defendants owed plaintiff a nondelegable duty and (2) that the hospital defendants are liable, even apart from agency principles, for the failure to obtain informed consent from plaintiff regarding anesthesia services. . . . [B]ecause of our resolution of this appeal, we need not address these alternative arguments. . . .

Notes: Hospital Vicarious Liability

1. *Employed Physicians.* Under modern law, there is universal agreement that hospitals are vicariously liable for their employed physicians and nurses. Principles of actual agency determine when doctors are hospital agents even when they are not official employees. Notice how the hospital in *Diggs* had carefully arranged its anesthesiology contract to avoid actual agency, following factors specified in an earlier N.C. appellate court decision. But, what about different contracts at other hospitals? In Adamski v. Tacoma General Hospital, 579 P.2d 970 (Wash. App. 1978), the court allowed a jury trial on actual agency for emergency room physicians when the hospital billed patients for their services, among other factors.

2. *Hospital Control.* Is it consistent with the law's prohibition of the "corporate practice of medicine" to hold a hospital responsible for the professional mistakes of its agent-physicians? The corporate practice of medicine doctrine holds that it is illegal for corporations to subject physicians to the control of lay management because this would constitute the unlicensed practice of medicine. If respondeat superior liability is premised on the principal's control of an agent's actions, how can it coexist with this prohibition of corporate control of physicians? One court, agreeing with this logic, surprisingly held that a health center cannot, as a matter of law, be held responsible for a physician's negligence. Daly v. Aspen Center for Women's Health, 134 P.3d 450 (Colo. App. 2005). Another decision, issued with respect to an HMO, found it necessary to declare the corporate practice of medicine doctrine "totally abolished" in order to hold the HMO vicariously liable for an employed physician's mistake. Sloan v. Metropolitan Health Council of Indianapolis, 516 N.E.2d 1104 (Ind. Ct. App. 1987). The court also reasoned, consistent with other decisions, that respondeat superior does not require actual control but merely a finding that the negligent acts occurred within the course and scope of employment. Otherwise, hospitals could not be held responsible for employed nurses, or airlines for employed pilots. Perhaps based on this thinking, other courts have not found it necessary to abolish the corporate practice of medicine doctrine in order

to hold hospitals liable for physicians' errors. See, e.g., McDonald v. Hampton Training School for Nurses, 486 S.E.2d 299 (Va. 1997) (vicarious liability attaches even though hospital does not control actual medical judgment); Dias v. Brigham Medical Associates, Inc., 438 Mass. 317 (2002) (same, for a medical group).

3. *"Captain of the Ship."* One hospital defense against vicarious liability that still remains is the "captain of the ship" or borrowed servant doctrine discussed at page 412. The effect of this doctrine is not only to hold physicians (usually surgeons) responsible for subordinate doctors and nurses, but sometimes also to relieve the hospital from vicarious responsibility. This occurs when a hospital employee's negligent acts are directed or supervised by a physician who is not an agent of the hospital; then, the independent physician can be found to have temporarily "borrowed" the hospital's employee. Courts usually find that the hospital and the physician in charge share the employee and therefore share liability. See, e.g., Tonsic v. Wagner, 329 A.2d 497 (Pa. 1974). However, courts sometimes hold the doctor solely liable if he instructs the nurse to perform an act that contravenes hospital policy. See, e.g., Hoffman v. Wells, 397 S.E.2d 696 (Ga. 1990). See also Restatement (Second) of Agency §227.

4. *Indemnification Agreements.* The principles of vicarious liability introduced here apply to other medical institutions than just hospitals. Materials below explore for instance how vicarious liability applies to HMOs. Earlier, it was observed that physician practice groups or clinics can be held liable as an entity for the negligence of one of their members. It is possible in all of these circumstances, however, to reallocate liability among the parties through the use of indemnification agreements. These agreements do not alter the rights of the injured patient, but they do affect which of several joint tortfeasors can seek contribution or indemnification from the others. Negotiating these indemnification agreements is a major aspect of contract drafting, especially in managed care settings.

5. *Ostensible Agency.* Even though the *Diggs* court claims that facts and circumstances matter, how different would the next case be if the surgical consent form refers to "*my* anesthesiologist" rather than "*the* anesthesiologists"? Or, what if the hospital were to have patients sign a separate disclaimer form acknowledging that all doctors are independent contractors and not hospital agents? In the emergency room context, most modern courts hold that hospitals are subject to a jury finding of ostensible agency for emergency room physicians regardless of the specifics of the arrangement. The courts' reasoning is reflected in the following cases: Gilbert v. Sycamore Municipal Hospital, 622 N.E.2d 788 (Ill. 1993) (hospital advertising itself as offering quality care contributes to the impression that doctors work for the hospital); Simmons v. Tuomey Regional Medical Center, 533 S.E.2d 312 (S.C. 2000) (patient did not specifically choose any of the emergency room physicians that treated her); Whitlow v. Rideout Memorial Hospital, 237 Cal. App. 4th 631 (2015) (disclaimer of agency in admission form and on wall signs may not have been adequate notice for patient in excruciating pain). To the contrary, see Frezados v. Ingalls Memorial Hosp., 991 N.E.2d 817 Illl. App. 2013) ("Nearly everyone who seeks emergency treatment is in some physical or emotional distress, and were we to hold that such distress could operate to nullify provisions in an otherwise duly signed treatment consent form, hospitals would always be required to proceed to trial on claims of vicarious liability.").

In non-emergency contexts like that in *Diggs*, where ostensible agency is applied to hospital-based specialists such as radiologists and anesthesiologists, some

courts are more open to argument both ways, depending on the facts and circumstances. See, e.g., Milliron v. Francke, 793 P.2d 824 (Mont. 1990) (providing radiologist with office, equipment, personnel, and billing is not sufficient to establish
agency relationship; in a rural setting, it is understood this is necessary to maintain
adequate staffing). However, most courts find their way to allowing the case to go
to trial. E.g., Burless v. West Virginia University Hospitals, Inc., 601 S.E.2d 85 (W.
Va. 2004) (disclaimer in a consent form was not sufficient to inform patient giving
birth that university physicians were not hospital employees); Sword v. NKC Hospitals, 714 N.E.2d 142 (Ind. 1999) (anesthesiologist could be found to be an apparent
agent of a hospital that "aggressively marketed its services to the public . . . [as]
'the most technically sophisticated birthplace in the region' and touted the 'full
availability of a special anesthesiology team, experienced and dedicated exclusively
to OB patients' "); York v. Rush-Presbyterian-St. Luke's Medical Center, 854 N.E.2d
635 (Ill. 2006) (similar, based on 28-page analysis of detailed testimony, even for a
patient who himself was a surgeon and who picked most of his own doctors).

6. *Office-Based Physicians.* Do you think the ostensible agency doctrine could
apply to specialists who are not entirely hospital based, such as surgeons or consultants referred by a patient's primary care physician? After all, hospitals also have
departments of cardiology and surgery, and patients often do not pick their own
surgeons or cardiologists (for instance, if their heart or surgical problem develops
while they're in the hospital for a different problem, or if they enter the hospital
through the emergency room before being transferred to a regular hospital room).
So far, only Puerto Rico courts have not gone this far, holding hospitals vicariously
liable whenever a patient "goes directly to the hospital seeking medical aid and the
hospital 'provides' the physicians who treat him [or her], . . . because [then] the
patient has entrusted his or her health to the hospital." Casillas-Sanchez v. Ryder
Memorial Hosp., 960 F.Supp.2d 362 (D.P.R. 2013). In contrast, this court held
that the hospital cannot be held vicariously liable "when the patient has first gone
directly to the physician's private office and then is treated at the hospital on the
physician's recommendation merely because said institution is one of several which
the physician has the privilege of using." At present, this is a distinctly minority
position, but a few other courts appear willing to expand vicarious liability to any
situation where "a patient seeks treatment from a hospital and not from a particular
physician of the patient's choosing." Syracuse v. Diao, 707 N.Y.S.2d 570 (App. Div.
2000) (allowing case to go to trial where a patient simply called a specialized surgery
center to request an appointment but did not ask for a particular physician).

7. *Enterprise Liability.* Notice the *Diggs* court's brief mention at the end of an
argument based on "non-delegable duty," also known as "enterprise liability." This
concept would hold hospitals automatically liable for all acts of negligence, either
within particular departments or for all physicians within their walls, regardless of
the specifics of actual or apparent agency—even if the doctor is conceded to be an
obvious independent contractor. The rationale for a nondelegable duty is that the
public policy supporting hospital responsibility is so strong that, as a matter of law,
the hospital may not avoid responsibility by delegating the function to an independent contractor. The classic example is an airline that attempts to shield itself from
liability by retaining pilots as independent contractors.

So far, this nondelegable duty concept has been applied in only a few cases
and only to emergency room care. The leading case is Jackson v. Power, 743 P.2d

1376 (Alaska 1987). Based on hospital licensing statutes and Joint Commission accreditation standards, the court observed that the hospital had assumed a duty to ensure adequate emergency room services. The court then concluded that a hospital "may not shield itself from liability by claiming that it is not responsible for the results of negligently performed health care when the law imposes a duty on the hospital to provide that health care. . . . We simply cannot fathom why liability should depend upon the technical employment status of the emergency room physician who treats the patient." Is this reasoning necessarily limited to emergency room care? So far, this is as far as courts have taken it. See Fletcher v. South Peninsula Hospital, 71 P.3d 833 (Alaska 2003) (refusing to extend the doctrine to surgeons).

8. *The Next Stage.* Falling between vicarious liability for some physicians and enterprise liability for all physicians is a position known as "direct institutional liability," in which hospitals are held liable even for acts of independent physicians, but only if the hospital management breached a duty of care owed directly to patients with respect to selecting or supervising the physician. That theory of liability is thought to have been introduced by the next case. See if you can discern in this case a major shift in liability, or instead whether its holding rests on a more conventional application of vicarious liability. To the extent it presages a new duty of hospitals, precisely what is the content of that duty?

■ DARLING v. CHARLESTON COMMUNITY MEMORIAL HOSPITAL
211 N.E.2d 253 (Ill. 1965), cert. denied, 383 U.S. 946 (1966)

Schaefer, Justice.

. . . On November 5, 1960, the plaintiff, who was 18 years old, broke his leg while playing in a college football game. He was taken to the emergency room at the defendant hospital where Dr. Alexander, who was on emergency call that day, treated him. Dr. Alexander, with the assistance of hospital personnel, applied traction and placed the leg in a plaster cast. A heat cradle was applied to dry the cast. Not long after the application of the cast plaintiff was in great pain and his toes, which protruded from the cast, became swollen and dark in color. They eventually became cold and insensitive. On the evening of November 6, Dr. Alexander "notched" the cast around the toes, and on the afternoon of the next day he cut the cast approximately three inches up from the foot. On November 8, he split the sides of the cast with a Stryker saw; in the course of cutting the cast the plaintiff's leg was cut on both sides. Blood was observed by the nurses and others, and there was a stench in the room, which one witness said was the worst he had smelled since World War II. The plaintiff remained in Charleston Hospital until November 19, when he was transferred to Barnes Hospital in St. Louis and placed under the care of Dr. Fred Reynolds, head of orthopedic surgery at Washington University School of Medicine and Barnes Hospital. Dr. Reynolds found that the fractured leg contained a considerable amount of dead tissue which in his opinion resulted from interference with the circulation of blood in the limb caused by swelling or hemorrhaging of the leg against the construction of the cast. Dr. Reynolds performed several operations in a futile attempt to save the leg but ultimately it had to be amputated eight inches below the knee.

The evidence before the jury is set forth at length in the opinion of the Appellate Court and need not be stated in detail here. The plaintiff contends that it established that the defendant was negligent in permitting Dr. Alexander to do orthopedic work of the kind required in this case, and not requiring him to review his operative procedures to bring them up to date; in failing, through its medical staff, to exercise adequate supervision over the case, especially since Dr. Alexander had been placed on emergency duty by the hospital, and in not requiring consultation, particularly after complications had developed. Plaintiff contends also that in a case which developed as this one did, it was the duty of the nurses to watch the protruding toes constantly for changes of color, temperature and movement, and to check circulation every ten to twenty minutes, whereas the proof showed that these things were done only a few times a day. Plaintiff argues that it was the duty of the hospital staff to see that these procedures were followed, and that either the nurses were derelict in failing to report developments in the case to the hospital administrator, he was derelict in bringing them to the attention of the medical staff, or the staff was negligent in failing to take action. Defendant is a licensed and accredited hospital, and the plaintiff contends that the licensing regulations, accreditation standards, and its own bylaws define the hospital's duty, and that an infraction of them imposes liability for the resulting injury.

The defendant's position is stated in the following excerpts from its brief:

> It is a fundamental rule of law that only an individual properly educated and licensed, and not a corporation, may practice medicine. . . . Accordingly, a hospital is powerless under the law to forbid or command any act by a physician or surgeon in the practice of his profession. . . . A hospital is not an insurer of the patient's recovery, but only owes the patient the duty to exercise such reasonable care as his known condition requires and that degree of care, skill and diligence used by hospitals generally in that community. . . . Where the evidence shows that the hospital care was in accordance with standard practice obtaining in similar hospitals, and Plaintiff produces no evidence to the contrary, the jury cannot conclude that the opposite is true even if they disbelieve the hospital witnesses. . . . A hospital is not liable for the torts of its nurse committed while the nurse was but executing the orders of the patient's physician, unless such order is so obviously negligent as to lead any reasonable person to anticipate that substantial injury would result to the patient from the execution of such order. . . . The extent of the duty of a hospital with respect to actual medical care of a professional nature such as is furnished by a physician is to use reasonable care in selecting medical doctors. When such care in the selection of the staff is accomplished, and nothing indicates that a physician so selected is incompetent or that such incompetence should have been discovered, more cannot be expected from the hospital administration.

The basic dispute, as posed by the parties, centers upon the duty that rested upon the defendant hospital. That dispute involves the effect to be given to . . . hospital regulations adopted by the State Department of Public Health under the Hospital Licensing Act, to the Standards for Hospital Accreditation of the American Hospital Association, and to the bylaws of the defendant. . . .

> The conception that the hospital does not undertake to treat the patient, does not undertake to act through its doctors and nurses, but undertakes instead simply to procure them to act upon their own responsibility, no longer reflects the fact.

Present-day hospitals, as their manner of operation plainly demonstrates, do far more than furnish facilities for treatment. They regularly employ on a salary basis a large staff of physicians, nurses and internes, as well as administrative and manual workers, and they charge patients for medical care and treatment, collecting for such services, if necessary, by legal action. Certainly, the person who avails himself of "hospital facilities" expects that the hospital will attempt to cure him, not that its nurses or other employees will act on their own responsibility. (Fuld, J., in Bing v. Thunig (1957), 2 N.Y.2d 656, 163 N.Y.S.2d 3, 11, 143 N.E.2d 3, 8.)

The Standards for Hospital Accreditation, the state licensing regulations and the defendant's bylaws demonstrate that the medical profession and other responsible authorities regard it as both desirable and feasible that a hospital assume certain responsibilities for the care of the patient.

We now turn to an application of these considerations to this case. . . . [W]e need not analyze all of the issues submitted to the jury. Two of them were that the defendant had negligently:

5. Failed to have a sufficient number of trained nurses for bedside care of all patients at all times capable of recognizing the progressive gangrenous condition of the plaintiff's right leg, and of bringing the same to the attention of the hospital administration and to the medical staff so that adequate consultation could have been secured and such conditions rectified; . . .

7. Failed to require consultation with or examination by members of the hospital surgical staff skilled in such treatment; or to review the treatment rendered to the plaintiff and to require consultants to be called in as needed.

We believe that the jury verdict [against the hospital] is supportable on either of these grounds. On the basis of the evidence before it the jury could reasonably have concluded that the nurses did not test for circulation in the leg as frequently as necessary, that skilled nurses would have promptly recognized the conditions that signalled a dangerous impairment of circulation in the plaintiff's leg, and would have known that the condition would become irreversible in a matter of hours. At that point, it became the nurses' duty to inform the attending physician, and if he failed to act, to advise the hospital authorities so that appropriate action might be taken. As to consultation, there is no dispute that the hospital failed to review Dr. Alexander's work or require a consultation; the only issue is whether its failure to do so was negligence. On the evidence before it the jury could reasonably have found that it was. . . .

Judgment affirmed.

■ JOHNSON v. MISERICORDIA COMMUNITY HOSPITAL
301 N.W.2d 156 (Wis. 1981)

COFFEY, Justice.

. . . This action arose out of a surgical procedure performed at Misericordia by Dr. Salinsky on July 11, 1975, in which he unsuccessfully attempted to remove a pin fragment from Johnson's right hip. During the course of this surgery, the plaintiff's common femoral nerve and artery were damaged causing a permanent paralytic condition of his right thigh muscles with resultant atrophy and weakness and loss of function. . . .

[T]he jury found that Salinsky was negligent with respect to the medical care and treatment he afforded the plaintiff and attributed 20 percent of the causal negligence to him and 80 percent to the hospital. . . . [T]he only facts material to this review are those connected with Misericordia Hospital in appointing Dr. Salinsky to the medical staff with orthopedic privileges.

The record establishes that Misericordia was formerly . . . a nursing home known as Downtown Nursing Home, Inc. Subsequently, . . . all of the nursing home services were discontinued and the name "Misericordia Community Hospital" was adopted. The hospital known as Misericordia Community Hospital was not and has not been accredited by the Joint Commission on Accreditation of Hospitals. . . .

Dr. Salinsky applied for orthopedic privileges on the medical staff. In his application, Salinsky stated that . . . his privileges at other hospitals had never "been suspended, diminished, revoked, or not renewed." In another part of the application form, he failed to answer any of the questions pertaining to his malpractice insurance. . . .

Mrs. Jane Bekos, Misericordia's medical staff coordinator (appointed April of 1973), testifying from the hospital records, noted that Salinsky's appointment to the medical staff was recommended by the then hospital administrator, David A. Scott, Sr., on June 22, 1973. Salinsky's appointment and requested orthopedic privileges, according to the hospital records, were not marked approved until August 8, 1973. This approval of his appointment was endorsed by Salinsky himself. Such approval would, according to accepted medical administrative procedure, not be signed by the applicant but by the chief of the respective medical section. Additionally, the record establishes that Salinsky was elevated to the position of Chief of Staff shortly after he joined the medical staff. However, the court record and the hospital records are devoid of any information concerning the procedure utilized by the Misericordia authorities in approving either Salinsky's appointment to the staff with orthopedic privileges, or his elevation to the position of Chief of Staff.

Mrs. Bekos, testified that . . . she failed to contact any of the references in Salinsky's case. . . . Further, Mrs. Bekos stated that an examination of the Misericordia records reflected that at no time was an investigation made by anyone of any of the statements recited in his application. . . .

Dr. A. Howell, the hospital's medical director, stated that the hospital did not have a functioning credentials committee at this time, and therefore the executive committee . . . assume[d] the responsibility of evaluating and approving applications for medical staff privileges. . . . [T]he minutes of [the June 21st] meeting list Salinsky as an attending member of the defendant's medical staff at the meeting despite the fact that Salinsky's application for staff privileges had neither been recommended for approval, nor approved by the committee as of this date. . . .

At trial, the representatives of two Milwaukee hospitals, . . . gave testimony concerning the accepted procedure for evaluating applicants for medical staff privileges. Briefly, they stated that the hospital's governing body, i.e., the board of directors or board of trustees, has the ultimate responsibility in granting or denying staff privileges. However, the governing board delegates the responsibility of evaluating the professional qualifications of an applicant for clinical privileges to the medical staff. The credentials committee (or committee of the whole) conducts an investigation of the applying physician's or surgeon's education, training, health, ethics and experience through contacts with his peers in the specialty in which he is seeking privileges, as well as the references listed in his application to determine the veracity of his statements and to solicit comments dealing with the applicant's credentials. Once the credentials committee (or committee of the whole) has conducted their investigation and reviewed all of the information bearing on the applicant's qualifications, it relays its judgment to the governing body, which, as noted, has the final appointing authority.

The record demonstrates that had the executive committee of Misericordia, in the absence of a current credentials committee, adhered to the standard and accepted practice of investigating a medical staff applicant's qualifications and thus examined Salinsky's degree, postgraduate training, and contacted the hospitals referred to in his application, it would have found, contrary to his representations, that he had in fact experienced denial and restriction of his privileges, as well as never having been granted privileges at the very same hospitals he listed in his application. This information was readily available to Misericordia, and a review of Salinsky's associations with various Milwaukee orthopedic surgeons and hospital personnel would have revealed that they considered Salinsky's competence as an orthopedic surgeon suspect, and viewed it with a great deal of concern. . . .

[W]e hold that a hospital has a duty to exercise due care in the selection of its medical staff. . . . [O]ur holding is supported by the decisions of a number of courts from other jurisdictions. See . . . Annot., 51 A.L.R.3d 981 (1973). These cases hold that a hospital has a direct and independent responsibility to its patients, over and above that of the physicians and surgeons practicing therein, to take reasonable steps to (1) insure that its medical staff is qualified for the privileges granted and/ or (2) to evaluate the care provided. . . .

The resolution of the issue of whether the hospital was negligent in granting Salinsky orthopedic surgical privileges and appointing him to its medical staff depends on whether Misericordia exercised that degree of care and skill as the average hospital exercises in selecting its medical staff. Applying this standard to the facts of this case, Johnson was only required to show that the defendant did not exercise reasonable care (that degree of care ordinarily exercised by the average hospital) to determine whether Salinsky was competent. . . . Therefore, the trial court's instruction that the hospital was required to exercise reasonable care in the granting of medical staff privileges and that reasonable care "meant that degree of care, skill and judgment usually exercised under like or similar circumstances by the average hospital," was proper.

Turning to the plaintiff's proof requirements, since the procedures ordinarily employed by hospitals in evaluating applications for staff privileges are not within the realm of the ordinary experience of mankind, we agree with the ruling of the appellate court that expert testimony was required to prove the same. . . .

There was credible evidence to the effect that a hospital, exercising ordinary care, would not have appointed Salinsky to its medical staff. Mr. Harden, administrator for Family Hospital, testified a hospital governing board with knowledge that an applicant for medical staff privileges had his orthopedic surgical privileges revoked at one hospital, on the recommendation of a panel of three orthopedic surgeons, and that his orthopedic privileges at another hospital were confined to simple operative procedures, would not, on the basis of this information, have granted him surgical privileges in that specialty. Dr. Sam Neeseman stated that a hospital's credentials committee, with knowledge of such events would not, in the exercise of ordinary care, have approved the applicant's request for orthopedic privileges. . . . Thus, the jury's finding of negligence on the part of Misericordia must be upheld as the testimony of Mr. Harden and Dr. Neeseman constituted credible evidence which reasonably supports this finding. . . .

[A]lthough [a hospital] must rely on the medical staff and in particular the credentials committee (or committee of the whole) to investigate and evaluate an applicant's qualifications for the requested privileges, . . . this delegation of the responsibility to investigate and evaluate the professional competence of applicants for clinical privileges does not relieve the governing body of its duty to appoint only qualified physicians and surgeons to its medical staff and periodically monitor and review their competency. . . . The facts of this case demonstrate that a hospital should, at a minimum, require completion of the application and verify the accuracy of the applicant's statements, especially in regard to his medical education, training and experience. Additionally, it should: (1) solicit information from the applicant's peers, including those not referenced in his application, who are knowledgeable about his education, training, experience, health, competence and ethical character; (2) determine if the applicant is currently licensed to practice in this state and if his licensure or registration has been or is currently being challenged; and (3) inquire whether the applicant has been involved in any adverse malpractice action and whether he has experienced a loss of medical organization membership or medical privileges or membership at any other hospital. The investigating committee must also evaluate the information gained through its inquiries and make a reasonable judgment as to the approval or denial of each application for staff privileges. The hospital will be charged with gaining and evaluating the knowledge that would have been acquired had it exercised ordinary care in investigating its medical staff applicants. . . . This is not to say that hospitals are insurers of the competence of their medical staff, for a hospital will not be negligent if it exercises the noted standard of care in selecting its staff.

Notes: Hospitals' Direct Liability; Risk Management Programs

1. *Direct vs. Vicarious Liability. Darling* is undoubtedly the most significant hospital liability case in the past 50 years. It is frequently referred to as a landmark decision in the field of hospital liability because it placed at least some degree of direct responsibility on the hospital for the maintenance of an acceptable standard of care of patients. Direct or "corporate" liability contrasts with vicarious liability in that it imposes on hospitals a duty of care owed directly to patients with respect to medical judgment. Conventional forms of direct liability entail primarily administrative, not medical, functions such as maintaining safe premises, sterile equipment, and adequate rules and regulations. *Darling* is recognized as extending direct corporate liability to substandard medical care rendered by independent doctors. Hospitals thus can be found liable for some act of negligence on their part with respect to patient care decisions made by independent doctors; vicarious liability, on the other hand, attaches regardless of the degree of hospital care but only when doctors are actual or apparent agents.

2. *Darling's Progeny*. Consider whether the *Darling* court actually intended to announce a new theory of liability. How else could the case have been reasoned, using principles from the previous case and notes? Commentators have observed that *Darling* achieved its status largely by virtue of the importance that academic commentators and subsequent decisions attached to it, and the vocal reaction of hospitals and physicians. The leading commentator was health law professor Arthur Southwick, in The Hospital's New Responsibility, 17 Clev.-Marshall L. Rev. 146 (1968); and The Hospital as an Institution—Expanding Responsibilities Change Its Relationship with the Staff Physician, 9 Cal. W. L. Rev. 429 (1973). See generally Annot., 62 A.L.R. 4th 692 (1988).

3. *Enterprise Liability and the Balance of Power*. What reaction to *Darling* would you expect from the medical profession and the hospital industry? Surprisingly, *Darling* was openly embraced by hospitals but vehemently attacked by physicians. It greatly influenced the standards of the Joint Commission and virtually became the official philosophy of the American Hospital Association. The AMA's reaction to the *Darling* decision was immediate and negative. In considering why this would be so, consider what *Darling* signals about the power relationship between hospitals and physicians. Would it be fair to impose hospital responsibility for patient care without allowing hospital authority? In its comment on the case in 12 Citation 82 (1965), the AMA said, "The effect of this decision is unfortunate since it appears to place a hospital in a position where it must exercise control over the practice of medicine by physicians on its attending staff in order to avoid liability. This is apt to encourage control of the practice of medicine by persons who are not licensed physicians."

A similar reaction occurred in 1993 when President Clinton's health care reform task force aired an idea for medical malpractice reform known as exclusive enterprise liability. As discussed at pages 518 and 543, exclusive enterprise liability would change existing law in two ways: (1) it would hold hospitals and HMOs vicariously liable for all negligent injuries caused by any member physician, regardless of status or contractual relationship with the institution; and (2) the institution would be solely liable, letting doctors entirely off the hook. Surprisingly, the hospital industry was interested in this idea but the AMA vehemently opposed it, causing the Clinton administration to quickly back away. Even though the AMA was clamoring for relief from medical malpractice, it viewed this proposal for abolishing physician liability as a Trojan Horse because of its implications for the relative power balance between doctors and medical institutions. See Frances Miller, Malpractice Liability and Physician Autonomy, 342 Lancet 973 (1993); Robert A. Berenson, Do Physicians Recognize Their Own Best Interests?, 13(2) Health Aff. 185 (1994).

Despite this hostility, some HMOs, most teaching hospitals, and virtually all government hospitals implement a de facto form of exclusive enterprise liability in which the institution pays for the physicians' malpractice insurance (usually as part of its own self-insured retention fund), defends all suits, and pays all judgments for claims arising from treatment at the institution. Reinforcing the policy argument in favor of a more general form of hospital enterprise liability, recall the readings at pages 312 and 321 explaining that many medical errors in hospitals are due to flaws in the system of care rather than purely individual physician mistakes, but that hospitals lack a sufficient "business case" to improve patient safety because they internalize only a small percentage of the costs of medical error. See also Michelle M. Mello et al., Who Pays for Medical Errors? An Analysis of Adverse Event Costs, the Medical Liability System, and Incentives for Patient Safety Improvement, 4 J. Empirical Legal Stud. 835 (2007).

For these reasons, most legal scholars strongly favor broader hospital enterprise liability. See, e.g., Kenneth Abraham & Paul Weiler, Enterprise Liability and the Evolution of the American Health Care System, 108 Harv. L. Rev. 381 (1994); Barry Furrow, Patient Safety and the Fiduciary Hospital, 1 Drexel L. Rev. 439 (2009); Philip G. Peters, Resuscitating Hospital Enterprise Liability, 73 Mo. L. Rev. 369-397 (2008).

4. *Duty to Supervise and Nursing Negligence. Darling* and its progeny identify two forms of hospital negligence with respect to physicians: negligent selection and retention, and negligent supervision. The first of these, which is developed in Johnson v. Misericordia Community Hospital, is much less controversial. Observe that it was recognized in passing even in *Schloendorff,* supra. It entails reviewing physicians' competency and performance history before admission to the medical staff and periodically (typically every two years) thereafter. Surprisingly, however, one modern court has refused to recognize a tort for negligent credentialing, reasoning that regulatory oversight of hospitals suffices. Paulino v. QHG of Springdale, Inc., 386 S.W.3d 462 (Ark. 2012).

The duty to supervise, in contrast, assumes *contemporaneous* supervision of daily treatment decisions *as they are made.* Several subsequent decisions have alluded to this duty of contemporaneous supervision, but few have squarely imposed it, distinct from the duty of care in selection and retention. Indeed, subsequent decisions in Illinois have expressly disavowed any such duty arising from *Darling.* See Essig v. Advocate BroMenn Medical Center, 33 N.E.3d 288 (Ill. App. Ct. 2015) ("the only logical inference from [plaintiffs'] argument is that [the hospital] should have appointed . . . a fully trained and licensed urologist to oversee [the surgeon] . . . and to veto the allegedly negligent course of treatment . . . . Of course, the law does not impose such a duty on hospitals").

Other courts, however, have rather explicitly imposed such a duty of active supervision, at least in dictum. See, e.g., Thompson v. Nason Hospital, 591 A.2d 703 (Pa. 1991). Usually, these are cases of gross negligence in which the departure from medical standards is so blatant that it is possible to attribute to hospital administrators' constructive knowledge of the error in progress. One route for attributing this knowledge is through nurses, under the logic that, at some point, nurses should object to or call to a supervisor's attention treatment that is going extremely badly. Because nurses are hospital employees, this theory essentially holds hospitals vicariously liable for nurses' failure to speak up or intervene. See Strubhart v. Perry Memorial Hospital, 903 P.2d 263 (Okla. 1995); T. Hardy, 61 Tul. L. Rev. 86 (1986) (the test under *Darling* should be "whether in a given situation a reasonable, prudent nurse would have spoken up about a physician's negligence"). Is this explanation consistent with the facts in *Darling?* Is it consistent with the practical realities of the doctor-nurse relationship? Recall Justice Cardozo's treatment of this very same theory of liability in *Schloendorff,* supra. See also Essig v. Advocate, supra ("it would be entirely inconsistent with both the scope of nursing practice and the applicable standard of care for an attending nurse to attempt to interfere with a surgeon, *in the midst of an ongoing surgery*").

5. *Risk Management.*

The newly created role in hospitals of "risk manager" marks the official recognition of a role that has become central to the way hospitals are run. Their role is clearly defined . . . "to avoid or minimize potential legal, and hence, financial loss for the health care provider." Although they may fulfill several different administrative functions, . . . I contend that current risk management practices in hospitals have risen to a pitch of near hysteria. They embody actions that are unprecedented in their intrusiveness into the doctor-patient relationship and are unethical in violating the rights of patients. . . . The typical responses of risk managers are wildly overactive. If people in ordinary life were to act in accordance with the minuscule probabilities on which risk management bases its decisions, we would all be in a constant state of paralysis. . . . Hospital administrators have refused to permit competent adult patients to reject burdensome treatment even when physicians concur with the patient's wish. It is not uncommon for administrators to request that a court order be obtained whenever there is a shred of doubt (which almost always exists) about what the law says. Where it was once physicians who overtreated patients because they believed it was their moral obligation to continue therapy, it is now hospital administrators and risk managers who more often insist on overtreatment out of fear of medical-legal liability. It is not a great exaggeration to view risk managers as enemies of patients. . . .

Who are these risk managers, and what is the origin of their role in the hospital? Some risk managers have law degrees, but most do not. Some are nurses who rose to the rank of supervisor and then moved into hospital administration, often after obtaining a master's degree. Others come from the ranks of hospital administrators, some with a degree in hospital or business administration. More rare are individuals with an advanced degree in a field such as sociology, and still others made their career in health planning or administration and were around long before the occupation of risk manager was invented. Large medical centers typically have an office of risk management in addition to in-house counsel. The staff of lawyers works together with risk management both in devising hospital policies that affect patients and in dealing with individual cases in which anyone suspects that there may be a risk of some sort.

The overall movement can be traced back to the late 1960s and early 1970s, when efforts were begun in industrial and other workplaces to reduce the costs of liability payments by underwriters and insurance companies. The trend widened, and in the 1980s risk management offices began to be established in hospitals . . . to deal with concerns about possible liability arising out of incident reports in the hospital: a patient falling out of bed, a visitor slipping in a puddle of water in the corridor, an inadvertent injury to a patient in the course of treatment. . . . The original worries about legal liability have now expanded to encompass everything that might place the hospital in a bad light. Risk managers are now charged with the task of minimizing risks other than those of liability. They look out for the projected risks of bad publicity, the actions of a disgruntled employee, or the possible political ramifications of a medical decision or hospital policy. . . . Even when the patient has no family, and there is no one around who would sue the hospital, risk management is brought into the case. One of the peculiar features of this situation is the nearly automatic response by many physicians to call risk management whenever the slightest uncertainty is voiced about an ethical matter or vaguely perceived to have legal implications. . . .

Ruth Macklin, Enemies of Patients (1993). Does this account confirm the fears of the AMA about the consequences for physicians of exposing hospitals to liability?

Hospitals are now required to have risk management programs by Joint Commission accreditation standards, and, in a few states, by hospital licensing laws. Risk management programs are now common also in nursing homes and HMOs. On their structure and content generally, see American Society for Healthcare Risk Management, Risk Management Handbook for Health Care Facilities (1990); B. Youngberg, Essentials of Hospital Risk Management (1990).

6. *Informed Consent Liability.* One form of physician supervision for which courts have been especially reluctant to impose hospital liability is the duty to obtain informed consent. One might suppose that it easily falls within the hospital's administrative functions to ensure that patients have signed the proper paperwork before major operations are conducted, especially since nurses usually have a central role in obtaining informed consent. Most courts, however, hold that informed consent is solely the responsibility of the physician because the delicate considerations of what exactly to tell the patient and when are matters "particularly calling for the exercise of medical judgment." Valles v. Albert Einstein Medical Center, 805 A.2d 1232 (Pa. 2002) (no liability even for employed physician because "a medical facility cannot maintain control over this aspect of the physician-patient relationship"). For a critique, see Robert Gatter, The Mysterious Survival of the Policy Against Informed Consent Liability for Hospitals, 81 Notre Dame L. Rev. 1203 (2006); Note, 1 Ind. Health L. Rev. 253 (2004).

7. *Self-Imposed Standards.* The hospital licensing regulations, accreditation standards, and hospital bylaws referred to in the *Darling* opinion contained statements such as the following:

[REGULATIONS]

The [hospital] board [of directors] shall be responsible for the maintenance of proper standards of professional work in the hospital and shall require that the medical staff function in conformity with reasonable standards of competency. . . .

[ACCREDITATION STANDARDS]

Maintaining high standards of medical care will depend upon the character of the [medical] staff and the effectiveness of its organization to carry out the following duties: 1. Selection of those recommended for staff appointments and hospital privileges. 2. Constant analysis and review of the clinical work done in the hospital. . . . It is the duty of the hospital [medical] staff through its chiefs of service and Executive Committee to see that members of the staff do not fail in the matter of calling consultants as needed.

[MEDICAL STAFF BYLAWS]

The purpose of this organization shall be to insure that all patients admitted to the hospital or treated in the outpatient department receive the best possible care.

Another important aspect of the court's holding is that standards such as these, to which the hospital subscribed or was bound, can be introduced as evidence, but not conclusive proof, of the customary standard of administrative care that prevails in the hospital industry. See also the discussion at page 393 of practice guidelines and other written standards used to establish the medical standard of care against physicians. Is the effect of these standards to make a hospital strictly liable for any mistakes that doctors make? How would you revise these standards in order to perform their intended function in these various legal documents while at the same time moderating their liability effect?

8. *Hospital Custom.* Most courts hold hospitals to a national standard of care in selecting medical staff members. Would a similar locality standard be more appropriate? Consider the history and accreditation status of Misericordia Community Hospital, which was a very small hospital with relatively few medical staff. Under the national standard, are these factors relevant to the "like or similar circumstances" qualifier? See Note, 1983 Wis. L. Rev. 453 (arguing that the *Misericordia* standards are too demanding for some hospitals). Observe, though, that the duty to fully investigate physicians' credentials is greatly eased now that hospitals can obtain records of past malpractice lawsuits and disciplinary actions by other hospitals from the National Practitioner Data Bank, described at page 478.

Hospital negligence cases are not as dependent on expert witnesses as are physician negligence cases, despite the *Johnson* court's holding on this point. Once the issue of physician negligence is established, issues of administrative care and proper oversight are subject to the "reasonable person" standard. Other courts sometimes hold that these issues are subject to commonsense understanding. If you were on a jury, would you consider a hospital negligent if it approved a physician who had been sued for malpractice three times in the past five years? If he had lost or settled two of the three suits for substantial amounts?

9. *Medical Staff Committees.* Observe the brief discussion at the end of *Johnson* concerning the legal effect of the hospital's delegating the task of medical staff credentialing to members and committees of the medical staff. Recall that medical staff members are, generally speaking, not agents of the hospital. Therefore, could a hospital not claim in a typical case, where it merely follows the medical staff's recommendation, that it is not responsible for their sloppiness or poor judgment? Assume the hospital board has no way to know that the medical staff did a poor job or made a bad decision. This defense does not work for two reasons: (1) Although medical staff members are independent contractors in their medical status as practicing doctors, they are agents of the hospital in their administrative status while sitting on medical staff committees. Therefore, ordinary respondeat superior applies to their committee mistakes. (2) The duty to screen medical staff members is considered nondelegable.

Distributing liability in the opposite direction, would it be possible to hold medical staff members individually liable for doing a poor job in evaluating an applicant? Alternatively, could the medical staff be held liable as an entity? In practice, physicians are not individually exposed since hospitals usually assume responsibility for liability arising from medical staff review activities. See generally J. Horty & D. Mulholland, The Legal Status of the Hospital Medical Staff, 22 St. Louis U. L.J. 485 (1978).

10. *Puzzles to Ponder.* In *Johnson,* the jury found Dr. Salinsky negligent. Is this necessary to hold the hospital liable for its own negligence? If a hospital negligently admits a bad doctor to the medical staff, shouldn't it be liable for any injury the doctor causes, under the notion that the hospital's negligence is distinct from the doctor's? This question seems to never have been addressed directly by the courts. Uniformly, they find hospital negligence only where the doctor is also negligent.

The best explanation for this limitation is one of proximate cause. A hospital's negligent screening of a physician is not sufficiently proximate to a patient's injury, even if it literally causes the injury, unless the injury results from the physician's own negligence as well.

Another doctrinal puzzle is whether hospitals who negligently credential a physician are liable to patients who are injured off premises in the doctor's private office. Although standard foreseeability and but-for causation tests would appear to be met, most courts hold that hospitals are liable only for injuries to hospital patients, even where the plaintiff can prove she relied on the hospital credentials in selecting the doctor. Again, the notion appears to be one of proximate cause, influenced by older notions of privity of contract. See Insinga v. LaBella, 543 So. 2d 209 (Fla. 1989) (no hospital liability for giving admitting privileges to a person masquerading as a physician, where injury occurred outside hospital). But see Copithorne v. Framingham Union Hospital, 520 N.E.2d 139 (Mass. 1988) (hospital duty extends to medical staff member who drugged and raped patient in her home). Should it make any difference if the doctor practices in a hospital-owned and -leased medical office building right next door? What if the hospital owns an HMO that the doctor and patient belong to?

11. Other important sources of hospital liability are surveyed at Chapters 2.A and 3.B. Of particular importance is the federal Emergency Medical Treatment and Labor Act (EMTALA), which creates a form of strict liability for hospitals that refuse to treat patients who are in labor or in a serious emergency condition. Much of the litigation under EMTALA has addressed whether it essentially federalizes malpractice actions arising out of the emergency room (or potentially anywhere in the hospital). For the most part, courts have said "no," holding that the statute was intended to apply only to purposefully refusing standard care, not to errors in judgment or skill in carrying out treatment. See page 79.

2. Managed Care Liability

We turn now to a new form of institution, one that combines medical delivery with medical financing. When confronted with HMOs' institutional liability, courts quickly applied the same structure of analysis that had developed for hospitals. Because HMOs differ in important respects from hospitals, however, the result of this analysis may not be the same. In the following materials, consider how different types of managed care entities and arrangements should be treated under the various theories and branches of no liability, vicarious liability, and direct liability.

■ BOYD v. ALBERT EINSTEIN MEDICAL CENTER
547 A.2d 1229 (Pa. Super. Ct. 1988)

OLSZEWSKI, Judge:

This is an appeal from the trial court's order granting summary judgment in favor of defendant/appellee, Health Maintenance Organization of Pennsylvania (hereinafter HMO). Appellant asserts that the trial court erred in granting the motion for summary judgment when there existed a question of material fact as to whether participating physicians are the ostensible agents of HMO. For the reasons stated below, we reverse the grant of summary judgment.

The facts, as averred by the parties in their pleadings and elicited through deposition testimony, reveal that at the time of her death, decedent and her husband were participants in the HMO. HMO is a medical insurance provider that offers an alternative to the traditional Blue Cross/Blue Shield insurance plan.[1] Decedent's husband became eligible for participation in a group plan provided by HMO through his employer. Upon electing to participate in this plan, decedent and her husband were provided with a directory and benefits brochure which listed the participating physicians. Restricted to selecting a physician from this list, decedent chose Doctor David Rosenthal and Doctor Perry Dornstein as her primary care physicians.

In June of 1982, decedent contacted Doctor David Rosenthal regarding a lump in her breast. Doctor Rosenthal ordered a mammogram to be performed which revealed a suspicious area in the breast. Doctor Rosenthal recommended that decedent undergo a biopsy and referred decedent to Doctor Erwin Cohen for that purpose. Doctor Cohen, a surgeon, is also a participating HMO physician. The referral to a specialist in this case was made in accordance with the terms and conditions of HMO's subscription agreement.[2]

On July 6, 1982, Doctor Cohen performed a biopsy of decedent's breast tissue at Albert Einstein Medical Center. During the procedure, Doctor Cohen perforated decedent's chest wall with the biopsy needle, causing decedent to sustain a left hemothorax. Decedent was hospitalized for treatment of the hemothorax at Albert Einstein Hospital for two days.

In the weeks following this incident decedent complained to her primary care physicians, Doctor David Rosenthal and Doctor Perry Dornstein, of pain in her chest wall, belching, hiccoughs, and fatigue. On August 19, 1982, decedent awoke with pain in the middle of her chest. Decedent's husband contacted her primary care physicians, Doctors Rosenthal and Dornstein, and was advised to take decedent to Albert Einstein Hospital where she would be examined by Doctor Rosenthal. Upon arrival at Albert Einstein emergency room, decedent related symptoms of chest wall pain, vomiting, stomach and back discomfort to Doctor Rosenthal. Doctor Rosenthal commenced an examination of decedent, diagnosed Tietz's syndrome,[3] and

1. A Health Maintenance Organization is an organized system of health care which provides or arranges for a comprehensive array of basic and supplemental health care services. These services are provided on a prepaid basis to voluntarily enrolled members living within a prescribed geographic area. Responsibility for the delivery, quality and payment of health care falls to the managing organization—the HMO.

2. Doctor Rosenthal admitted in his deposition that HMO limited specifically the doctors to whom decedent could have been referred.

3. Tietze's Syndrome is an inflammatory condition affecting the costochondral cartilage. It occurs more commonly in females, generally in the 30 to 50 age range.

arranged for tests to be performed at his office where decedent underwent X-rays, EKG, and cardiac isoenzyme tests.[4] Decedent was then sent home and told to rest.[5]

During the course of that afternoon, decedent continued to experience chest pain, vomiting and belching. Decedent related the persistence and worsening of these symptoms by telephone to Doctors Rosenthal and Dornstein, who prescribed, without further examination, Talwin, a pain medication. At 5:30 that afternoon decedent was discovered dead in her bathroom by her husband, having expired as a result of a myocardial infarction.

Appellant's complaint and new matter aver that HMO advertised that its physicians and medical care providers were competent, and that they had been evaluated for periods of up to six months prior to being selected to participate in the HMO program as a medical provider. The complaint further avers that decedent and appellant relied on these representations in choosing their primary care physicians. The complaint then avers that HMO was negligent in failing to

> qualify or oversee its physicians and hospital who acted as its agents, servants, or employees in providing medical care to the decedent nor did HMO of Pa. require its physicians, surgeons and hospitals to provide adequate evidence of skill, training and competence in medicine and it thereby failed to furnish the decedent with competent, qualified medical care as warranted.

Finally, appellant's new matter avers that HMO furnished to its subscribers documents which identify HMO as the care provider and state that HMO guarantees the quality of care.

Appellant's theory of recovery before the trial court was primarily one of vicarious liability under the ostensible agency theory. In granting defendant HMO's motion for summary judgment, the trial court found that plaintiff/appellant had failed to establish either of the two factors on which the theory of ostensible agency, as applied to hospitals in *Capan*, is based. On appeal, appellant contends that the evidence indicates that there exists a question of fact regarding whether HMO may be held liable under this theory. . . .

The group master contract provides that HMO "operates a comprehensive prepaid program of health care which provides health care services and benefits to Members in order to protect and promote their health, and preserve and enhance patient dignity." HMO was incorporated in 1975 under the laws of Pennsylvania and converted from a nonprofit to a for-profit corporation in 1981. HMO is based

---

4. HMO avers that decedent was returned to the doctor's office for testing because it was more comfortable and convenient for her. Appellant, however, asserts that the tests were performed in the doctor's office, rather than the hospital, in accordance with the requirements of HMO whose primary interest was in keeping the medical fees within the corporation.

5. Appellant contends that Doctor Rosenthal acted negligently in ordering the tests to be performed in his office when decedent exhibited symptoms of cardiac distress. The safer practice, avers appellant, would have been to perform the tests at the hospital where the results would have been more quickly available. Appellant further contends that, despite Doctor Rosenthal's diagnosis of Tietze's Syndrome, the nature of the tests he ordered indicates that he was concerned about the possibility of a heart attack.

on the individual practice association model (hereinafter IPA), which means that HMO is comprised of participating primary physicians who are engaged in part in private practice in the HMO service area. Under the plan, IPA contracts with HMO to provide medical services to HMO members. IPA selects its primary and specialist physicians and enters into an agreement with them obligating the physician to perform health services for the subscribers of HMO.

The primary physician's role is defined as the "gatekeeper into the health care delivery system." "An HMO member must consult with his primary physician before going to a specialist and/or the hospital." If the primary physician deems it necessary, he arranges a consultation with an HMO participating specialist, which constitutes a second opinion. "Basically, with the primary physicians 'screening' the members' illnesses, excessive hospitalization and improper use of specialists can be reduced."

Member-patients use a physician directory and choose a conveniently located office of a participating primary physician. HMO members will only receive reimbursement from nonparticipating providers when the condition requiring treatment was of an immediate nature. Determinations of immediacy are made by the HMO quality assurance committee. In any event, persons desiring emergency nonprovider benefits must notify HMO or their primary physician of the emergency within 48 hours and must give written proof of the occurrence within ninety days after service is rendered. . . .

Primary physicians are paid through a mechanism termed "capitation." Capitation is an actuarially determined amount prepaid by HMO to the primary physician for each patient who has chosen his office. The dollar amount is based upon a predetermined rate per age group. The primary physicians are paid 80 percent of the capitation amount and the remaining 20 percent is pooled by IPA and goes back into a pooled risk-sharing fund as a reserve against specialty referral costs and hospital stays. Each primary care office has its own specialist fund and hospital fund established by allocating a predetermined amount each month for each member who has chosen that primary care office. The surplus from the specialist fund is returned to the primary care office. The hospital fund, however, is governed by a hospital risk/incentive-sharing scheme which anticipates a number of inpatient days per members per year. If the actual hospital utilization is less than anticipated, the HMO and IPA each receive 50 percent of the savings. IPA must place the savings in the Special IPA risk-sharing account and must use the funds to offset losses resulting from unanticipated physician costs. If utilization is greater than anticipated, IPA is responsible for 50 percent of the loss up to the amount of uncommitted funds in the Special IPA risk sharing account. . . .

HMO asserts that because the theory of ostensible agency has been applied in Pennsylvania only to the relationship between hospitals and independent contractor physicians, the theory is not appropriate in the instant situation. We emphasize, however, that when this court introduced the concept of ostensible agency to this Commonwealth in *Capan*, supra, we based that decision in large part upon "the changing role of the hospital in society [which] creates a likelihood that patients will look to the institution" for care. Because the role of health care providers has changed in recent years, the *Capan* rationale for applying the theory of ostensible agency to hospitals is certainly applicable in the instant situation. . . .

We find that the facts indicate an issue of material fact as to whether the participating physicians were the ostensible agents of HMO. HMO covenanted that it would "[provide] health care services and benefits to Members in order to protect and promote their health. . . . " "HMOPA operates on a direct service rather than an indemnity basis." Appellant paid his doctor's fee to HMO, not to the physician of his choice. Then, appellant selected his primary care physicians from the list provided by HMO. Regardless of who recommended appellant's decedent to choose her primary care physician, the fact remains that HMO provides a limited list from which a member must choose a primary physician. Moreover, those primary physicians are screened by HMO and must comply with a list of regulations in order to honor their contract with HMO.

Further, as mandated by HMO, appellant's decedent could not see a specialist without the primary physician's referral. As HMO declares, the primary physician is the "gatekeeper into the health care delivery system." "An HMO member must consult with his primary physician before going to a specialist and/or the hospital." Moreover, appellant's decedent had no choice as to which specialist to see. In our opinion, because appellant's decedent was required to follow the mandates of HMO and did not directly seek the attention of the specialist, there is an inference that appellant looked to the institution for care and not solely to the physicians; conversely, that appellant's decedent submitted herself to the care of the participating physicians in response to an invitation from HMO. See comment (a), Restatement (Second) Agency §267. . . .

We conclude, therefore, that the trial court erred when it granted HMO's motion for summary judgment on the ground that the participating physicians were not the ostensible agents of HMO. . . .

McEwen, Judge, concurring.

I concur in the result reached by the majority since the author, after a very careful analysis of the issues presented in this appeal, reaches the quite basic principle that issues of material fact may not be resolved by summary judgment.

I write only because it appears to me that the learned trial court improperly resolved by summary judgment the basic factual issue of whether the literature, in which HMO "guaranteed" and "assured" the quality of care provided to its subscribers, had been distributed to appellant or to other subscribers of HMO.

It might also be mentioned that while the court was understandably uncertain as to the theories upon which plaintiff was proceeding,[1] it appears that the amended complaint of plaintiff does contain factual averments supporting a breach of warranty claim.

---

1. The trial court noted in its opinion that

the gravamen of plaintiff's complaint is that HMO of PA guaranteed or warranted the quality of care provided. . . . Plaintiff's theory of recovery . . . is not entirely clear. A reading of the complaint suggests Plaintiff is proceeding upon grounds of corporate liability. However, in his answer to the motion of HMO of PA for summary judgment, plaintiff contends HMO of PA is vicariously liable through ostensible agency.

■ WICKLINE v. STATE
239 Cal. Rptr. 810 (Cal. Ct. App. 1986)

ROWEN, Associate Justice.

[Lois Wickline, who was treated under California's Medicaid program (known as "Medi-Cal"), sued the State, but not her physician, for negligently causing her premature discharge from the hospital, resulting in complications that eventually necessitated amputation of her right leg. Wickline alleged that her premature discharge was the fault of Medi-Cal's erroneous withholding of its authorization for her continued hospitalization.] This is an appeal from a judgment for plaintiff entered after a trial by jury. For the reasons discussed below, we reverse the judgment.

Principally, this matter concerns itself with the legal responsibility that a third party payor, in this case, the State of California, has for harm caused to a patient when a cost containment program is applied in a manner which is alleged to have affected the implementation of the treating physician's medical judgment. . . .

I

Responding to concerns about the escalating cost of health care, public and private payors have in recent years experimented with a variety of cost containment mechanisms. We deal here with one of those programs: The prospective utilization review process.

At the outset, this court recognizes that this case appears to be the first attempt to tie a health care payor into the medical malpractice causation chain and that it, therefore, deals with issues of profound importance to the health care community and to the general public. For those reasons we have permitted the filing of amicus curiae briefs in support of each of the respective parties in the matter to assure that due consideration is given to the broader issues raised before this court by this case. . . .

Early cost containment programs utilized the retrospective utilization review process. In that system the third party payor reviewed the patient's chart after the fact to determine whether the treatment provided was medically necessary. If, in the judgment of the utilization reviewer, it was not, the health care provider's claim for payment was denied.

In the cost containment program in issue in this case, prospective utilization review, authority for the rendering of health care services must be obtained before medical care is rendered. Its purpose is to promote the well-recognized public interest in controlling health care costs by reducing unnecessary services while still intending to assure that appropriate medical and hospital services are provided to the patient in need. However, such a cost containment strategy creates new and added pressures on the quality assurance portion of the utilization review mechanism. The stakes, the risks at issue, are much higher when a prospective cost containment review process is utilized than when a retrospective review process is used.

A mistaken conclusion about medical necessity following retrospective review will result in the wrongful withholding of payment. An erroneous decision in a prospective review process, on the other hand, in practical consequences, results in the withholding of necessary care, potentially leading to a patient's permanent disability or death.

II

Though somewhat in dispute, the facts in this case are not particularly complicated. In 1976, Wickline a married woman in her mid-40's, with a limited education, was being treated by Dr. Stanley Z. Daniels (Dr. Daniels), a physician engaged in a general family practice, for problems associated with her back and legs. Failing to respond to the physical therapy type of treatment he prescribed, Dr. Daniels had Wickline admitted to Van Nuys Community Hospital (Van Nuys or Hospital) in October 1976 and brought in another physician, Dr. Gerald E. Polonsky (Dr. Polonsky), a specialist in peripheral vascular surgery, to do a consultation examination. Peripheral vascular surgery concerns itself with surgery on any vessel of the body, exclusive of the heart.

Dr. Polonsky examined plaintiff and diagnosed her condition as arteriosclorosis obliterans with occlusion of the abdominal aorta, more generally referred to as Leriche's Syndrome. . . .

According to Dr. Polonsky, the only treatment for Leriche's Syndrome is surgical. In Wickline's case her disease was so far advanced that Dr. Polonsky concluded that it was necessary to remove a part of the plaintiff's artery and insert a synthetic (Teflon) graft in its place.

After agreeing to the operation, Wickline was discharged home to await approval of her doctor's diagnosis and authorization from Medi-Cal for the recommended surgical procedure and attendant acute care hospitalization. It is conceded that at all times in issue in this case, the plaintiff was eligible for medical benefits under California's medical assistance program, the "Medi-Cal Act," which is more commonly referred to as Medi-Cal. (Welf. & Inst. Code, §§14000 et seq., 14000.4.)

As required, Dr. Daniels submitted a treatment authorization request to Medi-Cal, sometimes referred to as form "161," "MC-161" or "TAR." In response to Dr. Daniels' request, Medi-Cal authorized the surgical procedure and 10 days of hospitalization for that treatment.

On January 6, 1977, plaintiff was admitted to Van Nuys by Dr. Daniels. On January 7, 1977, Dr. Polonsky performed a surgical procedure in which a part of plaintiff's artery was removed and a synthetic artery was inserted to replace it. Dr. Polonsky characterized that procedure as "a very major surgery."

Later that same day Dr. Polonsky was notified that Wickline was experiencing circulatory problems in her right leg. He concluded that a clot had formed in the graft. As a result, Wickline was taken back into surgery, the incision in her right groin was reopened, the clot removed and the graft was resewn. Wickline's recovery subsequent to the two January 7th operations [was] characterized as "stormy." She had a lot of pain, some spasm in the vessels in the lower leg and she experienced hallucinating episodes. On January 12, 1977, Wickline was returned to the operating room where Dr. Polonsky performed a lumbar sympathectomy.

A lumbar sympathectomy is a major operation in which a section of the chain of nerves that lie on each side of the spinal column is removed. The procedure causes the blood vessels in the patient's lower extremity to become paralyzed in a wide open position and was done in an attempt to relieve the spasms which Wickline was experiencing in those vessels. Spasms stop the outflow of blood from the vessels causing the blood to back up into the graft. Failure to relieve such spasms can cause clotting.

Dr. Polonsky was assisted in all three surgeries by Dr. Leonard Kovner (Dr. Kovner), a board-certified specialist in the field of general surgery and the chief of surgery at Van Nuys. Dr. Daniels was present for the initial graft surgery on January 7, 1977, and for the right lumbar sympathectomy operation on January 12, 1977.

Wickline was scheduled to be discharged on January 16, 1977, which would mean that she would actually leave the hospital sometime before 1 P.M. on January 17, 1977. On or about January 16, 1977, Dr. Polonsky concluded that "it was medically necessary" that plaintiff remain in the hospital for an additional eight days beyond her then scheduled discharge date. Drs. Kovner and Daniels concurred in Dr. Polonsky's opinion.

Dr. Polonsky cited many reasons for his feeling that it was medically necessary for plaintiff to remain in an acute care hospital for an additional eight days, such as the danger of infection and/or clotting. His principal reason, however, was that he felt that he was going to be able to save both of Wickline's legs and wanted her to remain in the hospital where he could observe her and be immediately available, along with the hospital staff, to treat her if an emergency should occur.

In order to secure an extension of Wickline's hospital stay, it was necessary to complete and present to Medi-Cal a form called "Request for Extension of Stay in Hospital," commonly referred to as an "MC-180" or "180." . . .

At Van Nuys, Patricia N. Spears (Spears), an employee of the hospital and a registered nurse, had the responsibility for completing 180 forms. In this case, as requested by Dr. Polonsky, Spears filled out Wickline's 180 form and then presented it to Dr. Daniels, as plaintiff's attending physician, to sign, which he did, in compliance with Dr. Polonsky's recommendation. All of the physicians who testified agreed that the 180 form prepared by Spears was complete, accurate and adequate for all purposes in issue in this matter.

Doris A. Futerman (Futerman), a registered nurse, was, at that time, employed by Medi-Cal as a Health Care Service Nurse, commonly referred to as an "on-site nurse." . . .

Futerman, after reviewing Wickline's 180 form, felt that she could not approve the requested eight-day extension of acute care hospitalization. While conceding that the information provided might justify some additional time beyond the scheduled discharge date, nothing in Wickline's case, in Futerman's opinion, would have warranted the entire eight additional days requested and, for those reasons, she telephoned the Medi-Cal Consultant. She reached Dr. William S. Glassman (Dr. Glassman), one of the Medi-Cal Consultants on duty at the time in Medi-Cal's Los Angeles office. The Medi-Cal Consultant selection occurred randomly. As was the practice, whichever Medi-Cal Consultant was available at the moment took the next call that came into the office. . . .

After speaking with Futerman on the telephone, Dr. Glassman rejected Wickline's treating physician's request for an eight-day hospital extension and, instead, authorized an additional four days of hospital stay beyond the originally scheduled discharge date. . . .

After review of Wickline's 180 form, Dr. Glassman testified that the factors that led him to authorize four days, rather than the requested eight days, was that there was no information about the patient's temperature which he, thereupon, assumed was normal; nothing was mentioned about the patient's diet, which he then presumed was not a problem; nor was there any information about Wickline's bowel function, which Dr. Glassman then presumed was functioning satisfactorily. Further, the fact that the 180 form noted that Wickline was able to ambulate with help and that whirlpool treatments were to begin that day caused Dr. Glassman to presume that the patient was progressing satisfactorily and was not seriously or critically ill. . . .

In essence, respondent argues, Dr. Glassman based his decision on signs and symptoms such as temperature, diet and bowel movements, which were basically irrelevant to the plaintiff's circulatory condition for which she was being treated and did not concern himself with those symptoms and signs which an ordinary prudent physician would consider to be pertinent with regard to the type of medical condition presented by Wickline.

Complying with the limited extension of time authorized by Medi-Cal, Wickline was discharged from Van Nuys on January 21, 1977. Drs. Polonsky and Daniels each wrote discharge orders. At the time of her discharge, each of plaintiff's three treating physicians were aware that the Medi-Cal Consultant had approved only four of the requested eight-day hospital stay extension. While all three doctors were aware that they could attempt to obtain a further extension of Wickline's hospital stay by telephoning the Medi-Cal Consultant to request such an extension, none of them did so. . . .

At trial, Dr. Polonsky testified that in the time that had passed since the first extension request had been communicated to Medi-Cal, on January 16th or 17th, and the time of her scheduled discharge on January 21, 1977, Wickline's condition had neither deteriorated nor become critical. In Dr. Polonsky's opinion no new symptom had presented itself and no additional factors had occurred since the original request was made to have formed the basis for a change in the Medi-Cal Consultant's attitude regarding Wickline's situation. In addition, he stated that at the time of Wickline's discharge it did not appear that her leg was in any danger.

Dr. Polonsky testified that at the time in issue he felt that Medi-Cal Consultants had the state's interest more in mind than the patient's welfare and that that belief influenced his decision not to request a second extension of Wickline's hospital stay. In addition, he felt that Medi-Cal had the power to tell him, as a treating doctor, when a patient must be discharged from the hospital. Therefore, while still of the subjective, noncommunicated, opinion that Wickline was seriously ill and that the danger to her was not over, Dr. Polonsky discharged her from the hospital on January 21, 1977. He testified that had Wickline's condition, in his medical judgment, been critical or in a deteriorating condition on January 21, he would have made some effort to keep her in the hospital beyond that day even if denied authority by Medi-Cal and even if he had to pay her hospital bill himself. . . .

All of the medical witnesses who testified at trial agreed that Dr. Polonsky was acting within the standards of practice of the medical community in discharging Wickline on January 21, 1977. . . .

Wickline testified that in the first few days after she arrived home she started feeling pain in her right leg and the leg started to lose color. In the next few days the pain got worse and the right leg took on a whitish, statue-like marble appearance. Wickline assumed she was experiencing normal recovery symptoms and did not communicate with any of her physicians. Finally, when "the pain got so great and the color started changing from looking like a statue to getting a grayish color," her husband called Dr. Kovner. It was Wickline's memory that this occurred about the third day after her discharge from the hospital and that Dr. Kovner advised Mr. Wickline to give extra pain medicine to the plaintiff.

Thereafter, gradually over the next few days, the plaintiff's leg "kept getting grayer and then it got bluish." The extra medication allegedly prescribed by Dr. Kovner over the telephone did not relieve the pain Wickline was experiencing. She testified that "by then the pain was just excruciating, where no pain medicine helped whatsoever." Finally, Wickline instructed her husband to call Dr. Kovner again and this time Dr. Kovner ordered plaintiff back into the hospital. Wickline returned to Van Nuys that same evening, January 30, 1977, nine days after her last discharge therefrom. . . .

Attempts to save Wickline's leg through the utilization of anticoagulants, antibiotics, strict bed rest, pain medication and warm water whirlpool baths to the lower extremity proved unsuccessful. On February 8, 1977, Dr. Polonsky amputated Wickline's leg below the knee because had he not done so "she would have died." The condition did not, however, heal after the first operation and on February 17, 1977, the doctors went back and amputated Wickline's leg above the knee. . . .

In Dr. Polonsky's opinion, to a reasonable medical certainty, had Wickline remained in the hospital for the eight additional days, as originally requested by him and her other treating doctors, she would not have suffered the loss of her leg. . . .

Dr. Polonsky testified that in his medical opinion, the Medi-Cal Consultant's rejection of the requested eight-day extension of acute care hospitalization and his authorization of a four-day extension in its place did not conform to the usual medical standards as they existed in 1977. He stated that, in accordance with those standards, a physician would not be permitted to make decisions regarding the care of a patient without either first seeing the patient, reviewing the patient's chart or discussing the patient's condition with her treating physician or physicians.

III

From the facts thus presented, appellant takes the position that it was not negligent as a matter of law. Appellant contends that the decision to discharge was made by each of the plaintiff's three doctors, was based upon the prevailing standards of practice, and was justified by her condition at the time of her discharge. It argues that Medi-Cal had no part in the plaintiff's hospital discharge and therefore was not liable even if the decision to do so was erroneously made by her doctors. . . .

As to the principal issue before this court, i.e., who bears responsibility for allowing a patient to be discharged from the hospital, her treating physicians or the health care payor, each side's medical expert witnesses agreed that, in accordance with the standards of medical practice as it existed in January 1977, it was for the patient's treating physician to decide the course of treatment that was medically necessary to treat the ailment. It was also that physician's responsibility to determine whether or not acute care hospitalization was required and for how long. Finally, it was agreed that the patient's physician is in a better position than the Medi-Cal Consultant to determine the number of days medically necessary for any required hospital care. The decision to discharge is, therefore, the responsibility of the patient's own treating doctor.

Dr. Kaufman testified that if, on January 21, the date of the plaintiff's discharge from Van Nuys, any one of her three treating doctors had decided that in his medical judgment it was necessary to keep Wickline in the hospital for a longer period of time, they, or any of them, should have filed another request for extension of stay in the hospital, that Medi-Cal would expect those physicians to make such a request if they felt it was indicated, and upon receipt of such a request further consideration of an additional extension of hospital time would have been given.

Title 22 of the California Administrative Code §51110, provided, in pertinent part, at the relevant time in issue here, that: "The determination of need for acute care shall be made in accordance with the usual standards of medical practice in the community."

The patient who requires treatment and who is harmed when care which should have been provided is not provided should recover for the injuries suffered from all those responsible for the deprivation of such care, including, when appropriate, health care payors. Third party payors of health care services can be held legally accountable when medically inappropriate decisions result from defects in the design or implementation of cost containment mechanisms as, for example, when appeals made on a patient's behalf for medical or hospital care are arbitrarily ignored or unreasonably disregarded or overridden. However, the physician who complies without protest with the limitations imposed by a third-party payor, when his medical judgment dictates otherwise, cannot avoid his ultimate responsibility for his patient's care. He cannot point to the health care payor as the liability scapegoat when the consequences of his own determinative medical decisions go sour.

There is little doubt that Dr. Polonsky was intimidated by the Medi-Cal program but he was not paralyzed by Dr. Glassman's response nor rendered powerless to act appropriately if other action was required under the circumstances. If, in his medical judgment, it was in his patient's best interest that she remain in the acute care hospital setting for an additional four days beyond the extended time period originally authorized by Medi-Cal, Dr. Polonsky should have made some effort to keep Wickline there. He himself acknowledged that responsibility to his patient. It was his medical judgment, however, that Wickline could be discharged when she was. All the plaintiff's treating physicians concurred and all the doctors who testified at trial, for either plaintiff or defendant, agreed that Dr. Polonsky's medical decision to discharge Wickline met the standard of care applicable at the time. Medi-Cal was not a party to that medical decision and therefore cannot be held to share in the harm resulting if such decision was negligently made.

In addition, thereto, while Medi-Cal played a part in the scenario before us in that it was the resource for the funds to pay for the treatment sought, and its input regarding the nature and length of hospital care to be provided was of paramount importance, Medi-Cal did not override the medical judgment of Wickline's treating physicians at the time of her discharge. It was given no opportunity to do so. Therefore, there can be no viable cause of action against it for the consequences of that discharge decision. . . .

V

This court appreciates that what is at issue here is the effect of cost containment programs upon the professional judgment of physicians to prescribe hospital treatment for patients requiring the same. While we recognize, realistically, that cost consciousness has become a permanent feature of the health care system, it is essential that cost limitation programs not be permitted to corrupt medical judgment. We have concluded, from the facts in issue here, that in this case it did not.

For the reasons expressed herein, this court finds that appellant is not liable for respondent's injuries as a matter of law. That makes unnecessary any discussion of the other contentions of the parties.

Notes: Managed Care Liability

1. *The Components of Managed Care.* Managed care is a term that applies broadly to a wide variety of arrangements that restrict the generosity of traditional health insurance. Managed care (1) restricts choice of physicians through networks and gatekeepers, (2) alters discrete treatment decisions through utilization review and prior authorization requirements, and (3) creates cost-constrained financial incentives through capitation payments and risk-sharing pools. Each of these components has distinct liability implications and can exist separately from the others. For instance, "managed indemnity" insurance does (2) but not (1) or (3), simply by adding utilization review to traditional insurance. Preferred provider organizations (PPOs) do (1) but not (3), and may do (2) but not necessarily. HMOs are the fullest embodiment of managed care because they incorporate all three components. In analyzing these cases and others that are likely to arise in the future, however, be sure to think individually about each of these components and observe how they might arise in a variety of different institutional forms.

2. *HMO Immunity.* In a few jurisdictions, HMOs are immune from suit for negligent treatment, in some states by statute and in one state formerly by court decision. Williams v. Good Health Plus, Inc., 743 S.W.2d 373 (Tex. Ct. App. 1987), resonates with hospital decisions early in the century by holding that an HMO logically cannot be held liable because the corporate practice of medicine doctrine prevents it from controlling physicians' treatment decisions. That decision has since been overturned by statute, however. Comment, 30 Tex. Tech. L. Rev. 1227 (1999). But California, by statute, declares that health insurers may not be held vicariously liable for medical decisions by independent physicians. Martin v. PacifiCare of California, 198 Cal. App. 4th 1390 (2011). Economist Patricia Danzon is one who argues for HMO immunity under the theory that holding physicians individually liable is sufficient, unless the HMO agrees by contract to assume liability. Patricia M. Danzon, Tort Liability: A Minefield for Managed Care, 24 J. Leg. Stud. 491 (1997). Do you agree?

3. *Vicarious Liability.* There are two basic types of HMOs, with several permutations. The HMO type in *Boyd* was an Independent Practice Association (IPA), which is composed of a large contractual network of physicians who maintain practices in their own offices and see patients with many different types of insurance. For a decision similar to *Boyd*, see Villazon v. Prudential Health Care Plan, 843 So. 2d 842 (Fla. 2003). An agency relationship is much easier to establish with the other type of HMO, a staff or group model, in which a smaller number of physicians work exclusively for a single HMO in a centralized clinic. What about a PPO (preferred provider organization) or POS (point of service) plan with an open network in which patients are encouraged to stay with the designated physicians but are

free to go outside the network and select any doctor they want by paying a higher deductible or copayment? What about a closed network that is very large but has no gatekeeping restrictions, that is, patients can see anyone they want when they want, but only within the network? See generally Comment, Managed Health Care: HMO Corporate Liability, Independent Contractors, and the Ostensible Agency Doctrine, 15 J. Corp. L. 535 (1990).

How might an IPA HMO alter its structure or operations to avoid the attribution of agency and vicarious liability? See Chase v. Independent Practice Ass'n, 583 N.E.2d 251 (Mass. App. Ct. 1991) (vicarious liability rejected where HMO contract stated the IPA only "arranged for" services but did not provide services directly); Jones v. U.S. Healthcare, 723 N.Y.S.2d 478 (App. Div. 2001) (an HMO "cannot be held vicariously liable for defendant doctors' and hospital's alleged malpractice in discharging plaintiff and her baby prematurely, where the . . . Group Master Contract, membership card and Member Handbook clearly state that doctors and hospitals participating in defendant's health care program are independent contractors"). But see Petrovich v. Share Health Plan, 719 N.E.2d 756 (Ill. 1999) (exculpatory language in insurance documents does not control if the patient didn't actually read or understand the documents). Because IPAs are now the dominant form of HMOs, and because HMO lawyers have widely adopted these techniques, the working assumption among both plaintiff's and defense lawyers is that HMOs generally cannot be held vicariously liable simply by virtue of forming a network and requiring gatekeeping. This is also confirmed in several of the state managed care liability statutes discussed in the next note. See Agrawal & Hall, infra.

4. *HMO Direct Liability.* The focus of *Boyd* is vicarious liability, but HMOs have also been held to the same type of direct corporate liability ushered in by Darling v. Charleston Community Memorial Hospital, page 491. Recall that for hospitals, direct corporate liability takes two basic forms: a duty of care in the selection of physicians, and a duty of care in the contemporaneous supervision of physicians. The former is readily applicable to HMOs as well. Several courts have held that they have the same obligation hospitals do to review the credentials and competency of physicians that they select for their network. See, e.g., McClellan v. Health Maintenance Organization, 604 A.2d 1053 (Pa. Super. Ct. 1992); Pagarigan v. Aetna, 2005 WL 2742807 (Cal. Ct. App. 2005). HMOs are required under their own accreditation standards to engage in a hospital-like credentialing process, and increasingly they are required to do so by state regulation as well. Nevertheless, many managed care networks accept virtually "any willing provider," that is, anyone with a license who agrees to the network's payment terms. A "Dear Doctor" letter sent by one PPO to California physicians stated, "Welcome to the PPO network. You are now part of a carefully selected panel of more than 300 hospitals and 21,000 physicians." Robert A. Berenson, Beyond Competition, 16(2) Health Aff. 171, 175 (1997). Some states require by statute that HMOs accept any qualified provider. Does either voluntary or mandatory nonselectivity undermine the basis for a duty of care in selection?

Recall that the second branch of *Darling*—the duty of contemporaneous supervision—is highly controversial with respect to hospitals and is accepted in only a very limited fashion in most jurisdictions because it doesn't make sense to require hospital administrators to actively intervene in medical treatment decisions. Is the case for an HMO's duty to supervise any stronger? Even if there is no such mandatory duty, however, consider whether HMOs have voluntarily assumed such a duty through their utilization review function. Is this not the essential point of *Wickline*, that when insurance companies choose to intervene in treatment decisions, they assume a duty of care in doing so? Accord Shannon v. McNulty, 718 A.2d 828 (Pa. Super. Ct. 1998) ("When . . . an insurer interjects itself into the rendering of medical decisions affecting a subscriber's care it must do so in a medically reasonable manner.").

To remove any doubt about this issue, about a dozen states have adopted statutes that hold insurers liable for personal injuries caused by negligent or inappropriate administration of health insurance benefits. See Agrawal & Hall, infra; Note, 74 Temp. L. Rev. 507 (2001). It is unlikely, however, that these statutes can be applied to employer-provided health insurance, due to the federal preemption doctrine discussed in the following case.

5. *Medical Tourism.* Complex medical care can be quite good in some less developed countries such as India and Malaysia, but considerably less expensive, even factoring in travel costs — with net savings of tens of thousands of dollars per procedure for many common surgeries. See page 43. Thus, it may be just a matter of time before insurers, or self-insured employers, begin offering strong incentives (in the form of discounts or rebates) to people who opt to use "preferred providers" overseas. Would doing only that give rise to insurer liability for any medical injuries? If so, under what theory(ies) of institutional liability? And, what standard of care (domestic or foreign) should determine the provider's underlying negligence? For discussion, but no resolution, of these fascinating questions, see Glenn Cohen, Protecting Patients with Passports, 95 Iowa L. Rev. 1467 (2010).

6. Wickline's *Holding.* The precise holding or nonholding of *Wickline* has been a source of considerable confusion, both in the courts and among lawyers and commentators. This confusion is due in part to the unusual tactical decision by the plaintiff's lawyer not to sue the treating physicians. As a result, the plaintiff was able to use the treating physicians as experts for her side, but the physicians were unwilling to indict themselves by testifying that the four-day stay fell below a minimally acceptable standard of care. Without such testimony, the court was forced to find no liability. Without any basis in the clinical evidence for finding anyone liable, much of what the court said about the competing responsibilities of physicians and insurers was rendered dictum.

Nevertheless, *Wickline* is still the seminal case on the issues it addresses. In trying to make sense of what the opinion means for future disputes, distinguish these two issues: (1) whether insurers are potentially on the liability hook for making bad coverage decisions, and (2) whether physicians are off the liability hook when insurers are at fault. Realize it is possible to answer "yes" to (1) and "no" to (2); in other words, both can be held liable at the same time. Others sometimes interpret *Wickline* to mean, however, that the doctor's ultimate responsibility absolves the insurance company from blame. The most prominent instance of this reading of *Wickline* is a subsequent California decision, Wilson v. Blue Cross of Southern California, 271 Cal. Rptr. 876 (Cal. Ct. App. 1990). There, a psychiatric patient committed suicide after being released from the hospital when his private insurer stopped paying for his hospitalization benefits due to lack of medical necessity. The court found it necessary to distinguish and disapprove *Wickline* in order to allow the case to be tried against the insurer under a negligence theory. Is anything in *Wickline* opposed to such a holding? For a sampling of the extensive commentary on these two cases, see John Blum, An Analysis of Legal Liability in Health Care Utilization Review and Case Management, 26 Hous. L. Rev. 191 (1989); Comment, 52 Ohio St. L.J. 1289 (1991).

Under *Wickline*, could insurer liability be imposed not only based on the substance of the utilization review decision, but also based on the process? What flaws were present in Medi-Cal's UR process? How feasible would it be to improve on that process?

If insurers can be found liable for negligent failures to approve necessary care, can they also be held accountable for negligent approvals of harmful care?

7. *Bringing Liability and Payment into Sync.* Does the potential liability under *Wickline* make sense from the physician's perspective? Physicians complain that it is unfair to hold them responsible for failing to provide treatment that insurance will not pay for. See Note, 59 Duke L. Rev. 955 (2010). What realistic options did Mrs. Wickline's physicians have? How might the tort standard of medical appropriateness be brought more into sync with the insurance standard? One possibility is by referring to the law of abandonment, which is discussed in Chapter 2.B.3. There, we learn that physicians are able to terminate care in certain circumstances if they give proper notice and an opportunity to locate another physician. Whether lack of payment is a permissible reason to give this notice has not yet clearly been decided.

See also section B.2 for consideration of whether physicians practicing under managed care constraints should be held to a lower standard of care than under fee-for-service insurance.

8. *Few Cases but Big Verdicts.* One reason for the lack of clarity about the respective responsibilities of physicians and insurers is that there have been surprisingly few cases like *Wickline* and *Wilson* with decisions on the merits. This suggests that perhaps in practice insurers rarely deny coverage for care that is required by the minimal standard of medical practice. The paucity of suits may also be due to the preemption of state law by the federal ERISA statute, discussed in the next case. Others attribute the favorable malpractice record of staff model HMOs like Kaiser to their detailed programs of malpractice prevention and physician monitoring and to the availability of a grievance process for dissatisfied patients. These characteristics typically do not exist, however, in the broad network model HMOs that currently prevail in the market. Further explanation for the small number of suits comes from the fact that plaintiffs' lawyers are reluctant to name health insurers in medical malpractice suits since this greatly complicates the litigation and is usually unnecessary given the fact that the treating physician is "on the hook" in any event (for reasons explained in *Wickline*). Also, plaintiffs' lawyers report seeing few or no cases where harm results from health insurers' refusing to pay for treatment that physicians request. Agrawal & Hall, infra.

Although there have been few successful cases against health insurers, when plaintiffs have succeeded, they sometimes win very large punitive damages awards, in the range of $50 million to $100 million or more. For instance, in Fox v. Health Net (1993), a California jury awarded $77 million in punitive damages (plus $12 million compensatory) against an HMO that had refused to pay for an innovative cancer treatment, which the surviving family claimed resulted in the patient's death. This was eclipsed by the $120 million verdict in Goodrich v. Aetna U.S. Healthcare (1999), $116 million of which were punitive damages. Like *Fox*, the *Goodrich* verdict was based on an HMO's reluctance to authorize expensive, state-of-the-art treatment for terminal cancer that it considered to be experimental. Then, in 2013, a Nevada jury returned a whopping $524 million verdict against an HMO for contracting with a physician whose sloppy procedures resulted in infecting the patient with Hepatitis C, Meyer v. Health Plan of Nevada.

Does this track record of very few successful verdicts, but some that are extremely large, create appropriate incentives for plaintiffs to sue? Is it likely to send appropriate deterrence signals to health insurers? Does the small number of suits suggest a need to remove barriers to suing health plans? Would a "floodgate" of litigation threaten the viability of the managed care industry or of its core cost-containment practices? For discussion from various perspectives, see the literature cited in note 14.

9. *Financial Incentives.* Another potential basis for direct liability against HMOs and managed care arrangements is the use of financial incentives to encourage physicians to economize. An insurer might avoid the entire issue of liability for second-guessing medical judgment by paying doctors in a way that encourages them to economize in their own clinical decisionmaking. Using *Wickline*'s notion of "defects in the design or implementation of cost containment mechanisms," is it possible nevertheless to argue that some financial incentives are too strong per se, or that in practice they caused a physician to err? Answering "yes," see Pagarigan v. Aetna, 2005 WL 2742807 (Cal. Ct. App. 2005). Consider by analogy the suits in the 1990s against Domino's Pizza for pressuring its deliverers to drive too fast. As discussed in section B.1, financial incentives might also lead to claims for punitive damages in medical malpractice cases against physicians. Section B.2 discusses whether incentives give rise to a claim for breach of fiduciary duty.

10. *Breach of Contract.* The *Boyd* concurrence suggests that HMO liability might also be based on a contractual or quasi-promissory theory, such as warranty or fraud. This possibility is explored in the notes following Sullivan v. O'Connor, at page 406. Is there a difference between the nature of the promises an HMO makes and those made by typical hospitals or doctors? Professor Brewbaker argues that, because HMOs, unlike hospitals, sell medical services, they undertake an implied warranty of quality which, as with doctors, promises nonnegligent care. Therefore, he argues that HMOs should be automatically liable for any negligent care delivered under their auspices, regardless of whether they fall under the theories of liability devised for hospitals. William Brewbaker, Medical Malpractice and Managed Care Organizations: The Implied Warranty of Quality, 60 Contemp. Probs. 117 (Spring 1997).

11. *Employer Liability.* If insurers can be held liable for lack of care in selecting physicians and supervising treatment decisions, how about employers who construct their own managed care plans? Many large employers eliminate the "middle man" by contracting directly with hospitals and physicians on a self-insured basis. In doing so, an employer may either "rent a network," that is, contract with an existing network of providers, or it might form its own network. In either event, is it plausible to impose the same type of managed care liability on employers as on the insurers they have ousted? If such liability existed under state law, it would likely be preempted for reasons addressed in the following case. For discussion, see Dana M. Muir, Fiduciary Status as an Employer's Shield: The Perversity of ERISA Fiduciary Law, 2 U. Pa. J. Lab. & Emp. L. 391 (2000).

12. *Exclusive Enterprise Liability.* The furthest extension of the concepts of enterprise liability developed for hospitals, HMOs, and other forms of managed care would be to hold a network of hospitals, doctors, and insurers exclusively liable at the highest institutional level for any medical mistake that occurs within any component part. If the health care delivery system were to move toward an "integrated delivery system" structure, commentators have speculated whether these networks should or will be the final point of liability focus. So far, most networks are only loosely formed contractual affiliations in which the parties (hospitals, doctors, and insurers) agree on a nonexclusive basis to market their services collectively to employers or other insurers. Does this entail sufficient integration, coordination, selection, and supervision to justify imposition of enterprise liability? Consider whether it is feasible for integrated delivery systems to influence the quality of care if these affiliations are nonexclusive, that is, if doctors and hospitals belong to several such networks. As Mello & Kachalia, infra page 531, explain:

> [T]he plan's liability could be limited to injuries caused by physicians who receive the greatest share of their reimbursement from that payer, or could extend to any injury incurred by the plan's insured patients. The former would better peg liability to the plan's ability to influence the physician's practice, since the plan's threat not to contract with physicians in the future if they did not improve would have greater financial consequence for the physician. However, it could allow plans that did not have a large market share to evade liability altogether.

13. *Consumer-Driven Health Care.* As insurers recede from aggressive managed care, will these liability threats likewise recede, or will they be replaced with new theories of liability? According to one professor, consumer-driven health care opens up an entirely new arena of potential health plan liability in the form of failure to provide full or accurate information about health care options. Kristin Madison, ERISA and Liability for Provision of Medical Information, 84 N.C. L. Rev. 471-546 (2006). See also E. Haavi Morreim, High-Deductible Health Plans: Litigation Hazards for Health Insurers, 18 Health Matrix 1 (2008).

14. *Further Reading.* For commentary and analysis on **managed care liability** generally, see Haavi Morreim, Holding Health Care Accountable (2001); Jennifer Arlen & William MacLeod, Malpractice Liability for Physicians and Managed Care Organizations, 78 N.Y.U. L. Rev. 1929 (2003); Gail Agrawal & Mark Hall, What If You *Could* Sue Your HMO? Managed Care Liability Beyond the ERISA Shield, 47 St. Louis U. L.J. 235 (2003); Clark Havighurst, Vicarious Liability: Relocating Responsibility for the Quality of Medical Care, 26 Am. J.L. Med. 7 (2000); Peter Jacobson & Neena Patil, Managed Care Litigation: Legal Doctrine at the Boundary of Tort and Contract, 57 Med. Care Res. & Rev. 440 (2000); David Studdert et al., Expanded Managed Care Liability: What Impact on Employer Coverage?, 18(6) Health Aff. 7 (Dec. 1999); Richard A. Epstein & Alan O. Sykes, The Assault on Managed Care: Vicarious Liability, Class Actions, and the Patient's Bill of Rights, 30 J. Leg. Stud. 625 (2002).

On **enterprise liability** (note 12), see K. Abraham & P. Weiler, Enterprise Medical Liability and the Choice of the Responsible Enterprise, 20 Am. J.L. & Med. 29 (1994); Clark C. Havighurst, Making Health Plans Accountable for the Quality of Care, 31 Ga. L. Rev. 587 (1997); William Sage, Enterprise Liability and the Emerging

Managed Care Health Care System, 60 Law & Contemp. Probs. 159 (Spring 1997); Randall R. Bovbjerg & Robert Berenson, Enterprise Liability in the Twenty-First Century, *in* Medical Malpractice and the U.S. Health Care System (W. Sage & R. Kersh eds., 2006); Note, 121 Harv. L. Rev. 1192 (2008).

Problem: Enterprise Liability

Mike Mulligan is administrator of Florence Nightingale Hospital, a large facility in a metropolitan area. Mary Anne is the local lawyer. Mike has a plan to protect the hospital from the erosion of business that has resulted from managed care contracts taking more and more patients into the larger facilities nearby. Mulligan's plan is for the hospital to form its own managed care network. Mulligan would like to include as many of the local physicians as possible in the network. (Assume this is legal under antitrust law.) The network will then sell HMO-type insurance to local residents. The premium revenues will be split 50/50 between the hospital and the doctors, with the physician half going mostly to the primary care physicians. These primary care physicians will act as gatekeepers for hospitalization decisions, referrals to specialists in town, and referrals to larger hospitals for more complex care.

Mulligan consults Mary Anne about advice on the liability implications of this plan. The hospital has been named in a number of suits recently, and he is concerned at the formation stage about what new liability exposure the network will create and what steps are possible to manage or reduce that exposure. Taking the position of Mike Mulligan, how desirable would each of the following alternative ideas be from a business or practical perspective? Taking the position of Mary Anne, how desirable would each be from a legal perspective?

1. Automatically accept into the network any doctor with medical staff privileges at the hospital.
2. In contracting with doctors, insist on an indemnification clause that requires them to compensate the hospital system for any paid claims that arise from the doctor's own fault.
3. Agree to purchase malpractice insurance for network physicians, defend any claims brought by patients, and pay for any resulting liability. Consider this option both for hospital-based care only and for all medical care.
4. Increase the size and authority of the risk management department, school them in the techniques of quality assurance and "total quality management," and impose a passel of practice guidelines that cover liability-sensitive areas of medicine.
5. Write insurance contracts so as to notify subscribers that network physicians are independent contractors. Post similar statements in doctors' waiting rooms, at hospital entrances, on hospital admission forms, and on informed consent forms. Review stationery, billing forms, and uniform dress to avoid creating the unintended impression of an agency relationship between the hospital system and network physicians.
6. Have the risk management department and Mary Anne review all advertising and marketing materials to eliminate any statements that might create an expectation or image of receiving quality care.

7. Write insurance contracts so as to specifically promise an "adequate level
   of care, consistent with the coverage provided by this insurance and within
   the standards of care that prevail in other, similar locations in this state."

■AETNA HEALTH INC. v. DAVILA
542 U.S. 200 (2004)

Justice THOMAS delivered the opinion of the Court.

In these consolidated cases, two individuals sued their respective HMOs for
alleged failures to exercise ordinary care in the handling of coverage decisions,
in violation of a duty imposed by the Texas Health Care Liability Act (Texas Act).
We granted certiorari to decide whether the individuals' causes of action are completely preempted by the . . . Employee Retirement Income Security Act of 1974
(ERISA) . . .

[Davila was covered by Aetna through his employer, and Calad was covered
by CIGNA through her husband's employer.] Respondents both suffered injuries
allegedly arising from Aetna's and CIGNA's decisions not to provide coverage for
certain treatment and services recommended by respondents' treating physicians.
Davila's treating physician prescribed Vioxx to remedy Davila's arthritis pain, but
Aetna refused to pay for it. Davila did not appeal or contest this decision, nor did
he purchase Vioxx with his own resources and seek reimbursement. Instead, Davila
began taking Naprosyn, from which he allegedly suffered a severe reaction that
required extensive treatment and hospitalization. [Editors' note: The Court fails to
mention that Davila nearly died from bleeding ulcers and that, although Vioxx is
much more expensive than Naprosyn, it has fewer side effects relating to bleeding
ulcers.]

Calad underwent surgery, and although her treating physician recommended
an extended hospital stay, a CIGNA discharge nurse determined that Calad did not
meet the plan's criteria for a continued hospital stay. CIGNA consequently denied
coverage for the extended hospital stay. Calad experienced postsurgery complications forcing her to return to the hospital. She alleges that these complications
would not have occurred had CIGNA approved coverage for a longer hospital
stay.

[In separate state-court suits,] respondents . . . argued that petitioners' refusal
to cover the requested services violated their "duty to exercise ordinary care when
making health care treatment decisions," and that these refusals "proximately
caused" their injuries. Petitioners removed the cases to Federal District Courts,
arguing that respondents' causes of action fit within the scope of, and were therefore completely preempted by, ERISA . . . The United States Court of Appeals for
the Fifth Circuit consolidated their cases with several others raising similar issues . . .
After examining the causes of action available under [ERISA], the Court of Appeals
determined that respondents' claims could possibly fall under . . . §502(a)(1)
(B), which provides a cause of action for the recovery of wrongfully denied benefits. . . . [However, the court ruled that this case does not fall under ERISA because]
respondents "are not seeking reimbursement for benefits denied them," but rather
request "tort damages" arising from "an external, statutorily imposed duty of 'ordinary care.' " . . .

II

Congress enacted ERISA to "protect . . . the interests of participants in employee benefit plans and their beneficiaries" by setting out substantive regulatory requirements for employee benefit plans and to "provid[e] for appropriate remedies, sanctions, and ready access to the Federal courts." 29 U.S.C. §1001(b). The purpose of ERISA is to provide a uniform regulatory regime over employee benefit plans. To this end, ERISA includes expansive preemption provisions, see ERISA §514, which are intended to ensure that employee benefit plan regulation would be "exclusively a federal concern." ERISA's "comprehensive legislative scheme" includes "an integrated system of procedures for enforcement." . . . As the Court said in *Pilot Life Ins. Co. v. Dedeaux*, 481 U.S. 41 (1987):

> [T]he detailed provisions of §502(a) set forth a comprehensive civil enforcement scheme that represents a careful balancing of the need for prompt and fair claims settlement procedures against the public interest in encouraging the formation of employee benefit plans. The policy choices reflected in the inclusion of certain remedies and the exclusion of others under the federal scheme would be completely undermined if ERISA-plan participants and beneficiaries were free to obtain remedies under state law that Congress rejected in ERISA. The six carefully integrated civil enforcement provisions found in §502(a) of the statute as finally enacted . . . provide strong evidence that Congress did *not* intend to authorize other remedies that it simply forgot to incorporate expressly.

Therefore, any state-law cause of action that duplicates, supplements, or supplants the ERISA civil enforcement remedy conflicts with the clear congressional intent to make the ERISA remedy exclusive and is therefore pre-empted. . . . It follows that if an individual brings suit complaining of a denial of coverage for medical care, where the individual is entitled to such coverage only because of the terms of an ERISA-regulated employee benefit plan, and . . . if an individual, at some point in time, could have brought his claim under ERISA §502(a) . . . then the individual's cause of action is completely preempted by ERISA. . . .

III

The only action [Davila] complained of was Aetna's refusal to approve payment for Davila's Vioxx prescription. Further, the only relationship Aetna had with Davila was its partial administration of Davila's employer's benefit plan. Similarly . . . Calad contests only CIGNA's decision to refuse coverage for her hospital stay . . . It is clear, then, that respondents complain only about denials of coverage promised under the terms of ERISA-regulated employee benefit plans. Upon the denial of benefits, respondents could have paid for the treatment themselves and then sought reimbursement through a §502(a)(1)(B) action, or sought a preliminary injunction. . . .[1]

---

1. Respondents also argue that the benefit due under their ERISA-regulated employee benefit plans is simply the membership in the respective HMOs, not coverage for the particular medical treatments that are delineated in the plan documents. Respondents did not identify this possible argument in their brief in opposition to the petitions for certiorari, and we deem it waived.

Respondents contend, however, that the complained-of actions violate legal duties that arise independently of ERISA or the terms of the employee benefit plans at issue in these cases. Both respondents brought suit specifically under the Texas Act, alleging that petitioners "controlled, influenced, participated in and made decisions which affected the quality of the diagnosis, care, and treatment provided" in a manner that violated "the duty of ordinary care." . . . The Texas Act does impose a duty on managed care entities to "exercise ordinary care when making health care treatment decisions," and makes them liable for damages proximately caused by failures to abide by that duty. However, if a managed care entity correctly concluded that, under the terms of the relevant plan, a particular treatment was not covered, the managed care entity's denial of coverage would not be a proximate cause of any injuries arising from the denial. Rather, the failure of the plan itself to cover the requested treatment would be the proximate cause.[2] More significantly, the Texas Act clearly states that "[it] . . . create[s] no obligation on the part of the health insurance . . . entity to provide to an insured or enrollee treatment which is not covered by the health care plan of the entity." Hence, . . . interpretation of the terms of respondents' benefit plans forms an essential part of their [state law] claim, and [state law] liability would exist here only because of petitioners' administration of ERISA-regulated benefit plans. Petitioners' potential liability under the Texas Act in these cases, then, derives entirely from the particular rights and obligations established by the benefit plans. . . . [R]espondents bring suit only to rectify a wrongful denial of benefits promised under ERISA-regulated plans, and do not attempt to remedy any violation of a legal duty independent of ERISA. . . .

[T]he Court of Appeals found significant that respondents "assert a tort claim for tort damages" rather than "a contract claim for contract damages," and that respondents "are not seeking reimbursement for benefits denied them." But, distinguishing between preempted and non-preempted claims based on the particular label affixed to them would "elevate form over substance and allow parties to evade" the preemptive scope of ERISA simply "by relabeling their contract claims as claims for tortious breach of contract." . . . In [previous Supreme Court cases finding preemption], the plaintiffs all brought state claims that were labeled either tort or tort-like. . . .

Respondents also argue—for the first time in their brief to this Court—that the Texas Act is a law that regulates insurance, and hence that ERISA §514(b) (2)(A) saves their causes of action from preemption.[3] This argument is unavailing. . . . ERISA §514(b)(2)(A) must be interpreted in light of the congressional intent to create an exclusive federal remedy in ERISA §502(a). Under ordinary principles of conflict preemption, then, even a state law that can arguably be characterized as "regulating insurance" will be preempted if it provides a separate vehicle to assert a claim for benefits outside of, or in addition to, ERISA's remedial scheme.

---

2. To take a clear example, if the terms of the health care plan specifically exclude from coverage the cost of an appendectomy, then any injuries caused by the refusal to cover the appendectomy are properly attributed to the terms of the plan itself, not the managed care entity that applied those terms.

IV

Respondents, their *amici*, and some Courts of Appeals have relied heavily upon Pegram v. Herdrich, 530 U.S. 211 (2000), in arguing that ERISA does not preempt or completely preempt state suits such as respondents'. . . . *Pegram* cannot be read so broadly. In *Pegram*, the plaintiff sued her physician-owned-and-operated HMO (which provided medical coverage through plaintiff's employer pursuant to an ERISA-regulated benefit plan) and her treating physician, both for medical malpractice and for a breach of an ERISA fiduciary duty. The plaintiff's treating physician was also the person charged with administering plaintiff's benefits; it was she who decided whether certain treatments were covered. We reasoned that the physician's "eligibility decision and the treatment decision were inextricably mixed." We concluded that "Congress did not intend [the defendant HMO] or any other HMO to be treated as a fiduciary to the extent that it makes mixed eligibility decisions acting through its physicians." . . .

[I]it was essential to *Pegram*'s conclusion that the decisions challenged there were truly "mixed eligibility and treatment decisions," *i.e.*, medical necessity decisions made by the plaintiff's treating physician *qua* treating physician and *qua* benefits administrator. Put another way, the reasoning of *Pegram* "only make[s] sense where the underlying negligence also plausibly constitutes medical maltreatment by a party who can be deemed to be a treating physician or such a physician's employer." Cicio v. Does, 321 F.3d 83, 109 (C.A.2 2003) (Calabresi, J., dissenting in part). Here, however, petitioners are neither respondents' treating physicians nor the employers of respondents' treating physicians. Petitioners' coverage decisions, then, are pure eligibility decisions, and *Pegram* is not implicated. . . .

Justice GINSBURG, with whom Justice BREYER joins, concurring.

. . . [This] decision is consistent with our governing case law on ERISA's preemptive scope. I therefore join the Court's opinion. But, with greater enthusiasm . . . I also join "the rising judicial chorus urging that Congress and [this] Court revisit what is an unjust and increasingly tangled ERISA regime." DiFelice v. AETNA U.S. Healthcare, 346 F.3d 442, 453 (C.A.3 2003) (Becker, J., concurring). Because the Court has coupled an encompassing interpretation of ERISA's preemptive force with a cramped construction of the "equitable relief" allowable under §502(a)(3), a "regulatory vacuum" exists: "[V]irtually all state law remedies are preempted but very few federal substitutes are provided."

A series of the Court's decisions has yielded a host of situations in which persons adversely affected by ERISA-proscribed wrongdoing cannot gain make-whole relief [because] "there is a stark absence in [ERISA] itself and in its legislative history of any reference to an intention to authorize the recovery of extracontractual damages" for consequential injuries. . . . [F]resh consideration of the availability of consequential damages under §502(a)(3) is plainly in order. See 321 F.3d, at 106, 107 (Calabresi, J., dissenting in part) ("gaping wound" caused by the breadth of preemption and limited remedies under ERISA, as interpreted by this Court, will not be healed until the Court "start[s] over" or Congress "wipe[s] the slate clean"); DiFelice, 346 F.3d, at 467 ("The vital thing . . . is that either Congress or the Court act quickly, because the current situation is plainly untenable."); Langbein, What ERISA Means by "Equitable": The Supreme Court's Trail of Error in *Russell, Mertens,* and *Great-West*, 103 Colum. L. Rev. 1317, 1365 (2003). . . . The Government notes a potential amelioration. . . . [It] suggests that the Act, as currently written and interpreted, may "allo[w] at least some forms of 'make-whole' relief." . . . As the Court points out, respondents here declined the opportunity to amend their complaints to state claims for relief under §502(a). . . . But the Government's suggestion may indicate an effective remedy others similarly circumstanced might fruitfully pursue.

"Congress . . . intended ERISA to replicate the core principles of trust remedy law, including the make-whole standard of relief." *Langbein* 1319. I anticipate that Congress, or this Court, will one day so confirm.

Notes: ERISA Preemption

1. *Damages Under ERISA.* Under ERISA, patients who are wrongly denied health insurance benefits can recover compensation only for the costs of treatment, but not for consequential damages, pain and suffering, wrongful death, or punitive damages. Corcoran v. United Healthcare, Inc., 965 F.2d 1321 (5th Cir. 1992), dramatically illustrates the hardship caused by this restriction in available remedies. There, a woman miscarried late in her pregnancy due, she alleged, to the HMO's refusal to authorize hospitalization for pregnancy complications. The court limited her potential remedies under ERISA to an order for treatment or compensation for treatment costs. But, because the fetus had died, these remedies were meaningless. This restriction of damages is much more severe even than that imposed by ordinary contract law. See Sullivan v. O'Connor, page 401. Therefore, it is important to note the concurring Justices' argument in *Davila* that this limitation can and should be revisited. See Sarah Spisich, The Aftermath of *Davila*: Are Healthcare Enrollees Now in a Sinking Ship Without a Paddle?, 17(4) The Health Lawyer 22 (Aug. 2005); Comment, 2006 B.Y.U. L. Rev. 1589 (2007).

The majority in *Davila* appears to think the outcome makes perfect sense according to congressional intent. Legislative history, however, reveals that Congress wrote ERISA primarily with pension benefits in mind, and long before managed care health insurance existed. Do you see why limiting damages to the costs of treatment might have made a lot more sense under traditional insurance? Assuming, as the concurrence argues, that ERISA's remedies no longer make sense for managed care insurance, whose responsibility is it to fix the problem: Congress's or the courts'? See Andrews-Clarke v. Travelers Insurance Co., 948 F. Supp. 49 (D. Mass. 1997) ("Although the [failure of the utilization reviewer to approve hospitalization for a deeply troubled alcoholic who later committed suicide] is extraordinarily troubling, even more disturbing to this Court is the failure of Congress to amend a statute that, due to the changing realities of the modern health care system, has gone conspicuously awry from its original intent. Does anyone care? Do you?").

2. *ERISA Terminology Is Obscure and Confusing.* Essentially, an ERISA "plan" exists any time an employer pays for health insurance. If the employer simply purchases health insurance, then technically there may be a distinction between the "plan," which is the decision to purchase, and the insurance, which is the contracted-for benefit. Would it be possible, using this distinction, to argue that ERISA preempts only suits against employers for failing to provide insurance, but not suits against insurers for failing to provide the benefits covered by the insurance? Observe how *Davila* avoids this issue in footnote 2 of the opinion, but a few lower courts have adopted this

position. See, e.g., Washington Physicians Service Ass'n v. Gregoire, 147 F.3d 1039 (9th Cir. 1998) ("The mere fact that many [employers] choose to buy health insurance for their [employees] does not cause a regulation of health insurance automatically to 'relate to' any employee benefit plan—just as a decision to buy an apple a day for every employee, or to offer employees a gym membership, does not cause all state regulation of apples and gyms to 'relate to' employee benefit plans."). But see Hotz v. Blue Cross & Blue Shield of Massachusetts, 292 F.3d 57, 59-60 (1st Cir. 2002) ("Although the [employer plan/insurance plan] distinction is linguistically possible, it would mean that numerous past ERISA suits brought to secure payment for medical services from third-party providers under ERISA plans lacked a legal basis."). See generally Russell Korobkin, The Failed Jurisprudence of Managed Care, and How to Fix It: Reinterpreting ERISA Preemption, 51 UCLA L. Rev. 457 (2003).

Regardless, ERISA preemption would still apply to situations where the employer self-insures, that is, pays for health care directly out of its own funds. In that case, ERISA clearly preempts state law liability against the employer. So far, courts have applied ERISA preemption equally to both purchased and self-funded health insurance, where tort and contract claims are concerned. This distinction is relevant, however, for purposes of preemption of state insurance regulation.

3. *Which Claims Are Preempted?* The end of the *Davila* opinion briefly alludes to ERISA's effect on more conventional medical malpractice claims that arise under managed care insurance. Lower court decisions clarify the following: ERISA clearly does not apply to a malpractice claim against only the treating physician for a medical mistake that is unaffected by health insurance. . . . Likewise, courts usually find no preemption if a plaintiff attempts to hold a health insurer vicariously liable for a treating physician's mistake. Pacificare of Oklahoma v. Burrage, 59 F.3d 151 (10th Cir. 1995); Rice v. Panchal, 65 F.3d 637 (7th Cir. 1995). This helps to explain *Davila*'s reference to the fact that the plaintiffs' physicians in that case were not employees of the health plans.

The law is unsettled, however, when there is a medical treatment mistake and the plaintiff attempts to hold the insurer *directly* responsible because it selected bad physicians or influenced their treatment decisions. This is similar to the situation in Pegram v. Herdrich, 530 U.S. 211 (2000), which is discussed in *Davila*. There, the patient claimed that her doctor was influenced by profit distributions from the HMO and that this financial tie violates ERISA fiduciary standards. In the course of rejecting that claim under ERISA, the Court noted that the patient was free to pursue her claim in state court in the form of a medical malpractice suit. This strongly suggests that direct liability actions against HMOs for care provided by treating physicians are not preempted by ERISA, even after *Davila*.

In short, courts must distinguish between tort claims based on insurance coverage decisions, which are preempted, and medical malpractice liability, which is not preempted. In drawing this line, many lower courts have followed a rule of thumb that distinguishes between claims based on the *quantity* of care and those based on its *quality*. See, e.g., Dukes v. U.S. Healthcare, 57 F.3d 350 (3d Cir. 1995); Bauman v. U.S. Healthcare, Inc., 193 F.3d 151 (3d Cir. 1999). The *Davila* case makes no reference to this concept, however. Instead, it focuses on whether the insurer or the treating physician made the critical decision. Is that distinction likely to be sufficiently clear in most cases? What about situations where the treating physician is employed full time by an HMO, and the HMO instructs the physician that a particular treatment option is not approved, for instance, that women should not remain in the hospital longer than 48 hours following normal childbirth? That might be regarded as a quantity decision based on the insurance policy's medical appropriateness criteria, or it might be regarded as a form of direct HMO liability for interfering with physicians' ability to make good treatment decisions. Does *Davila* resolve which is the correct characterization?

One further complication: If it is possible to find an agency relationship between the HMO and the treating physician, should it matter that the HMO is not the physician's employer? Isn't the critical factor whether or not the physician agreed with, or acquiesced in, the HMO's decision? In *Davila*, the HMO refused to pay for treatments the physicians ordered, but, in many other cases, physicians may not order treatment they know the HMO won't pay for or that will cost the physician money under the HMO's payment incentives. Shouldn't patients be able to blame the HMO, at least in part, when this happens? In such cases, should *Davila* apply?

There is a large amount of academic literature discussing these issues, but most of it predates *Davila*. For subsequent analysis, see Aaron S. Kesselheim & Troyen A. Brennan, The Swinging Pendulum: The Supreme Court Reverses Course on ERISA and Managed Care, 5 Yale J. Health Pol'y L. & Ethics 451 (2005); Leonard A. Nelson, Aetna v. Davila: A Missed Opportunity, 31 Wm. Mitchell L. Rev. 843-896 (2005); Comment, 88 U. Colo. L. Rev. 1169 (2017); Note, 84 Tex. L. Rev. 1347-1383 (2006).

4. *Medicare Preemption.* Preemption issues might also arise under Medicare, which has a restrictive set of remedies for beneficiaries. One court has held that Medicare's administrative review process does not preempt a state tort action against a private HMO that contracted to deliver Medicare services. McCall v. Pacificare of California, Inc., 21 P.3d 1189 (Cal. 2001). But, a later court has disagreed, finding that Medicare's 2006 amendments preempt liability suits against private Medicare insurers. Morrison v. Health Plan of Nevada, 328 P.3d 1165 (Nev. 2014).

H. MEDICAL MALPRACTICE REFORM

■ McCALL v. UNITED STATES
134 So.3d 894 (Fla. 2014)

Lewis, J.

This case is before the Court to answer four questions of Florida law certified by the United States Court of Appeals for the Eleventh Circuit: [does the state's $1,000,000 cap on noneconomic damages in medical malpractice wrongful death cases violate any of four provisions of Florida's constitution: (1) the right to equal protection; (2) the right of access to the courts; (3) the right to trial by jury; and (4) the separation of powers? The court answered the first question in the affirmative, finding an equal protection violation, and so the court decided that it is unnecessary to answer the remaining constitutional questions.] . . .

FACTS AND PROCEDURAL HISTORY

[As described by the trial court, Michelle McCall was a "bright, beautiful, and healthy, 20-year-old woman" who, while living at home, became pregnant with her high school sweetheart. Because one or both parents were in the Air Force, she received care from military medical personnel. Tragically, during delivery, she bled to death because, as the trial court found, her nurses failed to recognize, or convey to the physicians in time, the seriousness of her blood loss over the span of two hours. Under Florida's wrongful death statute, the trial court awarded damages for economic loss of almost $1 million, plus noneconomic damages totaling $2 million — with $750,000 of the latter going to each of her parents and $500,000 going to her newborn son. Florida's malpractice reform statute, however, limits noneconomic damages to $1 million in wrongful death cases, regardless of the number of recovering family members. The federal court of appeals (11th Cir.) ruled that this limit does not violate the U.S. Constitution, but it certified to the Florida Supreme Court whether a different result obtains under the state's constitution.]

EQUAL PROTECTION

. . . The Florida Constitution provides, in pertinent part: "All natural persons, female and male alike, are equal before the law." . . . Unless a suspect class or fundamental right protected by the Florida Constitution is implicated by the challenged provision, the rational basis test will apply to evaluate an equal protection challenge. To satisfy the rational basis test, a statute must bear a rational and reasonable relationship to a legitimate state objective, and it cannot be arbitrary or capriciously imposed. . . The statutory cap on wrongful death noneconomic damages fails because it imposes unfair and illogical burdens on injured parties when an act of medical negligence gives rise to multiple claimants. . . Further, the statutory cap on wrongful death noneconomic damages does not bear a rational relationship to the stated purpose that the cap is purported to address, the alleged medical malpractice insurance crisis in Florida.

ARBITRARY DISTINCTIONS

. . . The plain language of this statutory plan irrationally impacts circumstances which have multiple claimants/survivors differently and far less favorably than circumstances in which there is a single claimant/survivor. . . Applying the cap, the federal court then reduced the amounts of damages so each claimant would receive only half of his or her respective damages. . . [T]he greater the number of survivors and the more devastating their losses are, the less likely they are to be fully compensated for those losses.

Other state supreme courts have struck down caps on noneconomic damages based upon a similar rationale. . . The Supreme Court of New Hampshire condemned on equal protection grounds a $250,000 cap on noneconomic damages in medical malpractice cases, concluding that it is "simply unfair and unreasonable to impose the burden of supporting the medical care industry solely upon those persons who are most severely injured and therefore most in need of compensation." Carson v. Maurer, 120 N.H. 925, 424 A.2d 825, 837 (1980). [The Florida cap likewise] has the effect of saving a modest amount for many by imposing devastating costs on a few — those who are most grievously injured, those who sustain the greatest damage and loss, and multiple claimants for whom judicially determined noneconomic damages are subject to division and reduction simply based upon the existence of the cap. . .

Our holding today is not inconsistent with the decisions in . . . University of Miami v. Echarte, 618 So.2d 189 (Fla.1993) . . . . [I]n Echarte this Court considered whether a $250,000 cap on noneconomic damages for medical malpractice claims where a party requested arbitration violated the access to courts provision of the Florida Constitution. . . In upholding the constitutionality of the cap in medical malpractice arbitration proceedings, this Court in Echarte noted that arbitration provided commensurate benefits in exchange for the cap, such as saving the expense of attorney fees and expert witnesses. Conversely, under [the wrongful death cap], survivors receive absolutely no benefit whatsoever from the cap on noneconomic damages, but only arbitrary reductions based upon the number of survivors. . . .

THE ALLEGED MEDICAL MALPRACTICE CRISIS

In addition to arbitrary and invidious discrimination between medical malpractice claimants, the cap on noneconomic damages also violates the Equal Protection Clause of the Florida Constitution because it bears no rational relationship to a legitimate state objective. . . The Florida Legislature attempted to justify the cap on noneconomic damages by claiming that "Florida is in the midst of a medical malpractice insurance crisis of unprecedented magnitude." The Legislature asserted that the increase in medical malpractice liability insurance premiums has resulted in physicians leaving Florida, retiring early from the practice of medicine, or refusing to perform high-risk procedures, thereby limiting the availability of health care. . .

Although assertions of a malpractice insurance crisis are often accompanied by images of runaway juries entering verdicts in exorbitant amounts of noneconomic damages, one study revealed that in Florida cases which resulted in payments of $1 million or more over a fourteen-year period, only 7.5 percent involved a jury trial verdict [citing Vidmar et al., page 473 supra]. . . . Not only do jury trials constitute only a small portion of $1 million payments, [but] the settlements following verdicts tend to be substantially less than the jury awards." According to the authors, with one exception, cases with verdicts in excess of $4 million settled for, on average, 37 percent less than the verdict. Thus, available data indicates the Task Force's finding that noneconomic damage awards by juries are a primary cause of the purported medical malpractice crisis in Florida is most questionable.

Even the Task Force whose report was relied upon by the Florida Legislature . . . recognized that there are other explanations for the dramatic rise in medical malpractice insurance premiums. For example, the Task Force Report notes that, [according to one witness]:

[T]his so-called "crisis" is nothing more than the underwriting cycle of the insurance industry, and driven by the same factors that caused the "crises" in the 1970s and 1980s. According to . . . [this witness], with each crisis, there has been a severe drop in the investment income for insurers, which has been compounded by sever [sic] under-pricing of insurance premiums in the prior years. . . . [D]uring years of high interest rates or excellent insurer profits that are invested for maximum return, the insurance companies engage in fierce competition for premium dollars by selling under-priced premiums and insuring very poor risks. Then . . . when investment income drops, either due to increases in interest rates or the stock market, or due to low income resulting from unbearably low premiums, the insurance industry responds by sharply increasing premiums and reducing coverage. . . The tort reform changes in the 1980s had nothing to do with the flattening of rates. The flattening was caused instead by modulations in the insurance cycle throughout the country. . .

See also Tom Baker, THE MEDICAL MALPRACTICE MYTH 53-54 (2005) ("[T]he two most recent medical liability insurance crises did not result from sudden or dramatic increases in medical malpractice settlements or jury verdicts. . . . [T]he crises resulted from dramatic increases in the amount of money that the insurance industry put in reserve for claims. Those reserve increases were so big because the insurance industry systematically underreserved in the years leading up to the crisis."). . . Based upon these statements and reports, although medical malpractice premiums in Florida were undoubtedly high in 2003, we conclude the Legislature's determination that . . . Florida was in the midst of a bona fide medical malpractice crisis, threatening the access of Floridians to health care, is dubious and questionable at the very best.

THE IMPACT OF DAMAGE CAPS ON THE ALLEGED CRISIS

Even if these conclusions by the Legislature are assumed to be true, . . . [r]eports have failed to establish a direct correlation between damages caps and reduced malpractice premiums. [Various insurance officials testified during legislative deliberations that, if a cap were enacted, they would not necessarily reduce malpractice premiums immediately, or would do so only slightly, in part because they would need to see if the cap survives in court.] . . . While the cap on noneconomic damages limits the amount of money that insurance companies must pay injured victims of medical malpractice, [it] does not require insurance companies to use the acquired savings to lower malpractice insurance premiums for physicians. . . . [Although Florida's insurance regulator required insurers to take the cap into account in formulating their rates], [t]here was no mandated rate reduction [and Florida's malpractice premiums remain high compared to other states, with Florida insurers earning substantial profits.]. . . . With such impressive [profits], the insurance industry should pass savings onto Florida physicians in the form of reduced malpractice insurance premiums.[10] . . .

THE CURRENT STATUS OF MEDICAL MALPRACTICE IN FLORIDA

Lastly, even if a "crisis" existed when [the cap] was enacted, a crisis is not a permanent condition. Conditions can change, which remove or negate the justification for a law, transforming what may have once been reasonable into arbitrary and irrational legislation. . . Having evaluated current data, we conclude that no rational basis exists to justify continued application of the noneconomic damages cap . . . . [M]edical malpractice filings in Florida have decreased significantly, [more than

10. Despite such increases in net income, in 2012 one medical malpractice insurance company nonetheless charged obstetricians in Miami–Dade County more than $190,000 for $1 million of coverage. The company charged obstetricians in other Florida counties approximately $98,000 for the same coverage. During 2012, the same company charged orthopedists in Miami–Dade County more than $115,000 for $1 million of coverage, whereas orthopedists in other Florida counties were charged approximately $59,000.

60 percent since 2003-2004. Moreover, the number and amount of malpractice claims paid by insurers has dropped about 30 percent.] . . .

Based on the foregoing, we . . . hold that the cap on wrongful death noneconomic damages violates the Equal Protection Clause of the Florida Constitution. We defer answering the remaining certified questions.

[One other Justice joined this opinion. Three other justices concurred only in the result, making this merely a plurality opinion, because: "Although this Court is not bound to blindly defer to all legislative findings, I disagree with the plurality's independent evaluation and reweighing of reports and data . . . ."].

POLSTON, C.J., with CANADAY, J., dissenting.

. . . On appeal, the Eleventh Circuit . . . reasoned as follows [under the U.S. Constitution]:

> Plaintiffs ask us to second guess the legislature's judgment in enacting a "per incident" rather than "per claimant" statutory cap. However, equal protection is not a license for courts to judge the wisdom, fairness, or logic of legislative choices. The legislature identified a legitimate governmental purpose in passing the statutory cap, namely to reduce the cost of medical malpractice premiums and health care. The means that Florida chose, a per incident cap on noneconomic damages, bears a rational relationship to that end. The Florida legislature could reasonably have concluded that such a cap would reduce damage awards and in turn make medical malpractice insurance more affordable and healthcare more available. . .

[Similarly], multiple state courts have rejected equal protection challenges to statutory caps on noneconomic damages. . . In fact, it is hard to conceive a more rational means of assuaging the fear of huge damage awards and reining in insurance costs in the case of a victim's death than by limiting noneconomic wrongful death damages. More specifically, the Florida Legislature could have rationally believed that the cap on noneconomic damages would reduce malpractice damage awards, which would thereby increase predictability in the medical malpractice insurance market and lead to reduced insurance premiums. . . In fact, the Governor's Task Force, upon which the Legislature expressly relied, concluded as much:

> [I]mposing caps on non-economic damages in medical malpractice cases will significantly reduce the exposure of Florida healthcare providers to risk of loss from jury awards of inherently subjective damages. Such a reduction of risk will make malpractice losses much more predictable, and thereby lead to stability in malpractice insurance premium rates. A reduction in potential liability and resulting stability will encourage more malpractice insurers to participate in the Florida market. This, along with the reduced exposure to risk, will permit insurers to charge lower premiums, on a sound financial basis . . .

The Task Force received specific testimony indicating that "[i]n Georgia, physicians pay from $5,000 to $6,000 for $1,000,000 of coverage. Thirty miles south, in Jacksonville, that costs $27,000." And the Task Force . . . found that "[i]n Miami, evidence reflects that 80 percent of the OB/GYNs carry no insurance and those who do are paying over $207,000 per year for $1 million dollars worth of coverage." . . . The Task Force also described testimony indicating that, as a result of these issues, over half the doctors in Florida that carry insurance can only afford to carry a $250,000 policy . . . .

The Task Force also stated its belief that "caps on non-economic damages are particularly effective, because they limit the escalation of awards for pain and suffering, which fuels large increases for all awards and settlements." In fact, the Task Force thought that a cap on noneconomic damages was so important to alleviating the crisis and lowering premiums that it recommended a $250,000 per incident cap on noneconomic damages, rather than the $1 million per incident cap at issue in this case. . .

Justice Lewis notes that medical malpractice filings have decreased significantly since fiscal year 2003–04 and that Florida, according to a 2011 report, is now retaining a fairly high percentage of Florida-trained medical students. While he uses this information to support the plurality's argument that the statutory caps are no longer justified because a medical malpractice crisis does not currently exist, this information just as easily (and perhaps more likely) supports the argument that the cap has had its intended effect and that, if the cap is eliminated, the medical malpractice crisis would return in full force. . .

While the plurality clearly would have come to a different policy choice than the Legislature based upon the hardly unambiguous data that the plurality could cull from the record and the Internet, that is not the point. Instead, our precedent dictates that we employ the rational basis test, which is a relatively easy test for a statute to pass. . .

[For various reasons, the dissent also reasoned that the cap does not infringe the right of access to the courts; the right to trial by jury; or the separation of powers.]

■ EVALUATION OF OPTIONS FOR MEDICAL MALPRACTICE SYSTEM REFORM
Michelle M. Mello & Allen Kachalia*
Report to the Medicare Payment Advisory Commission, 2010

The objective of this report is to evaluate the prospects for several leading medical malpractice reform proposals to positively affect the performance of the medical liability system and the system's impact on health care. . . . This report describes the essential features of each proposed reform [in Table 1] and synthesizes the best available evidence about the likely effects of each of 6 outcome variables:

1. **Claims:** malpractice claim outcomes, including the number of claims filed, including the ease and equity with which patients receive compensation, and claims costs

2. **Overhead costs:** malpractice system administrative costs, including litigation costs and insurers' overhead expenses

*This excerpt contains a few passages from the authors' updated version of this report, Medical Malpractice: Evidence on Reform Alternatives and Claims Involving Elderly Patients (MedPac, 2016).

Table 1.
Reform Options Evaluated

Reform	Basic Description
Traditional State Reforms	*Reforms that have been widely implemented at the state level*
Caps on noneconomic damages	Limit the amount of money that a plaintiff can take as an award for noneconomic losses, or "pain and suffering," in a malpractice suit. The cap may apply to the plaintiff, limiting the amount she may receive, or to each defendant, limiting the total amount for which each may be liable.
Pretrial screening panels	Panel reviews a malpractice case at an early stage and provides an opinion about whether a claim has sufficient merit to proceed to trial. Typically, a negative opinion does not bar a case from going forward, but can be introduced by the defendant as evidence at the trial.
Certificate of merit	Requires a plaintiff to present, at the time of filing the claim or soon thereafter, an affidavit certifying that a qualified medical expert believes that there is a reasonable and meritorious cause for the suit.
Attorney fee limits	Limits the amount of a malpractice award that a plaintiff's attorney may take in a contingent-fee arrangement. The limitation is typically expressed as a percentage of the award; it may also incorporate a maximum dollar value.
Joint-and-several liability reform	In cases involving more than one defendant, such as a physician and a hospital, this reform limits the financial liability of each defendant to the percentage fault that the jury allocates to that defendant. Without this reform, the plaintiff may collect the entire amount of the judgment from one defendant if the other(s) default on their obligation to pay, even if the paying defendant bore only a small share of the responsibility for what happened to the plaintiff.
Collateral-source rule reform	Eliminates a traditional rule that if an injured plaintiff receives compensation for her injury from other sources, such as health insurance, that payment should not be deducted from the amount that a defendant who is found liable for that injury must pay.
Periodic payment	Allows or requires insurers to pay out malpractice awards over a long period of time, rather than in a lump sum. This enables insurers to purchase annuities (sometimes called "structured settlements") from other insurance companies which cost less than paying the whole award up front. Insurers are also able to retain any amounts that the plaintiff does not actually collect during her lifespan.
Statutes of limitations/repose	

Reform	Basic Description
Innovative Reforms	*Reforms that have had limited or no implementation in the U.S.*
Schedule of noneconomic damages	A hierarchy or tiering system is created for purposes of categorizing medical injuries and creating a relative ranking of severity. A dollar value range for noneconomic damages is then assigned to each severity tier. The schedule is used by juries and judges either as an advisory document or as a binding guideline.
Administrative compensation systems or "health courts"	Routes medical injury claims into an alternative adjudication process involving specialized judges, decision and damages guidelines, neutral experts, and (under most proposals) a compensation standard that is broader than the negligence standard.
Disclosure-and-offer programs	Institutional programs that support clinicians in disclosing unanticipated care outcomes to patients and that make rapid offers of modest compensation in appropriate cases.
Enterprise medical liability	Broadens the prospects for holding health care organizations, such as hospitals and managed care organizations, directly liable for medical injuries, in addition to or instead of holding individual clinicians liable.

3. **Liability costs:** malpractice liability costs for health care providers (i.e., malpractice insurance premiums)

4. **Defensive medicine:** defensive medical practices and overall health care spending and utilization

5. **Supply:** health care provider supply and patient access to care, including health insurance coverage and cost

6. **Quality of care:** potential to foster evidence-based care and improve patient safety

TRADITIONAL STATE REFORMS

CAPS ON NONECONOMIC DAMAGES

. . . The rationale for this reform is to reduce the number of multi-million dollar awards, which are difficult for liability insurers to plan for and pay and which may pose special difficulties for health care facilities that are self-insured. It is also motivated by a desire to reduce the high degree of variation and perceived arbitrariness in jury awards for "pain and suffering." Twenty-six states currently impose a cap on noneconomic damages and 6 cap total damages. Medical professional societies strongly desire to see noneconomic damages caps adopted in the remaining states, through state legislation or imposition of a federal cap. . . .

Although the oldest and most widely publicized example of a noneconomic damages cap, California's, is $250,000, most states have found it politically difficult to implement such a stringent cap in more recent rounds of reform. It is more common for states to set the cap at $500,000 or more, and to opt for a tiered cap in which different amounts apply to different kinds of injuries. The appeal of a flat cap is its simplicity and, when set at a low amount, greater potential for cost control. The appeal of a tiered cap is its greater vertical equity—that is, more severe injuries are eligible for a higher award. . . .

The evidence increasingly suggests that noneconomic damages caps are associated with a statistically significant decrease in the frequency of claims, whether the measure used is paid claims or all claim filings. Six studies have returned such findings, 22, 26-31, while two have found no association. Mechanistically, the . . . link is that caps discourage plaintiff's attorneys from filing claims by lowering the expected value of the case, which in a contingent-fee system affects the attorney's expected return on investment. Overall, the evidence is too equivocal at this time to support a conclusion about the effect of caps on claim frequency.

Most studies of the effects of caps on claims payouts have found a significant effect, typically on the order of a 20 to 30 percent reduction in average award size. . . . The effect of damages caps on malpractice insurance premiums has been the subject of intense controversy. The issue has been exhaustively studied, with mixed findings among well-designed studies. [Five] studies have identified significant effects of caps, while four older studies found no effect. A reasonable conclusion based on strong, recent studies is that caps moderately constrain the growth of premiums over time, with an effect on the order of 6 to 13 percent. . . .

[Regarding defensive medicine, there] is good, but not uniform, evidence that damages caps are associated with lower rates of utilization of services that are considered to be indicators of defensive medicine [such as cesarean sections and evaluation for heart problems]. . . . [A] fairly large evidence base suggests that non-economic damages caps effect statistically significant increases in the supply of physicians in a state—though some evidence suggests the effect may be concentrated among high-risk specialist physicians, rural areas, and/or caps at the most stringent level (around $250,000). . . Examining the studies with positive findings, the effect sizes have varied dramatically, but have clustered around 2-5%. . . .

Overall, the . . . weight of the evidence suggests that caps reduce claims frequency, achieve substantial savings in average claims payments, modestly constrain the growth of malpractice insurance premiums, moderately improve physician supply, and reduce at least some defensive medical practices. Evidence concerning their effects on health insurance and quality of care is too limited or equivocal to support firm conclusions. . . .

PRETRIAL SCREENING PANELS

The function of pretrial screening panels is to review a malpractice case at an early stage and provide an opinion about whether or not the claim has sufficient merit to proceed to trial. Typically, a negative opinion does not bar a case from going forward, but can be introduced by the defendant as evidence at the trial. The rationale for this reform is to reduce the number of nonmeritorious malpractice claims, and the litigation expenses incurred in defending them, by bringing expert judgment to bear before a large amount of legal expenses are incurred. Additionally, panel decisions can provide juries with a neutral source of expertise in cases that go to trial. About 20 states currently have pretrial screening panels of some kind. Screening panels have been repealed in at least 7 states and overturned by courts on constitutional grounds in at least another 5. . . .

A handful of well-designed studies have examined the effects of pretrial screening panels, and the weight of the evidence suggests that they are not effective in reducing claims costs, claim frequency, or malpractice insurance premiums. They may help reduce defensive medicine. The evidence concerning their effects on defense costs, physician supply, health insurance premiums, and quality of care is too limited or equivocal to support conclusions about those relationships. Panels involve their own administrative costs.

CERTIFICATE OF MERIT

Certificate of merit (COM) reforms require the plaintiff in a malpractice suit to present, at the time of filing the claim or soon thereafter, an affidavit certifying that a qualified medical expert believes that there is a reasonable and meritorious cause for the suit. Like pretrial screening panels, the rationale for COM requirements is to reduce the number of nonmeritorious malpractice claims and associated expenses by bringing expert judgment to bear early in the litigation. At least 11 states have adopted COM requirements, but Washington State's COM law was recently struck down on constitutional grounds. . . .

Only one methodologically-strong study has examined the effects of COM requirements and did not find an effect on the number of paid claims or payment amounts on large claims. On their face, COM requirements add a modest amount to the cost of litigation. Theoretically, the prospects for affecting the key outcome variables appear quite weak.

ATTORNEY FEE LIMITS

Attorney fee limits cap the amount of a malpractice award that a plaintiff's attorney may take as a contingency fee. Nearly all medical malpractice cases are handled by plaintiff's attorneys on a contingent-fee basis. . . . The rationale for attorney fee limits is to discourage plaintiff's attorneys from accepting cases of marginal or no merit by altering the attorney's expected return on investment in the case. Sixteen states currently have limits on attorney fees in medical malpractice cases. . . . [The evidence shows weak or no effects for this and the remainder of the "traditional" reforms. See Table 3 below.]

INNOVATIVE REFORMS . . .

ADMINISTRATIVE COMPENSATION SYSTEMS OR "HEALTH COURTS"

The use of administrative compensation systems or "health courts" for medical injury has frequently been proposed over the last 40 years. Proposals for administrative systems or health courts can contain several differing features, but most fit into one of two general models. In one model, often described as a *medical court*, a jury is replaced with a . . . medically trained judge to adjudicate the negligence determination. Most of the other features of the present tort process are kept without much change. In the second model, an administrative agency investigates and adjudicates claims for medical injury. . . . The medical court model is a smaller departure from the present tort system than an administrative model . . . [in that] most medical court proposals [change only the adjudicator but] keep the remainder of the tort process intact. This model is rooted in the notion that better equipped judges and fact-finders would make quicker and more accurate decisions. The objective is not necessarily to improve patient access to compensation, but rather to handle the claims filed more accurately and efficiently.

In the administrative model, . . . the agency would act as a neutral fact-finder and adjudicator so that the process would not be slowed down by an adversarial fact-finding process. Decisions could theoretically be rendered more cost-effectively because neither attorneys nor experts to represent each point of view would be required. Because filing a claim should be easier, administrative models can have the additional benefit of increasing the number of patients with access to the compensation system. To further boost access to compensation, most administrative models call for the use of a compensation standard broader than negligence, such as "avoidability." . . . A no-fault standard would not compensate all injuries caused by medical care, but just those that are not "necessary and ordinary to" medical care (e.g., the loss of hair due to chemotherapy would not be compensable but a post-surgical infection would be). A no-fault standard would, however, be more expensive because a greater proportion of claims would be paid. It also would not align as well with patient safety principles that focus on preventability of harm. . . .

The design of an administrative compensation system will need to include whether or not limits on damages (economic, noneconomic, or punitive) will be applied. One option is to . . . create a schedule of noneconomic damages and award full or close to full economic damages. . . .

[Another key design question is] whether the system will be patients' only legal remedy for malpractice, or whether claimants can opt to pursue their claims in the administrative system or in the courts. . . . A detailed constitutional analysis [of a mandatory design] is beyond the scope of this report, but . . . [o]ther exclusive administrative systems, such as workers' compensation systems, have been successfully designed and implemented while withstanding constitutional challenges. A voluntary design avoids these constitutional difficulties for the most part, but has other disadvantages. Due-process rights would still require that a mechanism for informing patients about their choice and eliciting informed consent to participation be developed. Laws in some states may prohibit such pre-injury agreements. . . . [Also, providing a choice] perpetuates the current inefficiencies of the tort system and essentially creates two tracks for compensation, leading to greater complexity. . . . Additionally, legal wrangling may arise over whether a particular claim meets the defined categories for jurisdiction. . . .

Very little actual experience on administrative systems for medical injury in the United States exists, but . . . modeling has predicted that total costs in an administrative compensation system may remain unchanged or slightly decline as compared to the negligence based tort system. Total costs, nevertheless, will vary based on the compensation standard and award limits (if any). Effects on defensive medicine and quality of care are likely to be positive, while effects on insurance premiums and physician supply are difficult to predict.

DISCLOSURE-AND-OFFER PROGRAMS

Disclosure and offer (D&O) [or apology] programs support clinicians in disclosing unanticipated care outcomes to patients and make rapid offers of compensation in appropriate cases. [These are also known as "communication and resolution" programs.] Presently, they are operated by a [limited number] of hospitals and liability insurers (predominantly self-insured hospital systems). . . . D&O programs vary in their structures and processes, but contain some common elements: When an unanticipated outcome occurs, clinicians are asked to promptly report it to . . . patients and/or their families. A disclosure occurs when a provider reveals and explains an adverse event and apologizes. . . . A rapid investigation into the cause of the error is conducted, and further disclosures are made regarding the findings of the investigation. . . . The institution makes an expedited decision about whether compensation in some form is appropriate, based on the compensation standard it has adopted. If the standard is met, an offer is made to the patient. Incidents not resolved through settlement after this process can go on to become malpractice claims in the tort system. . . .

D&O programs . . . appeal to many clinicians because they are consonant with principles of medical ethics (fiduciary duty, patient autonomy, and justice). . . . On the other hand, [l]iability risk is widely regarded to be among the chief barriers, and the number of institutions with formal D&O programs remains limited. Other barriers to disclosure include the emotional difficulty of the conversation, shame and guilt, the stress of a possible lawsuit, potential consequences in credentialing processes, and reputational harm. . . .

[T]he evidence base for evaluating the effects of such programs on the key outcome variables is [small]. However, . . . the available reports suggest that [these programs] are a highly promising approach, which can return substantial benefits in terms of reductions in claim frequency, payouts, and overhead costs and at the same time improve patient access to compensation and patient safety. . . , there is some risk associated with experimentation with this approach. . . . [P]oorly executed disclosures or inadequate offers of compensation may inflame patients and families, prompting additional claims. . . .

ENTERPRISE MEDICAL LIABILITY

Enterprise medical liability is a legal doctrine assigning liability to a health care organization for tortious injuries that occur within its facilities or are caused by its clinical staff affiliates, including but not limited to its employees. Under this system, the liability of individual physicians and other clinicians is reduced or eliminated. . . . Although some judicial loosening in this area has been visible over time, it remains difficult to hold health care facilities directly liable for medical malpractice outside of a few narrow circumstances. . . .

The two most important rationales for imposing enterprise medical liability are economic efficiency and fairness. In the malpractice context, enterprise medical liability addresses the perceived unfairness of holding individual health care providers liable for "systems failures" within an organization that lead to preventable injuries and that the individuals have little or no ability to control. The efficiency rationale is that placing liability on the organization provides economic incentives for the organization—which does have control over the "systems failures" and is in a position to prevent injuries at a lower cost than the clinician—to invest in cost-justified changes to improve patient safety. Future injuries will therefore be prevented at a socially efficient level. Without enterprise medical liability, the tort system sends an economic signal to actors who arguably are not in a good position to effect the kind of changes that are needed to prevent injuries. . . .

A fourth rationale is that enterprise medical liability permits more effective use of experience rating in insurance. Experience rating is the practice of pricing insurance premiums to reflect the insured's past claims experience. This is actuarially difficult to do for individual physicians because they are sued so infrequently, but it is considerably easier at the level of the health care organization. The advantages of experience rating are that it more fairly apportions insurance costs to those who create losses and that it more accurately targets the "deterrent signal" of the tort system to those who most need to modify their behavior in order to prevent injuries. . . .

A proposal for demonstration projects of health-plan-based enterprise medical liability was part of the Clinton health reform package. However, the proposal did not advance due to adverse reactions, ranging from disinterest to strong opposition, on the part of key stakeholder groups, including physician organizations, liability insurers, plaintiff's attorneys, and managed care organizations. . . .

Some proposals for enterprise medical liability have focused on health plans as the locus of liability, while others have suggested that hospitals and other health care provider organizations serve as the responsible enterprise. Today, the latter formulation receives more attention in policy debates, largely due to the ascendency of network-model managed care organizations in the market, which have less control over their affiliated physicians than closed-panel HMOs. The "accountable care organization" (ACO) is another, more modern concept with potential applicability for this reform. Economic theory suggests that liability should be placed on an organization that can realistically be expected to have the power to institute systemic patient safety improvements within health care systems and influence individual physician behavior. . . . Health insurers' leverage may vary considerably depending on their market share and the nature of their affiliation with physicians, and many community hospitals (as opposed to academic medical centers) may not have close relationships with the physicians they credential. On the other hand, placing liability on health plans is argued to serve as a counterweight to health plans' extant incentives to provide less care than might be medically optimal. . . .

Most proposals for enterprise medical liability specify that there would no longer be any liability for individual clinicians. An alternative would be to greatly expand the potential for holding health care organizations liable while retaining the possibility of holding individuals liable as well. Different rules could be imposed depending on whether the care was rendered within the walls of a hospital or other health facility as opposed to a non-hospital-affiliated physician office. . . . [An] argument against retaining individual liability is that pure enterprise medical liability [is] a simpler regime that avoids fights among defendants in a malpractice case about who was responsible for the injury. . . .

Enterprise medical liability is generally discussed in the literature as a mandatory scheme imposed by statute. An alternative is that health plans or health care facilities could voluntarily elect to assume liability for some or all of their affiliated physicians, with the physicians agreeing by contract to the necessary financial adjustments to finance the new arrangement. . . . One drawback would be . . . the fragmentation of incentives that would occur if not all physicians affiliated with the sponsoring hospital or health plan agreed to participate in the new arrangement. . . .

[In summary, enterprise medical liability] is promising on theoretical grounds, but existing examples of this arrangement in the U.S. are limited and have not been evaluated in a way that supports inferences about its effect on any of the key out-come variables.

CONCLUSIONS

The findings of this analysis concerning the effects of traditional and innova-tive tort reforms are summarized in Tables 3 and 4 [on the next two pages, which have been edited somewhat]. . . . [T]he evidence base for evaluating most *traditional* state tort reforms is large and mature. However, studies have generated limited or no evidence that most reforms have significant effects on the key outcome variables examined in this report. The exception is caps on noneconomic damages, which have well-documented effects on several of the outcomes. . . .

The Congressional Budget Office (CBO) recently estimated the cost of a package of 5 reforms implemented together in all states: a $250,000 noneconomic damages cap, a punitive damages cap of $500,000 or twice the economic damages award, collateral-source offsets, a 1-year statute of limitations for adults and 3-year limit for children, and joint-and-several liability reform. . . . Its current cost model estimates that nationwide implementation of [this package of 5 reforms] would result in a 0.5 percent decrease in total national health care expenditures. . . .

The evidence base for evaluating the *innovative* tort reforms is extremely small. . . . However, based on theoretical predictions and the limited evidence avail-able, most of these reforms show sufficient promise for impacting some of the key outcome variables to merit controlled experimentation, such as through demon-stration projects. . . .

In closing, tort reform in the states to date has been characterized by a pattern of imitation of reforms implemented in other jurisdictions—even in the absence of evidence that they are effective in achieving their goals. Reform initiatives have often been driven by health care providers' and insurers' urgent demands that pol-icy makers do something to ameliorate the effects of highly volatile liability environ-ments. Today, most states are experiencing at least a moderate easing of the "crisis" conditions of the last decade. This environment presents more favorable conditions for experimentation with more novel reforms.

Notes: Medical Malpractice Reform Statutes

1. *Deja Vu All Over Again.* With each previous edition of this casebook, it seems we were in the midst of, or just exiting from, yet another crisis in medical liability. But, for whatever reason, this issue has not flared up much over the past decade. Malpractice reform was not included as part of President Obama's Affordable Care Act. Prior to that, President George W. Bush proposed a national set of reforms sim-ilar to those in California, but Congress failed to act. In 2003, Prof. Bill Sage aptly commented that "it is striking . . . that Congress is actively debating whether to adopt [a package of reforms] enacted in California in 1975, . . . [yet] the health care system has undergone revolutionary change since [then]. It is as if Rip van Winkle awoke from his twenty-year nap and went about his business equipped with antique weap-ons and dressed in yesteryear's fashions without the current townspeople thinking anything was amiss." William M. Sage, Unfinished Business: How Litigation Relates to Health Care Regulation, 28 J. Health Pol. Pol'y & L. 387, 392 (2003).

Table 3.
Summary of Evidence Concerning the Effects of Traditional Tort Reforms

	Claims frequency and costs	Overhead costs	Liability costs	Defensive medicine	Supply	Quality of care
Caps on noneconomic damages	↓ for frequency ↓↓ for costs	↑	↓ for premiums	↓	↑ for physician supply 0 for health insurance premiums	0
Pretrial screening panels	0	↑	0	↓	0	0
Certificate of merit	0	↑	0	0	0	0
Attorney fee limits	0	↑	0	0	0	0
Joint-and-several liability reform	0	0	0	0	0 for physician supply 0 for health insurance premiums	0
Collateral-source rule reform	0	0	0	0	0 for physician supply 0 for health insurance premiums	0
Periodic payment	0	0	0	0	0	0
Shorter statute of limitations/repose	0	0	↓	0	0	0

Notes: Effects are classified as large increase (↑↑), modest increase (↑), no change (0), modest decrease (↓), or large decrease (↓↓). [This table is updated with information from the authors' 2016 report.]

Table 4.
Summary of Probable Effects of Innovative Tort Reforms

	Claims frequency and costs	Overhead costs	Liability costs	Defensive medicine	Supply	Quality of care
Schedule of noneconomic damages	0 (highly dependent on award levels)	↓	↓	↓	0	0
Administrative compensation systems or "health courts"	Medical court model: 0 / Administrative model: ↑↑ for frequency, 0 for costs	Medical court model: ↓ / Administrative model: ↓	0	Medical court model: 0 / Administrative model: ↓	0	Medical court model: 0 / Administrative model: ↑
Disclosure-and-offer programs	↓	↓↓	↓	0	0	↑
Safe harbors for adherence to evidence-based practice guidelines	0	↓	0	↓↓		↑↑
Enterprise liability	0	↓	↓	↓	0	↑

Notes: Effects are classified as large increase (↑↑), modest increase (↑), no change (0), modest decrease (↓), or large decrease (↓↓).

2. *Statutory Scope.* An important legal issue created by all malpractice reform statutes is precisely which actions they apply to and whether plaintiffs can state their claims in a manner that avoids these restrictions. These statutes typically are written to apply to professional negligence actions against practitioners of the healing arts. One route for avoiding them that appeared open for a while was the federal anti-dumping legislation discussed in Chapter 2.A. Some state limitations do not apply to actions under the federal statute. See Draper v. Chiapuzio, 9 F.3d 1391 (9th Cir. 1993). But courts have restricted the federal anti-dumping statute so that, for the most part, it does not apply to garden-variety malpractice complaints. Other avoidance techniques include framing the action with an alternative common-law theory, such as breach of contract, fraud, or battery, or as institutional rather than professional negligence. See, e.g., Atkinson v. Lammico Insurance Co., 63 So. 3d 1176 (3d Cir. 2011) (malpractice reform statute does not apply to physician's failure to advise testing the patient's son for genetic disease since the victim was not the doctor's patient); David v. Our Lady of the Lake Hospital, Inc., 849 So. 2d 38 (La. 2003). Courts also sometimes find that these statutes do not apply to nonphysicians. See, e.g., Lane v. Health Options, Inc., 796 So. 2d 1234 (Fla. App. 2001) (negligence action against an HMO is not a medical malpractice action). Another court found that a damages cap does not apply to a physician's professional corporation because the corporation is not a licensed professional, even though the doctor was a sole practitioner and the liability of his wholly owned corporation was purely vicarious. Schwartz v. Brownlee, 482 S.E.2d 827 (Va. 1997). However, courts are sharply split on most of these issues, and courts sometimes apply reform statutes even to suits that do not relate to patient care. E.g., Texas West Oaks Hospital v. Williams, 371 S.W.3d 171 (Tex. 2012) (malpractice statute applies to suit by employee over unsafe work conditions). See generally Annots., 12 A.L.R. 5th 1 (1993); 89 A.L.R. 4th 887 (1992).

3. *Constitutional Challenges.* Damages caps have received the most constitutional scrutiny, with well over half the states having a supreme court decision on point. The cases are split approximately evenly, and some states have reversed themselves, e.g., Watts v. Lester E. Cox Medical Centers, 376 S.W.3d 633 (Mo. 2012) (overruling earlier case that upheld noneconomic damage cap of $350,000). See the casebook Web site, www.health-law.org, for the latest. See also Annot., 26 A.L.R. 5th 245 (1995), and note 8.

Other reform elements generally fare better in the courts, but nevertheless encounter substantial opposition. The usual objections are either of the equal protection stripe, or are based on separation of powers (protecting inherently judicial functions) or on a constitutional right to court access and to a jury trial, which were mentioned in *McCall.* See, e.g., Zeier v. Zimmer, 152 P.3d 861 (Okla. 2006) (declaring unconstitutional the requirement to obtain a certificate of merit prior to filing suit); Putman v. Wenatchee Valley Medical Center, 166 Wn. 2d 974, 216 P.3d 374 (Wash. 2009) (same).

One maneuver to avoid constitutional objections is for the legislature to authorize parties to elect an alternative dispute resolution mechanism by contract. This is already common in the form of arbitration statutes. This could also be done for damages caps, limitations periods, and all the rest. See, e.g., Ralph Peeples & Catherine T. Harris, Learning to Crawl: The Use of Voluntary Caps on Damages in Medical Malpractice Litigation, 54 Cath. U. L. Rev. 703 (2005). Is there any constitutional barrier to the legislature authorizing the enforcement of contracts that courts would ordinarily find to be unconscionable adhesion contracts? Note the *McCall* court's discussion of an earlier decision in that state which upheld a damage cap that applies to voluntary arbitration.

4. *Public Policy Rhetoric vs. Evidence.* Consider again the complaints that doctors typically make against the legal system. How accurate are they, in light of the notes and materials in sections A and F, as well as the facts and figures mentioned in *McCall?* And, as the *McCall* court asks, how likely are any of these reforms to abate these criticisms? One reputable national survey reports that variation across states in doctors' concerns about malpractice risk have no obvious relationship to objective indicators of actual risk, or to the extent of statutory reforms. Emily Carrier et al., Physicians' Fears of Malpractice Lawsuits Are Not Assuaged by Tort Reforms, 29(9) Health Aff. 1585 (Sept. 2010).

If a convincing case for reform cannot be made based on these arguments, how about one based simply on the need to contain overall health care spending? As the *McCall* decision documents, malpractice insurance premiums vary considerably by location and by physicians' practice specialties. Overall, malpractice premiums total roughly $10 billion (hospitals and doctors combined, in 2008), but this is substantially less than 1 percent of all health care spending. Of potentially greater significance are the "shadow" costs of malpractice litigation that occur in the form of defensive medical practices. Doctors argue they cannot hold down the costs of treatment as long as they are exposed to the potential liability for omitting expensive but marginally beneficial care. Review the notes at page 370 to consider whether this is a compelling argument, and see Michelle Mello et al., National Costs of the Medical Liability System, 29(9) Health Aff. 1569 (Sept. 2010).

5. *Screening Panels.* Why do you think advisory screening panels have been so ineffective? As Mello and Kachalia mention, their purpose is to give litigants a more accurate view of the merits of their case in order to promote settlement. Consider that these panels usually are composed of lawyers and doctors. How helpful are their views on the merits likely to be in predicting jury verdicts? In some states, plaintiffs' lawyers simply refuse to show up during the screening panel process, believing the information is not worth the time and effort and that any negative finding will not be that damaging even if it comes to the attention of the jury. Two states have declared screening panels unconstitutional based on evidence of their poor performance in practice. See note 8.

6. *Exclusive Enterprise Liability.* As Mello and Kachalia note, even if exclusive enterprise liability is not officially enacted, it already exists in "virtual" form through private agreement. Some HMOs and many government and teaching hospitals purchase insurance for all their doctors and defend all lawsuits arising from treatment under their auspices. The HMO or hospital assuming full responsibility for all negligent medical care within the institution has the same effect as shifting liability entirely from the doctor. See Kenneth S. Abraham & Paul C. Weiler, Enterprise Liability and the Evolution of the American Health Care System, 108 Harv. L. Rev. 381 (1994).When Harvard's teaching hospitals implemented this scheme, the liability insurer began to monitor patterns of litigation and noticed recurring problems in anesthesia. The insurer asked the Harvard anesthesiologists to analyze the causes. Rather than blaming others or acting defensively, the group devised new techniques and equipment to lower the risk of mishap. As a result, anesthesia

mortality dropped tenfold, and the Harvard anesthesia protocols have become standard across the country. Based on experiences such as this, some scholars advocate that newly emerging "Accountable Care Organizations" should also take on enterprise liability, in order to encourage better teamwork among care providers. Laura Hermer, Aligning Incentives in Accountable Care Organizations: The Role of Medical Malpractice Reform, 17 J. Health care L. & Pol'y 271 (2014) ("It remains to be seen, however, whether physicians would be prepared to accept the impact these changes may have on professional autonomy . . .").

7. *What You See Depends on Where You Stand.* What perspectives do you think each of the following groups has on what are the fundamental social purposes of malpractice litigation and how well they are being achieved: (1) injured patients and their lawyers; (2) doctors; (3) patients who have not been injured (but some day may be), that is, the general public? Try answering this question in terms of these three purposes: (1) compensating injured patients; (2) making wrongdoers pay for their harms; and (3) improving the quality of medicine.

8. *Bibliography.* On **the purposes of malpractice liability** generally (note 7), see Michael J. Saks et al., A Multiattribute Utility Analysis of Legal System Response to Medical Injuries, 54 DePaul L. Rev. 277 (2005); Roger B. Dworkin, The Process Paradigm: Rethinking Medical Malpractice, 41 Wake Forest L. Rev. 509 (2006); Alex Stein, Toward a Theory of Medical Malpractice, 97 Iowa L. Rev. 1201 (2012).

On the **malpractice crisis generally**, see Michelle Mello et al., The New Medical Malpractice Crisis, 348 New Eng. J. Med. 2281 (2003); Marc A. Rodwin et al., Why the Medical Malpractice Crisis Persists Even When Malpractice Insurance Premiums Fall, 25 Health Matrix 163 (2015). Advocating for a stronger federal role in reform, see Abigail R. Moncrieff, Federalization Snowballs: The Need for National Action in Medical Malpractice Reform, 109 Colum. L. Rev. 844 (2009). On malpractice **insurance premiums**, see Bernard Black, et al., Medical Liability Insurance Premia: 1990-2016 Dataset, with Literature Review and Summary Information, 14 J. Empirical Leg. Stud. 238 (2017).

For additional reviews of or proposals for both **traditional and innovative reforms** and their effects, see Daniel Kessler, Evaluating the Medical Malpractice System and Options for Reform, 25 J. Econ. Perspect. 93 (2011); Myungho Paik et al., Will Tort Reform Bend the Cost Curve?, 9 J. Empirical Legal Stud. 173 (2012); Leonard Nelson et al., Medical Liability and Health Care Reform, 21 Health Matrix 443 (2011); Jan Ambrose & Anne Carroll, Medical Malpractice Reform and Insurer Claims Defense, 32 J. Health Pol. Pol'y L. 843 (2007); Michelle Mello & Troyen Brennan, Medical Malpractice, 350 New Eng. J. Med. 283 (2004); Ronen Avraham & Max Schanzenbach, The Impact of Tort Reform on Private Health Insurance Coverage, 12 Am. L. & Econ. Rev. 319 (2010); Mary Coombs, How Not to Do Medical Malpractice Reform: A Florida Case Study, 18 Health Matrix 373 (2008); Frank Sloan & Lindsey M. Chepke, Ill-Suited? Medical Malpractice at a Crossroads (2008); W. Sage & Rogan Kersh eds., Medical Malpractice and the U.S. Health Care System (2006); Symposium, 37 U. Mem. L. Rev. 455 (2007); Symposium, 59 Vand. L. Rev. 1017 (2006); Symposium, 27 J. Leg. Med. 1 (2006); Symposium, 33 J.L. Med. & Ethics 414 (2005); Symposium, 5 Yale J. Health Pol'y L. & Ethics 341 (2005); Symposium, 23(4) Health Aff. (Aug. 2004); Symposium, 54 DePaul L. Rev. 203 (2005); Symposium, 26 N. Ill. U. L. Rev. 439 (2006); David Studdert, Note, 56 Duke L.J. 611 (2006).

On **constitutional challenges** (note 3), see Carly Kelly & Michelle Mello, Are Medical Malpractice Damages Caps Unconstitutional?, 33 J.L. Med. & Ethics 515 (2005); Elizabeth Stewart Poisson, Addressing the Impropriety of Statutory Caps on Pain and Suffering Awards in the Medical Liability System, 82 N.C. L. Rev. 759 (2004); Michelle M. Mello et al., Policy Experimentation with Administrative Compensation for Medical Injury: Issues Under State Constitutional Law, 45 Harv. J. on Legis. 59 (2008).

On **screening panels** (note 5), see Jona Goldschmidt, Where Have All the Panels Gone? A History of the Arizona Medical Liability Review Panel, 23 Ariz. St. L.J. 1013 (1992); Catherine Struve, Doctors, the Adversary System, and Procedural Reform in Medical Liability Litigation, 72 Fordham L. Rev. 943 (2004).

Problem: Malpractice Reform Legislation

Look up the various components of the medical malpractice reform statute in your (or another) state in an annotated statute book. Categorize these components according to the chart on page 532. Which interest groups appear to have prevailed with the legislature — doctors, personal injury lawyers, or insurers? What has been the judicial reaction? When was the statute first enacted, and have there been subsequent amendments?

Glossary of Organizational Terms and Acronyms

In previous generations, it was necessary to learn a specialized vocabulary to study law and medicine. This is still true, but in the past that vocabulary was purely medical. Today, it includes many obscure organizational terms as well. This is a selected glossary of organizational terms and acronyms, adapted from Prospective Payment Assessment Commission, 1996 Report to Congress.

ACA	Affordable Care Act of 2010
ACO	Accountable Care Organization
AHA	American Hospital Association
AHRQ	Agency for Health Care Research and Quality
AMA	American Medical Association
CDHC	Consumer-Directed (or Driven) Health Care
CMS	Center for Medicare and Medicaid Services
COBRA	Consolidated Omnibus Budget Reconciliation Act of 1985
DHHS	*See* HHS
ERISA	Employee Retirement Income Security Act of 1974
ESRD	End-Stage Renal Disease
FDA	Food and Drug Administration
HCFA	Health Care Financing Administration, now CMS
HHS	Health and Human Services, Department of
HIPAA	Health Insurance Portability and Accountability Act
HIV	Human Immunodeficiency Virus
HMO	Health Maintenance Organization
HRA or HSA	Healthcare Reimbursement or Health Savings Account (*see also* MSA)

IDS	Integrated Delivery System
IPA	Independent Practice Association
JCAHO	Joint Commission on Accreditation of Healthcare Organizations
MSA	Medical Savings Account
NCQA	National Committee for Quality Assurance
OBRA	Omnibus Budget Reconciliation Act
POS	Point of Service
PPACA	Patient Protection and Affordable Care Act
PPO	Preferred Provider Organization
PPS	Prospective Payment System
SNF	Skilled Nursing Facility
SSI	Supplemental Security Income
UR/UM	Utilization Review, or Utilization Management

Accountable Care Organization (ACO) — An organization or network of physicians and/or hospitals that is able to receive payment from public or private insurers on a bundled basis that holds the provider group collectively responsible for the cost and quality of patients' care.

Consumer-Driven Health Care — An alternative to managed care, which seeks to activate patients to be cost-conscious consumers at the point of treatment, by requiring them to pay more out of pocket, and by providing better information about treatment options and costs.

Cost Shifting — Increasing revenues from some payers to offset uncompensated care losses and lower net payments from other payers.

Fee-for-Service — A method of reimbursing health care providers in which payment is made for each unit of service rendered.

Health Maintenance Organization (HMO) — A managed care plan that integrates financing and delivery of a comprehensive set of health care services to an enrolled population. HMOs may contract with, directly employ, or own participating health care providers. Enrollees are usually required to choose from among these providers and in return have limited co-payments. Providers may be paid through capitation, salary, per diem, or prenegotiated fee-for-service rates.

Health Savings Account (HSA) — A tax-sheltered account, similar to an IRA, and also known as a Healthcare Reimbursement Account (HRA) or Medical Savings Account (MSA), that is used to pay for medical expenses. It is coupled with high-deductible or "catastrophic" insurance, such that the HSA can pay for most ordinary expenses and insurance is used only for very expensive treatment.

Integrated Delivery System (IDS) — Any number of different arrangements among doctors, hospitals, other medical facilities, and insurers in which a full range of medical services is offered to employers, subscribers, or insurers. Includes conventional arrangements such as HMOs, as well as more innovative arrangements known as PHOs, PSNs, or MSOs, which are discussed in Chapter 10.

Managed Care — Any system of health service payment or delivery arrangements in which the health plan or provider attempts to control or coordinate health service use to contain health expenditures, improve quality, or both. Arrangements often involve a defined delivery system of providers having some form of contractual relationship with the plan.

Point-of-Service (POS) — A health plan allowing the enrollee to choose to receive a service from a participating or a nonparticipating provider, with different benefit levels associated with one or the other types of providers.

Preferred Provider Organization (PPO) — A health plan with a network of providers whose services are available to enrollees at lower cost than the services of non-network providers. PPO enrollees may self-refer to any network provider at any time.

Prospective Payment — A method of paying health care providers in which rates are established in advance. Providers are paid these rates regardless of the costs they actually incur.

Uncompensated Care — Care rendered by hospitals or other providers without payment from the patient or a government-sponsored or private insurance program. It includes both charity care, which is provided without the expectation of payment, and bad debts, for which the provider has made an unsuccessful effort to collect payment due from the patient.

Utilization Review (UR) — A review of services delivered by a health care provider to evaluate the appropriateness, necessity, and quality of the prescribed services. The review can be performed on a prospective, concurrent, or retrospective basis.

Table of Cases

Primary cases are indicated by italics.

Index